Client/Server Application Development with
PowerBuilder

Jan L. Harrington

I(T)P International Thomson Publishing

Cambridge • Albany • Bonn • Boston • Cincinnati • London • Madrid • Melbourne • Mexico City
New York • Paris • San Francisco • Singapore • Tokyo • Toronto • Washington

Client/Server Application Development with PowerBuilder is published by CTI.

Managing Editor	Wendy Welch Gordon
Associate Product Manager	Richard Keavney
Production Editor	Christine Spillett
Text and Cover Designer	Kim Munsell & Doug Goodman
Cover Illustrator	Doug Goodman

© 1996 by CTI.
A Division of Course Technology – I(T)P

For more information contact:

Course Technology
One Main Street
Cambridge, MA 02142

International Thomson Publishing Europe
Berkshire House 168-173
High Holborn
London WCIV 7AA
England

Thomas Nelson Australia
102 Dodds Street
South Melbourne, 3205
Victoria, Australia

Nelson Canada
1120 Birchmount Road
Scarborough, Ontario
Canada M1K 5G4

International Thomson Editores
Campos Eliseos 385, Piso 7
Col. Polanco
11560 Mexico D.F. Mexico

International Thomson Publishing GmbH
Künigswinterer Strasse 418
53227 Bonn
Germany

International Thomson Publishing Asia
211 Henderson Road
#05-10 Henderson Building
Singapore 0315

International Thomson Publishing Japan
Hirakawacho Kyowa Building, 3F
2-2-1 Hirakawacho
Chiyoda-ku, Tokyo 102
Japan

All rights reserved. This publication is protected by federal copyright law. No part of this publication may be reproduced, stored in a retrieval system, or transmitted in any form or by any means, electronic, mechanical, photocopying, recording, or otherwise, or be used to make a derivative work (such as translation or adaptation), without prior permission in writing from Course Technology.

Trademarks
Course Technology and the open book logo are registered trademarks of Course Technology.
I(T)P The ITP logo is a registered trademark under license.
Microsoft and Windows 95 are registered trademarks of Microsoft Corporation.
Some of the product names and company names used in this book have been used for identification purposes only and may be trademarks or registered trademarks of their respective manufacturers and sellers.

Disclaimer
Course Technology reserves the right to revise this publication and make changes from time to time in its content without notice.

ISBN 0-7600-3560-1

Printed in the United States of America

10 9 8 7 6 5 4 3 2 1

This book is dedicated to

Mr. Francis Murray

who, during the 1966-67 school year, taught me to write.

He also taught me a great deal about teaching, and I will be

forever grateful to him for his excellence.

PREFACE

Back in 1991, I wrote a book to teach students to use a database development environment so they could complete a semester-long database design and development project. That book was based on R:BASE 3.1. At the time, I felt it was pedagogically the best DBMS for supporting the theory that was being taught in the classroom. It also had good development tools that could be used by relatively technologically unsophisticated users to create stand-alone applications. Boy, have things changed...

The most overwhelming trend in database management today is the move toward client-server processing. SQL, which was already a standard in 1991, has become the lingua franca of data management. End-user products such as R:BASE are more and more becoming front-end tools that communicate with database servers.

It became clear about a year ago that I had to change what I was doing in my database courses. (I've been teaching graduates and undergraduates for more than ten years now.) A survey of what was actually happening in business today brought forth the name of one product: PowerBuilder. PowerBuilder is overwhelmingly the development environment of choice for client-server application programs. It is a powerful, sophisticated development environment.

Being popular or powerful isn't enough reason to choose software for classroom use. The software must be pedagogically sound; it must support the concepts being taught in the classroom. Fortunately, when you purchase PowerBuilder, you also get a single-user version of WatcomSQL, a relatively standard SQL-based DBMS that supports the extensions to SQL that support primary and foreign keys. The coupling of the power of PowerBuilder with a capable SQL DBMS makes PowerBuilder very suitable for classroom use.

At the time this book was written, PowerBuilder Desktop was available for lab use direct from PowerSoft for $75 a copy (including the single-user version of WatcomSQL). A six-user network version of WatcomSQL cost $149. A student purchase program is also available. For details, contact PowerSoft directly.

Scope of the Book

PowerBuilder is an enormous product. There is no way a student can be expected to master the entire product in a semester, especially when the course he or she is taking is focused on the theory and concepts of database management and not on a software product. Therefore, this book doesn't attempt to be comprehensive. Instead, it gives students a grounding in basic PowerBuilder skills. By the time they have finished working through the tutorials, students will be able to complete a database design and implementation project.

This means that this book places emphasis on getting data into and out of a database with a clean, easy-to-use interface. It rarely mentions tools that make the user interface "pretty," although many students will discover drawing tools on their own.

How This Book is Organized

This book is divided into three parts. The first (Chapters 1–5) contains introductory material, including a discussion of what a client-server DBMS is, a review of relational database concepts, and an overview of the PowerSoft programming language. In addition, the introductory material contains a tour of the PowerBuilder development environment and instructions on how to connect to PowerBuilder databases. These last two chapters are tutorial, while the first three are conceptual only.

The second part contains tutorials that cover direct interaction with the database using PowerBuilder as a front-end. This is where students learn to create database structure (tables, views, indexes, and so on), to display and modify data without an application, and to issue SQL commands directly to a database.

The tutorials in the third part of the book cover basic application development skills. Students learn to create windows that form an application framework and then add content to those windows for displaying and retrieving data in a variety of ways.

What Readers Need to Know

The unfortunate reality of any software development environment as powerful as PowerBuilder is that students need to have some background in computing before they can begin working with the product. For that reason, this book assumes that readers have the following knowledge and experience:

- Familiarity with the GUI under which they will be using PowerBuilder (typically Windows 3.1, Windows 95, or Macintosh). This includes skills such as working with a basic text processing application and using the mouse to manipulate menus and objects (for example, dragging objects).

- Familiarity with the principles of relational database design. (These principles are reviewed in Chapter 2, however.)

- A working knowledge of the SQL SELECT command. (I've had to change the order in which I present course material in my own classes to accommodate this requirement. Instead of leaving SQL to midway through the semester, I'm teaching it very early, right after presenting the concepts of the relational data model. Normalization and relational algebra now come after SQL.)

- Fluency in a high-level programming language. (A one-semester programming course should be sufficient.) Although object-oriented concepts are introduced in Chapter 3 and covered throughout this book, experience with an object-oriented language will make learning PowerBuilder easier. The general syntax of the PowerSoft language is introduced in Chapter 3; reference materials describing the language syntax in depth can be found in Appendix D.

Case Studies and Exercises

Two case studies run though this book. The first, Pinehill Software, is used for exercises within the tutorials. The Pinehill Software database tracks trade shows that the company attends to market its products, looking at scheduling, expenses, and sales leads gathered at the shows. There are two versions of the database on the instructor's disk that is available to adopters of this book. The first (tcomp) is a complete working version of the application that is used in the guided tour of the PowerBuilder environment. The second (tshows) contains tables with data from which the tutorials build the entire tshows application.

The second case study, College & University Rentals, forms the basis for the end-of-chapter exercises. A portion of the database (curents) is contained on the instructor's disk. Some tables have been created and already loaded with data. The remainder of the data for this database is supplied as text files. Students will create the tables during their exercises and then load the data. This organization has two advantages: One, students don't waste time doing data entry; two, they learn how to import data.

The exercises at the end of each tutorial chapter give students the chance to practice the same techniques they've just experienced in the step-by-step tutorials. However, the exercises simply state a goal rather than explain the process for achieving that goal (for example, create a window that does *x*) and therefore force the students to transfer the procedures outlined in the tutorials to a different environment. In my experience, this is the best way to make sure students actually learn software skills. Just keystroking through tutorials isn't enough.

Conventions Used in the Tutorials

There are some conventions used throughout the tutorials in this book to make your work easier, including the following:

- Menu selections are written using the name of the menu, followed by an arrow, followed by the menu option. For example, selecting the Close option from the File menu is written File -> Close. If the menu option has a submenu, then another arrow separates the menu option choice from the submenu option choice, as in File -> Connect -> Tshows.

- Because most of the mouse use with PowerBuilder involves only the left button on the typical PC mouse, references to the mouse button, clicking, and double-clicking mean the left mouse button. In those few instances where the right mouse button is required, the right mouse button will indicated specifically with the phrase "Right-click."

Acknowledgements

It takes a big group of people to put together a book like this, and I'd like to take this opportunity to thank them. First, all the folks at Course Techology:

- Wendy Welch Gordon, Managing Editor
- Richard Keaveny, Associate Product Manager
- Susan Roche, Editorial Assistant
- Patty Stephan, Production Manager
- Christine Spillett, Production Editor
- Kim Munsell and Doug Goodman, Text Designers
- Doug Goodman, Cover Designer

There were a host of freelancers who helped as well:

- Robert Epp, Willow New Media Services Developmental Editor
- Jane Pedicini, Copy Editor
- Susan Gall, Proofreader
- Gex, Inc., Prepress Services

And let's not forget the reviewers:

- Nate Bryer
- David Paradice, Texas A&M University

And last, but certainly not least, Cecile Roche and Rachael Stockton, our liaisons at PowerSoft, who provided software and arranged permission for us to reprint portions of the PowerBuilder documentation.

Thanks everyone!

JLH

CONTENTS

Part One: Introduction

Chapter One: Client-Server Database Management

Client-Server Versus Centralized Database Management .4

    The Centralized Database Management Environment 4

    The Client-Server Environment 5

Deciding to Switch to Client-Server 7

Benefits of Client-Server Architectures 7

Drawbacks to Client-Server Architectures 8

PowerBuilder and Client-Server Database Management 9

    PowerBuilder Middleware 9

Looking Ahead 10

Chapter Two: Relational Database Concepts

Databases and Data Relationships 14

    Types of Data Relationships 14

    The Relational Data Model 16

Relations 16

Integrity Rules 17

    Primary Key Constraints 18

    Referential Integrity 19

    Domain Constraints 20

Designing Good Relations 21
    Insertion Anomalies 21
    Deletion Anomalies 22
    Modification Anomalies 23
    The Cause of Most Anomalies 23
    Normalization 24
    Performing Relational Design 26
Views 26
Query Languages 27
The Data Dictionary 28
Pinehill Software 28
    Design of the Pinehill Software Trade Show Database 29
College and University Rentals 33
Looking Ahead 36

Chapter Three: PowerBuilder Software Concepts

The Object-Oriented Programming Model 38
    Classes and Objects 38
    Information Hiding 39
    Inheritance 40
    Polymorphism 41
PowerBuilder and the Object-Oriented Model 41
    Application Libraries 41
    Application Objects 42
    Window Objects 42
    DataWindow Objects 42
    Other Types of Objects 42
    Communicating with Objects 43

Events and Scripts 44

Inheritance 44

Transactions 45

Introducing PowerScript 46

General Statement Syntax 47

Variables 47

Embedded SQL 48

Looking Ahead 49

Chapter Four: Getting Started

Launching PowerBuilder 52

Opening an Application 52

Creating a New Application 54

Exiting PowerBuilder 57

Connecting to a Database 58

Configuring the ODBC Driver 59

Looking Ahead 64

Chapter Five: Introducing PowerBuilder

Viewing a Working Application 66

The General Work Environment 71

Customizing the Toolbars 77

Displaying Button Text 78

Configuring Other Toolbars 79

The Library Painter and Deleting Objects 80

Getting Help 82

Looking Ahead 87

Part Two: Interacting Directly with a DBMS

Chapter Six: Managing Database Structure

Creating the Database 92

Creating Tables 94

    Rules for Naming Tables and Columns 95

    PowerBuilder's Column Data Types 95

    Defining a New Table 96

    Defining a Foreign Key 103

Modifying a Schema 110

    Altering Table Definitions 110

    Dropping Tables 112

Indexes 113

    Deciding Which Indexes to Create 113

    Creating Indexes 114

    Dropping Unwanted Indexes 118

Looking Ahead 118

Chapter Seven: Direct Data Manipulation

The Data Manipulation Painter 124

    Entering the Data Manipulation Painter 124

    Exiting the Data Manipulation Painter 125

Filtering Data 125

Sorting Data 127

Modifying Data 128

    Editing Existing Data 128

    Inserting Rows 130

    Deleting Rows 131

Loading Data From Text File 132

Issuing SQL Commands Directly to the Database 133

Views 136

    Creating a View 136

    Looking at View Data 142

    Dropping a View 142

    Views with Grouping Queries 143

Looking Ahead 145

Chapter Eight: Extended Data Attributes

The Scope of Extended Attributes 148

Adding Column Comments 149

Column Headers and Labels 151

Setting Default Alignment and Width 154

Display Formats 155

Edit Formats 157

    The Default Edit Format 157

    Setting an Edit Mask for a Date Column 160

    Character Column Edit Styles 162

    Check Boxes 164

    Radio Buttons 166

    Dropdown Lists 169

Column Validation 171

    Specifying Validation Rules 172

    Providing Default Values 174

Looking Ahead 175

Part Three: Database Access Using an Application

Chapter Nine: Building Windows as an Application Framework

- Planning the Application 180
- Basic Application Actions 182
  - Transaction Objects 182
  - Deciding When to Connect and Disconnect 184
- PowerBuilder Window Types 185
- Creating "Main" Windows 186
- Changing Window Characteristics 188
- Saving and Naming the Window 193
- Application Scripts 194
  - Application Events 194
  - Writing an Application Open Script 194
- Main Window Scripts 197
  - Main Window Events 198
  - Writing a Window Open Script 198
  - Writing a Window Close Script 199
- Adding More Windows and Button Controls 200
  - Adding the Next Level Windows 200
  - Introducing Button Controls 201
  - Drawing Command Button Controls 202
  - Writing Simple Button Control Scripts 206
  - Creating Picture Buttons 207
- Completing the Application FrameWork 212
- Viewing the Object Hierarchy 216
- Looking Ahead 217

Chapter Ten: Introducing DataWindows

- Creating a Simple DataWindow Object 220
  - Configuring a Quick Select 220
  - Configuring the DataWindow 225
- Placing a DataWindow Control 229
- Getting Data into a DataWindow Control 234
  - Understanding the Script 236
- Overriding Edit Formats 239
  - Copying a Script 242
- Basic Computed Fields and Duplicate Suppression 244
  - Specifying a Quick Select with a Join 245
  - Suppressing Duplicate Values 246
  - Adding the Computed Field 246
  - Placing the DataWindow Control 249
- Looking Ahead 250

Chapter Eleven: DataWindows and Queries

- DataWindows and the Select Painter 252
  - Beginning the Select 252
  - Creating an Input Argument 253
  - Modifying the Formatting 255
  - Adding a Summary Value 257
  - Placing the DataWindow Control 258
- Enabling a Response Window 259
  - Creating the Response Window 260
  - Writing Response Window Scripts 264
  - Modifying the Application Window Script 265
  - Understanding the Scripts 265

Picking From a List 267
    Understanding the Scripts 270
Handling Complex Queries 271
Looking Ahead 275

Chapter Twelve: Control Break Reports

Using the Group Presentation Style 278
    Creating the DataWindow Object 278
    Adding Summary Calculations 282
    Modifying the DataWindow's Appearance 283
    Placing the DataWindow Control 285
    Enabling Printing 286
Defining Groups Through a DataWindow 287
    Preparing the View 288
    Creating the Initial DataWindow Layout 288
    Adding the Groups 289
    Adding Summary Calculations 291
    Placing the DataWindow Control 295
Looking Ahead 295

Chapter Thirteen: Inheritance

When to Use Inheritance 298
What You Can Do to a Descendant 299
    Control Modifications 299
    Script Modifications 300
Preparing the Ancestor Application Window 300
    The DataWindow Object 301
    The Control 302

Creating the Ancestor Response Window 304

    Changing the Tab Order 306

Duplicating and Modifying the DataWindow Objects .307

    Creating the First Descendant Window 307

    Creating the Descendant Response Window .311

    Creating the Second Pair of Descendants 313

Making Changes 314

Inherited Objects and the Object Hierarchy 315

Looking Ahead 316

Chapter Fourteen: Enabling Data Modification Capabilities

Enabling Single-Row Modification 320

    Creating a Single-Row DataWindow 321

    Understanding the Scripts 324

    Using a Response Window to Find a Row for Modification 325

Picking Values From DropDown DataWindows 328

    Single-Column DropDown DataWindows 328

    Multi-Column DropDown DataWindows 336

Implementing Sequential Access 341

Autonumbering Columns 344

Using Related DropDown DataWindows 345

    Introducing Child DataWindows 346

    Creating the DataWindow Objects 347

    Putting the Window Together 347

    Understanding the itemchanged Event Script 349

Looking Ahead 350

Chapter Fifteen: Connecting DataWindows

Creating Nested Reports 352

Creating Windows with Updatable 1:M DataWindows .358

    Adding Running Totals 363

    Catching Unsaved Changes 365

Creating Windows with Updatable M:1 DataWindows .368

    Building the DataWindows 369

    Laying Out the Window 371

    Adding the Radio Buttons 372

    Writing the Scripts 376

Looking Ahead 382

Chapter Sixteen: Dynamic DataWindows

Hiding and Showing DataWindows 386

Changing a DataWindow's Query 390

    Understanding the Script 392

Looking Ahead 395

Chapter Seventeen: Creating Menus

Creating a Main Application Menu 398

    Setting Up Menu Items and Options 398

    Previewing the Menu 402

    Adding Cascading Menus 403

    Writing Scripts for Menu Options 405

    Attaching the Menu Object to a Window 408

Creating a Menu for an Application Window 409

Contents

Using Inheritance to Create a Menu 410

    Developing the Ancestor Menu 10

    Developing the Descendant Menu 412

Wrapping Up 413

Appendix A: Building Executables

Creating a Quick Executable 416

Creating Executables Using the Project Painter 418

Appendix B: Using PowerBuilder Macintosh

Keyboard Changes for Macintosh Users 422

Window Painter Changes 423

    Font Issues 424

Menu Painter Changes 424

    Cross-Platform Menu Issues 425

Project Painter Changes 426

Appendix C: Function Reference   429

Appendix D: PowerScript Language Reference   501

Appendix E: Complete Design for C&U Rentals   549

Glossary   553

Index   559

PART ONE

Introduction

CHAPTER ONE

CLIENT-SERVER DATABASE MANAGEMENT

CHAPTER TWO

RELATIONAL DATABASE CONCEPTS

CHAPTER THREE

POWERBUILDER SOFTWARE CONCEPTS

CHAPTER FOUR

GETTING STARTED

CHAPTER FIVE

INTRODUCING POWERBUILDER

CHAPTER ONE

Client-Server Database Management

IN THIS CHAPTER YOU WILL:

- Learn about the difference between client-server and more traditional architectures for database systems
- Discover the advantages and disadvantages of client-server environments
- Understand where PowerBuilder fits into a client-server database application development environment

As you read this book, there is a major change occurring in the way many organizations structure their database management environment. They are moving from a centralized environment where all processing is done on a single computer (often a mainframe) to a decentralized environment where processing is shared between several, usually smaller, computers. This new environment is known as *client-server*. The way in which the various components of the environment are configured is often called a *client-server architecture*.

In this chapter you will read about the differences between a client-server environment and the more traditional centralized database processing environment. You will also learn about the costs and benefits of making such a switch. Finally, this chapter looks at the support PowerBuilder provides for client-server database management.

Client-Server Versus Centralized Database Management

The fundamental difference between a centralized database environment and a client-server database environment is where the actual processing of the data takes place. To help make the contrast clearer, let's look at two sample hardware configurations: one for a centralized environment and one for a client-server environment.

The Centralized Database Management Environment

In Figure 1.1 you can see hardware that might be used for a centralized database environment. All of the data manipulation takes place on the host processor (usually a mainframe or minicomputer). Terminals are connected to the host through some form of data communications channel. Today, this usually means a local area network for users at the same site as the host and modems for remote users.

The "terminals" that access the data can be dumb terminals, which have no processing capabilities of their own, or they can be desktop computers. Although desktop computers have processing capabilities, when interacting with a centralized host-based database management system (DBMS), they run terminal emulation software that makes them appear to the host as dumb terminals. In other words, the desktop computers do no processing of the data.

The price of desktop computers has dropped so much that they cost only a few hundred dollars more than a dumb terminal. For that reason, many companies are purchasing desktop computers instead of dumb terminals for host-based environments, primarily because the stand-alone computers provide much greater capabilities at nearly the same cost.

Data manipulation requests are sent from a terminal to the host, which processes the request and formats the output. The DBMS and all application programs (including interactive query processing programs such as those that accept SQL commands directly from a user) run on the host's CPU. Formatted output is sent back to a terminal for display. The terminal—whether it be a dumb terminal or a desktop computer emulating a dumb terminal—simply shows on its screen whatever it receives from the host.

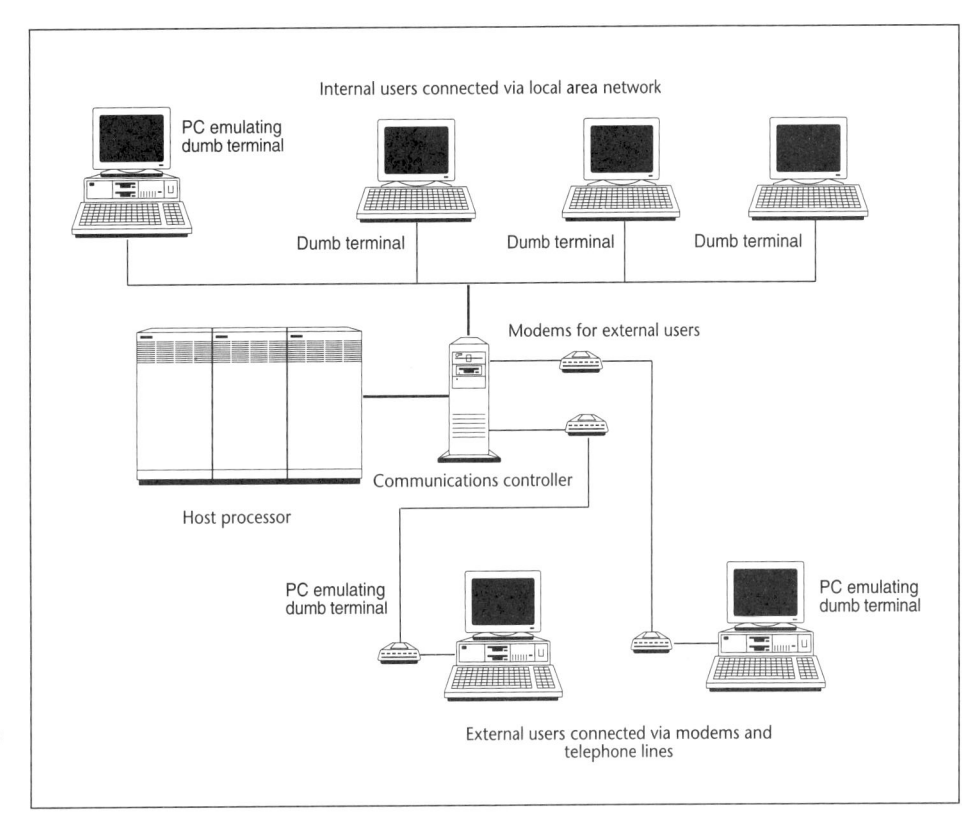

Figure 1.1
A centralized database architecture

The Client-Server Environment

In direct contrast to a centralized environment, a client-server environment distributes the chores of processing data among multiple computers. As you can see in Figure 1.2, each piece of hardware connected to the network is a computer in its own right; dumb terminals can't be used because every computer that is part of the environment must have some processing capabilities.

A special type of DBMS, called a *database server*, runs on a computer dedicated to this task. The software accepts data manipulation requests from other computers on the network—the *clients*—and returns the result of the request. The client computers complete processing the data, including formatting output for display on the client computer's screen. In a client-server environment, the data processing is shared between the clients and the server.

There are three general types of software that can run on the client machines: a stand-alone application program, a query language processor for interactive database queries, or another DBMS. When the client software is another DBMS, the environment usually requires software called *middleware* that translates data manipulation requests framed in the client DBMS's language into syntax that the database server can understand (see Figure 1.3). The advantage to using a client DBMS (for example, Access, dBase, FoxPro, or Paradox) is that many of these products have application development tools that end users can use to create their own database applications.

The hardware that runs the database server software is also usually called a *database server*. The computer acting as a server can be any size: a mainframe, minicomputer, or high-end microcomputer. In fact, there is no reason that a

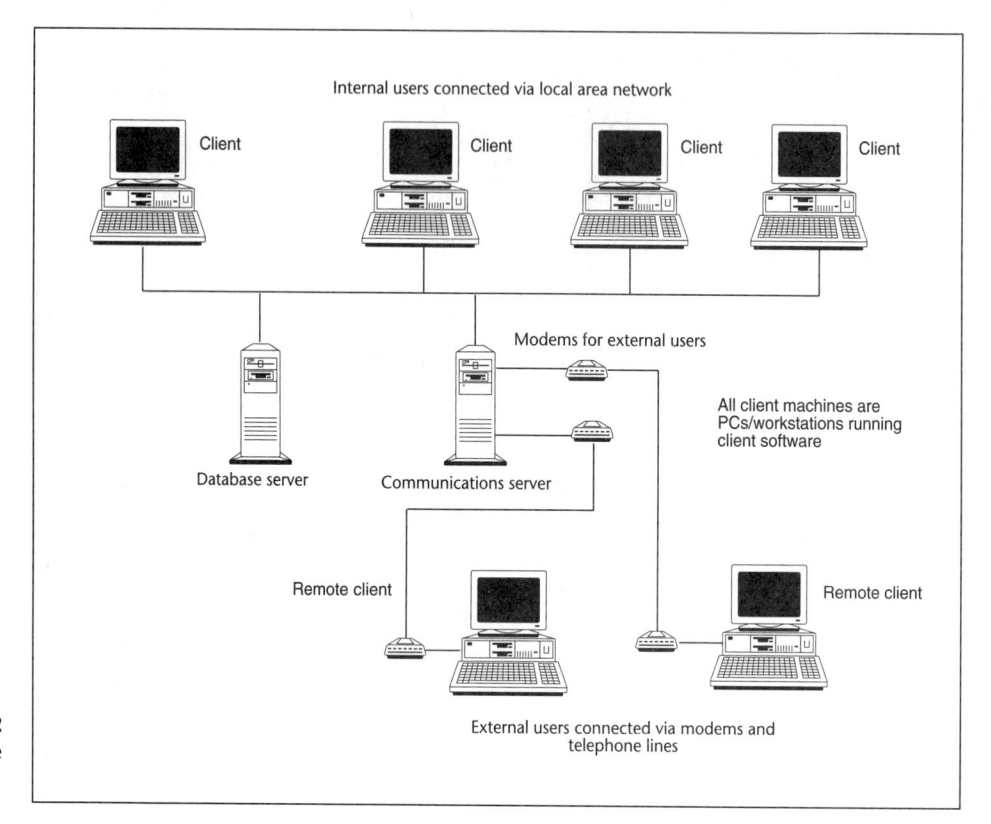

Figure 1.2
A client-server database architecture

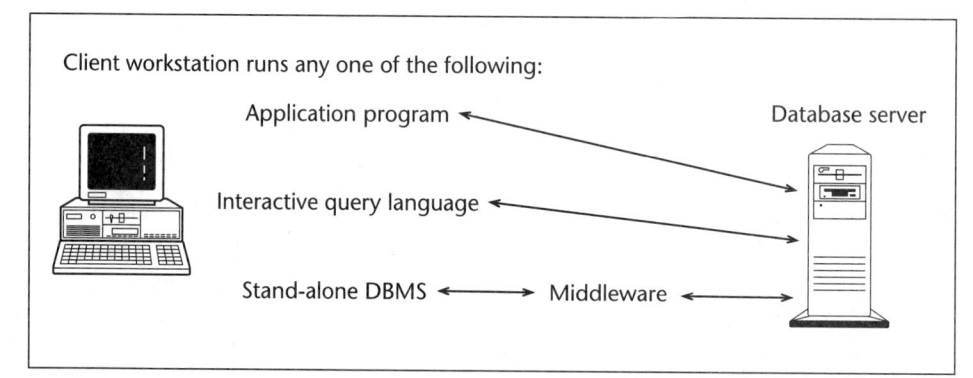

Figure 1.3
The interaction between client software and a database server

mainframe that originally acted as a host for a centralized database environment can't be reconfigured as a database server.

A client-server environment in which there is only a single database server does not constitute a distributed database. A database server stores a complete database and all its data. The processing of that data is distributed, but the data are still centralized. To have a distributed database, you must be storing data on more than one server.

Deciding to Switch to Client-Server

When might an organization decide to make the switch to a client-server architecture? Because the switch means such a fundamental change in the way an organization handles its data, it is rare that such a change will be made simply because client-server is the "latest thing." There must be compelling reasons to undertake such a project.

The basic reason can be summed up fairly simply: An organization's current system doesn't meet the organization's current and/or future needs. The current system's shortfalls may include (but are not limited to) any of the following areas:

- Cost: The current system is costing too much to maintain and/or upgrade.
- Strategic position in the marketplace: The current system no longer provides the capabilities necessary to provide the organization with a strategic advantage.
- Operational capabilities: The current system cannot provide the information users need to do their jobs on a daily basis.
- Application backlog: Application development tools available for the current system aren't capable of supporting the timely creation of application programs. Users are waiting too long for applications needed to perform their jobs.
- System support: The current system is so old that the hardware and/or software vendors are either out of business or no longer providing technical support.

Benefits of Client-Server Architectures

Given that so many organizations have switched to client-server environments, there must be some significant benefits to doing so. Many companies have expected the following benefits:

- Cost savings: Because client-server architectures usually involve smaller computers than centralized architectures, the costs of obtaining, maintaining, and upgrading hardware are less. For example, the cost of RAM for a desktop machine is less the one-tenth the cost of RAM for a mainframe (assuming purchase of the same amount of memory).
- Increased flexibility in hardware selection: Hardware purchases can be tailored to the needs of the individual user.
- Expanded usefulness of hardware: The desktop machines purchased to connect to a client-server database are multi-purpose machines. They can be used for graphics, word processing, multimedia, spreadsheet financial analysis, and so on, as well as interacting with a database. In this way, an organization gets more productivity from its investment in hardware than it would if the hardware were unable to be used for anything besides database access.

To be perfectly fair, the preceding benefits are also why many organizations no longer purchase dumb terminals, which can do nothing but sit idle when a user isn't interacting with a host computer.

- Better development tools: Client-server development tools are generally cheaper, easier to use, and often more powerful than development tools for large systems. Development of a client-server application is therefore usually easier and faster than development of a large-system application. When you consider that users typically wait six months to two years for application development in a centralized, host-based environment, anything that speeds up such development is a major benefit.
- Better software user interfaces: Client-server development tools provide better support for graphic user interfaces (GUIs), client-server applications tend to be more user-friendly than many large system applications. A good interface cuts down on the time and money it takes to train new users and on the time needed to support users.
- End-user development opportunities: End users can avail themselves of easy-to-use application development tools to create their own programs, relieving an Information Systems (IS) staff of some of its application development burden.

Drawbacks to Client-Server Architectures

As with any data processing environment, a client-server architecture can have some drawbacks, which include the following:

- Cost savings: The cost savings over a centralized host-based architecture that were originally anticipated haven't materialized. However, there is no evidence that a client-server environment costs *more* than a centralized environment.
- Loss of control: Because data processing is distributed, a centralized IS department loses some control over the data and over users. This can lead to inconsistencies in data handling, where the same data are viewed and processed differently in different parts of the organization. In addition, when application development takes place without the knowledge of the IS staff, it can be very difficult for the IS staff to support and keep track of those applications.
- Slower I/O: The desktop computers used as servers for most of today's client-server DBMSs aren't as fast as larger computers, such as mainframes. Although the CPUs of desktop computers are as fast as the CPUs of larger machines, the desktop computers can't match the larger machines' I/O performance. A client-server database system may therefore be slower than a centralized host-based system, especially during peak access periods when a local area network is heavily loaded with database users.
- End-user development complications: Users who develop their own applications can be a source of problems. The time used to develop an application is time taken away from the user's ordinary job responsibilities. In addition, there is no control over the accuracy of the results produced by a user-developed application; users working with their own software may be basing job decisions on inconsistent or inaccurate data analysis.

PowerBuilder and Client-Server Database Management

PowerBuilder is a database application development tool. It is not a client-server DBMS but is instead intended to be used to create programs that interact with a wide range of database server software, including the following:

- WatcomSQL: A single-user version of WatcomSQL, which isn't a client-server product, ships with PowerBuilder. The purpose of this DBMS is to test your PowerBuilder applications. A multi-user, client-server version of WatcomSQL is also available.
- SQLServer: SQLServer (from Microsoft) is a client-server DBMS. Versions prior to 6.0 run in a DOS/Windows environment. Version 6.0 runs under Windows NT only.
- Sybase: Sybase (from Sybase) is also a client-server DBMS. It is primarily aimed at UNIX environments, but will run in a DOS/Windows environment as well.

Powersoft, the company that developed PowerBuilder, is now owned by Sybase. The purchase also included the WatcomSQL DBMS, which Sybase has positioned as its entry-level product in the client-server database market and retained the Sybase DBMS as its heavy-duty product.

- SQLBase: SQLBase, a product of the Gupta Corporation, is designed for Intel-based servers.
- Oracle (versions 6 and 7): Oracle (from Oracle Corporation) is the most widely used DBMS today, in large measure because it runs on virtually every hardware and operating system platform.
- Informix: Informix (Informix Corporation) is a UNIX-oriented DBMS that is also available for Intel PCs.
- DB2/2: IBM's DB2/2 is a workstation-based version of its DB2 mainframe software.

In addition, PowerBuilder can develop applications for desktop DBMSs such as Access, dBASE, Paradox, and FoxPro.

PowerBuilder Middleware

The most typical way to interact with a database server using PowerBuilder is through Microsoft's *Open Database Connectivity* (ODBC) interface. As you can see in Figure 1.4, ODBC takes care of connecting to database, handles errors generated by database access, and stores data about the structure of the database. To work with PowerBuilder, a DBMS must either have a PowerBuilder ODBC driver or be one of the DBMSs for which PowerBuilder provides a native database driver. Products in this latter category include Sybase, Oracle, and Informix.

PowerBuilder ships with ODBC drivers for the DBMSs listed above. You may also be able to obtain drivers from other vendors, although Powersoft doesn't test or verify third-party drivers.

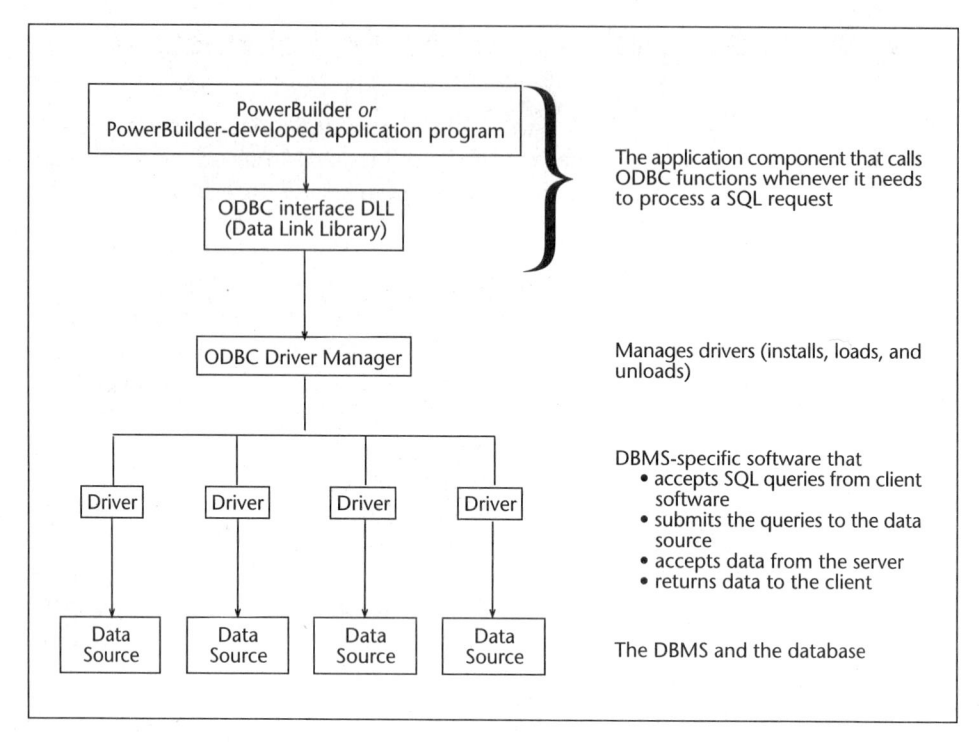

Figure 1.4
Use of ODBC drivers to access data sources

```
PowerBuilder or
PowerBuilder-developed application program
    ↓
ODBC interface DLL
(Data Link Library)
```
} The application component that calls ODBC functions whenever it needs to process a SQL request

```
ODBC Driver Manager
    ↓
Driver   Driver   Driver   Driver
  ↓        ↓        ↓        ↓
Data     Data     Data     Data
Source   Source   Source   Source
```

Manages drivers (installs, loads, and unloads)

DBMS-specific software that
- accepts SQL queries from client software
- submits the queries to the data source
- accepts data from the server
- returns data to the client

The DBMS and the database

Information describing databases about which PowerBuilder knows is stored in two files: *ODBC.INI* and *PB.INI*. An entry for a database must exist in those files before PowerBuilder can connect to the database and use it. You will learn to configure ODBC so that it can recognize a database created on another computer in Chapter 4.

Looking Ahead

In this chapter you have been introduced to the framework in which a client-server database exists. This is one of the three foundations of the PowerBuilder environment. In Chapter 2 you will get an overview of the second foundation: relational database concepts. (The third PowerBuilder foundation is the development software, which is discussed in Chapter 3.)

EXERCISES

The following exercises will give you a chance to think about the characteristics and impacts of switching to client-server computing. You will also get a chance to examine the computing environment that you will be using as you learn PowerBuilder.

1. A corporate credit union with three branches is considering switching from their current time-sharing system to an in-house client-server system.

Under the current arrangement, the credit union pays the company from which they lease computer time for all software development.

  a. List the characteristics of this business that might make it a good candidate for a client-server system.
  b. List the reasons why this business might want to stay with their current arrangement.

2. An advertising firm has a PC on almost every employee's desk. At this time, the PCs are networked only for e-mail. However, the firm would like to modify the system to support a database of "boilerplate" (prewritten paragraphs that can be used repeatedly) and artwork.

  a. List the characteristics of this business that make it a good candidate for a client-server system.
  b. List the drawbacks, if any, to using a client-server architecture for this firm.
  c. Assuming the firm has 15 artists, 3 clerical workers, and 4 managers—each of whom has a PC—draw a sample configuration for a client-server architecture.

3. Research the computing facilities at your school that will be supporting your work in this class, and answer the following questions:

  a. Can the network be classified as a client-server architecture? Why or why not?
  b. Can a user dial-in to the network from off-campus? If so, is working as an off-campus user any different from working as an on-campus user? Why or why not?
  c. What DBMSs (if any) are available on the network? Are they client-server or centralized DBMSs?

4. Consider the DBMS you are using for this course.

  a. Is your DBMS a client-server DBMS? Why or why not?
  b. How many concurrent users will your DBMS support?
  c. Diagram the network over which your DBMS is being used.

Chapter Two

Relational Database Concepts

IN THIS CHAPTER YOU WILL:

- Review the important relational database concepts that form the underpinnings of the PowerBuilder application development environment
- Discuss the case studies that are used as examples and exercises throughout this book

CHAPTER TWO RELATIONAL DATABASE CONCEPTS

This second introductory chapter contains a review of database concepts, the relational data model, and the terminology PowerBuilder uses to describe them. The intent is not to teach relational database theory, but to help you connect the theory you have learned in your database course with the PowerBuilder environment. At the end of this chapter, you will also be introduced to the case studies that are used as examples and exercises throughout this book.

Databases and Data Relationships

A *database* is a collection of data and definitions of the relationships between those data. The data in a database are stored in disk files, but a file is not a database. To be considered a database, a set of files must not only include stored data, but information about how the data are logically related.

A database user looks at the data stored in files through a DBMS. The DBMS translates data manipulation requests framed in terms of the logical relationships between data into commands that will access the data stored in files.

Types of Data Relationships

When relationships are captured in a database system, the relationships are between entities, the things about which we store data. An *entity* symbolizes a physical object, a person, an event, a place, and even the relationship between other entities.

There are three kinds of relationships in the real world, two of which are generally represented in databases. The three relationships are: 1) one-to-one, 2) one-to-many, and 3) many-to-many relationships. Relationships between entities are often represented graphically using an entity-relationship diagram (E-R diagram). In such a diagram, each entity is represented by a box; relationships are indicated by diamonds. The following discussion and illustrations of the three types of data relationships introduce the use of the E-R model for each type of relationship.

One-to-one Relationships   Assume that a software company has four employees and four computers. (You will be introduced to this software company—Pinehill Software—throughout this chapter; an in-depth description of their database appears toward the end of the chapter.) Each computer is used by one and only one employee; each employee uses one and only one computer. A one-to-one relationship therefore exists between computers and employees.

The E-R diagram representation of the one-to-one relationship between employees and computers is drawn as in Figure 2.1. The diagram is read as:

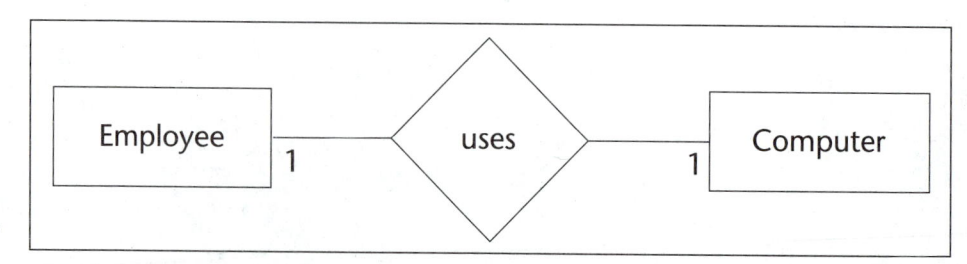

Figure 2.1
Drawing a one-to-one relationship

[Employee] —1— ⟨uses⟩ —1— [Computer]

"One employee uses no computer or one computer" or "One computer is used by no employees or one employee." Notice the small numbers that appear outside the entity boxes. These indicate the type of relationship (i.e., 1:1).

One-to-many Relationships Assume that Pinehill Software receives some computers that are prototypes of new machines that are not yet being marketed. Each new computer is assigned to one employee for testing; the employee is to use the new computer along with the computer that he or she has already been assigned to use. In this case, all computers are used by only one person, but some people use more than one computer. The presence of the new computers means that there is a one-to-many relationship between employees and computers.

This employee to computer relationship is one-to-many because it is possible for a person to use more than one computer. It does not mean that every person must use more than one computer. In fact, as long as Pinehill Software believes that a person may use more than one computer, the relationship should be generalized as one-to-many. The instances where a person uses only one computer are therefore not one-to-one relationships, but examples of a one-to-many relationship where the "many" is just one computer.

The E-R diagram for the one-to-many relationship is drawn as in Figure 2.2. It is read as "One employee uses no computers, one computer, or many computers" or "A computer can be used by no employees or one employee." The difference between this diagram and the one-to-one diagram is the M that appears next to the Computer box. This indicates the one-to-many relationship (i.e., 1:M).

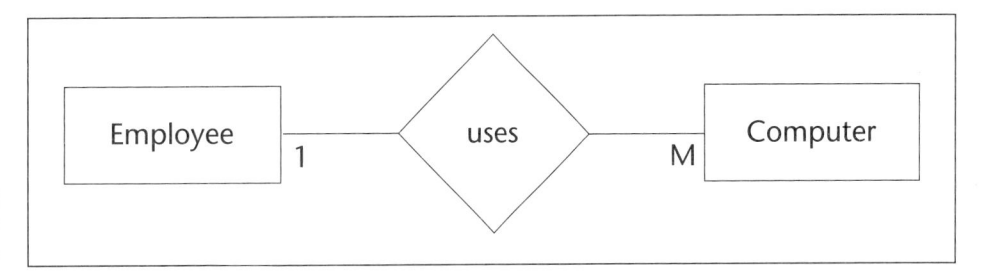

Figure 2.2
Drawing a one-to-many relationship

Many-to-many Relationships Pinehill Software purchases three new computers that will form the backbone of a local area network. These computers are shared by everyone who works for the company. In other words, many people use each computer and each computer is used by many people. This is an example of a many-to-many relationship.

The E-R diagram for the many-to-many relationship is drawn as in Figure 2.3, which is read as "One employee can use no computers, one computer, or many computers" or "A computer can be used by no employees, one employee, or many employees." The M:N next to the entity boxes represent the many-to-many relationship.

The "N" in M:N is from mathematics and represents some unknown quantity greater than or equal to zero.

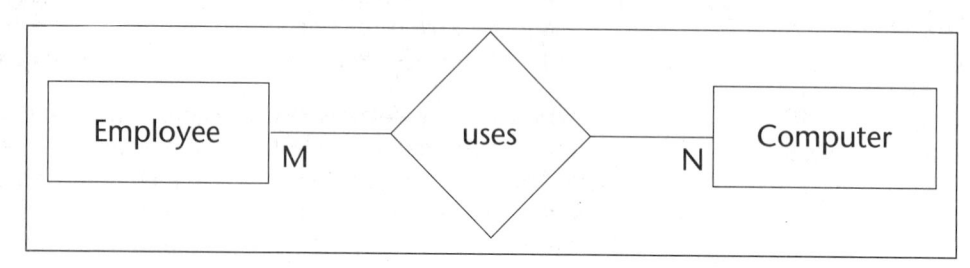

Figure 2.3
Drawing a many-to-many relationship

The Relational Data Model

The data relationships stored in a database system are expressed using one of three data models: hierarchical, network, and relational. All three are available in mainframe and minicomputer DBMSs; with only a few exceptions, microcomputer DBMSs are relational.

The *relational data model* uses only one data structure—a two-dimensional table made up of columns (*attributes*) and rows (*tuples*). This table is known as a *relation*. The term "relational" comes from mathematical set theory, where a two-dimensional table is called a relation.

> *DBMSs that use "pointers" or "links" between tables violate the fundamental principle of relational database theory. In particular, many desktop DBMSs (for example, Access, dBase, and FileMaker Pro 3.0) fall into this trap. The drawback to requiring pointers between tables is that data retrieval is limited to those predefined relationships. If a user needs a relationship that hasn't been anticipated by the database designer, then the designer must modify the database structure to include that relationship. In contrast, the relational data model is founded on the idea of ultimate flexibility, where relationships need not be defined in advance and can be used whenever needed without making any changes to the database structure. Desktop DBMSs that require predefined relationships are still DBMSs and may be very useful products; they just aren't relational.*

Relations

Although it is accurate to say that a relation is a two-dimensional table, that definition is somewhat incomplete. Relations have some characteristics that distinguish them from a rectangular area on a spreadsheet or a flat file. These characteristics begin with the following:

- Each row has a unique primary key. The *primary key* is a column or combination of columns whose values uniquely identify each row in the table. When no single column contains values unique to every row, then multiple columns are required as the primary key. A multiple-column key is known as a *concatenated key*.

Any column or set of columns that might serve as the primary key of a relation is known as a *candidate key*. When there are multiple candidate keys in a relation, you should generally choose the one that:

- requires the fewest number of columns.
- is least likely, over time, to be null. (*Null* is a value meaning "unknown." It is not the same as a zero or a blank.)
- is least likely, over time, to be duplicated.

In many cases, relations are given arbitrary unique primary keys, such as employee ID numbers and student ID numbers. These are more convenient than long concatenated keys. (Social security numbers do not necessarily make good primary keys; there is always the chance that someone may not have one.) Rules specific to primary keys are discussed in the next section of this chapter.

In addition to being required to have a unique primary key, a relation has the following characteristics:

- Each row in a relation is unique (i.e., there are no duplicate rows). Most DBMSs, including SQL-based DBMSs, do not enforce this characteristic. Database developers usually enforce unique primary keys to obtain the same result.
- Only one value is stored at the intersection of any column and row. In other words, each intersection of column and row cannot be multivalued.
- A column contains only one type of data. For example, if a column is named Salary, then it contains only the amount of money employees are paid.
- Each column has a *domain*, a statement of the permissible values for the column. A domain may be very broad (e.g., "all human names") or very narrow (e.g., "dates in the format MM/DD/YY"), depending on the type of data being stored.
- The order in which the rows in a table are viewed is unimportant. The rows may be reordered for display as needed.
- The order in which the columns in a table are viewed is unimportant. The columns may be reordered for display as needed.

Integrity Rules

One of the worst things that can happen to a database system is for "bad data" (inaccurate, inconsistent, meaningless data) to creep in. Bad data undermines the reliability of an organization's data management and consumes valuable data processing resources to correct the problem. If at all possible, an organization should prevent bad data from ever getting into a database system. The most common way of doing so is to impose a set of integrity rules, or constraints, that data must meet during data modification operations. Integrity rules can be divided into three major groups: primary key constraints, referential integrity, and domain constraints.

Primary Key Constraints

There are two primary key constraints:

- Each primary key must be unique.
- No part of a primary key may be null. This constraint is known as *entity integrity*.

The reason these constraints are important may not be obvious. First consider the issue of primary keys. Assuming that primary key values in a relation are unique, then a user can retrieve any piece of data in the database by knowing the name of the table in which it is stored, the name of its column, and the primary key of its row. If, however, primary keys are not unique, then supplying the table, column, and primary key will retrieve some row with that primary key, but not necessarily the correct row.

To see the problem with not having a unique primary key, compare Table 2.1 (the Shows table) and Table 2.2 (the Calendar table). These tables might be used in the database that Pinehill Software uses to manage its trade show activities. The Shows table describes trade shows at which Pinehill Software may choose to exhibit. Because each of these trade shows occurs many times (sometimes more than once a year), no dates are included in this table. The schedule for trade shows is stored in Calendar. This table includes the name of the show and its starting and ending dates.

Table 2.1 Shows table

S_name	Producer
PCExpo	Expo Mgmt Group
MacWorld Expo	Mitch Hall Associates
North East Business Fair	Business Fair Inc.
West Coast Business Fair	Business Fair Inc.

Table 2.2 Calendar table

S_name	Start_date	End_date
PCExpo	02/12/96	02/14/96
PCExpo	10/10/96	10/12/96
North East Business Fair	03/15/96	03/18/96
North East Business Fair	09/22/96	09/25/96
North East Business Fair	03/12/97	03/15/97
West Coast Business Fair	01/27/96	01/31/96
West Coast Business Fair	09/30/96	10/03/96
West Coast Business Fair	12/02/96	12/05/96
MacWorld Expo	01/14/96	01/17/96
MacWorld Expo	08/11/96	08/14/96
MacWorld Expo	01/13/97	01/17/97

> *NOTE: The actual design of the trade show database is slightly different from the tables that are being used as examples in the first part of this chapter. These early examples are intended only to illustrate some specific points of relational database design. You will see the design that is actually implemented a bit later in this chapter.*

Assume, for example, that the S_name column is selected as the primary key of the Calendar table. Theoretically, all that's needed to find the starting date of a trade show would be the name of the table (Calendar), the name of the column (Start_date), and the primary key of the row (some value in the S_name column). However, the Calendar table contains multiple rows for each value of S_name. For example, if a search is made using the S_name value "PCExpo," the result will be two starting dates (02/12/96 and 10/10/96). There is no way to retrieve one specific starting date.

Entity integrity is a direct corollary of the requirement for unique primary keys. Because null means "unknown," one row with a primary key of null might be permitted. However, when more than one row has a value of null anywhere within the key, then the primary key loses its property of uniqueness. It is therefore simpler to require that no part of a primary key be null.

Primary key constraints should be defined in the database structure and enforced automatically by the DBMS during data modification. As you will see early in this book, you will identify primary keys when you define the structure of your tables. Once the DBMS knows which columns comprise the primary key, you can leave enforcing of primary key constraints up to the software.

Referential Integrity

The primary key of the Shows table in Table 2.1 is S_name (the name of the show); the correct primary key for the Calendar table in Table 2.2 is S_name and Start_date (the starting date of the show). As discussed earlier, S_name is not a sufficient primary key for Calendar (each value for show name appears in more than one row). Calendar therefore requires a key whose values are found in more than one column (a *concatenated key*). The pairing of S_name with Start_date does produce unique values in every row.

The S_name column in Calendar is a foreign key. A *foreign key* is a column that is the same as the primary key of another table. Keep in mind that a foreign key may be part of the primary key of its own table, as it is in this case, or it may be a column that is not part of the primary key (a nonkey column). In this example, S_name in Calendar references S_name in Shows. The relationship is in one direction only. In other words, S_name in Shows is not a foreign key referencing S_name in Calendar.

Referential integrity is an integrity constraint that states that every nonnull foreign key must reference an existing primary key. This constraint is vital to ensuring the consistency of data through a relational database. To understand why this is so, consider what happens when referential integrity is not enforced.

Assume that a Pinehill Software employee adds rows to Calendar describing two Comdex trade shows. Calendar will then appear as it does in Table 2.3. Notice that no record for Comdex currently exists in Shows.

Shortly after adding the row to Calendar, a Pinehill Software employee would like to find the names of the producers of trade shows that will be held during

Table 2.3 Calendar table

S_name	Start_date	End_date
PCExpo	02/12/96	02/14/96
PCExpo	10/10/96	10/12/96
North East Business Fair	03/15/96	03/18/96
North East Business Fair	09/22/96	09/25/96
North East Business Fair	03/12/97	03/15/97
West Coast Business Fair	01/27/96	01/31/96
West Coast Business Fair	09/30/96	10/03/96
West Coast Business Fair	12/02/96	12/05/96
MacWorld Expo	01/14/96	01/17/96
MacWorld Expo	08/11/96	08/14/96
MacWorld Expo	01/13/97	01/17/97
Comdex	04/20/96	04/27/96
Comdex	09/16/96	09/23/96

September 1996. To perform this query, the DBMS must first select rows from Calendar where the starting date of the trade show is between 09/01/96 and 09/30/96. It must then match the show names in the selected rows with show names in Shows to identify the correct producer name.

There will be no problem in locating a producer for the North East Business Fair (starting date of 9/22/96) or the West Coast Business Fair (starting date of 9/30/96). Both of these shows have matching records in Shows. However, Shows contains no row for Comdex. The DBMS therefore cannot retrieve a name for Comdex's producer.

Because referential integrity was not enforced during data modification operations, the database is unable to provide information that Pinehill Software needs. Ideally, referential integrity should be defined within the structure of a relational database and enforced automatically by the DBMS. You will be able to do so when you create your tables, either through PowerBuilder or directly using your DBMS.

Domain Constraints

Although relational theory requires only the two primary key constraints and referential integrity, database designers often impose additional constraints to validate data. These fall into the general category of *domain constraints* because they express the permissible values for a column.

Domain constraints are most practical for columns that contain a small number of distinct values or whose values can be expressed by a range. For example, a table describing the merchandise sold by a T-shirt company would include a column named Size. The permissible sizes are S, M, L, and XL. A simple domain constraint would allow only those values, and prevent data modification if some other value was present.

Columns that contain numeric values often can be validated by using a domain constraint that restricts the permitted range of values. For example, a company that publishes a magazine might have a table containing the ending dates of current subscriptions. Assuming that no subscription is longer than three years, a domain constraint could be written to ensure that any termination date that was entered or modified was between the current year and three years hence.

When you define the columns for a table, a DBMS asks you to select a data type for each column. A data type is a broad sort of domain constraint, limiting the values in a column to, for example, text (generally any character you can type from the keyboard), numbers, dates, and times. In addition, many DBMSs and application development environments let you impose more restrictive domain constraints.

Designing Good Relations

For any given set of attributes that describes a database environment, there are many ways to group attributes into tables. Some arrangements are "better" than others because they avoid problems known as anomalies. An *anomaly* is an unexpected, and usually undesirable, property. There are three types of common anomalies that occur in tables: insertion, deletion, and modification.

Insertion Anomalies

An *insertion anomaly* occurs when the design of a table makes it impossible to insert data because you do not have data for all of the columns that are part of the table's primary key. (Remember, no part of a primary key may be null.) As an example, consider the relation in Table 2.4, drawn again from Pinehill Software's trade show database.

S_name	Start_date	End_date	Producer	P_phone
PCExpo	02/12/96	02/14/96	Expo Mgmt Group	212-555-1234
PCExpo	10/10/96	10/12/96	Expo Mgmt Group	212-555-1234
North East Business Fair	03/15/96	03/18/96	Business Fair Inc.	212-555-4567
North East Business Fair	09/22/96	09/25/96	Business Fair Inc.	212-555-4567
North East Business Fair	03/12/97	03/15/97	Business Fair Inc.	212-555-4567
West Coast Business Fair	01/27/96	01/31/96	Business Fair Inc.	212-555-4567
West Coast Business Fair	09/30/96	10/03/96	Business Fair Inc.	212-555-4567
West Coast Business Fair	12/02/96	12/05/96	Business Fair Inc.	212-555-4567
MacWorld Expo	01/14/96	01/17/96	Mitch Hall Associates	617-555-3456
MacWorld Expo	08/11/96	08/14/96	Mitch Hall Associates	617-555-3456
MacWorld Expo	01/13/97	01/17/97	Mitch Hall Associates	617-555-3456

Table 2.4 Calendar2: A table with an insertion anomaly

The primary key of this table is the show name concatenated with the starting date. That being the case, consider what happens if Pinehill Software gets a mailer from someone who is producing a new trade show. Although the trade show has a name, the dates for the first show have not been set. Unfortunately, no data can be inserted into Calendar2 about the new show. The starting date for the show is unknown (i.e., null); there is no way to provide a complete primary key for a new row. (An integrity rule that enforces entity integrity will prevent a row without both a show name and a starting date from being inserted into the table.) The inability to store data about shows without a starting date constitutes the insertion anomaly.

Deletion Anomalies

A *deletion anomaly* occurs when the deletion of data from a table causes all or part of the primary key to become null, forcing a removal of an entire row and the loss of data that should otherwise be kept. Assume that one date is established for the new trade show (ComputerFaire), as in Table 2.5.

S_name	Start_date	End_date	Producer	P_phone
PCExpo	02/12/96	02/14/96	Expo Mgmt Group	212-555-1234
PCExpo	10/10/96	10/12/96	Expo Mgmt Group	212-555-1234
North East Business Fair	03/15/96	03/18/96	Business Fair Inc.	212-555-4567
North East Business Fair	09/22/96	09/25/96	Business Fair Inc.	212-555-4567
North East Business Fair	03/12/97	03/15/97	Business Fair Inc.	212-555-4567
West Coast Business Fair	01/27/96	01/31/96	Business Fair Inc.	212-555-4567
West Coast Business Fair	09/30/96	10/03/96	Business Fair Inc.	212-555-4567
West Coast Business Fair	12/02/96	12/05/96	Business Fair Inc.	212-555-4567
MacWorld Expo	01/14/96	01/17/96	Mitch Hall Associates	617-555-3456
MacWorld Expo	08/11/96	08/14/96	Mitch Hall Associates	617-555-3456
MacWorld Expo	01/13/97	01/17/97	Mitch Hall Associates	617-555-3456
ComputerFaire	06/15/97	06/19/97	Trade Shows Inc.	415-555-0987

Table 2.5 Calendar2: A table with a deletion anomaly

Unfortunately, a month after Pinehill Software enters the new data into the Calendar2 relation, Trade Shows Inc. loses its funding and the ComputerFaire is cancelled. The Pinehill Software staff would like to remove the dates of the show. At the same time, they would like to leave the producer, its phone number, and the name of the show in the database, just in case the producer is able to reschedule the show. Unfortunately, deleting the starting date causes part of the primary key to become null; the row can no longer be left in the table. When the row is deleted, Pinehill Software loses the name of the show, the producer, and the producer's phone number. The loss of this information constitutes the deletion anomaly.

Modification Anomalies

Both of the relations in Table 2.4 and Table 2.5 suffer from *modification anomalies*. Assume, for example, that Business Fair Inc. must change its name because a trademark search revealed another corporation with the same name. Given the current design of the relation, the name of a trade show producer is repeated every time one of that producer's shows is scheduled. The modification must therefore be made more than once (in this case, six times). In this situation, where data are duplicated unnecessarily, it is possible that Business Fair Inc.'s name may be inadvertently changed in some rows, but not all. If that occurs, the database is left in an inconsistent state. The unnecessary duplication of data often leads to modification anomalies of this type.

The Cause of Most Anomalies

The cause of most anomalies can be described more precisely than simply saying that the design of a relation is poor. They are, in fact, tied directly to the special kind of relationships that exist between the attributes in a database environment. These relationships are known as functional dependencies.

A *functional dependency* is defined formally in the following manner:

"Attribute B is functionally dependent on Attribute A if, for each unique value of Attribute A, there exists only one value of Attribute B in the relation at any one time."

To help understand how this works, consider the relationship between a trade show name and its producer's name in the Shows table. Each trade show has only one producer associated with it because each trade show is produced by only one producer. In other words, the producer's name is functionally dependent on the trade show. The name of the trade show is known as a *determinant* because it has at least one other attribute dependent on it.

Functional dependency is a one-way relationship. It's not true, for example, that the trade show is functionally dependent on the producer. As you can see from the Shows table, a given producer may produce more than one trade show. In other words, a producer can be associated with more than one trade show. Therefore, no functional dependency exists.

Figure 2.4 is a bubble diagram that represents all of the functional dependencies in Table 2.4. Each attribute (column) in the table appears in its own bubble. A line is drawn from each determinant to the attributes it determines (the arrow points toward the attribute that is functionally dependent on the determinant). Concatenated determinants are grouped together behind a brace.

There are three determinants in Figure 2.4. The first is the concatenation of the show name and the starting date. For each combination of the two columns there will be only one ending date. Second, for each show name there will be only one producer and one producer's phone number. Finally, for each producer, there will be only one producer's phone number.

The anomalies arise in Calendar2 because there are determinants in the relation (S_name and Producer) that aren't the *candidate keys* (eligible to fill the role of the primary key) of the relation. The relationship between S_name and the producer and producer's phone number is a partial dependency. In other words, Producer and P_phone are dependent on part of the primary key, but not the entire primary key.

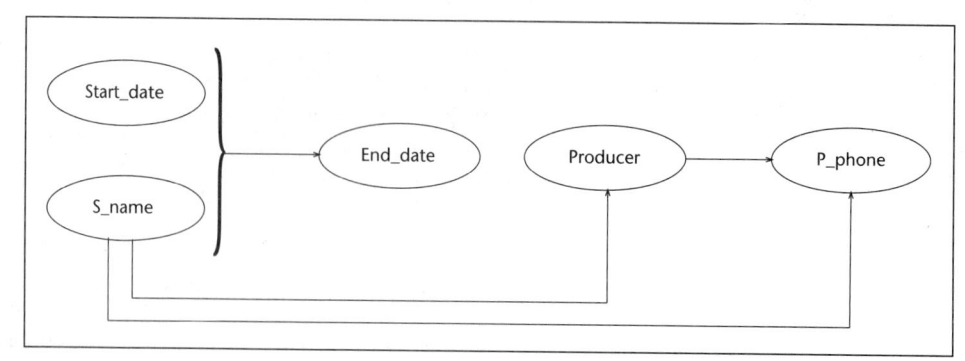

Figure 2.4
A bubble diagram for the Calendar2 relation in Table 2.4

The relationship between Producer and P_phone is called a *transitive dependency*. The term arises from the mathematical concept "if a > b and b > c then a > c." In this case, S_name determines Producer, which in turn determines P_phone. As a result, S_name determines P_phone as well. In other words, A determines B and B determines C; therefore A determines C. This transitive dependency arises because Producer, which is a determinant, isn't a candidate key for the relation.

Normalization

The solution to the problems caused by anomalies is to break the relation into a group of smaller relations (*decompose* it) so that every determinant is the primary key of its own table, effectively removing both the partial and the transitive dependencies. This process is known as *normalization*.

For the Pinehill Software trade show tables, the result would be a set of bubble dependency diagrams like those in Figure 2.5. Notice that these diagrams contain the same attributes as Figure 2.4, but that each determinant now belongs to its own diagram, along with the attributes it determines.

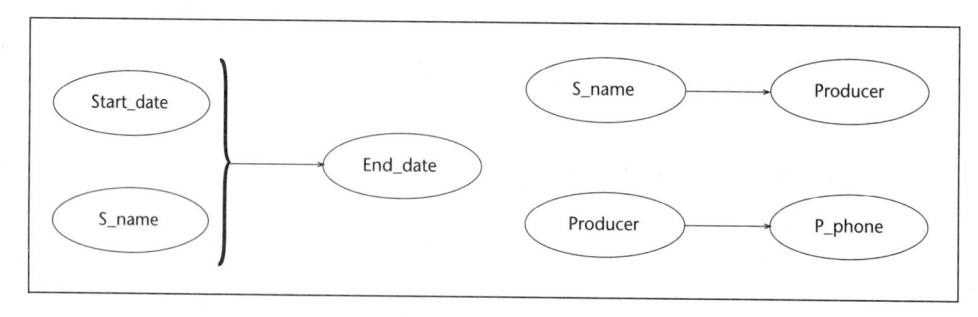

Figure 2.5
A revised set of bubble diagrams eliminating the partial and transitive dependencies

Table 2.6
Calendar table in third normal form

S_name	Start_date	End_date
PCExpo	02/12/96	02/14/96
PCExpo	10/10/96	10/12/96
North East Business Fair	03/15/96	03/18/96
North East Business Fair	09/22/96	09/25/96
North East Business Fair	03/12/97	03/15/97
West Coast Business Fair	01/27/96	01/31/96
West Coast Business Fair	09/30/96	10/03/96
West Coast Business Fair	12/02/96	12/05/96
MacWorld Expo	01/14/96	01/17/96
MacWorld Expo	08/11/96	08/14/96
MacWorld Expo	01/13/97	01/17/97

When we translate the bubble diagrams to tables, we get a relational design like that in Table 2.6, Table 2.7, and Table 2.8. If you can design your relations in this way—all nonkey attributes are functionally dependent on the *entire* primary key (no partial dependencies) and all transitive dependencies have been removed—you will avoid most design problems.

Table 2.7
Shows table in third normal form

S_name	Producer
PCExpo	Expo Mgmt Group
North East Business Fair	Business Fair Inc.
West Coast Business Fair	Business Fair Inc.
MacWorld Expo	Mitch Hall Associates

Table 2.8
Producers table in third normal form

Producer	P_phone
Expo Mgmt Group	212-555-1234
Business Fair Inc.	212-555-4567
Mitch Hall Associates	617-555-3456

Relational database theory contains a set of increasingly stringent rules called *normal forms* to which relations must conform. The higher the normal form whose rules a relation meets, the better the design of that relation is generally considered to be. There are seven normal forms, the first three of which are generally considered to be of practical use:

- First normal form: the data are expressed as a two-dimensional table with no repeating groups (in other words, only one value is stored at the intersection of each column and row).
- Second normal form: the relation is in first normal form, and all nonkey attributes are fully functionally dependent on the primary key (in other words, there are no partial dependencies).
- Third normal form: the relation is in second normal form, and there are no transitive dependencies (in other words, the only determinants are candidate keys).

Of the remaining normal forms, Boyce-Codd normal form is very similar to third normal form. It handles the special case of relations that have multiple overlapping concatenated keys. As long as all determinants are candidate keys, then the relation is in Boyce-Codd normal form.

Fourth normal form handles problems that rarely arise. Fifth normal form and Domain-Key normal form are of purely theoretical interest and are rarely used when designing production databases. The bottom line is that if you can put your database in third normal form, you will have eliminated most of the problems that arise from poor relational design.

Performing Relational Design

Despite the complicated theory, good relational database design doesn't have to be difficult. The trick is to understand the relationships between the data in the database environment. In other words, if you can identify the functional dependencies, you're 80% of the way there.

A procedure that works well for designing good relations is as follows:

1. Analyze the database environment to determine the data that must be stored in the database. It may help to create a list on paper that specifies each attribute and its meaning. (Actually, this is the hard part of database design.)
2. Identify the functional dependencies between the attributes. Express them in bubble diagrams. (This will bring you to second normal form, since you will have identified the determinants and what is dependent upon them.)
3. Examine the bubble diagrams for transitive dependencies. Where one occurs, split the diagram into two parts. Remember to keep the second determinant (for example, Producer in Figure 2.5) as part of the first diagram. (This will bring you to third normal form.)
4. Create one table for each bubble diagram. The determinant becomes the primary key; the attributes it determines become the nonkey columns.

Views

The tables that are stored on disk (the tables in which the data actually reside) are called *base tables*. However, in most business implementations, users do not work directly with those tables. Instead, they work with *views*. A view is a *virtual table* (a table that exists temporarily in main memory rather than on disk) created by executing a data retrieval request.

No data are stored in the definition of a view. Instead, the database system's data dictionary stores a data retrieval query expressed in the DBMS's query language. (See the next section of this chapter for more information about query languages.) The name of the view is used in data manipulation requests just as the name of a base table might be. Whenever the view name is invoked, the DBMS executes the stored view query and assembles the virtual table for the user. The user, however, is unaware that he or she is using a view rather than a base table.

Views are useful for two reasons. First, they are used to enforce database security. Because a view can limit the tables, columns and/or rows that a user sees, a database application developer can create views that are tailored to the access rights of a specific user. For example, all employees in an organization should probably be allowed to see the names, office locations, and office telephone extensions of other employees from the Employees table. However, most employees shouldn't see the content of that table's Salary column. The database developer prevents access to the base table and creates two views (one with just the names, office locations, and office telephone extensions and another with all the data in the table). All employees can then be given rights to the first view; only Human Resources employees receive rights to the second.

Second, a view can simplify complex queries that must be issued repeatedly. Once a complex query is developed and tested, it can be stored as a view and then executed simply by using its name. SQL queries that are candidates for storing as views include those with nested subqueries, multiple joins, or complex logical expressions in their WHERE clause.

Query Languages

To be considered fully relational, not only must a DBMS store everything in tables, but it must also have a query language. A *query language* is a syntax through which data modification and retrieval requests are communicated to the DBMS. As far as relational database theory is concerned, a query language must be able to:

- Define the structure of the database (e.g., define tables)
- Define integrity rules, including both entity and referential integrity
- Perform data modification operations on more than one row at a time
- Perform data retrieval operations
- Define views
- Define *transactions* (units of work that are submitted to the database for processing)

Data modification and retrieval must be supported both interactively and from within an application program.

Most of today's relational DBMSs, including those that can interface with PowerBuilder, support a query language called SQL (originally called "Sequel" and often still pronounced that way). SQL (Structured Query Language) has been accepted by ANSI (the American National Standards Institute) as a national standard query language for relational databases. However, it is far from perfect. Although it can be used to define tables and enforce primary key constraints, the ANSI standard does not include specifications for referential integrity verification. For that reason, many current SQL implementations do not support referential integrity. Others have added extensions to SQL to do so.

The Data Dictionary

The structure of a relational database is stored in a *data dictionary*, or catalog. The relational data model specifies that the data dictionary should be a set of tables that can be queried just like any other tables in the database.

Most relational DBMSs are data dictionary driven. This means the DBMS goes through the data dictionary before going to the base tables. For example, whenever a data manipulation request is issued, a DBMS first checks the appropriate data dictionary table to be certain that the user has been granted permission to perform the requested operation. In addition, when a request is made to add or update data, the DBMS checks the data dictionary table that stores integrity rules to determine if any primary key or foreign key integrity rules have been defined. If rules are present, the DBMS will ensure that the rules are met before data modification is performed. Remember also that views are stored in data dictionary tables. Any data manipulation request that includes a view must consult the table that stores view definitions to obtain the query that defines the view.

Pinehill Software

Beginning with Chapter 4, each chapter in this book is organized in a similar manner. The major portion of the chapter describes a related set of techniques for working with PowerBuilder. Because learning to work with computer software is nearly impossible without good examples, each technique will be illustrated with examples drawn from the data management activities of Pinehill Software.

Pinehill Software is a corporation that develops and markets microcomputer software. Its major products include a property management system and an accounting subsystem. Although the accounting system is part of the property management system, it is also sold to other software developers as a module around which they can build their own applications.

Pinehill's products target two very different markets. The property management system is aimed at real estate users. It is therefore advertised in real estate magazines and shown at real estate trade shows. The accounting subsystem is sold to a wider range of users: software developers and businesses. Marketing efforts include advertisements in the more general microcomputer magazines and appearances at microcomputer trade shows.

Trade shows are an extremely important marketing tool in the computer industry. Although trade shows do hold conference sessions with formal speakers, a large portion of the business takes place in the exhibit hall. The exhibit halls are usually divided into 8' x 10' booths. A standard booth is open at the front, draped on the back by a 6' curtain wall, and draped on the sides by 3' curtain walls. The price of the booth rental varies from one show to another, from as little as $250 to more than $2500.

However, the price of the booth itself is only a fraction of the cost of exhibiting at the trade show. Carpeting for the booth is extra, as is the cost of running electricity to the booth and installing a telephone. (A cellular phone isn't an economical alternative. Cellular phones are very costly, especially since Pinehill needs to be able to use the telephone for credit card authorizations.)

Most software companies also rent hardware (rather than bringing their own). Some also rent two or more adjacent booths to gain a larger exhibit area. In addition, booth furniture must be either rented or shipped into the exhibit hall by the exhibitor. For most major shows, labor (e.g., moving items from the shipping dock to the booth) must be performed by union workers and therefore paid for at union rates.

Aside from the cost of the booth itself, a company exhibiting at a trade show must also pay for shipping their product and product literature, transportation for booth personnel, and food and lodging for booth personnel. A company may also decide to provide giveaway items, such as pens or custom printed plastic bags, to attract people to their booth. A major show easily can cost a company anywhere between $30,000 and $150,000.

Late on a Friday afternoon in June, Pam Nathan, president of Pinehill Software, sat at her desk reviewing a report provided by Ray, the corporate accountant. The report summarized the expenses from a recent trip to exhibit at Comdex, a major microcomputer trade show. Going to the show was certainly expensive—nearly $60,000— but it wasn't simply the cost figure that was troubling. Ms. Nathan realized that she had no way of evaluating whether the trip had paid off in increased sales. Before she authorized the spending on another trade show, she wanted some mechanism in place for tracking both costs and benefits of the trade shows.

The following Monday morning, Ms. Nathan called Richard Lake, her administrative assistant, into her office. Richard was a student at a nearby college who worked 20 hours a week for Pinehill. Although he was majoring in business, his minor was Computer Information Systems. Richard was currently taking a database management course, and Ms. Nathan felt that he was well prepared to develop an application for monitoring trade show activities.

She explained to Richard the problem with trying to do cost/benefit analysis of trade show attendance without complete data. Ms. Nathan had already designed the logical structure of the database. She handed Richard a data dictionary containing the relations and notations about what the columns in the relations should contain.

Richard's assignment was to begin implementing the database. Initially, Ms. Nathan wanted him to create the relations, establish data integrity rules, define data entry forms, enter some preliminary data, and practice data retrieval. She would decide which reports would be needed at a later date. Eventually, Richard would be creating a menu-driven application that could be used by Pinehill employees without a great deal of computer experience.

Design of the Pinehill Software Trade Show Database

An entity-relationship diagram for Pinehill Software's database appears in Figure 2.6. Notice that the Show entity represents a trade show (e.g., Comdex) that is presented many times. The Scheduled Show entity (a *composite entity*, shown as a diamond within a box to indicate that it stands for the relationship between two other entities—in this case, Show and Show Location) represents a given trade show scheduled to be held on specific dates.

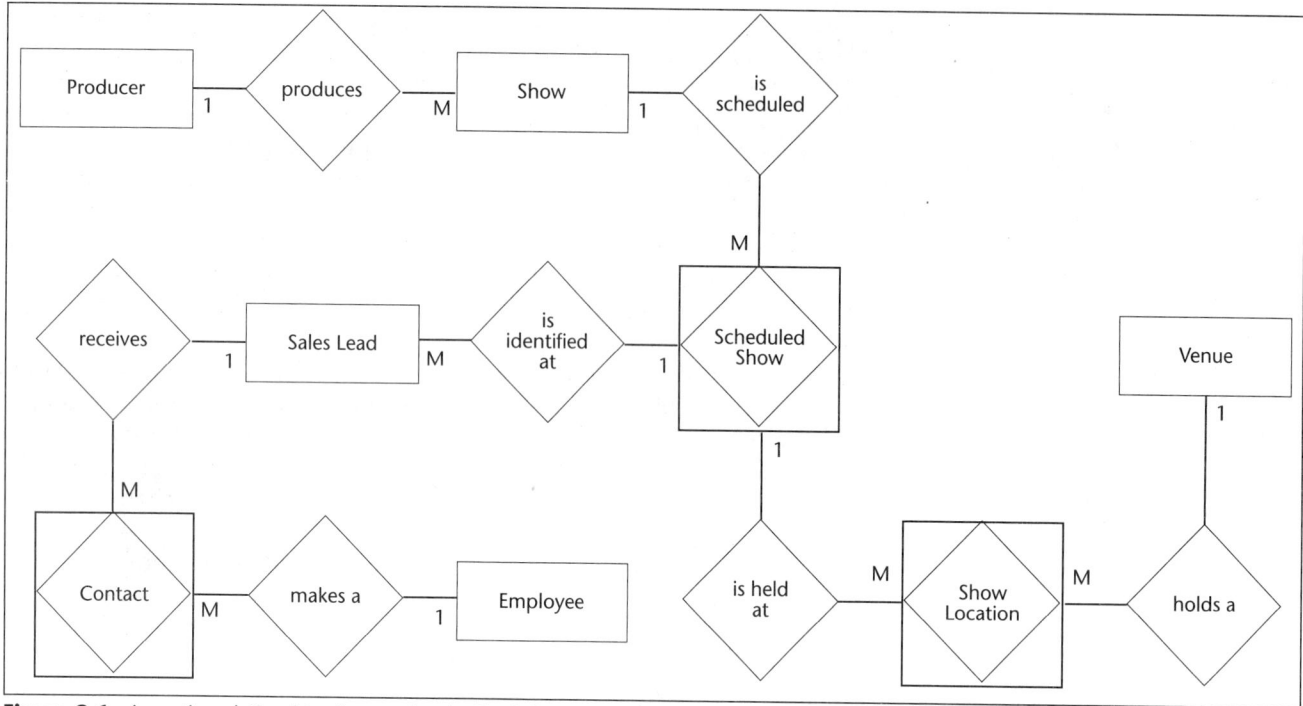

Figure 2.6 An entity relationship diagram for the Pinehill Software trade show database

Because a single show can be held at more than one location, there is a many-to-many relationship between a Scheduled Show and a Venue. This means that the database design needs another composite entity. This composite entity—Show Location—stands for the relationship between a scheduled show and a venue.

The third composite entity in the diagram is Contact. Contact represents an activity such as a telephone call or visit that a Pinehill employee makes to a sales lead. Data such as the date of the contact, the type of the contact, and the result of contact (e.g., did it generate any revenue) apply to the contact itself, not to either the employee who made the contact or the sales lead who received it.

Although this diagram contains an entity for an employee making a sales contact, Pinehill Software is not concerned with who makes specific contacts. The name of the employee is therefore not stored in the database. However, an E-R diagram represents the relationships between entities in the data environment (including the employees who make sales contacts) and does not necessarily have a one-to-one correspondence with the tables in the database design or the data items stored in those tables.

The tables that Ms. Nathan gave Richard to use for the trade show monitoring database are listed below using the notation Table_name (Column1, Column2 ...).

The functional dependencies between the attributes in each relation appear in the bubble diagram in Figure 2.7. You may wish to verify that these tables are indeed in third normal form.

CHAPTER TWO RELATIONAL DATABASE CONCEPTS 31

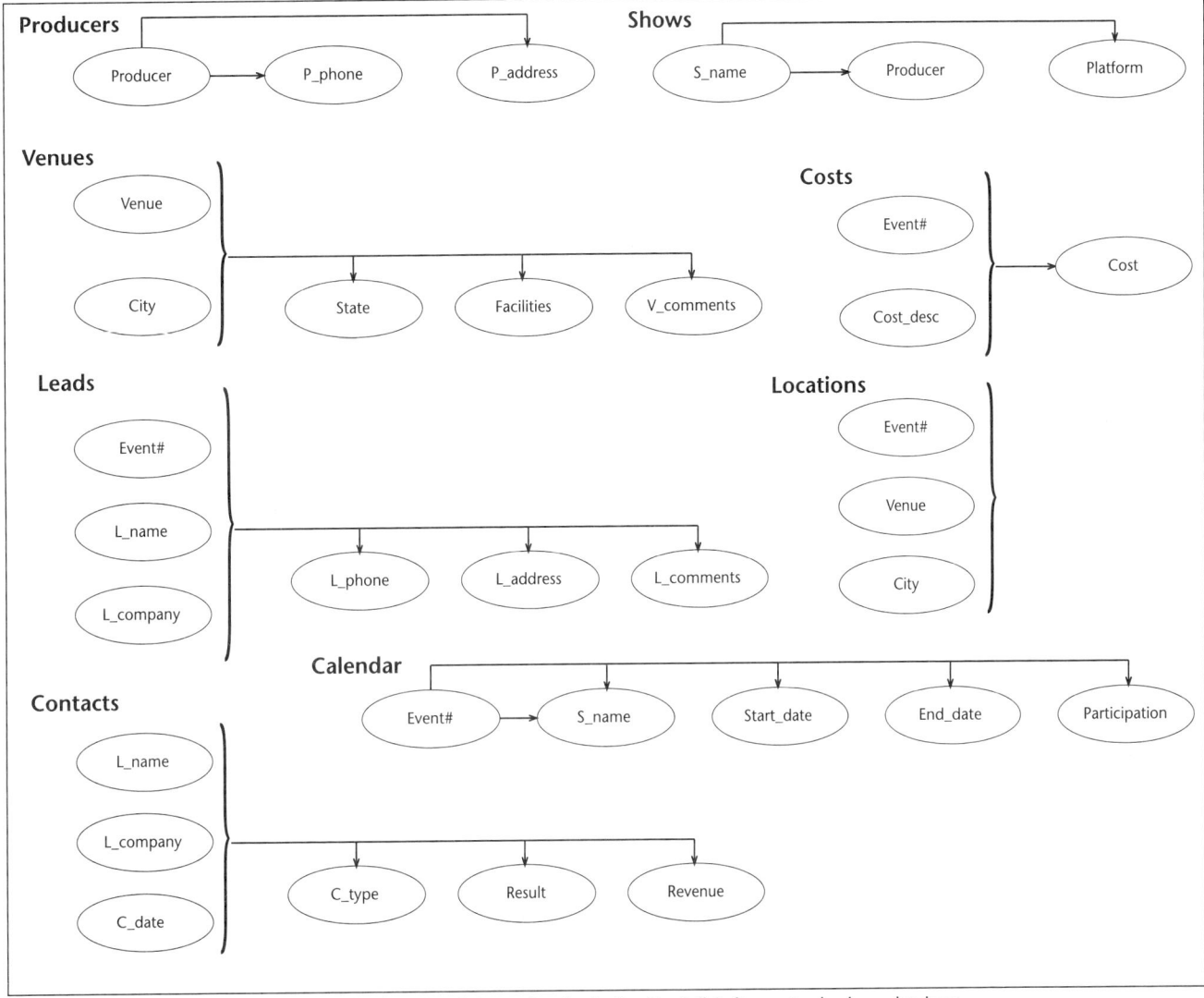

Figure 2.7 Bubble diagrams showing the functional dependencies in the Pinehill Software trade show database

- *Producers* (Producer, P_phone, P_address)
  Producer: person in charge of the trade show.
  P_phone: phone number at which a show's producer can be reached.
  P_address: address at which a show's producer can be found.

- *Shows* (S_name, Producer, Platform): descriptions of the trade shows at which Pinehill Software exhibits.
  S_name: the name of a trade show. Although show names are unique, the same show is held at varying dates and in varying locations from one year to another.
  Platform: Types of hardware featured at the trade show. There are three possible values: PC, Mac, and Both.

- *Venues* (Venue, City, State, Facilities, V_comments): descriptions of the locations where trade shows are held.
  Venue: location at which trade show exhibits are scheduled. Because many trade shows have grown so large, it is possible that a single show may use more than one location for exhibits. The names of venues are not unique between cities. For example, both New York City and Boston have World Trade Centers.
  City: city where a venue can be found. Because trade shows are held in major cities, the names of cities in which the venues are located do not duplicate.
  State: state where a venue can be found.
  Facilities: text description of the exhibition facilities available at a given venue.
  V_comments: unrestricted comments about the venue.

- *Calendar* (Event#, S_name, Start_date, End_date, Participation): names and dates of trade shows that Pinehill Software might possibly attend.
  Event#: an arbitrary, unique key that identifies a scheduled trade show. The presence of this key simplifies foreign key references to shows throughout the database.
  Start_date: starting date of a show.
  End_date: ending date of a show.
  Participation: a true/false value that indicates whether Pinehill Software attended or plans to attend a specific show.

- *Costs* (Event#, Cost_desc, Cost)
  Cost_desc: type of cost associated with exhibiting at a trade show. Trade show costs include items such as the fee for the booth on the exhibit floor, electricity at the booth, union labor, shipping for furniture used in the booth, equipment rental, and travel, lodging, and food for personnel.
  Cost: amount spent for a given type of cost.

- *Leads* (L_name, L_company, Event#, L_phone, L_address, L_comments): information taken from business cards left at a trade show booth.
  L_name: name of a person who left a business card at the booth (a "lead").
  L_company: place of employment for a lead.
  L_phone: phone number of a lead.
  L_address: address of a lead.
  L_comments: comments about a lead. Comments may include, for example, notations about the product in which a lead is most interested or what time is the best to call.

- *Contacts* (L_name, L_company, C_date, C_type, Result, Revenue): information about all contacts made with sales leads.
  C_date: date on which a lead is either contacted by a Pinehill employee or on which a lead contacts Pinehill.
  C_type: type of contact (e.g., phone call, letter).
  Result: result of the contact. The preferred result is the sale of a product.
  Revenue: amount of income from the contact.

- *Locations* (Event#, Venue, City): information about where a scheduled event is to be held.

There are six foreign keys in the Pinehill Software database:

1. Producer in the Shows table is a foreign key referencing the primary key of the Producers table.
2. S_name in the Calendar table is a foreign key referencing the primary key of the Shows table.
3. Event# in the Costs table is a foreign key referencing the primary key of the Calendar table.
4. Event# in the Locations table is a foreign key referencing the primary key of Calendar.
5. Event# in the Leads table is a foreign key referencing the primary key of Calendar.
6. Venue and City in the Locations table are a concatenated foreign key referencing the primary key of Venues.

In addition, there is one cross-reference that, while it does not strictly meet the definition of a foreign key, should be validated in the same manner to maintain data integrity:

- The concatenation of L_name and L_company in Contacts should reference one or more existing rows in Leads.

College and University Rentals

The end of each chapter in this book contains a set of exercises that will give you a chance to practice the techniques presented in the body of the chapter. The exercises involve data management for College and University Rentals, a company that rents items such as refrigerators and microwave ovens to students living in college dormitories. A description of the way in which College and University Rentals does business appears below, followed by an Exercises section, which gives you a chance to understand and develop the design of their database.

Janice Murphy and Carol Steinberg were juniors when they were fortunate enough to be assigned to their college's new dormitory in the fall of 1968. This particular dorm was organized in clusters of four bedrooms, a shared bathroom, and a shared living room with a balcony. Looking at their cluster's living room, Janice and Carol decided that something was definitely missing—a refrigerator.

Janice approached her father, who owned an appliance store, about obtaining a small refrigerator. Rather than having his daughter and her roommate spend their money on something they would probably use only for a couple of years, he offered to purchase the refrigerator and rent it to them. When Janice and Carol graduated, he would rent it to some other student. Janice and Carol accepted the offer and the refrigerator was installed in the cluster's living room.

Within a few days of its appearance, visitors to the cluster were asking its residents where they had obtained the refrigerator. As Janice and Carol listened to what their friends were saying, they realized that many people would be interested in renting refrigerators as well. Janice went back to her father, expecting him to be interested in opening a new sideline to his existing business. Stan Murphy, however, had an altogether different idea.

"Why don't you start a refrigerator rental business," he suggested. "I'll make you a loan to purchase your initial inventory. The two of you will be responsible for advertising, delivery at the start of the semester, collecting the rental fees, and pickup at the end of the semester. There's enough space in my warehouse for summer storage, if you like."

Janice and Carol were ecstatic. Neither was happy with her current part-time job; this seemed a bit riskier—a big loan was involved—but it also seemed more lucrative. The roommates agreed to Stan's proposal.

After obtaining the permission of the college housing office, Janice and Carol placed flyers advertising their refrigerator rental service in every student mailbox in their dorm. The response overwhelmed them—over 80% of the clusters wanted refrigerators. Stan placed a rush order for the appliances. Using some of the rental prepayments, Janice and Carol rented a truck and hired two of their friends to help with the deliveries. The fledgling business—named College and University Rentals—became an instant success.

For the next 15 years, Janice and Carol continued to run C&U Rentals as a sideline business, providing refrigerators to three colleges and two universities in their city. Both completed their undergraduate degrees. Janice took a full-time job as an accountant; Carol went on to graduate school, earned a Master of Library Science degree, and was working as a corporate librarian for a large pharmaceutical company.

Everything changed with the introduction of the microwave oven. Suddenly, Janice and Carol saw another product that could be rented to students. They added microwaves to their inventory and business more than doubled. With the expansion of their business, keeping other full-time jobs became impossible. Janice and Carol quit their jobs, rented office space, hired an assistant, and entered the appliance rental business with the intention of making it their careers.

Currently, C&U Rentals handles more than just refrigerators and microwave ovens. In particular, its inventory has expanded to include furniture. The target market is still students attending the more than 75 colleges and universities within a 50 mile radius of the company's warehouse.

C&U Rentals will be installing a microcomputer-based database system to manage inventory and its efforts to obtain permission to rent items to additional schools in the area. The data that will be stored in the database are:

- IC#: A unique inventory control number assigned to each appliance or piece of furniture that C&U Rentals rents. The IC# is permanently affixed to the appliance or piece of furniture in some way. The C&U Rentals staff refers to each individual appliance or piece of furniture as an "item."
- MERCH#: A code number identifying a type of merchandise. The merchandise number refers to a specific type of appliance or piece of furniture, made by one manufacturer, with one model number. C&U Rentals owns many of each type of merchandise.
- MERCH_DESC: A text description of the merchandise. For example, "mattress and boxspring" or "kitchen table and four chairs."
- MANUFACTURER: The manufacturer of a piece of merchandise.

- MODEL#: The model number assigned by the manufacturer of a piece of merchandise.
- SIZE: The size of a piece of merchandise. In terms of appliances, size is generally expressed in cubic feet. For furniture, size includes things such as the length of a couch in inches or the size of a mattress and boxspring.
- FINISH: The finish of a piece of merchandise. For appliances, the finish refers to the type of material on the exterior of the appliance and its color. For furniture, the finish may refer to the type of wood or the type of cloth in which the item is upholstered.
- WEIGHT: The shipping weight of a piece of merchandise. This is of particular importance in determining how many items can be loaded into a given truck and in determining how many people to send on a delivery.
- SEMESTER_FEE: The amount of money charged to rent a piece of merchandise for a semester.
- YEARLY_FEE: The amount of money charged to rent a piece of merchandise for an entire school year (generally less than twice the semester fee).
- INVENTORY_LEVEL: The number of items owned by C&U Rentals of a given piece of merchandise.
- AVAILABLE: The number of items in the warehouse, available for rent, of a given piece of merchandise.
- STATUS: The status of an individual item. An item may be in the warehouse, out for repair, or rented.
- CUST#: An arbitrary unique number for a customer.
- CUSTOMER: The name of a student who is responsible for an item.
- ADDRESS: The address at which an item has been placed.
- PHONE: The phone number where a customer can be reached.
- SCHOOL: The college or university that a customer attends.
- STUDENT#: A customer's student ID#. C&U Rentals requires the name of a customer's school and his or her student ID# to provide an additional way of contacting the student if problems arise with the rental.
- RENTAL_PERIOD: The period for which an item has been rented (either a semester or an academic year).
- DELIVERY_DATE: The date on which an item was delivered or is scheduled to be delivered.
- RETURN_DATE: The date on which an item was picked up or is scheduled to be picked up. For current rentals, the return date will be in the future.
- FEE_PAID: The amount of money paid for the rental. This value will be zero if the rental fee has not been paid.
- SCHOOL: The name of a college or university where C&U Rentals rents items or where the company would like to rent items.
- DORM: The name of a dormitory at a school where C&U Rentals would like to obtain permission to rent merchandise (a "possible" school) or where C&U Rentals currently rents merchandise.
- H_PHONE: The phone number of the housing office at a possible school.
- H_PERSON: The name of the individual to speak with at the housing office of a possible school.
- DORM_ADDRESS: The address of a dormitory at a current school or a possible school.
- ROOMS: Number of rooms in a dormitory.
- CONTACT_DATE: The date on which a contact is made with a possible school.

- ACTIVITY: The type of contact made with a possible school (e.g., speaking with the head of the housing office, writing a letter to the Board of Trustees).
- RESULT: The result of a contact made with a possible school.

Looking Ahead

At this point, you have read about client-server architecture and reviewed relational database design concepts. You are now ready to learn about PowerBuilder software development in Chapter 3, the final building block in the PowerBuilder application development environment. You will be introduced to the concepts of object-oriented programming and see how PowerBuilder uses those concepts. Once you've finished Chapter 3, you'll be ready to begin working with PowerBuilder.

EXERCISES

Before getting into the meat of this book, try your hand at designing a group of third normal form relations for C & U Rentals.

1. Draw bubble diagrams showing the relationships between the data items described above. These will form the columns in your tables.
2. Identify any transitive dependencies. Redraw the diagrams in which they appear, removing the transitive dependencies.
3. Write the relations in the database design. Use the notation:

    Table_name (Column1, Column2, ...)

    a. Underline the column(s) that are part of the primary key of each table. Place the primary column(s) immediately after the opening parenthesis so they are easy to identify.
    b. Place a double underline under each foreign key. Draw an arrow from the foreign key to the primary key it references.

4. Check your relations with those in Appendix D. (Appendix D contains the relations that will be used for exercises throughout the rest of this book.)

    a. Identify the differences between your design and those in the Appendix.
    b. What assumptions on your part may have been responsible for those differences? What does this tell you about the importance of "meaning" in the design of a relational database?

CHAPTER THREE

PowerBuilder Software Concepts

IN THIS CHAPTER YOU WILL:

- Read about the basic concepts behind the object-oriented software paradigm
- Learn how PowerBuilder uses the object-oriented paradigm to organize database applications
- Learn how transactions organize database application activities
- Read about the basic concepts behind the PowerSoft scripting language

Along with client-server architectures, another major theme running through today's computing is the *object-oriented paradigm*, a method of organizing the elements of an application environment. Object-oriented concepts can form the foundation of the structure of an application program, represent data relationships in a database, or be used as the basis for systems analysis.

In this chapter you will first read about some of the underlying principles of the object-oriented paradigm as it applies to application programs. You will then be introduced to the elements of that model used by PowerBuilder. (If you are familiar with an object-oriented programming language, you can just skim the first part of the chapter.) The third section of this chapter provides an introduction to database transactions and how they are used to control and organize the way an application interacts with a database. Finally, you will read about the basic concepts behind the PowerSoft scripting language.

The Object-Oriented Programming Model

When applied to programming, the object-oriented model provides an alternative to structured programming for the overall organization of a program. Languages such as C++, SmallTalk, and Eifel are designed for object-oriented software development. You may also encounter versions of Pascal and COBOL that have been augmented with object-oriented features.

Regardless of which language you use, there are a number of features of the object-oriented environment that you should expect an object-oriented development tool to support. In the first part of this chapter, we will look at those features and explore how they support the object-oriented model. In the latter part of the chapter, we'll see which features are actually used by PowerBuilder.

Classes and Objects

An object-oriented program views its environment as a collection of objects. An *object* is a data structure that contains data that describe the object along with definitions of procedures the object knows how to perform. For example, an object might be a program menu. In that case, the data that describe the object would include the menu's title, a list of the items in the menu, and the menu's status (enabled or disabled). The procedures a menu might know how to perform include drawing itself in the menu bar, dropping down to expose its items when the user places the mouse pointer in the appropriate position, and identifying the item chosen by the user.

A customer could also be an object, with data including a customer number, a name, an address, a phone number, an account number, and the amount of money owed. The things a customer object knows how to do might include listing itself in a variety of formats, identifying the amount of money owed by a customer, and identifying a customer's name and phone number.

In each of the preceding examples, a program is likely to have many objects of the same type (in other words, many menus and many customers), each with its own data and links to the procedures it knows how to perform. The pattern for the object—the data structure that describes what data an object will store and that describes the object's behaviors—is called a *class*. It often helps to think of a class as a template from which objects are stamped out.

Class Declarations The declaration of a class contains two types of elements: declarations of the variables that will hold an object's data and declarations of the member functions (or methods) that will describe the behaviors an object knows how to perform. The specific syntax of the declaration depends on the programming language being used.

Class *variables* are declared like other program variables. They are given names and data types. However, you can initialize a program variable when it is declared, you can't initialize a class variable in the class declaration. You will need to use a member function to do so.

Member functions are self-contained modules of program code that usually perform one task. Data that the function needs to perform its task are passed into the function as *parameters*. In most cases, a member function returns one value to the program element that called it.

Member functions are the same as functions in C and C++ and take the place of both procedures and functions in Pascal. There is no equivalent in COBOL, although the same effect can be gained using COBOL subroutines.

One of the most important characteristics of the object-oriented model is that data and operations on the data are stored together, rather than being separated as they are in structured programs. This provides one of the model's major benefits: When data and procedures are stored together in a self-contained module, they can be easily reused in many programs.

There is a major irony in this idea of storing data and procedures together. Although the high-level structure of the program involves combining data and procedures, the member functions themselves are written using standard structured programming techniques.

Class declarations become part of the data definitions for an object-oriented program, just like other variables, records, or structures used by the program. An object-oriented program creates objects from its classes as needed. Each object is given its own storage space in main memory, which can be referenced by the object's name (much as you use a variable) or by a pointer to that storage space.

Information Hiding

Parts of a class are *public* (accessible to other parts of the program using an object created from the class); other parts are *private* (accessible only within an object created from the class). The class's variables and member functions used only by other member functions within the class remain private. The public portion of a class usually includes the declaration of the class's member functions: the names of the functions and the parameters needed for the function to perform its task. This gives other program elements enough information to call the member functions, invoking them to act upon their objects.

Although the public portions of a class include member function declarations, the bodies of the member functions—the code that actually does the work of a function—are hidden, along with the class's variables. This characteristic of the object-oriented model (*information hiding* or *encapsulation*) provides another one of the model's major benefits: A programmer can change the body of a member function or a class's variables without affecting any program element that calls the member function.

Inheritance

Many times a program uses classes that differ only slightly. For example, a program might contain a generic menu class that includes variables for the window's title, size, and initial position on the screen. However, the program also needs to have classes for specific types of windows, such as document windows with scroll bars and close boxes, and dialog boxes with close buttons.

Rather than working with two completely different classes for document windows and dialog boxes, an object-oriented program uses three window classes: a generic window class that contains variables and member functions that can be shared by all windows, a class for document windows, and a class for dialog boxes. The document window class and the dialog box class, however, don't duplicate the window properties found in the generic window class. Instead, they *inherit* the contents of the generic window class.

Inheritance brings two major benefits to a program. First, it provides a way to organize related classes. Second, it helps avoid duplication between classes. If you can write a member function once in a base class, you may not have to rewrite it again for a class derived from that base class. This saves the programmer time and effort, as well as cutting down on duplicated code.

To better understand what inheritance means, take a look at Figure 3.1. Each box represents a class and contains the class's variables. Notice that the three classes are arranged in a hierarchy, with the document window and dialog box classes below the window class box. The window class's variables flow down the arrows to the classes below. Therefore, whenever you create an object from a class at the bottom of the hierarchy, the object has not only its own class's variables, but also the variables of the classes above it in the hierarchy.

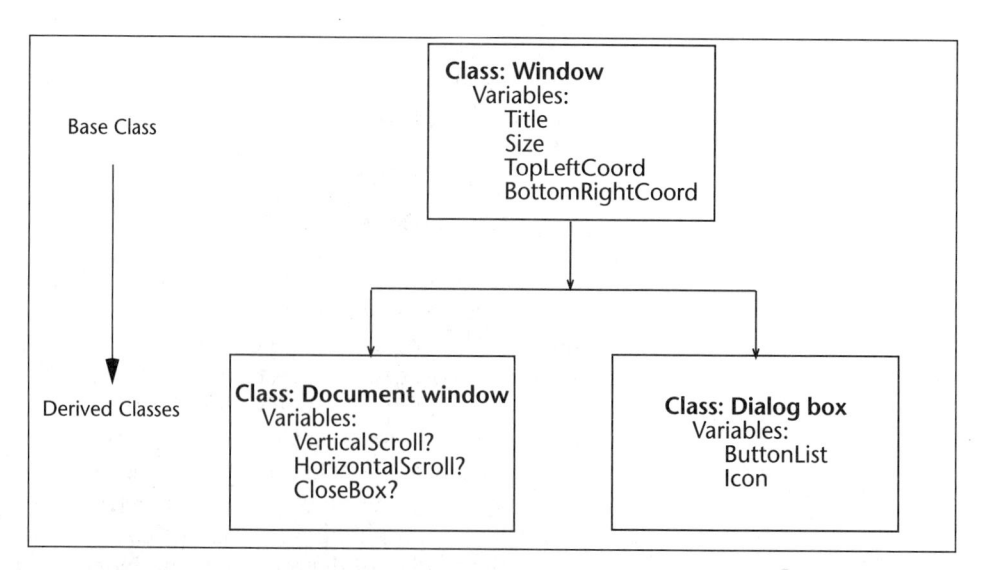

Figure 3.1
An inheritance hierarchy

Base Class

Class: Window
Variables:
Title
Size
TopLeftCoord
BottomRightCoord

Derived Classes

Class: Document window
Variables:
VerticalScroll?
HorizontalScroll?
CloseBox?

Class: Dialog box
Variables:
ButtonList
Icon

In this hierarchy, the window class is known as a *base class* because it has other classes that inherit from it. The document window class and the dialog box class are *derived classes* because they inherit from the window class.

Although it is possible to create objects from base classes, it is not uncommon to use them only for inheritance purposes, never actually using them to generate objects. This strategy forces programmers to create derived classes and therefore clarifies program structure. In other words, when a programmer is forced to derive classes, there won't be any confusion as to which objects are created directly from the base class and which are created from derived classes. Objects will therefore behave consistently, making the program easier to understand.

Member functions as well as variables are inherited. Although in most cases all variables are inherited, the rules for which member functions are inherited are somewhat complex and to some extent are dependent upon the language with which you are working.

Polymorphism

The objects manipulated by an object-oriented program communicate with each other and with other program elements by passing messages. A *message* contains the name of an object, the name of a member function to be executed, and values for the parameters required by the member function. One way an object-oriented program can help simplify a programmer's job is by creating member functions for classes in the same inheritance hierarchy that react differently when they receive the same message.

For example, consider the simple window class hierarchy we were discussing earlier. The document window and dialog box classes each have a member function that draws the window on the screen. Both functions are declared to have the same name and the same parameter list. They are therefore invoked with the same message. However, the windows produced by these functions look very different so the code in the body of the two functions must also be different. Nonetheless, as far as the programmer is concerned, using the two functions is identical.

The ability to have objects of different classes in the same inheritance hierarchy respond differently to the same message is called *polymorphism*. Polymorphism is implemented using *virtual functions*, functions that are first declared in a base class and then redefined in derived classes, which give them their distinctive bodies.

PowerBuilder and the Object-Oriented Model

PowerBuilder supports many of the object-oriented concepts about which you have been reading. Not only does it view the components of an application as objects and provide for object inheritance, but its programming language has many object-oriented characteristics. To begin the discussion, we'll be looking at how PowerBuilder stores an application and then we'll turn to the objects that form the application.

Application Libraries

The components of a PowerBuilder application are stored in one or more application libraries. An *application library* is a disk file with a *.pbl* (pronounced "pibble") extension that contains data about one or more applications. (Yes, you read the preceding correctly: An application can be spread throughout many application libraries, and at the same time an application library can contain data for many applications.) As you will see beginning in Chapter 4, the first step in working with PowerBuilder is to open an application library and an application within that library.

Application Objects

Each PowerBuilder application has one *application object* that contains data that pertain to the application as a whole, including the following:

- The application libraries in which the application is stored.
- The default fonts to be used throughout the application.
- Program modules (scripts) that are to be executed when the application is started and ended.
- Global variables, whose contents are accessible to entire application.

Window Objects

The basic object through which users interact with a PowerBuilder application is a window object. *Window objects* contain *controls*, elements that accept input from a user and present output for a user to see, such as places to enter data, places to view data, buttons, and dropdown lists. An application generally contains many window objects.

DataWindow Objects

A *DataWindow object* defines an area in which data can be displayed or modified. It can present data in a listing format or as a data entry form through which the user can manipulate one row at a time. An application will typically contain many DataWindow objects, each of which is designed to manipulate data returned by one SQL query.

DataWindow objects aren't placed directly on windows. Instead, you place a *DataWindow control* on a window object. The control acts as an interface between the user and the DataWindow. Use of the control also makes it possible to use the same DataWindow object on many different windows.

Other Types of Objects

In addition to application, window, and DataWindow objects, a PowerBuilder application uses several other objects, including the following:

- User objects: Completely configured objects stored for reuse.
- Projects: The libraries and objects in those libraries needed for an executable PowerBuilder application.
- Transaction objects: Objects used as an interface between the application and a DBMS. Transactions are discussed later in this chapter; transaction objects are covered in Chapter 9.
- Menus: The names of menus in a menu bar and the options in menus.
- Functions: Functions written by programmers and stored for reuse.
- Structures: Data structures designed by programmers and stored for reuse.

Notice that there is a single theme running through all these types of objects: An object provides an encapsulated application component that can be reused throughout multiple applications. Although PowerBuilder isn't completely object-oriented, it does support information hiding and software reuse, which are two of the major benefits of the object-oriented model.

Communicating with Objects

An object-oriented software development environment must provide some way for objects to communicate. The portion of a program that is using a given object must be able to retrieve the contents of an object's variables and change the values in an object's variables. A program must also be able to execute an object's member functions.

Accessing Object Attributes   PowerBuilder uses the term *attributes* to describe the containers for its objects' properties. For example, controls that are placed in Window objects have attributes that describe whether the control is visible or invisible, enabled or disabled.

A PowerBuilder application can change attribute contents with an assignment statement. However, because each object of the same type has attributes of the same name, an application must know exactly which object the program wants to affect. PowerBuilder therefore uses what is known in object-oriented terminology as *dot notation* to identify the object to which an attribute applies. Dot notation includes the name of the object, followed by a period, followed by the name of the attribute:

```
object_name.attribute_name
```

For example, if you wanted to enable a control (an object with which a user interacts, such as a button, check box, or scroll bar) named `cb_button` (in other words, make the button active so a user could select it), you might write:

```
cb_button.enabled = TRUE
```

Invoking Member Functions   PowerBuilder objects have many member functions. For example, a DataWindow control object can retrieve data using the `Retrieve` member function. The syntax used to execute a member function certainly varies from one language to another. Nonetheless, there is a basic format for such function calls that is shared by C, C++, and PowerBuilder's scripting language. To invoke a member function—to make it act on an object—you use dot notation: the name of the object, followed by a period, followed by the name of the function and a list of its input parameters:

```
object_name.function_name (parameter_list)
```

In the preceding example, notice that the parameter list is surrounded by parentheses. If a data window control object were named `dw_list`, for example, you could retrieve data to display in that window using the following:

```
dw_list.Retrieve()
```

You will learn a great deal about the `Retrieve` *function throughout this book. In the preceding example, it takes no parameters. However, whether parameters are required depends on the way in which the DataWindow object has been defined.*

Events and Scripts

PowerBuilder applications are controlled by modules of program code called *scripts,* which are attached to objects and controls. Each script is triggered by a specific type of application behavior, known as an *event*. Events include just about everything that happen in a PowerBuilder environment, including opening windows, making window selections, modifying data, clicking buttons, and so on.

Because scripts are attached to PowerBuilder objects and controls, the program code that controls a PowerBuilder application may look very different from other programs you may have written, in which all the code was part of a single continuous executable file. In a scripting environment, each script is self-contained and triggered not by an instruction from another module of code, but by some action the user takes.

For example, when you start a PowerBuilder application, the first event that occurs is an Open event for the application object. PowerBuilder therefore runs the script that is associated with the object's Open event, performing whatever actions the script tells the application to do.

The PowerBuilder scripting language—PowerScript—is a relatively simple language. Some basic concepts behind its syntax are covered at the end of this chapter. You will also find reference materials about the portions of the language used in this book in Appendix C.

Inheritance

PowerBuilder inheritance is somewhat more flexible than inheritance in the strictest sense. Any window or menu can inherit from (be a *descendant* of) any other object of the same type (the *ancestor*). In other words, any window can inherit from any other window; any menu can inherit from any other menu. There doesn't need to be any logical relationship between ancestor and descendent; they simply need to be the same type of object.

A descendant object inherits all of its ancestor's properties, including controls and scripts. However, once you have created the descendant object, you can change the object as needed. You can *override* an ancestor script (replacing the ancestor script with a different script) or add to the ancestor script. You can also move or change the appearance of items, and so on. You won't be able to remove any items, but there is a variety of techniques for hiding unwanted inherited elements.

The beauty of PowerBuilder inheritance is that descendant objects remain linked to their ancestor. If you make a change to the ancestor, then that change is passed down to all of the ancestor's descendants. The exception is that if you've changed an element in a descendant, that change overrides any change you make to that same element in the ancestor.

Why use inheritance? Two reasons. First, it can cut down on the amount of work you have to do by eliminating the need to create duplicates of similar objects from scratch. Second, it can make modification of objects much easier by eliminating the need to make similar modifications many times. You will be introduced to PowerBuilder inheritance in Chapter 13.

Transactions

A *transaction* is a series of data manipulation activities that are presented to a database as a unit. The entire transaction—including all modifications it makes to the database—must be completed successfully. If even one part of the transactions fails (for example, an action taken by the transaction violates an integrity constraint), then the entire transaction fails.

An example will help you understand why this "all or nothing" approach is so essential. Assume that you have the following two tables in your database:

```
Student (Student-name, Birthdate, ...)
Grades (Student-name, Course, Grading-period, Grade)
```

Notice that the Student_name column is a foreign key in the Grades table, referencing the primary key of Student. Suppose that a student named Leslie Jones changes his or her name to Leslie Smith. To maintain referential integrity, every row in the Grades table for the former Leslie Jones must changed along with the row for the student in the Student table.

The transaction that a program creates to make the needed changes to the student database first makes the change to the Student table. It then turns to the Grades table and begins by retrieving all ten rows for Leslie Jones. The transaction then attempts to update the rows, one by one. The update of the first five rows is successful. However, when the transaction attempts to update the sixth row, the power to the computer fails. If we leave the database the way it is, Leslie Smith will have lost five of his or her ten courses because the sixth through tenth courses are still under the old name.

After the failure, we are faced with a serious referential integrity problem: There is no primary key reference for those rows where the student name is Leslie Jones. Making matters worse, there is no way for the database to know what the correct value for the student name should be. The only solution is to undo the changes that have been made—restoring the database to a consistent, accurate state—and then redo the entire transaction.

This primary key/foreign key modification problem is a very good example of why you should avoid using meaningful data for primary keys. "Meaningful data" includes things such as names or codes in which meaning has been embedded. For example, there is a video store that creates customer ID numbers out of the customer's zip code, the first three letters of the last name, and a sequence number within the zip code. When a customer moves, the customer number becomes invalid, requiring a change not only to the Customer table but to the tables that store data about the customer's purchases. As you can see, you will have much less trouble with referential integrity if you never have to change primary key values.

A transaction can end in one of two ways: It can be *committed* or it can be *rolled back*. Committing a transaction makes permanent any modifications made by the transaction to the database. In contrast, rolling back a transaction undoes everything the transaction did, restoring the database to the state it was in before the transaction began. A rollback effectively eliminates any trace of the transaction's presence; the database appears as if the transaction never ran at all.

To be able to perform a rollback, a DBMS must keep track of every action taken by a transaction. This information is kept in a *before-image file*. When an application commits a transaction, the transaction's data are removed from the before-image file and the space released for use by another transaction. However, when an application rolls back a transaction, the DBMS uses the data in the before-image file to perform the transaction's actions in reverse order, thus undoing everything done by the transaction. Once the rollback is complete, the transaction is removed from the before-image file.

Traditionally, transactions have been characteristic of program-based interaction with a database. However, as you will see first-hand in Chapter 7, PowerBuilder supports transactions even when you are working interactively. Any changes that you make to a database directly through PowerBuilder—without using an application—can either be saved (committed) or discarded (rolled back).

In most cases, a DBMS does not automatically decide to commit or roll back a transactions. That decision is under user control. In other words, a user—or an application program—must explicitly issue a command to either commit or roll back.

There can be two exceptions to the rule that a DBMS doesn't roll back a transaction. If the database goes down (for example, from a power failure), the DBMS restart procedure may undo anything it finds partially done in the before-image file. In addition, a DBMS may roll back a transaction when transactions are deadlocked (unable to proceed because two or more transactions are each waiting for data to which the others have been given exclusive access).

A PowerBuilder application cannot interact with a database without a transaction. You will therefore be writing scripts that configure transaction objects and then commit a transaction or roll back a transaction.

Introducing PowerScript

This section presents some of the basic concepts behind the PowerScript scripting language (in particular, those aspects of the language that probably are different from other languages you know). A complete syntax reference can be found in Appendix C.

If you are very comfortable with programming in a structured, high-level language such as Pascal, COBOL, C, or C++, then you will find that you can pick up enough PowerScript to complete a database project just by looking at the sample scripts throughout this book. You will probably find that you need to consult Appendix C just to verify some syntax details. On the other hand, if you feel your programming skills aren't solid, you should spend some time reading Appendix C before you get to Part Three of this book.

General Statement Syntax

PowerScript statements end with a carriage return. This means that if you need to break a statement onto more than one line to keep the line from disappearing off the side of the screen, you must end each line in the statement—with the exception of the last line—with the *continuation character* (&). For example, the statement

```
MessageBox("Sample Alert","See how it works?")
```

is equivalent to

```
MessageBox ("Sample Alert", &
    "See how it works?")
```

You can actually break a literal string if you place the continuation character inside a pair of single or double quotes:

```
MessageBox ("Sample Alert", "See how &
    it works.")
```

However, you should avoid doing so because reading the code can be confusing. If you must continue a literal string, break the string into chunks that are concatenated together. Notice in the example below that the first line closes the string, uses a plus sign for concatenation, and then reopens the string on the following line:

```
MessageBox ("Sample Alert","See how " +&
    "it works.")
```

PowerScript statements are not case-sensitive. Unlike C or C++, names of tables, columns, objects, object attributes, variables, and functions can use any case. For example, PowerScript sees the following as identical:

```
MessageBox
messagebox
MESSAGEBOX
messageBox
```

Variables

Like other high-level programming languages, PowerScript supports a number of variable data types (for example, integers, long integers, and strings). However, the scope of PowerScript variables is somewhat different from that used by Pascal, C, or C++.

If you are a COBOL programmer, then you are used to working in an environment where all variables are global. In other words, all variables declared in a program's DATA DEFINITION section are available to the entire program. However, in Pascal, C, C++, and PowerScript, variables may be restricted to a portion of a program, depending on where and how the variables are defined. The portion of a program to which a variable is accessible is known as the scope of that variable.

PowerScript variables have one of the following scopes:

- Global: Global variables are accessible to the entire application. Once initialized, global variables keep their values until either the application run ends or a script assigns another value to the variable.
- Instance: By default, instance variables are accessible to all scripts attached to the same object. They are particularly useful when all the scripts used in a window object need to share a value. An instance variable is created when its object is created and initialized (for example, when the window is opened). The variable, and its value, are destroyed when the object is destroyed (for example, when the window is closed).
- Shared: Shared variables are accessible to all objects of a given type. For example, a shared variable can be declared so that all menu objects can use it. A shared variable is created and initialized when the first object of its type is created (in this example, when the first menu is displayed) and keeps its value until either it is changed by an assignment statement or the application run ends.
- Local: A local variable is accessible only within the script in which it is declared. It is created and initialized when the script is executed; it is destroyed when the script ends.

As you will see throughout this book, there are circumstances under which global variables are necessary and instance variables are desirable. However, because global, instance, and shared variables take up application memory, use them only when necessary.

Local variables are declared by including the variable declaration in a script. The other three types of variables aren't tied to a script and therefore are declared in dialog boxes designed for that purpose. You will learn how to declare them in Chapter 13.

Embedded SQL

To gain direct access to a DBMS, you can embed SQL statements in a PowerScript script. The specific syntax of an embedded SQL statement depends to some extent on the DBMS with which you are working. However, there is a general syntax issue that you should keep in mind.

Although PowerScript statements end with a carriage return and require a continuation character when split onto multiple lines, embedded SQL statements end with a semi-colon and should not use the continuation character. The following SQL statement is therefore correct:

```
SELECT employee_name
INTO :name_of_employee
FROM EMPLOYEES
WHERE employee_number = 306;
```

Looking Ahead

Until now, you have been reading about the concepts that underlie the PowerBuilder environment. Beginning in Chapter 4, you'll see how those concepts are actually used. In the next chapter, you'll learn how to enter the PowerBuilder development environment, how to open an application, and how to get PowerBuilder to recognize a database created on another computer.

EXERCISES

In these exercises you'll get a chance to explore object-oriented software concepts and to think about the implications of object-orientation on application development.

1. Compare and contrast the concept of a class with the concept of a database entity. How are they alike? How are they different?

2. List some of the benefits that scripting brings to the application development process. List some drawbacks to working with scripts instead of traditional programs.

3. Some programmers believe that it is easier to always use global variables. What is the purpose of having variables with different scopes? Why should you bother to use instance, shared, and/or local variables in a script rather than making all variables global?

4. As you read in this chapter, a database application program has control of the start and end of a transaction. Should a transaction be long or short? What is the major drawback to having very long transactions? What is the major drawback to having very short transactions?

5. List some of the advantages and disadvantages of connecting and disconnecting from a database each time an application issues a SQL statement. List some of the advantages and disadvantages of connecting once at the beginning of an application run and disconnecting once at the end of the application run.

Chapter Four

Getting Started

IN THIS CHAPTER YOU WILL:

- Create a new PowerBuilder application
- Configure PowerBuilder to recognize a database that wasn't the last database used on your computer
- Make a connection between PowerBuilder and a database so that PowerBuilder can manipulate stored data

In this chapter you will learn the basics of working with PowerBuilder applications and the databases (*data sources*) used by those application. You will learn how to launch, exit, and restart PowerBuilder as well as how to connect to databases. You will also learn how to open and create applications and application libraries.

It may seem a bit strange that we're creating applications and connecting to databases without having a broad overview of PowerBuilder first. However, you can't do anything with PowerBuilder unless you are working with an application. The tour of PowerBuilder that we're going to take in Chapter 5 also requires that you be connected to a database.

Connecting to a database can be a bit tricky if you aren't working on the same computer that was used to create a database. You will learn how to deal with this problem at the end of this chapter.

At the time this book was written, there were two versions of PowerBuilder in general use: 4.0 and 5.0. Where the two versions are the same, the screen shots you see have been taken from version 4.0. In that case, you may find some minor differences (for example, window background coloring), but the content will be the same. Where the two versions differ substantially, you will find screen shots for both versions (identified by the icons you see in the margin to the left of the paragraph) and separate instructions in the text. When there are two sets of instructions, the version 4.0 instructions always precede the version 5.0 instructions.

PowerBuilder 4.0   PowerBuilder 5.0

Launching PowerBuilder

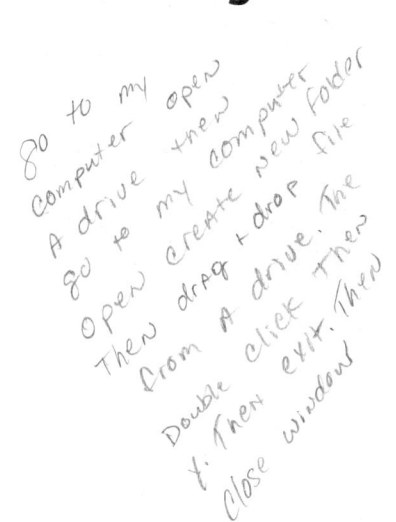

Even if all you want to do with PowerBuilder is work directly with a database—modifying its structure or directly modifying data in base tables—you must still open a PowerBuilder application library and an application stored within that library. When you launch PowerBuilder, it automatically opens the last application used. If you want to work with a different application, you will need to open it explicitly.

Opening an Application

To open a different application, you must enter the Application painter, open the application library, and then open the application from within the library.

To launch PowerBuilder and open an application:

1 Double-click the **PowerBuilder** icon to launch PowerBuilder. Wait while PowerBuilder automatically opens the last used application and database.

If PowerBuilder can't find the last used application, it will ask you to locate an application to use. In that case, PowerBuilder displays dialog boxes for choosing a library and an application. If the Select Application Library dialog box appears immediately after completing the preceding Step 1, skip directly to Step 3.

2. Click the **Application** button in the toolbar just below the menu bar to enter the Application painter (Figure 4.1). The Application painter opens.

Figure 4.1
Using the Application painter button

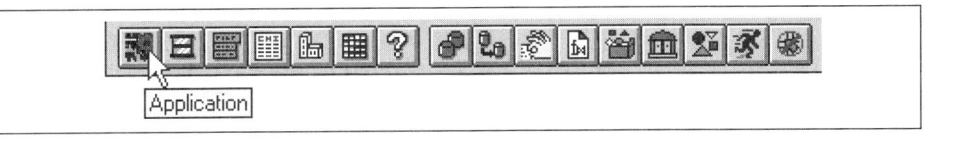

Because PowerBuilder gives you a great deal of control over the appearance and location of its toolbars, your tool bar may not look exactly like the one you see Figure 4.1. You should therefore look for a button who's icon matches the Application button in Figure 4.1, regardless of where it may appear. If you can't find the button, press Shift+F1, the keyboard shortcut for entering the Application painter.

3. Choose **File -> Open**. The Select Application Library dialog box appears (Figure 4.2). Note that the *.pbl* files you see listed at the left of the dialog box will vary, depending on what is installed on your disk.

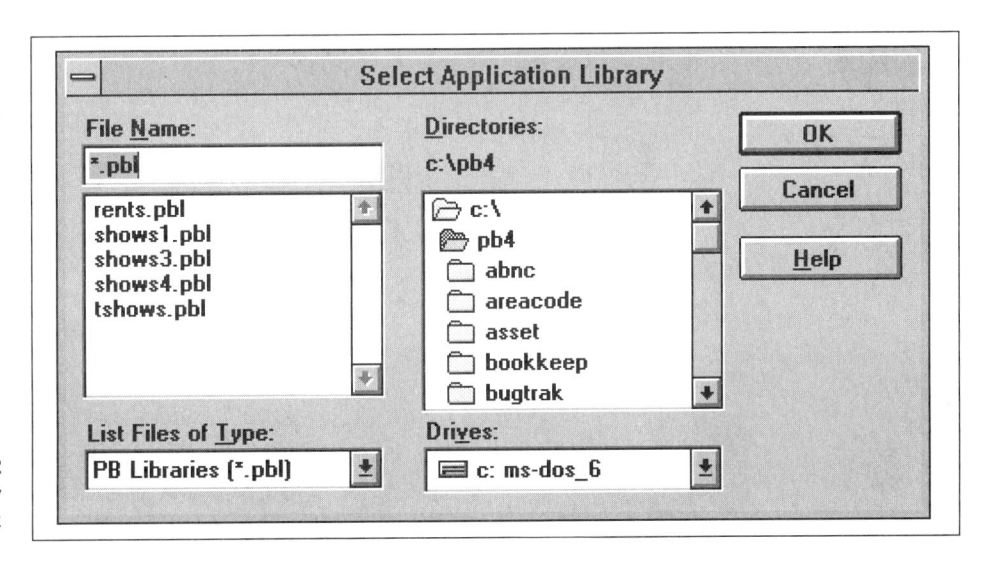

Figure 4.2
Select Application Library dialog box

4. If necessary, use the Drives list at the bottom center of the dialog box to choose the drive on which the sample files that accompany this book are stored.

5. If necessary, use the Directories list to choose the directory in which the sample files that accompany this book are stored. When you have located the correct drive and directory, the File Name list should look like Figure 4.2.

6. Double-click **tshows.pbl**. PowerBuilder opens the application library and displays the Select Application dialog box so you can choose the

application (Figure 4.3). The first application in the library is highlighted.

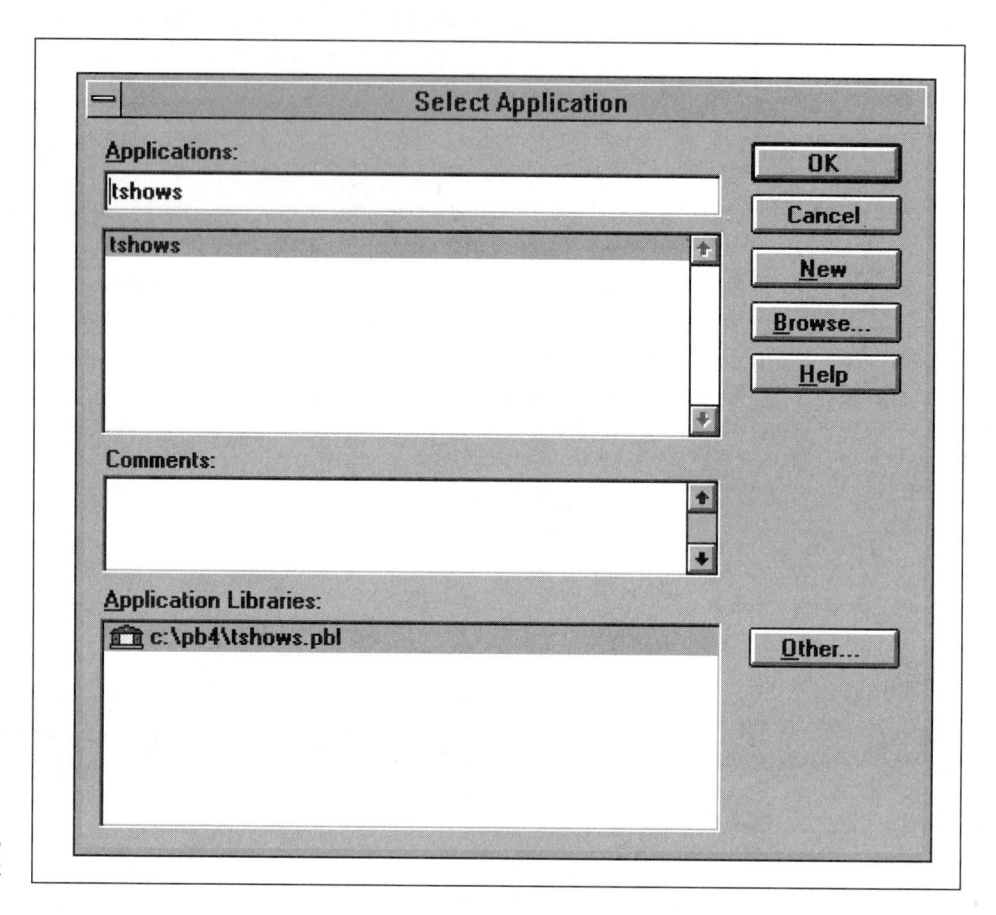

Figure 4.3
Select Application dialog box

7   Click the **OK** button or press the **Enter** key to select the *tshows* application. PowerBuilder opens the application.

Opening an application doesn't connect to the database used by the application. You must either connect to the database from the Database painter or have a script in your application that performs the connection. You'll learn how to connect later in this chapter.

Creating a New Application

Once you have an application open in the Application painter, you can create a new application. For this exercise, you will be creating an application named *shows1*, to which you will be adding tables in Chapter 6.

CHAPTER FOUR   GETTING STARTED   **55**

To create the new application:

1. If necessary, launch PowerBuilder and enter the Application painter.
2. Choose **File -> New**. The Select New Application Library dialog box appears.
3. Type **shows1.pbl** as the file name.
4. If necessary, use the Drives list to select the drive on which the new library will be stored (see Figure 4.4).

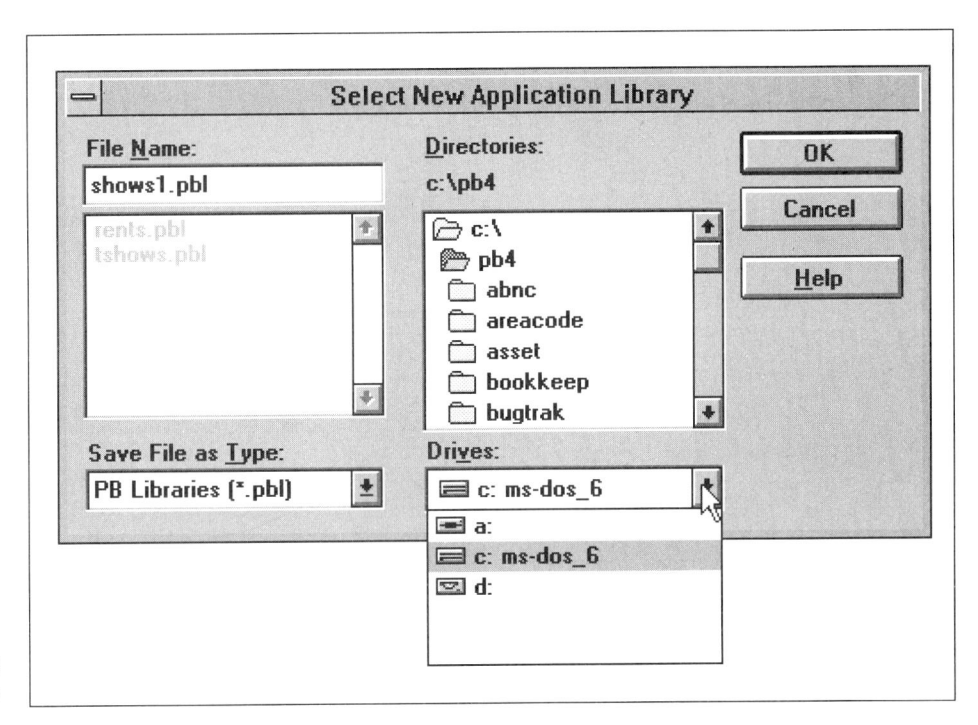

Figure 4.4
Creating a new application library

5. If necessary, use the Directories list to select the directory in which the new library will be stored.
6. Click the **OK** button. PowerBuilder displays the Save Application dialog box.
7. Type **shows1** as the name of the application.

Application names can be up to 40 characters long. They can contain letters, numbers, and some special characters (for example, the underscore (_), the dollar sign, and the pound sign).

8. Type **A first application that we'll use to learn to create a new database.** in the Comments box (see Figure 4.5 on the following page).
9. Click the **OK** button or press the **Enter** key. PowerBuilder asks whether you want an application template (Figure 4.6 on the next page).
10. Click the **No** button or press the **Enter** key. PowerBuilder creates the application and the application library. PowerBuilder also closes the

Figure 4.5
Save Application dialog box

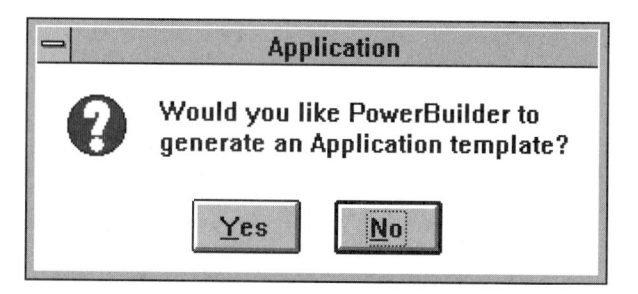

Figure 4.6
Deciding whether to create an application template

Save Application and Select New Application Library dialog boxes. The Application painter workspace displays information about the new application (Figure 4.7 on the following page).

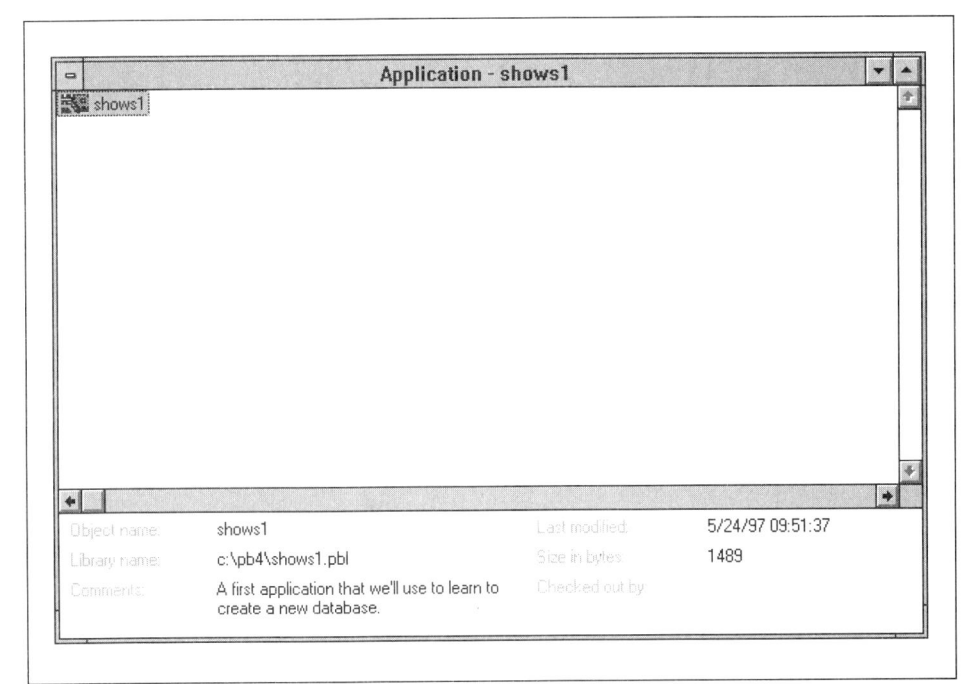

Figure 4.7
Application painter workspace for a new application

Exiting PowerBuilder

At this point, you know how to launch PowerBuilder and how to create a new application library. Although you can certainly continue working with that application, you should also know how to exit the software. This way you can stop whenever you need to without ever feeling trapped in the PowerBuilder environment.

To exit PowerBuilder under Windows 3.1, double-click the control box in the upper-left corner of the PowerBuilder window's title bar. If you are working under Windows 95 or using the Macintosh version of PowerBuilder, click the close box in the upper-left corner of the PowerBuilder window's title bar. Alternatively, choose File -> Close from the Windows menu bar.

Because the way in which you close a window varies slightly depending on the operating system with which you are working, the instructions in this book will be based on Windows 3.1. If you are using Windows 95 or the Macintosh Operating System, keep in mind that references to double clicking a window's control box mean that you should click the window's close box.

If you are storing your files on a floppy disk, leave the disk in the drive until you return to the desktop. PowerBuilder must close files as it exits. Therefore, if you remove the disk too soon, you run the risk of damaging your files and preventing PowerBuilder from returning to the operating system. If you are working in a lab and want to be to kind the next person who uses the copy of PowerBuilder you are exiting, connect to a database on the computer's hard disk (for example, the PowerBuilder demo database) before returning to the desktop.

You can exit PowerBuilder at any time. If there are any unsaved changes in your work, PowerBuilder will ask you if you want to save them. Although the tutorials in this book rarely explicitly instruct you to exit PowerBuilder, you can also safely do so at the end of any group of numbered steps.

Connecting to a Database

When you run a PowerBuilder application, an application script takes care of connecting to the database. However, if you want to work directly with the database—to modify data or to add tables, indexes, or views— or create portions of an application that need access to a database, you must connect manually. Nonetheless, regardless of how you connect, PowerBuilder must be able to find a database profile for your database. A *database profile* contains three elements needed to complete the connection: the path name of the database file, the user name, and the password. PowerBuilder also keeps track of the databases about which it knows in its *PB.INI* file.

To be completely accurate, when you work on a part of an application that requires database access, PowerBuilder connects automatically to the last database used. However, if that database doesn't happen to be the one you want, you must connect to the correct database manually.

If you have used a database with a particular copy of PowerBuilder in the past, then PowerBuilder will have both a database profile and an entry in *PB.INI* for the database and be able to connect without a problem. However, if you are using a copy of PowerBuilder that you haven't used before, then there are some steps you must take so that PowerBuilder can access the database. Because the sample databases that accompany this book were created on a computer other than the one you're using, you must use this procedure at least the first time you work with each database. If you always work on the same computer, then you need only to do it once for each database. However, if you are working in a lab where you can't count on using the same computer each time, then you must use this procedure each time you sit down to work with PowerBuilder.

In addition to *PB.INI*, PowerBuilder uses two other files to manage connections to ODBC databases: *ODBC.INI* and *ODBCINST.INI*. *ODBCINST.INI* contains a list of the ODBC drivers installed in the /SYSTEM directory, including the full path name of each driver. *ODBC.INI* contains information about all the data sources known to PowerBuilder.

PB.INI, ODBC.INI, and ODBCINST.INI are text files that can be viewed and edited by any text editor. However, you should avoid the temptation to modify those files. The result could be inaccessible databases or a copy of PowerBuilder that doesn't work. You'll then need to reinstall PowerBuilder and reconfigure ODBC for every database you need to use.

The basic strategy for getting PowerBuilder to recognize a new database is to configure an ODBC driver for the database, at the same time creating a database profile for the database and writing an entry for it in *PB.INI* and modifying *ODBC.INI* and *ODBCINST.INI* as needed. Once the database profile is available, you can connect manually to the database or run an application that connects to the database.

Configuring the ODBC Driver

To configure an ODBC driver for a database and then connect to that database:

1. If necessary, launch PowerBuilder choose an application library and application. (Any one will do.)
2. Click the **Database** button in the toolbar below the menu bar to switch to the Database painter (Figure 4.8). PowerBuilder opens the Database painter and attempts to connect to the last used database (the "current" database in *PB.INI*).

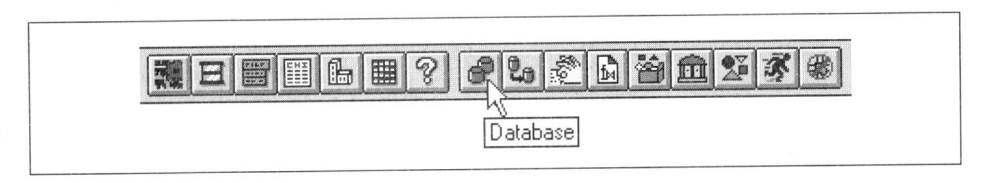

Figure 4.8
Entering the Database painter

If you can't find the Database painter button, press Shift+F7, the Database painter's shortcut key.

If PowerBuilder can't find the last used database, it displays a sequence of error messages. Exactly which messages you see depends on where the last used database was stored. For example, if the last used database was stored on a floppy disk and no disk is present in the disk drive, you may first see the error message in Figure 4.9. Clicking the OK button to dismiss the error message brings up a second error message (Figure 4.10 on page 60). Alternatively, you may see the fairly common "Unable to connect" message in Figure 4.11 on page 60.

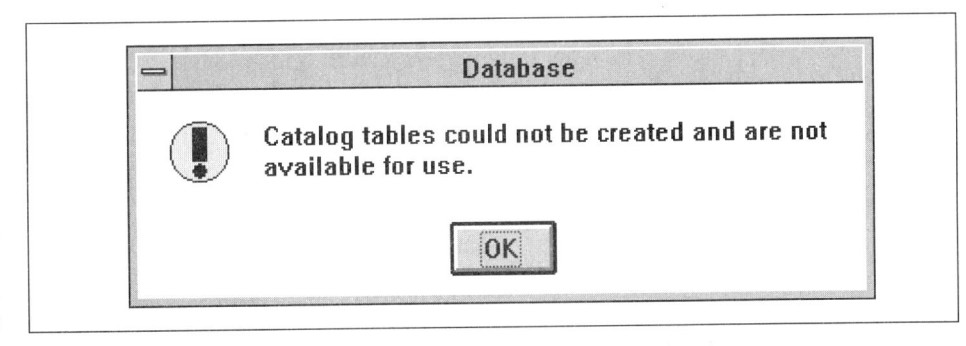

Figure 4.9
The first error message generated when PowerBuilder cannot find a floppy disk

Because there are so many possible places that the last used database could be stored, there is no way to be certain exactly what error message PowerBuilder will show you if it can't connect automatically. Therefore, you should simply dismiss any error messages that appear by clicking on the OK button in the message's dialog box. Then you must connect to some database that

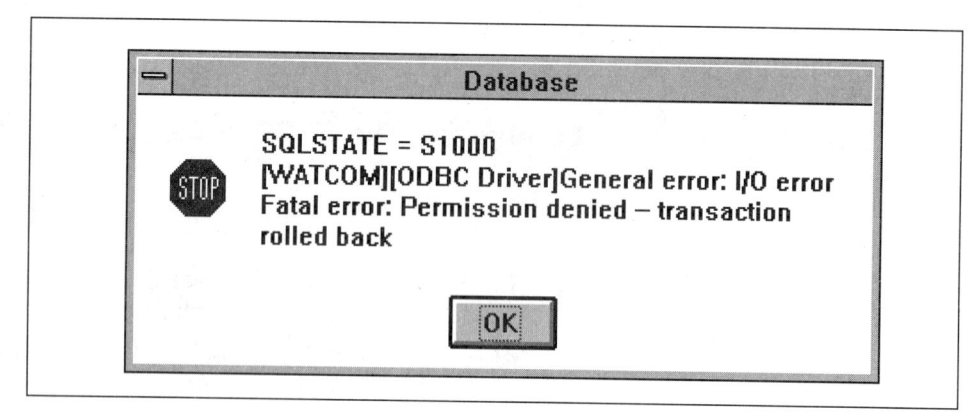

Figure 4.10
The second error message generated when PowerBuilder cannot find a floppy disk

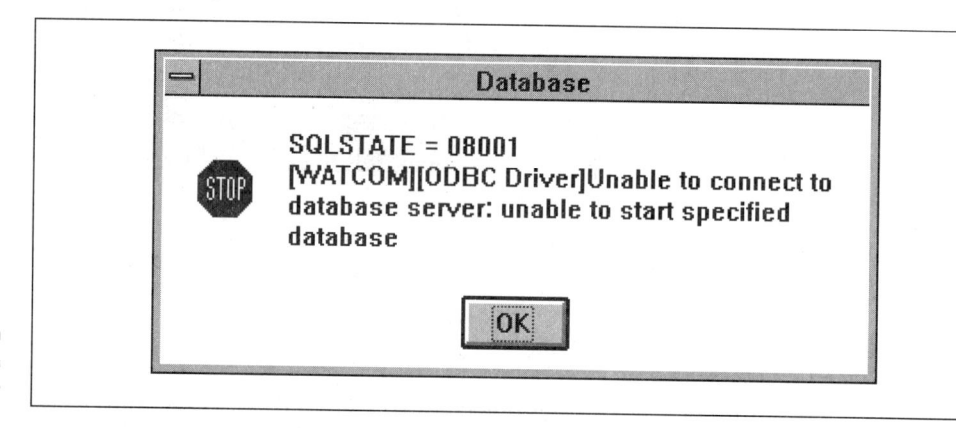

> **Database**
>
> SQLSTATE = S1000
> [WATCOM][ODBC Driver]General error: I/O error Fatal error: Permission denied – transaction rolled back

Figure 4.11
The error message that appears when PowerBuilder cannot connect to a database

> **Database**
>
> SQLSTATE = 08001
> [WATCOM][ODBC Driver]Unable to connect to database server: unable to start specified database

PowerBuilder can find. (You must either be connected to *something* or create a new database before you can do any work in the Database painter.)

For this exercise, you will connect to the PowerBuilder Demo DB, which is installed when PowerBuilder is installed:

3 Choose **File** -> **Connect** -> **Powersoft Demo DB**.

The method you just used to connect to the Powersoft Demo DB can be used to connect to any database for which a database profile and an entry in the PB.INI file exists.

4 Choose **File** -> **Configure ODBC**. The Configure ODBC dialog box appears (Figure 4.12 on the following page). PowerBuilder lists all ODBC drivers installed in the Installed Drivers list. If WatcomSQL 4.0 (used by PowerBuilder 4.0) or SQL Anywhere (used by PowerBuilder 5.0) is the only installed driver, it will be highlighted.

When Powersoft released PowerBuilder 5.0, Watcom SQL was renamed SQL Anywhere. SQL Anywhere is therefore an upgraded version of Watcom SQL 4.0.

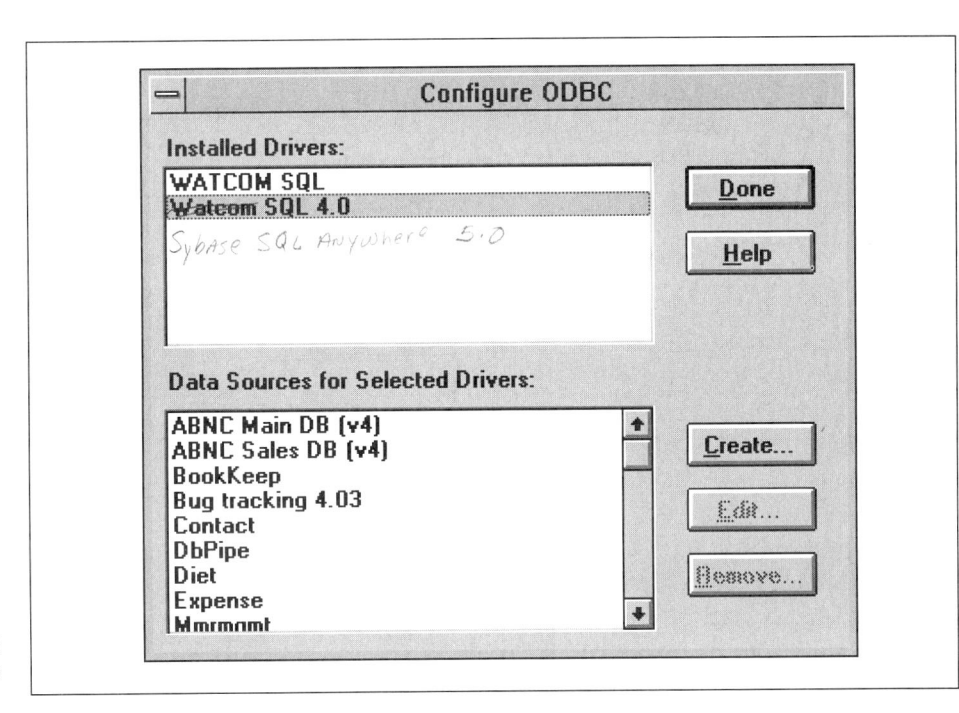

Figure 4.12
Configure ODBC dialog box

[Configure ODBC dialog box showing Installed Drivers: WATCOM SQL, Watcom SQL 4.0, with handwritten annotation "Sybase SQL Anywhere 5.0". Data Sources for Selected Drivers: ABNC Main DB (v4), ABNC Sales DB (v4), BookKeep, Bug tracking 4.03, Contact, DbPipe, Diet, Expense, Mgrmgmt. Buttons: Done, Help, Create, Edit, Remove.]

5   If necessary, click on the name of the DBMS you are using (Watcom SQL 4.0 or SQL Anywhere) in the Installed Drivers list to highlight it.

6   Click the **Create** button. A dialog box for configuring a driver for your particular DBMS appears. If you are using Watcom SQL, you will see the Watcom SQL ODBC Configuration dialog box in Figure 4.13 on page 62. If you are using SQL Anywhere, you will see Figure 4.14 on page 63.

7   Click the **Browse** button. The Select Database dialog box appears (Figure 4.15). A list of database files (files with a *.db* extension) appears in the File Name list at the left of the window.

8   If necessary, use the Drives list to select the drive on which the database is stored.

9   If necessary use the Directories list to select the directory in which the database is stored.

10   Click **tshows.db** to select the name of the database.

11   Click the **OK** button. PowerBuilder closes the Select Database dialog box and fills in the name of the database.

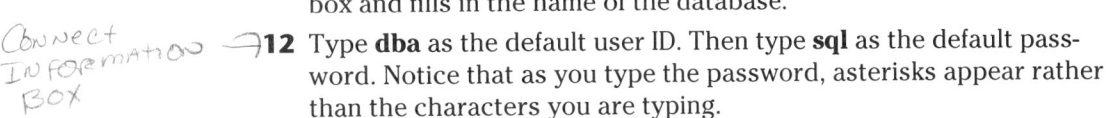

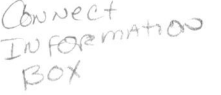

[handwritten: Connect Information Box]

12   Type **dba** as the default user ID. Then type **sql** as the default password. Notice that as you type the password, asterisks appear rather than the characters you are typing.

> **WARNING**
> *PowerBuilder uses the user ID and password in the database profile to connect to the database. If you have forgotten either one, you will be unable to configure PowerBuilder to access your database. For the purposes of this book, you should therefore always use "dba" as the user name and "sql" as the password. This will avoid the problem of a database becoming inaccessible.*

62 CHAPTER FOUR GETTING STARTED

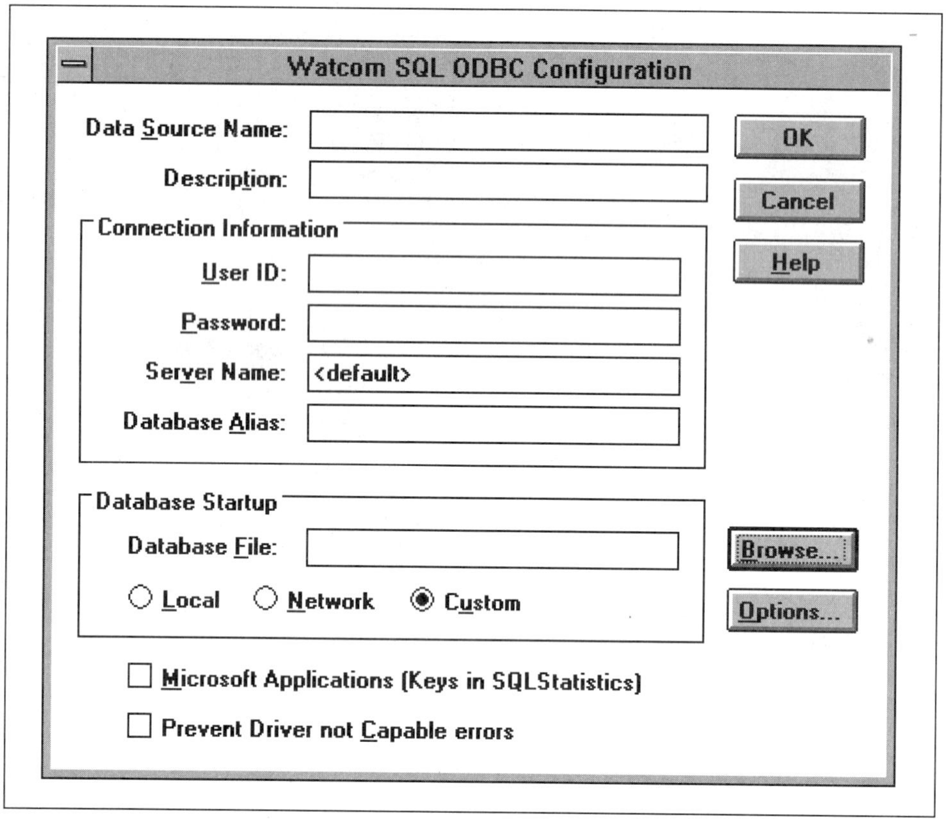

Figure 4.13
Watcom SQL ODBC Configuration dialog box (4.0)

13 Click the **OK** button. PowerBuilder closes the dialog box, creates a database profile for the database, and writes information about it to *PB.INI*.

Now that PowerBuilder has a database profile for the database and an appropriate entry in *PB.INI*, you can connect to the database.

14 Choose **File** -> **Connect** -> **tshows**. PowerBuilder connects to the database and presents you with a list of tables in the database (Figure 4.16 on page 64).

15 Click each of the table names one at a time so that all are highlighted.

16 Click the **Open** button. PowerBuilder closes the database and opens the tables in the Database painter.

You can open tables one at a time by double-clicking on table names. When all tables are opened, PowerBuilder automatically closes the Select Tables dialog box. If you don't want to open all the tables, you can use the Cancel button or the dialog box's control box at any time.

You don't necessarily have to open any tables to work with the Database painter. If you are creating a new database, for example, you can simply click the Cancel button or use the control box to dismiss the Select Tables dialog box without ever selecting a table.

Figure 4.14
The Watcom SQL ODBC Configuration dialog box (5.0)

Figure 4.15
The Select Database dialog box

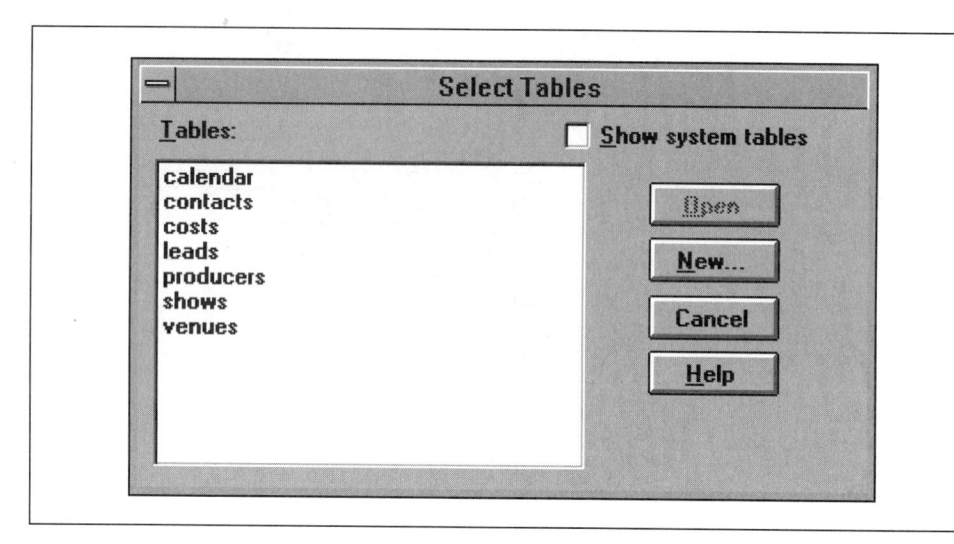

Figure 4.16
The Select Tables dialog box

Looking Ahead

Now that you can enter and exit the PowerBuilder development environment, you're ready to take a look at exactly what a PowerBuilder application can do. Therefore, in Chapter 5 you'll take a tour of the completed trade show application. This will help you see what you can expect a PowerBuilder application to be able to do.

EXERCISES

You will be using two versions of the College and University Rentals database for the tutorial exercises in this book (*rents* and *curents*). Each is accompanied by an application (*rents.pbl* and *curents.pbl*). Configure ODBC for both databases. These exercises will make sure that you can open the applications and connect to the databases.

The following hints should help you along:

- Open the application first.
- Enter the Database painter. Let PowerBuilder connect to whichever database was last used. If PowerBuilder can't find the last used database, select the PowerBuilder demo database.
- Once PowerBuilder is connected to an existing database, you can begin configuring ODBC for the new database.
- Use the Configure ODBC dialog box's Browse button to help you locate the database for which you are creating a database profile.
- Use "dba" as the default user ID and "sql" as the default password.

1. Configure ODBC for the *rent* database. Connect to the database. What tables are part of this database? (*Hint*: You'll find them listed in the Select Tables dialog box, which appears when you connect to the database.)

2. Configure ODBC for the *curents* database. Connect to the database. What tables are part of this database?

CHAPTER FIVE

Introducing PowerBuilder

IN THIS CHAPTER YOU WILL:

- Navigate through the PowerBuilder development environment
- Learn about the elements of a PowerBuilder application

In this chapter you'll get your first look at the environment that PowerBuilder provides for its users. This overview is intended to give you a broad picture of how PowerBuilder's tools are organized. In addition, you'll take a tour of a completed PowerBuilder application to get a feeling for the user interface elements that you will be able to create when you've finished working through the tutorials in this book.

If you find yourself suffering from "icon overload" as you read, don't worry; it's a common problem for people starting out with PowerBuilder. Although PowerBuilder uses hundreds of icons, you'll find that you will soon be able to focus on those that you need to use frequently and tune out those that you don't need at all. In fact, once you decide which buttons you really need, you can customize the toolbars to remove buttons you don't need and leave just those you want to keep handy.

Viewing a Working Application

To get started, let's first take a look at a working PowerBuilder application. This will give you an overview of what you can expect to be able to do on your own when you've finished working through the tutorials in this book.

To tour a PowerBuilder application:

1 Launch PowerBuilder.

2 Open the *tcomp* application library (*tcomp.pbl*) and choose the *tshows* application. This is a complete, working version of the Pinehill Software trade show database.

You will be building most of this application throughout this book. You are welcome to use the look and feel of the completed version as a guide, but don't feel constrained by it. There are certainly many ways to present a clear and understandable interface to users; this sample is by no means the only way to design the components of this application. In fact, database application programmers differ considerably in what they believe to be an effective user interface. Although there are some major guidelines to which you will be introduced throughout this book, interface design is to some extent a matter of personal choice and esthetics.

3 Using the technique you learned in Chapter 4, configure ODBC to recognize the *tcomp* database.

4 Click the **Run** button in the toolbar below the menu bar (Figure 5.1 on page 67). PowerBuilder runs the *tcomp* application, displaying the opening screen in Figure 5.2 on page 67.

If you can't find the Run button, choose File -> Run or press Ctrl+R.

5 Choose **Costs** -> **Costs for One Show** from the opening screen's menu bar, as in Figure 5.3 on page 67. A window appears from which you can choose the show whose costs you want to see (Figure 5.4 on page 68).

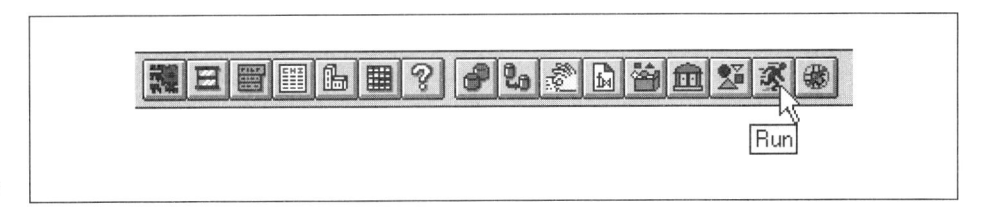

Figure 5.1
Run button

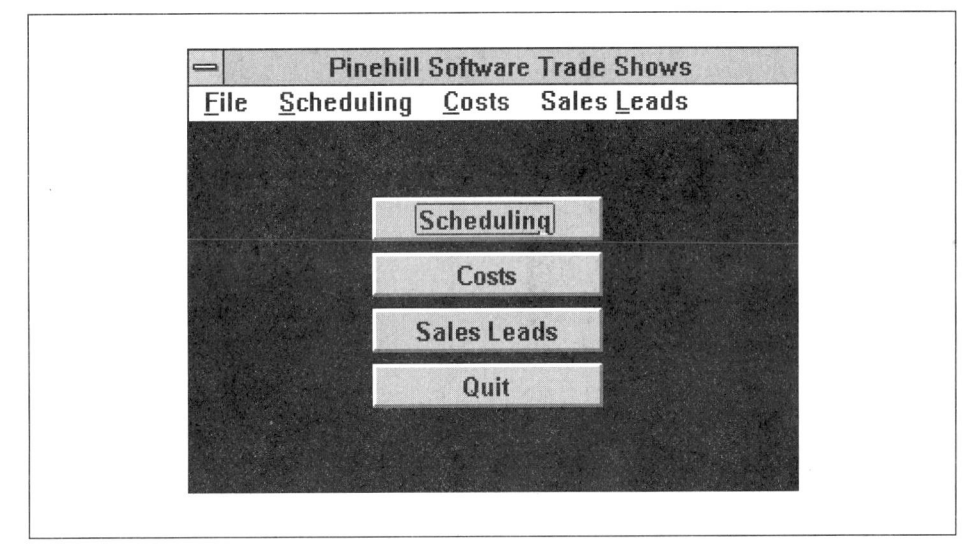

Figure 5.2
The trade show application's opening screen

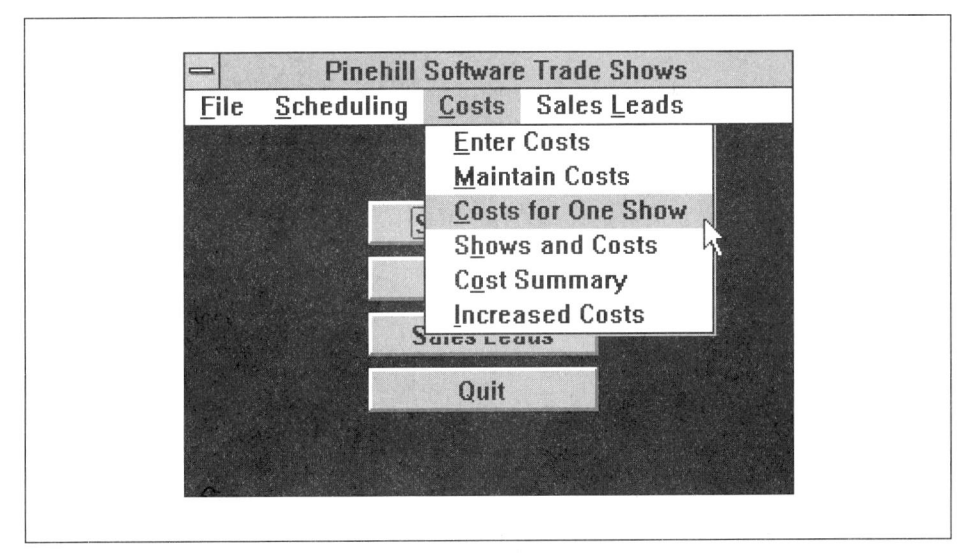

Figure 5.3
Making a choice from a PowerBuilder application's menu

The first show in the list of scheduled shows is already highlighted. This is the show for which you want to see costs.

6 Click the **OK** button. The Choose Show window disappears and the window listing the costs for the chosen show appears (Figure 5.5 on page 68).

7 Scroll down the listing until you can see the total costs at the bottom.

68 CHAPTER FIVE INTRODUCING POWERBUILDER

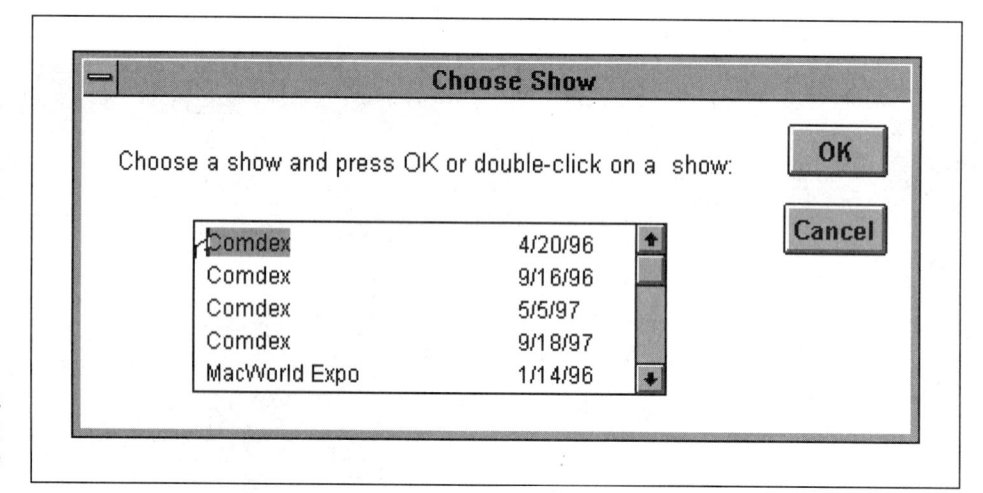

Figure 5.4
Choosing a show whose costs you want to see

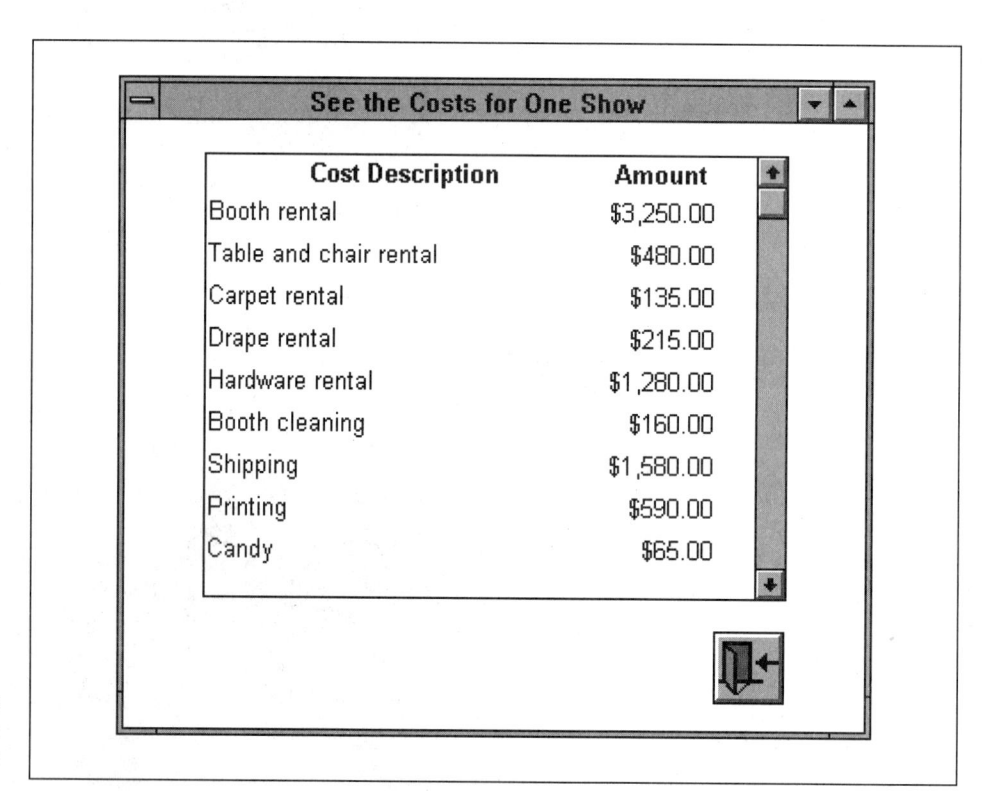

Choose Show	
Choose a show and press OK or double-click on a show:	OK / Cancel
Comdex	4/20/96
Comdex	9/16/96
Comdex	5/5/97
Comdex	9/18/97
MacWorld Expo	1/14/96

Figure 5.5
Viewing the costs to attend a trade show

See the Costs for One Show

Cost Description	Amount
Booth rental	$3,250.00
Table and chair rental	$480.00
Carpet rental	$135.00
Drape rental	$215.00
Hardware rental	$1,280.00
Booth cleaning	$160.00
Shipping	$1,580.00
Printing	$590.00
Candy	$65.00

8 Click the button with a picture of a closing door in the lower-right corner of the window. This closes the window and makes the opening screen visible again.

9 Click the **Scheduling** button. A window containing a button menu of scheduling functions appears (Figure 5.6 on page 69). Using a series of windows containing buttons is an alternative to using a cascading menu, such as that in Figure 5.7 on page 69.

10 Click the **Calendar** button. A window containing a button menu of functions related to the schedule of trade shows appears (Figure 5.8 on page 69).

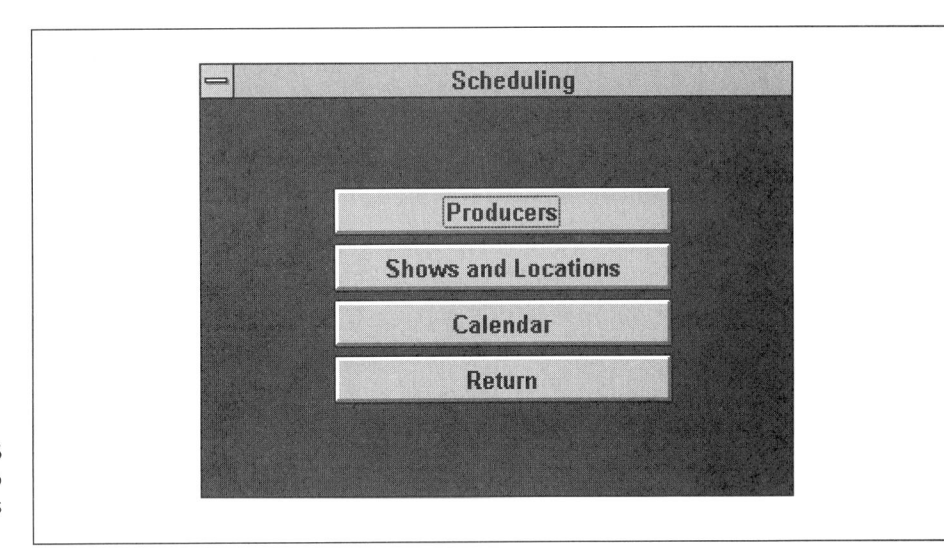

Figure 5.6
A button menu providing access to scheduling functions

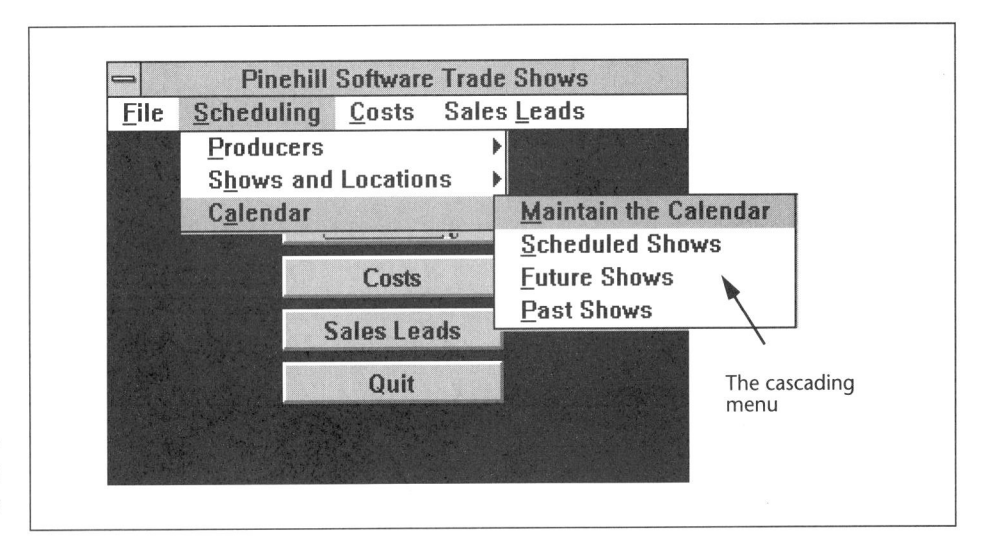

Figure 5.7
Cascading menu with related functions

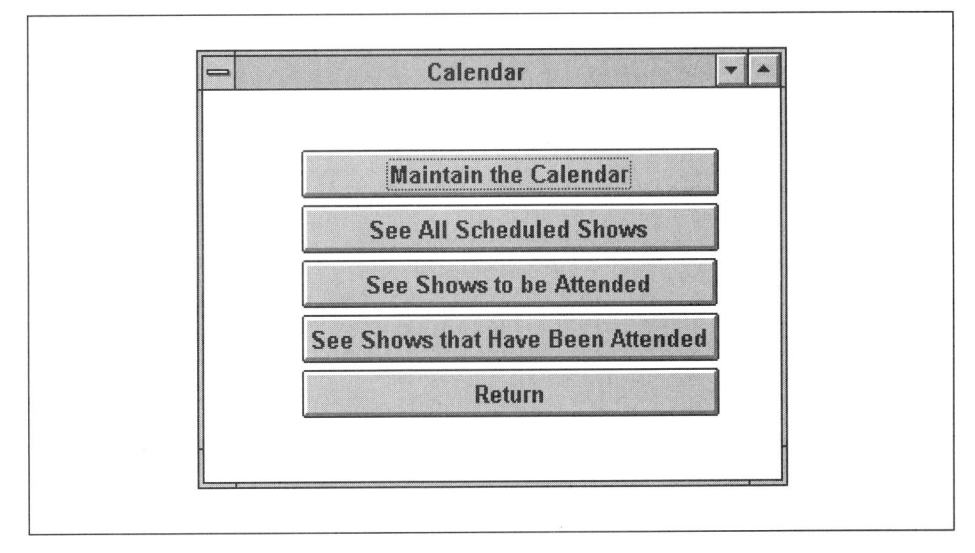

The cascading menu

Figure 5.8
A button submenu of functions related to the calendar of trade shows

11 Click the **See All Scheduled Shows** button. A window for entering dates appears. The values collected by this window will be used to restrict the rows that appear in the report.

12 Type **1/1/96**, press the Tab key, then type **12/31/96**. Your window should now look like Figure 5.9.

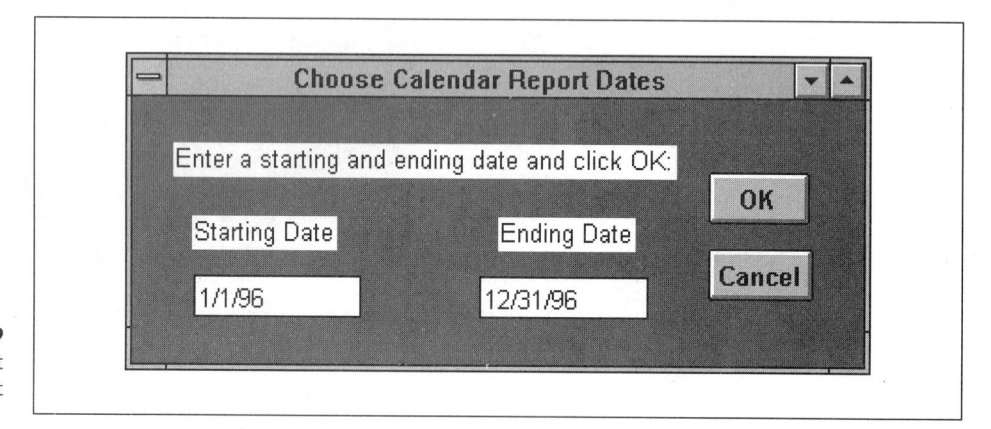

Figure 5.9
Entering a range of dates to restrict rows that appear in a report

13 Click the **OK** button. A listing of shows scheduled within the range of dates you entered appears (Figure 5.10).

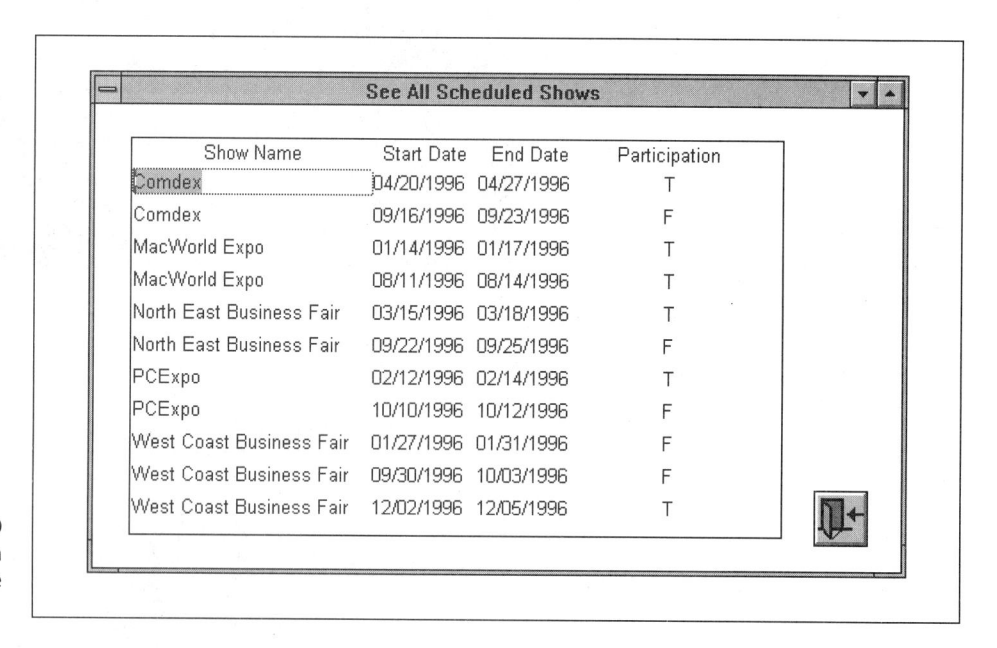

Figure 5.10
A listing of scheduled shows in a specified date range

14 Double-click the window's control box to close it.
15 Click the **Return** button in the Calendar window to close it.
16 Click the **Return** button in the Scheduling window to close it.

17 Explore any other parts of the application you choose. You can either make choices from the opening screen's menu bar or click on the buttons that appear in the middle of the button menu windows.

18 Click the **Quit** button on the opening screen to close the window, end the application, and return to PowerBuilder.

Now that you have a taste of how a PowerBuilder application looks when it is running, it's time to explore the environment in which that application was developed.

The General Work Environment

Although PowerBuilder is a complex environment, there are many consistent elements about its tools. In this section you will be introduced to those elements to provide you with a framework for all the work you will be doing throughout this book.

To explore the PowerBuilder development environment:

1 If necessary, launch PowerBuilder.

2 Open the *tcomp* application library and choose the *tshows* application.

The toolbar that appears, by default, below the menu bar is known as the *PowerBar*. It contains buttons that let you navigate among the components of the PowerBuilder development environment. The PowerBar also lets you run an application, use the debugger, and access PowerBuilder Help. Figure 5.11 provides an enlarged and labeled version of the default PowerBar.

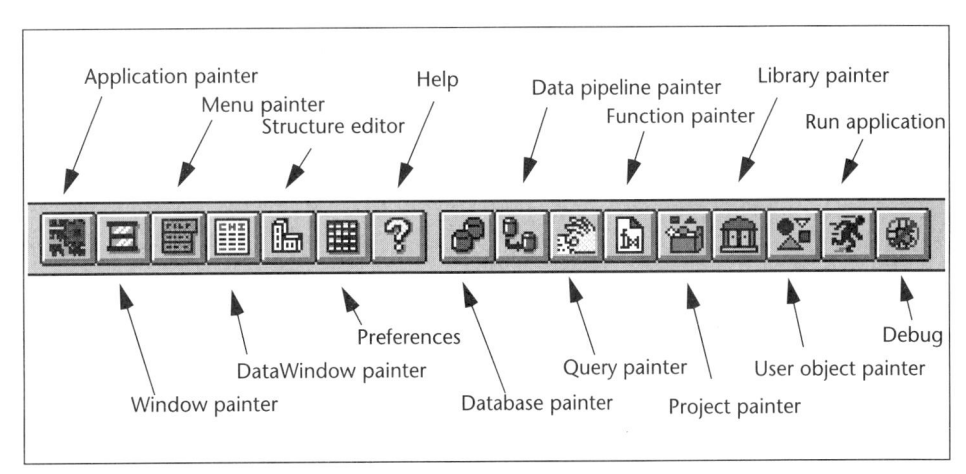

Figure 5.11
The buttons in the default PowerBar

3 Click the **Database** button in the PowerBar.

The Database painter with which you have been working is only one example of a PowerBuilder painter. A *painter*, which provides a way for PowerBuilder to group related tools, is designed to work with one type of PowerBuilder object, such as an application, a window, or a DataWindow. Some painters—such as the Application painter and the Database painter—are accessible from the PowerBar; others are accessible only from within other painters.

4 Connect to the database.

5 Exit the Database painter. The window that you see should have a menu bar and a toolbar across the top, as in Figure 5.12. The exact size of the buttons and whether there is text below each button depends on current PowerBuilder settings. You may even find that the specific buttons in the toolbar are different. (You will see how to make changes of this type later in this chapter.)

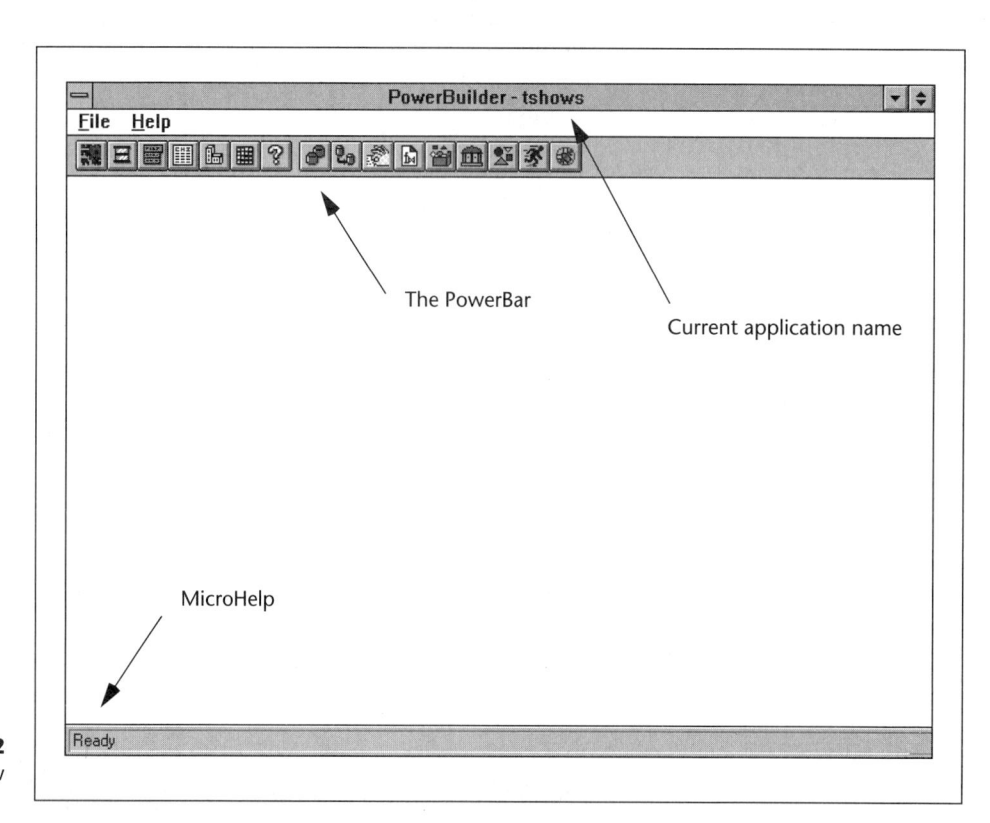

Figure 5.12
PowerBuilder opening window

The bottom line of the window displays Microhelp messages, which provide PowerBuilder status messages while you are working. Microhelp also identifies the object with which you are working at any given time. (As you will discover as you work with PowerBuilder, this can be very helpful, especially when you are dealing with a window that contains many objects.)

You can also access many of the painters in the default PowerBar with the keyboard by using the list of Shift and function key combinations in Table 5.1.

Table 5.1 Keyboard equivalents to enter PowerBuilder painters

Application painter	Shift+F1
Window painter	Shift+F2
Menu painter	Shift+F3
DataWindow painter	Shift+F4
Structure editor	Shift+F5
Database painter	Shift+F7
Query painter	Shift+F8
Function painter	Shift+F9
Library painter	Shift+F10
User object painter	Shift+F11

Each PowerBuilder painter has unique characteristics. However, all painters share some common elements.

To explore the elements of PowerBuilder painters:

1 Click the **Window** button in the PowerBar (Figure 5.13). (Don't worry if your PowerBar doesn't show the little label that appears in Figure 5.13. Just choose the button that contains the Window icon.)

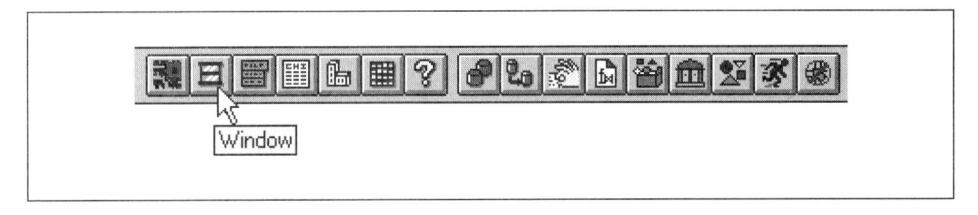

Figure 5.13
Window button in the PowerBar

The Select Window dialog box appears, as in Figure 5.14 on page 74. The layout of this dialog box is typical of those throughout PowerBuilder that let you open an object of a single type in its painter or create a new object of that type.

2 Scroll down the list of window names until you see w_manage_calendar.

3 Click **w_manage_calendar** to highlight it.

4 Click the **OK** button. PowerBuilder opens w_manage_calendar in the Window painter.

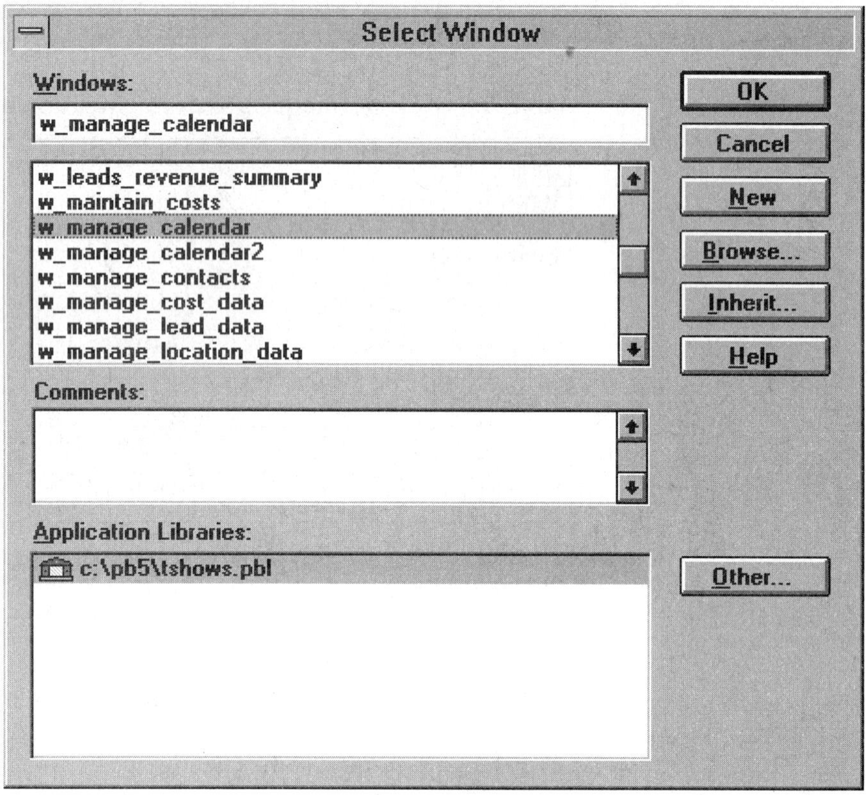

74 CHAPTER FIVE INTRODUCING POWERBUILDER

Figure 5.14
Select Window dialog box

As you can see in Figure 5.15 on page 75, the painter not only has the Power-Bar across the top, but also has a second toolbar down the left side. This is the *PainterBar*, which contains buttons specific to the current painter. (On your system, the PainterBar may be displayed underneath the PowerBar, at the top or bottom of the window, or in a floating palette.) Because a toolbar can be customized, changing which buttons appear, the PainterBar in your copy of Power-Builder may not match exactly with Figure 5.15.

The contents of a painter's *workspace*—the area between the scroll bars in which you define the contents of a PowerBuilder object—varies considerably from one painter to another. In this particular example, the window contains the window itself and three types of controls (a DataWindow control, a picture button control, and three command button controls).

The top of the workspace window in many painters is occupied by the *Style Bar*, which is used to set text characteristics. When a control that has text is selected, that text appears at the left edge of the Style Bar, as in Figure 5.16 on page 75. In fact, one way to change the text is to edit it directly in the Style Bar. You can also use the Style Bar to choose a font, set the type size, choose a font style (boldface, italic, and/or underlined), and text alignment.

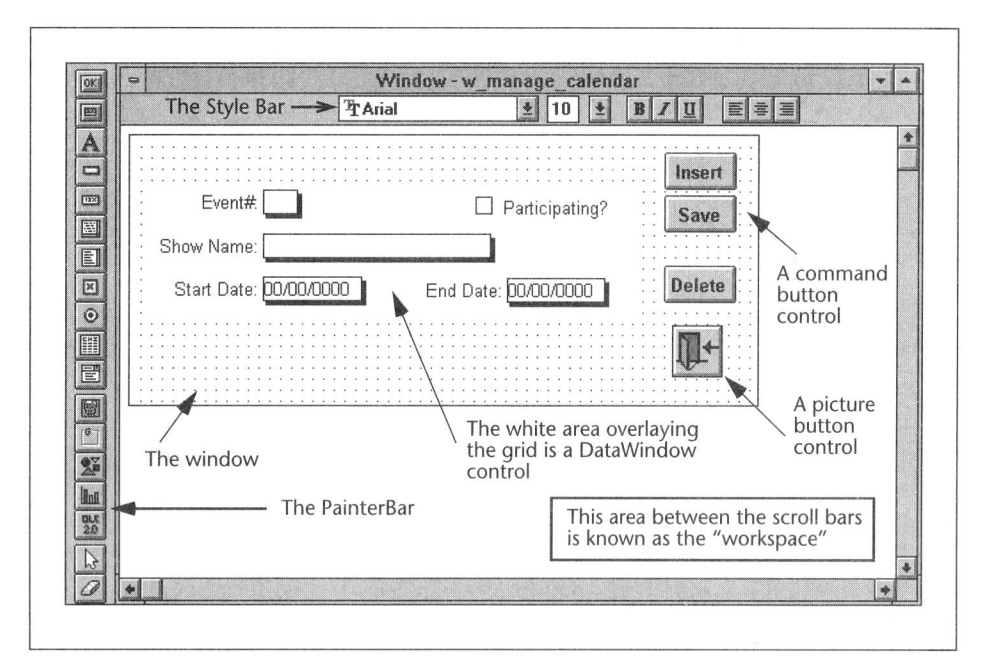

Figure 5.15
A typical painter

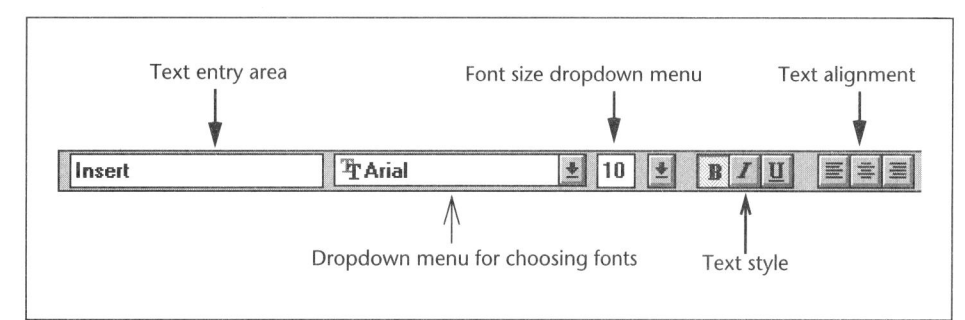

Figure 5.16
Style Bar

Each of the elements in Figure 5.15's workspace can have scripts attached to it. To view or modify a script, you enter the Script painter (a painter that is accessible only from within another painter).

To enter the Script painter:

1 Most objects in a painter workspace have popup menus that provide access to options that configure the behavior and appearance of the object. Right-click in the window in any place that isn't occupied by a control. The window's popup menu appears. In version 4.0 (Figure 5.17 on page 76), an object's properties are listed individually in the popup menu. However, in version 5.0 (Figure 5.18 on page 76), the properties are collected into a single Properties dialog box, and the popup menu therefore contains the Properties option rather than the names of the individual properties.

2 Choose **Script** from the popup menu. The Script painter appears, as you can see in Figure 5.19 on page 77.

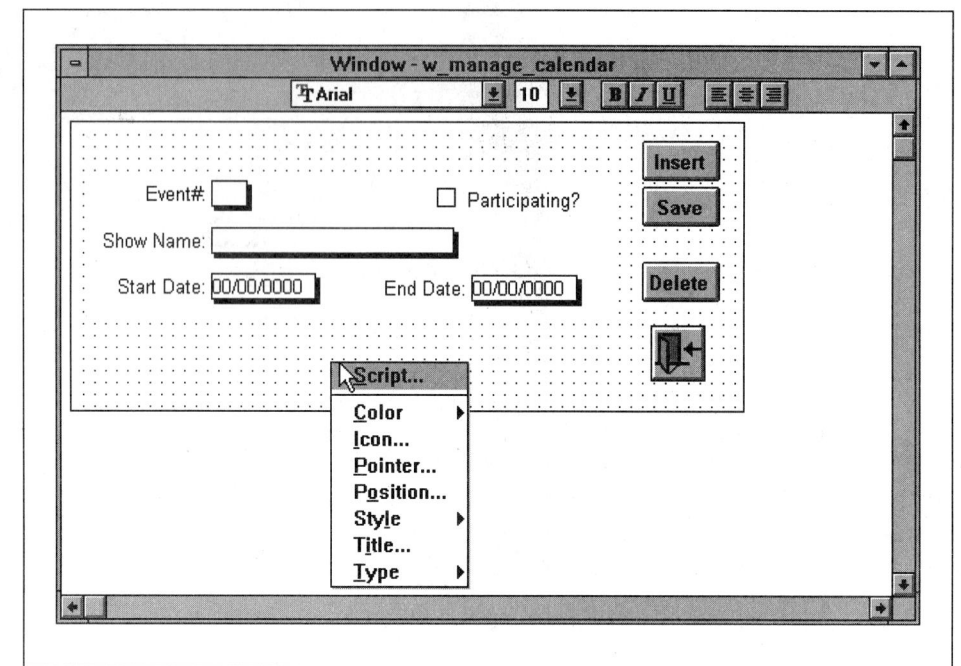

Figure 5.17
A popup menu in the workspace (4.0)

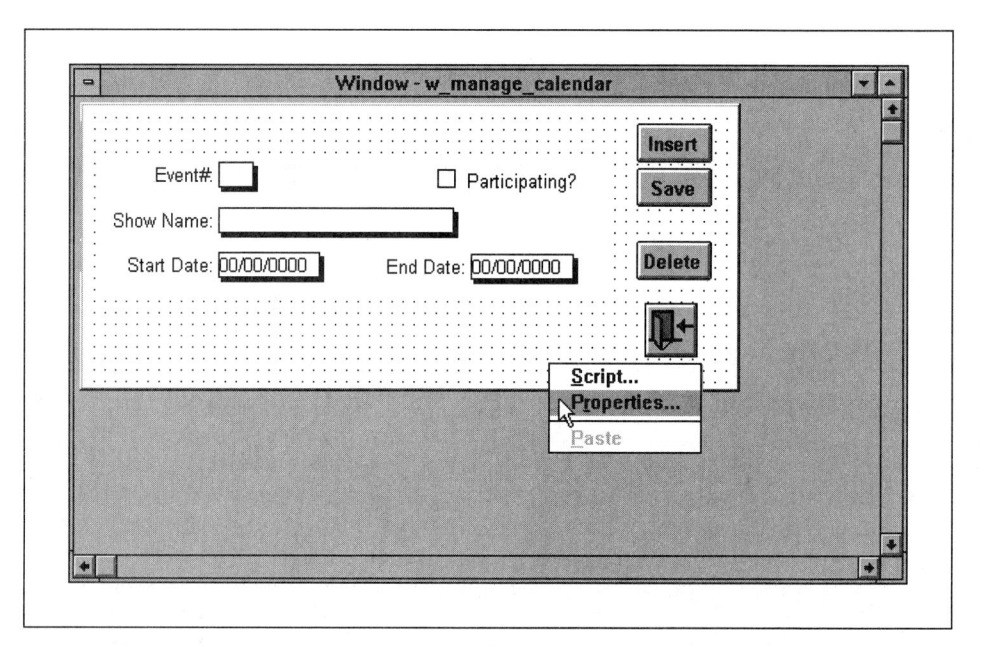

Figure 5.18
A popup menu in the workspace (5.0)

Version 5.0 includes syntax coloring. If you have a color monitor, by default data types appear in purple, comments in blue, keywords in green, and string constants in brown. This coloring can help you avoid errors by avoiding such problems as the use of keywords as variable names and unterminated strings.

Like any other painter, the Script painter has its own PainterBar. It also has four dropdown menus displayed across the top of the workspace. The Select Event menu lists all the events that can be triggered by the object to which the

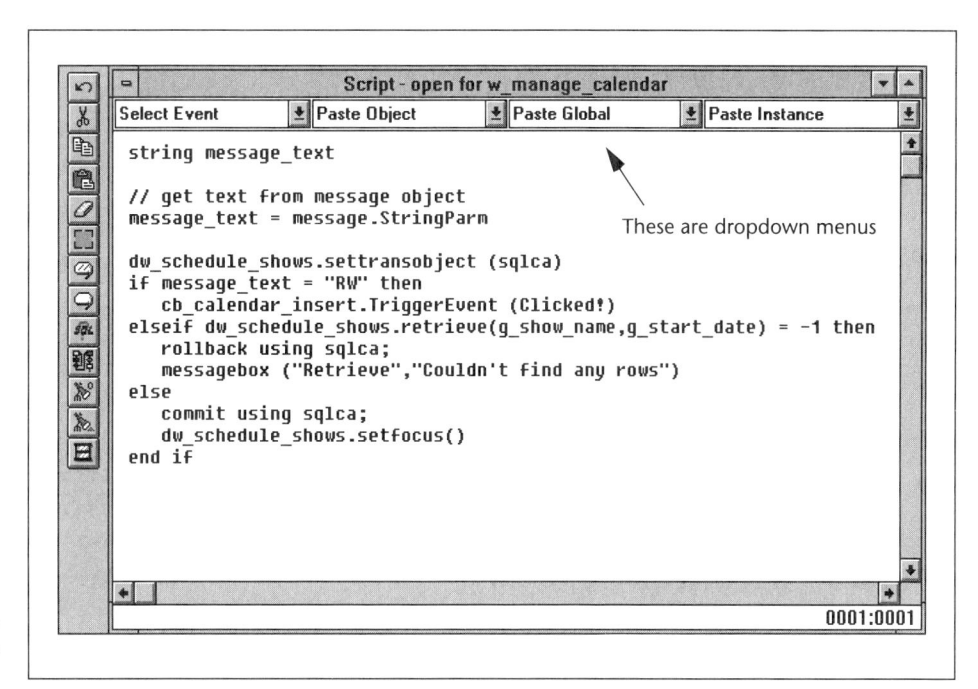

Figure 5.19
Script painter

```
string message_text

// get text from message object
message_text = message.StringParm

dw_schedule_shows.settransobject (sqlca)
if message_text = "RW" then
   cb_calendar_insert.TriggerEvent (Clicked!)
elseif dw_schedule_shows.retrieve(g_show_name,g_start_date) = -1 then
   rollback using sqlca;
   messagebox ("Retrieve","Couldn't find any rows")
else
   commit using sqlca;
   dw_schedule_shows.setfocus()
end if
```

These are dropdown menus

script is being attached. The event to which the current script applies appears in the workspace window's title bar (in this example, the open event, which is triggered when the window is opened).

The remaining three menus let you paste text into the Script painter's workspace. The Paste Object menu contains the names of all objects in the current painter. Global variables can be copied from the Paste Global menu; instance variables can be copied from the Paste Instance menu.

The Script painter's workspace is a simple text editor. Unlike a word processor, it doesn't perform word wrap. However, it does support cut, copy, paste, and undo operations.

3 Double-click the Script painter's control box to exit the Script painter and reenter the Window painter.

4 Double-click the Window painter's control box to exit the Window painter.

Customizing the Toolbars

If the copy of PowerBuilder you are using is shared by more than one person, a previous user may have changed the way in which the toolbars appear. In this section you will learn to change the appearance and placement of the toolbars. You will also be introduced to the situations in which special configurations of the toolbars make it easier to work with PowerBuilder.

Displaying Button Text

The first decision you need to make about the toolbars is whether you want to see text in the button, whether you want text to appear when you move the mouse pointer over a button (as it does with the figures in this chapter), or whether you don't want any text at all.

To change button text and see the effect of your changes:

1   If necessary, launch PowerBuilder and open the *tshows* application from the *tcomp* application library. (You won't be using an application in this exercise, but as you know, you can't work with PowerBuilder without opening an application.)

2   Choose **File -> Toolbars**. The Toolbars dialog box appears. In Figure 5.20, it is configured to show the PowerBar under the menu bar and to display the name of the button when the mouse pointer passes over it This type of label is known as a *PowerTip*.

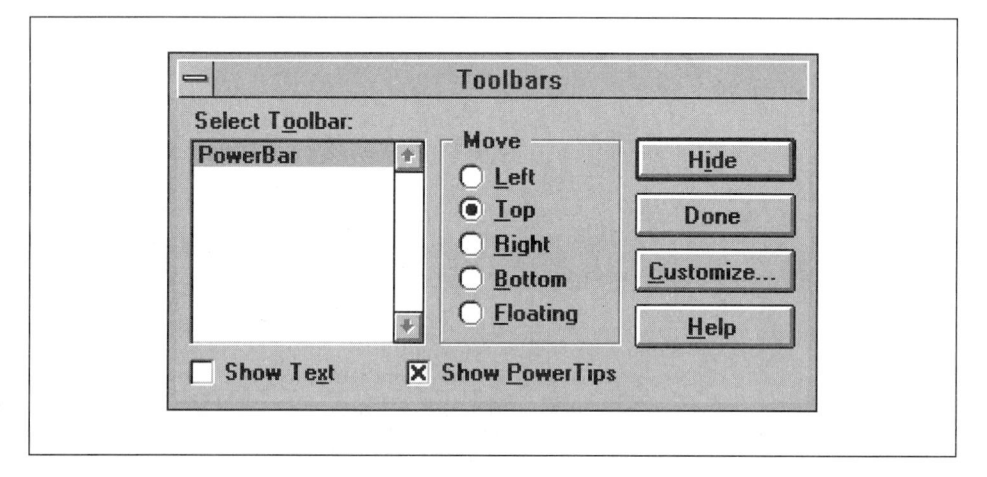

Figure 5.20
Toolbars dialog box

If a painter is open, use Window -> Toolbox rather than File -> Toolbars.

3   Click the **Show Text** check box. The PowerBar changes immediately to include larger, labeled buttons (Figure 5.21). The major drawback to displaying text under the buttons is that the buttons become so large that some of them disappear off the right edge of a 640 by 480 resolution monitor. Since there is no way to scroll the toolbar, buttons that disappear in this way are inaccessible.

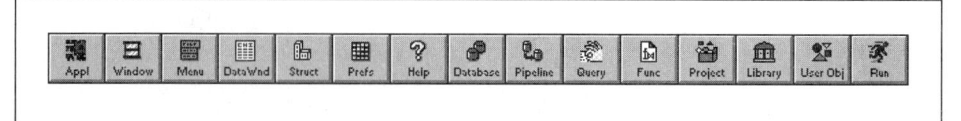

Figure 5.21
A toolbar with text under the buttons

4 Click the **Floating** radio button in the Toolbars dialog box. The Power-Bar immediately turns into a floating palette (Figure 5.22). This solves the disappearing button problem.

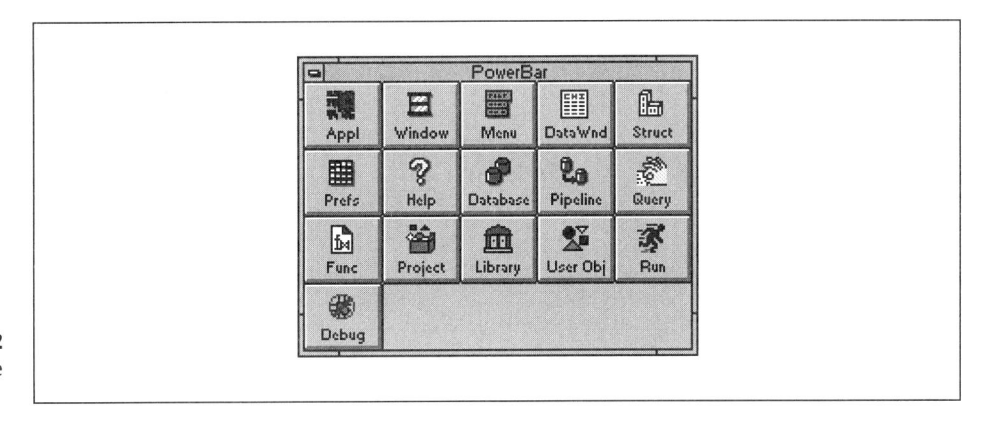

Figure 5.22
A floating PowerBar palette

5 Click the **Done** button to close the Toolbars dialog box.
6 Experiment with moving the PowerBar palette by dragging its title bar.

Configuring Other Toolbars

When you aren't working in a painter, the Toolbars dialog box provides access only to the PowerBar. However, there are three other toolbars that are available when a painter is open.

To experiment with the other painters:

1 Click the **DataWindow** button in the PowerBar palette to open a window in the Window painter. The Select Window dialog box appears.
2 Click the **OK** button to open the first DataWindow in the list. (For what you're going to be doing, it doesn't matter which DataWindow is open in the Window painter.)
3 Choose **Windows -> Toolbars**. The Toolbars dialog box reappears. Notice that there are now four toolbars listed.
4 If necessary, click **PowerBar** to highlight it. Click the **Top** radio button, and remove the X from the Show Text check box by clicking the check box again. If you want the PowerTips to show (the text that appears when the pointer passes over a button), make sure that there is an X in the Show PowerTips check box. In most cases, you will leave the PowerBar across the top of the window so that it doesn't overlay the workspace.
5 In contrast, look at the PainterBar. Even with the smaller buttons, some of them still can't be seen on a 640 by 480 monitor. Therefore, you might want to display the PainterBar in a palette. To see what it looks like, click **PainterBar** in the list of toolbars; then click the **Floating** radio button.

6   Click the **Done** button to close the Toolbars dialog box. Notice that not only can you now see all the buttons in the toolbar, but you have also gained extra width in the workspace.

7   If you are working with version 4.0, right-click in the title bar of the PainterBar palette. The Toolbars popup menu appears, as you can see in Figure 5.23. (This feature is not available in version 5.0).

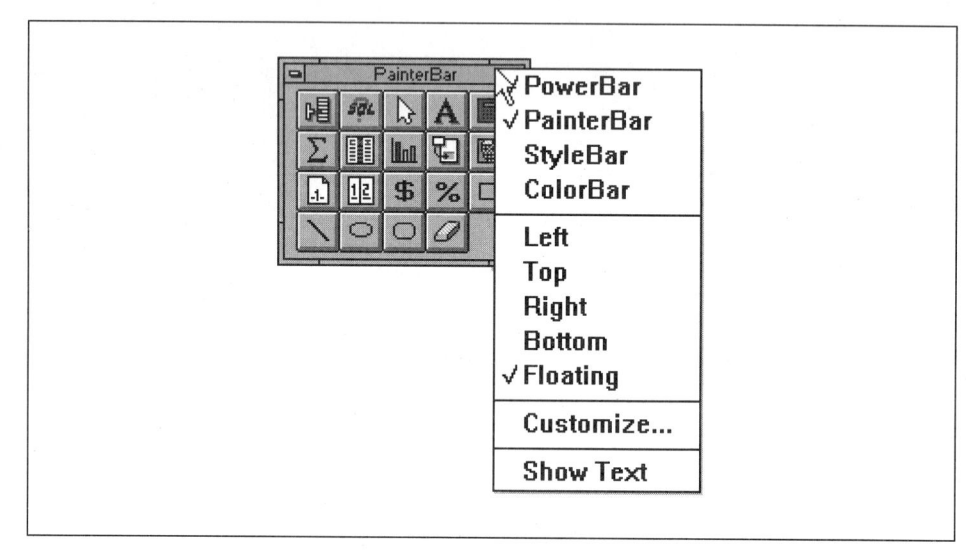

Figure 5.23
Toolbars popup menu

8   Choose **Left** from the popup menu. The PainterBar returns to the left side of the window.

You can display the Toolbars popup menu for any toolbar by right-clicking in a toolbar in any place not occupied by a button. The Left, Top, Right, Bottom, and Floating settings apply to the toolbar in which you right-clicked. The listing of toolbars at the top lets you choose which toolbars are visible. Choose a checked toolbar to make it invisible; choose an unchecked toolbar to make it visible.

9   Double-click the workspace window's control box to close it.

The Library Painter and Deleting Objects

There are many ways to create and modify objects using PowerBuilder. However, there is only one way to delete objects: through the Library painter. The Library painter also gives you an overview of all the objects in your application.

To enter the Library painter and delete an object:

1   Click the **Library** button in the PowerBar (Figure 5.24 on page 81). The Library painter appears, showing the contents of the current library, similar to what you see in Figure 5.25 on page 81. The display shows

CHAPTER FIVE   INTRODUCING POWERBUILDER   **81**

all libraries in the current directory. The contents of the current application library appear in alphabetical order.

Figure 5.24
Library button in the PowerBar

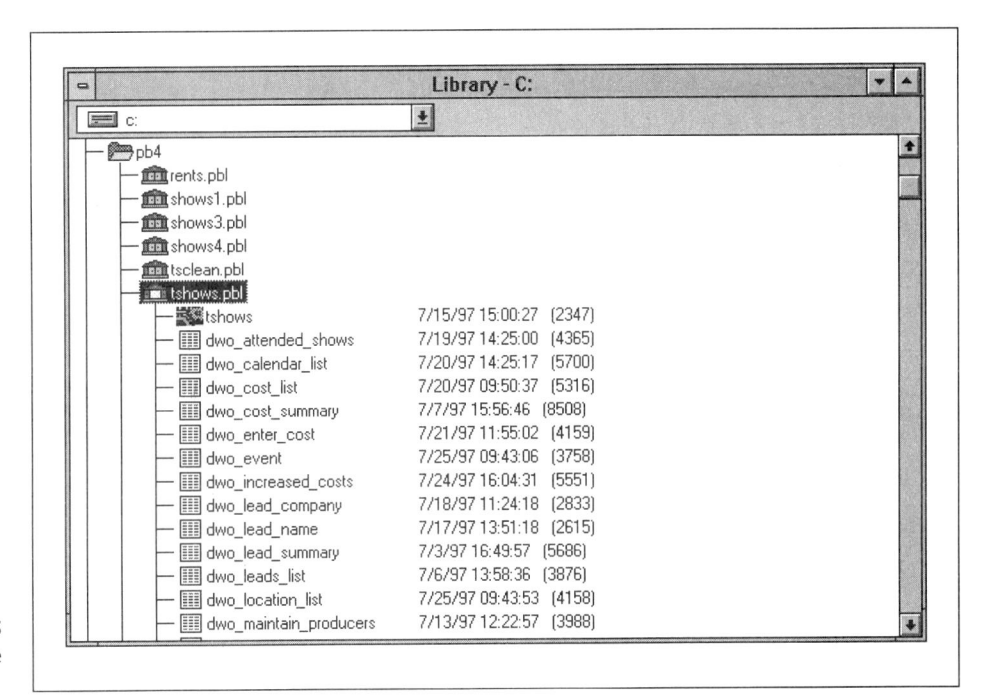

Figure 5.25
Library painter workspace

2   Scroll down the window until you see the object *for_deletion*.

3   Click **for_deletion** to select it.

4   Click the **Delete** button in the PainterBar (Figure 5.26 on page 82). PowerBuilder displays a dialog box asking you to confirm the deletion (Figure 5.27 on page 82).

5   Click the **Yes** button. Powerbuilder completes the deletion and removes the deleted object from the display.

Although PowerBuilder does ask you to confirm a deletion, it doesn't verify that the object you are deleting isn't used anywhere in the application. This means that you could accidentally delete something whose absence would affect another part of the application. Mistakenly deleting an object can be particularly destructive if you happen to delete an object from which other objects inherit. Therefore, be careful that you only delete objects that aren't being used in the application.

6   Double-click the Library painter workspace's control box to exit the painter.

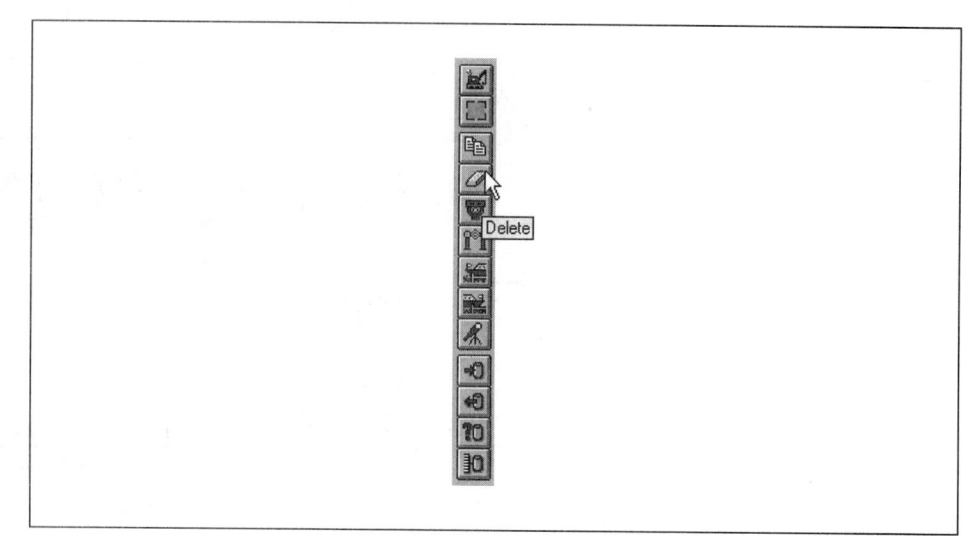

Figure 5.26
The Library painter's Delete button

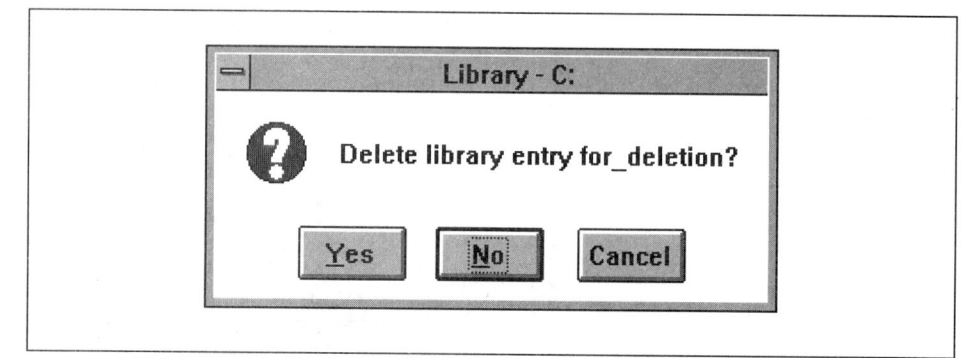

Figure 5.27
Dialog box confirming the deletion of a PowerBuilder library entry

Getting Help

If you are working in a lab environment, you may not have access to a full set of PowerBuilder manuals. Don't despair! PowerBuilder's online Help facility is quite extensive and can provide much of the information you need.

To use PowerBuilder's online Help:

1   If necessary, launch PowerBuilder and open the *tshows* application in *tcomp.pbl*.
2   Click the **Help** button in the PowerBar (Figure 5.28 on page 83). The PowerBuilder Help contents window appears, as in Figure 5.29 on page 83 (version 4.0) or Figure 5.30 on page 83 (version 5.0).

PowerBuilder Help is a stand-alone application. This means you can quit PowerBuilder and leave Help running.

3   Click the button to the left of "Getting started with PowerBuilder." The topic expands to show you more detailed topics underneath, as in Figure 5.31 (version 4.0) or Figure 5.32 (version 5.0).

CHAPTER FIVE   INTRODUCING POWERBUILDER   **83**

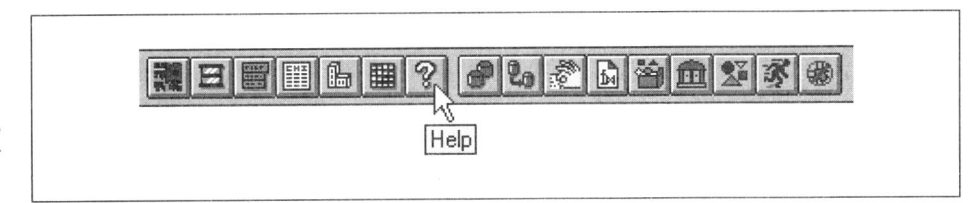

Figure 5.28
Help button in the PowerBar

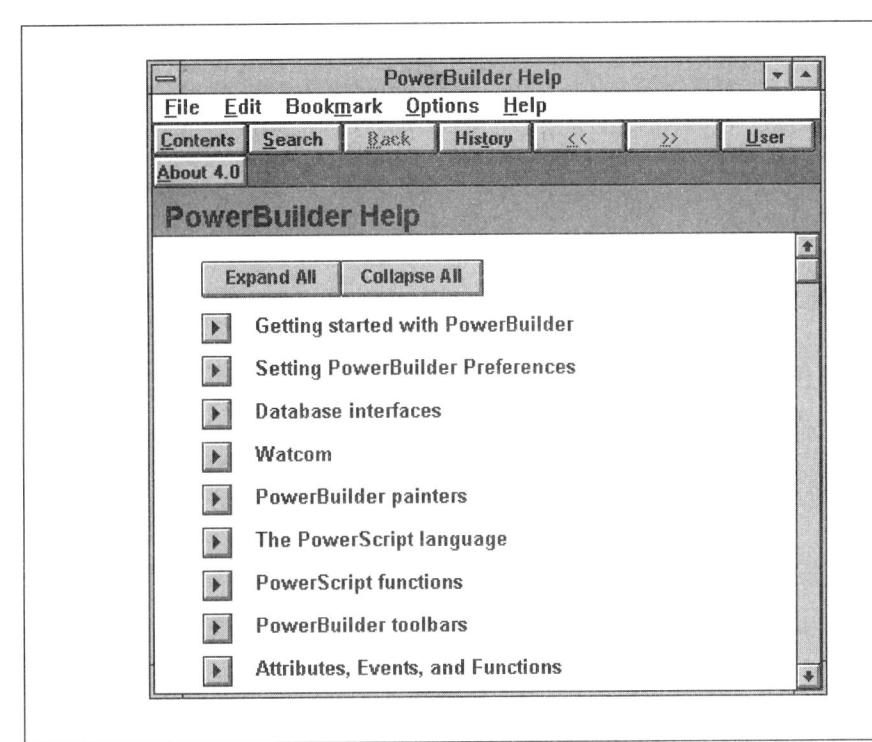

Figure 5.29
PowerBuilder Help contents screen (4.0)

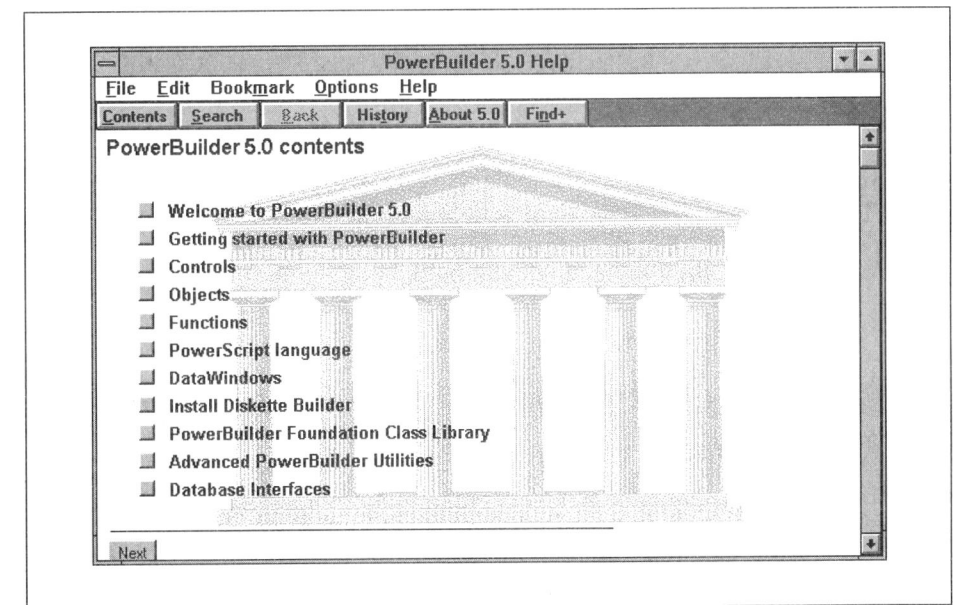

Figure 5.30
PowerBuilder Help contents screen (5.0)

84 CHAPTER FIVE INTRODUCING POWERBUILDER

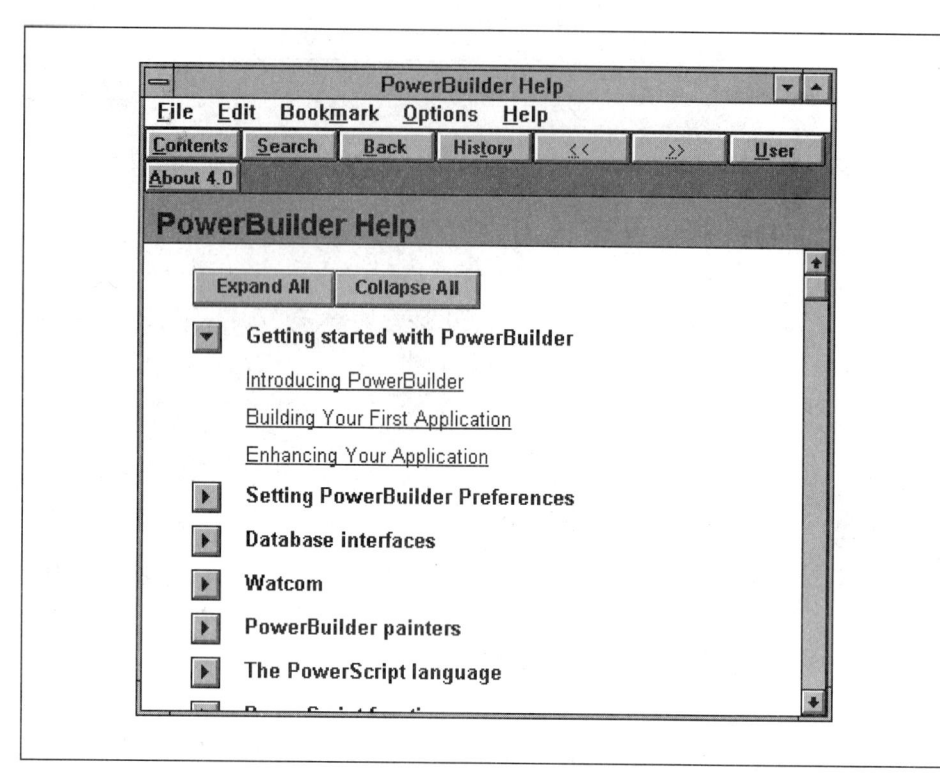

Figure 5.31
Expanded Help contents (4.0)

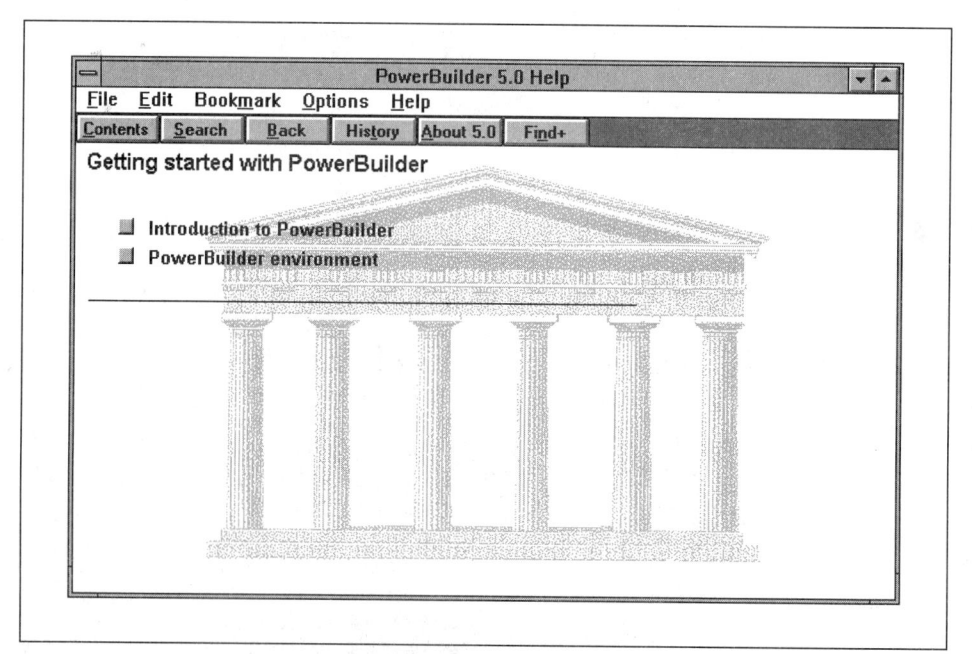

Figure 5.32
Expanded Help contents (5.0)

4   Move the pointer over "Introducing PowerBuilder." The pointer changes to a hand with a pointing finger.

5   Double-click **Introducing PowerBuilder** (version 4.0) or click the button to the left of "Introduction to PowerBuilder" (version 5.0).

CHAPTER FIVE   INTRODUCING POWERBUILDER   **85**

The article appears (Figure 5.33 for version 4.0 and Figure 5.34 for version 5.0).

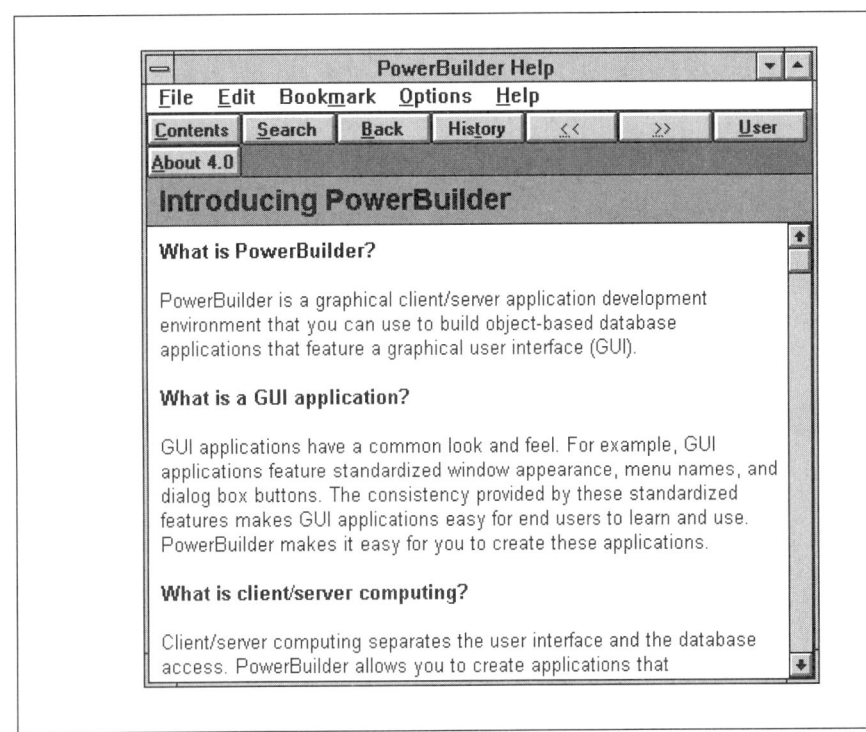

Figure 5.33
A PowerBuilder Help article (4.0)

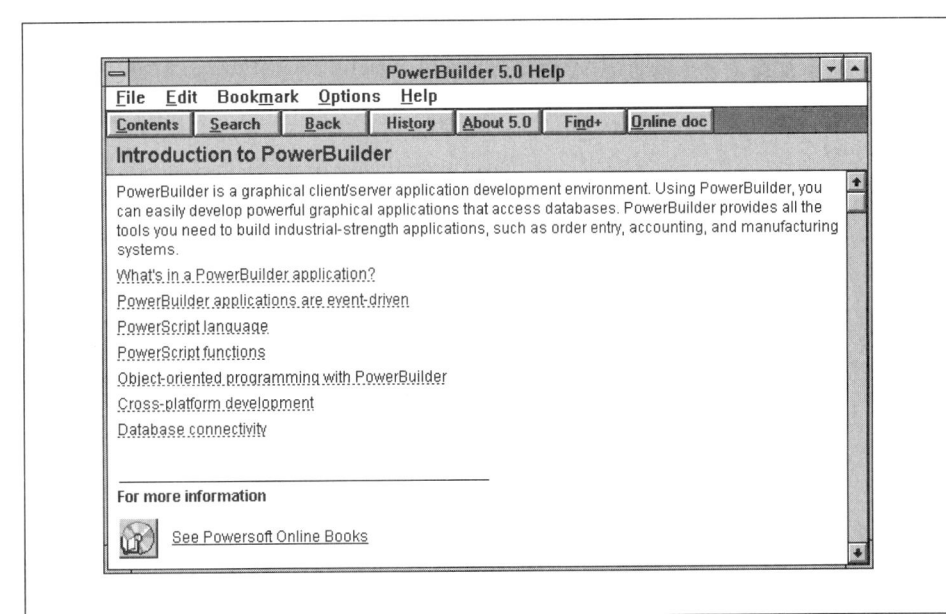

Figure 5.34
A PowerBuilder Help article (5.0)

6 Click the **Back** button to return to the previous screen.

7 Click the **History** button. PowerBuilder displays a window that shows you—in most recent to least recent order—all the Help windows

86 CHAPTER FIVE INTRODUCING POWERBUILDER

you've viewed (Figure 5.35). You can use this window at any time to quickly go back to a previous article.

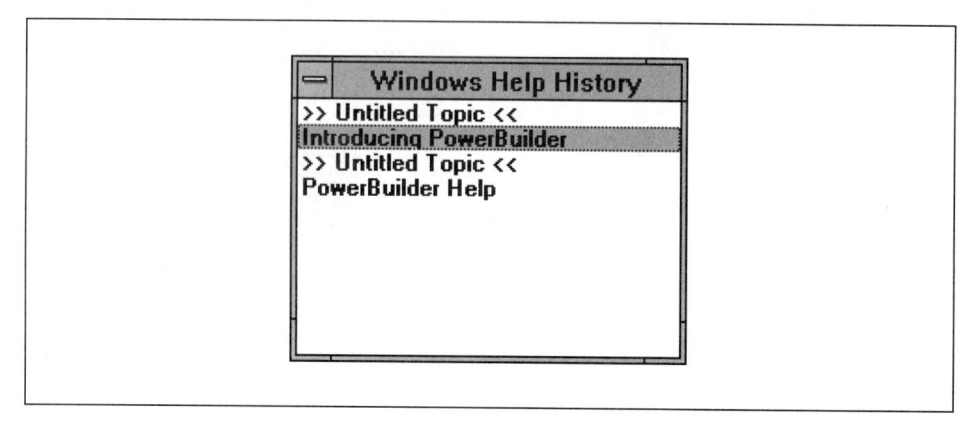

Figure 5.35
Help History window

8 Double-click the History window's control box to close the window.
9 Click the **Search** button. The Search dialog box appears (Figure 5.36). The edit box at the top of the dialog box is for entering a search string. The list directly below contains all topics in PowerBuilder Help. Articles about selected topics appear in the list at the bottom of the dialog box.

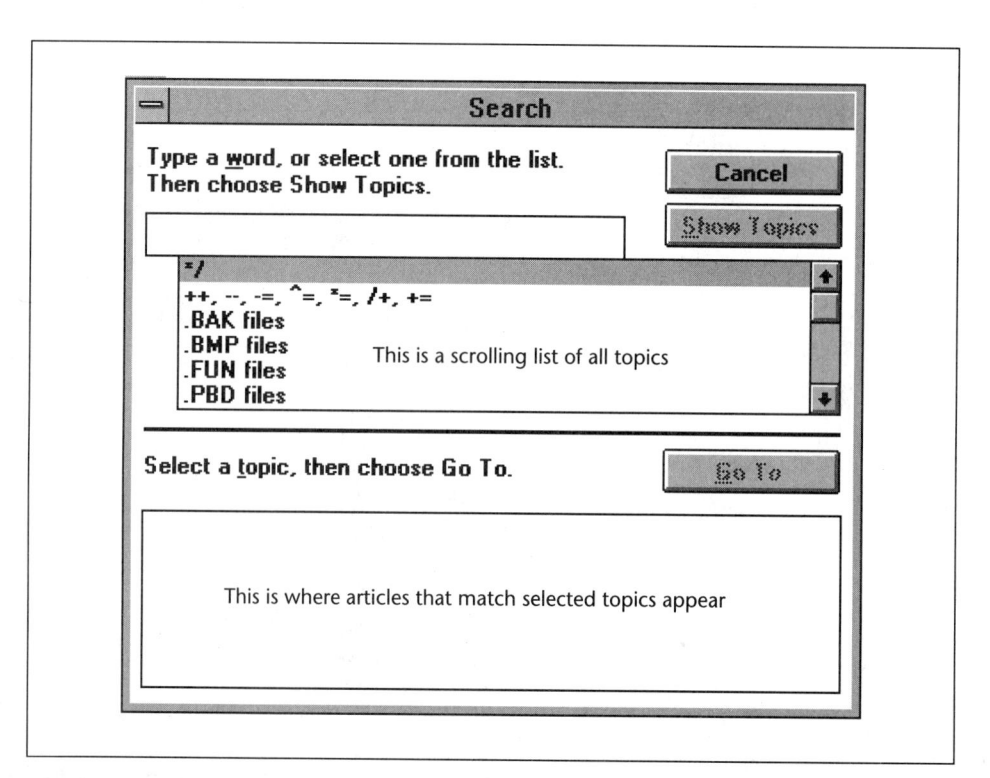

Figure 5.36
PowerBuilder Help's Search dialog box

10 Type **d**. Notice that the list of topics scrolls to the first topic beginning with "d."

11 Type **atawindow**. The list of topics has now scrolled to topics that begin with "DataWindow."

12 Double-click **DataWindow**. The names of the two articles associated with that topic appear in the list at the bottom of the window, as in Figure 5.37.

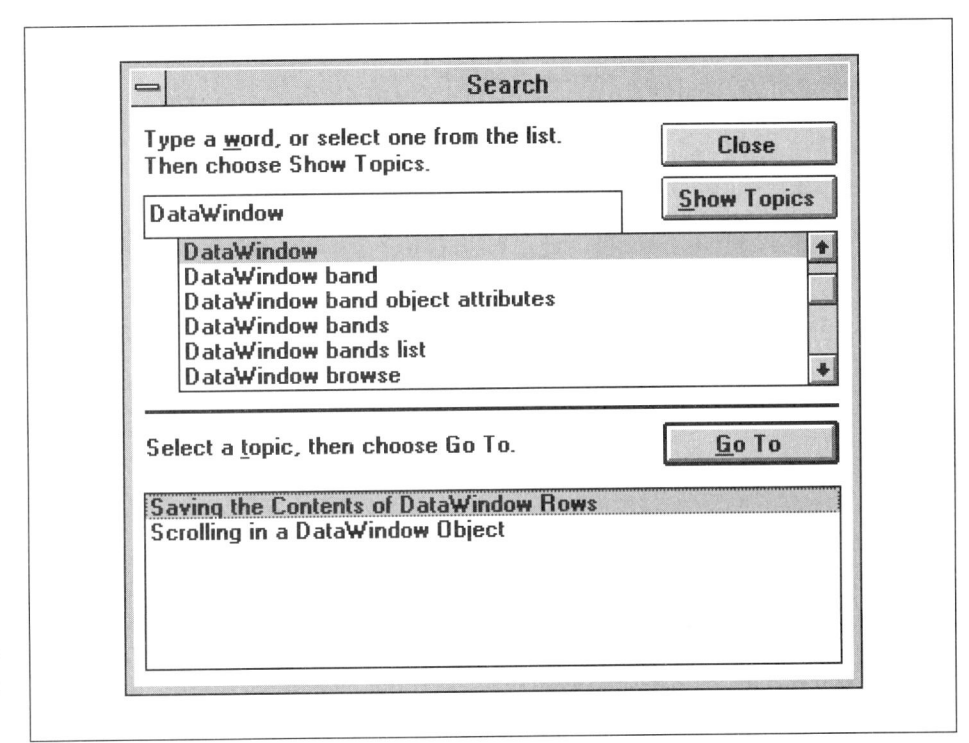

Figure 5.37
A completed search

13 Click the **GoTo** button. PowerBuilder Help displays the selected article.

14 Double-click on the PowerBuilder Help window's control box to close the window.

At this point, PowerBuilder Help might not seem very useful. This is because you haven't learned enough yet to identify the topics to enter into the search window. However, as you work through the tutorials in this book, you will learn PowerBuilder terminology and therefore be able to quickly extract much information from the Help facility.

Looking Ahead

Now that you've had some basic experience with the PowerBuilder environment, you can begin to use it for data manipulation. In Part Two of this book, you'll learn about PowerBuilder's features for interacting directly with a database without running an application. Although PowerBuilder's primary strength is application development, as you will see, it can also function as an interactive data manipulation tool.

EXERCISES

In these exercises you'll get a chance to explore the PowerBuilder environment and to experiment with tailoring it to your personal working preferences.

1. Launch PowerBuilder and open the Database painter. (Any application and database will do.) Explore different arrangements for the toolbars. Which arrangement do you prefer? Why?

2. Use PowerBuilder Help to search for articles about transaction objects.
   a. How many articles do you find?
   b. What is the title of the article that discusses a transaction object's attributes?
   c. Which article discusses combining transactions and embedded SQL?
   d. What does the SQLCode value of -1 mean? (You can find this in one of the articles retrieved by your search.)

3. Use PowerBuilder Help to find the answers to the following questions:
   a. What is the purpose of the `MessageBox` function? What parameters are required? What parameters are optional?
   b. How do you add the current page number to a window? How do you add a count of the total number of pages in a report to a window?
   c. How would you include the value π in a calculation?
   d. How do you give a menu option an accelerator key?
   e. Describe PowerBuilder's graphing capabilities.
   f. What support does PowerBuilder provide for "drag and drop" operations?
   g. What is a "band"?
   h. What syntax would you use to change the font in which the contents of a column appear?
   i. What is a PowerBuilder "string"?
   j. How can you change the tab order in a window?

4. Open the *rents* application and connect to the *rents* database. Look at the application in the Library painter.
   a. How many objects are currently part of this application?
   b. List at least two reasons why you might want to use the Library painter's hierarchical view of objects when maintaining the contents of an application library.

PART TWO

Interacting Directly with a DBMS

CHAPTER SIX

MANAGING DATABASE STRUCTURE

CHAPTER SEVEN

DIRECT DATA MANIPULATION

CHAPTER EIGHT

EXTENDED DATA ATTRIBUTES

> # CHAPTER SIX

Managing Database Structure

IN THIS CHAPTER YOU WILL:

- Use PowerBuilder to create database tables, views, and indexes
- Add integrity rules to tables
- Include basic data formatting in table definitions

The most common use of PowerBuilder is to develop an application program for end users. However, you can also use PowerBuilder as an interface for direct interaction with a client-server DBMS. You can use PowerBuilder to create tables, views, and indexes; you can also add, modify, and delete data.

In this chapter you will be introduced to PowerBuilder's data definition capabilities. You will get a chance to create a new database, define its tables, and add some integrity rules and formatting characteristics. You will also create indexes to help speed data retrieval performance.

Creating the Database

To create a new database, you must first have an application that will be used to interact with that database. Although the application can be empty (no windows or menus defined), it must exist and be open. The following exercise therefore uses an empty version of the *tshows* application stored in the application library *tshows1.pbl*. We'll be defining a database with the same name.

To create the new database:

1   Launch PowerBuilder. Then, open the *tshows* application within the *tshows1.pbl* application library.
2   Click the **Database** button in the PowerBar (Figure 6.1). The Select Tables dialog box appears, listing the tables in the current database (Figure 6.2 on page 93).

Figure 6.1
Database button in the PowerBar

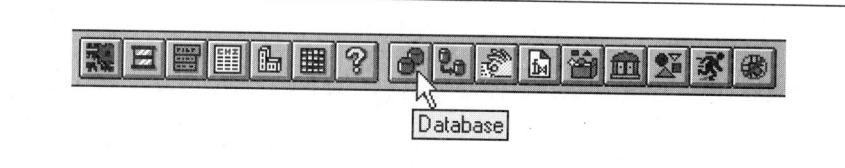

3   Click the **Cancel** button to dismiss the dialog box.
4   Choose **File -> Create Database**. The Create Local Database dialog box appears (Figure 6.3 on page 93).

PowerBuilder fills in a default user ID of "DBA" and a command to be used when you connect to the database (the start command). Although you see only three asterisks, the default password is "sql". Do not change the user ID, password, or start command.

If you change the user ID or password and happen to forget the new values, your database will be inaccessible. Therefore, for purposes of this book, leave the defaults in place.

5   Type **tshows1** as the database name.

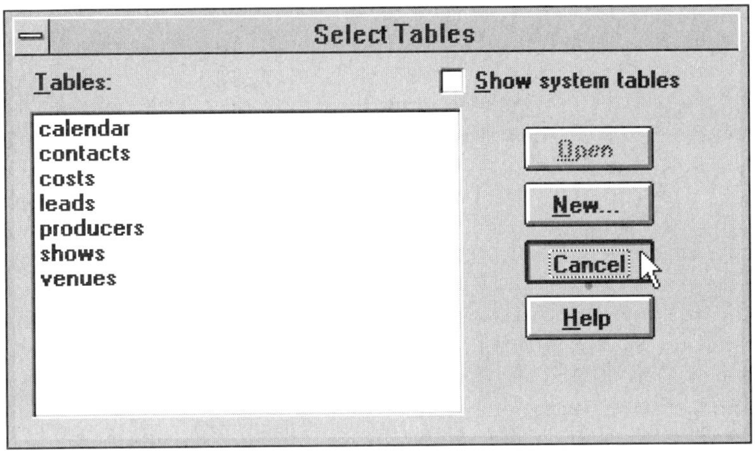

CHAPTER SIX   MANAGING DATABASE STRUCTURE   **93**

Figure 6.2
Select Tables dialog box

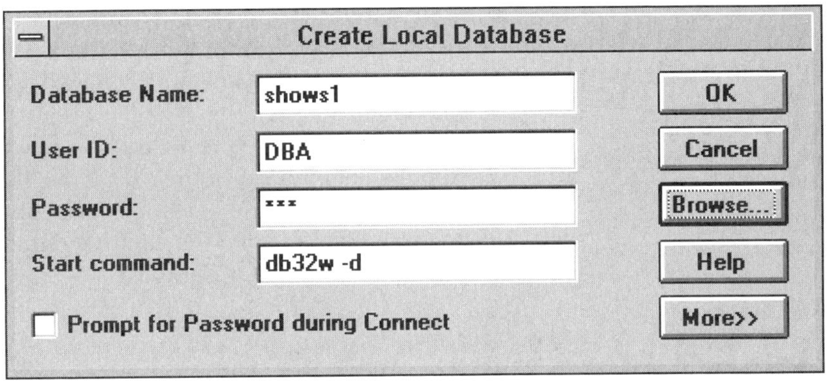

Figure 6.3
Create Local Database dialog box

6. If you want to store the database file somewhere other than the directory in which PowerBuilder is stored, click the **Browse** button. A second Create Local Database dialog box appears (Figure 6.4 on page 94). Select the drive on which you want to store the database from the Drives list at the bottom of the dialog box. Double-click the subdirectory (if any) in the Directories list. When you have identified the location for your database file, click the **OK** button to close the dialog box. The first Create Local Database dialog box will again be accessible.

7. Click the **OK** button. PowerBuilder closes the dialog box and creates the *tshows1* database. At this point, the database exists but contains no tables.

PowerBuilder does four things when you create a new database:

- Creates a database file with the extension *.db* in the current directory. This file contains the database's data dictionary, data, and indexes.

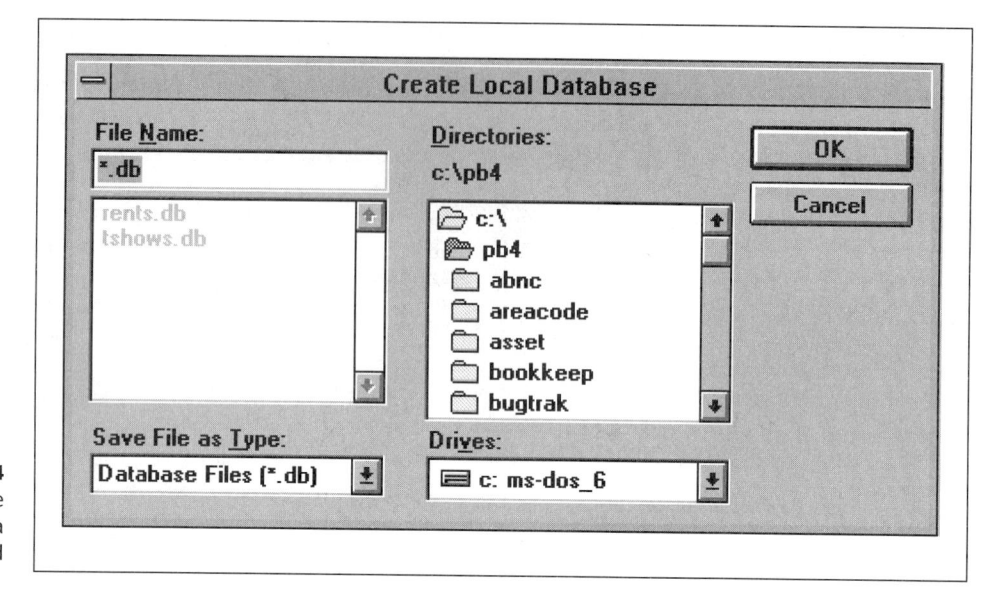

Figure 6.4
The second Create Local Database dialog box, used to indicate where a database file should be stored

- Writes information about the new data source to the *ODBC.INI* file. If *ODBC.INI* already contains a database with the same name, a suffix is appended to the name of the new database to distinguish it from the existing database.
- Creates a database profile for the new database and writes information about the database to the *PB.INI* file. If *PB.INI* already contains a database with the same name, a suffix is appended to the name of the new database to distinguish it from the existing database.
- Connects to the new database.

Creating Tables

Data in a relational database are stored in tables that provide a structure for the organization of those data. Before data can be stored, the columns that make up a table must be defined. Creating a new table involves the following tasks:

- Naming the table
- Naming the columns
- Assigning data types to the columns
- Where required, assigning sizes to the columns
- Indicating whether a column can be null
- Defining a primary key for the table
- Where required, defining foreign keys
- If desired, adding basic display formatting to the tables

Rules for Naming Tables and Columns

The rules that govern table and column names are dependent on the DBMS with which PowerBuilder is interacting. If you are using WatcomSQL or another SQL-based database server, then the following naming rules hold:

- Table names must be unique within the database.
- Column names must be unique within the table.
- Table and column names must begin with a letter or an underscore (_).
- Table and column names can contain letters, numbers, pound signs (#), dollar signs ($), and underscores (_).

If you are working with another type of DBMS, such as Microsoft Access, then you should consult the DBMS's documentation to determine its naming rules.

Although it isn't required, database management is easier if foreign key columns have the same names as the primary key columns they reference.

PowerBuilder's Column Data Types

Each column must be assigned a data type. A column *data type* is a broad type of domain constraint, because it restricts the data that can be stored in the column. As with naming rules, the available column data types depend on the DBMS with which you are working. If you are using WatcomSQL, then you can choose from among the following:

- *char* or *varchar*: A char or varchar column holds up to 32,767 bytes of text data. When defining either type of column, you must specify the maximum number of characters that can be stored in the column.
- *long varchar*: A long varchar column holds a theoretically unlimited amount of text data. The current limit is 2Gb, the maximum size of a database.
- *date*: A date column holds a date (month, day, and year).
- *time*: A time column holds a time (hour, minutes, seconds, and fractions of seconds).

Although a SQL-based DBMS stores fractions of seconds in a time column, the DBMS can't query on those fractions. You should never use time columns as comparison values in the WHERE clause of a SQL SELECT; the DBMS will never be able to match the values in the query with stored times.

- *int* or *integer*: Int and integer columns store 32-bit integers.
- *smallint*: Smallint columns store 16-bit integers.
- *decimal* or *numeric*: Decimal and numeric columns store numbers that can include decimal fractions. When defining either type of column, you specify the *precision* (total number of digits) and the *scale* (number of places to the right of the decimal point).
- *float* or *real*: Float or real columns store floating point values in the range $1.175494351 * 10^{-38}$ to $3.402823466 * 10^{38}$.
- *double*: A double column holds a double precision floating point value in the range $2.22507385850720160 * 10^{-308}$ to $1.79769313486231560 * 10^{308}$.

- *binary*: A binary column, also known as a *blob* (binary large object), holds up to 32,767 bytes of binary data. Typical uses for binary columns include storing graphic images, digitized movies, and digitized sounds. Binary columns can also be used to store documents created and formatted by other applications.
- *long binary*: A long binary field holds a theoretically unlimited amount of binary data. The current limit is 2Gb, the maximum size of a database.
- *timestamp*: A timestamp column stores a combined date and time. The primary use for this type of column is to mark table rows with the date and time of some occurrence. Because the comparison of a timestamp column in a query would include both the date and time components, timestamp columns are rarely used for simple date storage.

As a rule of thumb, always use the char or varchar data type unless you have a good reason for doing otherwise. Consider, for example, what happens if you store a zip code in an integer column. For most of the country, there won't be a problem. However, zip codes in New England start with zeros. Because columns defined to store numbers omit leading zeros, New England zip codes stored in an integer column will be only four digits long. If zip codes are stored as text, the leading zeros are retained.

PowerBuilder requires foreign keys to have the same data types as the primary keys they reference. You must therefore make sure that primary key/foreign key column definitions are consistent.

Defining a New Table

Tables are added to an existing database using the Database painter. As a first example, you'll be creating the Shows table in the *tshows1* database that you created earlier.

To create the structure of the table:

1. Make sure that you are working with the Database painter and that *tshows1* is the current database.
2. Click the **New** button in the PainterBar (Figure 6.5 on page 97). The Create Table dialog box appears. In version 4.0, you are still within the Database painter. However, in version 5.0, you have entered the Table painter.
3. If you are working with version 4.0, type **shows** as the name of the table (Figure 6.6 on page 97).

   If you are working with 5.0, you will name the table later. As you can see in Figure 6.7 on page 97, the new table is currently "untitled."

Regardless of how you capitalize a table or column name, PowerBuilder translates all your characters to lowercase.

4. If you are working with version 4.0, press the **Tab** key. The cursor moves down into the space where you can enter the name of the first column.

   If you are working with version 5.0, the cursor is already in the space for the name of the first column.

CHAPTER SIX MANAGING DATABASE STRUCTURE **97**

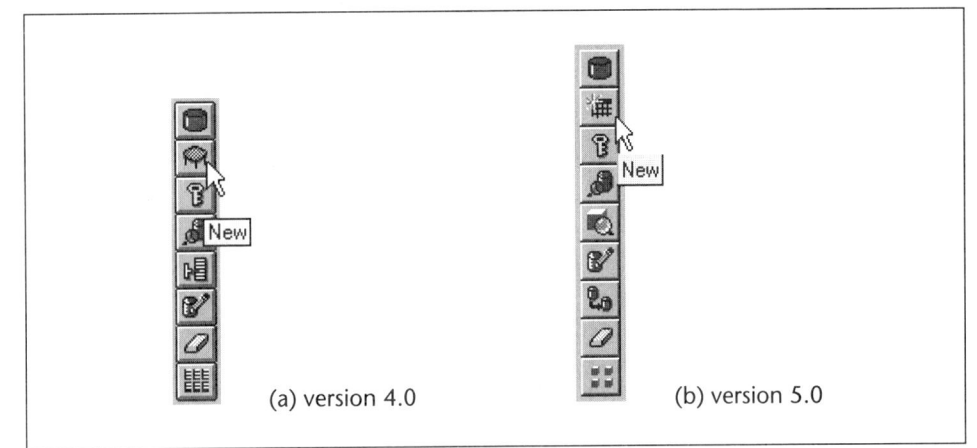

Figure 6.5
New button in the PainterBar

(a) version 4.0

(b) version 5.0

PowerBuilder 4.0

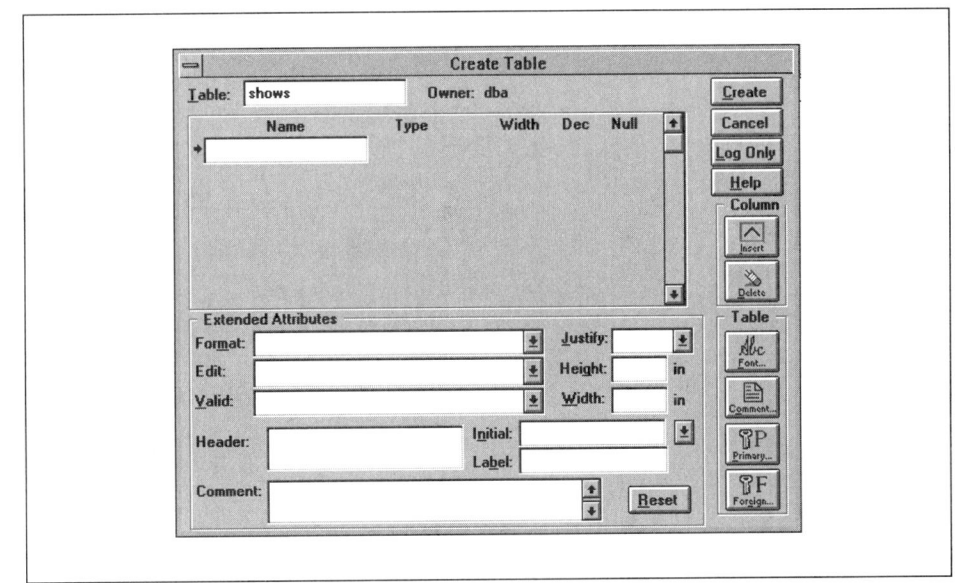

Figure 6.6
Entering the name of a new table (4.0)

PowerBuilder 5.0

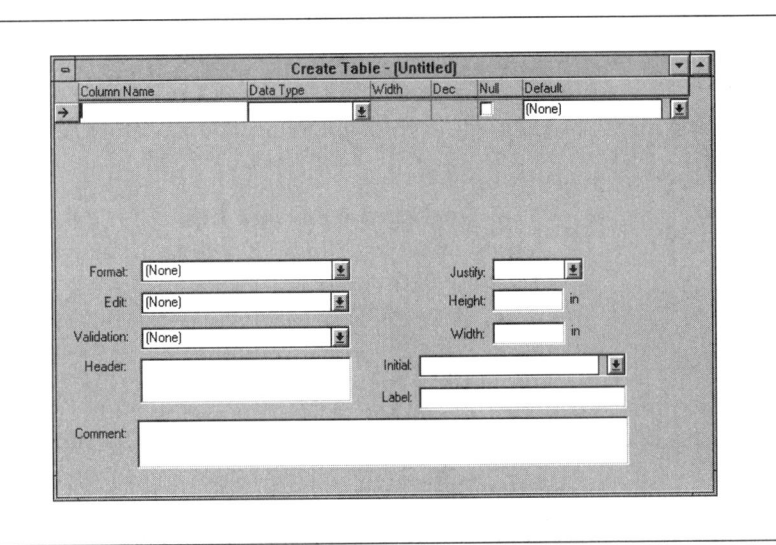

Figure 6.7
Creating a new table (5.0)

5   Type **show_name** as the name of the first column. As you begin to type, PowerBuilder fills in default values for the column's data type and width. PowerBuilder also assumes that the column can't be null (Figure 6.8).

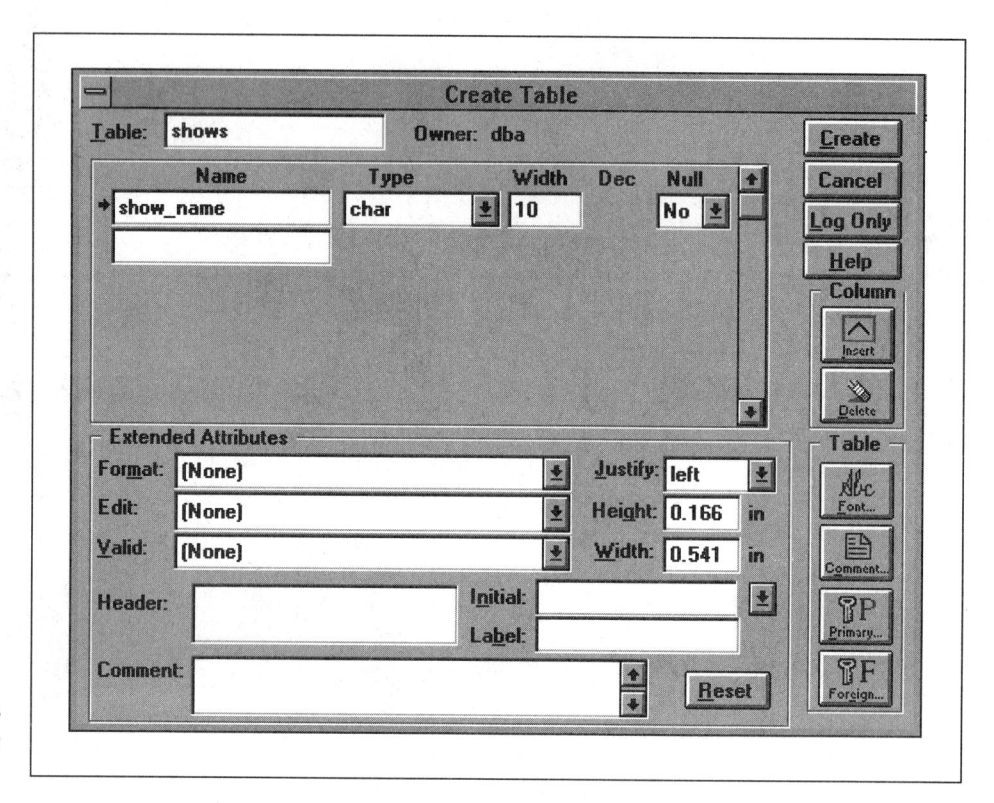

Figure 6.8
Entering a column name

6   Press the **Tab** key twice to accept the default column data type and highlight the contents of the Width box.

7   Type **25** to allow up to 25 characters in the column.

8   Press the **Tab** key twice to accept the default null status and move to the Name box in the line below.

9   Repeat Steps 5 through 8 for the second column in the table, making the column name **producer**, the data type **char**, and the width **25**.

Adding the Primary Key   The SQL-based DBMSs that PowerBuilder supports can store primary key definitions in their data dictionaries. Whenever you modify data in a table that has a primary key, the DBMS automatically verifies that each primary key is nonnull and that its value is unique. Once you've defined the columns in a table, you can declare the primary key.

To add a primary key for the Shows table:

1 If you are working with version 4.0, click the **Primary** button in the lower-right corner of the dialog box. The Primary Key Definition dialog box appears (Figure 6.9).

If you are working with version 5.0, click the **Properties** button in the PainterBar (Figure 6.10), or choose **Edit->Table Properties** to display the Table Properties dialog box. Click the **Primary Key** tab at the top of the dialog box to display the Primary Key panel (Figure 6.11).

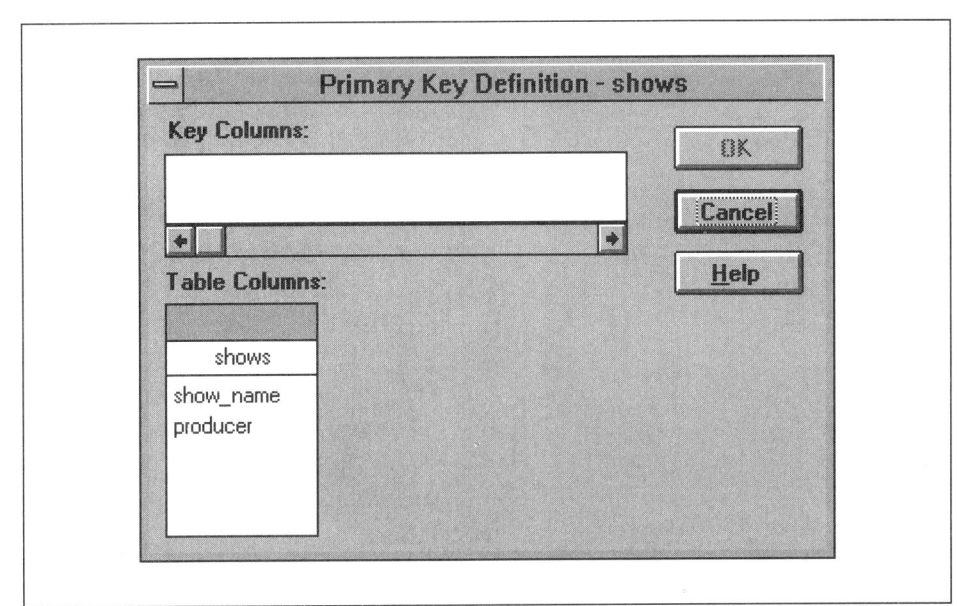

Figure 6.9
Declaring a primary key (4.0)

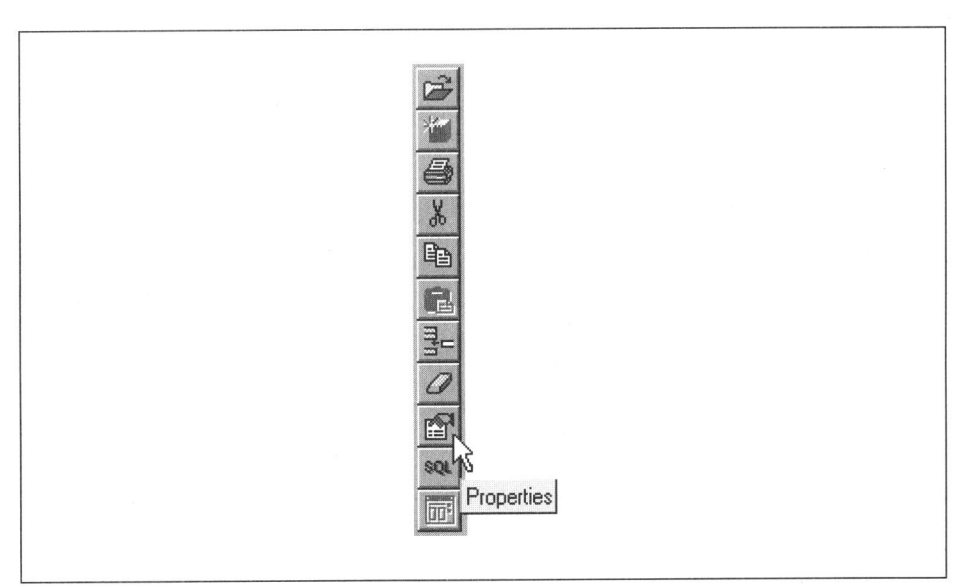

Figure 6.10
Properties button in the PainterBar (5.0)

100 CHAPTER SIX MANAGING DATABASE STRUCTURE

PowerBuilder 5.0

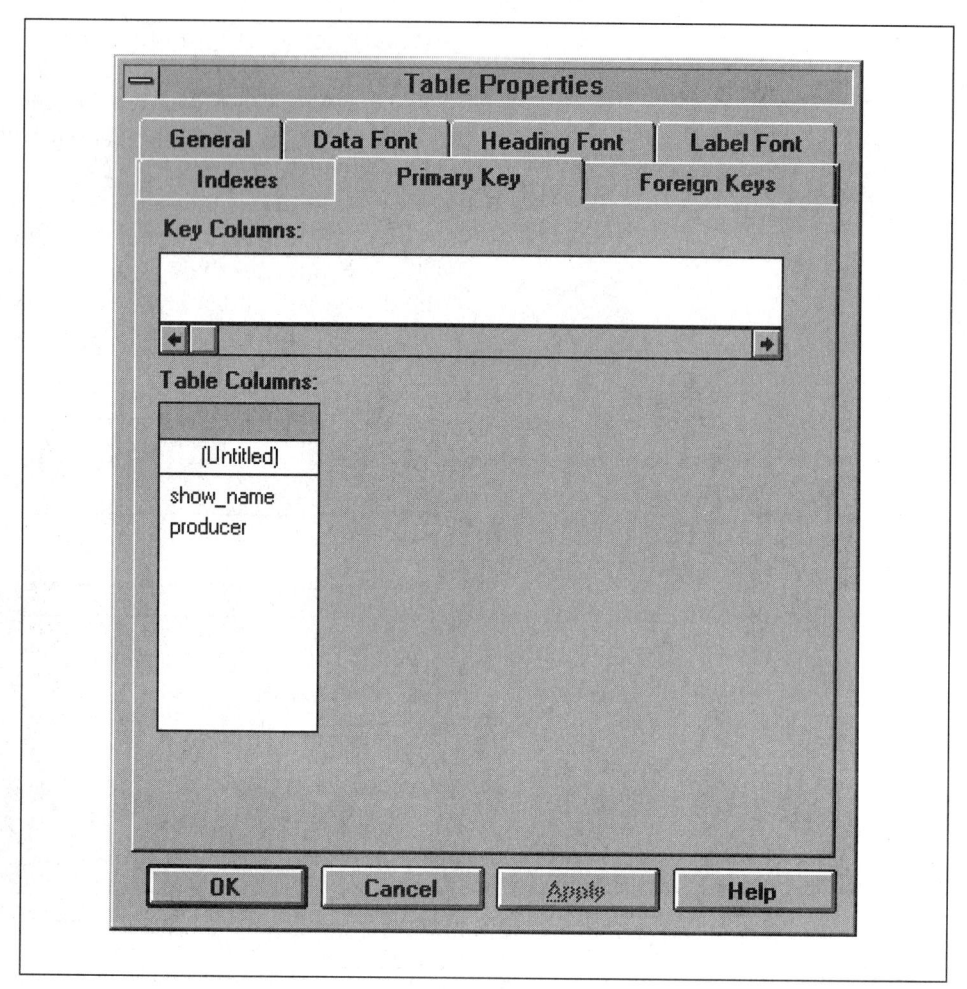

Figure 6.11
Declaring a primary key (5.0)

PowerBuilder 5.0

With version 5.0, the Primary Key panel appears in the Table Properties dialog box only when the table hasn't been saved. To change the primary key of an existing table, click the Primary Key button in the PainterBar to display the Primary Key definition dialog box.

2 Click **show_name** in the Table Columns list. The selected column appears in the Key Columns box as the first column of the primary key.

3 If there were additional columns in the primary key, you would repeat Step 2 for each column. In this particular example, the primary key was complete after executing Step 2.

4 Click the **OK** button to close the dialog box.

Although Watcom SQL and other similar database servers can store and enforce primary key constraints, they don't require you to declare a primary key for a table. Because it is possible to have a table without a primary key, today's DBMSs still don't provide complete primary key support.

5. If you are working with version 4.0, click the **Create** button in the Create Table dialog box. PowerBuilder closes the dialog box and creates the table.

   If you are working with version 5.0, double-click the Create Table window's control box. PowerBuilder asks you if you want to save the new table (Figure 6.12). Click the **Yes** button or press the **Enter** key to display the Create New Table dialog box. Type **shows** as the name of the table. Then click the **OK** button (Figure 6.13).

   If you are working with version 4.0, the table and its primary key appear in the Database painter's workspace (Figure 6.14 on page 102).

Figure 6.12
Deciding whether to save a new table (5.0)

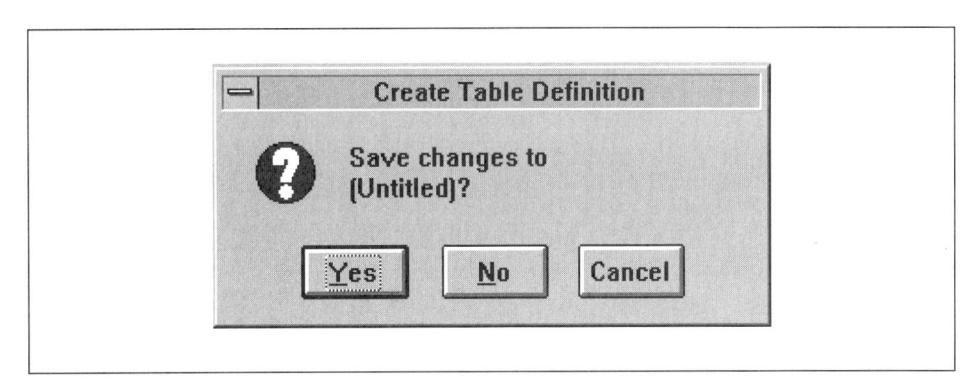

Figure 6.13
Naming and saving a new table (5.0)

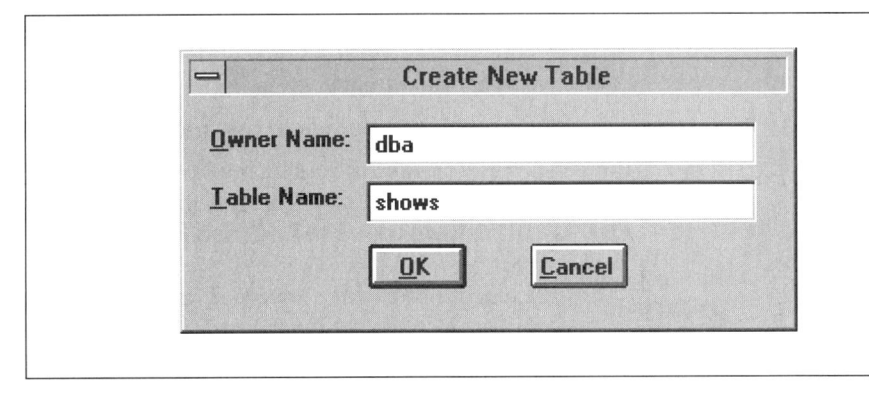

Because version 5.0 uses the separate Table painter to create tables, new tables do not automatically appear in the Database painter workspace. To open the new table, you must click on the Open button in the PainterBar to display the Select Table dialog box and then double-click the table name, just as you would to open any other table.

Setting Column Data Types To explore changing column data types, you will create a second table for the *tshows1* database. This table—Costs—stores data about how much Pinehill Software spent at a trade show.

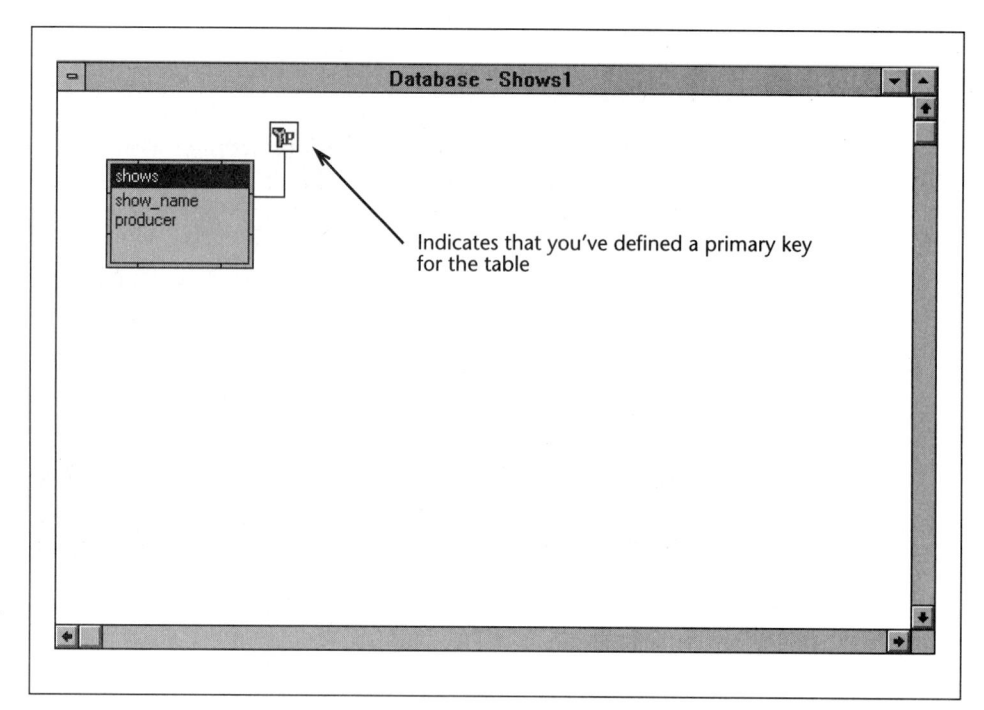

Figure 6.14
A table in the Database Painter workspace

[Screenshot: Database - Shows1 window showing a "shows" table with columns show_name and producer, with an arrow pointing to a key icon labeled "Indicates that you've defined a primary key for the table"]

To create the new table:

1. Click the **Create Table** button in the PainterBar.
2. Type **costs** as the name of the table.
3. Type **event#** as the name of the first column.
4. Click the **down arrow** next to the Type box.
5. Choose **smallint** from the dropdown menu (Figure 6.15 on page 103). If you are working with version 5.0, you will need to scroll the dropdown menu to find "smallint."

You can choose a value from a dropdown list by typing the first letter of the value. For example, to select "smallint," you could just press the letter "s". If more than one item in the list begins with the same letter, your first keypress selects the first item in the list that matches. Press the same key again to select the next item that matches, and so on until you reach your choice.

6. Type **cost_description** as the name of the second column. Make the column 50 characters wide. It should also be nonnull.
7. Type **amount** as the name of the third column.
8. Click the **down arrow** next to the amount column's Type box.
9. Choose **numeric** from the dropdown menu.
10. Press the **Tab** key.
11. Type **9** as the number of digits in the value.
12. Press the **Tab** key.

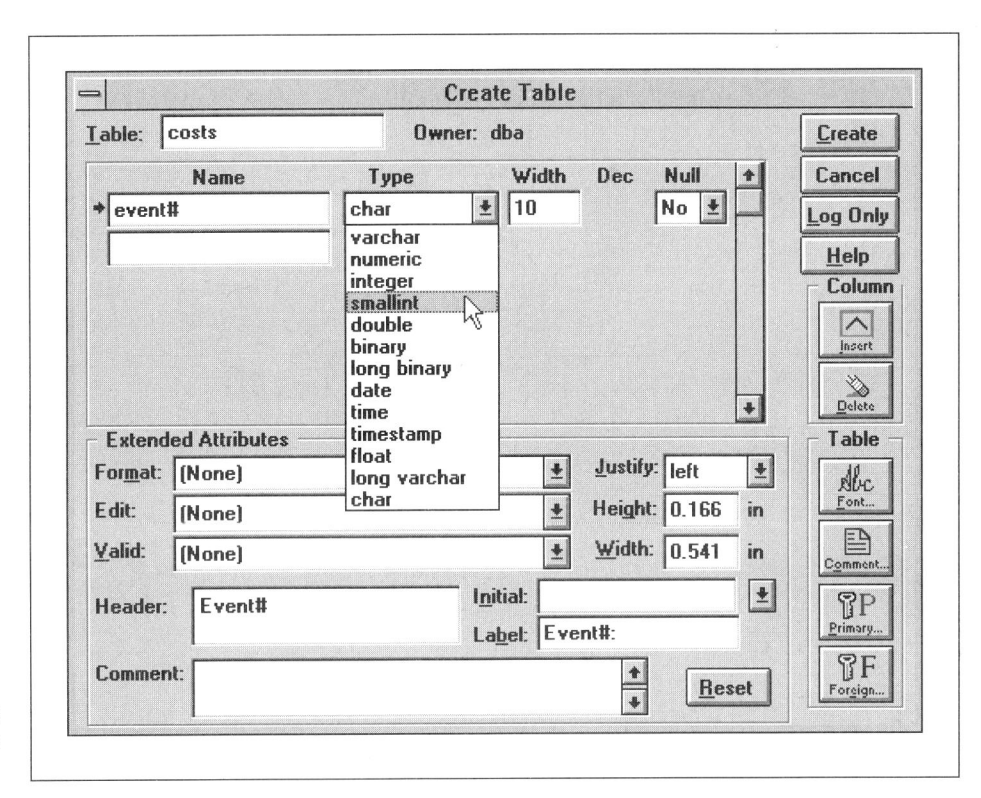

Figure 6.15
Choosing a column data type

13 Type **2** as the number of digits to the right of the decimal point. At this point, your Create Table dialog box should look like Figure 6.16 on page 104.

14 If you are working with version 4.0, click the **Primary** button to open the Primary Key Definition dialog box.

If you are working with version 5.0, click the **Properties** button in the PainterBar to open the Properties dialog box. Then click on the **Primary Key** tab to display the Primary Key panel.

15 Click **event#** and **cost_description** (in that order) as the primary key.

16 Close the Primary Key Definition dialog box.

Defining a Foreign Key

The linchpin of this entire database is really the Calendar table, which contains data about scheduled trade shows. There are three other tables that have foreign key references to Calendar's primary key (event#). To get experience with creating foreign keys, you should therefore next create the Calendar table using the information in Table 6.1.

The Costs table is one of the three tables that has event# as a foreign key. You should therefore declare a foreign key reference from the Costs table to the Shows table.

104 CHAPTER SIX MANAGING DATABASE STRUCTURE

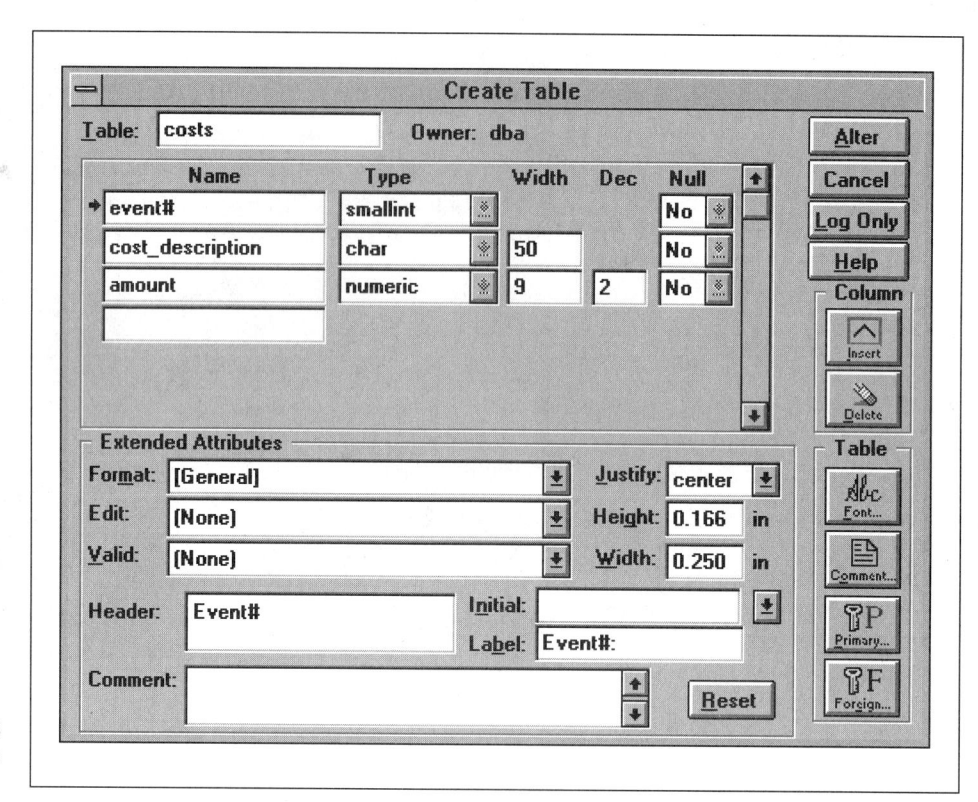

Figure 6.16
The completed costs table

Table 6.1
Specifications for the Calendar table

		COLUMN NAME	DATA TYPE	LENGTH
Table: Calendar		event#	smallint	
		show_name	char	25
Primary key:		start_date	date	
event#		end_date	date	
		participation	char	1

To define the foreign key:

1 If you are working with version 4.0, double-click the **Costs** table in the Database painter workspace. An Alter Table dialog box appears, which looks very much like the Create Table dialog box. However, some of the options are unavailable because some characteristics of a table can't be changed after the table has been created.

   If you are working with version 5.0, click the **Properties** button in the PainterBar to display the Table Properties dialog box.

2 If you are working with version 4,0, click the **Foreign** button in the lower-right corner of the Alter Table dialog box. The Foreign Key Selection dialog box appears (Figure 6.18 on page 105).

   If you are working with version 5.0, click the **Foreign Keys** tab to display the Foreign Keys panel (Figure 6.17 on page 105).

CHAPTER SIX MANAGING DATABASE STRUCTURE **105**

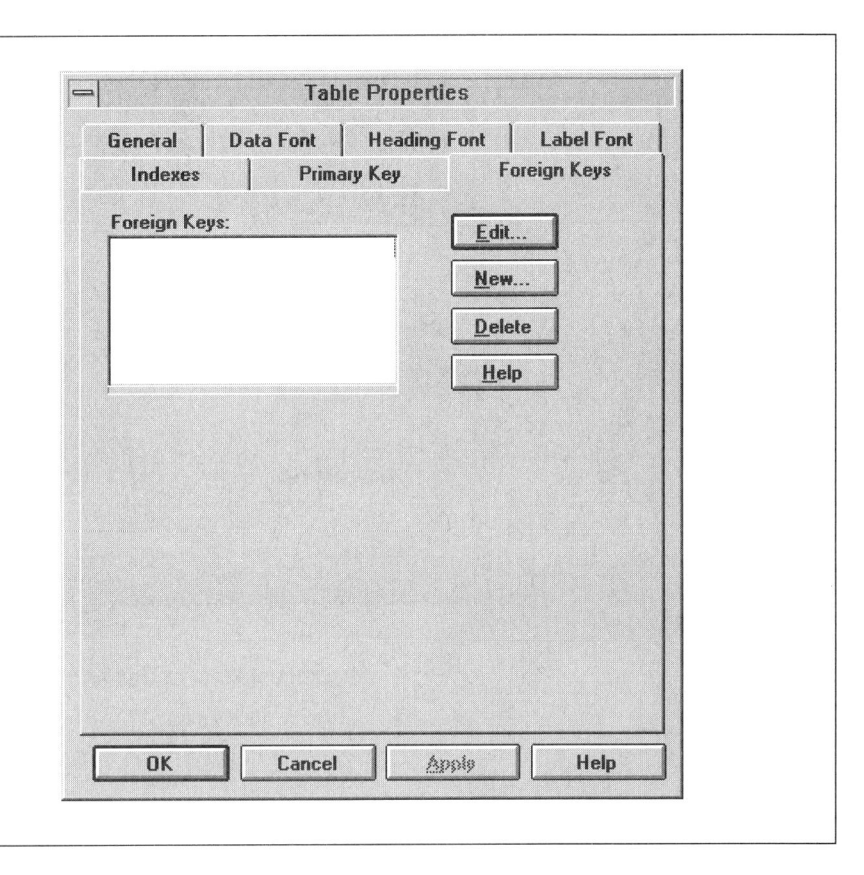

Figure 6.17
Foreign Keys panel in the Table Properties dialog box (5.0)

With version 5.0, the Foreign Keys panel appears only in the Table Properties dialog box until a table has been saved. To add a foreign key to an existing table, use the Foreign Key button in the PainterBar to display the Foreign Key definition dialog box.

3 Click the **New** button. The Foreign Key Definition dialog box appears (Figure 6.19 on page 106).

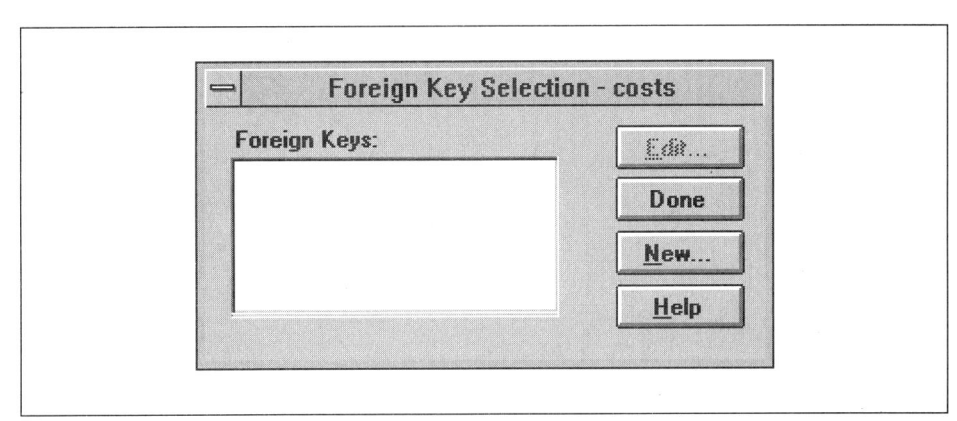

Figure 6.18
Foreign Key Selection dialog box (4.0)

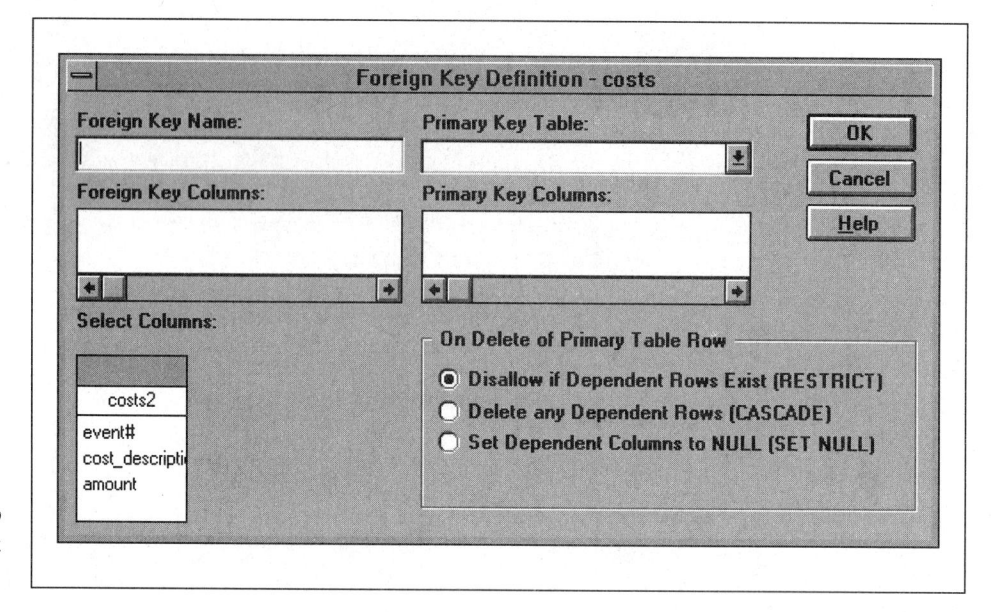

Figure 6.19
Foreign Key Definition dialog box

4. Type **costs2calendar** as the name of the foreign key.
5. Choose **calendar** from the Primary Key Table dropdown menu. PowerBuilder displays the primary key column of the Shows table in the Primary Key Columns box.
6. Click **event#** in the Select Columns list. The column name appears in the Foreign Key Columns box. At this point, the dialog box should look like Figure 6.20.

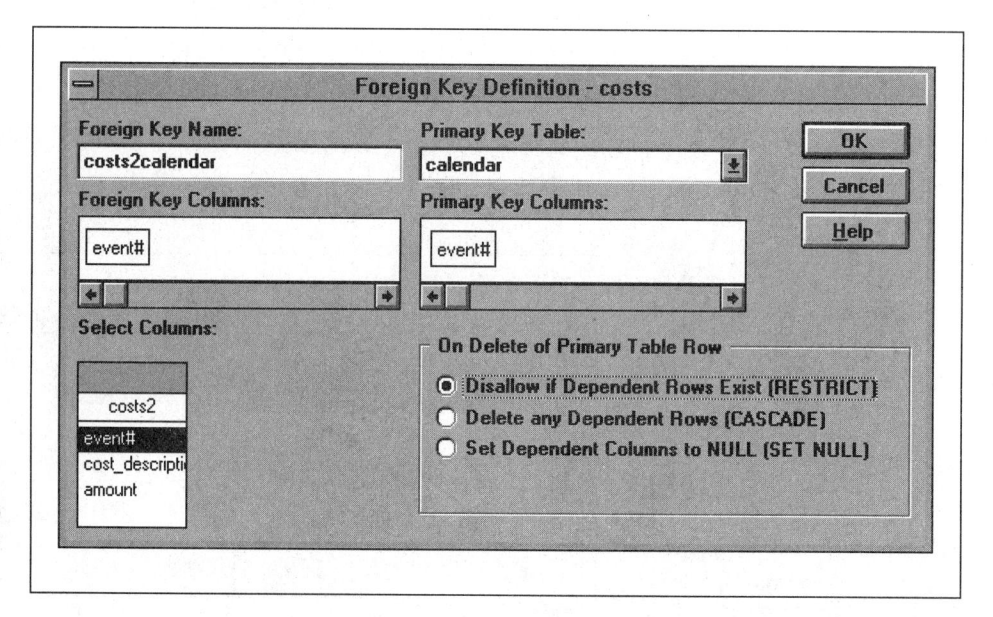

Figure 6.20
Completed foreign key definition

In the lower-right corner of the Foreign Key Definition dialog box there are three radio buttons that control what happens to rows in the foreign key table

CHAPTER SIX   MANAGING DATABASE STRUCTURE   **107**

when the primary key table row is deleted. There are three possible actions if referential integrity is to be maintained:

- RESTRICT: Prevent the deletion of the row from the primary key table when foreign key references exist.
- CASCADE: Delete all matching rows from the foreign key table when the primary key is deleted.
- SET NULL: Set the foreign key values to null when the primary key row in the primary key table is deleted. This is possible only when the foreign key isn't part of the primary key of its table.

In this particular case, the money spent on a trade show has little meaning if we can't retrieve information about the show itself. Therefore, leave the default RESTRICT option selected.

To finish creating the foreign key and the table:

1. Click the **OK** button to close the Foreign Key Definition dialog box. If you are working with version 4.0, the name of the foreign key now appears in the Foreign Key Selection dialog box.

   If you are working with version 5.0, the name of the foreign key appears in the Foreign Keys panel of the Table Properties dialog box.

2. If you are working with version 4.0, click the **Done** button to close the Foreign Key Selection dialog box. Then click the **Alter** button to close the Alter Table dialog box and add the foreign key to the table.

   If you are working with version 5.0, double-click the close box of the Table Properties dialog box to close the dialog box.

   As you can see in Figure 6.21, the Database painter workspace now shows all three tables along with their keys.

PowerBuilder doesn't always display foreign key references in the database painter workspace immediately after you close the Create or Alter Table dialog box in which the foreign key was defined. Something needs to trigger an update event in the workspace window so that the foreign key will be drawn. If you don't see the foreign key relationship that you created in the preceding Step 3, try clicking the Costs or Calendar table window.

Although the Database painter draws lines between foreign keys and the primary keys they reference, this doesn't mean that the database actually stores pointers for such "links." The lines are visible only for your reference; they aren't stored in the data dictionary.

Finishing the Schema   Repeat the procedure you have learned for creating tables and their keys for the remaining tables in the Pinehill Software schema. To create these tables as a part of the *tshows1* database, use the table and column information in Table 6.2 on page 109. Create foreign keys as needed. Depending on which foreign keys you decided to create, your completed Database painter workspace will include all the tables and many of the cross-reference lines in Figure 6.22 on page 108. Your arrangement of the table icons, however, will almost certainly be different.

108 CHAPTER SIX MANAGING DATABASE STRUCTURE

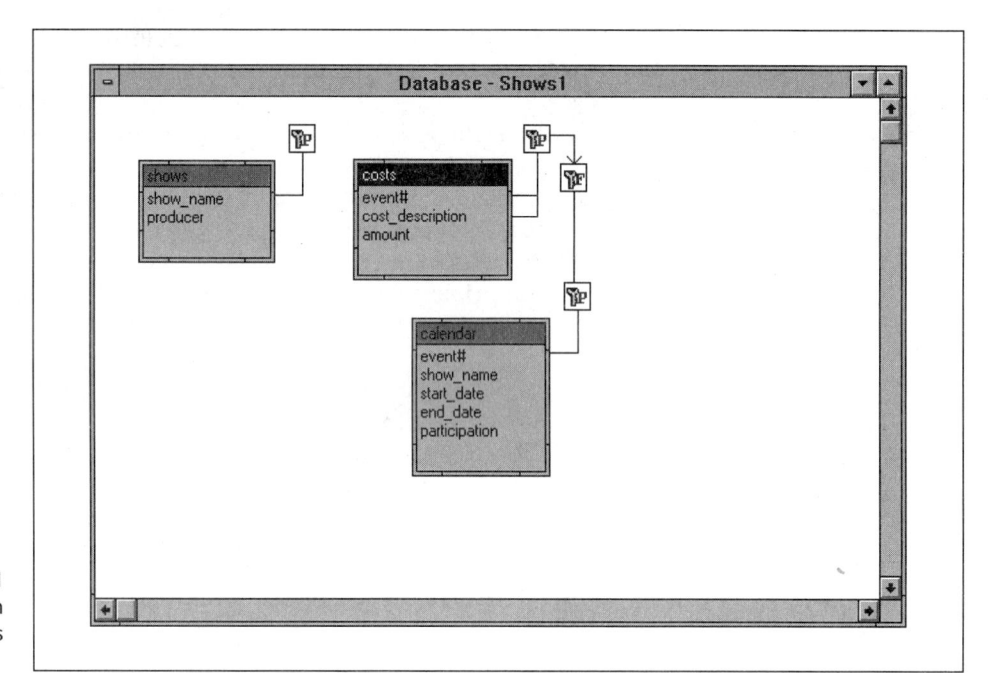

Figure 6.21
Database painter workspace with related tables

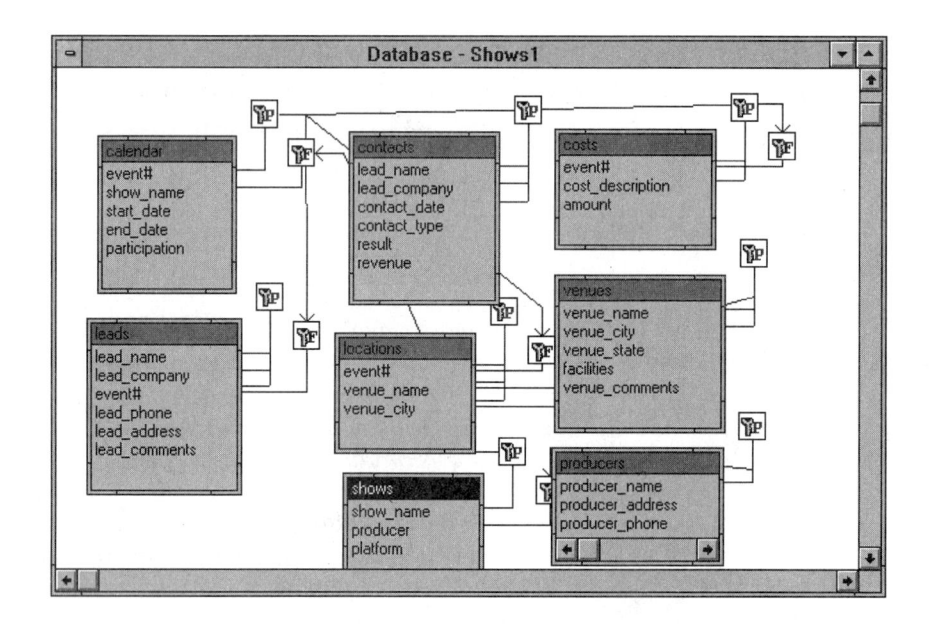

Figure 6.22
The complete *tshows1* schema

If you're having trouble identifying the foreign keys, look back at page 33 in Chapter 2.

	COLUMN NAME	DATA TYPE	WIDTH
Table: Leads	lead_name	char	25
	lead_company	char	25
Primary key:	event#	smallint	
lead_name	lead_phone	char	12
lead_company	lead_address	char	60
	lead_comments	char	256
Table: Contacts	lead_name	char	25
	lead_company	char	25
Primary key:	contact_date	date	
lead_name	contact_type	char	20
lead_company	result	char	128
contact_date	revenue	numeric	8, 2
Table: Producers	producer_name	char	25
	producer_phone	char	12
Primary key:	producer_address	char	40
producer_name			
Table: Venues	venue_name	char	25
	venue_city	char	20
Primary key:	venue_state	char	2
venue_name	facilities	char	256
venue_city	venue_comments	char	256
Table: Locations	event#	smallint	
	venue_name	char	25
Primary key:	venue_city	char	20
event#			
venue_name			
venue_city			

Table 6.2
Column definitions for the remaining tables in the *tshows1* database

> **NOTE** *In concept, having primary keys and foreign key references illustrated in the Database painter workspace is great. However, as you can see in Figure 6.22, once you get more than a few tables and cross-references on the screen, the display becomes so crowded that it's not very useful. (You can increase the resolution of your monitor or purchase a larger monitor to give you more room on your screen, but those options aren't always available.)*

> *If you aren't happy with where PowerBuilder places tables in the Database painter workspace, you can move the tables to new locations. Simply hold the left mouse button down over a table name and drag. PowerBuilder will redraw foreign key reference lines as needed. Alternatively, you can let PowerBuilder arrange them. To do so, click the Arrange button in the PainterBar (see Figure 6.23 on page 110) with version 4.0 or choose Window- >Arrange Icons with version 5.0.*

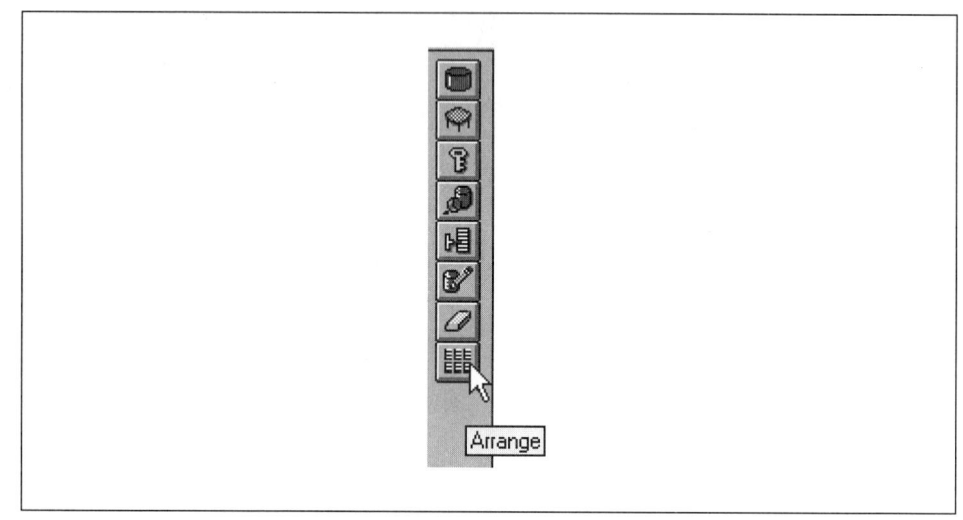

Figure 6.23
Arrange button in the PainterBar

Modifying a Schema

Over time, an organization's needs change, and the design of that organization's database must therefore change to meet new requirements. You must therefore be able to make alterations to a database schema as needed. As you would expect, you can add tables at any time; you can also delete (or *drop*) tables. However, as you will see in the next section, the modifications you can make to an existing table are rather limited.

Altering Table Definitions

Once a table has been created, there are only a few changes you can make to its structure. You can:

- Add a column (which must allow null values) to the end of a table
- Add foreign keys
- Change the table's extended attributes
- Make a column wider
- Allow nulls in a column that was previous nonnull (but not the opposite)

The last two options above are dependent on the DBMS. They are supported by Watcom SQL, but not by every database server. Even using Watcom SQL there are restrictions. For example, you can't make a primary key column wider.

CHAPTER SIX   MANAGING DATABASE STRUCTURE   **111**

> *If you want to make any other changes, you must create a new table, copy data from the original table into the new one using a SQL insert command (if possible), and then drop the original table. You will learn how to issue SQL commands directly to a database at the end of Chapter 7.*

For this exercise, you will be adding a column to the Shows table to indicate the type of hardware featured at a particular trade show.

To add the column:

1. Make sure that you are working with the *tshows1* database.
2. Enter the Database painter.
3. Open the Shows table.
4. Double-click the **Shows** table in the Database painter workspace. The Alter Table dialog box appears.
5. Click in the Name box (version 4.0) or Column Name box (version 5.0) below the producer column.
6. Type **platform** as the column name. Chose **char** from the Type drop-down menu. Then type **10** as the width. At this point your dialog box should look like Figure 6.24.

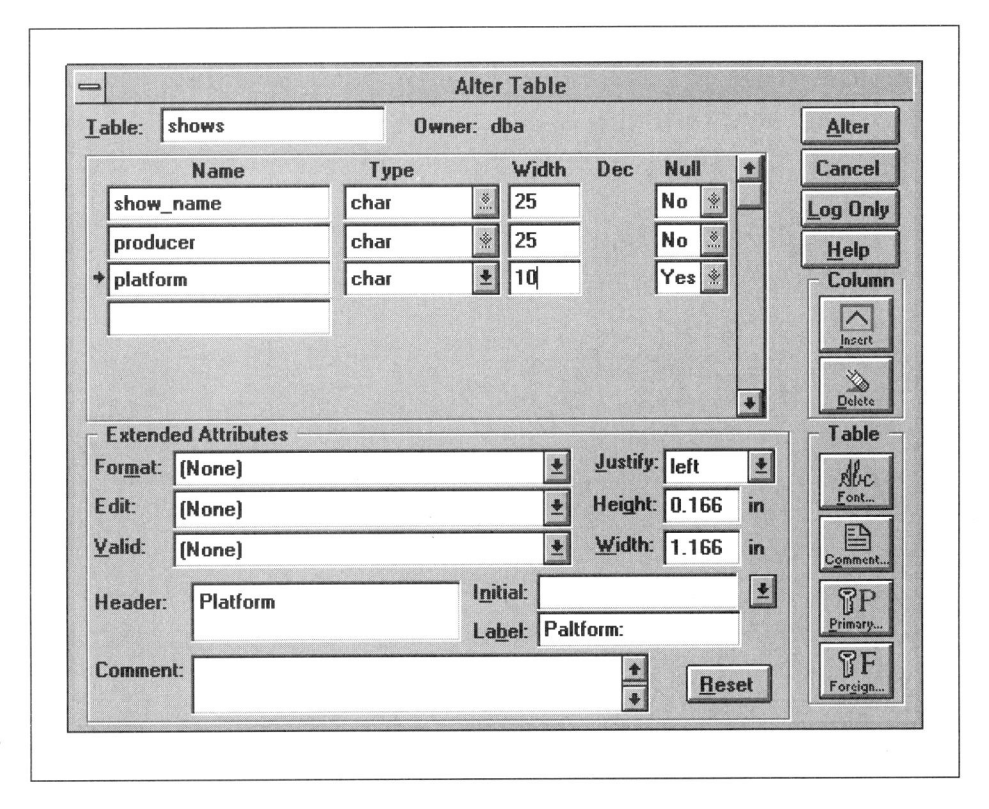

Figure 6.24
Adding a column to an existing table

7. Click the **Alter** button. PowerBuilder closes the Alter Table dialog box and adds the column to the Shows table. The new column appears at the bottom of the Shows table in the Database painter workspace.

Dropping Tables

To remove a table from the database, you drop the table. Although the procedure for dropping tables is easy, the consequences are serious. When you drop a table, the DBMS removes it completely, including the data and the structure of the table.

There is no way to undo a drop; once the table is gone, it's gone. The lesson here, of course, is that you should be very sure that you mean it when you give the command to drop a table.

For this exercise, you'll be dropping a table from *tshows1*. Since *tshows1* has no data, nothing is lost but the definitions of the columns in the table.

To drop a table:

1 Make sure that you are working with the *tshows1* database, that the Database painter is open, and that the for_deletion table is open in the workspace.

2 Click the **for_deletion** table window to select it.

3 Click the **Drop** button in the PainterBar (see Figure 6.25). A confirmation dialog box appears (Figure 6.26).

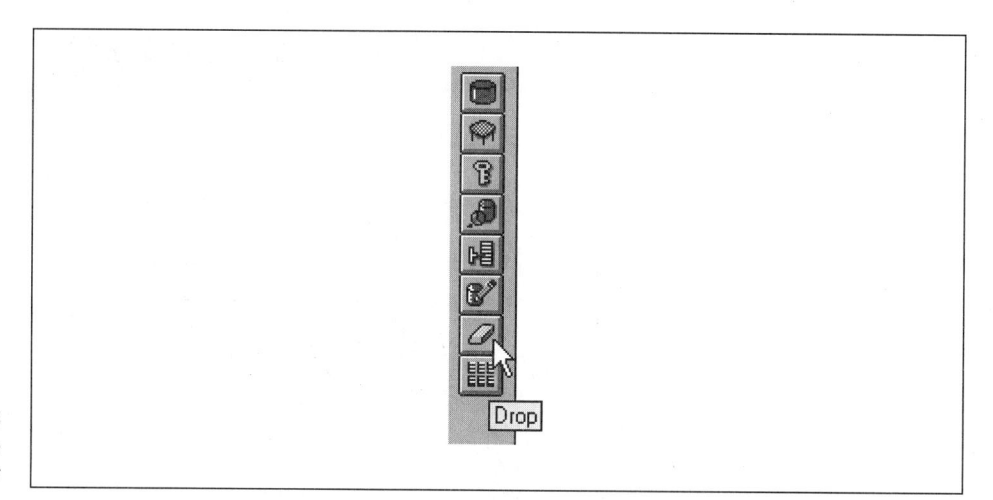

Figure 6.25
Drop button in the Database painter PainterBar

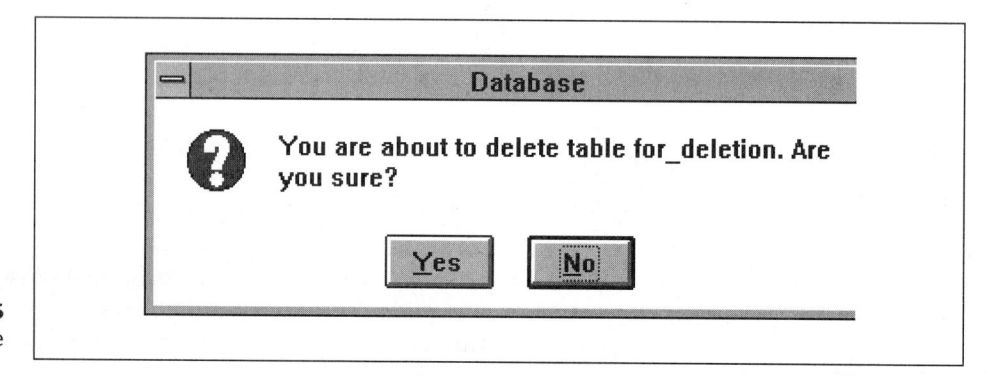

Figure 6.26
Confirming the drop of a table

4   Click the **Yes** button to complete dropping the table. PowerBuilder removes the table from the database and the workspace display.

Indexes

An *index* on a column or combination of columns in a table is like an index to a book. A book index contains an ordered list of key values (index terms in alphabetical order) to where information corresponding to the key is stored. Because we understand alphabetical order, we can search the ordered index very rapidly. In the same way, an index on data in a table can speed up searching.

Once an index is created, a DBMS will use that index whenever it determines that the index can help speed up a search. Aside from creating them, you will not need to deal directly with indexes in any way.

When you declare a primary key, PowerBuilder automatically builds an index on that key. This index has two purposes: it speeds access using the primary key and makes it possible to enforce primary key uniqueness. You can build indexes on other columns, or combinations of columns, to achieve the same two effects.

Deciding Which Indexes to Create

Indexes can indeed speed up searching, but at the same time, they consume disk space and slow down data modification. Each index stores a copy of the values in the column or columns on which the index is based as well a pointer to where each row can be found in the base table (for example, Figure 6.27). This means that the values in the index column or columns are stored twice, doubling the amount of disk space occupied by the columns in question. In addition, there is no limit to the number of indexes in which a column can be used, possibly adding to the data duplication.

The values in an index are ordered (alphabetically for character data, numerically for number columns, chronologically for date and time columns, and so on). The ordering allows a DBMS to use fast search techniques on the index, rather than slowly searching the base table sequentially. However, the fast search techniques are effective only if the index remains in the correct order. The index must therefore be updated whenever data are entered, updated, or deleted. If a table has thousands of rows and several indexes, the time needed to update the indexes may noticeably slow data modification. The bottom line is that it takes extra time to maintain indexes, as well extra space to store the indexes.

Because indexes speeds searching but use additional disk space and slow data modification, there is a performance and storage trade-off that you need to consider when deciding to create an index. In general, you should create indexes when any of the three following statements are true:

- A column or combination of columns make up a foreign key, especially one that will be used frequently to join tables.
- Columns are used frequently in row selection criteria.

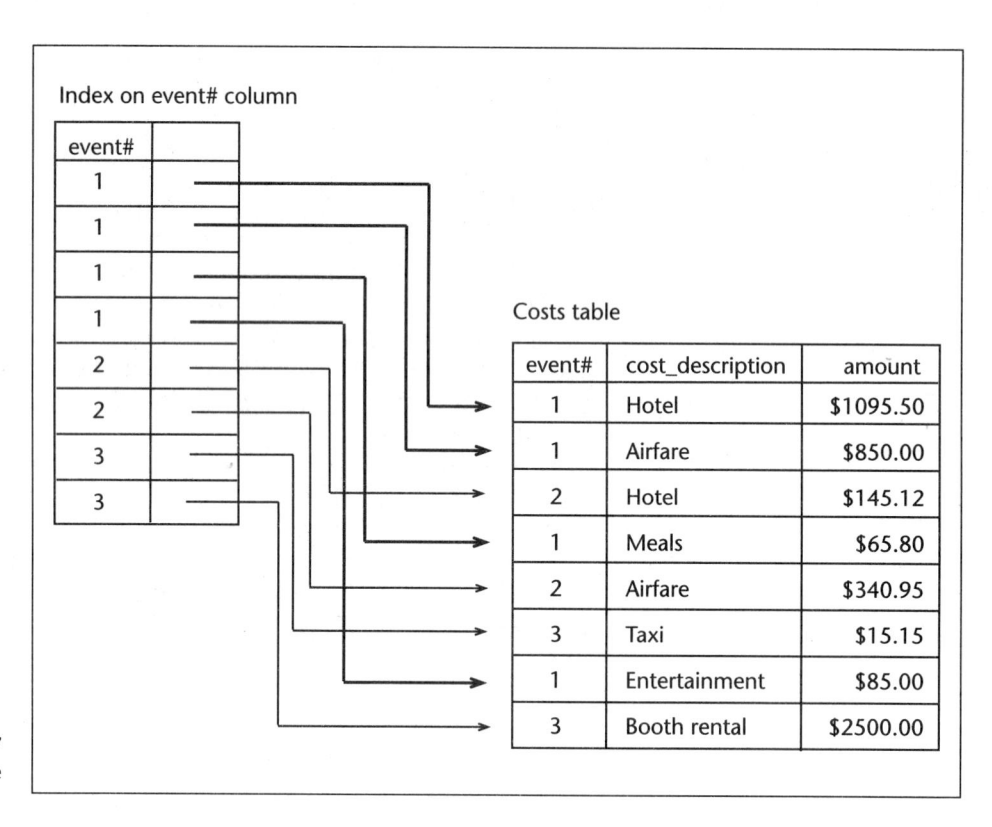

Figure 6.27
Function of an index to a table

[Diagram showing Index on event# column with values 1,1,1,1,2,2,3,3 mapping via arrows to the Costs table with columns event#, cost_description, amount:]

Costs table

event#	cost_description	amount
1	Hotel	$1095.50
1	Airfare	$850.00
2	Hotel	$145.12
1	Meals	$65.80
2	Airfare	$340.95
3	Taxi	$15.15
1	Entertainment	$85.00
3	Booth rental	$2500.00

- The values in a column or combination of columns must be unique although the column or columns aren't the primary key of the table. In most cases, these will be candidate keys.

Creating Indexes

As you explore the creation of indexes, you will be working with the *tshows* database, a version of the trade show database that contains all of the tables populated with sample data. This database will be used throughout the rest of this book.

To build an index on the event# column in the Locations table:

1 Enter the Database painter and connect to the *tshows* database. Display all the tables in the workspace.

2 Click the **Locations** table window to select it.

3 Click the **Index** icon in the PainterBar (see Figure 6.28 on page 115). The Create Index dialog box appears, as in Figure 6.29 on page 115.

4 Type **locations_event#** in the Create Index box as the name of the index.

5 Click the **Duplicate** radio button. (There will be duplicate values for event# in this table.)

CHAPTER SIX   MANAGING DATABASE STRUCTURE   **115**

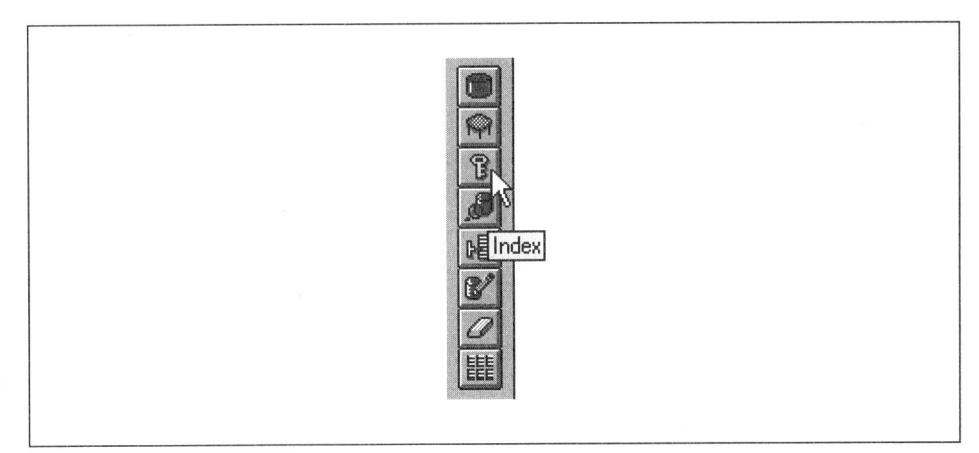

Figure 6.28
Index button in the PainterBar

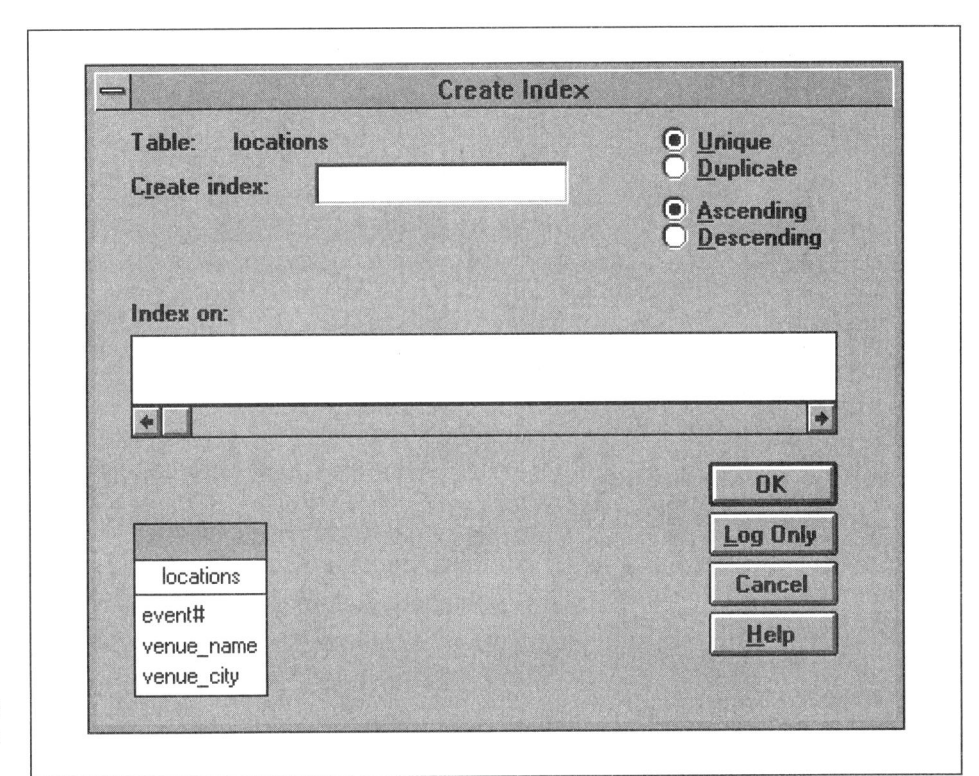

Figure 6.29
Create Index dialog box

6   The Ascending/Descending radio buttons determine whether indexing goes for high to low values or low to high values. Make sure the Ascending option is selected.

7   Click **event#** in the list of column names in the lower-left corner of the dialog box. The column name appears in the Index on box.

8   Click the **OK** button to create the index. PowerBuilder displays the presence of the duplicate index in the workspace. (In Figure 6.30 on page 116, look for the icon with two keys.)

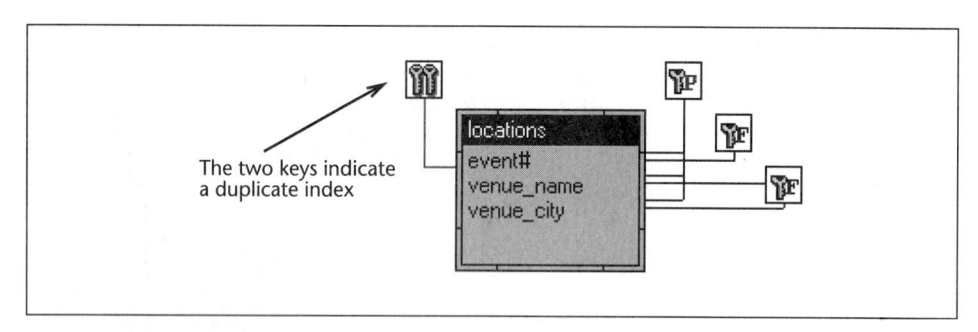

Figure 6.30
Column with a duplicate index

The two keys indicate a duplicate index

As with the display of foreign key references, PowerBuilder may need a bit of a jolt to update your display with the index you just created. Therefore, if the index doesn't appear in the Database painter workspace, do something that forces PowerBuilder to update the display, such as opening an Alter Table dialog box by double-clicking a table name.

To return to the Create Index dialog box, click the key icon that represents the index in the workspace.

A unique index allows only one occurrence of each key value. If you attempt to insert a a new row with a duplicate key or value or update data so that a key value becomes a duplicate, the DBMS will prevent the data modification. This is the way in which SQL-based DBMSs enforce unique primary keys. The important thing to recognize is that although the effect is to ensure that there are no duplicate keys in the base table, the check for uniqueness is being made in an index, not in the base table.

To create a unique index for a candidate key in a table that isn't a primary key:

1 Click the Calendar table window in the workspace to select it.
2 Click the **Index** button in the PainterBar.
3 Type **calendar_name_date** as the name of the index.
4 Make sure the Unique radio button is selected.
5 Make sure the Ascending radio button is selected.
6 Click the **show_name** and **start_date** columns. The completed dialog box should look like Figure 6.31 on page 117.
7 Click the **OK** button. PowerBuilder closes the dialog box and creates the index. The unique index appears in the workspace as a single key icon (see Figure 6.32 on page 117).

When you create a unique index for a table that already contains data, PowerBuilder verifies that the data meet the constraint imposed by the index (index values will be unique) before creating it.

For additional practice, create the remaining indexes for the *tshows* database. Descriptions of those indexes can be found in Table 6.3 on page 117. All indexes are duplicate (in other words, they allow duplicate index key values).

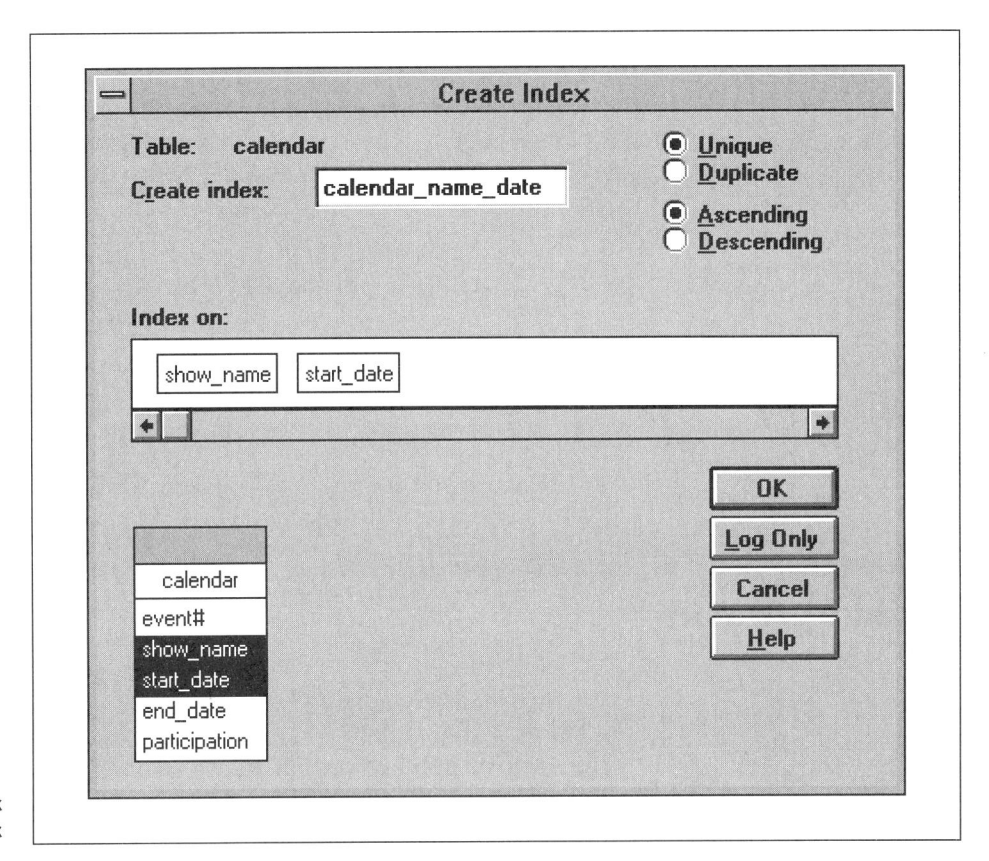

Figure 6.31
Completed Create Index dialog box for a unique index

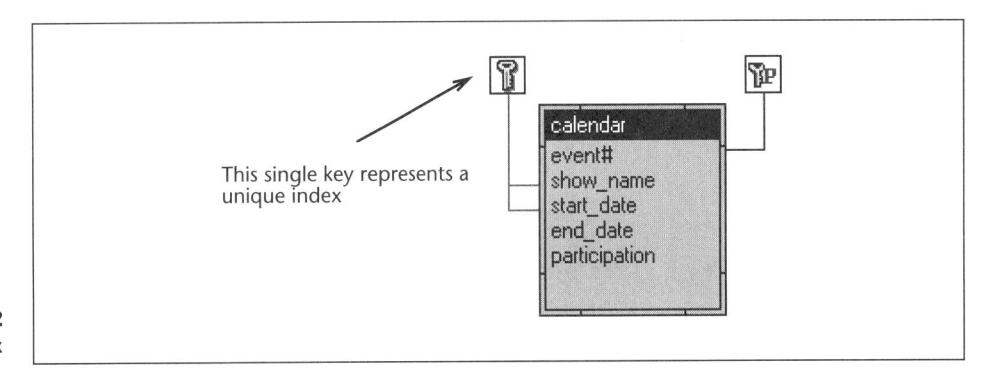

Figure 6.32
Column with a unique index

This single key represents a unique index

TABLE	INDEX NAME	COLUMNS
Contacts	contacts_name_company	lead_name
		lead_company
Locations	locations_name_city	venue_name
		venue_city
Leads	leads_event#	event#
Costs	costs_event#	event#
Shows	shows_producer	producer

Table 6.3
Additional indexes for the *tshows* database

Dropping Unwanted Indexes

Removing an unwanted index is even easier than dropping a table.

To drop an index:

1. Make sure that you are working with the *tshows* database and that all tables are displayed in the Database painter workspace.
2. Click the **key** icon of any index to select it.
3. Click the **Drop** button in the PainterBar. PowerBuilder deletes the index.

Because you are going to continue working with the *tshows* database, you should re-create the index you just dropped.

Looking Ahead

In this chapter you have learned to create the initial structure of a database. The next step in data manipulation is to add data to that database. As you develop an application, you may also find that you need to retrieve data to test queries that will become part of the application. You will learn how to add, modify, and delete data as well as how to issue direct queries to a database in the next chapter.

EXERCISES

As you may have discovered, the *rents* database that accompanies this book is incomplete because it has only four tables. The remaining three—Schools, Dorms, and Contacts—have been left for you to create in the following exercises. The first exercise takes you step by step through the table creation process; the remaining exercises leave you on your own.

1. Create the Schools table.
    a. Launch PowerBuilder and open any application.
    b. Connect to any database.
    c. Enter the Database painter.
    d. If necessary, configure ODBC for the *rents* database.
    e. Connect to *rents*.
    f. Open all the tables currently in the database.
    g. Click the New button in the PainterBar.
    h. Type "schools" as the name of the table. Then press the Tab key.
    i. Type "school_name" as the name of the first column. Choose "varchar" as the column's data type. Make it 30 characters wide. Do not allow nulls.

CHAPTER SIX MANAGING DATABASE STRUCTURE

j. Type "housing_office_phone#" as the name of the second column. Choose "char" as the column's data type. Make it 12 characters wide. Nulls are allowed.
k. Type "housing_officer" as the name of the third column. Choose "char" as the column's data type. Make it 30 characters wide. Nulls are allowed.
l. Create a primary key using "school_name" as the single primary key column.
m. Click the Create button to create the table and return to the Database painter.

2. Create the Dorms table using the data types and lengths in Table 6.4. Use school_name and dorm_name as the primary key. Create a foreign key that references the primary key of the Schools table and create an index on the school_name column.

COLUMN NAME	DATA TYPE	WIDTH
school_name	varchar	30
dorm_name	char	50
dorm_address	char	75
how_many_rooms	integer	

Table 6.4 Specifications for the Dorms table

It is essential that you adhere to the preceding column order, data types, and lengths. In later chapters you will load data into this table from a text file. The load will not work properly if the columns are in a different order or if they are too short to contain the data.

3. Create the Contacts table using the data types and lengths in Table 6.5. Use school_name and contact_date as the primary key. Create a foreign key that references the primary key of the Schools table and create an index on the school_name column. As with the Schools and Dorms tables, be sure to adhere to these column orders, data types, and lengths.

COLUMN NAME	DATA TYPE	WIDTH
school_name	varchar	30
contact_date	date	
activity	char	30
result	char	256

Table 6.5 Specifications for the Contacts table

4. Now that you have created all the tables for the *rents* database, you should add some additional foreign key references and indexes.

   a. Customer table: Create an index on the school_name column. Create a foreign key reference to the primary key of the School table.

b. Item table: Create an index on the merchandise# column.

c. Rentals table: Create an index on the customer# column.

d. Identify any other foreign keys or places where indexes might be useful. If you are able to find some, create the necessary foreign keys and indexes.

The exercises below make such significant modifications to the database structure that it will be unsuited for use in the exercises in other chapters. Therefore, connect to the CURents database beginning any of the following exercises. You will be using this database only for these exercises; you can delete it after you have finished. **USE CURents ONLY in the remaining exercises; put rents away!**

5. Change the name of the delivery_date column in the Rentals table to d_date.

6. Change the name of the school_name column in the Customer table to name_of_school. What affect does this have on the school_name column in the Schools, Dorms, and Contacts tables? What does this tell you about the need for foreign key columns to have the same names as the primary key columns they reference?

7. Attempt to change the width of the school_name column in the Customer table to 50. Does PowerBuilder permit this change? Why or why not? What does this tell you about the need for foreign key columns to have the same lengths of the primary key columns they reference?

8. Attempt to change the width of the school_name column in the School table to 15. Does PowerBuilder permit this change? Why or why not?

9. PowerBuilder will not allow you to change the data type of an existing column. Instead, you must create a new table and then drop the old one. (Typically you copy data from the old table to the new, but we'll leave out that step for now.) To see how this works, do the following:

   a. Create a new table named Customer2 using the specifications in Table 6.6. The table's primary key is customer#; also create a foreign key for the school_name column.

COLUMN NAME	DATA TYPE	WIDTH
customer#	integer	
first_name	char	15
last_name	char	15
street	char	30
city	char	15
state	char	2
zip	char	5
customer_phone	char	12
school_name	char	30

Table 6.6 Specifications for the Customer2 table

b. Drop the Customer table. What affect does this have on foreign keys from other tables that reference the primary key of this table?
c. Open the Alter Table dialog box for each table that lost a foreign key reference to the original Customer table. Edit the foreign key reference to reestablish it with the new Customer2 table.
d. Rename the Customer2 table as Customer. What affect does this have on foreign keys from other tables that reference the primary key of this table?

Chapter Seven

Direct Data Manipulation

IN THIS CHAPTER YOU WILL:

- Use the Data Manipulation painter to view and modify data
- Create views
- Use PowerBuilder's interface for formulating SQL queries

Although PowerBuilder's primary purpose is application development, it can also be used to interact directly with the data stored in base tables. In this chapter, you learn about how you can view and modify data using the Data Manipulation painter. You will then learn to create views that, among other things, can help make the Data Manipulation painter more flexible. As you learn to create views, you will also learn to use PowerBuilder's interface for formulating SQL queries.

The Data Manipulation Painter

The Data Manipulation painter is accessed from the Database painter. Its purpose is to let you view and manipulate the data in one base table at a time. As you will see throughout this chapter, its retrieval capabilities are rather limited and it is therefore best suited for quick checks of data during application development rather than day-to-day activities, which are typically most easily performed using an application.

The Data Manipulation painter can also be reached from the PowerBar if the painter's button has been added to the default PowerBar.

Entering the Data Manipulation Painter

To enter the Data Manipulation painter:

1. Launch PowerBuilder, open the *tshows* application in *tshows1.pbl*, enter the Database painter, and connect to the *tshows* database.
2. Open the Costs table in the workspace.
3. Click the **Preview** button in the PainterBar (Figure 7.1). PowerBuilder switches to the Data Manipulation painter and retrieves the data in the table, displaying it in a listing format, as in Figure 7.2. Notice that the Data Manipulation painter has its own PainterBar, different from that of the Database painter. Notice also that the MicroHelp bar in the lower-left corner of the window shows you which rows are being displayed.

You can see the contents of a view as well as a table in the Data Manipulation painter.

4. Click the **down arrow** in the vertical scroll bar once to scroll the window. Notice how many rows are scrolled into view.
5. Press the **Page Down** key to scroll the window. Notice how many rows are scrolled into view.

If the screen isn't wide enough to display all the columns in the table, use the horizontal scroll bar to move the display left and right.

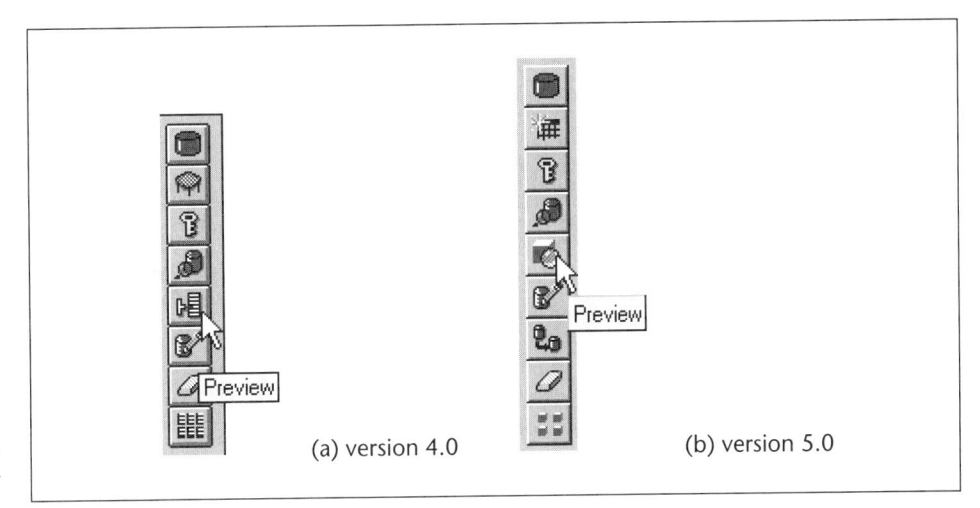

Figure 7.1
Preview button in the PainterBar

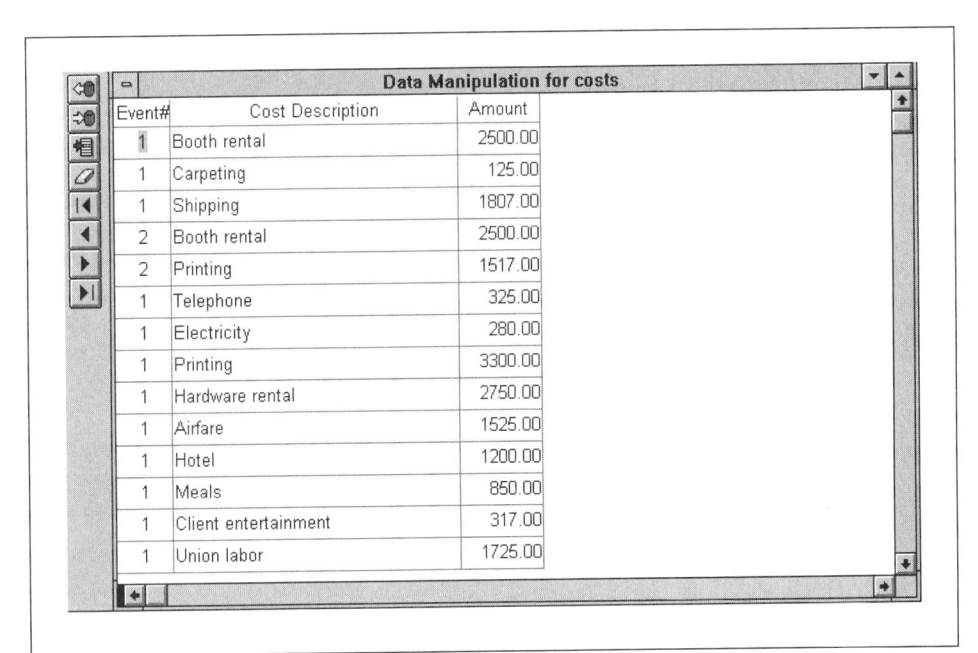

(a) version 4.0   (b) version 5.0

Figure 7.2
TData in a base table displayed in the Data Manipulation painter workspace

Exiting the Data Manipulation Painter

To exit the Data Manipulation painter, double-click the control box in the upper-left corner of the workspace window. You are returned to the Database painter.

Filtering Data

When you enter the Data Manipulation painter, PowerBuilder shows you every row in the table or view with which you're working. However, the Data Manipulation painter does let you supply some simple retrieval criteria to restrict what you see.

To create a data filter:

1. Display the Costs table in the Data Manipulation painter workspace.

Because a data filter can affect only one table or view, if you want to work with data that are stored in more than one table, you must be working with a view that performs the needed joins. Creating views is discussed later in this chapter.

2. Choose **Rows -> Filter** to display the Specify Filter dialog box.
3. Type **amount > 300** in the box in the upper-left corner of the dialog box, as in Figure 7.3.

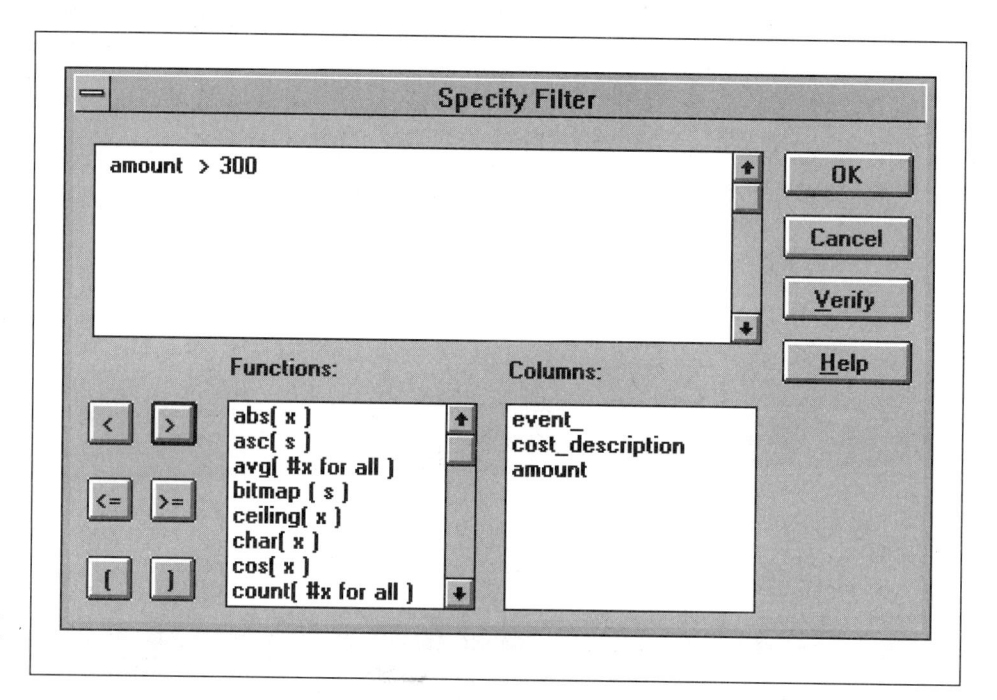

Figure 7.3
Specifying a data filter

4. Click the **OK** button. PowerBuilder closes the dialog box and applies the filter to the data in the table or view with which you are currently working.
5. Exit the Data Manipulation painter.
6. Reenter the Data Manipulation painter. Notice that PowerBuilder did not retain the data filter; all rows in the table will appear.

The logical expression that you type in the Specify Filter dialog can contain any number of simple logical expressions, linked by AND and OR. As you look at Figure 7.3, notice that as an alternative to typing every part of the expression, you can click the column names, function names, and some of the operators. However, because the operator buttons only provide some of the operators you might want to use, it's often easier just to type the expression.

NOTE *To remove a data filter without exiting the Data Manipulation painter—restoring the display to all the rows in the table or view—open the Specify Filter dialog box and delete the contents of the filter. When you close the dialog box, PowerBuilder redisplays every row.*

Sorting Data

In addition to performing simple queries on base tables, the Data Manipulation painter will also sort the contents of the table or view displayed in its workspace. Keep in mind that this sorting is done only in the computer's main memory (RAM); it does not affect the order in which data are stored in the base tables.

To sort the contents of a table:

1 If necessary, display the contents of the Costs table from the *tshows* database in the Data Manipulation painter.

2 Choose **Rows** -> **Sort**. The Specify Sort Columns dialog box appears (Figure 7.4).

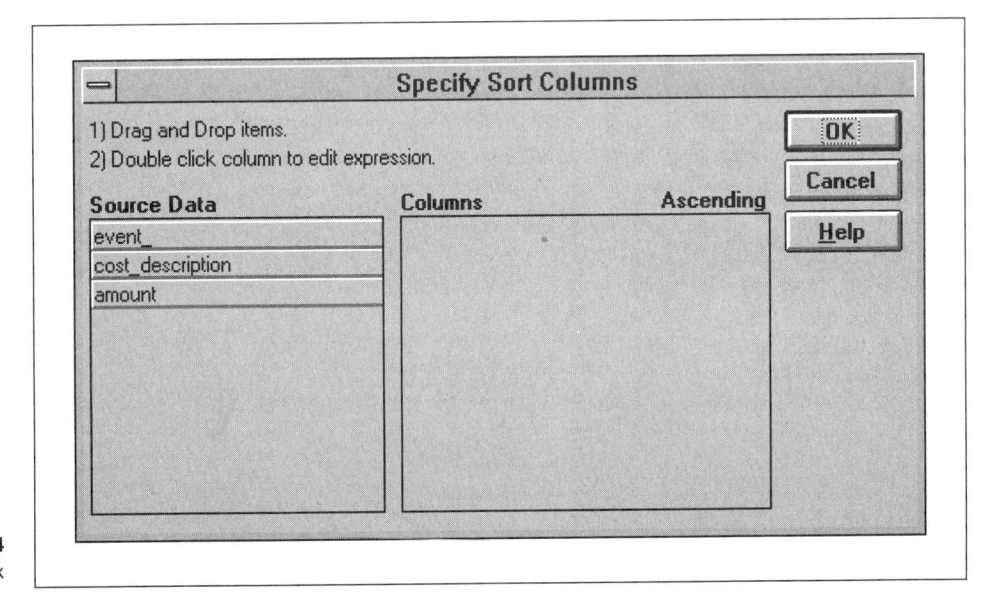

Figure 7.4
Specify Sort Columns dialog box

3 Drag the **amount** column name from the Source Data list at the left of the dialog box to the **Columns** list in the middle of the dialog box. A small rectangle moves with the pointer as you drag. Release the mouse button when that rectangle is in the **Columns** list.

4 By default, sorting is in ascending order. For this example, remove the X from the Ascending check box. Your completed dialog box should look like Figure 7.5.

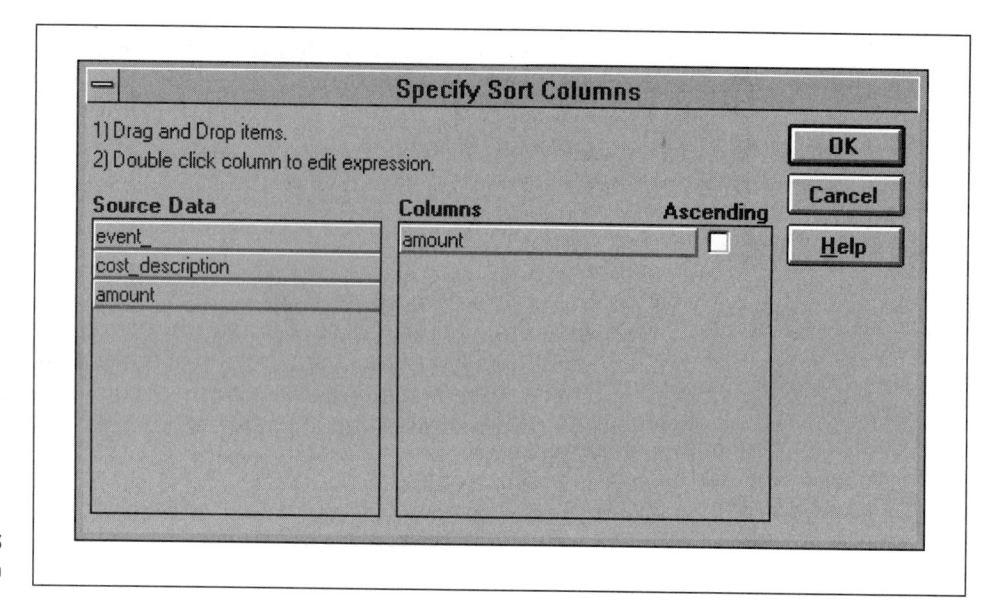

Figure 7.5
Completed sort specification

5   Click the **OK** button. PowerBuilder closes the Specify Sort Columns dialog box, sorts the data in the workspace, and displays the result.
6   Exit the Data Manipulation painter.

As with data filters, PowerBuilder does not retain sort specifications when you leave the Data Manipulation painter. The sorting and data filter capabilities provided by the Data Manipulation painter are therefore only suited for simple, ad hoc work.

Modifying Data

The Data Manipulation painter lets you modify data directly in base tables. Although it doesn't present a particularly user-friendly interface, it's convenient for quick data maintenance.

You cannot use the Data Manipulation painter to modify data displayed in views, even if the view meets the view updatability criteria described later in this chapter. You also will not be able to edit data in a table that doesn't have a primary key.

When you enter the Data Manipulation painter, PowerBuilder opens a transaction. As you will see shortly, you can commit the transaction at any time. If there are uncommitted changes when you leave the Data Manipulation painter, PowerBuilder asks if you want to save them.

Editing Existing Data

If you need to make simple changes to data, you can make them directly through the Data Manipulation painter. As you will see, this type of data modification is tedious, particularly because all operations are manual. Nonetheless, you may need to use PowerBuilder's direct data modification capabilities to correct inaccurate data or make other small modifications during application development.

To edit data already stored in a table:

1. Display the Calendar table from the *tshows* database in the Data Manipulation painter.
2. Click in the row and column you want to edit. In this case, click the **Start Date** column for any event. PowerBuilder highlights the contents of the row and column intersection and places a flashing insertion point at the left of the data.
3. Move the insertion point to the left of the character where modification is to begin. For this exercise, press the **right arrow** key four times to move the cursor to the left of the second digit of the day portion of the date.

If an entire data value is highlighted after clicking, be careful not touch the Backspace or any other character key before using an arrow key to move the insertion point. If you do, you will delete all of the highlighted data.

4. Press the **Delete** key to delete the character to the right of the insertion point.
5. Type the replacement value of **1**. PowerBuilder inserts the new character.

Once the intersection of a column and row is highlighted, you can also move the insertion point by clicking the pointer in the location you want it to appear.

6. Click the **Save Changes** button in the PowerBar (Figure 7.6) to commit the transaction, making the change to the database permanent.

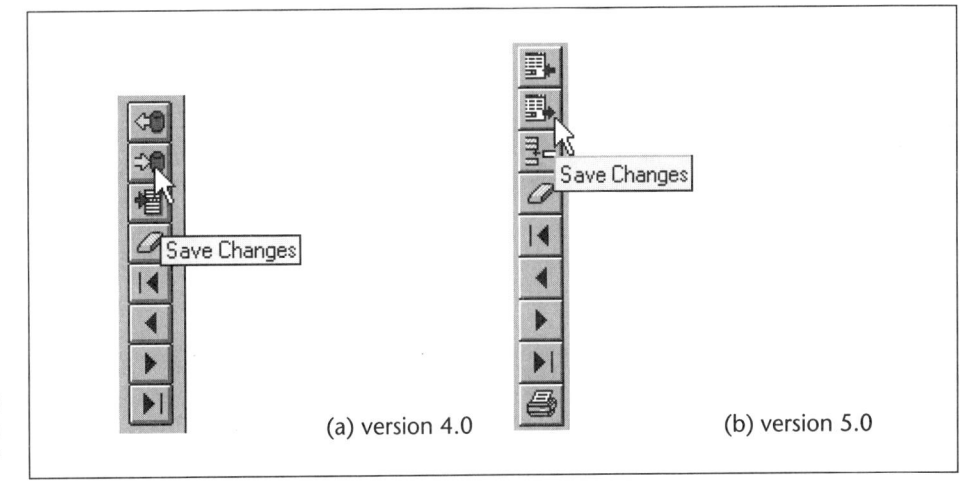

Figure 7.6
Save Changes button in the PainterBar

(a) version 4.0

(b) version 5.0

Inserting Rows

Like the direct modification of data, inserting data directly into a base table can be tedious. However, when you are developing an application, you need to be able to enter data on which you can test your application. Using the Data Manipulation painter is the only way to do so.

To use the Data Manipulation painter to add a new row to a table:

1. Display the Calendar table on the Data Manipulation painter. (If you've been working through this chapter without stopping, the table should already be displayed.)
2. Click the pointer anywhere in the row above which you want a new row inserted. In this case, click in the second row from the top.
3. Click the **Insert Row** button in the PowerBar (Figure 7.7). PowerBuilder inserts an empty row (see Figure 7.8) that contains a null in every column. Although the nulls look like spaces, if you save the row without entering any data in any given column, the database will store a null in that column.

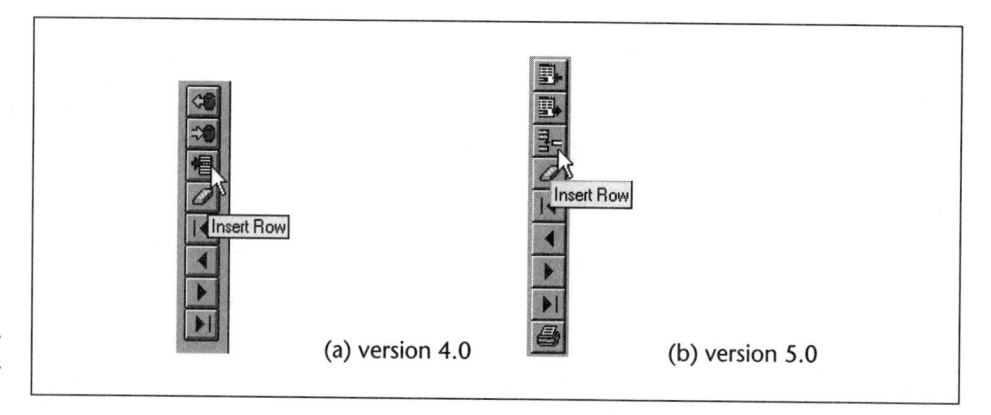

Figure 7.7
Insert Row button in the PainterBar

(a) version 4.0 (b) version 5.0

Figure 7.8
Empty row ready for new data

4 Type data for the new row. In this case, replace the nulls with the following data:

Event#	**20**
Show Name	**PCExpo**
Start Date	**2/18/97**
End Date	**2/22/97**
Participation	**T**

5 Double-click the Data Manipulation painter's close box. PowerBuilder asks you whether you want to save your changes, as in Figure 7.9.

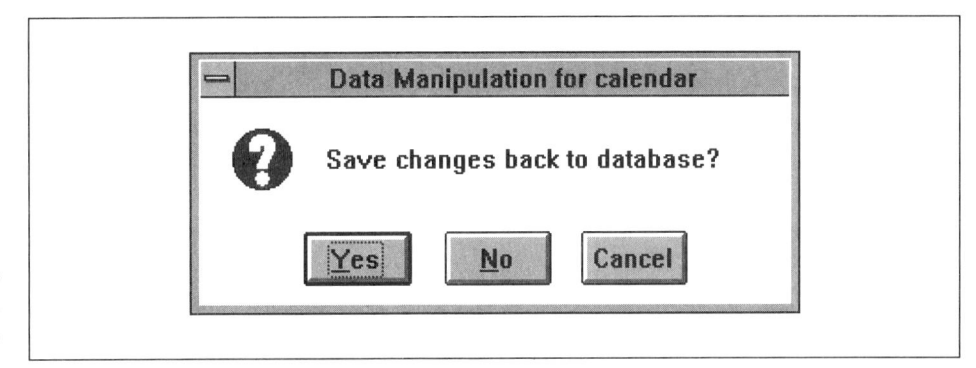

Figure 7.9
Deciding whether to save database modifications

6 Click the **Yes** button. PowerBuilder returns you to the Database painter.

7 Display the Calendar table once more in the Data Manipulation painter. Notice that the row you inserted isn't in the same place it was when you added the row. In fact, although you seem to specify where you want a new row to appear when you click the Insert Row button, there is no way to easily predict exactly where the row will be added. This is because the location of a new row is determined by the way in which a DBMS internally maintains its tables.

Deleting Rows

Deleting a row using the Data Manipulation painter requires placing the insertion point in the row to be deleted and issuing a delete command.

To delete a row:

1 If necessary, open the Calendar table from the *tshows* database in the Data Manipulation painter.

2 Click in the row you added during the preceding exercise.

3 Click the **Delete Row** button in the PowerBar (Figure 7.10 on page 132). PowerBuilder deletes the row.

4 Exit the Data Manipulation painter, saving your changes.

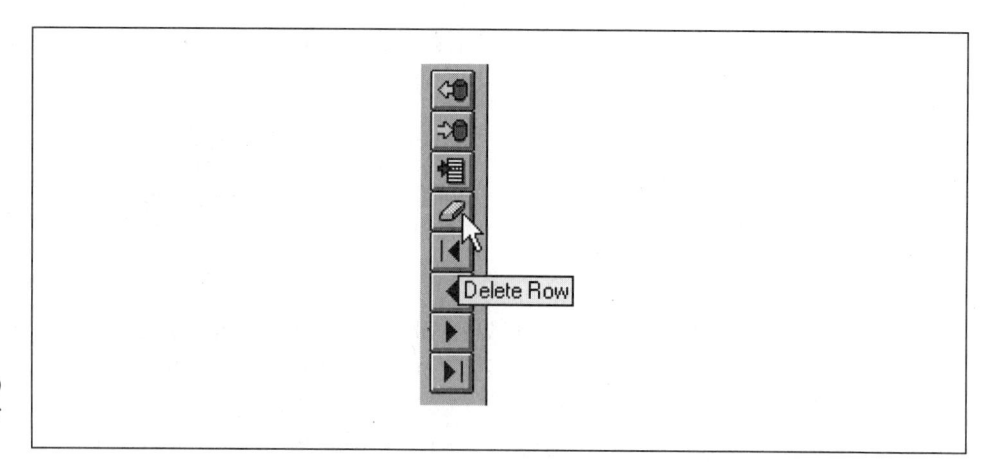

Figure 7.10
Delete Row button in the PainterBar

A SQL-based DBMS can't undo a committed transaction. Once you delete a row and commit the transaction containing that deletion, there is no way to recover the deleted row. If you accidentally delete a row, exit the Data Manipulation painter without saving changes, thereby rolling back the transaction and undoing all changes made during the transaction.

Loading Data From Text Files

Entering large volumes of data can be a tedious process. For example, you may want to load data stored in another DBMS's database into the database you are manipulating with PowerBuilder. Retyping the data by hand is always an alternative, albeit not one that is very efficient. A better alternative is to transfer the data from an existing disk file.

PowerBuilder can read files created by an xBase database (for example, dBase or FoxPro). Such files have a *.DBF* extension. In addition, PowerBuilder can work with *tab-delimited text files*, files in which there is a tab character between the data for each column within a row and in which each row ends with a carriage return.

It might be tempting to use a text editor to create import files. However, many text editors—including the DOS text editor—replace tab characters with spaces before saving a file. Be very certain that your file contains the ASCII code for a tab between columns before attempting to use the file for data import.

Before loading data from a text file, you must know the order of the columns within each row in the text file, which must be exactly the same as the order of the columns into which the data will be loaded. Although column order is largely irrelevant when you are working with a relational database, loading data from a text file is one major exception.

To load data from a tab-delimited text file:

1 Connect to the *tshows* database and open the Producers table.
2 Display the Producers table in the Data Manipulation painter.
3 Choose **Rows** -> **Import**. The Select Import File dialog box appears.

4   Click **pddat.txt** in the File Name list to select it as the source data file (Figure 7.11).

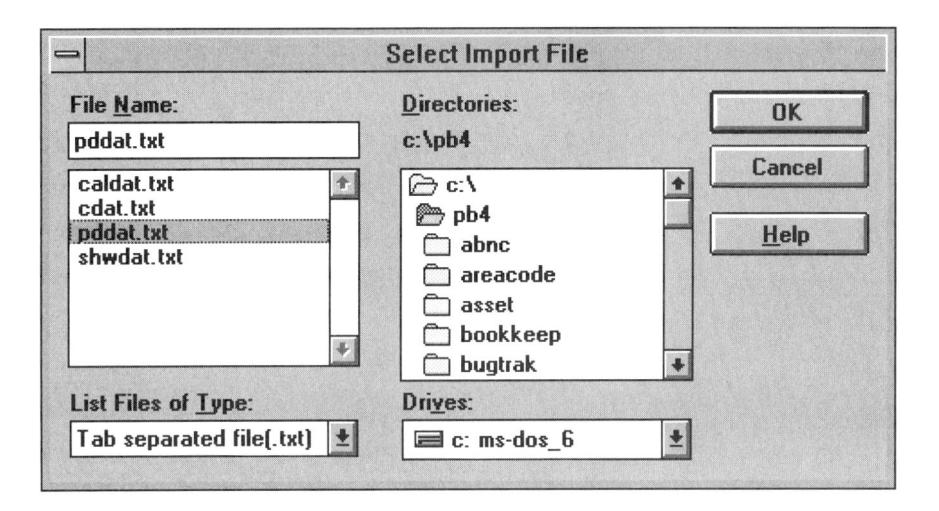

Figure 7.11
Choosing a source file for data import

5   Click the **OK** button. PowerBuilder imports the rows.
6   Exit the Data Manipulation painter, saving the changes to the database.

When you attempt to save the changes to a table into which you have imported data, the DBMS applies any integrity rules that are defined for the table. If, for example, the table contains foreign keys, matching primary keys must exist for those foreign keys before the transaction will be successfully committed. This is why you loaded data into the Producers table rather than any of the other tables in the database, most of which have foreign keys.

Issuing SQL Commands Directly to the Database

If you are already fluent in SQL and want to do some interactive querying or modification of your database, you can do so without leaving PowerBuilder by using the Database Administration painter. (If you are just learning SQL, you can still perform the exercises in this section.) Like the Data Manipulation painter, the Database Administration painter is accessible only from the Database painter (unless you explicitly place its button in the PowerBar).

To issue direct SQL commands:

1   Connect to the *tshows* database and enter the Database painter.
2   Click the **Admin** button in the PainterBar (Figure 7.12). As you can see in Figure 7.13, the Database Administration painter has its own

134 CHAPTER SEVEN DIRECT DATA MANIPULATION

PainterBar and a blank workspace into which you can type a SQL query. The coordinates in the lower-right corner of the window indicate the current position of the insertion pointer in the format *row#:column#*.

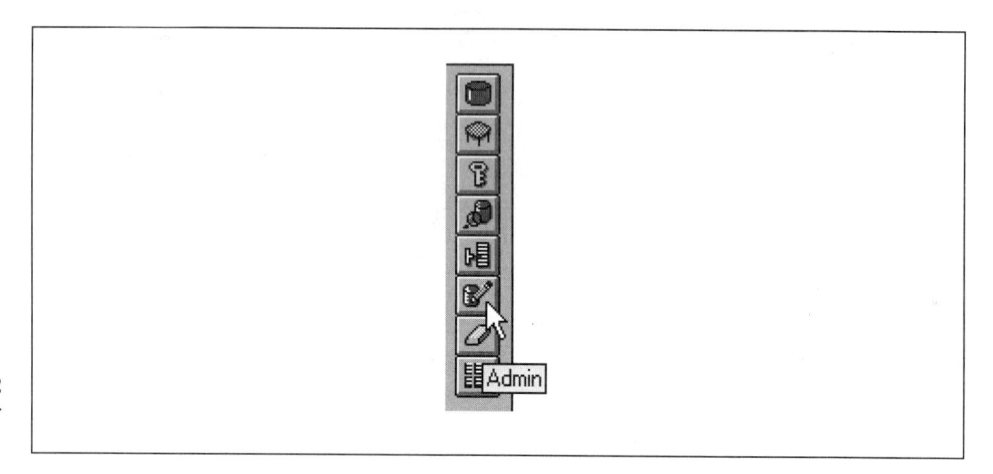

Figure 7.12
Admin button in the PainterBar

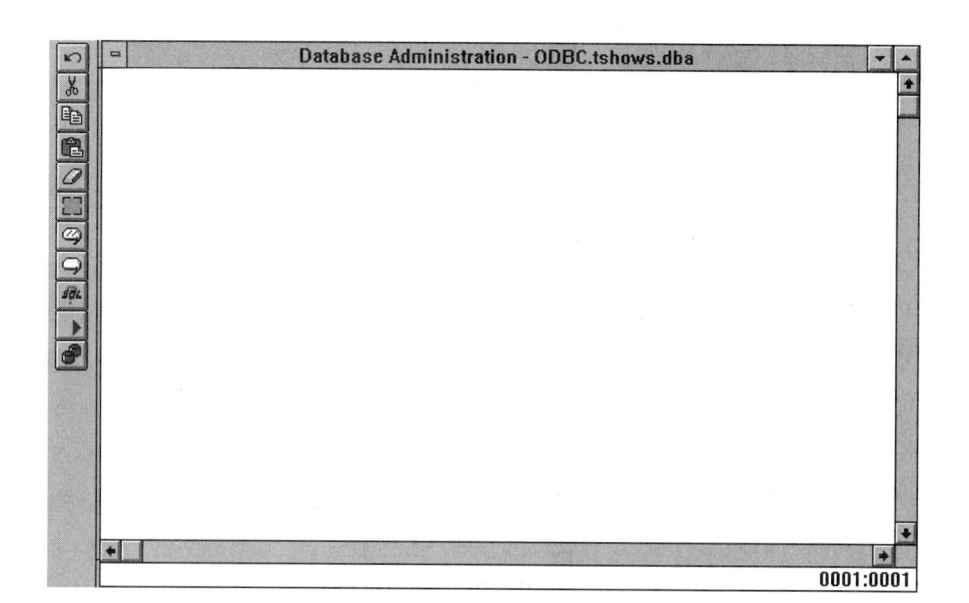

Figure 7.13
Database Administration painter

3 Type the following SQL command into the Database Administration painter workspace:

```
SELECT calendar.event#, show_name, venue_name,
  venue_city
FROM calendar, locations
WHERE calendar.event# = locations.event#;
```

4   Click the **Execute** button in the PainterBar (Figure 7.14). PowerBuilder submits the query to the database server, which processes the query and returns the results to PowerBuilder. PowerBuilder displays the results in the Data Manipulation painter.

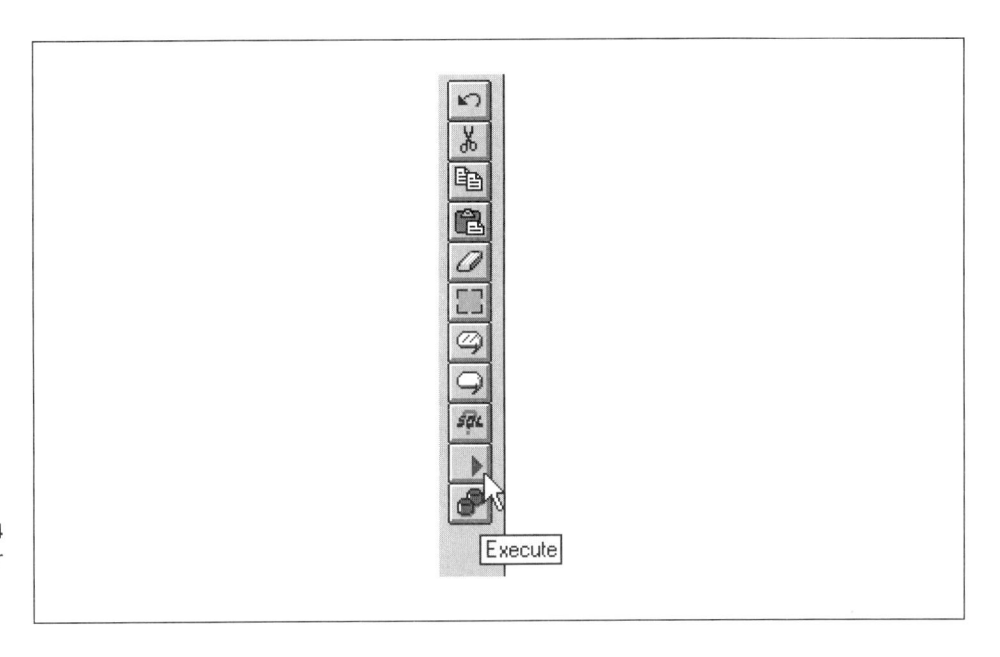

Figure 7.14
Execute button in the PainterBar

5   Exit the Data Manipulation painter. Notice that you are returned to the Database Administration painter.

6   Exit the Database Administration painter by double-clicking its control box.

You can also exit the Database Administration painter by using the Return button (the bottom button in the PainterBar).

7   When PowerBuilder asks if you want to save the contents of the Database Administration painter's workspace, click the **No** button.

The contents of the Database Administration painter workspace are saved as a text file. Should you need to reissue a SQL query frequently, you may wish to save it so that you can simply open the file the next time you need the query, instead of having to retype it.

When you use the Database Administration painter to make changes to the structure of a database (for example, creating a table or a view), those changes aren't reflected in the Database painter workspace.

Views

As you will remember from Chapter 2, in its broadest sense, the term *view* refers to the portion of the database with which a user works at any time. Relational database theory, however, more strictly defines the term. A relational view is a virtual table that is the result of executing a relational query. The definition of the view is stored with a name and the query that specifies the data that should be included in the virtual table. Database servers use this latter definition.

A view is a SQL query with a name. Once the view has been created and its definition stored in a database's data dictionary, the view appears in the Database painter workspace like a table and can be used—with some exceptions where updating is concerned—as if it were a base table. You can display and filter data in view in the Data Manipulation painter. As you will see in Part Three of this book, you can also base DataWindow objects on views.

When the view is used, the database executes the query on which the view is based and creates the virtual table. Even if the table or tables in the view's query have been modified since the last time the view was used, rebuilding the virtual table whenever the view is used ensures that the contents of the view are current. In this way, the data in a view are always correct.

There are at least four good reasons to create views:

- A view can avoid the creation of a complex SQL query, making it possible to easily execute the query without retyping it.
- A view lets you see the result of complex SQL queries in the Data Manipulation painter. In this case, a view functions much like a SQL query that you have saved in a Database Administration painter workspace file. However, a query saved from the Database Administration painter is unconnected to your database while a view is a part of the database structure.
- A view lets you display the result of complex SQL queries in a DataWindow.
- A view can be used to implement database security. First, you prevent users from accessing base tables. Then, you create views that contain exactly the data that a user can see and give the user access to those views.

Not all views can be used to update data. Although the specific rules of which views are updatable are DBMS-specific, the following rules are common:

- Only views based on one table can be used to update data.
- Only views that contain all nonnull columns from the underlying table can be used to update data.

Creating a View

Because the definition of a view becomes a part of your database's structure, you create views using the Database painter. However, defining a view also requires creating a SQL query, the query that will be stored in the database's data dictionary and will be used to retrieve the view's data whenever you access the view. In this section you will learn to use the interface that PowerBuilder provides for building SQL queries. This knowledge will be used throughout your work with PowerBuilder.

CHAPTER SEVEN DIRECT DATA MANIPULATION **137**

To create a view:

1 Connect to the *tshows* database and enter the Database painter.

2 Click the **View** button in the PainterBar (Figure 7.15). PowerBuilder enters the View painter and displays a Select Table dialog box.

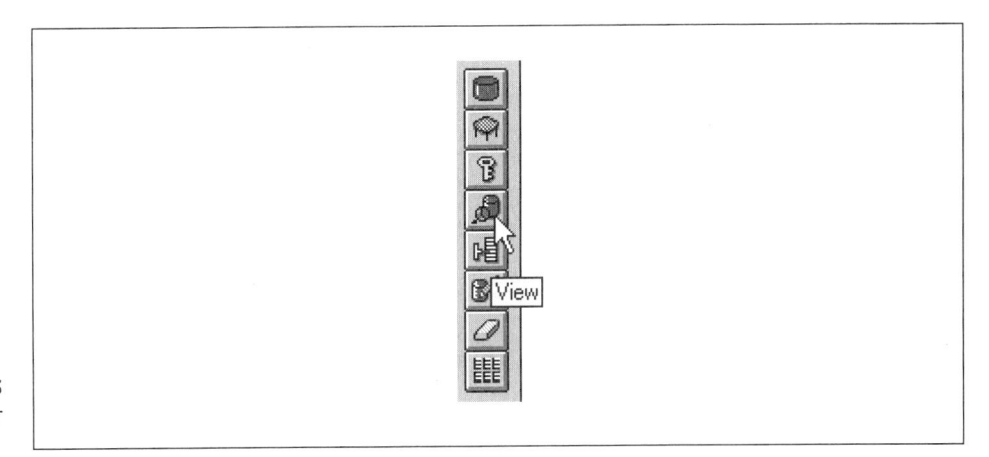

Figure 7.15
View button in the PainterBar

3 Open the Calendar and Costs tables. As you can see in Figure 7.16, the tables appear in the workspace. PowerBuilder automatically joins the two tables by placing an equal sign between primary and foreign keys (event#).

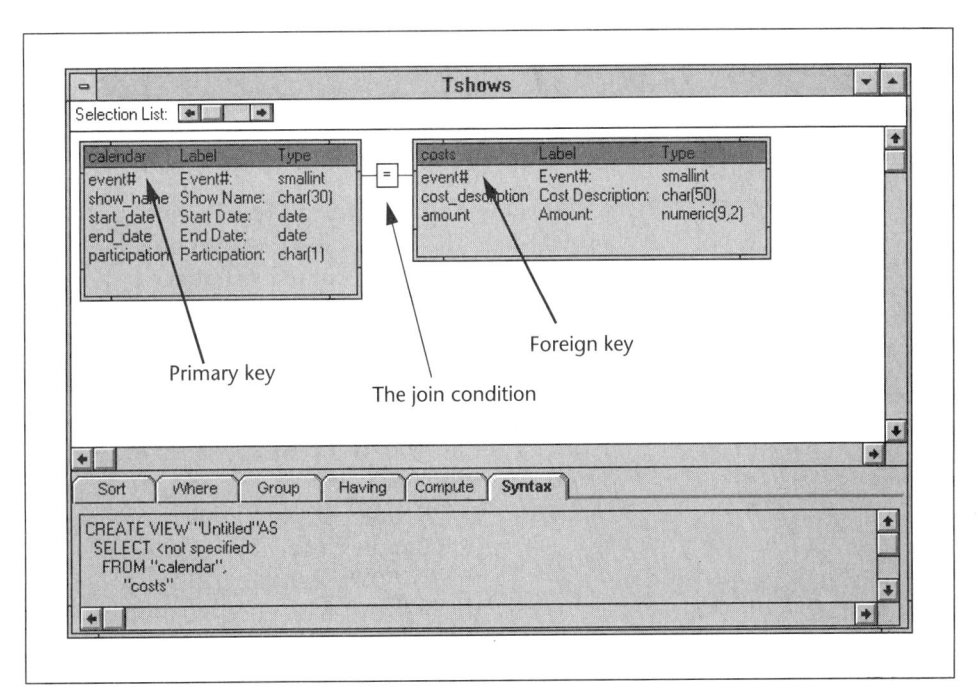

Figure 7.16
View painter

When you click on the Syntax tab, the bottom of the workspace displays the SQL query that is being built to define the view. The tabs switch among tools used to develop that query.

4   By default, PowerBuilder establishes a natural join between primary and foreign keys. To see alternative join conditions, click the **equal sign** box. As you can see in Figure 7.17, joins can be performed using any of the standard relationship operators. Notice also that the second two joins are outer joins (joins in which rows that don't match in the tables being joined are included in the result table with NULLs in the columns where matching values aren't present.)

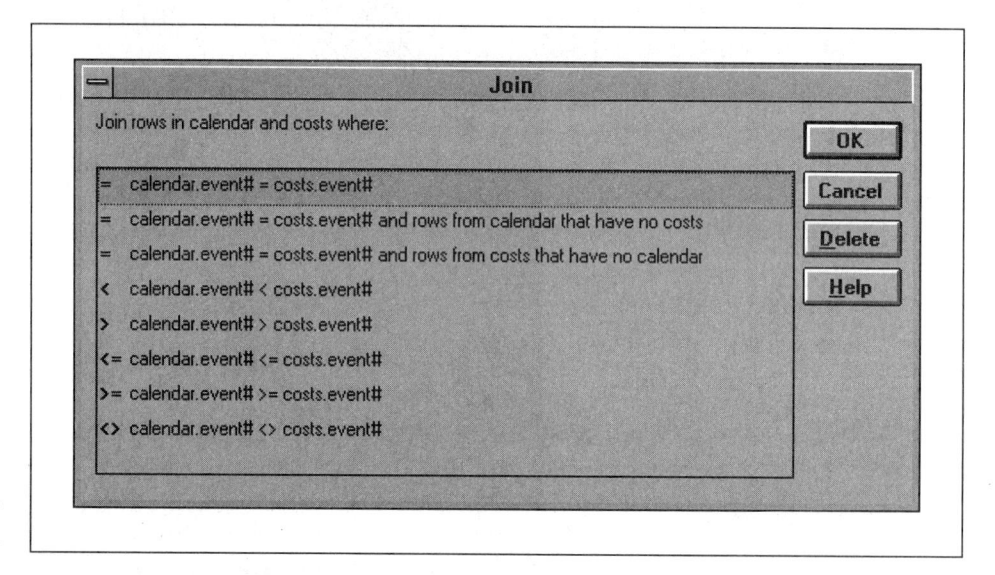

Figure 7.17
Join dialog box

5   Click the **Cancel** button to accept the natural join for this view.

Choosing Columns for a View   Once you've added your tables to a view and confirmed the default joins, you should indicate which column you want for the view. To choose the columns that are to appear in the view, you click their names in the View painter workspace.

To choose columns for a view:

1   Click the **show_name**, **start_date**, and **end_date** columns in the Calendar table. Click on the **cost_description** and **amount** columns in the Costs table. Three things happen as you click: the column names are highlighted in the workspace, the column names appear at the top of the workspace in the Selection List, and the column names appear in the SQL CREATE VIEW statement displayed at the bottom of the window.

By default, the columns appear in the Selection List in the order in which you clicked on them. However, you can change the order as needed.

2 Click on the **Columns** button in the PainterBar (Figure 7.18). The pointer changes to a hand.

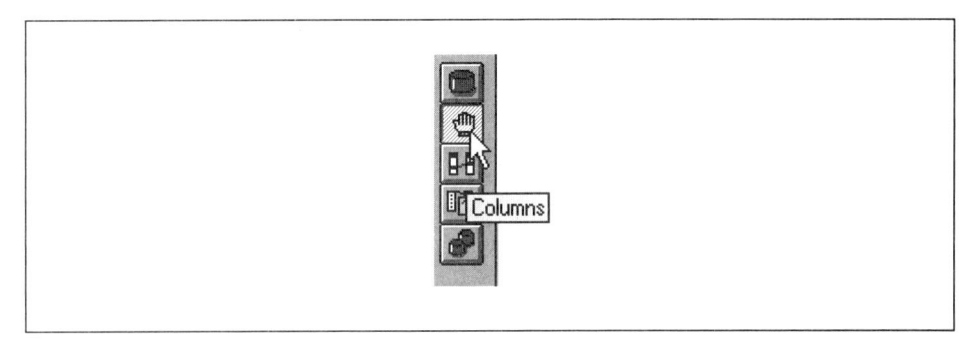

Figure 7.18
Columns button in the PainterBar

To move a column, you drag it with the hand pointer from its current position in the Selection List to the position in which you want it to appear.

3 Drag **start_date** to the right end of the list. Then drag **end_date** to the right edge of the list.
4 Scroll the SQL Syntax window to see the entire SQL query. Notice that although the view is still unnamed, the selected columns and the join condition are present.

Adding Row Selection Criteria Although PowerBuilder adds a WHERE clause automatically to a CREATE VIEW statement when it joins tables, you may also want to include additional row selection criteria in a view. These must be added manually to the view definition.

To add row selection criteria to a view definition:

1 To add row selection criteria, you enter specifications for a WHERE clause. Begin by clicking the **Where** tab in the SQL Toolbox at the bottom of the window.
2 Click in the first line below the word "Column." A down arrow indicating a dropdown menu appears.
3 Click the **down arrow** to display a list of the columns in the tables in the View painter workspace.
4 Click **"calendar"."show_name"**, as in Figure 7.19. The name of the selected column appears under Column and the default operator (equal to) appears under Operator. For this example, leave the default operator in place.
5 Click in the first row under Value. Type **MacWorld Expo**.
6 Click in the first row under Logical. A down arrow indicating a dropdown menu appears.

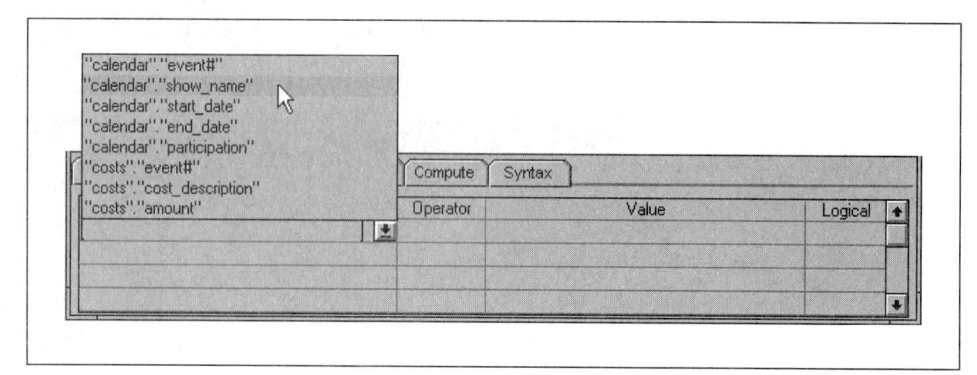

Figure 7.19
Choosing a column for a WHERE clause

7 Click the down arrow to display a list of logical operators (AND and OR).

8 Click **OR**. This will link two simple logical expressions into a complex logical expression.

9 Click in the second line under Column. Click **"calendar"."show_name"** again. Let the symbol for equal to (the equal sign) remain as the operator.

10 Type **PC Expo** as the comparison value in the Value column. Because this is the last simple expression in the WHERE clause, no logical operator is required.

There is theoretically no limit to the number of simple logical expressions you can combine in a single WHERE clause using AND and OR.

11 Click the **Syntax** tab to view the entire CREATE VIEW statement as it now exists.

Sorting the Rows in a View Unless the view definition directs otherwise, the rows in the view table will appear in the DBMS's default order. To change the order, you need to add an ORDER BY clause to the CREATE VIEW statement.

There is a bug in the initial 4.0 release of WatcomSQL that prevents the DBMS from accepting view definitions that include ORDER BY clauses. You will need to upgrade to Watcom SQL 4.0a or later and PowerBuilder 4.0.01 or later for the following steps to work. Free upgrade patches are available from Powersoft's ftp site: ftp.powersoft.com.

To add sort criteria to a view definition:

1 Click the **Sort** tab in the SQL Toolbox.

To indicate sort columns, drag the columns from the column list on the left to the sort list on the right.

2 Drag **show_name**, followed by **start_date** to the sort list on the right. Notice that as you drag, the column appears as a bar (see Figure 7.20 on page 141).

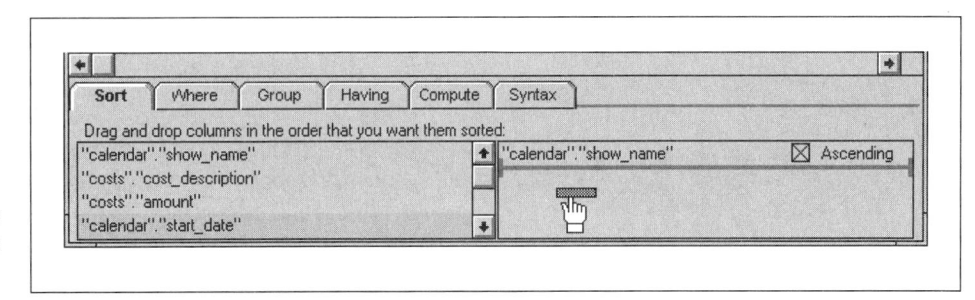

Figure 7.20
Dragging and dropping sort columns

By default, sorting is in ascending order. To sort in descending order, click the Ascending check box to remove the X.

3 Click the **Ascending** check box for the start_date column to change the sort order.

4 Click the **Syntax** tab to view the entire CREATE VIEW statement as it now exists.

Saving and Naming the View Now that the view definition is complete, you can submit it to the database server to create the view and install it in your database's data dictionary. You will also be naming the view at this point.

To finish creating the view:

1 Double-click the View painter workspace control box. A dialog box appears asking whether you want to save the view.

2 Click the **Yes** button or press the **Enter** key. The Save View Definition dialog box appears.

3 Type **macworld** as the name of the view, as in Figure 7.21.

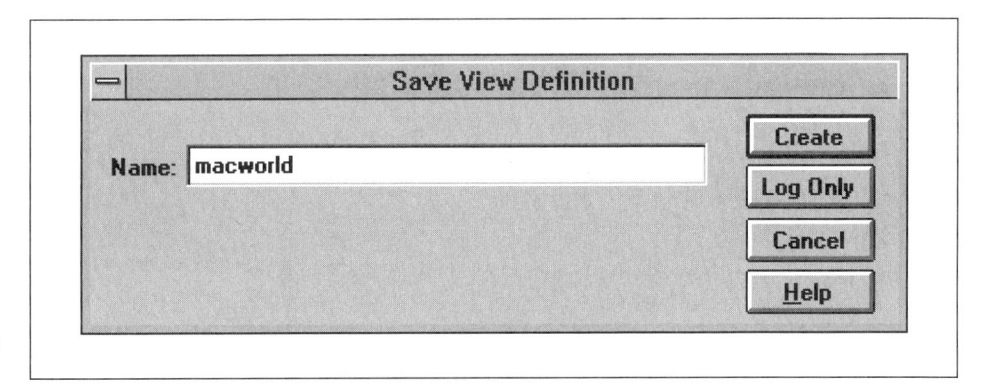

Figure 7.21
Saving and naming a view

4 Click the **Create** button or press the **Enter** key. PowerBuilder submits the CREATE VIEW statement to the DBMS, which stores the view definition in the database's data dictionary. PowerBuilder closes the View painter and returns you the Database painter. The newly created view appears in the Database painter workspace like the database's tables.

Its name will also appear in the Select Tables dialog box whenever you open tables in the database.

Is this view updatable? Probably not: Its definition contains a join. Most of today's DBMSs do not allow updates of views based on more than one table.

Looking at View Data

You can see the data retrieved by a view in the Data Manipulation painter, just as you can see data from base tables. If the view is updatable, you can also perform data updates from the Data Manipulation painter. Because views behave like base tables, you can apply data filters to view data displayed on the Data Manipulation painter, just as you applied data filters to base table data earlier in this chapter.

In most ways, a view behaves just like a base table. This means that once a view is defined and is available in the Database painter workspace, you can base other views on it; you can create views from views.

To access a view's data:

1 Connect to the database and display the view in the Database painter's workspace. In this case, use the *tshows* database. Make sure the macworld view is visible.
2 Click the **macworld** view to highlight it.
3 Click the **Preview** button in the PowerBar. PowerBuilder submits the data retrieval request to the DBMS, which performs the query that defines the view and displays the data in the Data Manipulation painter.
4 Double-click the Data Manipulation painter control box to return to the Database painter.

Dropping a View

Once created, the definition of a view can't be changed. If you need to modify a view, you must drop it and re-create it. Dropping a view is just like dropping a table.

To drop a view:

1 Connect to the *tshows* database and enter the Database painter.
2 Click the **macworld** view in the workspace.
3 Click the **Drop** button in the PainterBar.

Views with Grouping Queries

A *grouping query* is a query that identifies and collects rows with matching data. The query can count the number of members in a group and compute summary values (for examples, totals or averages) based on group members. Although a view with a grouping query can't be updated, it can provide a quick way to obtain an overview of data.

Creating the Initial View To explore using PowerBuilder to create a view that contains a grouping query, you will be creating a view that summarizes the revenue generated by all sales leads from each company in the database.

To create the view of revenue generated by sales leads:

1 Connect to the *tshows* database, and make sure you are in the Database painter.
2 Click the **View** button in the PainterBar.
3 Choose the **leads** and **contacts** tables. Notice that PowerBuilder automatically joins the tables on the lead name. However, for this view, the join should be on the company name.
4 Click the **equal sign** box that represents the join. The Join dialog box appears with the current join condition highlighted.
5 Click the **Delete** button to remove the join.
6 Click the **Join** button in the PainterBar (Figure 7.22).

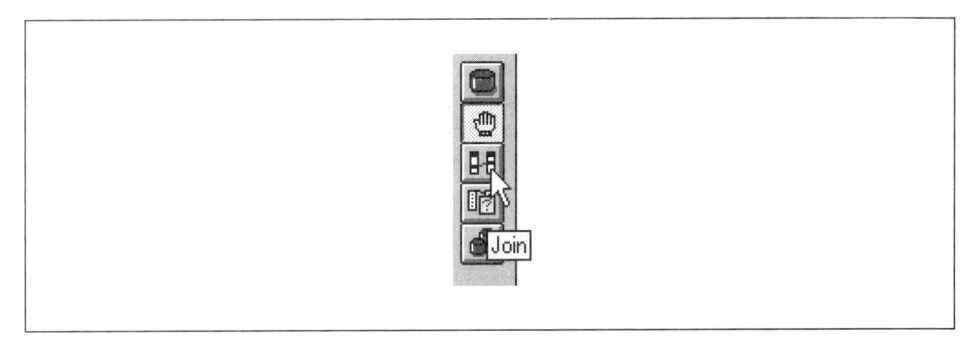

Figure 7.22
Join button in the PainterBar

7 Click **lead_company** in the Contacts table. Then click **lead_company** in the Leads table. PowerBuilder places an equal sign between them to indicate that they are joined.
8 Click the **Columns** button in the PainterBar.
9 Click the **lead_company** column in the Contacts table. You'll be adding a column for the total revenue generated from that company shortly.

Adding Grouping Columns The next step in the process of creating a grouping query is to indicate the column or columns that should be used to form the groups. When the query is executed, the DBMS then forms rows that have matching values on the chosen columns.

To group rows by the name of the company:

1. Click the **Group** tab in the SQL toolbox at the bottom of the screen.
2. Drag **"contacts"."lead_company"** from the list on the left to the right, so that the window appears as in Figure 7.23.

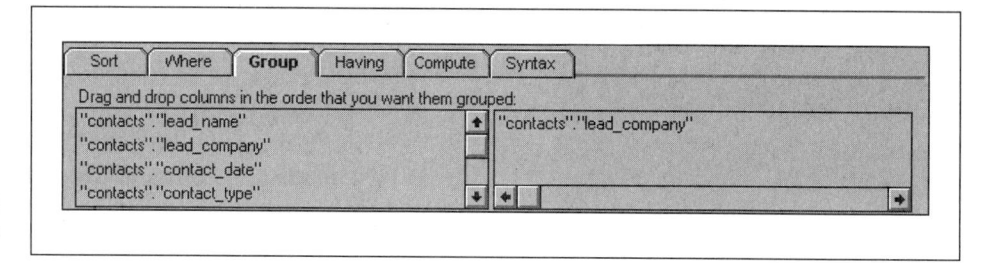

Figure 7.23
Choosing grouping columns

3. Click the **Syntax** tab to see the CREATE VIEW statement as it appears at this point.

Adding Computed Columns As you have studied SQL, you have learned that a SQL query can perform computations and display the result of the computation in a column that appears in a virtual result table. Such a column is simply called a *computed column*, which is a column whose contents aren't stored in the database but are assembled for output by manipulating data according to the formula that defines the column.

For queries that don't perform grouping, the computations are performed on one row at a time. However, grouping queries perform computations on each group. Nonetheless, the basic PowerBuilder procedure for appending a computed column to the result table is the same.

For this example, you will add a column that sums the revenue generated by each company.

To add the computed column:

1. Click the **Compute** tab in the SQL toolbox.
2. Type **sum(revenue)** in the first row under Computed Columns. This is the expression that defines the contents of the computed column. Unless you assign an alias to the column, the column's expression will also appear as the column's name when you look at the contents of the view in the Data Manipulation painter.

3   Type **Total_Revenue** in the first row under Alias. This will give the column a more meaningful display name. Your screen should now look like Figure 7.24.

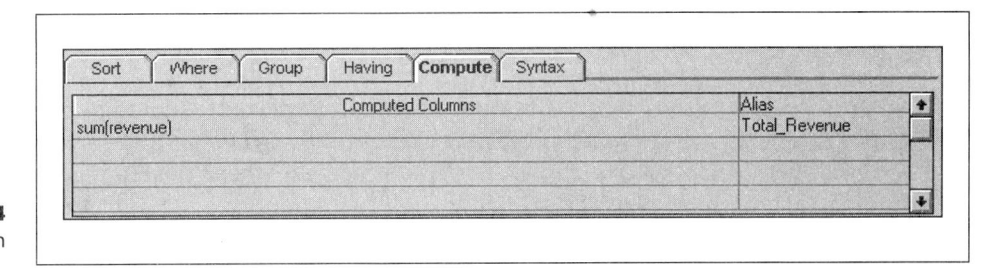

Figure 7.24
Adding a computed column

Keep in mind that computed columns are for display only. They exist only in main memory as part of the virtual result table; they aren't stored in the database and don't affect the base tables.

4   Save the view and name it "sum_revenue."
5   Display the contents of the view on the Data Manipulation painter. Notice that there is one row for each unique company name and that the underscores in the names of the columns have been replaced with spaces.

Is the view updatable? No: Its definition contains a GROUP BY clause. The rows in this view do not correspond directly to a base table, but instead are summaries of multiple rows in a base table. Therefore, there is no way for a DBMS to accurately pass updates down to stored data.

Looking Ahead

In this chapter you've acquired the skills to use PowerBuilder to manipulate data stored in a database's base tables directly. One of the things that makes doing so rather tedious is that by default the Data Manipulation painter doesn't have many of the data entry aids—dropdown menus, radio buttons, and so on—that are common to application programs. In Chapter 8 you will add extended data attributes, which can provide significant data entry help, even when working directly with base tables. Extended data attributes will also simplify the process of application development.

EXERCISES

The exercises that follow will give you practice in working with the Data Manipulation painter using the *rents* database. You will be displaying and filtering data from base tables. You will also be creating views and filtering data from those views.

1. College and University Rentals would like to see data about all customers who attend Brandt College. To see this data, first display the contents of the Customer table in the Data Manipulation painter. Then apply a filter to restrict the rows.

2. Create a view that displays the name and phone numbers of all customers who have unpaid bills. (*Hint*: Join the Customer and Rentals tables. Then choose rows in Rentals where the fee paid is 0.)

3. Create a view that displays the status of any type of merchandise. Use this view to find the status of all end tables.

4. Create a view that will display a name, school, return date, and merchandise description for all rentals. Display the contents of the view in the Data Manipulation painter and then add a data filter to restrict the display to those rentals that are for a semester (rental_period = 'semester'.) Can you apply the filter given the way in which the view is constructed? If not, what will you have to do so that you can perform the needed row restrictions?

5. Create a view that will display the inventory control number and merchandise type for of all items that have not been rented (status = warehouse). Use this view to find the inventory control numbers of all microwave ovens in the warehouse.

6. Create a view that will display the return date of rented merchandise. Order the view by return date. Display the contents of the view in the Data Manipulation painter to verify that it works correctly.

7. C&U Rentals would like a view that lets it see the names and phone numbers of customers who have rented specific types of merchandise (for example, portable washers and dryers). Create a view that can be used for this purpose. First, join the *four* tables that are needed. Then display the contents of the view in the Data Manipulation painter and apply a filter to restrict the rows to portable washers and portable dryers.

8. Create a view that computes the average semester rental fee for a type of merchandise. Display the contents of the view in the Data Manipulation painter and apply a filter to restrict the output to microwave ovens.

9. Create a view that will count the number of items of each type of merchandise that have been rented. Display the contents of the view in the Data Manipulation painter to make sure that it works correctly.

10. Create a view that computes the total fee owed by customers for their rentals. Display the contents of the view in the Data Manipulation painter to make sure that it works correctly. Then apply a data filter to see the fees for "Petronella, Lori."

11. Consider all the views that you have created for the exercises in this chapter. For each view, indicate whether it is updatable. If a view is not updatable, state why it is not.

Chapter Eight

Extended Data Attributes

IN THIS CHAPTER YOU WILL:

- Add self-documentation to the structural elements of a database
- Set default formats for columns
- Add validation rules to columns

If you look at either the Create Table or Alter Table dialog boxes, you'll notice that the bottom portion of the dialog box is reserved for Extended Attributes. While the table characteristics you have defined to this point are stored in the data dictionary, as a part of your database, *extended attributes* are PowerBuilder properties unrelated to the capabilities of a specific DBMS.

In this chapter you will learn how to configure extended attributes. Because you now know how to view data in the Data Manipulation painter, you will be able to see the results of your changes to tables immediately.

The Scope of Extended Attributes

The general purpose of extended attributes is to allow you to set some default column characteristics that can clarify displays on the Data Manipulation painter workspace and simplify the creation of DataWindow objects. In addition, the presence of extended attributes makes it easier to work with data in the Data Manipulation painter.

Specifically, extended attributes let you do the following:

- Add comments to columns. These comments show up in the Database painter to help you remember what is being stored in a column.
- Add default headers and labels to columns, which appear whenever you display the column in a DataWindow object or in the Data Manipulation painter workspace.
- Specify the default alignment and width for data display.
- Specify default data formats, such as formats for numbers, telephone numbers, or dates.
- Specify default data display styles, such as check boxes, radio buttons, or lists.
- Define validation rules that aren't covered by primary and foreign key constraints. For example, although Watcom SQL doesn't have a Boolean data type that can be used to restrict values to true or false, you can place a validation rule on a column that will have the same effect. You will be doing this shortly for the Calendar table's participation column.

As you will see, there are two ways to access a column's extended attributes using PowerBuilder 4.0. The first is from the Create Table or Alter Table dialog box. The second is directly from a column's popup menu. You'll explore both methods in this chapter. If you are working with version 5.0, you can also access column attributes from the Create Table or Alter Table dialog boxes. In addition, the column's popup menu provides access to a Column Properties dialog box, which provides a single access point for all extended attributes in a manner similar to the Table Properties dialog box.

Extended attributes set up defaults for many column characteristics. However, you can override those defaults when you are creating DataWindow objects.

Adding Column Comments

To begin exploring extended column attributes, you will add comments to the columns in the Shows table.

To add comments to the columns in the Shows table:

1. Launch PowerBuilder and open the *tshows* application in *tshows1.pbl*. Connect to the *tshows* database. Open all the tables in the database so that they appear in the Database painter workspace.
2. Double-click the **Shows** table. The Alter Table dialog box appears.
3. Click the **show_name** column's Name box to make it the current column.
4. Click in the Comment box at the bottom of the dialog box.
5. Type **The name of a trade show at which we might exhibit** (Figure 8.1).

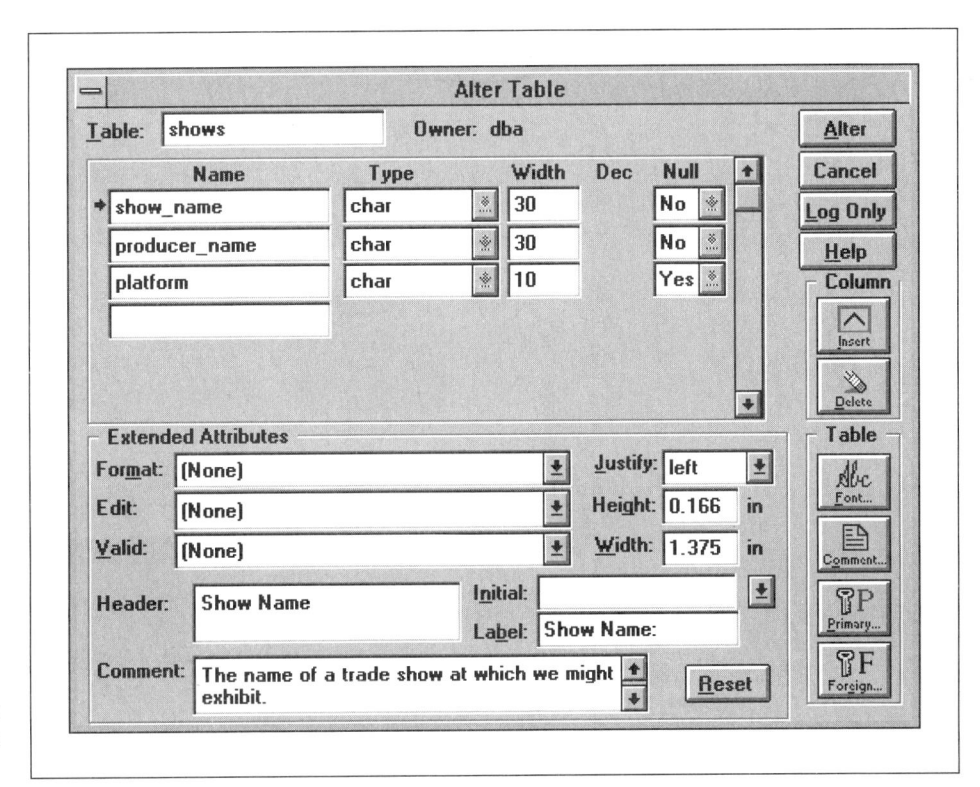

Figure 8.1 Entering a column comment

6. Click the **producer_name** column's Name box.
7. In the Comment box, type **The name of the company that produces the trade show**.
8. Click the **platform** column's Name box.
9. In the Comment box, type **The hardware platform featured at the show. The three possible values are PC, Mac, and Both.**

150 CHAPTER EIGHT EXTENDED DATA ATTRIBUTES

10 If you are working with version 4.0, click the **Alter** button to close the dialog box. PowerBuilder closes the dialog box and saves the comments.

If you are working with version 5,0, double-click the Alter Table dialog box's control box. PowerBuilder asks whether you want to save your changes (Figure 8.2). Click the **Yes** button.

For both versions, PowerBuilder expands the table in the workspace to show the entire comment (see Figure 8.3).

Figure 8.2
Deciding whether to save changes to a table definition (5.0)

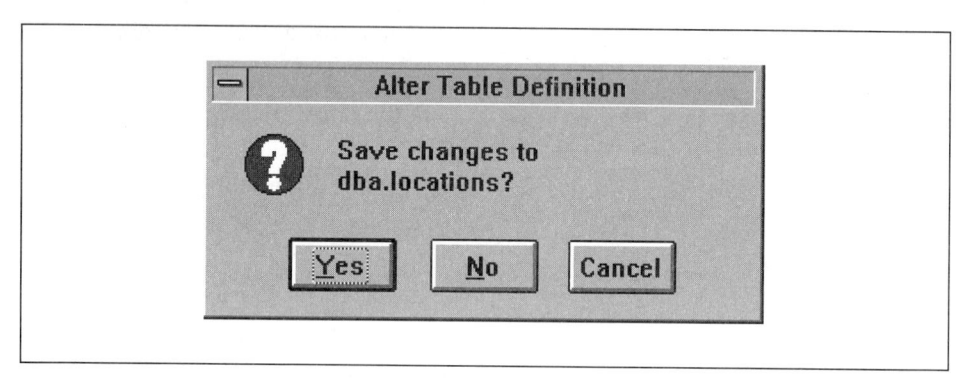

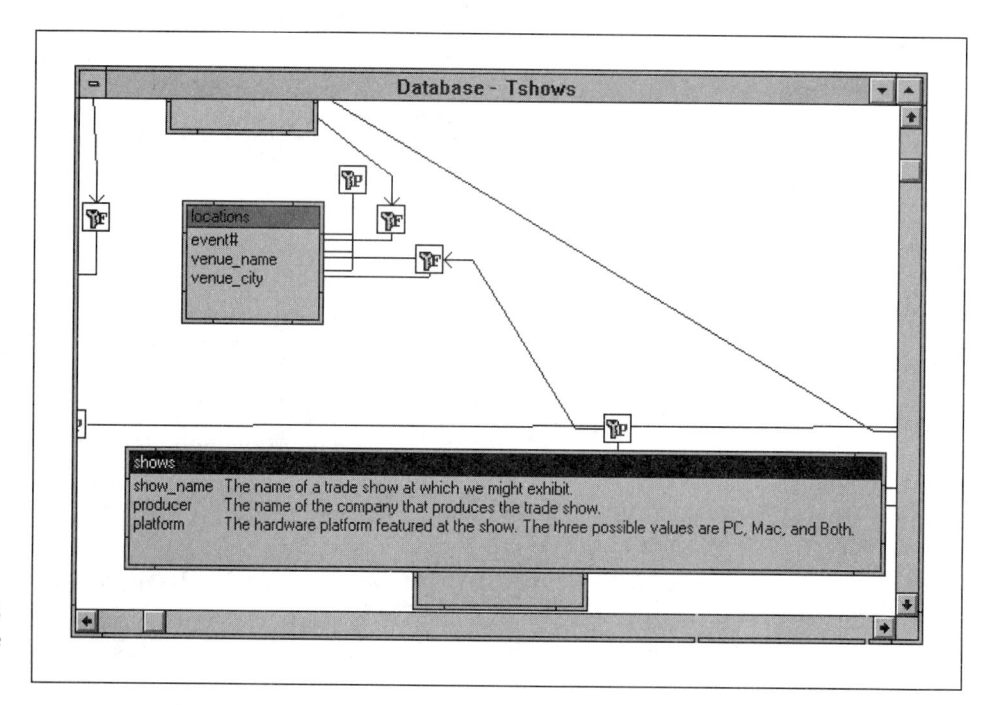

Figure 8.3
Long comments in the workspace

11 Resize the Shows table window as small as PowerBuilder will allow by placing the pointer over the right edge of the table's window, holding down the left mouse button, and dragging to the left. As you can see in Figure 8.4 on page 151, PowerBuilder adds scroll bars to the table window so you can see the comments as needed.

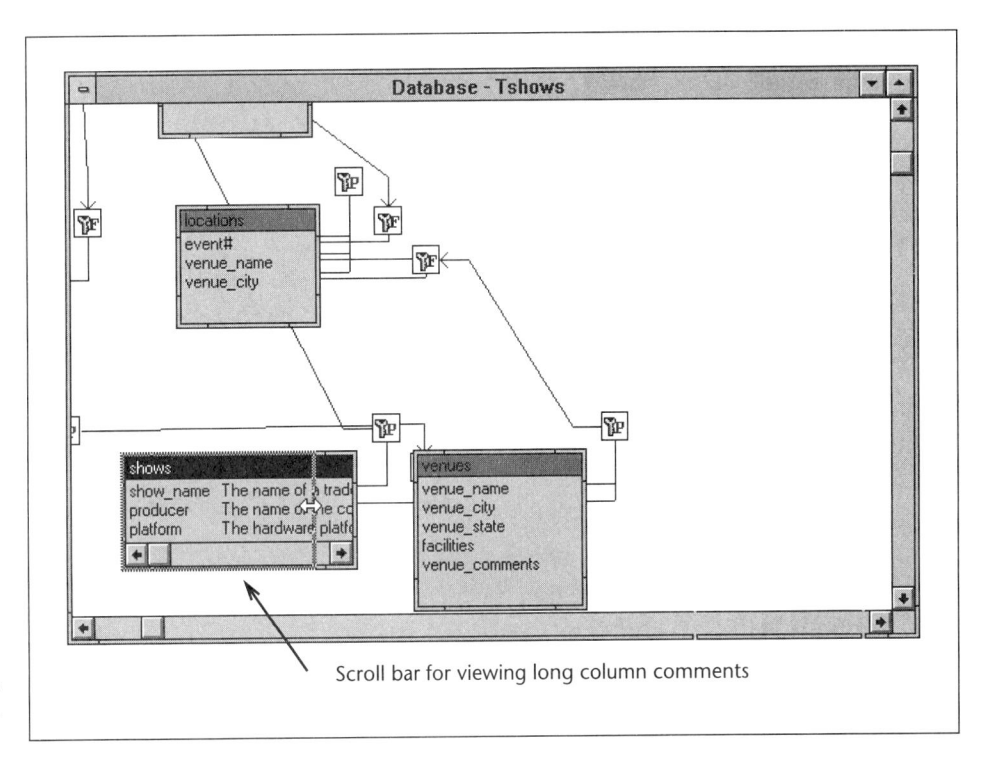

Figure 8.4
Resizing a window with comments

Scroll bar for viewing long column comments

Although you have resized the Shows table window to hide most of the comments, the window will return to its full size the next time you open it in the Database painter. You may therefore wish to return to the table's Alter Table dialog and remove the comments. To do so, highlight each comment in the Comment box and then press the Backspace key.

Column Headers and Labels

Column headers are words that appear at the top of a column in the Data Manipulation painter workspace or on a list of data in a DataWindow object. *Labels* are words that appear on freeform DataWindow objects (for example, those that are used for data entry). If you use underscore characters to separate the words in your column names, PowerBuilder can identify where words end and can therefore create good column headers and labels for you.

To explore column labels, we'll be working with the Locations table. You'll be using a column's menu to access the extended attributes, rather than displaying the Alter Table dialog box.

To access a column's extended attributes:

1 Click in the Locations table window to select it.

2 Right-click **event#** in the list of column names. The column's popup menu appears (Figure 8.5 on page 152 for version 4.0, Figure 8.6 on page 152 for version 5.0).

152 CHAPTER EIGHT EXTENDED DATA ATTRIBUTES

Figure 8.5
A column popup menu (4.0)

Figure 8.6
A column popup menu (5.0)

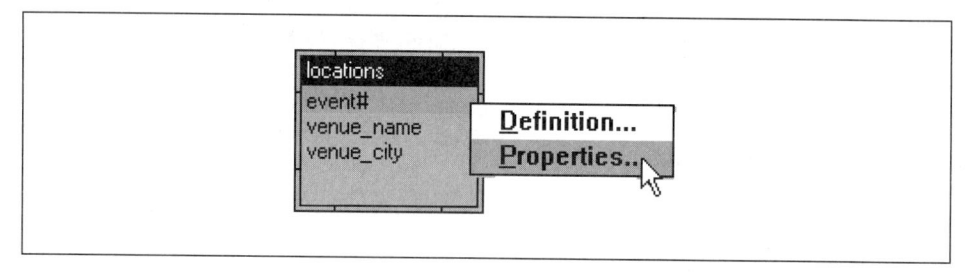

3 If you are working with version 4.0, choose **Header** from the popup menu. The Column Header dialog box appears (Figure 8.7).

If you are working with version 5.0, choose **Properties** from the popup menu to display the Column Properties dialog box. Click on the **Headers** tab to display the Headers panel (Figure 8.8 on page 153).

Notice that because there are no underscores in the column name, PowerBuilder uses the entire column name as a heading and the entire column name followed by a colon as a label.

Figure 8.7
Column Header dialog box (4.0)

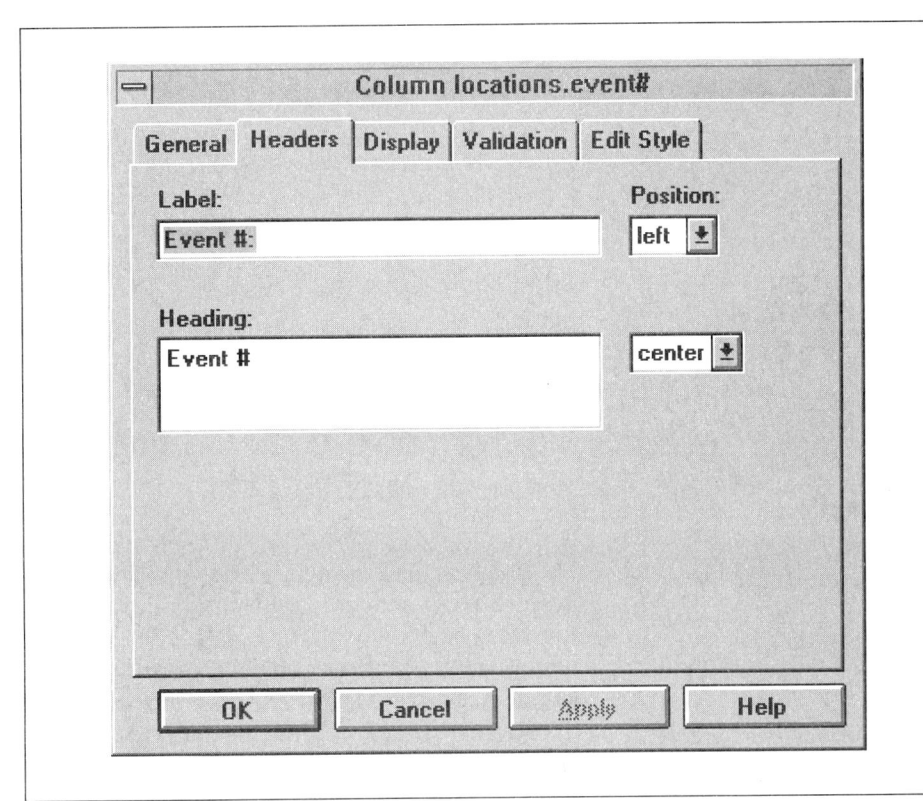

Figure 8.8
Headers panel (5.0)

4   Insert a space between the *t* and the # in both the label and the heading.
5   Click the **OK** button to close the dialog box.
6   Repeat Steps 2 and 3 for the venue_name column. Notice in Figure 8.9 that in both the label and the heading PowerBuilder has substituted a space for the underscore. PowerBuilder has also placed a capital letter at the beginning of each word.

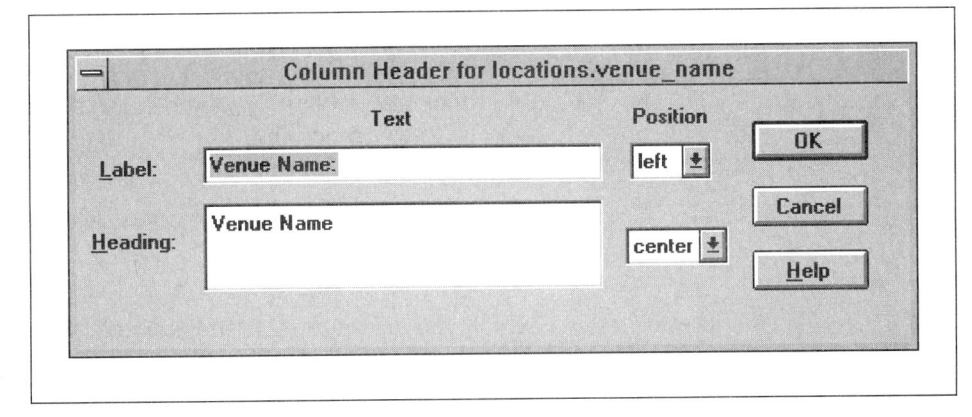

Figure 8.9
A two-word column header created from a column name that includes an underscore character

7   Because this label and heading are acceptable, simply close the dialog box by clicking either the **OK** or **Cancel** button.

8 Display the contents of the Locations table in the Data Manipulation painter to see your altered heading.

As you can see, when you use a column's popup menu (version 4.0) or the Column Properties dialog box (version 5.0) to access an extended attribute, you are working with one attribute for one column at a time. When you use the Create Table or Alter Table dialog boxes, you have access to all the extended attributes for an entire table at one time. It would therefore seem to make sense to work with either the Create Table or Alter Table dialog box unless you need to set only a single attribute. However, as you will see throughout the rest of this chapter, there are some features that are available only from a column popup menu or the Column Properties dialog box.

Setting Default Alignment and Width

As you saw in Chapter 7, when you view data in the Data Manipulation painter, PowerBuilder sets column widths that you cannot change. Often that width is too small to display all the data in the column. In addition, when you add a column to a DataWindow control, PowerBuilder gives that column a default width. (Remember that a DataWindow control is an object based on a DataWindow that is placed on a window for data display and/or modification.) Although a column width in a DataWindow control can certainly be changed, it makes your work easier if the default is usually the width that you want. You can therefore use a column's extended attributes to override PowerBuilder's choices to column width and alignment.

To explore these attributes, we'll be working with the Locations table again.

To set the column width and alignment:

1 Double-click the **Locations** table in the Database painter workspace to open the Alter Table dialog box.

2 Click the **event#** column's Name box to make event# the current column.

3 Change the column's alignment to **Center** using the Justify dropdown menu, as in Figure 8.10 on page 155.

4 Click in the **venue_name** column's Name box to make venue_name the current column.

5 Type **1.5** in the Width box to change the column's default width.

6 Click in the **venue_city** column's Name box to make venue_city the current column.

7 Type **1.5** in the Width box to change the column's default width.

8 If you are working with version 4.0, click the **Alter** button to close the Alter Table dialog box.

If you are working with version 5.0, double-click the Alter Table dialog box's control box. Click the **Yes** button to indicate that you want to save your changes. PowerBuilder stores the extended attributes.

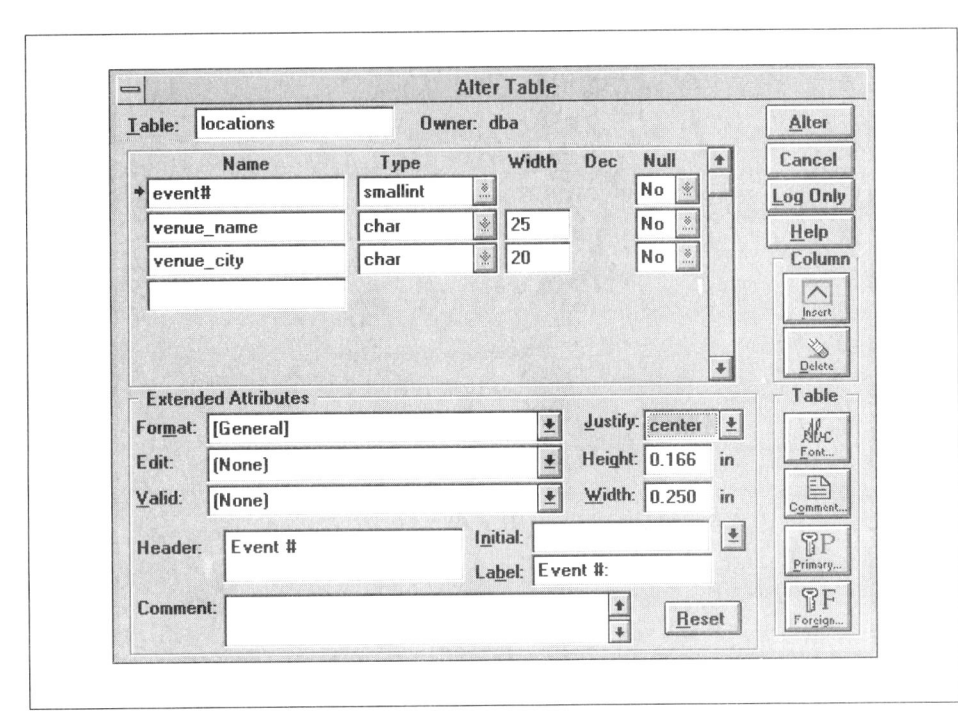

Figure 8.10
Changing the default alignment for a column

9 Display the contents of the table in the Data Manipulation painter to verify that the columns are now wide enough to show all of their data.

Display Formats

Display formats affect the way in which data are displayed in a window. We use them to make data more understandable. For example, phone numbers are usually grouped into an area code and a three-digit exchange, followed a four-digit number, as in (555) 555-1234. Dates and currency values also have recognizable formats that can make an application's output more understandable and easier to read.

Display formats are really intended only for data viewing. They can't be used to set up patterns for data entry. Edit formats, which affect both data display and data entry, are more flexible. You will be introduced to them later in this chapter.

PowerBuilder's display formats are expressed as patterns into which data must fit. These patterns, known as *display masks*, contain placeholders for data. For example, when formatting a number field a # represents any digit; a 0 represents a digit that must display. You might therefore create a number mask for a number of six or less digits as:

#,##0.00

The comma and the period are both literal characters that will always display as part of the number. If the number is less than three characters, the places

156 CHAPTER EIGHT EXTENDED DATA ATTRIBUTES

represented by 0s will be filled with 0. Therefore, the value .5 will appear as 0.50.

A column can have more than one format. Specifically, number columns can have up to four formats, separated by semicolons. In order, they represent the format for a positive value, a negative value, a value of zero, and a value of null. For example, the following format displays a plus sign (+) in front of a positive number and surrounds a negative number with parentheses:

```
+#,##0.00;(#,##0.00)
```

To explore number formats, you'll format the amount column in the Costs table so that it displays as typical U.S. currency.

To format the amount column:

1. Make sure that you are working with the *tshows* database and that the Costs table is open in the Database painter. (Any application will do at this point.)
2. Open the Alter Table dialog box for the Costs table.
3. Click in the **amount** column's Name box to make amount the current column.
4. Choose the format you see in Figure 8.11 from the Format dropdown menu. Notice that this particular format begins with a dollar sign and places parentheses around negative values. Because there is no display mask for the zero format, a value of zero uses the positive format. (Zero is a positive number.) If the value is null, the column will simply appear empty.

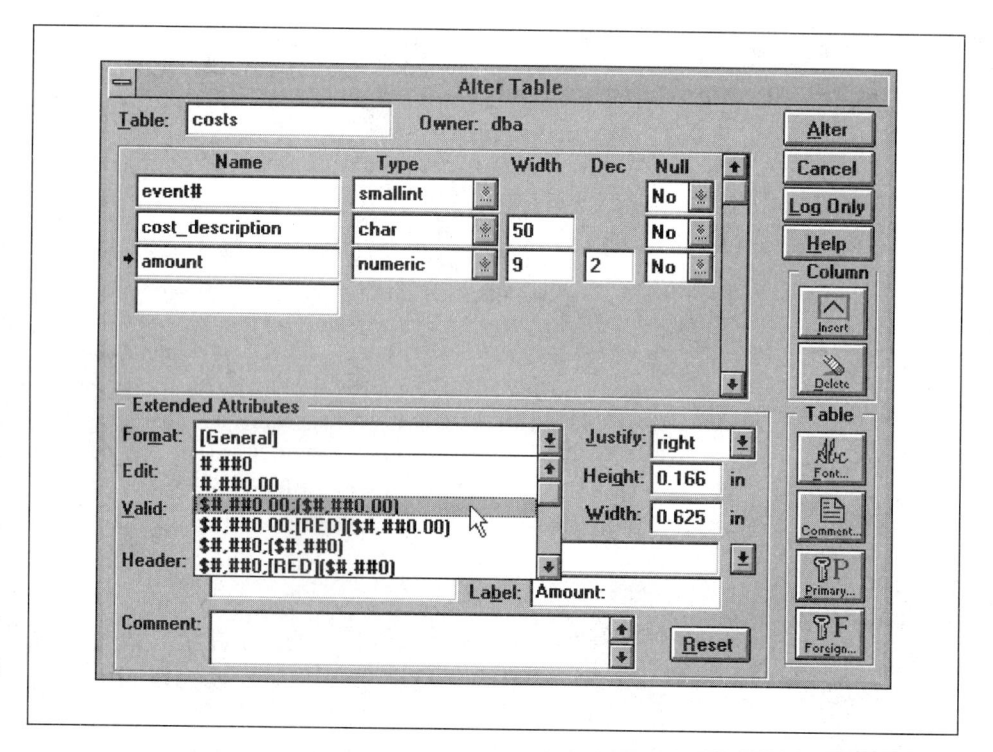

Figure 8.11
Choosing a default number format

5 If you are working with version 4.0, click the **Alter** button to close the dialog box and save the format.

If you are working with version 5.0, double-click the Alter Table dialog box's control box. Click the **Yes** button when PowerBuilder asks if you want to save your changes.

6 Display the contents of the table in the Data Manipulation painter to see the results of applying the display format.

Edit Formats

As you read earlier, an edit format affects not only how data are viewed, but also what the user sees during data entry. Although you can access PowerBuilder's built-in edit masks from the Alter Table dialog box, if you want an edit format that doesn't exist already, you'll need to build your own from the Edit Style dialog box.

The Default Edit Format

Unless you specify otherwise, PowerBuilder assigns each column the default Edit edit style. It's not a typographic error: The default edit style is named "Edit." You can modify this default style somewhat to adjust data display and editing. As an example, you'll add a vertical scroll bar to a column:

To add a vertical scroll bar to a column:

1 If necessary, connect to the *tshows* database and open the Leads table. (Any application will do at this point.)

2 If you are working with version 4.0, right-click the **lead_comments** column and choose **Edit Style** from the popup menu. The Edit Style dialog box appears (Figure 8.12 on page 158).

If you are working with version 5.0, right-click the **lead_comments** column and choose **Properties** from the popup menu to display the Column Properties dialog box. Click the **Edit Style** tab at the top of the Column Properties dialog box to display the Edit Style panel (Figure 8.13 on page 158).

3 Click the **New** button. A second Edit Style dialog box appears (Figure 8.14 on page 159 for version 4.0 and Figure 8.15 on page 160 for version 5.0).

4 Click the **H Scroll Bar** check box. This will place a horizontal scroll bar in the column when it is part of a DataWindow object.

5 Type **Horizontal scroll** in the Name box to give the edit style a name.

6 Click the **OK** button. PowerBuilder returns you to the original Edit Style dialog box/panel. The new edit style is highlighted in the list of style names.

7 Click the **OK** button to apply the highlighted edit style to the lead_comments column.

158 CHAPTER EIGHT EXTENDED DATA ATTRIBUTES

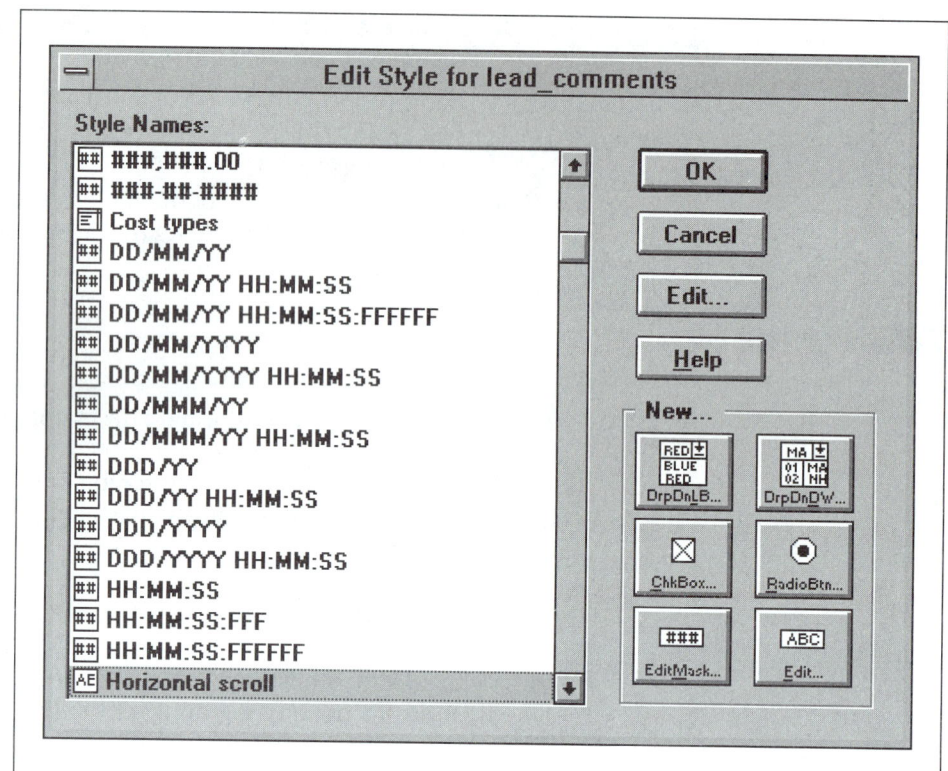

Figure 8.12
Edit Style dialog box (4.0)

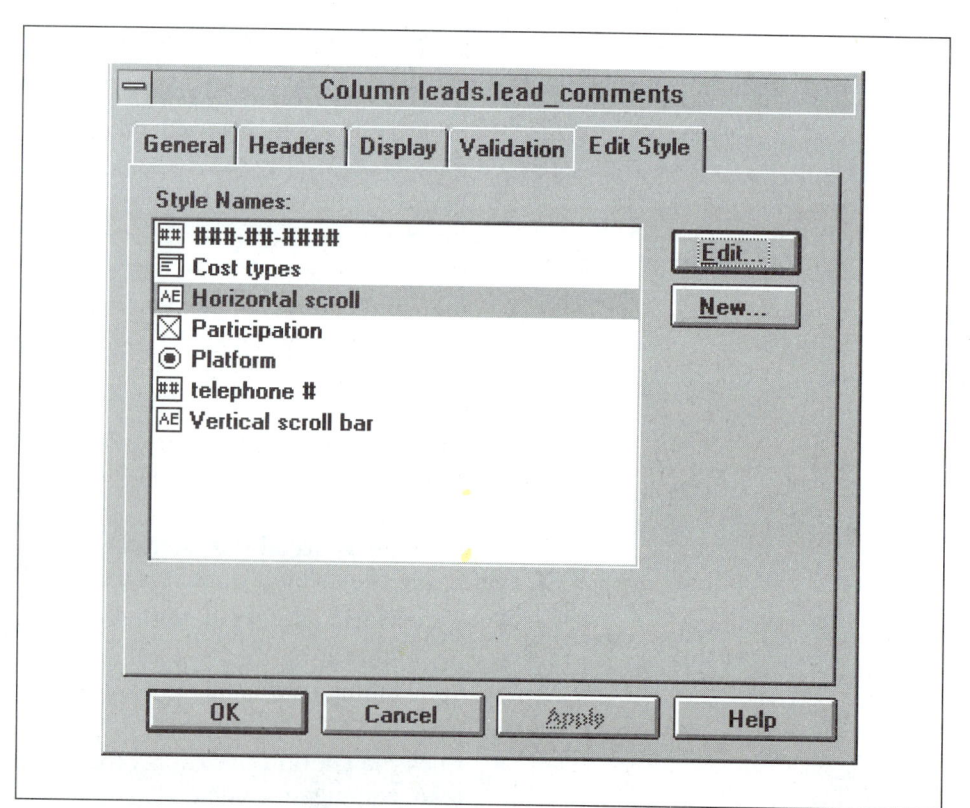

Figure 8.13
Edit Style panel (5.0)

Figure 8.14
Default Edit Style dialog box (4.0)

The scroll bar can't be seen in the Data Manipulation painter. You'll have to wait until you create a DataWindow using the lead_comments column before the scroll bar will appear.

The default Edit Style dialog box that appears in Figure 8.14 and Figure 8.15 can be used to set a variety of formatting characteristics, including the following:

- *Limit*: Specifies the maximum number of characters that can be entered in a column. The default value of 0 means that there is no limit.
- *Case*: Converts characters to either all uppercase or all lowercase. The default value of Any accepts characters as they are typed without performing any case conversion.
- *Accelerator*: Establishes a keyboard equivalent for selecting the column. In a Windows environment, this establishes an "ALT-*letter*" combination for the column. To set an accelerator, type an ampersand (&) followed by the letter that will be combined with ALT to select the column.
- *Password*: Translates characters as they are entered into asterisks so the entered value doesn't appear on the screen.
- *Display Only*: Allows data to be displayed but prevents data modification.

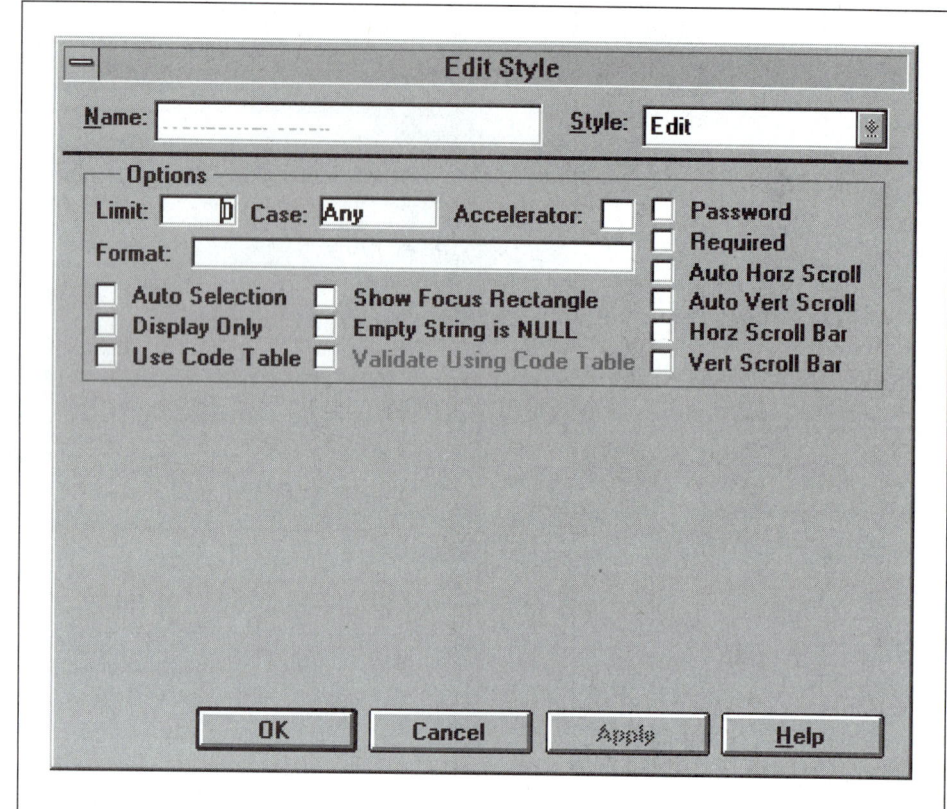

Figure 8.15
Default Edit Style dialog box (5.0)

- *Show Focus Rectangle*: Displays a border around the column whenever the column is active (in other words, has "focus") in a DataWindow.

The idea of focus is important in PowerBuilder applications. It refers to the row and column that PowerBuilder is currently using in a DataWindow. You will learn how to detect changes in focus (focus change events) throughout Part Three of this book.

Setting an Edit Mask for a Date Column

Date columns can have two display masks: one for the date and one for a null value. The placeholders in those formats include *d* for a day character, *m* for a month character, and *y* for a year character. For example, *d* produces a day without leading zeros, *dd* produces a two-digit day (adding a leading zero if necessary), *ddd* produces an three-character abbreviation for the day (for example, Mon, Tues, or Wed), and *dddd* produces the full name of the day. A date display mask can also include literal characters such as - and / that are commonly used to format dates.

To explore setting a date format:

1 If necessary, connect to the *tshows* database and open the Calendar table. (Any application will do at this point.)

CHAPTER EIGHT EXTENDED DATA ATTRIBUTES **161**

2 Right-click the **start_date** column.

3 If you are working with version 4.0, choose **Edit Style** from the popup menu. The Edit Style dialog box appears.

If you are working with version 5.0, choose **Properties** from the popup menu. Click the **Edit Style** tab to display the Edit Style panel.

As you can see in Figure 8.16, the dialog box/panel provides a list of predefined edit masks.

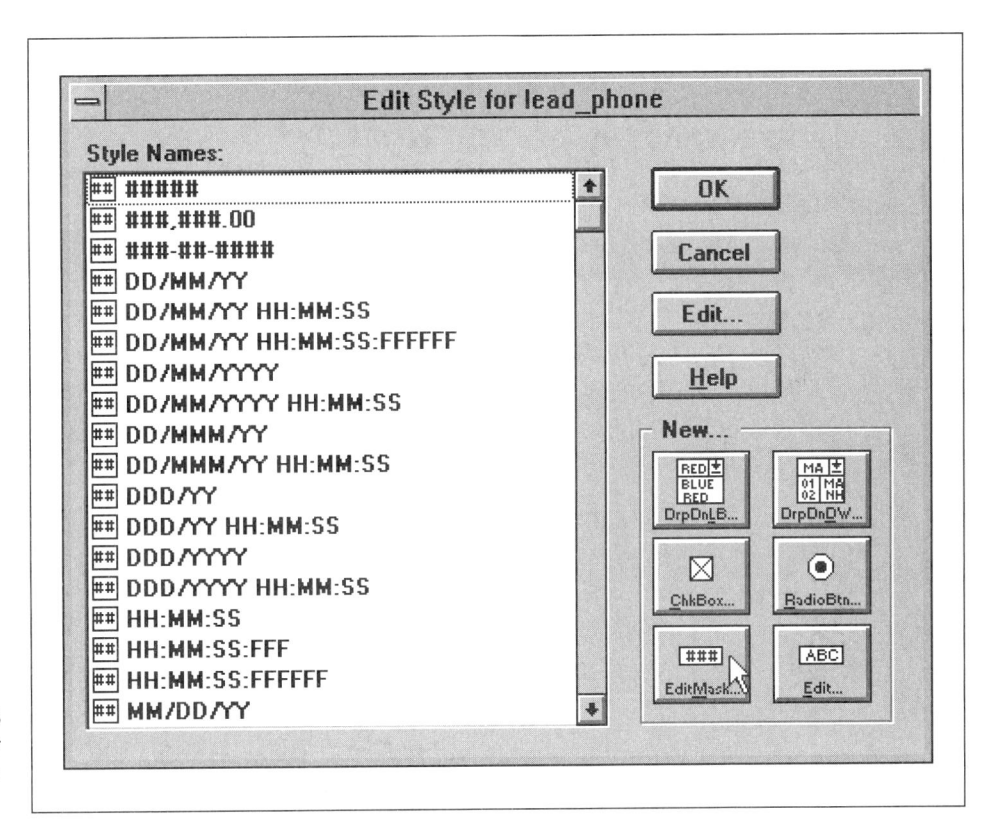

Figure 8.16
Edit Style dialog box for a date or time column

The list of edit styles in Figure 8.14 is accessible only from the column's popup menu (version 4.0) or the Column Properties dialog box (version 5.0). You won't find these styles in the Alter Table dialog box.

4 Click the **MM/DD/YYYY** format to highlight it. (You may need to scroll down the list of style names to see it.) Given that we are so close to the turn of the century, it makes sense to use four-digit years.

5 Click the **OK** button.

6 Repeat Steps 2 through 5 for the **end_date** column.

7 Display the contents of the Calendar table in the Data Manipulation painter to see the effect of your formatting.

8 Apply the same edit style to the **contact_date** column in the Contacts table.

> *Edit styles for dates have two major advantages. First, they relieve the user from having to type the delimiters between the parts of the date. Second, they ensure that dates appear in a consistent format throughout the database. This latter is particularly important as we near the turn of the century: You can force a user to enter a four-digit year.*

Character Column Edit Styles

In most cases, the list of predefined edit styles doesn't provide a mask that is suitable for a character column. You will therefore need to create a custom edit style. To explore creating your own edit styles, you will be defining a format for a telephone number.

To define a format for a telephone number:

1 Click the **Leads** table in the Database painter workspace to select it.

2 If you are working with version 4.0, right-click the **lead_phone** column and choose **Edit Style** from the popup menu. The Edit Style dialog box appears.

If you are working with version 5.0, right-click the **lead_phone** column and choose **Properties** from the popup menu to display the Column Properties dialog box. Click the **Edit Style** tab to display the Edit Style panel.

3 If you are working with version 4.0, click the **EditMask** button in the lower-right corner of the dialog box. The Edit Mask dialog box appears. Notice that the characters that you can use as placeholders in the mask appear in the lower-left corner of the dialog box.

If you are working with version 5.0, click the New button to display the Edit Style dialog box. Choose **EditMask** from the Style popup menu. The dialog box changes to appear as in Figure 8.17 on page 163. In this version, the characters that you can use a placeholders appear in the scrolling list labeled "Masks."

4 Type **telephone #** as the name of the edit mask. Once defined, this new edit style will appear in the Edit Style dialog box under its name. You'll be able to apply it to other columns without redefining the mask.

5 Drag the pointer across the contents of the Mask box to highlight them. (Alternatively, you can double-click on the contents of the box.) Press the **Backspace** key to delete them.

6 Type **(###) ###-####** in the Mask box, as in Figure 8.18 on page 163. This mask will automatically place parentheses around an area code and a dash in the middle of the telephone number, just as they usually appear.

7 Click the **OK** button to close the dialog box. Notice that the new edit style now appears in the Edit Style dialog box/panel. It is highlighted.

8 Click the **OK** button to apply the style.

9 Display the Leads table in the Data Manipulation painter. Notice that the column for the lead_phone column is no longer wide enough to display an entire phone number.

Figure 8.17
Edit Style dialog box used to create a new edit mask (5.0)

Figure 8.18
Creating an edit style for a character column

10 Change the width of the lead_phone column to **1** inch.

11 Display the Leads table once more in the Data Manipulation painter. The lead_phone column is now large enough to show all the data.

12 Click the **Insert Row** button in the PainterBar. (*Hint*: If you're not sure where it is, turn on PowerTips so that labels appear when you pass the pointer over each button.) Notice that the parentheses and the dash—the literal characters in the edit mask—appear in the column.

164 CHAPTER EIGHT EXTENDED DATA ATTRIBUTES

13 Click the **lead_phone** column. Then type **1015551234**. Notice that the digits are spaced properly in the mask, without requiring you to type the parentheses, any spaces, or the dash.

14 Exit the Data Manipulation painter *without* saving your changes.

Character column edit styles are appropriate when you want to enforce a consistent format (for example, the telephone number for which you just created an edit style) and when you want to simplify data entry for the user.

Check Boxes

A *check box* is a square box that can represent two values. PowerBuilder views the check box as being in one of two states (off or on); you assign exactly which two values are stored for each state. A user can then click the check box to change its state. In the on state, the box contains an X; clicking it removes the X and changes the state to off. When the check box is in the off state, clicking i the empty box changes the state to on and displays an X.

Check boxes are particularly appropriate for columns that can hold a value of true or false. For example, the participation column in the Calendar table should store *T* if Pinehill Software is exhibiting at a trade show and *F* if it is not.

To format the participation column so that it is displayed as a check box:

1 Select the Calendar table from the *tshows* database in the Database painter workspace.

2 If you are working with version 4.0, right-click the **participation** column and choose **Edit Style** from the popup menu. The Edit Style dialog box appears.

If you are working with version 5.0, right-click the **participation** column and choose **Properties** from the popup menu to display the Column Properties dialog box. Click the **Edit Style** tab to display the Edit Style panel. Click the **New** button to create a new edit style.

3 If you are working with version 4.0, click the **ChkBox** button in the lower-right corner of the dialog box. The CheckBox Style dialog box appears.

If you working with version 5.0, choose **CheckBox** from the Style popup menu.

4 Type **Participation** as the name of the edit style.

5 Type **Participating?** in the Text field as the label that will appear to the left of the check box.

6 Type **T** as the On data value and **F** as the Off data value. Your completed dialog box should look like Figure 8.19 on page 165 (version 4.0) or Figure 8.20 on page 165 (version 5.0).

7 Click the **OK** button. The new edit style is added to the list of available styles in the Edit Style dialog box and is highlighted.

8 Click the **OK** button to apply the style.

9 Change the width of the participation column to **1.25** inches.

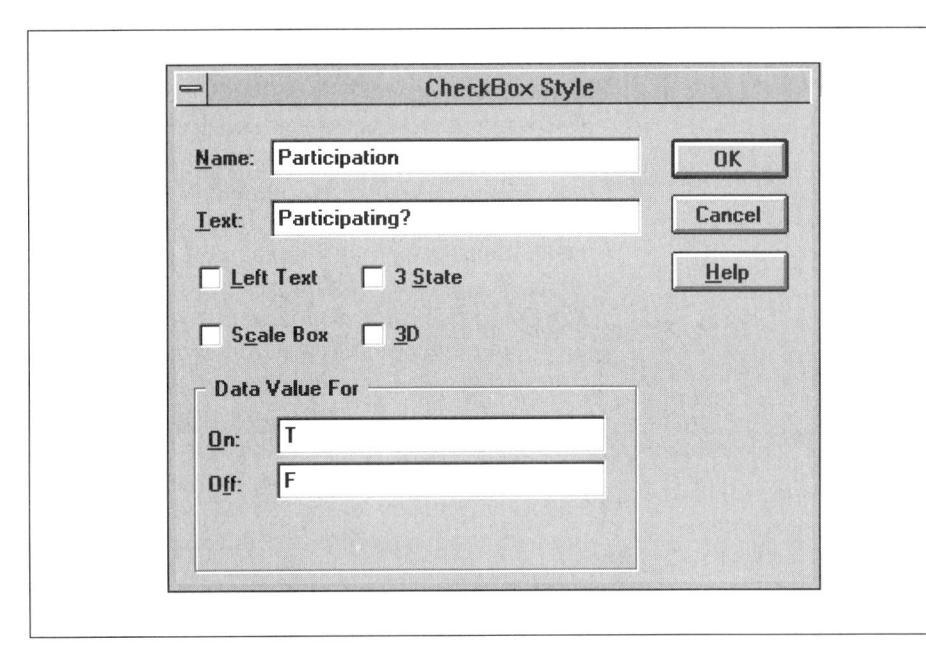

Figure 8.19
A check box edit style (4.0)

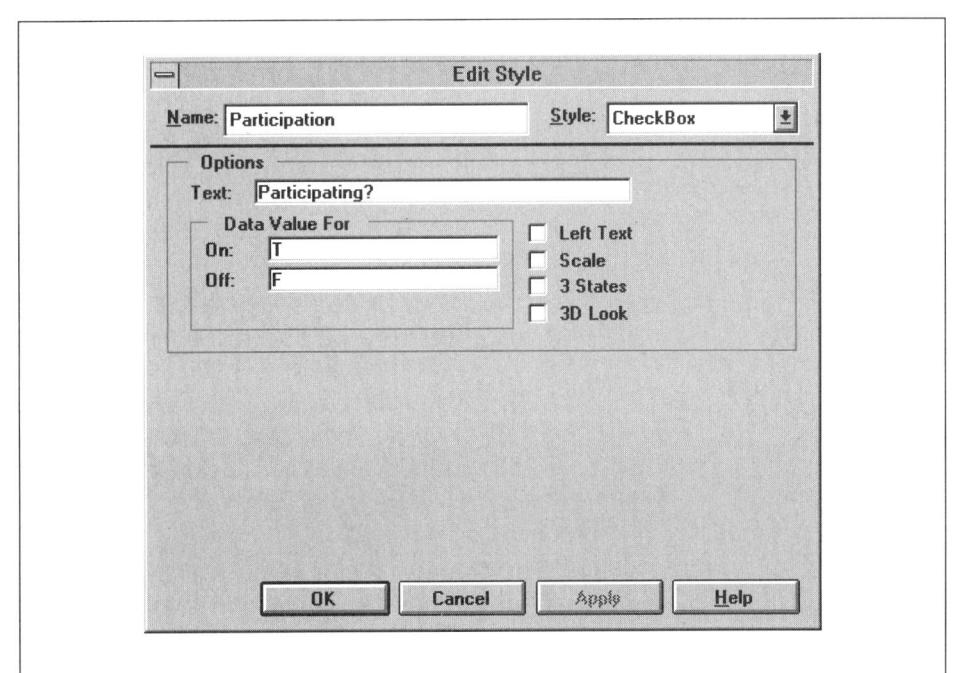

Figure 8.20
A check box edit style (5.0)

10 Display the Calendar table in the Data Manipulation painter to see the effect of the check box style.

To be completely accurate, a check box can actually represent a third value ("other"), which means that the check box isn't either off or on. To set up a check box that can hold three values, choose a 3 States check box. A check box whose value is unknown (null) will then appear as gray.

Radio Buttons

Radio buttons provide a mutually exclusive set of values from which a user can choose. In practice, this means that only radio button in a group of related radio buttons can be active. When the user selects one member of a group, PowerBuilder deselects the member of the group that was previously active. If a column can take no more than three or four values, then radio buttons can make it easier for the user to enter data.

NOTE *More than four radio buttons can be confusing to the user. If you have a set of more than four fixed values from which a user can choose only one, use a dropdown list, which is discussed in the next section.*

The platform column in the Shows table can take only three values: PC, Mac, or Both. It is therefore an excellent candidate for display using radio buttons. The radio buttons mean that all the user will need to do is click once, rather than be required to type a value, which might be entered incorrectly.

To create a set of radio buttons for the Platform column:

1. Select the Shows table from the *tshows* database in the Database painter workspace.
2. If you are working with version 4.0, right-click the **platform** column and choose **Edit Style** from the popup menu. The Edit Styles dialog box appears.

    If you are working with version 5.0, right-click the **platform** column and choose **Properties** from the popup menu to display the Column Properties dialog box. Click the **Edit Style** tab to display the Edit Style panel.

3. If you are working with version 4.0, click the **RadioBtn** button in the lower-right corner of the dialog box. The RadioButton Style dialog box appears (Figure 8.21 on page 167).

    If you are working with version 5.0, click the **New** button to create a new edit style. Choose **RadioButtons** from the Style popup menu. The panel changes to appear as in Figure 8.22 on page 167.

4. Type **Platform** as the name of the edit style.

The Columns Across value determines how many radio buttons will appear in a line. If you leave the value at 1, the radio buttons will appear in a vertical list.

5. Make sure the value is **1**.

The values that appear on the screen next to the radio buttons and the values that are actually stored in the database are entered in the thin-bordered rectangle in the lower-left corner of the dialog box. A right-pointing hand indicates the value with which you will be working.

6. Type **PC** as the first display value.
7. Press the **Tab** key. Then type **PC** as the first data value.

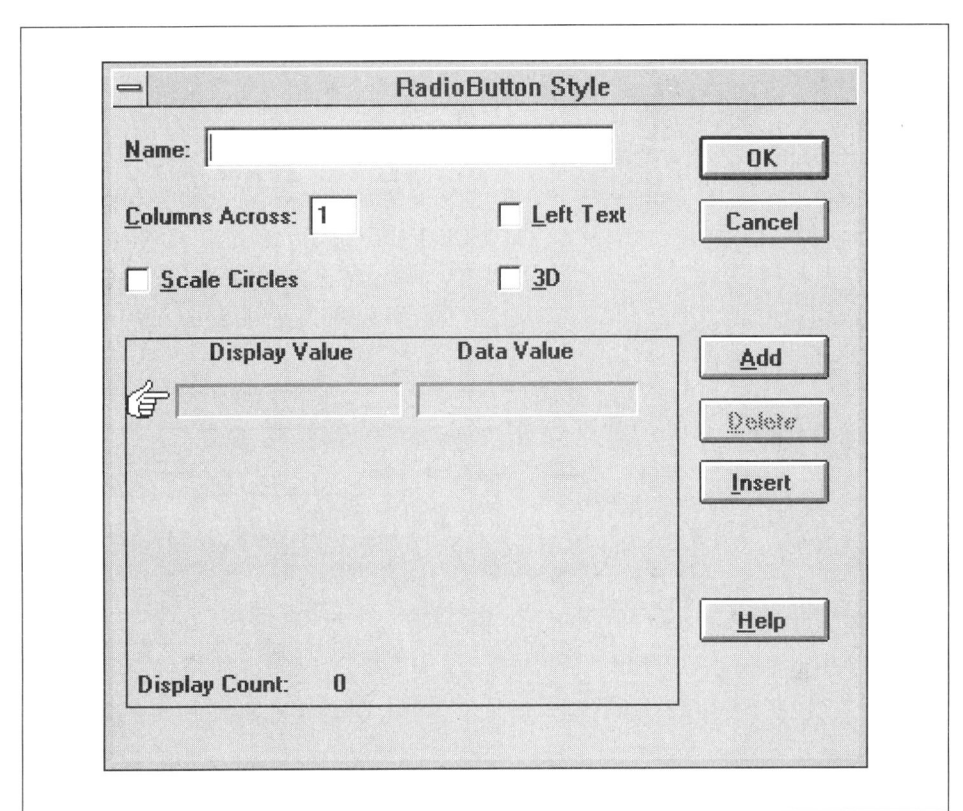

Figure 8.21
RadioButton Style dialog box (4.0)

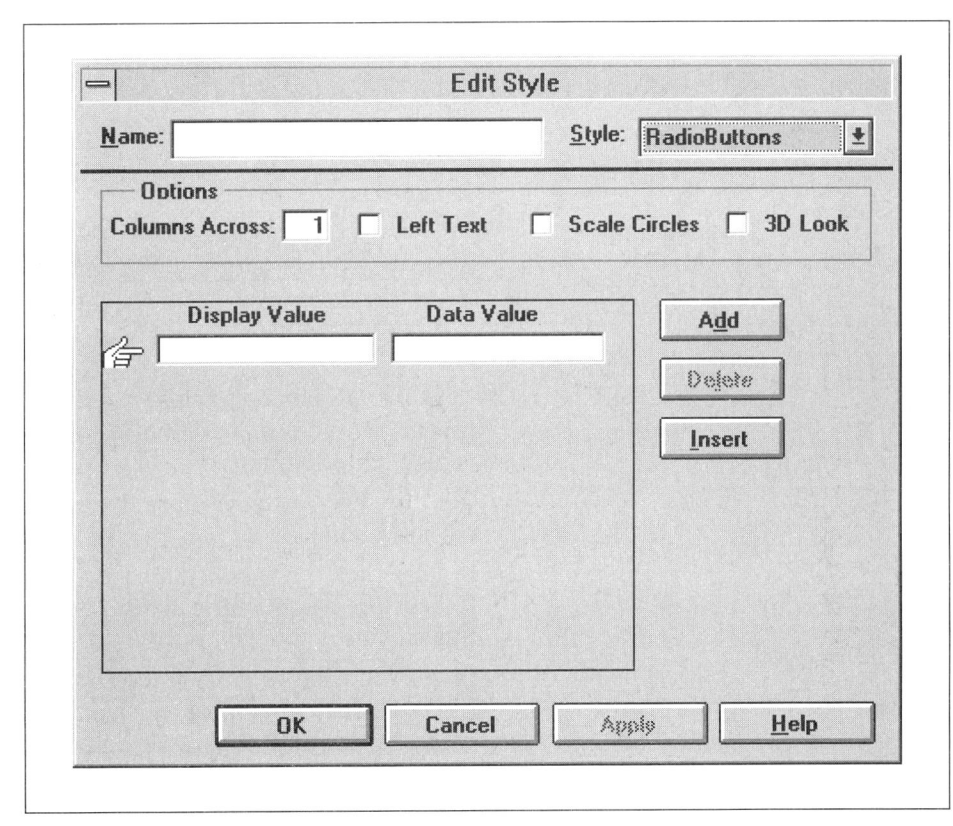

Figure 8.22
Creating a new radio button edit style (5.0)

168 CHAPTER EIGHT EXTENDED DATA ATTRIBUTES

> *Although this example uses identical display and data values, the two needn't be the same. For example, you might display "Personal Computer" and store "PC" to save space.*

8 Click the **Add** button.

9 Type **Mac** as the second display and data values.

10 Click the **Add** button.

11 Type **Both** as the third display and data values. Your completed dialog box should look like Figure 8.23.

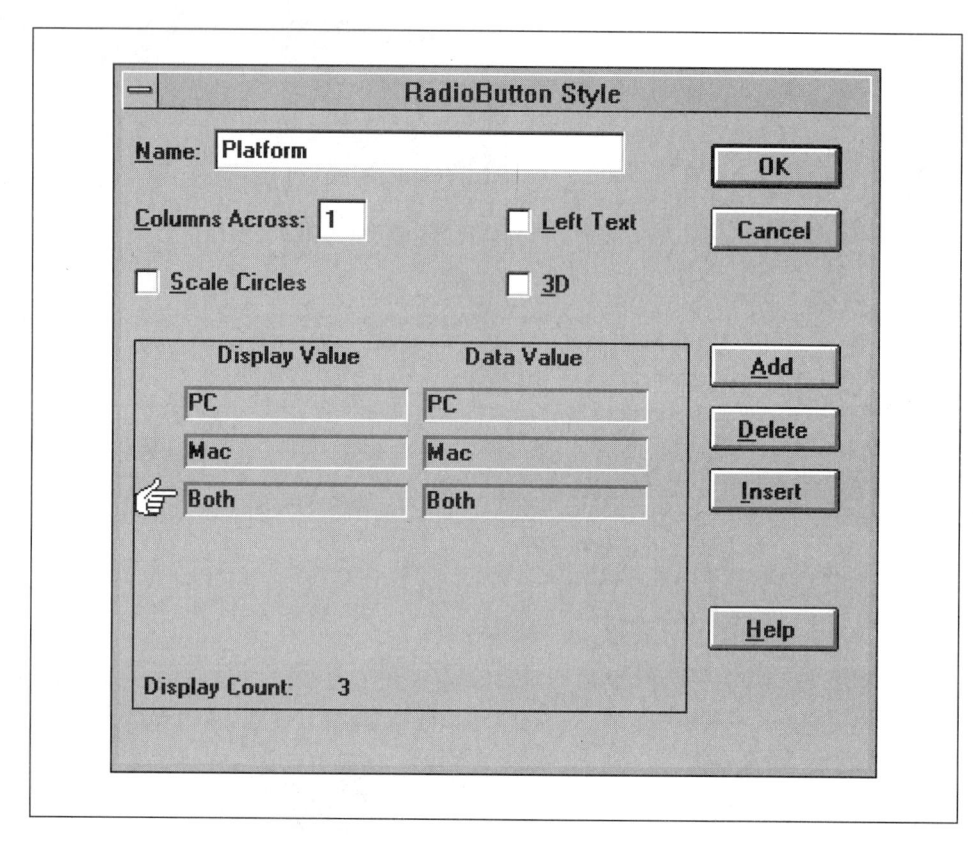

Figure 8.23
Completed RadioButton Style dialog box

12 Click the **OK** button to close the dialog box and add the new style to the list of styles in the Edit Style dialog box. Notice that the new style is highlighted in the list.

13 Click the **OK** button to close the dialog box and apply the style to the platform column.

14 Double-click the **Shows** table to open its Alter Table dialog box. Change the height of the platform column to **1** inch. (If you don't make this change, you won't be able to see all the radio buttons.)

15 Display the Shows table in the DataManipulation painter to see how the radio buttons appear. Click an empty radio button to change a value. Notice that clicking on an empty radio button automatically removes the highlight from the previously highlighted button in that row and places it in the button you clicked.

Dropdown Lists

A *dropdown list* provides a longer list of fixed values from which a user can choose than is practical with radio buttons. Like radio buttons, a dropdown list means a user doesn't need to type a value, removing the chance that a value might be mistyped.

> **NOTE** *Why do we seem to care so much about mistyped values? Because when you are searching for data, the DBMS matches data character-by-character. Although PC and Personal Computer mean the same thing to most of us, they aren't the same as far as a DBMS's search is concerned. In fact, an error of only one character (and sometimes even a mismatch in terms of case) means that a DBMS won't identify two items as the same, therefore missing rows that should be retrieved by a search. To ensure the most accurate data retrieval possible, we need to enforce accurate, consistent data storage.*

To create a dropdown list by creating a list of values for the cost_description column in the Costs table:

1. Open the Costs table from the *tshows* database in the Database painter workspace.
2. If necessary, click the **Costs** table to select it.
3. If you are working with version 4.0, right-click the **cost_description** column and choose **Edit Style** from the popup menu. The Edit Style dialog box appears.

    If you are working with version 5.0, right-click the **cost_description** column and choose **Properties** from the popup menu to display the Column Properties dialog box. Click the **Edit Style** tab to display the Edit Style panel. Click the **New** button to create a new edit style.

4. If you are working with version 4.0, click the **DrpDnLB** button in the lower-right corner of the dialog box. The DropDownListBox Style dialog box appears (Figure 8.24 on page 170).

    If you are working with version 5.0, choose **DropDownListBox** from the Style popup menu. The dialog box changes to appear like Figure 8.25 on page 170.

    Notice that both the version 4.0 and version 5.0 dialog boxes are very similar to the RadioButton Style dialog box.

5. Type **Cost types** as the name of the edit style.
6. Click the **Sorted** check box so that the items in the list will be sorted alphabetically.
7. Click the **Auto H Scroll** check box so that the items in the list will scroll horizontally as the pointer moves down the list.
8. Click the **Always Show Arrow** check box so that the arrow that indicates the presence of a dropdown list is always visible.

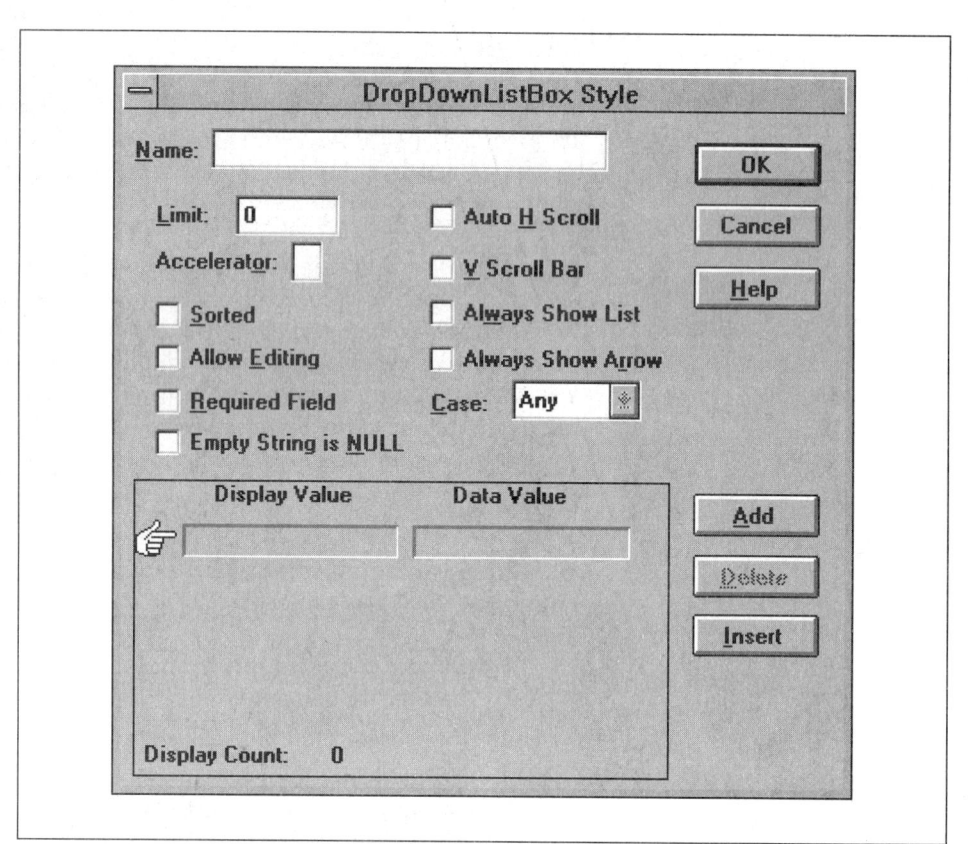

Figure 8.24
DropDownListBox Style dialog box (4.0)

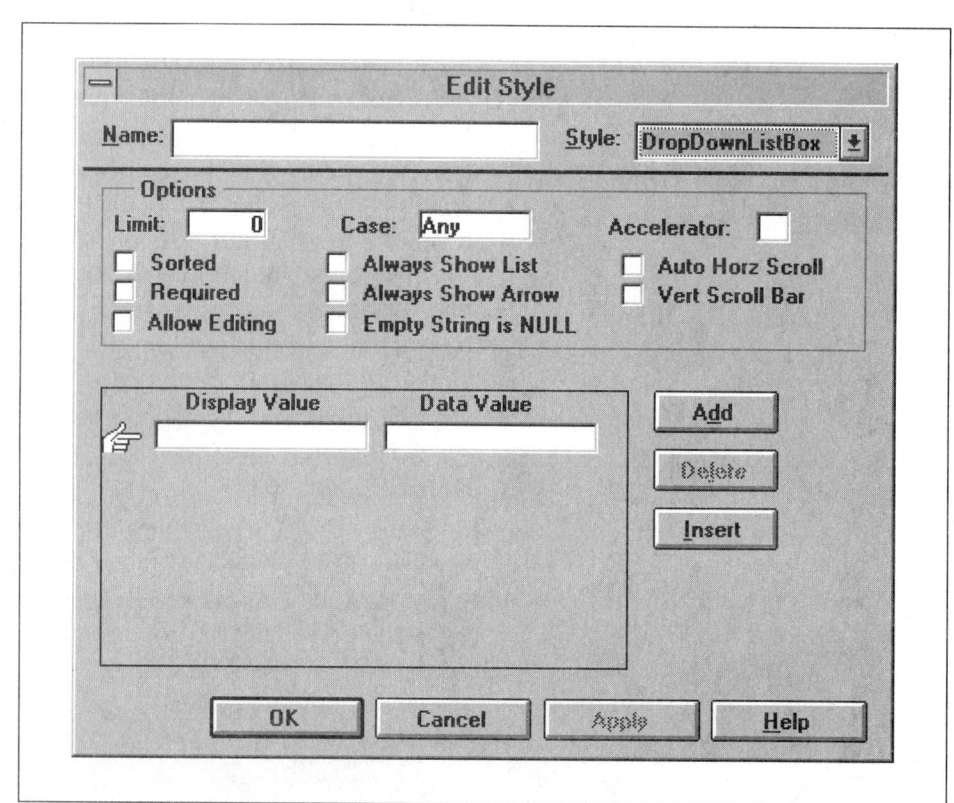

Figure 8.25
Creating a new DropDownListBox edit style (5.0)

9   Type the display and data values in the list below. Don't forget to use the Add button between each pair of values.

Display Value	Data Value
Hotel	Hotel
Meals	Meals
Airfare	Plane
Train fare	Train
Car expenses	Car
Registration	Fees
Ground transportation	Ground
Booth rental	Booth
Booth electricity	Electricity
Booth furnishings	Furnishings
Booth cleaning	Cleaning
Booth equipment	Equipment
Shipping	Shipping
Union labor	Labor
Booth telephone	Telephone

10 Click the **OK** button to close the DropDownListBox Style dialog box and return to the edit style dialog box. Notice that the Cost types style has been added to the list of styles and is highlighted.

11 Click the **OK** button to close the edit style dialog box and apply the highlighted style to the cost_description column.

12 Display the Costs table in the DataManipulation painter to see the dropdown list. Notice that you must pick a value from the list; you can't type a completely new value.

If you want to allow users to enter their own values while giving them a list from which to choose, click the Allow Editing check box in the DropDownListBox Style dialog box.

Dropdown lists have one major drawback: They aren't dynamic. If the values from which you want the user to pick change, then you must reenter the PowerBuilder development environment and modify the application. The alternative is a dynamic list that looks up values from a table or view in the database. You will learn how to create dynamic lists using dropdown DataWindows in Chapter 14.

Column Validation

As you created the structure for the *tshows* database, you defined primary and foreign key constraints to enforce data integrity. In addition, when you defined data types for columns you established broad domain constraints for the data to be stored in those columns. Using check boxes, radio buttons, and dropdown lists can also help ensure that users enter correct values. In addition, you can often create additional domain constraints that can accurately test the validity of data. Such *validation rules* are applied to individual columns and are expressed as logical criteria that data in a column must meet. In this section you will learn how to create validation rules. In addition, you will learn how to use the data validation facility to provide a default value for a column.

Specifying Validation Rules

To specify a validation rule, you construct a logical expression by combining three elements: a placeholder for a column value, operators (arithmetic and logical), and values (expressed as functions or constants). The placeholder for a column name begins with @ and is followed by the column name. For example, the event# column would appear as `@event#`. Functions are represented by their names, followed by a list of input parameters surrounded by parentheses.

For example, assume that you wanted to verify that every time someone entered a new row into the Calendar table, the starting date of the trade show was after the current date. An expression for this rule is:

```
@start_date > today()
```

The current system date is retrieved with the `today()` function, which requires no parameters.

To install the validation rule for the start_date column:

1. Open the Calendar table from the *tshows* database in the Database painter.

2. If you are working with version 4.0, right-click the **start_date** column and choose **Validation** from the popup menu. The Column Validation dialog box appears.

    If you are working with version 5.0, right-click the **start_date** column, and choose **Properties** from the popup menu to display the Column Properties dialog box. Click the **Validation** tab to display the Validation panel.

3. Click the **New** button. The Input Validation dialog box appears.

4. Type **date>today** as the name of the rule.

5. Click the **@start_date** button to enter the placeholder for the column in the Rule Definition box.

6. Type **> today()** in the Rule Definition box to complete the rule.

7. Change the Validation Error Message so that it reads **'Starting date of a trade show must be after today.'** The single quotation marks around the text of the message are required. At this point, your dialog box should look like Figure 8.26 on page 173.

Rather than typing a function, you can choose it from the Functions list in the lower-right corner of the Input Validation dialog box. However, because the list of functions is rather long, it is usually easier just to type the function.

8. Click the **OK** button to close the Input Validation dialog box. The validation rule appears highlighted in the Validation Rules dialog box.

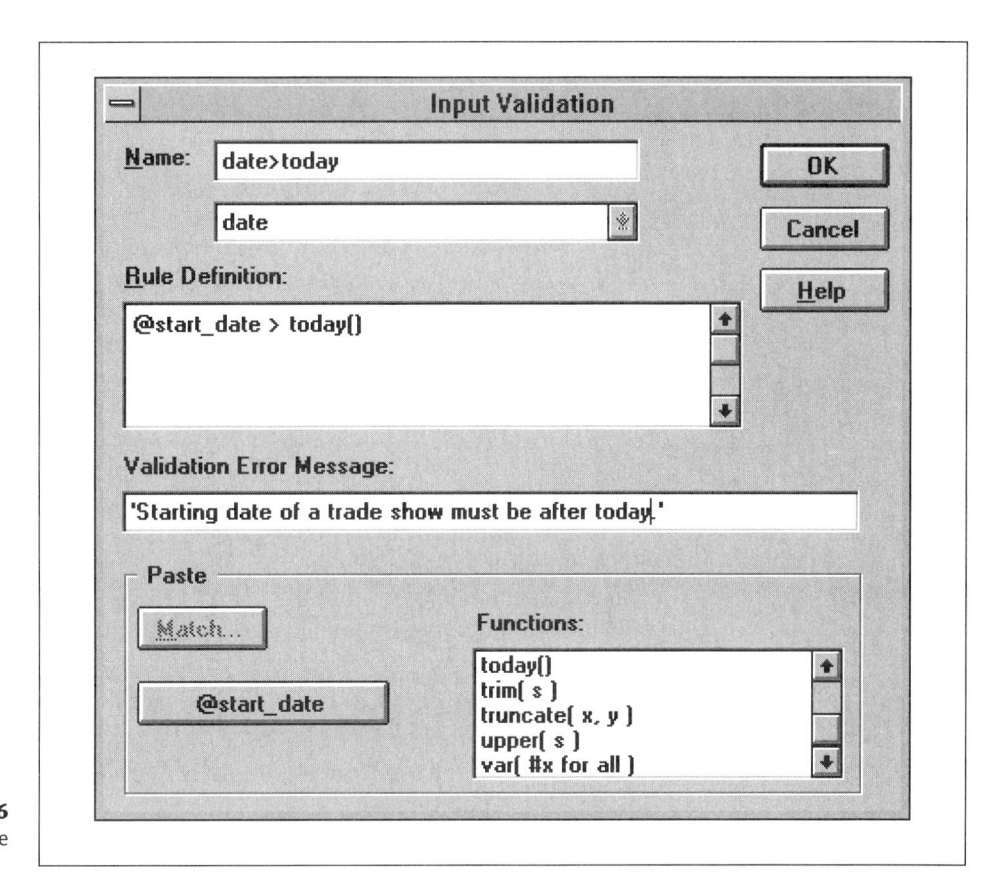

Figure 8.26
Defining an input validation rule

9. Click the **OK** button to close the Validation Rules dialog box and apply the validation rule to the start_date column.
10. Display the Calendar table in the Data Manipulation painter workspace.
11. Insert a new row and type a starting date of **05/16/91**.
12. Press the **Tab** key in an attempt to move to the end_date column. PowerBuilder displays a dialog box containing the error message you stored in the validation rule. Notice that you are unable to proceed until you enter valid data for the column.
13. Exit the Data Manipulation painter *without* saving changes.

There is a major limitation to validation rules: a validation rule can affect only one column. For example, PowerBuilder will not allow you to construct a validation rule that verifies that the Calendar table's end_date column is greater than the start_date column. Validation rules restrict you to expressions involving a single column and constant or computed values.

PowerBuilder maintains one set of validation rules for each column data type in the database. For example, if you define a validation rule for a date column, that rule is available for use with all other date columns in the database. When you apply the rule to a column other than the one for which the rule was originally defined, PowerBuilder substitutes the name of the column getting the rule for the column name placeholder used when the rule was defined. For example, if a validation rule is defined as `@contact_date >= today()` for the contact_date column and the rule is applied to the end_date column, PowerBuilder changes the rule to `@end_date >= today()`.

Providing Default Values

A *default value* is a common value that a database application assigns automatically to a column. Should the actual value be different, the user can replace the default. However, because the default is usually the most common value for the column, in most cases the user won't need to enter any data.

To enter a default value for a column, you use the Validation Rules dialog box. At the bottom of the dialog box is an edit box for entering the default value. The edit box also has a dropdown menu with some common defaults from which you can choose. If the column is a character column, then you can enter a specific value, choose to fill the column with spaces, or choose to set the column to null. If the column holds a numeric value, you can enter a specific value, choose the set the column to zero, or choose to set the column to null. Because we commonly want to fill a date column with the current system date, a date column also provides that option.

To enter the current system date into a date column:

1. Open the Contacts table from the *tshows* database in the Database painter.
2. If you are working with version 4.0, right-click the **contact_date** column and choose **Validation** from the popup menu. The Column Validation dialog box appears.

   If you are working with version 5.0, right-click the **contact_date** column, and choose **Properties** from the popup menu to display the Column Properties dialog box. Click the **Validation** tab to display the Validation Rules panel.
3. Choose **Set to Today** from the Initial Value popup menu (Figure 8.27 on page 175).
4. Click the **OK** button to return to the Database painter.
5. Display the Contacts table in the Data Manipulation painter workspace.
6. Click the **Insert Row** button in the PainterBar to insert a new row. Notice that the current system date automatically appears in the contact_date column.
7. Exit the Data Manipulation painter *without* saving changes.

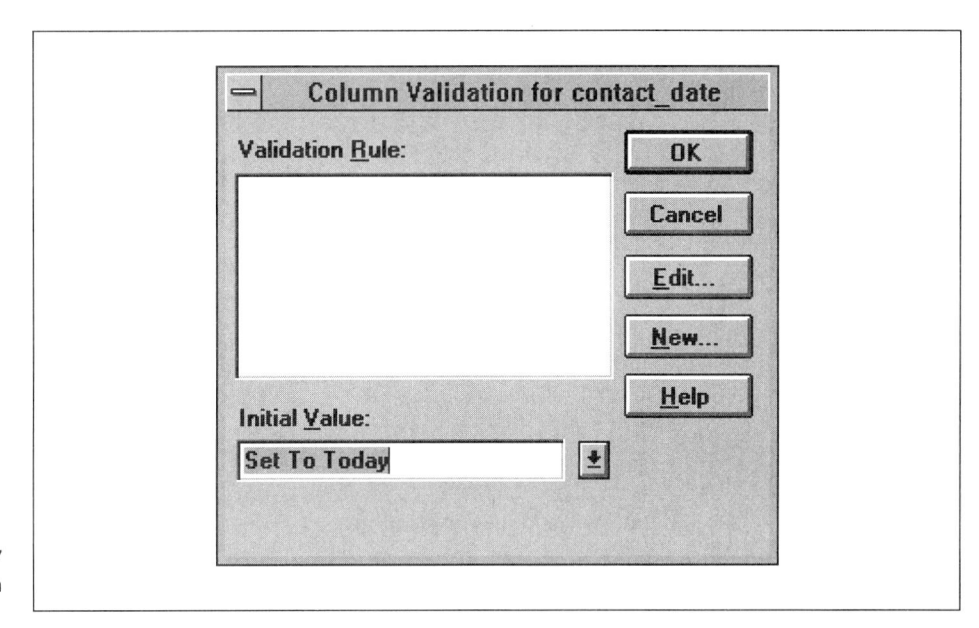

Figure 8.27
Setting a default value for a column

Looking Ahead

In this chapter you've had your first experience with the ways in which Power-Builder helps you enhance the data formatting and validation capabilities provided by a DBMS. The techniques you've learned here will be useful throughout the rest of this book, as we now turn to creating applications for end users that will keep them from having to deal with the details of direct database manipulation.

EXERCISES

The following exercises are based on the *rents* database and assume that you have completed the exercises at the end of Chapter 6, creating the tables that weren't present when you first started working with the database.

As you work through these exercises, be sure to look at the results of your modifications in the Data Manipulation painter workspace. Change the display size of columns as necessary to show all your formatting.

1. Add comments to each of the columns in the Item table to explain the meaning of the columns. Verify that the comments appear correctly in the Database painter workspace. If you are unhappy with the presence of the comments (in other words, you don't like the width of the table when the comments are present), remove the comments.

2. Check the labels and headers for each table in the *rents* database. Make any changes necessary to make the default labels and headers understandable by a user. For example, you might want to change *merchandise#* to *Merchandise #*, inserting a space between the word and the pound sign.

3. Assign edit formats to the following columns so that they include four-year dates: Delivery_date (Rentals table), Return_date (Rentals table), Contact_date (Contacts table).

4. Assign edit formats to the following columns so that appear as currency: Semester_fee (Merchandise table), Yearly_fee (Merchandise table), Fee_paid (Rentals table).

5. Create an edit format for a telephone number and assign it to the Phone (Customers table) and Housing_office_phone# (Schools table) columns.

6. Create a set of radio buttons for the Status column in the Item table. (*Hint:* Check the data in the table to determine the values used for that column.)

7. Identify at least one column in the *rents* database for which a dropdown list will simplify data entry. Create the dropdown list for the column or columns you chose.

8. Add vertical scroll bars to the Result column in the Contacts table. (Keep in mind that you won't be able to see these scroll bars in the DataManipulation painter.)

9. The domain constraints—validation rules—that are placed on a database are up to the database designer.

    a. List at least four domain constraints that make sense for the C&U Rentals database. (*Hint:* Consider those columns that have a small number of values or that have a restricted range.)

    b. Create and apply validation rules for each of the domain constraints you listed.

PART THREE

Database Access Using an Application

CHAPTER NINE
BUILDING WINDOWS AS AN APPLICATION FRAMEWORK

CHAPTER TEN
INTRODUCING DATAWINDOWS

CHAPTER ELEVEN
DATAWINDOWS AND QUERIES

CHAPTER TWELVE
CONTROL BREAK REPORTS

CHAPTER THIRTEEN
INHERITANCE

CHAPTER FOURTEEN
ENABLING DATA MODIFICATION CAPABILITIES

CHAPTER FIFTEEN
CONNECTING DATAWINDOWS

CHAPTER SIXTEEN
DYNAMIC DATAWINDOWS

CHAPTER SEVENTEEN
CREATING MENUS

CHAPTER NINE

Building Windows as an Application Framework

IN THIS CHAPTER YOU WILL:

- Plan an application before beginning application development
- Learn about the basic actions performed by all applications
- Create application windows and place button controls on them
- Write scripts for transaction control and to connect and disconnect from a database
- Write scripts that open and close application windows

The starting place for a PowerBuilder application is an application window. You can attach menus and buttons to an application window to control the flow of the application. You can place DataWindow controls on an application window to provide access to data.

However, you can't design your application windows until you have spent some time deciding how your completed application should be structured. This chapter therefore begins with a brief overview of the structure of the *tshows* application. That structure will provide the blueprint for all the development activity that will follow throughout the rest of this book.

You will then learn to create the application window that controls the *tshows* application and how to use it to access other application windows that will serve as locations for DataWindow controls. You will add scripts that perform basic actions performed by all applications (including connecting to and disconnecting from a database), along with buttons controls that navigate between windows and scripts to make those button controls function.

Planning the Application

The functions that an application will provide should be planned *before* you begin working with PowerBuilder. If you are working in a traditional IS environment, then specifications for the application will be made during the systems design phase of the Systems Development Life Cycle. Alternately, if you are working in an environment where system requirements aren't well known ahead of time, you may be given a list of requirements and asked to create a *prototype* (a working model of the application that will be modified as users test it).

The environment in which the *tshows* application is being developed is very dynamic and all the requirements for the application can't be specified in advance. However, the Pinehill employees who will be using the application have assembled a list of functions they know that they want in the first version of the software:

- Enter, update, and delete data about producers.
- Display data about producers.
- Enter, update, and delete data about shows.
- Display data about shows.
- Enter, update, and delete data about scheduled shows (the calendar).
- Display the calendar in at least three ways: all scheduled shows, scheduled shows that Pinehill is planning to attend, and scheduled shows that Pinehill has attended.
- Enter, update, and delete data about costs.
- Display the costs for one show.
- Display a summary of costs, organized by show, including cost totals.
- Enter, update, and delete sales leads.
- Display a list of sales leads that should be called.
- Display a list of sales leads, organized by company.
- Display a summary of revenue generated by sales leads, organized by show.

The job of the application designer is to organize these functions in some way that they make sense to the user. This usually means grouping similar functions together, using menus to provide access to each part of the application. A menu can be a pulldown menu, such as those used by Windows, or can be assembled from a group of buttons that are placed on application windows. Regardless, of which types of menus you choose for your application, you should draw a plan of what those menus will look like before you proceed to interact with PowerBuilder.

There are no simple rules for designing a menu structure because applications are specific to a given database environment. However, the following guidelines can help make an application easier to use:

- Wherever possible, limit the number of options in a menu to five or six (not including an option to exit the menu and return to the preceding menu).
- Choose names for main menu options that represent groups of related activities. For example, the main menu for the trade show database will need to have four options: Scheduling, which handles all activities related to trade show schedules, including producers, venues, shows, locations, and the calendar; Costs, which handles trade show costs; Sales Leads, which handles sales leads made at the trade shows; and Quit, which ends the application and returns to the operating system.
- Define menu option in terms of the actions they perform, rather than in terms of the table, view, or DataWindow name they invoke. For example, the option "View a cost summary" is more meaningful to a user than "View dw_cost_sum."

Because applications generally use many menus with many options, it helps to create the menu structure on paper. In Figure 9.1 you will see a sample menu tree for the *tshows* application. Each menu option in the main menu appears in boldface. Menu options that display a submenu are also in boldface, followed by an arrow (->). Menu options that invoke application functions appear in plain text. Keep in mind that this menu tree includes only application-specific menus. The typical GUI File and Edit menus will also be present in the menu bar.

Given the state of the cross-platform versions of PowerBuilder at the time this book was written, there is a good chance that you are doing your PowerBuilder work using some version of Windows. Nonetheless, PowerBuilder has been ported to the Macintosh and UNIX GUI environments. You will therefore need to tailor the content of standard File and Edit menus to a given GUI. However, application-specific menus can usually remain the same. For more information on Macintosh-specific issues, see Appendix B.

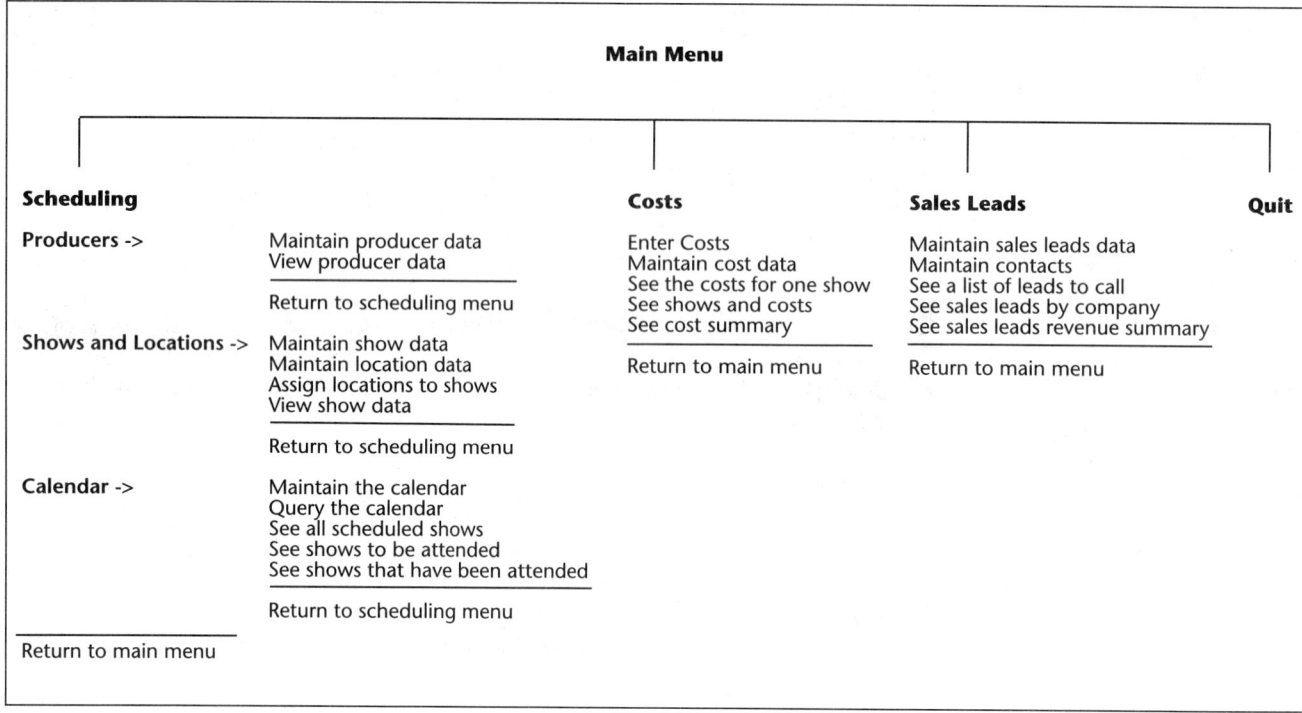

```
                                    Main Menu
        ┌──────────────────┬──────────────────────┬──────────────────┬──────┐
Scheduling                  Costs                  Sales Leads              Quit
Producers ->    Maintain producer data    Enter Costs                Maintain sales leads data
                View producer data        Maintain cost data         Maintain contacts
                                          See the costs for one show See a list of leads to call
                Return to scheduling menu See shows and costs        See sales leads by company
                                          See cost summary           See sales leads revenue summary
Shows and Locations -> Maintain show data
                Maintain location data    Return to main menu        Return to main menu
                Assign locations to shows
                View show data

                Return to scheduling menu
Calendar ->     Maintain the calendar
                Query the calendar
                See all scheduled shows
                See shows to be attended
                See shows that have been attended

                Return to scheduling menu

Return to main menu
```

Figure 9.1 The structure of the *tshows* application

Basic Application Actions

Although the details of the processing performed by an application vary tremendously based on the nature of the application, the general activities that occur during interaction with a database are the same. When an application wants to interact with a database, it does the following:

- Configures a transaction object. (Transaction objects are discussed in the next section.)
- Connects to the database.
- Connects the transaction object to the DataWindow control in which data manipulation will be taking place.
- Processes data in some way.
- Ends the transaction by either committing it or rolling it back.
- Disconnects from the database.

There are some decisions an application programmer has to make with regard to be preceding activities. As you will see shortly, you have options as to when you connect and disconnect from the database.

Transaction Objects

PowerBuilder communicates with a DBMS through a *transaction object*, an object that stores information about the database with which an application is interacting. Assuming that you are working with a single database, then an application uses only one transaction object at a time.

A transaction object has one major purpose: It contains references to data that make it possible for the application to connect to the database, including the name of the database, the user name, and the password. Rather than storing the actual data values in the transaction object, the transaction object contains the name of fields in an *INI* file where the data can be found. Assuming that you have configured ODBC to recognize your database, your transaction object will be taking its data from *PB.INI.*

PowerBuilder supplies a global transaction object called *SQLCA.* Unless you are using multiple databases, this transaction object is sufficient for everything you do. The script that begins your application must therefore tell SQLCA that it can find a description of your database in *PB.INI.*

SQLCA stands for SQL Communications Area. If you write a program in a procedural language (for example, COBOL or C) and include SQL statements in that program, SQLCA is a data structure that acts as a conduit between the application program and the database, passing configuration information into the database and returning the result of database interactions to the program.

Handling Database Errors SQLCA makes it possible for an application to trap and handle database errors. When you work interactively with a DBMS, issuing data manipulation requests directly to a DBMS without an application program, you see error messages generated by the database and respond to them. However, when database interaction is controlled by an application program, errors aren't automatically passed through to the user. Instead, they are returned to the program through variables that are part of SQLCA (or any other transaction object being used). It is therefore up to the application programmer to check for errors and to program the application to handle them.

One of the variables of SQLCA that you will use frequently when trapping program errors is SQLCODE, which contains a numeric code corresponding the result of a SQL command that was submitted to the database. If SQLCODE contains 0, then the command was completed successfully. In most cases, if SQLCODE isn't 0, then some error has occurred and an application should display a message to the user that all isn't well.

The easiest way to get a message to the user is to use the PowerBuilder MessageBox function, which places an alert on the screen along with message text and up to three buttons. For example, if an update fails (perhaps because it violates an integrity rule), a script could contain:

```
if SQLCA.SQLCODE <> 0 then
    MessageBox ("Update Failed",SQLCA.SQLERRTEXT)
    return
end if
```

There are several important elements in the preceding script:

- A PowerBuilder if statement.
- A statement to stop execution of the script (return).
- A call to a function that displays a message to the user: The MessageBox function requires at least two parameters. In the preceding example, the first is the name of the alert window, which appears in the window's menu bar. The second parameter is text that explains what error occurred. In this case, the text of the error message comes from another attribute of SQLCA:

SQLERRTEXT, which contains the DBMS's explanation of what occurred. Like many computer-generated error messages, a SQLERRTEXT message is generally cryptic and often confusing to the user. If you find that the SQLERRTEXT isn't clear enough, you can certainly use a literal string to provide a better error message.

Other than 0, which means that no problem has occurred, and 100, which means that a SQL statement couldn't find any rows, the actual values returned by SQL-CODE and the meanings of those values (including the contents of SQLERRTEXT) vary considerably from one DBMS to another. This means that if you want your application to determine specifically what error occurred so that it can take action based on that error, you must check the value in SQLCODE against the values that are actually used by the specific DBMS with which the application will be interacting. If the application is ported for use with another DBMS, you must check the error trapping code, modifying SQLCODE values as needed. Where do you find this list of SQLCODE values? Usually in one of the DBMS manuals.

General database application programming wisdom holds that you should check the result of every attempted database access. In other words, every time a PowerBuilder script performs a SQL command to access the database, the script should check to make certain that all is well. If something undesirable occurred, the application should then take action to determine what happened and alert the user.

Deciding When to Connect and Disconnect

Connecting to a database establishes an application as a user of that database. Most database servers have a limit to the number of users that can simultaneously be connected. This means that if an application is running in a very active environment, connecting and staying connected to the database the entire time the application is running may seriously impact the overall performance of the database system by preventing other users from connecting.

For small applications, including those you will be creating for this book, it is acceptable to connect to the database when the application is launched and to disconnect just before returning to the operating system. However, in a large active environment, where there are significantly more users than the number of concurrent user licenses available, an application should connect to the database just before displaying an application window that contains a DataWindow control and disconnect when closing that application window.

The difference between the two strategies affects the object to which scripts are attached rather than the content of those scripts. In the case of the small environment, where an application will be staying connected, the connection script is usually attached to the first window opened by the application. If an application will be connecting and disconnecting repeatedly, then scripts are attached to each window that contains a DataWindow control.

PowerBuilder Window Types

PowerBuilder provides six types of windows, each of which has different uses:

- Main: A *main window* is a stand-alone window. It can overlap other windows and in turn can be overlapped. It can appear anywhere on the screen and can be displayed whenever needed. In most cases, the first window opened by a PowerBuilder application is a main window. More than 90% of the windows in the *tshows* application are main windows. This is an appropriate type of window to use for data entry, data display, and (if desired) button menus in a small application.
- Popup: A *popup window* is a window that is opened by another window. The window that opens the popup window becomes the popup's *parent*. Although you can move a popup window outside its parent's boundaries, the parent window cannot overlay the popup. The popup is also hidden when its parent is minimized and closes when its parent is closed. The most typical use of a popup window is to display detail information about an item in a list. For example, an application could present a user with a list of customers. When the user double-clicks a customer name, a popup menu appears to show all customer information. The *tshows* application does not use popup windows.
- Child: A *child window* is a window that is opened by either a main or a popup window, which becomes its parent. Unlike a popup window, a child cannot overlap its parent. It can only be moved within its parent and closes when its parent is closed. Although the *tshows* application does not create child windows directly, it does use dropdown DataWindows (lists of data from which users can choose during data entry), which are child windows and can be accessed using techniques designed for manipulating child windows.
- Response: A *response window* is a stand-alone window typically used to collect information. Response windows are *modal*, which means that no other windows are accessible until the user closes the response window. Because the modal nature of response windows interferes with the benefits a multi-window environment, you should use them sparingly. You will see examples of response windows beginning in Chapter 11, where they are used to collect values to restrict the rows returned by the SQL queries that underlie DataWindows.
- MDI frame: An *MDI* (multiple document interface) *frame* is a window that acts as a container for other windows. Once the MDI frame is on the screen, you can open multiple windows within it (*sheets*). MDI frames are typically used for large applications and are beyond the scope of this book.
- MDI frame with MicroHelp: MicroHelp is a line of text that appears in the lower-left corner of a window to provide information to the user. An MDI frame with MicroHelp window provides the MicroHelp capability to an MDI application.

There is no reason that an application can't use a combination of main windows and MDI frames. Such combination applications are appropriate for applications of moderate size. A combination application may evolve naturally as a small application grows to a point where the number of independent main windows becomes unwieldy. Rather than redoing the entire application using MDI frames, the developer adds MDI frames to so that the application can continue to use existing windows and scripts.

Creating "Main" Windows

The first window in the *tshows* application will provide access to the main menu. As you have read, that menu can be implemented either as a set of drop-down menus attached to a single menu bar or as a menu of buttons. When you took your tour of the *tshows* application in Chapter 5, you saw and used both types of menus.

To get started, you will be using buttons as menus. Those windows that function as menus will contain buttons that open other windows and return to the main menu window; those windows that will contain DataWindow controls will have buttons that close themselves. Although all it will do is open and close windows, you will have a working application.

Main windows are created in the Window painter. Using the Window painter, you can create new windows, change window formats, and write window scripts.

To begin, you will create the window that will serve as the application's main menu. This will be the first window that the user sees when the application is launched.

To create a window:

1 Open the *tshows* application in *tshows1.pbl* and connect to the *tshows* database.

2 Click the **Window** button in the PowerBar (Figure 9.2). The Select Window dialog box appears (Figure 9.3 on page 187).

Figure 9.2
Window painter button in the PowerBar

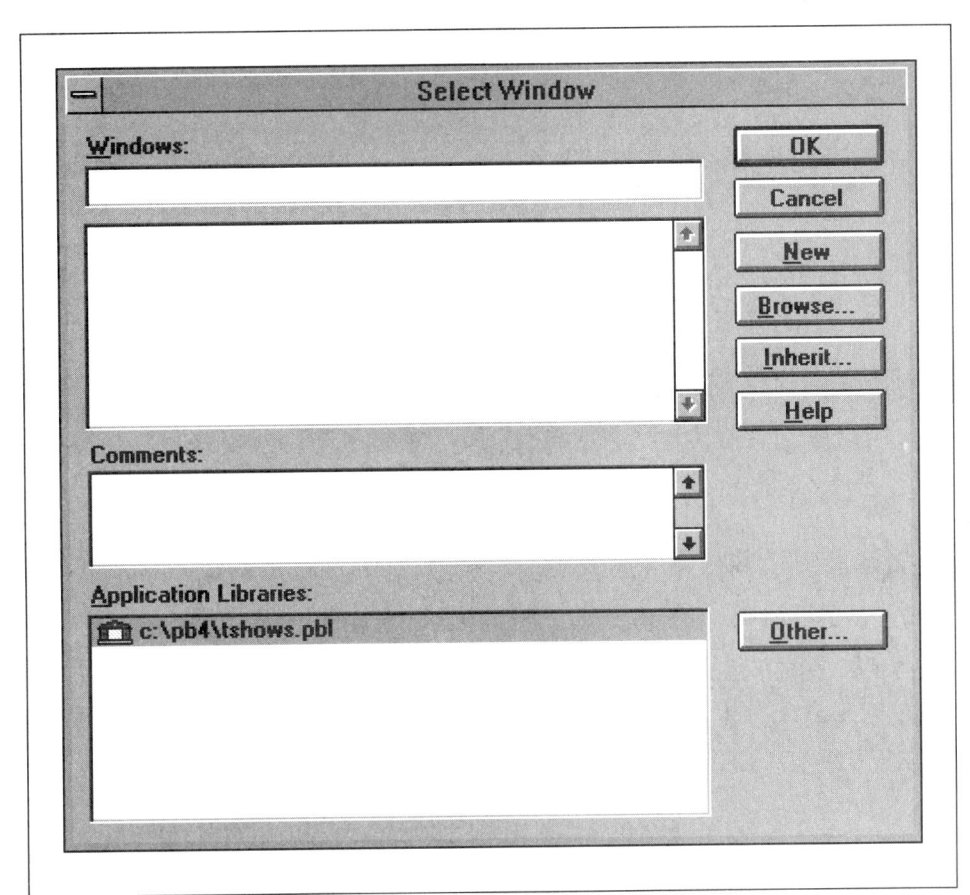

CHAPTER NINE   BUILDING WINDOWS AS AN APPLICATION FRAMEWORK   **187**

Figure 9.3
Select Window dialog box

3 Click the **New** button. The Window painter workspace appears (Figure 9.4 on page 188). As you can see, the version 4.0 PainterBar contains tools for placing items in a window, including buttons, text, and graphics. The window rectangle is the area filled with dots.

The default version 5.0 Window painter PainterBar has fewer buttons. The tools for placing items in the window are present but hidden in a palette that you expose when you click the top button in the PainterBar. You will learn to access those tools throughout this chapter.

The dots that fill the window area in Figure 9.4 constitute a grid that can help you place items in the window. If you want to get rid of the grid so that you have an empty window, choose Design -> Grid to display the Alignment Grid dialog box. Remove the X from the Show Grid check box. Alternatively, if you want objects to be automatically aligned with the nearest grid points, place an X in the Snap to Grid check box.

In Figure 9.4, the window background is white. However, if the Default to 3D option has been selected in the Options menu, the background will be gray. The figures in this book have been created without selecting the Default to 3D option.

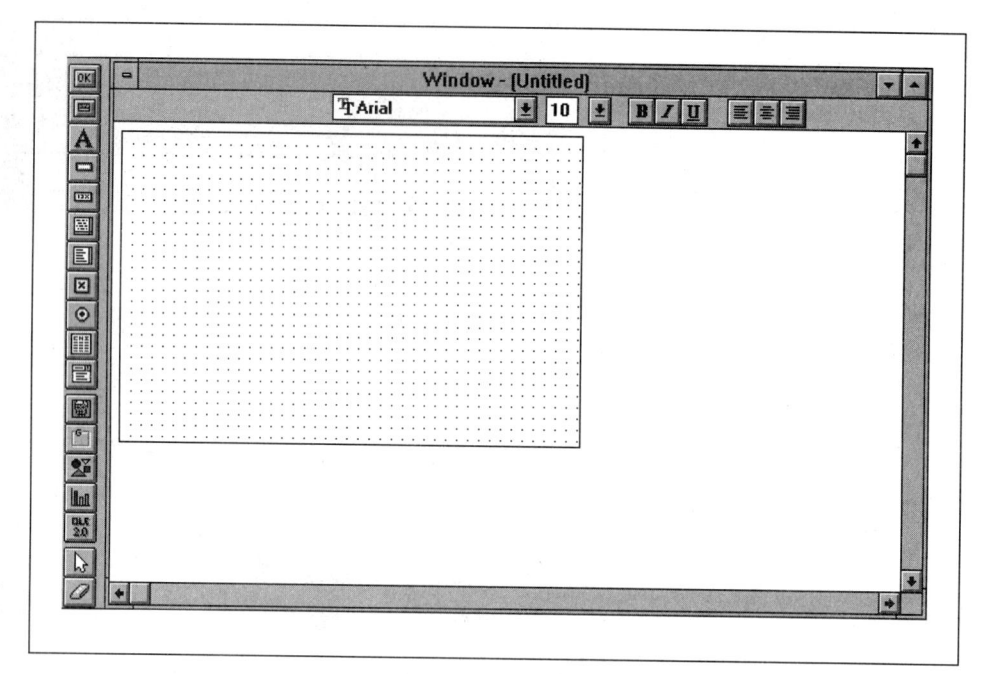

188 CHAPTER NINE BUILDING WINDOWS AS AN APPLICATION FRAMEWORK

Figure 9.4
Window painter workspace

4. Position the pointer in the lower-right corner of the window rectangle so that it appears as a diagonal double-headed arrow, as in Figure 9.5.

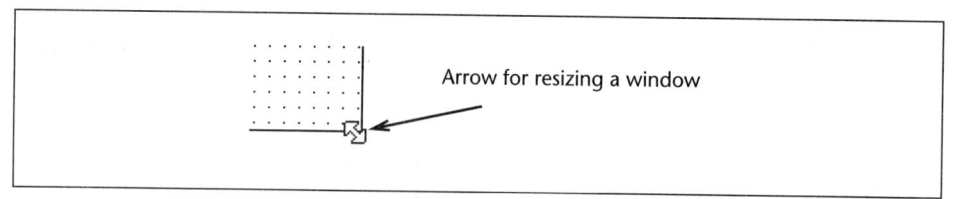

Figure 9.5
Resizing a window rectangle

5. Hold down the **mouse button** and drag the lower-right corner of the window rectangle down and to the right so that the window fills the Window painter workspace. Then release the mouse button. At this point, you are ready to begin customizing the window.

The window you just created hasn't been saved. Be sure to proceed with the next set of exercises before quitting.

Changing Window Characteristics

The Window painter sets many characteristics of a window, including its type, its title, whether it can be moved or resized, and whether it has scroll bars. The Window painter also sets a window's background color and where it first appears on the screen.

CHAPTER NINE BUILDING WINDOWS AS AN APPLICATION FRAMEWORK **189**

To explore setting window styles:

1 If you are working with version 4.0, choose **Design -> Window Style**. The Window Style dialog box appears (Figure 9.6). Notice that a sample of the window appears just to the left of the dialog box's buttons. The rest of the dialog box sets various window characteristics.

If you are working with version 5.0, choose **Design -> Properties** or click the **Properties** button in the PainterBar. The Window Properties dialog box appears with the General panel visible (Figure 9.7). Unlike the version 4.0 dialog box, the General panel doesn't show a sample window.

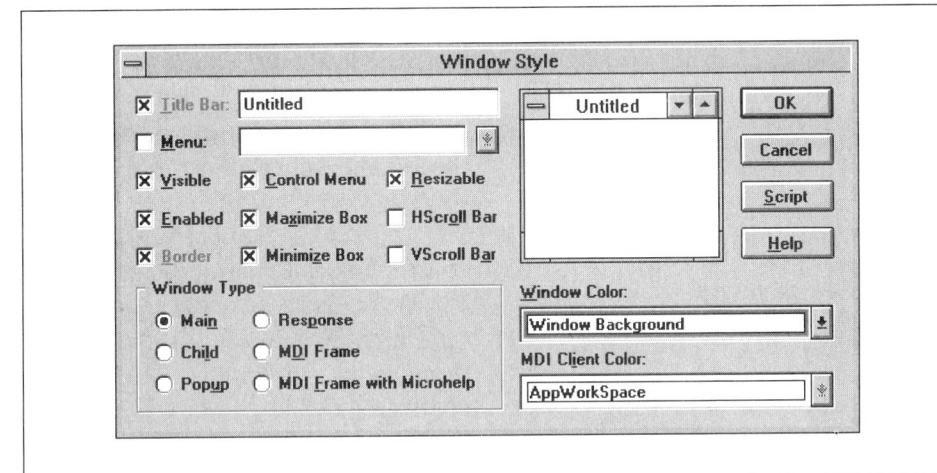

Figure 9.6
Window Style dialog box (4.0)

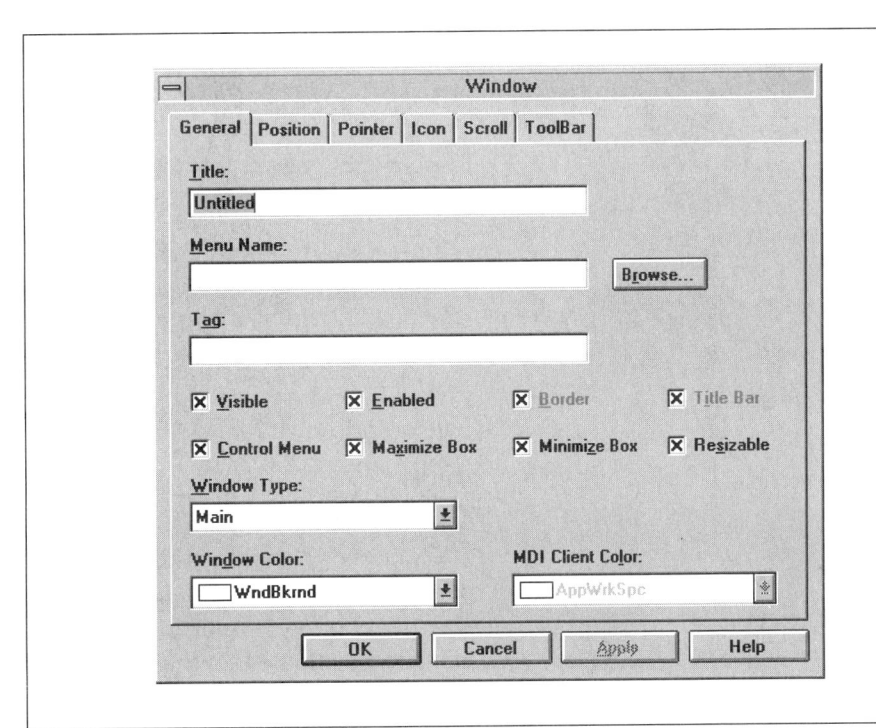

Figure 9.7
General panel in the Window Properties dialog box (5.0)

2 By default, a window has a title of "Untitled." Replace this with **Pinehill Software Trade Shows**.

3 If you are working with version 4.0, press the **Tab** key to move to the next field in the dialog box. Notice that the new title you entered in Step 2 replaces "Untitled" in the small window sample.

Setting the window title is not the same as giving the window a name. The window title is what appears in the window's title bar when the window is on the screen. The window's name is the unique name by which it is known within the application. While the title can contain spaces, the name must adhere to PowerBuilder's naming rules for objects.

4 By default, PowerBuilder sets the Window type to "Main." In this case, do not change the default.

5 Click the **Resizable** check box to remove the X. This will prevent the user from changing the window's size.

6 Click the **Maximize Box** check box to remove the X. Do the same for the Minimize check box. This will also prevent the user from changing the window's size.

7 The Control Menu check box determines whether the window has a control box and an associated menu. For this example, leave the Control Menu check box checked.

8 Click the **down arrow** to the right of the Window Color box. Scroll the dropdown menu until you can see the color choices. Select a bright color.

9 Click the **OK** button to close the dialog box and to apply the change you've made.

10 Choose **Design -> Preview** to see the window as it will appear on the screen (for example, Figure 9.8 on page 191).

You can also preview a window by pressing Ctrl+W.

11 Double-click the control box to close the window.

When you previewed the window, it wasn't centered on the screen, but instead was offset to the right. Because this window will be the application's opening screen, it should be centered: There's no reason the user should have to move it to see the entire window.

To change a window's initial position on the screen:

1 If you are working with version 4.0, choose **Design -> Window Position**. The Window Position dialog box appears, showing an outline of the window's current screen position (Figure 9.9).

If you are working with version 5.0, choose **Design->Properties** to display the Window Properties dialog box. Click the **Position** tab to display the Position panel (Figure 9.10).

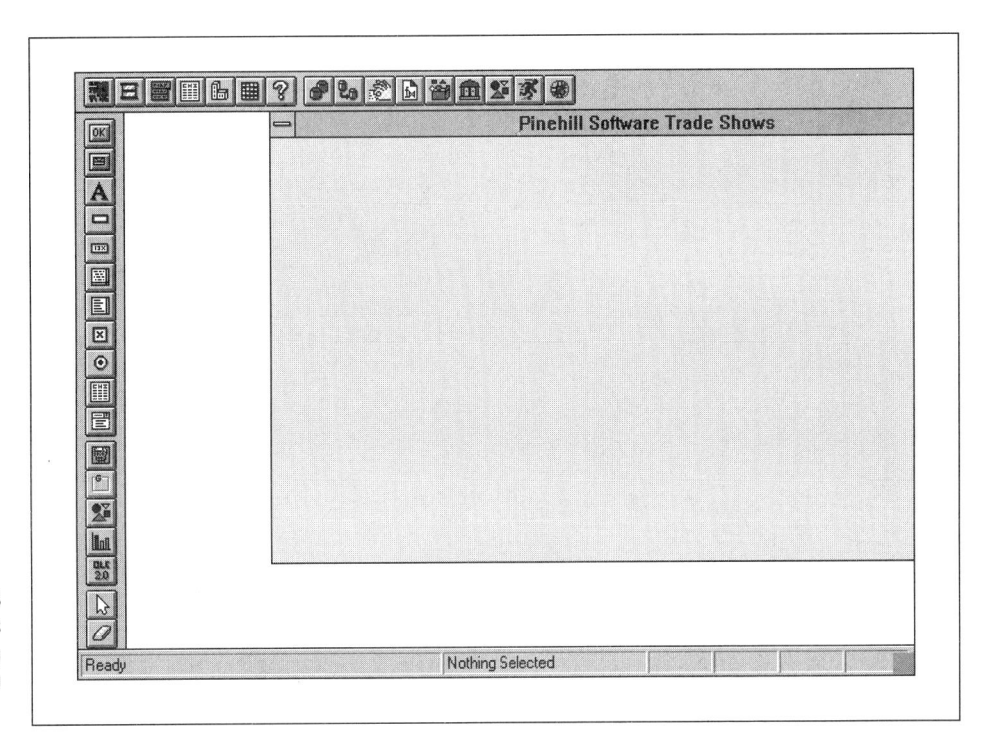

CHAPTER NINE   BUILDING WINDOWS AS AN APPLICATION FRAMEWORK   **191**

Figure 9.8
The initial window that will serve as the trade show application's opening screen and menu

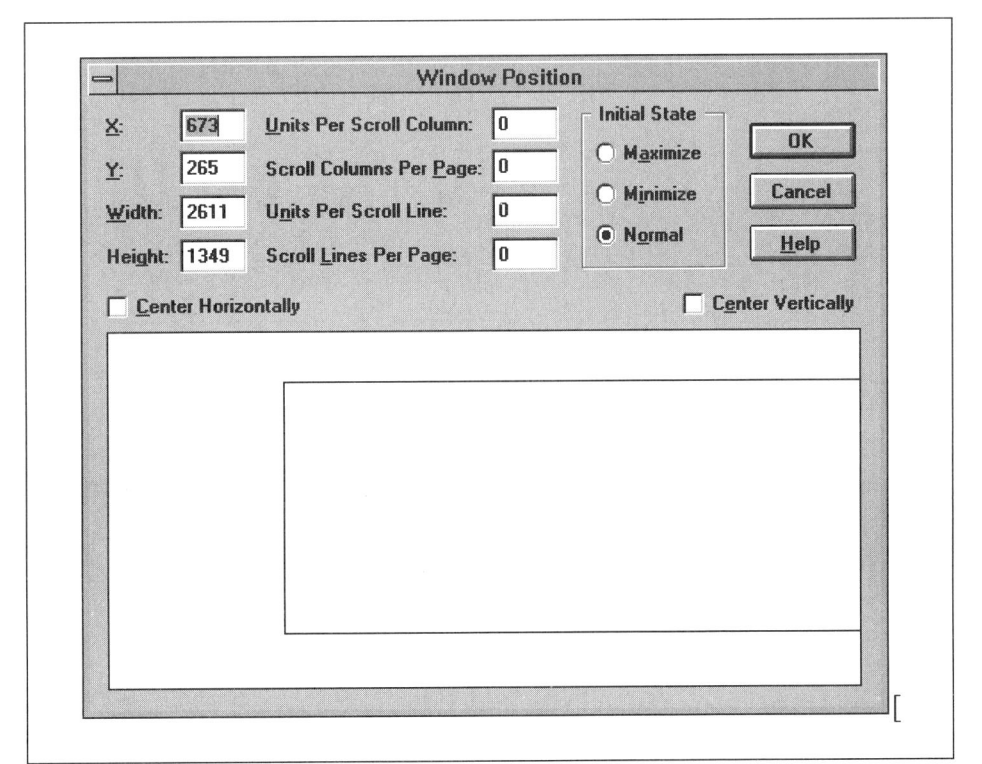

Figure 9.9
Window Position dialog box (4.0)

2 If you are working with version 4.0, click the **Center Horizontally** check box and the **Center Vertically** check box. As you click the check boxes, the outline of the window moves to the new position (centered on the screen).

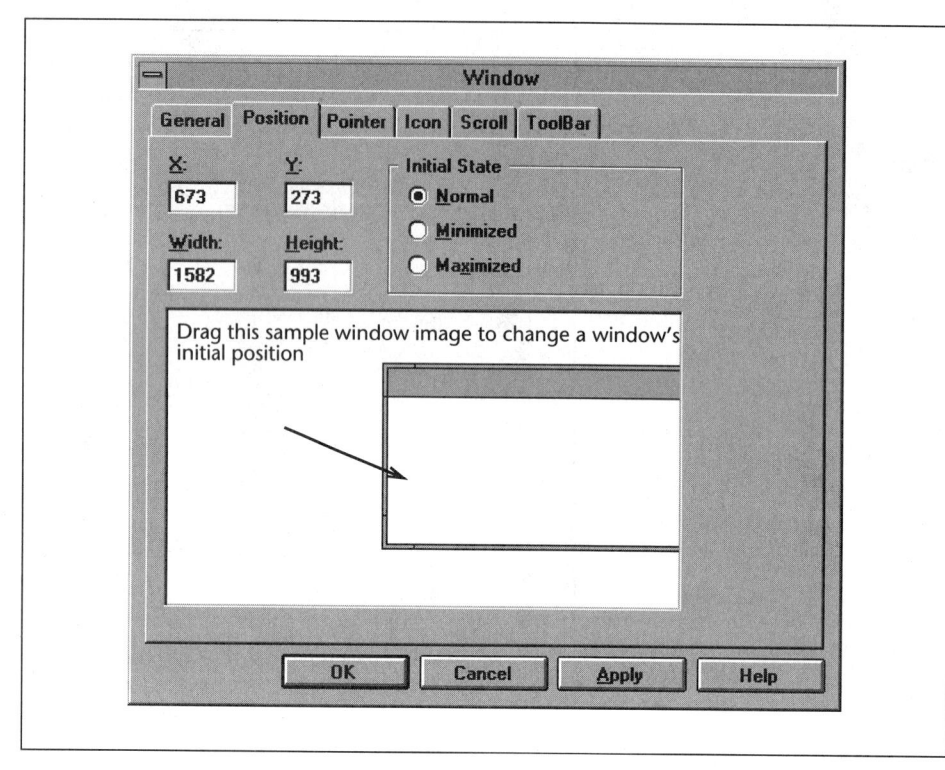

Figure 9.10
Window Position panel (5.0)

If you are working with version 5.0, drag the sample window image that appears in the middle of the Position panel to the center of the window in which it appears.

3 Click the **OK** button to close the dialog and to apply the changes.

4 Preview the window once more to see where it appears on the screen (for example, see Figure 9.11).

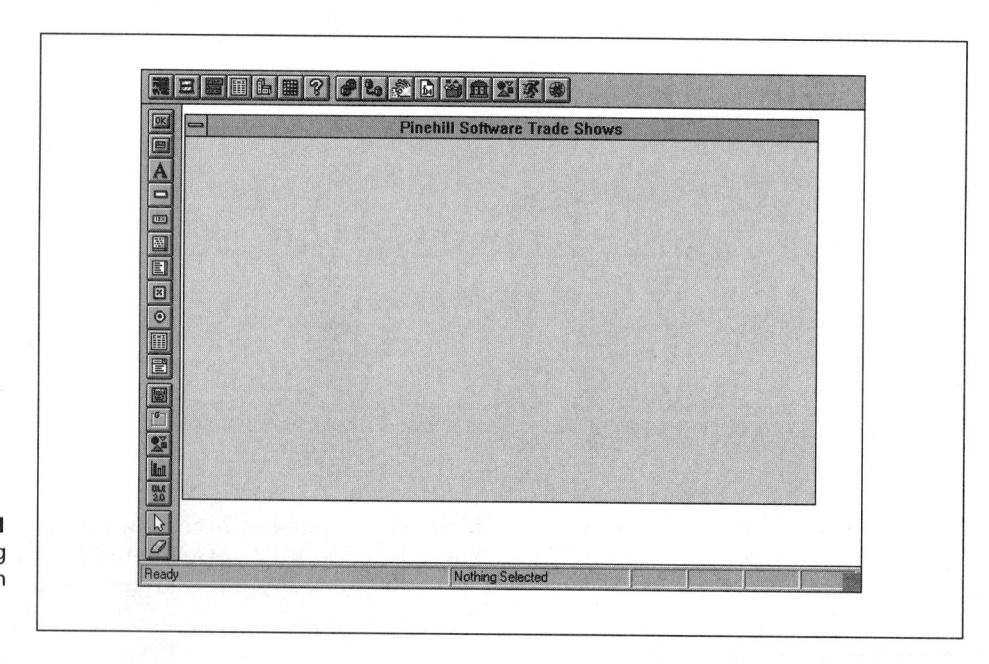

Figure 9.11
The trade show application opening window, centered on the screen

Saving and Naming the Window

A window definition is stored in an application library. When you exit the Window painter after creating a new window, you save and name the window.

To store a window:

1 Double-click the Window painter control box. A dialog box asking whether you want to save your changes appears.
2 Click the **Yes** button. The Save Window dialog box appears with the insertion point flashing in the Windows box.
3 Type **w_opening_screen** in the Windows box (Figure 9.12).

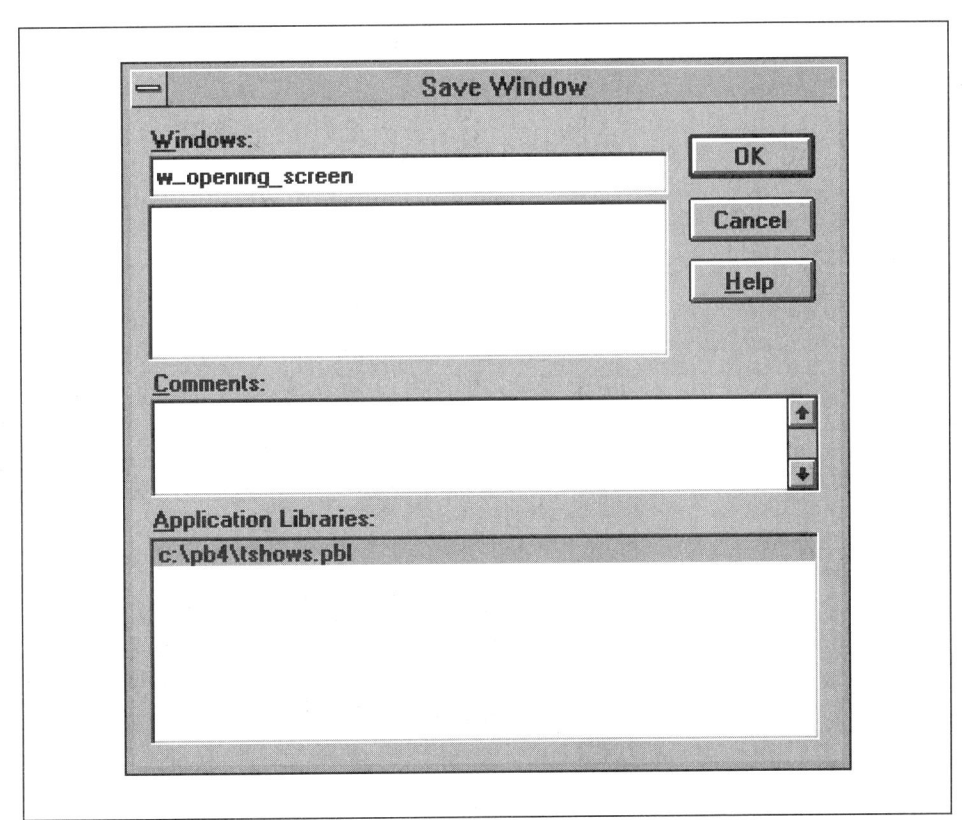

Figure 9.12
Save Window dialog box

> *The name of the window you just created isn't arbitrary. Most PowerBuilder applications follow a naming convention to make it easier to distinguish one type of object from another. Window object names, for example, typically begin with "w_". There is certainly no hard and fast rule that requires you to adhere to PowerSoft's suggested naming rules, but it does make it easier to understand the contents of a large application if you have some consistent way of naming your objects.*

4 Click the **OK** button to close the dialog box and to exit the Window painter.

> *Where you end up when you close the Window painter depends on where you were before you entered the Window painter. For example, if you entered the Window painter from the Database painter, you will be returned to the Database painter; if you entered from the Application painter, you will be returned to the Application painter.*

Application Scripts

The controlling force behind any PowerBuilder application is the scripts that open windows, close windows, and perform data manipulation. At this point in the application development process, you will need to write at least one script that belongs to the entire application. It will be triggered by an event that affects the application as a whole.

Application Events

As you know, an event is something that happens in an application's environment. It can be triggered by the direct action of a user, such as making a choice from a menu with the mouse or the keyboard. An event can also be triggered by another program. For example, a DBMS generates an event when it sends the result of a SQL command back to a PowerBuilder application. Operating systems also trigger events related to system activities, such as the opening of a file or a system error. Finally, a program can trigger its own events, such as those that occur when the application is idle and neither the user or other programs are interacting with the application.

Each type of PowerBuilder object has a specific set of events that it recognizes. When PowerBuilder detects an event appropriate to an object and sends an event message to an object, the object checks to see if it has a script associated with that event. If there is a script, PowerBuilder executes it. If there is no script, PowerBuilder does nothing.

A PowerBuilder application can respond to four events:

- **close**: triggered when the application exits to the operating system
- **idle**: triggered when the application sits idle for a specified period of time
- **open**: triggered when the application is launched
- **systemerror:** triggered when a system error occurs

At a minimum, an application needs an open script to display the application's first window and to configure a transaction object for the application. Whether other application scripts are needed depends on the specific requirements of the application.

Writing an Application Open Script

All scripts are entered using the PowerScript painter, which is similar to the editor you used to enter SQL commands directly to the database. How you access the PowerScript painter depends on the object to which the script is being attached.

CHAPTER NINE BUILDING WINDOWS AS AN APPLICATION FRAMEWORK **195**

To enter an open script for an application:

1 Make sure that you are working with the *tshows* application in *tshows1.pbl*, and enter the Application painter.

2 Click the **Script** button in the PainterBar (Figure 9.13). The PowerScript painter appears, as in Figure 9.14. Look carefully at the title of the window: It tells you the event that will trigger any script you enter and the name of the object to which the script will be attached.

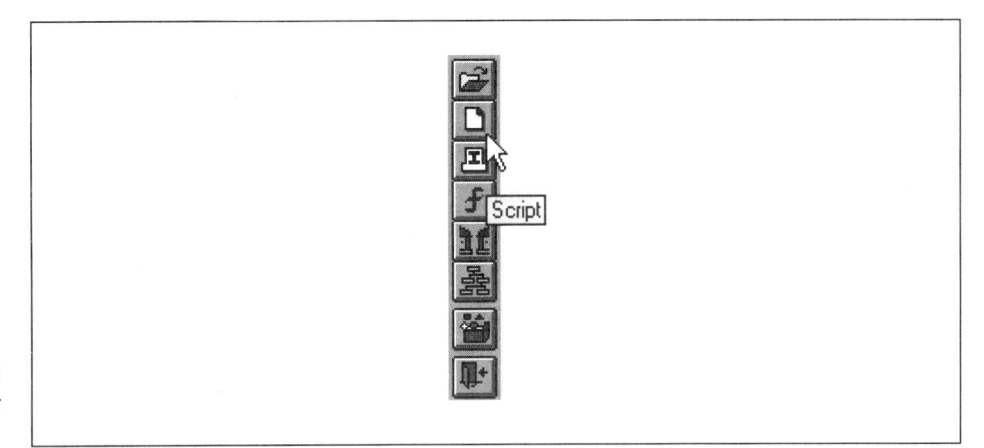

Figure 9.13
Script button in the PainterBar

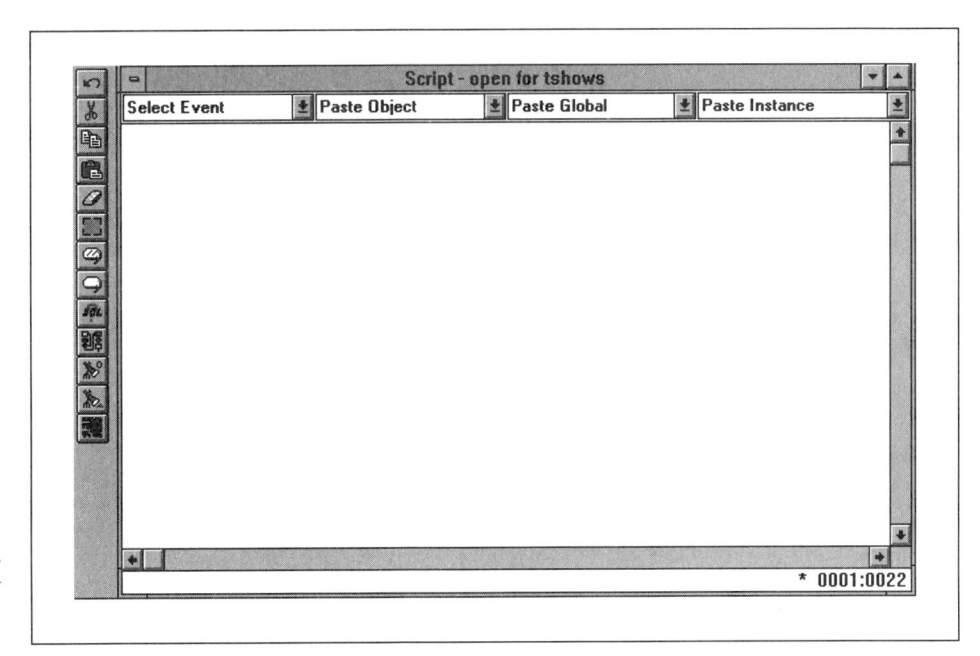

Figure 9.14
Script painter

3 Notice that there are four menus across the top of the PowerScript painter workspace. Display the Select Event menu, which lists all the events recognized by the type of object with which you are working. Although the PowerScript painter defaults to the open event, you can change to another event by making a choice from this menu. For this example, the default open event is what we want.

4   Type the following in the workspace exactly as it appears, including spacing and capitalization:

```
SQLCA.DBMS = "ODBC"
SQLCA.dbParm = "ConnectString = 'dsn=tshows'"
open (w_opening_screen)
```

The first two statements assign values to the SQLCA object. The first identifies the type of database, in this case, one that uses the ODBC middleware (WatcomSQL). The second statement identifies the data source (the database) that the application will be using by assigning the name used by ODBC to reference the database to a variable named ConnectString. The assignment operation within double quotation marks is in turn assigned, as a string of text, to SQLCA's dbParm attribute. To work with a different database, such as the *rents* database used for the exercises in this book, simply substitute the name of the database for *tshows*.

> **WARNING**
>
> *Be very careful when typing the dbParm line. The 'dsn=tshows' portion must be exactly as it appears, including capitalization and spacing. Be sure to surround it with single quotation marks and the entire expression on the right side of the assignment operator in double quotation marks.*

The third statement in the script calls the PowerBuilder open function, which, in its simplest form, takes a single parameter: the name of the window you want to open. For this example, the application will open the window you created earlier in this chapter.

5   Double-click the workspace window control box. PowerBuilder asks if you want to save your changes.

6   Click the **Yes** button. PowerBuilder saves the script and returns to the Window painter. At this point, you can actually run your application to see the action of the script you have just written.

> **TIP**
>
> *If you want to save a script and return to the painter for the object to which the script is attached, you can do so in one step by clicking the Return button in the PainterBar (for example, Figure 9.15). This saves the script and closes the Script painter window. The Return button is always the bottom button in the Script painter PainterBar. The button's icon varies, however, depending on the painter to which you will be returning.*

> **NOTE**
>
> *The PowerBuilder 4.0 documentation states that PowerBuilder "compiles" scripts. The scripts are indeed compiled into binary. However, each script is compiled separately rather than producing a single binary file as does a high-level language compiler. To create an executable application using version 4.0, you must go through a separate procedure for creating an executable file, which is discussed in Appendix A. PowerBuilder version 5.0, contains a true compiler.*

7   Click the **Run** button in the PowerBar (Figure 9.16).

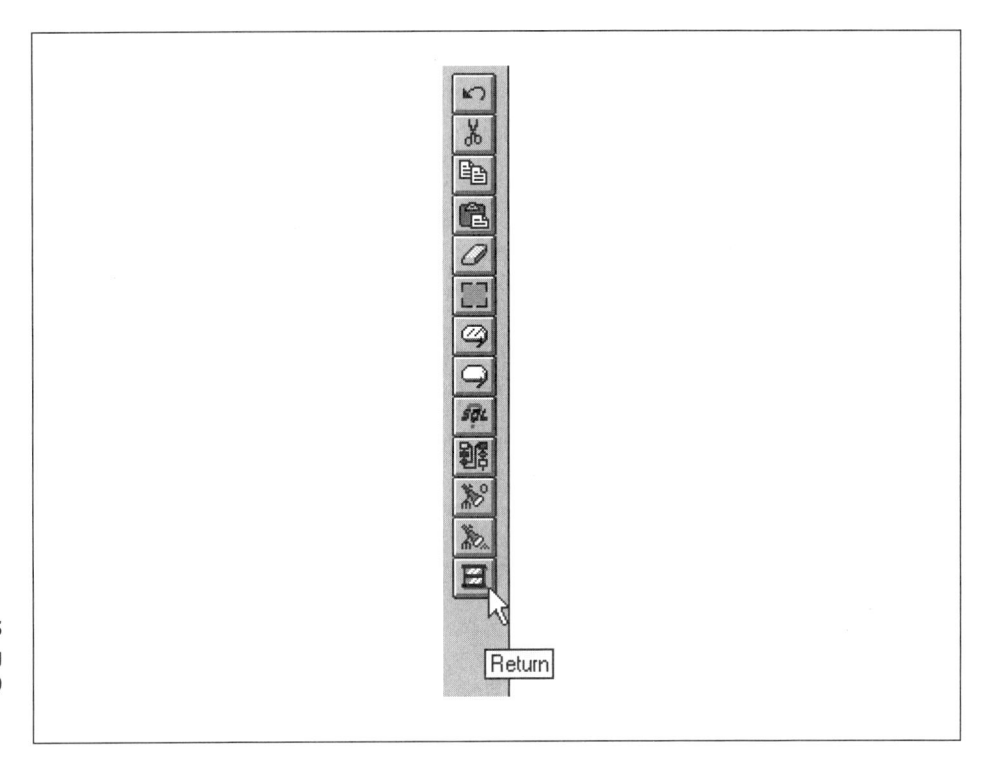

Figure 9.15
Return button (icon varies depending on the painter)

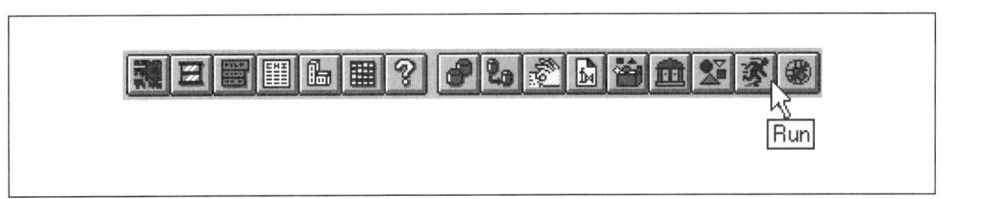

Figure 9.16
Run button in the PowerBar

8   PowerBuilder asks you if you want to save the changes to the application library. Click the **Yes** button. PowerBuilder then hides the PowerBuilder development environment and then displays the application's single window.

9   Double-click the window's control box. PowerBuilder stops the application and returns to the development environment.

Main Window Scripts

The scripts attached to a main window are triggered when events happen to the window, rather than to the contents of the window. For example, if you resize a window, or open a window, or click the right mouse button while the pointer is over the window (*not* any of its contents), the window responds to the event and triggers the associated script. At least one window in an application must have an open script to configure a transaction object and connect to the database. By the same token, there must be at least one script to disconnect from the database.

Main Window Events

Main windows respond to 29 events. The most commonly used include the following:

- **clicked**: triggered when the left mouse button is clicked an area of the window that doesn't contain any other object
- **close**: triggered when the window is closed
- **doubleclicked**: triggered when the left mouse button is double-clicked in an area of the window that doesn't contain any other object
- **triggered** when a key is pressed
- **mousedown**: triggered when the left mouse button is pressed and held down
- **mousemove**: triggered when the mouse pointer is moved
- **open**: triggered when the window is opened
- **rbuttondown**: triggered when the right mouse button is pressed and held down in an area of the window that doesn't contain any other object
- **resize**: triggered when the window is resized

Keep in mind that you don't need to have a script for every event that an object recognizes. If an event occurs for which there is no script, the application simply ignores the event. For example, if you press a key which an application window is the active window and that window has no script for a key event, nothing happens.

Writing a Window Open Script

One of the typical actions that takes place when a window opens is to connect to the database. In fact, an application must be connected before it can perform any data manipulation.

To write a script that connects to a database when a window is opened:

1. Click the **Window** button in the PowerBar. PowerBuilder displays the Select Window dialog box.
2. Because there is currently only one window in the application, PowerBuilder automatically highlights the window's name. Click the **OK** button to select the w_opening_screen window.
3. Right-click anywhere in the window. A window menu pops up (Figure 9.17 on page 199).
4. Choose **Script** from the popup menu. The Script painter appears.
5. Type the code in Listing 9.1 on page 199. Notice that in this case, the `if` statement contains the PowerBuilder command `halt`. Unlike `return,` which merely stops the execution of the current script, `halt` exits the application. In this situation—where the application can't even connect to the database—there is no point in attempting to continue.

The first statement in Listing 9.1 is a SQL statement. It is therefore followed by a semicolon. In a PowerBuilder application, all SQL state-

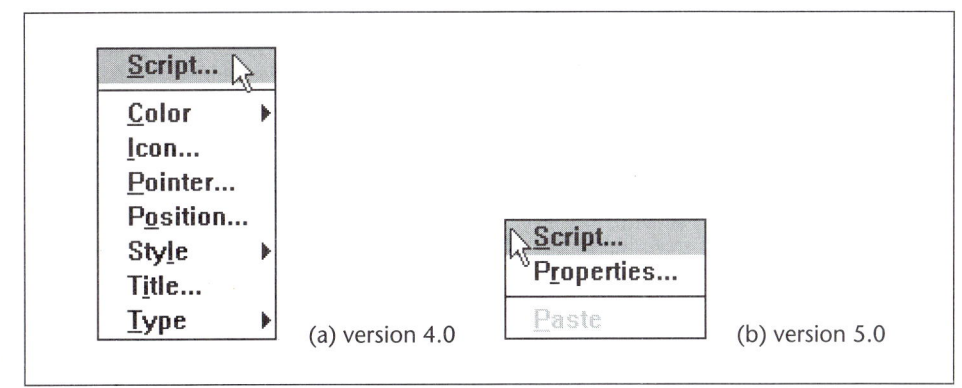

CHAPTER NINE BUILDING WINDOWS AS AN APPLICATION FRAMEWORK **199**

Figure 9.17
Window popup menu

(a) version 4.0   (b) version 5.0

stays same

Listing 9.1
Open script for an application's initial window

```
connect using SQLCA;
if SQLCA.SQLCODE <> 0 then
   MessageBox ("Connect Error","Couldn't connect to the database")
   halt
end if
```

ments end with a semicolon; PowerBuilder language statements do not end with a semicolon.

6 Double-click the Script painter control box. PowerBuilder asks you if you want to save your changes.

7 Click the **Yes** button.

8 Click the **Run** button in the PowerBar. PowerBuilder asks you if you want to save the changes to the application library.

9 Click the **Yes** button. As before, w_opening_window should appear on the screen.

10 Double-click the window's control box to return to the PowerBuilder development environment.

Writing a Window Close Script

Disconnecting from a database usually takes place when a window is closed or when an application terminates. The process is nearly the opposite of connecting to a database. However, if a disconnect fails, an application should roll back the transaction object. There is no way to be certain what caused the disconnect failure. Therefore, to avoid the risk of bad data being introduced into the database, the script should ask for a rollback.

To enter a window close script that performs a disconnect:

1 Make sure that you are working with the *tshows* application in *tshows1.pbl*.

2 Enter the Window painter and open the w_opening_screen window.

3 Open the Script painter for the w_opening_screen window.

4. Choose **Select Event -> Close**. Notice that the name of the workspace window changes to reflect the event with which you are now working.
5. Type the code in Listing 9.2. There are two SQL statements in this script. The first—disconnect—requests the disconnection from the database. The second—rollback—asks the DBMS to undo the current transaction. Notice again that both statements are terminated by a semicolon.

Listing 9.2
Close script for an application's initial window

stays same

```
disconnect using SQLCA;
if SQLCA.SQLCODE <> 0 then
    rollback using SQLCA;
    MessageBox ("Disconnect Error","Couldn't disconnect cleanly.")
end if
```

6. Double-click the Script painter control box. PowerBuilder asks you if you want to save your changes.
7. Click the **Yes** button. You are returned to the Window painter.
8. Click the **Run** button in the PowerBar. PowerBuilder asks if you want to save the changes to the window.
9. Click the **Yes** button. The window named opening_screen should appear on the screen as before.
10. Double-click the control box to close the window. If your close event script was entered properly, you will be successfully returned to the Window painter.

> **NOTE** *The scripts that you have seen to this point are scripts that will be present in just about every PowerBuilder application you create. Although they don't perform any data manipulation, they do perform essential management tasks without which you can't interact with the database.*

Adding More Windows and Button Controls

At this point in the application development process, a developer often establishes the structure of the application by creating windows for all menus and menu options. Although the windows won't contain any DataWindow controls to manipulate data, they will contain button controls that make it possible to navigate through the menu tree.

Adding the Next Level Windows

Before you can add button controls to open windows, the windows need to exist. The next step in the process is therefore to create the windows that will be opened by buttons on the window named w_opening_screen.

Script : open for rents returns (None)

```
SQLCA.DBMS = "ODBC"
SQLCA.dbParm = "ConnectString = 'dsn=curents'"
open (w_open_screen)
```

If you look back at Figure 9.1, you'll notice that the main menu has four options, three of which bring up other menus and one of which quits the application. This means that the application needs three windows to hold the next level submenus.

To create three windows:

1. Make sure that you are working with the *tshows* application in *tshows1.pbl* and that you are in the Window painter.
2. Click the **Window** button in the PowerBar. The Select Window dialog box appears.
3. Click the **New** button. PowerBuilder opens a new Window workspace.

Unless you've closed it by double-clicking its control box, the w_opening_screen window workspace is still open. You can see a list of all open windows by displaying the Window menu. To switch to an open window, click its name in the Window menu.

4. Leave this window in its original size. Do not allow the user to resize it. Give it a background color of your choice; name it **Scheduling**. Center the window on the screen.
5. Choose **File** -> **Save As**. The Select Window dialog box appears.
6. Save the window as **w_scheduling**.

As noted earlier, although you can save PowerBuilder objects under any names you choose, many developers adhere to naming conventions originated by Power-Soft. Should you decide to follow that naming scheme, application windows should be given names that begin with "w_".

7. Create two more windows with the same characteristics as the window you just created. Name them **Costs** (saved as w_costs) and **Sales Leads** (saved as w_sales_leads).

Introducing Button Controls

As you know, a PowerBuilder control is an object that has some associated behavior when it is placed on an application window. *Buttons controls* are live areas on a window that perform their actions in response to some event. There are two major types of button controls: command buttons and picture buttons. The difference between the two is that a command button displays text while a picture button displays a picture (see Figure 9.18).

A button control responds to 11 events, including the following:

- clicked: triggered when the button is clicked
- rbuttondown: triggered when the right button is pressed and held down in the control
- constructor: triggered just before an open event in the window that contains the control
- destructor: triggered just after a close event for the window that contains the control

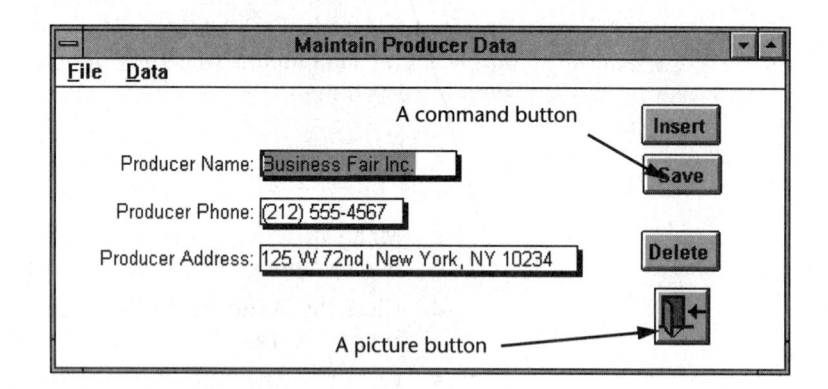

Figure 9.18
Command and picture buttons

As you might expect, the clicked and rbuttondown events are those you are most likely to use for simple applications.

Drawing Command Button Controls

The simplest button controls are command buttons that open and close windows. To become familiar with how they work, you will use command buttons to connect the trade show application's windows.

The first step in implementing command button controls is to draw the buttons on the window.

To draw a button on a window:

1 Open the w_opening_screen window in the Window painter.

2 If you are working with version 4.0, click the **CommandButton** button in the PowerBar (Figure 9.19(a) on the next page).

If you are working with version 5,0, you should also click the **CommandButton** button. However, when you do, notice that a palette of controls appears (Figure 9.19(b) on the next page). Click the **CommandButton** button in the upper-left corner of the palette.

3 Drag to place a button anywhere in the w_opening_screen window, as in Figure 9.20 on page 203. Notice that the button is selected, with a dark square at each corner. These squares are called *handles*, and are used to resize the button.

4 Drag the lower-right handle to the right so that the button is approximately 2-inches wide (for example, Figure 9.21 on page 204).

5 Drag the pointer across the "none" at the top of the workspace to highlight it. Type **Scheduling**. Your typing replaces the highlighted text.

6 Click the **B** button in the at the top of the workspace to make the text boldface. At this point, your button should look like Figure 9.22.

7 Right-click the button to display the command button menu (Figure 9.23 on page 204). Notice that this menu provides access to the button's Script painter as well as to dialog boxes that set a variety of button characteristics (version 4.0) or a Properties dialog box (version 5.0).

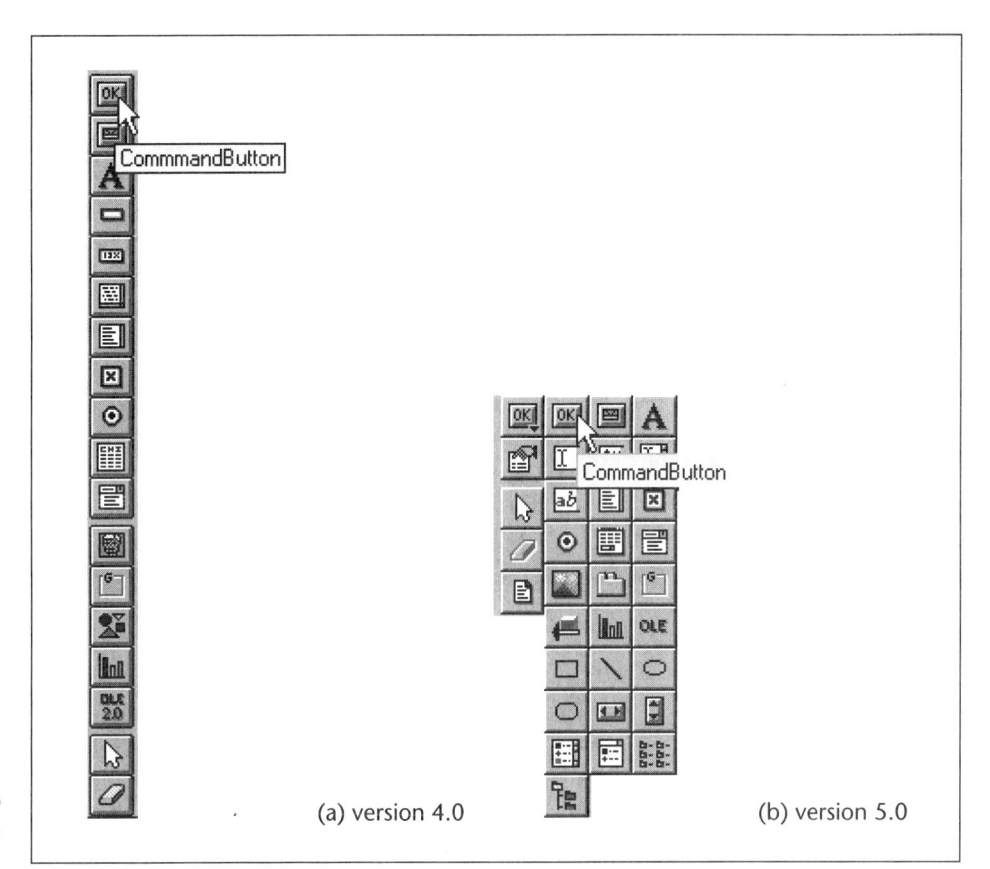

CHAPTER NINE   BUILDING WINDOWS AS AN APPLICATION FRAMEWORK   **203**

Figure 9.19
CommandButton button

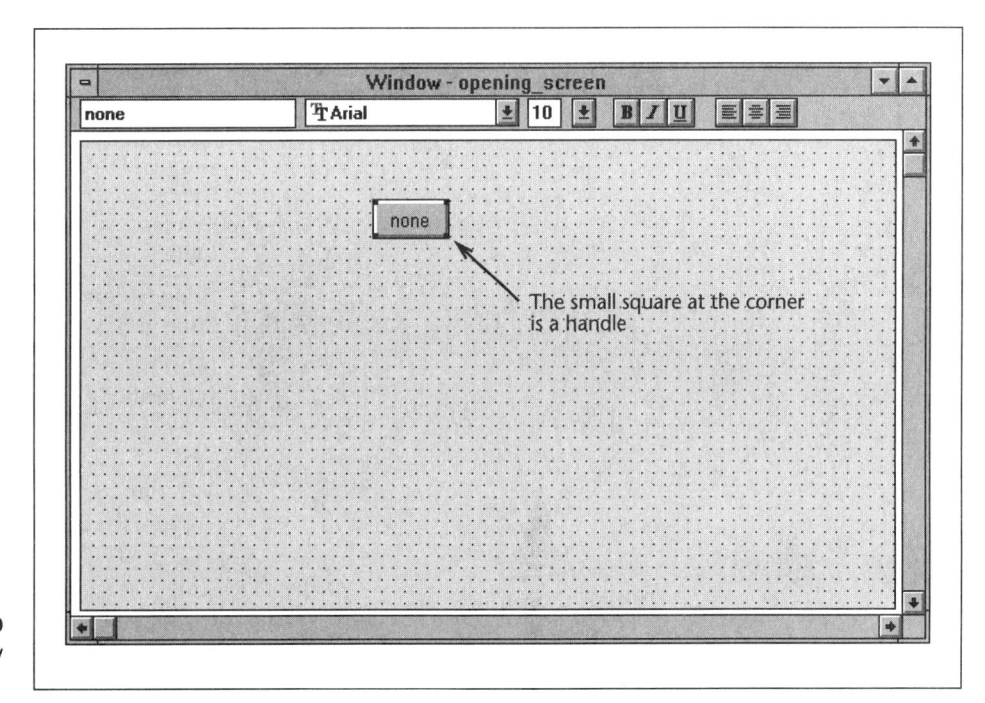

(a) version 4.0

(b) version 5.0

Figure 9.20
New command button in a window

204 CHAPTER NINE BUILDING WINDOWS AS AN APPLICATION FRAMEWORK

Figure 9.21
Resizing a button

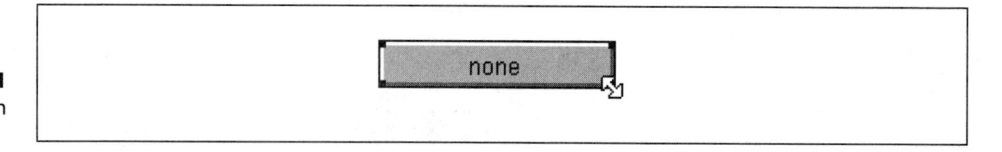

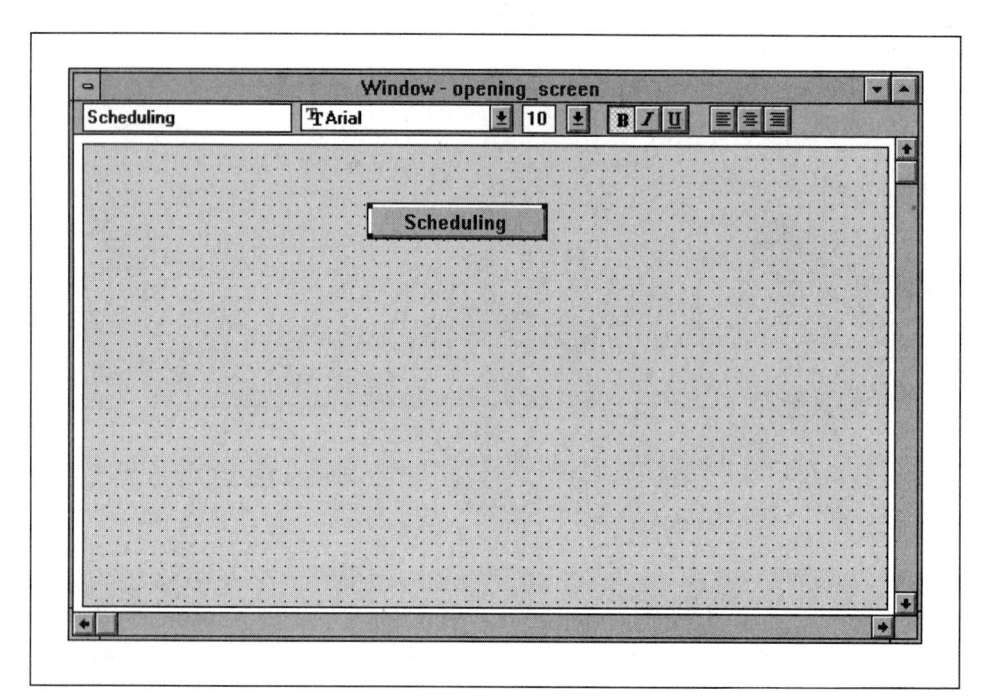

Figure 9.22
Renamed command button

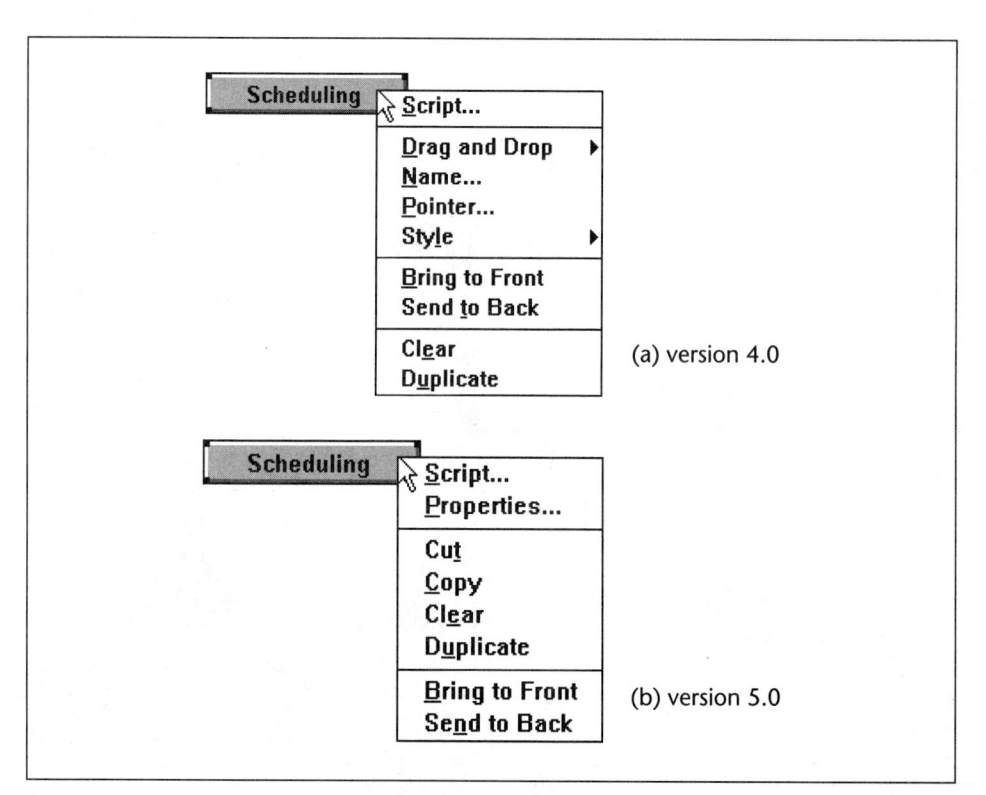

Figure 9.23
Command button menu

(a) version 4.0

(b) version 5.0

CHAPTER NINE   BUILDING WINDOWS AS AN APPLICATION FRAMEWORK   **205**

8 If you are working with version 4.0, choose **Name** from the popup menu. The CommandButton dialog box appears.

If you are working with version 5.0, choose **Properties** to display the CommandButton Properties dialog box. The General panel is visible.

Most objects in version 5.0 have a properties dialog box. There are two ways to gain access to it. The first is the method you have just used: choosing the Properties option from the object's popup menu. The second method is to double-click the object.

9 PowerBuilder has given the button a default name of cb_1. Replace the "1" with **scheduling**, so that your dialog box looks like Figure 9.24 (version 4.0) or Figure 9.25 (version 5.0).

Figure 9.24
CommandButton dialog box (4.0)

Figure 9.25
CommandButton General properties panel (5.0)

10 Click the **OK** button to save the name assigned to the button.

11 Right-click the button again. This time, choose **Duplicate** from the popup menu. A second, identical button appears under the Scheduling button, as in Figure 9.26 on page 206.

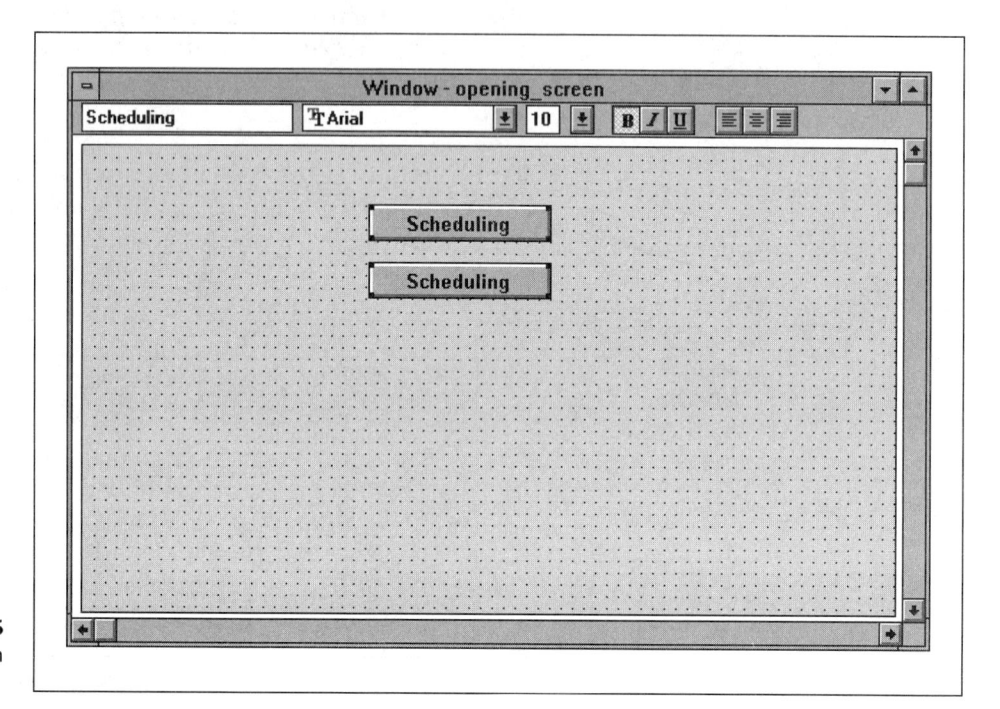

Figure 9.26
Duplicated command button

When you duplicate an object, you duplicate all of the object's characteristics, including the original object's script. You can therefore save considerable development time by duplicating similar objects and then modifying the duplicate.

12 Change the button's text to **Costs**. Change its name to **cb_costs**.

13 Create another duplicate buttons with the text **Sales Leads** and the name **cb_sales_leads**.

14 Create a final duplicate button with the text **Quit** and the name **cb_quit**.

15 Drag a rectangle around all four buttons, as in Figure 9.27. When you release the mouse button, all four command buttons will be selected.

16 Drag the buttons so that they are centered in the window.

Writing Simple Button Control Scripts

If you were to run the *tshows* application right now, you would see the command buttons on the opening window, but clicking them wouldn't do anything because the buttons don't have any scripts. The next step in the process is therefore to give each button a script so that it performs some action.

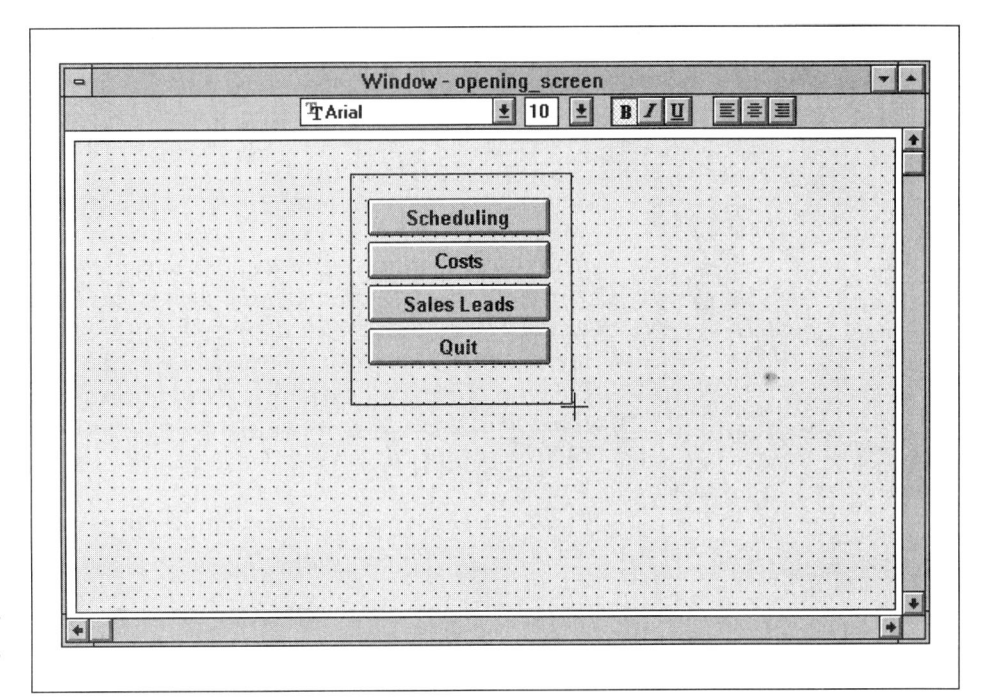

Figure 9.27
Dragging to select multiple objects

To add a script to a command button control:

1. Make sure that you are working in the Window painter with the w_opening_screen window.
2. Choose **Script** from the Scheduling button's popup menu. Notice that the default event for the button is "clicked." This event is triggered when the user clicks the button.
3. Type **open (w_scheduling)** in the PowerScript painter workspace.
4. Exit the Script painter and save the script.
5. Type **open (w_costs)** as a script for the Costs button.
6. Type **open (w_sales_leads)** as a script for the Sales Leads button.
7. Type **close (parent)** as a script for the Quit button.
8. Click the **Run** button in the PowerBar to run the application. Don't forget to answer **Yes** when PowerBuilder asks you if you want to save your changes.
9. Test each button on the opening screen. If the buttons are working properly, each of the first three should open an appropriately titled window. (Double-click each window's control box to close it.) Clicking the Quit button should stop the application and return you to the application development environment.

Creating Picture Buttons

A picture button is similar to a command button. However, rather than seeing text, the user sees a picture that suggests the button's function. In most cases, a picture button works best on a window that performs data manipulation rather than as part of a button menu. Therefore, as part of your initial experience with a picture button, you will be adding a window to the *tshows* application that will eventually be used to interact with the database. This window will contain a picture button that closes the window with a single click (one less click than it takes to close the window using a control box).

Should you have both a control box and a close button on a window? The answer to this type of interface question varies depending on with whom you're talking. Many windows have more than one way to do the same thing. For example, under Windows 3.1 a PowerBuilder dialog box has OK and Cancel buttons that close the window along with a control box. This type of design is typical of PowerSoft's sample applications as well. However, some application designers feel that the close button is redundant when the control box is present. Because interface design relies to a large extent on personal preference and experience, there is no single right answer to this issue.

To create a window that will hold the picture button and make that window accessible to the application:

1. Make sure that you are working with the *tshows* application in *tshows1.pbl* and that you are in the Window painter.
2. Create a new window with the title **Maintain Cost Data**. Save it under the name **w_manage_cost_data**. Size the window so that it nearly fills the workspace; center the window on the computer screen. At this point, leave the rest of the window's characteristics alone; you will be modifying them later.
3. Open the window named w_costs.
4. Place a command button on the window with the text **Maintain Cost Data** and the name **cb_manage_cost_data**.
5. Create an open event script for the button that opens the w_manage_cost_data window.
6. Run the application. Test the command button you added to w_costs to make certain that the new window (w_manage_cost_data) appears.

At this point, you're ready to add the picture button to the new window.

To add a picture button to the window:

1. Display the w_manage_cost_data window in the Window painter.

If you haven't closed any of the Window painter windows that you've opened, then you can display the w_manage_cost_data window by selecting its name from the list of open windows at the bottom of the Window menu.

2. If you are working with version 4.0, click the **PictureButton** button in the PainterBar (Figure 9.28 on the next page).

   If you are working with version 5.0, click the **CommandButton** button to expose the controls palette. Then click the **PictureButton** button (Figure 9.28 on the next page).

3. Click the lower-right corner of the window. An new picture button control appears, as in Figure 9.29 on page 209.

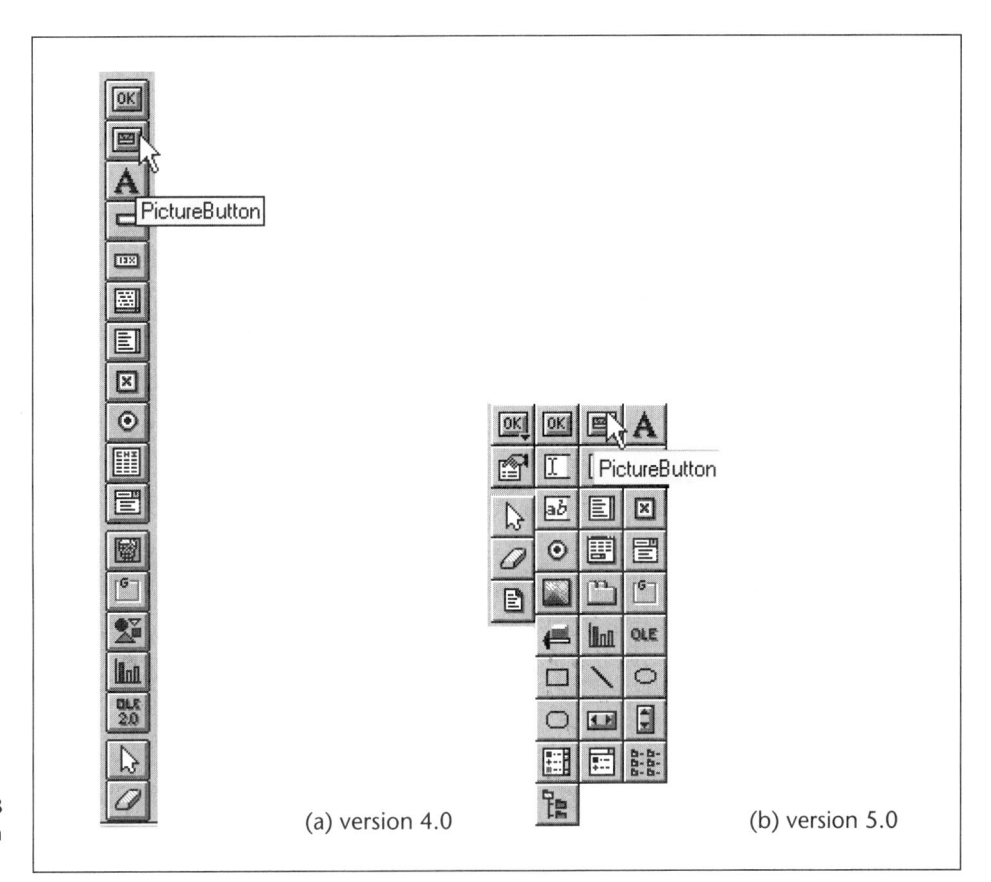

CHAPTER NINE BUILDING WINDOWS AS AN APPLICATION FRAMEWORK **209**

Figure 9.28
PictureButton button

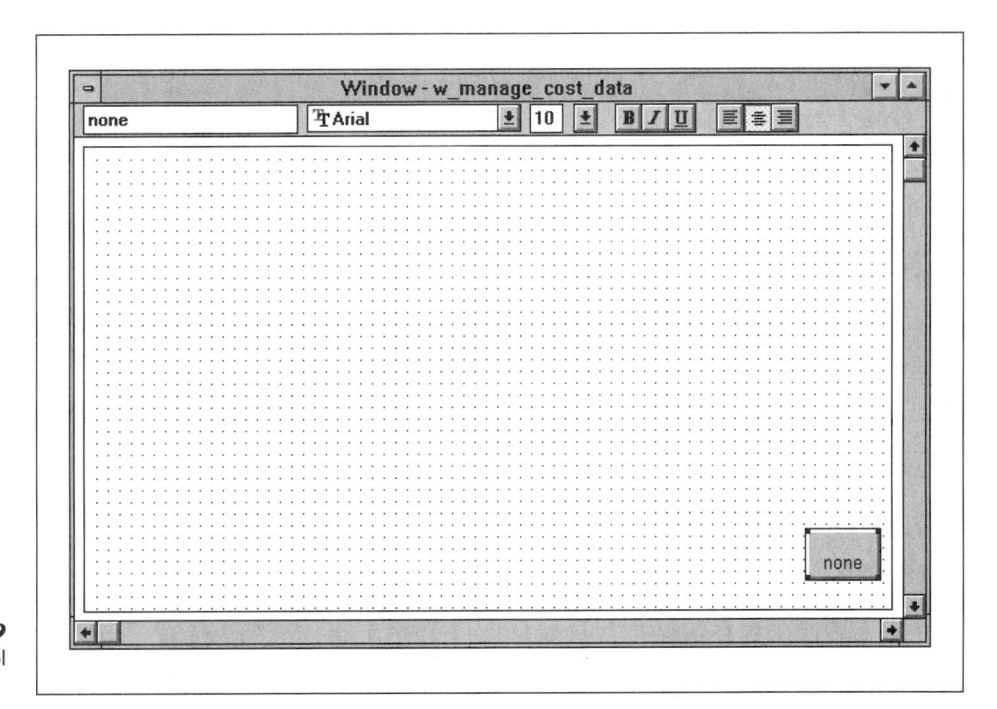

(a) version 4.0

(b) version 5.0

Figure 9.29
New picture button control

4 Remove the default text **none** from the text box above the Window painter workspace. This removes the text from the picture button.

5 Double-click the picture button. If you are working with version 4.0, the Select Picture dialog box appears.

If you are working with version 5.0, the PictureButton Properties dialog box appears, displaying the General panel. Click the **Browse Enabled** button to display the Select Picture dialog box.

6 If you have installed the PowerBuilder tutorial files, there are four bit-mapped images in the \pb4 or \pb5 directory. If you are working with version 4.0 and \pb4 is not the current directory, make it current so that you see a file listing similar to Figure 9.30.

If you are working with version 5.0, make \pb5 the current directory.

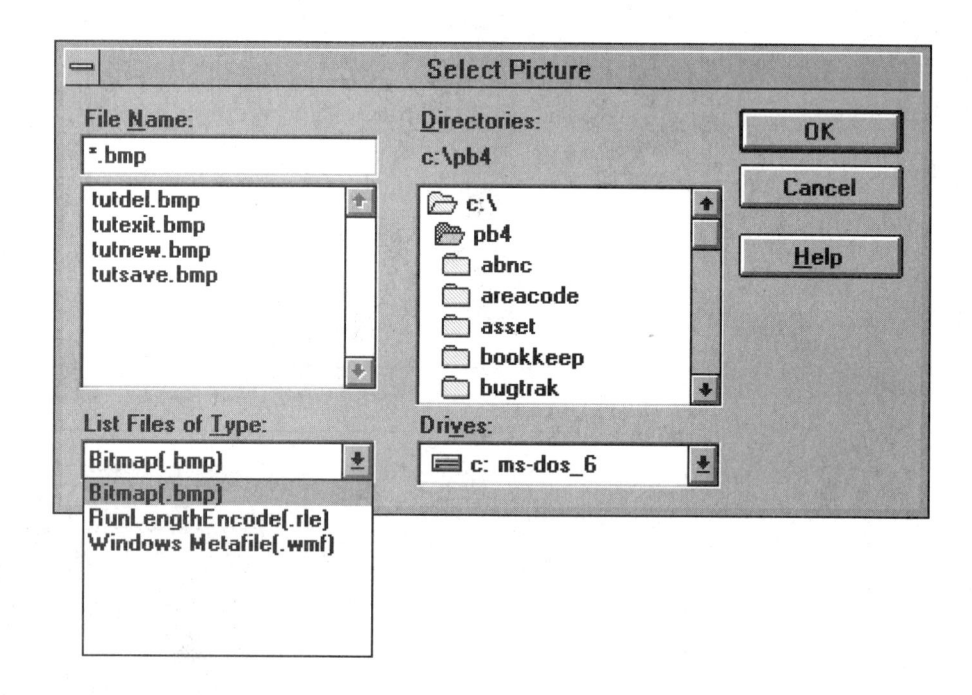

Figure 9.30
Select Picture dialog box

7 Click **tutexit.bmp** to select the file.

Where do the pictures for picture buttons come from? From any program that can save bitmapped images in any of the formats that you can see in Figure 9.30. If you're not an artist, you can get pictures from clip art collections. Many bitmapped images are also available in the public domain.

Pictures are linked to picture buttons. This means that the images aren't stored within the application. Instead, the application stores the path to an image's file. When you move an application from one computer to another, make sure you move image files as well and maintain the same relative path from the application to the files.

CHAPTER NINE   BUILDING WINDOWS AS AN APPLICATION FRAMEWORK   **211**

8 Click the **OK** button. PowerBuilder closes the Select Picture dialog box and installs the selected picture as part of the button. If you are working with version 4.0, PowerBuilder opens the PictureButton dialog box.

If you are working with version 5.0, PowerBuilder returns you to the General panel of the PictureButton Properties dialog box.

9 Change the button's default name to **pb_close**.

10 Click the **Original Size** check box. This will automatically resize the picture button so that it can hold the image at the image's original size. At this point, your dialog box should look like Figure 9.31 (version 4.0) or Figure 9.32 (version 5.0).

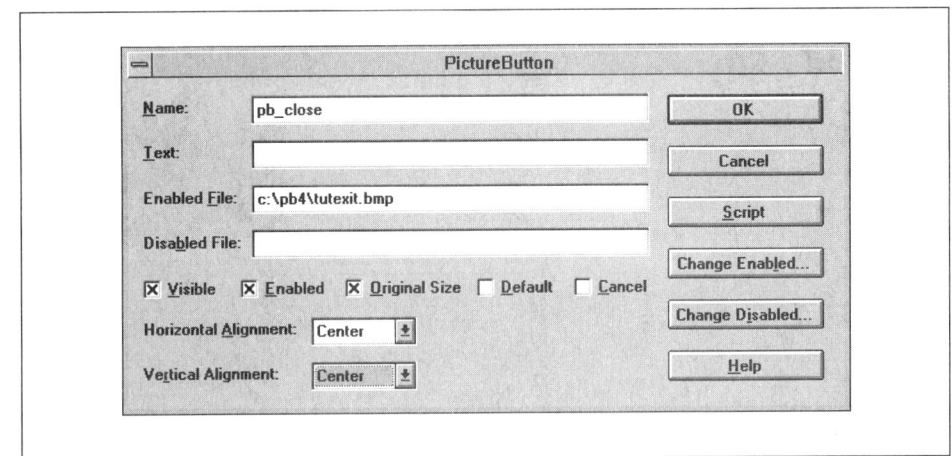

Figure 9.31
PictureButton dialog box (4.0)

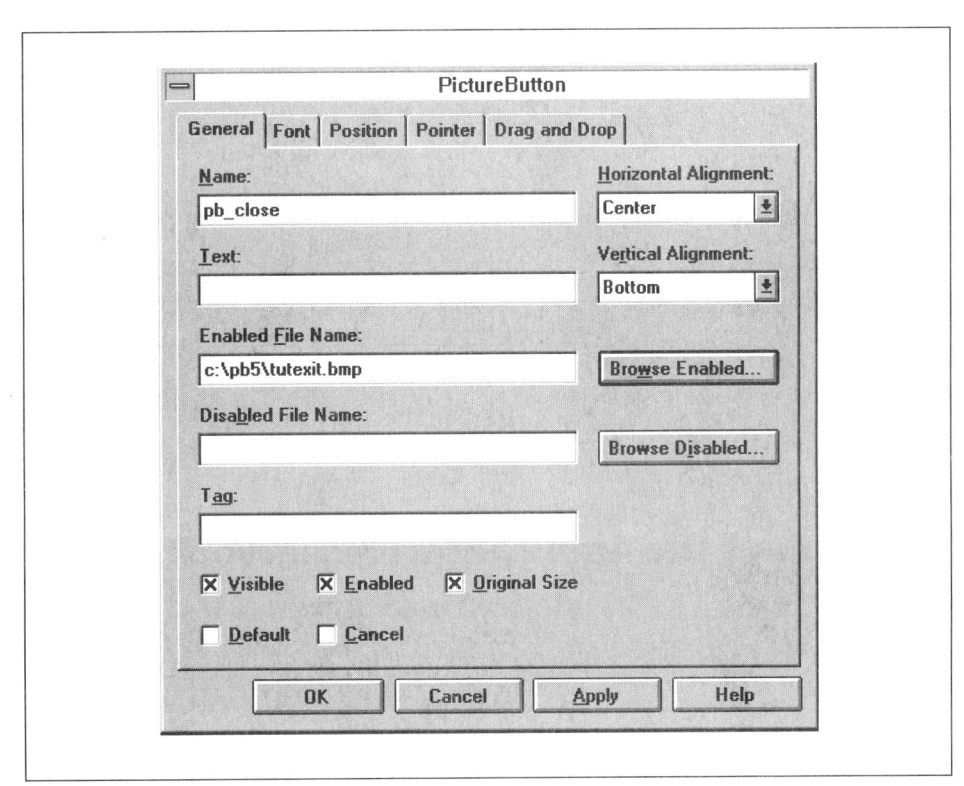

Figure 9.32
PictureButton General Properties panel (5.0)

212 CHAPTER NINE BUILDING WINDOWS AS AN APPLICATION FRAMEWORK

11 If you are working with version 4.0, click the **Script** button in the PainterBar to open the PowerScript painter.

If you are working with version 5.0, click the **OK** button to close the PictureButton Properties dialog box. Right-click the picture button to display its popup menu. Choose **Script** from the menu to enter the Script painter.

12 Type **close (parent)** as the picture button's script. The `close` function closes a window. Its single parameter is the name of the window to be closed. The special keyword `parent` closes the window containing the control.

13 Exit the Script painter, saving your changes. If you are working with version 4.0, you are returned to the Picture Button dialog box. Click the **OK** button to close the PictureButton dialog box.

If you are working with version 5.0, you are returned to the window painter. At this point, you should see something like Figure 9.33.

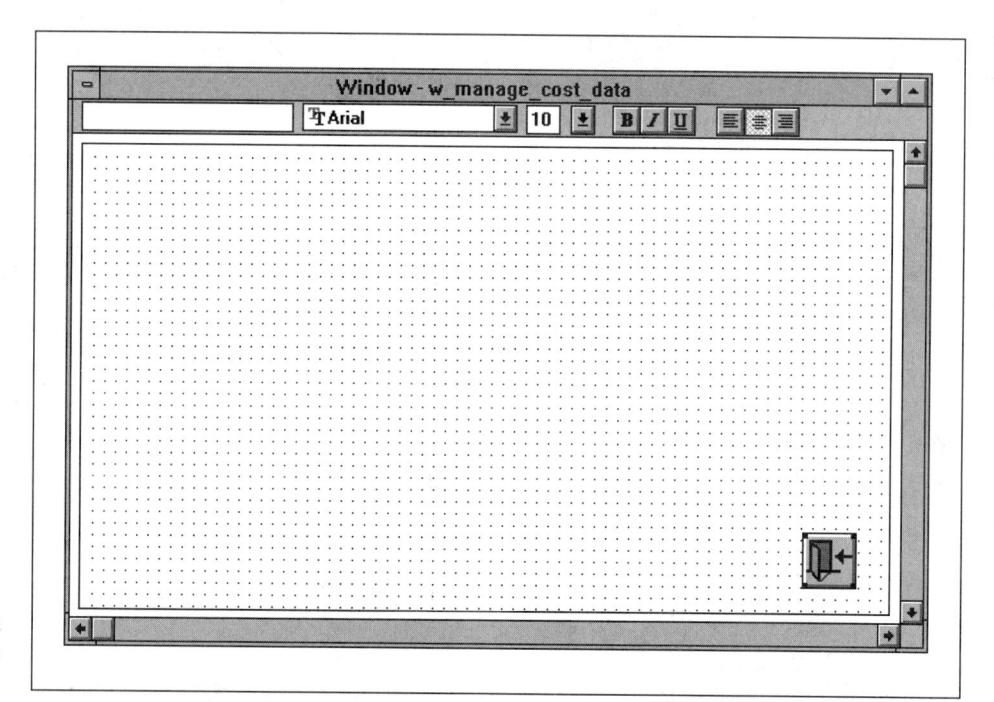

Figure 9.33
Completed picture button

14 Run the application and test the action of the picture button. Make sure you save all changes when prompted to do so by PowerBuilder.

Completing the Application FrameWork

For many developers, the next step in the application development process would be to complete the application framework for the *tshows* application. The windows and their contents can be found in Table 9.1. As you read this table, keep in mind that anything that begins with cb is a command button; pb is a picture button. Button names appear first, followed by their titles in parentheses. Anything that begins with W is a window object.

Creating all these windows and buttons can be a very tedious task. They have therefore been created for you and stored in the *tshows* application in the application library file *tshows2.pbl*. If you don't care to create the application framework yourself, you can switch to *tshows2.pbl* for the remainder of the work you will be doing with this book.

Should you choose to create the application framework yourself, look through Table 9.1 very carefully before you begin working. Many of the windows are the same with the exception of their names and titles. This means that you can save yourself a great deal of work if you duplicate an existing window and then change the copy's name and title as needed.

To save a copy of a window under another name:

1. Open the window you want to duplicate in the Window painter. For this example, open w_manage_cost_data, the window you created in the previous exercise.
2. Choose **File -> Save As**. The Save Window dialog box appears.
3. Type **w_lead_revenue_summary** as the new name for the window.
4. Click the **OK** button. PowerBuilder closes—but does not delete—the original window, creates a new window, and stores it under the new name.
5. Use the window's popup menu to change its title to **See Sales Leads Revenue Summary**.
6. Choose **File -> Save** to save the change you've just made to the new window.

Keep in mind that when you copy objects in this way, PowerBuilder makes an exact duplicate of the saved object, including all controls and associated scripts. In this case, that it precisely what you want to do

The windows in Table 9.1 are listed in top-down order. In other words, windows that are at the top of the hierarchy appear first. This makes it easier for you to understand how the table is organized. However, if you create windows in that order, the script compiler will warn you whenever you reference a window that doesn't exist. You have two alternatives. The first is to work from the bottom of the table forward. The second is to respond Yes when PowerBuilder asks if you want to ignore the compiler warnings. If compiler warnings bother you, start from the bottom of the table, which is the way tshows2.pbl was built.

The similarity of many of the windows in Table 9.1 might suggest to you that we are looking at a situation where inheritance could help. However, keep in mind that the windows that will be used for data manipulation have only a single characteristic—a title—and contain only a single control. They will be significantly different from one another once we start filling them with DataWindows and other controls.

WINDOW TITLE	WINDOW NAME	CONTENTS	SCRIPT ACTIONS
Scheduling	w_scheduling	cb_producers (Producers)	clicked event: open w_producers
		cb_shows_locations (Shows and Locations)	clicked event: open w_shows_locations
		cb_calendar (Calendar)	clicked event: open w_calendar
		cb_return (Return)	clicked event: close parent window
Producers	w_producers	cb_manage_producer_data (Maintain Producer Data)	clicked event: open w_manage_producer_data
		cb_see_producer_data (View Producer Data)	clicked event: open w_see_producer_data
		cb_return (Return)	click event: close parent window
Shows and Locations	w_shows_locations	cb_manage_show_data (Maintain Show Data)	clicked event: open w_manage_show_data
		cb_manage_location_data (Maintain Location Data)	clicked event: open w_manage_location_data
		cb_assign_locations (Assign Locations to Shows)	clicked event: open w_assign_locations
		cb_see_show_data (View Show Data)	clicked event: open w_see_show_data
		cb_return (Return)	clicked event: close parent window
Calendar	w_calendar	cb_manage_calendar (Maintain the Calendar)	clicked event: open w_manage_calendar
		cb_calendar_query (Calendar Query)	clicked event: open w_calendar_query
		cb_see_all_shows (See All Scheduled Shows)	clicked event: open w_see_all_shows
		cb_see_future_shows (See Shows to be Attended)	clicked event: open w_see_future_shows
		cb_see_past_shows (See Shows that Have Been Attended)	clicked event: open w_see_past_shows
		cb_return (Return)	clicked event: close parent window
Costs	w_costs	cb_enter_costs (Enter Costs)	clicked event: open w_enter_costs
		cb_manage_costs (Maintain Cost Data)	clicked event: open w_maintain_costs

Table 9.1 Windows for the *tshows* application framework

WINDOW TITLE	WINDOW NAME	CONTENTS	SCRIPT ACTIONS
		cb_see_one_show_costs (See the Costs for One Show)	clicked event: open w_see_one_show_costs
		cb_see_shows_and_costs (See Shows and Costs)	clicked event: open w_see_shows_and_costs
		cb_see_cost_summary (See Cost Summary)	clicked event: open w_see_cost_summary
		cb_see_increased_costs (See Increased Costs)	clicked event: open w_increased_costs
		cb_return (Return)	clicked event: close parent window
Sales Leads	w_sales_leads	cb_manage_lead_data (Maintain Sales Leads Data)	clicked event: open w_manage_lead_data
		cb_manage_contacts (Manage Contacts)	clicked event: open w_manage_contacts
		cb_see_leads2call (See a List of Leads to Call)	clicked event: open w_see_leads2call
		cb_leads_by_company (See Sales Leads by Company)	clicked event: open w_leads_by_company
		cb_leads_revenue_summary (See a Sales Leads Revenue Summary)	clicked event: open w_leads_revenue_summary
		cb_return (Return)	clicked event: close parent window
Maintain Producer Data	w_manage_producer_data	pb_close	clicked event: close parent window
View Producer Data	w_see_producer_data	pb_close	clicked event: close parent window
Maintain Show Data	w_manage_show_data	pb_close	clicked event: close parent window
Maintain Location Data	w_manage_location_data	pb_close	clicked event: close parent window
Assign Locations to Shows	w_assign_locations	pb_close	clicked event: close parent window
View Show Data	w_see_show_data	pb_close	clicked event: close parent window
Maintain the Calendar	w_manage_calendar	pb_closer	clicked event: close parent window
Query the Calendar	w_calendar_query	pb_close	clicked event: close parent window
See All Scheduled Shows	w_see_all_shows	pb_close	clicked event: close parent window

Table 9.1 (Continued) Windows for the *tshows* application framework

WINDOW TITLE	WINDOW NAME	CONTENTS	SCRIPT ACTIONS
See Shows to be Attended	w_see_future_shows	pb_close	clicked event: close parent window
See Shows that Have Been Attended	w_see_past_shows	pb_close	clicked event: close parent window
Enter Cost Data	w_enter_costs	pb_close	clicked event: close parent window
See the Costs for One Show	w_see_one_show_costs	pb_close	clicked event: close parent window
See Shows and Costs	w_see_shows_and_costs	none	
See Cost Summary	w_see_cost_summary	pb_close	clicked event: close parent window
See Increased Costs	w_increased_costs	pb_close	clicked event: close parent window
Maintain Sales Lead Data	w_manage_lead_data	pb_close	clicked event: close parent window
Maintain Contacts	w_manage_contacts	pb_close	clicked event: close parent window
See a List of Leads to Call	w_see_leads2call	pb_close	clicked event: close parent window
See Sales Leads by Company	w_leads_by_company	pb_close	clicked event: close parent window
See Sales Leads Revenue Summary	w_leads_revenue_summary	pb_close	clicked event: close parent window

Table 9.1 (Continued)   Windows for the *tshows* application framework

When you've finished creating the application framework, be sure to test all of the button controls to make certain that you can navigate properly through the windows.

Viewing the Object Hierarchy

As you add windows to an application, PowerBuilder keeps track of the window hierarchy you establish when you use scripts to open windows. You can see that hierarchy in the Application painter.

To view the object hierarchy for the *tshows* application framework:

1. If you have created your own application framework, continue working with the *tshows* application in *tshows1.pbl*. Otherwise, open the *tshows* application in *tshows2.pbl*.

CHAPTER NINE   BUILDING WINDOWS AS AN APPLICATION FRAMEWORK **217**

> **WARNING**
>
> *This is a change of application library. Unless have you completed the application framework yourself, make sure you are using tshows2.pbl rather than the file tshows1.pbl that you have been using to this point!*

2   Click the **Application** button in the PowerBar to enter the Application painter.

3   Double-click the **tshows** icon in the workspace. The hierarchy expands to show you an icon for the opening_screen window.

4   Double-click the **w_opening_screen** window icon in the workspace. Icons appear for the three windows opened by controls on the opening_screen window.

5   Continue clicking icons until no more windows appear. The top portion of the hierarchy should appear like Figure 9.34. Scroll the window to see the rest of the hierarchy.

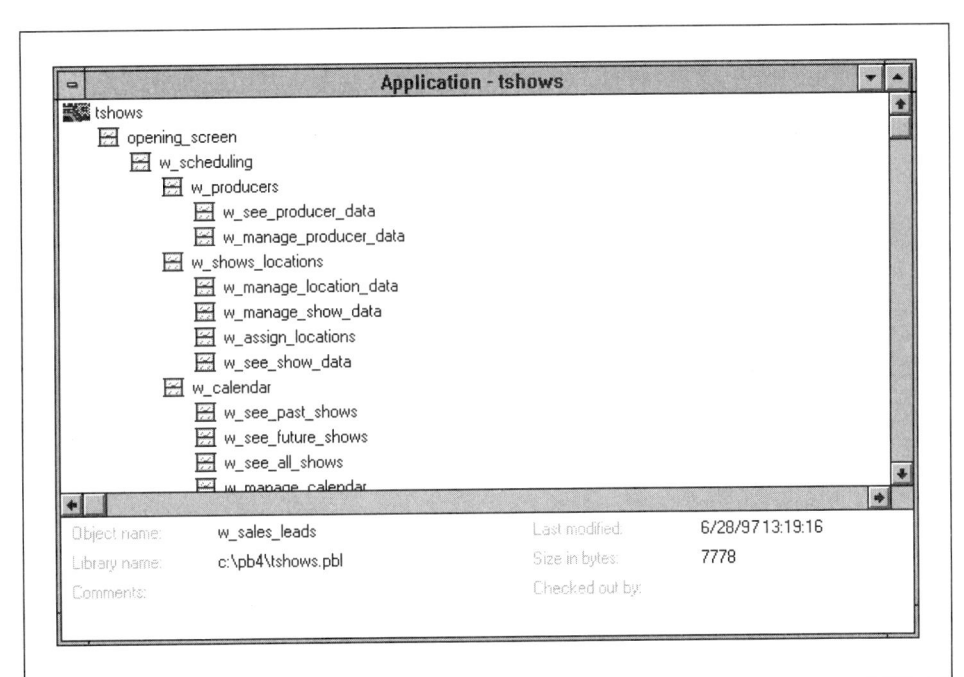

Figure 9.34
Expanded object hierarchy

Looking Ahead

In this chapter you have begun the process of developing a PowerBuilder application from the top down. You have designed the application's structure and seen the structure of the windows that will hold either menus or DataWindow objects for data manipulation. In Chapter 10, you will be introduced to DataWindow objects and how you can use them to display listings of data. In addition, you will learn how to add computed columns to DataWindow objects to summarize data for output purposes.

EXERCISES

The staff of College and University Rentals has assembled the following list of functions that they want their database application to perform:

- Enter, modify, and delete data about merchandise.
- View a list of types of merchandise.
- Enter, modify, and delete data about items.
- View a list of all merchandise items.
- View merchandise items organized by type of item.
- View merchandise items that are out for repair.
- View merchandise items of one type that are available for rental.
- Enter, modify, and delete data about schools.
- View a list of all schools.
- View a list of all customers at one school.
- Enter, modify, and delete data about customers.
- View a list of all customers.
- View a list of customers who haven't paid their rental fees.
- Find one customer and view all the customer's rentals.
- Enter, modify, and delete data about contacts with housing officers.
- Enter, modify, and delete data about rentals.
- View a list of deliveries that are to be made on a given day, organized by dorm within school.
- View a list of rentals that are due to be returned in the next week.
- View a rental revenue summary organized by type of merchandise.
- View a rental revenue summary organized by school.
- Enter, modify, and delete data about dorms.
- View a list of rentals that are due to be returned in a given period, organized by dorm within school.

1. Develop a menu tree similar to that in Figure 9.1 for the structure of an application for C&U Rentals. The tree should include all of the functions in the preceding list. In addition, fee free to add any other functions that you feel the application should perform.

2. Create an application framework for the application structure you created in Exercise 1. Create a window for each function; create additional windows to hold the menus that organize the windows. Include command and/or picture buttons as necessary to make it possible to navigate between all your windows. Test the application thoroughly to make sure that it works.

CHAPTER TEN

Introducing DataWindows

IN THIS CHAPTER YOU WILL:

- Identify the difference between DataWindow objects and DataWindow controls
- Create "quick" DataWindows based on SQL SELECT commands
- Pace DataWindow controls on windows and change the format of those controls
- Ceate computed fields

A PowerBuilder application interacts with a database through a DataWindow control that has been placed on an application window. A DataWindow control is an *instance* (a specific occurrence of) a DataWindow object. This arrangement provides a significant amount of flexibility in the creation of windows and in the development of applications.

Once you define a DataWindow object, you can place that same object on many windows by creating a different DataWindow control for each window. The beauty of this arrangement is that when you need the same input or output layout, you only need to create the layout once. You can then reuse it as necessary by creating many controls from the same object.

By the same token, the DataWindow object that is associated with a DataWindow control isn't fixed. An application can change the DataWindow while it is running. This means that both the data that appear in a window and the layout of that data can change as needed.

In this chapter you will learn to use the DataWindow painter to create DataWindows whose contents are generated by a simple SQL SELECT. You will extend the behavior of your SELECT by adding computed fields to a DataWindow. You will then place DataWindow controls on some of the windows in the *tshows* application framework and associate those controls with the DataWindow objects you have created.

> *People who are learning to use PowerBuilder often find the difference between a DataWindow object and a DataWindow control to be a bit of a mystery. It helps to think of a DataWindow control as a container into which a copy of a DataWindow object can be placed. Because the DataWindow control is a container, its contents can be changed. Because the DataWindow control conceptually contains a copy of a DataWindow object, the same DataWindow object can be placed in many DataWindow controls. (To be completely accurate, DataWindow objects are "linked" to DataWindow controls so that an application only needs to maintain one copy of each DataWindow object.)*

Creating a Simple DataWindow Object

The simplest type of DataWindow object for displaying data is one that is based on a SQL SELECT that requires no user input. In other words, you can completely specify the query's WHERE clause without requiring any values from the user or the application environment (a *Quick Select*). The *tshows* application can use this type of DataWindow, for example, to display all data stored in the Producers and Shows tables.

Configuring a Quick Select

To create a DataWindow object that displays the contents of the Producers table, you must first configure the Quick Select.

To configure the Quick Select:

1. Make sure you are working with the *tshows* application in *tshows2.pbl* and that you are connected to the *tshows* database.

> *Because DataWindow objects interact directly with a database, PowerBuilder needs to know which database to access when you are creating a DataWindow object. When you enter the DataWindow painter, PowerBuilder automatically connects to whichever database was last used on the computer that you are using. To be sure you are using the correct database, connect to it before you enter the DataWindow painter.*

2. Click the **DataWindow** button in the PowerBar (Figure 10.1). The Select DataWindow dialog box appears, as in Figure 10.2.

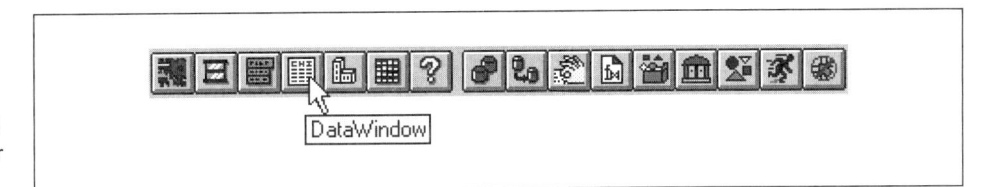

Figure 10.1
DataWindow button in the PowerBar

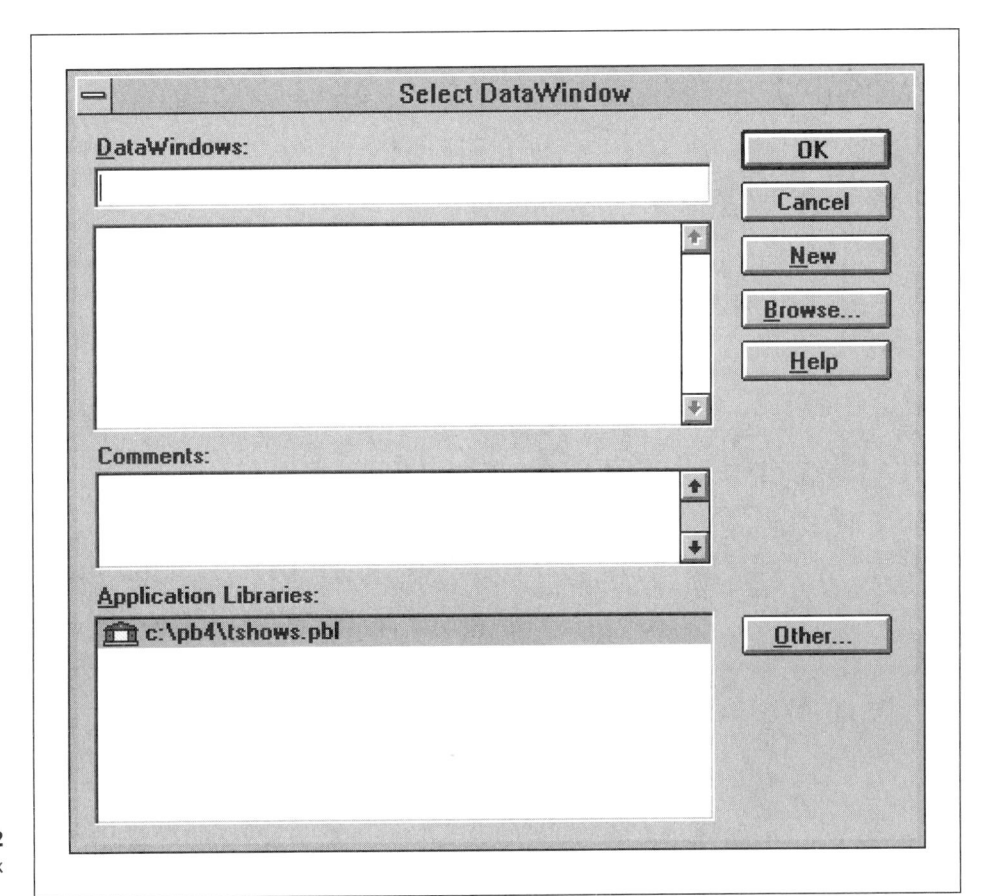

Figure 10.2
Select DataWindow dialog box

3. Click the **New** button. The New DataWindow dialog box appears (Figure 10.3 on page 222 for version 4.0 and Figure 10.4 on page 222 for version 5.0).

222 CHAPTER TEN INTRODUCING DATAWINDOWS

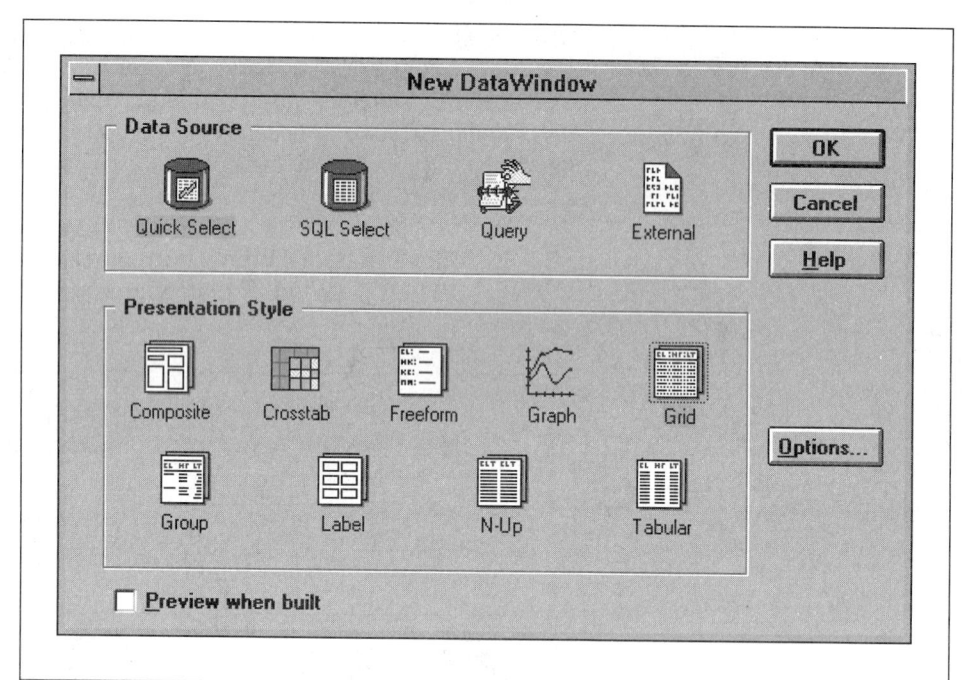

Figure 10.3
New DataWindow dialog box (4.0)

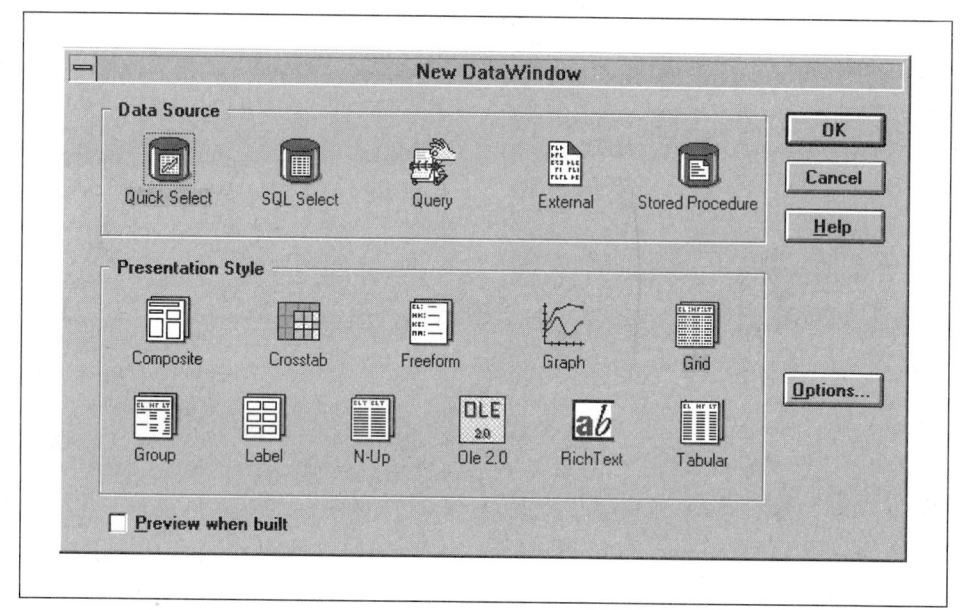

Figure 10.4
New DataWindow dialog box (5.0)

The Stored Procedure data source is not available with all DBMSs. For example, it is part of SQL Anywhere but not Watcom SQL 4.0.

The top third of the dialog box (the Data Source section) contains options for specifying how an application will obtain the data that will be displayed in a DataWindow. The data must be generated by a SQL query (the QuickSelect, SQL Select, or Query options) or must be loaded from some other source (the External or Stored Procedure options).

To use a Quick Select as a source for DataWindow data:

4 Click the **Quick Select** icon in the New DataWindow dialog box.

The bottom two-thirds of the dialog box determines the basic layout for data in the DataWindow (Presentation Style).

5 Click the **Grid** icon.

6 Click the **OK** button. The Quick Select dialog box appears (Figure 10.5).

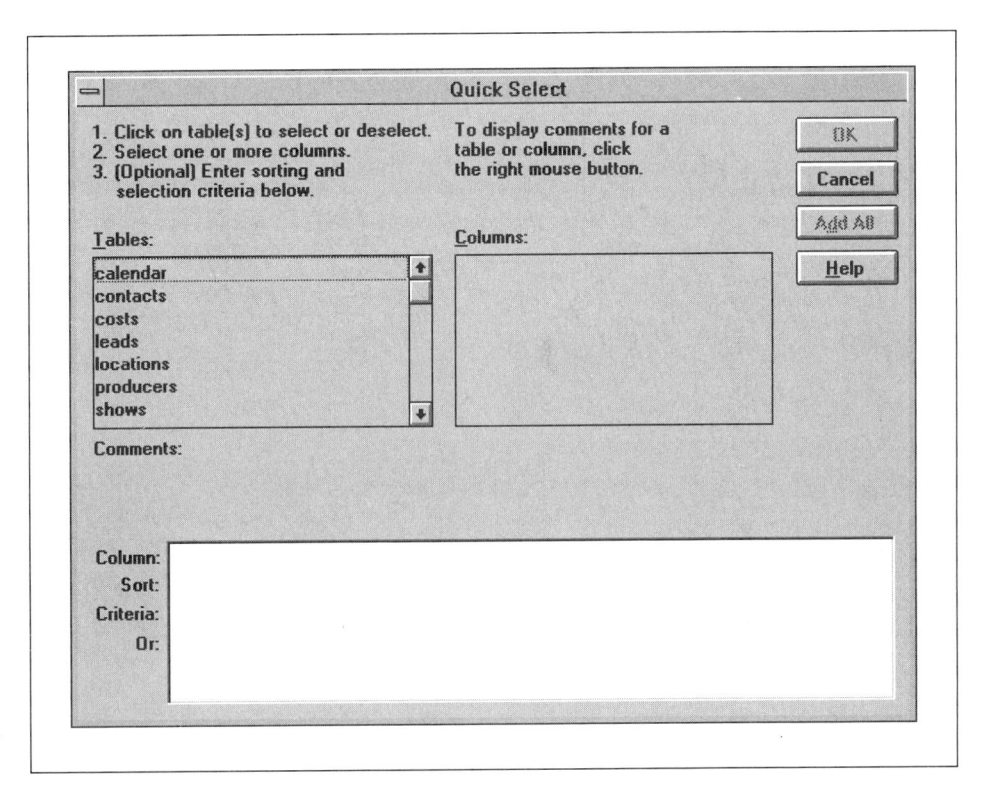

Figure 10.5
Quick Select dialog box

The instructions in the dialog box tell you to choose a table and the columns you want to see from that table. WHERE and ORDER BY clauses for the SELECT you are building are optional.

7 Click **producers** in the list of tables. PowerBuilder displays the columns in the table you just clicked, as in Figure 10.6 on page 224. It also indicates tables that contain foreign key references to the table you selected (for example, the Shows table in Figure 10.6). You can use existing foreign key/primary key relationships to automatically join tables to retrieve related data.

8 Click the **producer_name**, **producer_phone**, and **producer_address** columns in the Producer table. PowerBuilder places the three columns in a grid at the bottom of the Quick Select dialog box (see Figure 10.7 on page 224).

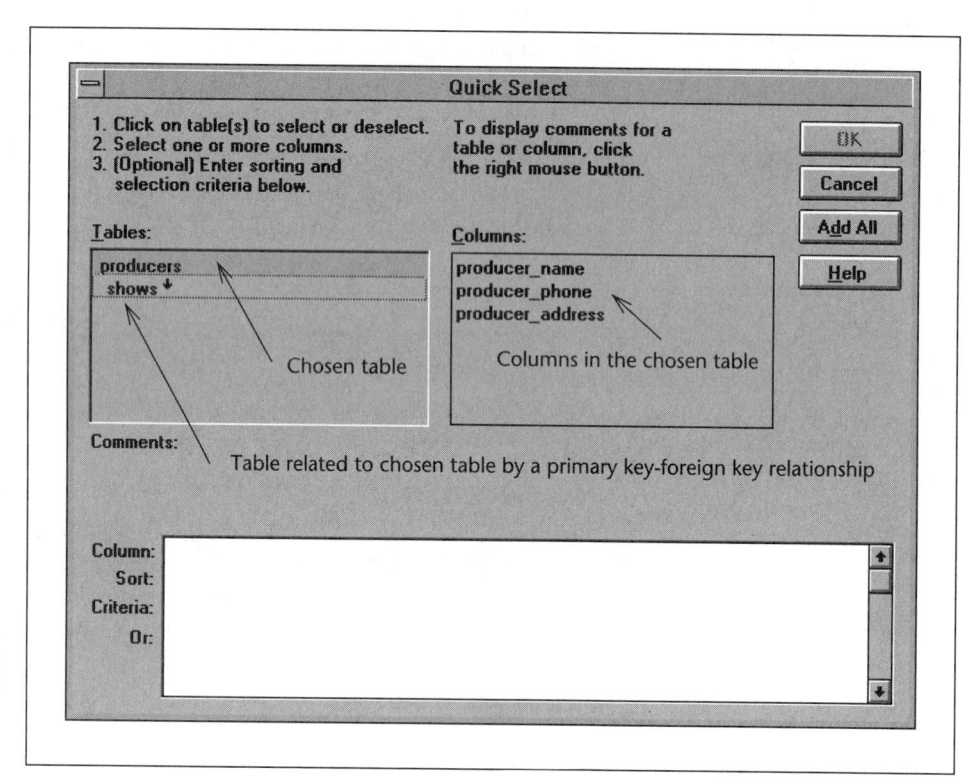

Figure 10.6
Table chosen in the Quick Select dialog box

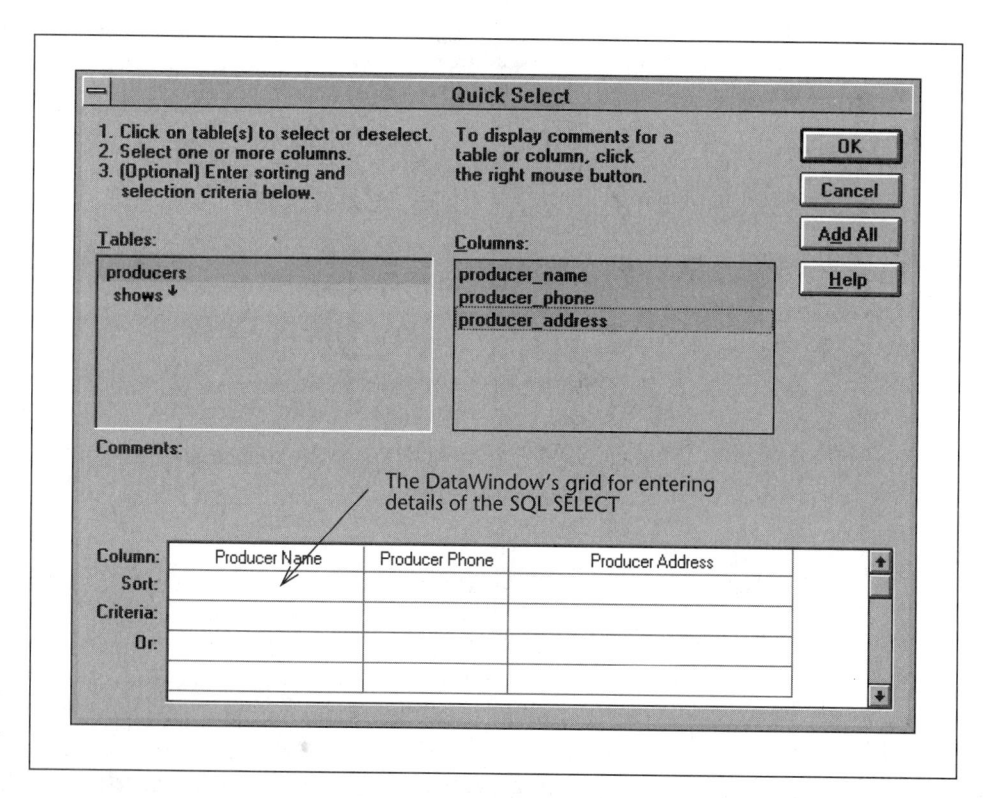

Figure 10.7
Columns chosen in the Quick Select dialog box

CHAPTER TEN   INTRODUCING DATAWINDOWS   **225**

9   Click the Sort line under the Producer Name column in the grid to display a list of possible sort orders.

10 Choose **Ascending** from the dropdown menu, as in Figure 10.8. Because the query requires no additional criteria, the Quick Select is complete.

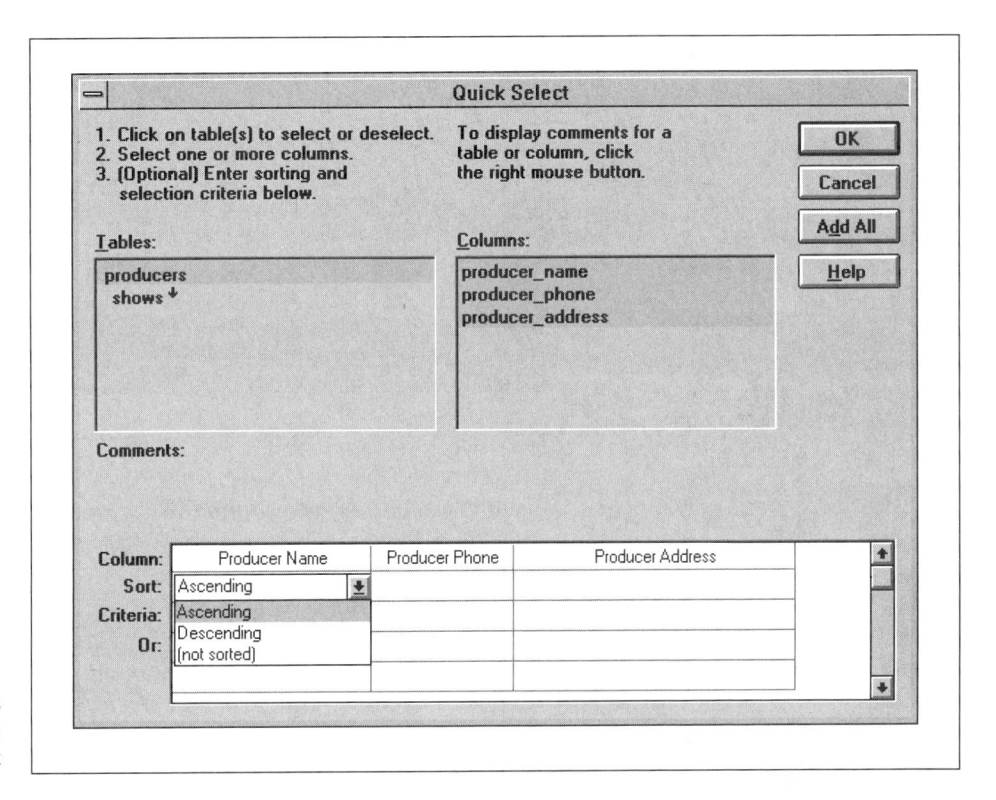

Figure 10.8
Choosing a sort order for a column in a Quick Select

11 Click the **OK** button. PowerBuilder displays the layout for the DataWindow object in the DataWindow painter (Figure 10.9).

Configuring the DataWindow

In Figure 10.9 on page 226 you can see many of the characteristics of the DataWindow painter. The most important thing to notice is that the workspace is divided into *bands*, each of which represents a part of the DataWindow's display. In this simple DataWindow object, there are four bands:

- Header: The contents of the header band appear once at the top of the DataWindow. If the DataWindow scrolls, the header stays put. A header is therefore useful for a report title and column headers.
- Detail: The contents of the detail band are repeated once for every row in the virtual result table produced by the query on which the DataWindow is based.
- Summary: The contents of the summary band appear once at the bottom of the DataWindow, above anything in the footer band. In the current example, you won't be placing anything in the summary band. However, it will be

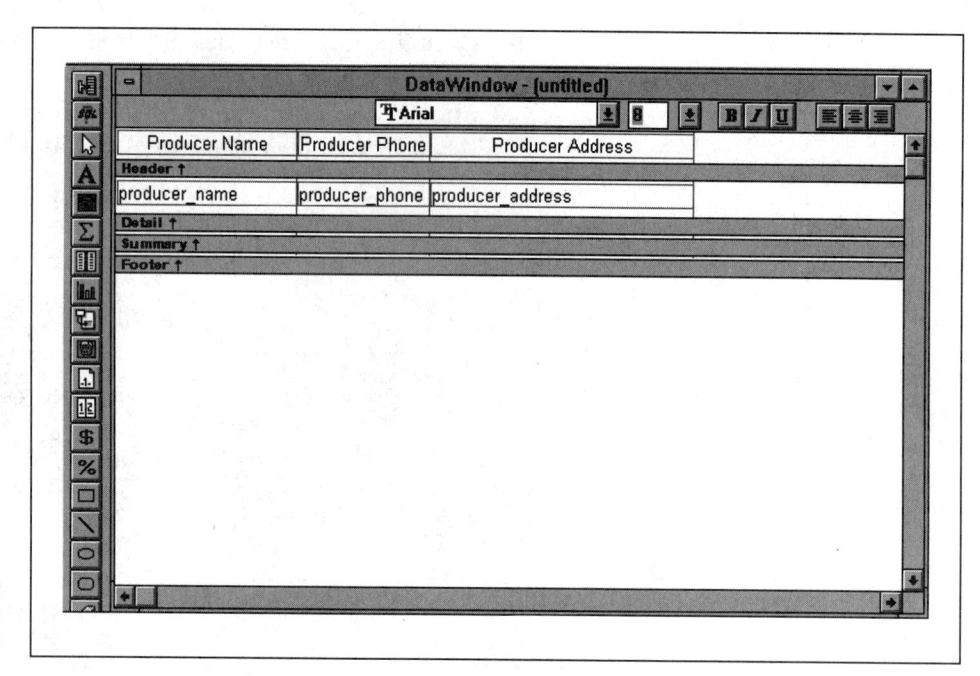

Figure 10.9
Quick Select DataWindow object in the DataWindow painter workspace

used when you create *control break reports* (reports that form groups of data based on matching data values and compute summary values about the groups) in Chapter 12.
- Footer: The contents of the footer band appear once at the very bottom of the DataWindow. If the DataWindow scrolls, the footer stays in place. A footer therefore provides a convenient place to display information that you want to remain in view, such as a page number or the current date.

The columns in the DataWindow object use the data formats you established in the Database painter. However, you can use the DataWindow painter to change the appearance of those formats. In addition, you can add display text and graphic objects, change fonts and type styles, add computed columns, and so on. For this example, you will be enlarging columns and changing the type style to make the output more readable.

To modify the appearance of the DataWindow object:

1. Click the Preview icon in the PainterBar to preview the DataWindow object to see what it currently looks like. (*Hint:* It's the same Preview button that you used in the Data Administration painter. In this case, it's at the very top of the PainterBar.) The DataWindow object appears in the Data Manipulation painter workspace. As you can see in Figure 10.10 on page 227, the Producer Address column is too narrow to display all the text.

If the values in the Producer Phone column aren't formatted as you see in Figure 10.10, then the Telephone# edit style hasn't been applied to the field in the Database painter. To fix the problem, first close preview by double-clicking on its control box. Then open the Producers table in the Database painter. Display the table's Alter Table dialog box, click the producer_phone column, and choose

CHAPTER TEN   INTRODUCING DATAWINDOWS   **227**

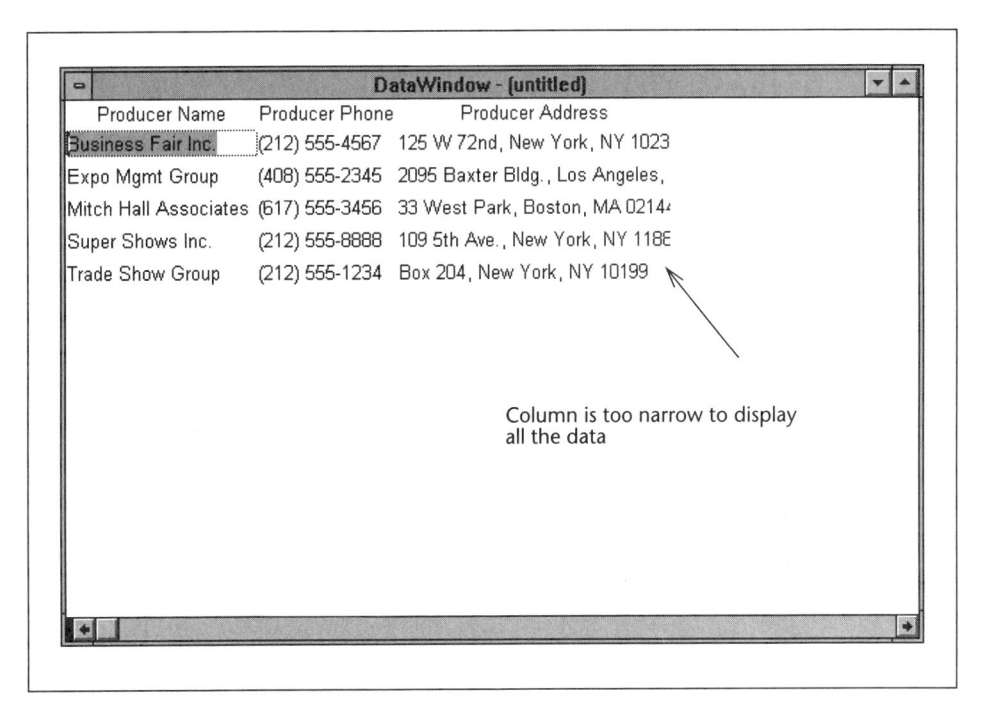

Figure 10.10
Previewing a DataWindow object based on a QuickSelect

Telephone# as its edit style. Save the changes and return to the DataWindow painter. Preview the DataWindow object again. This time the values in the Producer Phone column should be properly formatted.

2 Click the **Design** button in the PainterBar (Figure 10.11) to return to the DataWindow painter.

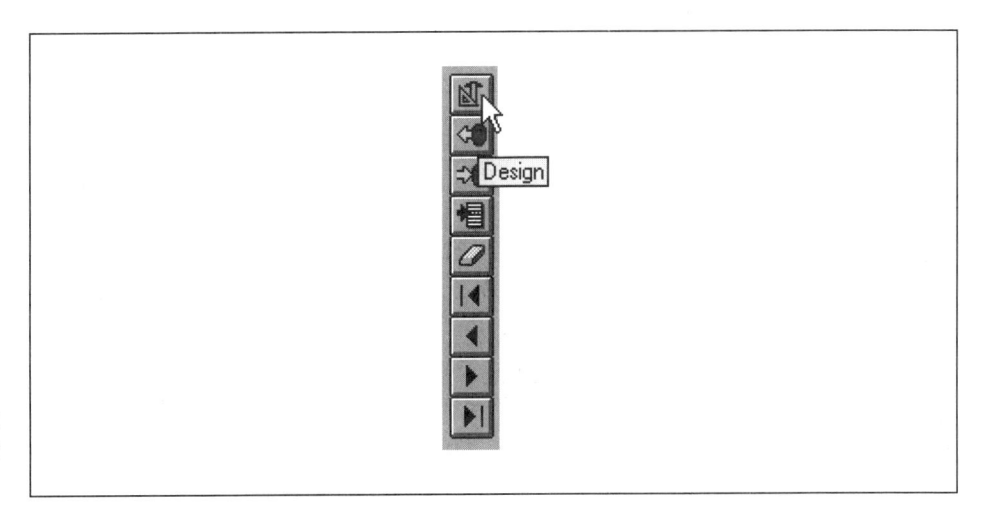

Figure 10.11
Design button in the PainterBar

3 Click the rectangle for the producer_address in the detail band.

4 Move the pointer over the right border of the rectangle. Notice that the pointer changes to a double-headed arrow when it is over the border.

5 Drag the right border of the rectangle to the right, as in Figure 10.12. Notice that the header for the column is enlarged as you change the width of the column. The text in the header remains centered in its rectangle.

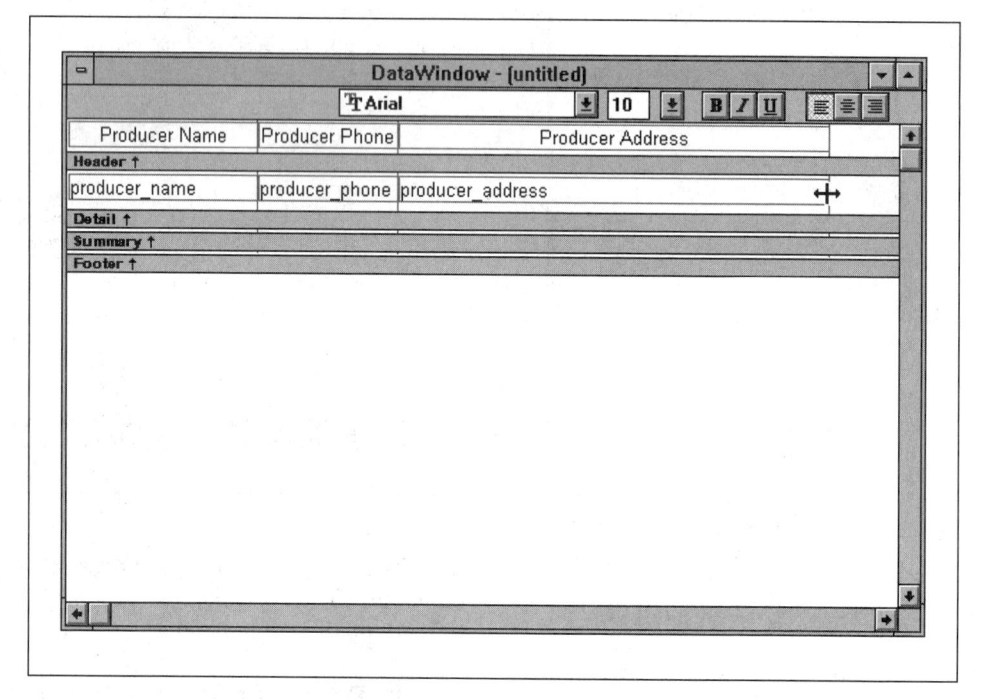

Figure 10.12
Changing the display width of a column

6 Preview the DataWindow object again to be certain that the Producer Address column is wide enough.

7 Click the **producer_phone** rectangle in the detail band to select it.

8 Make the producer_phone column slightly wider. Notice that as you drag its right boundary, the Producer Address moves over to make space for it. At the end of this step, the producer_phone column should still be selected in the detail band.

9 Click the **Center** button in the Style Bar to center the telephone number in the Producer Phone column (see Figure 10.13).

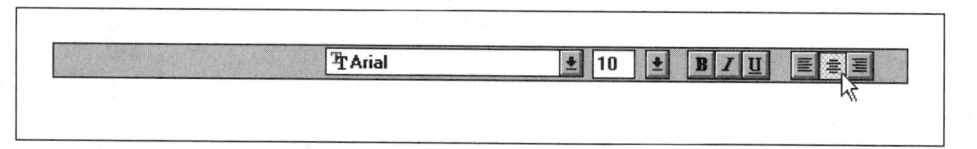

Figure 10.13
Changing a column's alignment

10 Click the **Producer Name** rectangle in the header band. Press the **Ctrl** key and click the **Producer Phone** rectangle in the header band. Press the **Ctrl** key and click the **Producer Address** rectangle in the header band. All three should be selected.

You have now seen two ways to select multiple objects in a workspace. The first is to drag the pointer with the right mouse button depressed across the objects. This selects all objects that are completely contained in the area across which the pointer is dragged. The second method is to click the first object and then Ctrl-click the remaining objects.

11 Click the **B** button in the Style Bar to make all three headers boldface.

12 Preview the completed DataWindow to see the effect of your changes.

13 Double-click the Data Manipulation painter control box. PowerBuilder asks if you want to save your changes.

14 Click the **Yes** button. The Save DataWindow dialog box appears.

15 Type **dwo_see_producers** to name the DataWindow, as in Figure 10.14. Click the **OK** button to close the dialog box and save the changes.

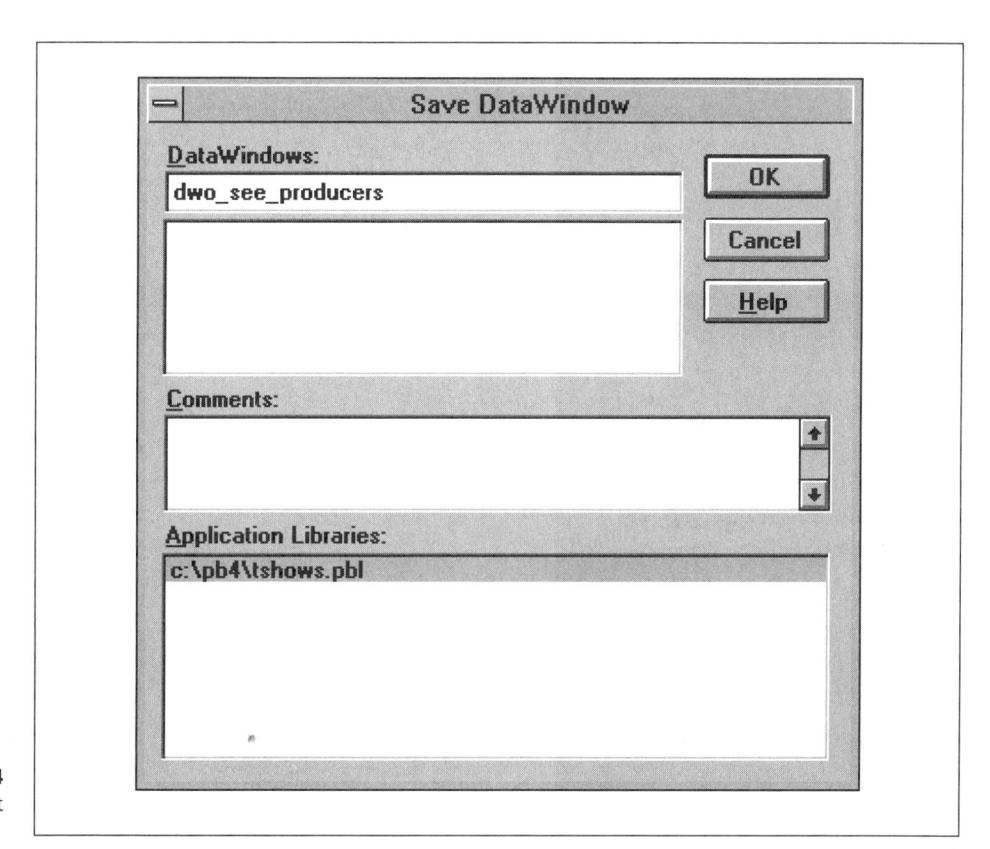

Figure 10.14
Saving a new DataWindow object

Placing a DataWindow Control

To use a DataWindow object, you must create a DataWindow control from the object and place the control on an application window. At that point, you can make additional changes in the format of the control.

230 Chapter Ten Introducing DataWindows

To create a DataWindow control:

1 Open the w_see_producer_data window in the Window painter. (*Hint:* Click the Window button in the PainterBar and then select the window by name from the list of window's already created.)

2 Click the **DataWindow** button in the PainterBar (Figure 10.15).

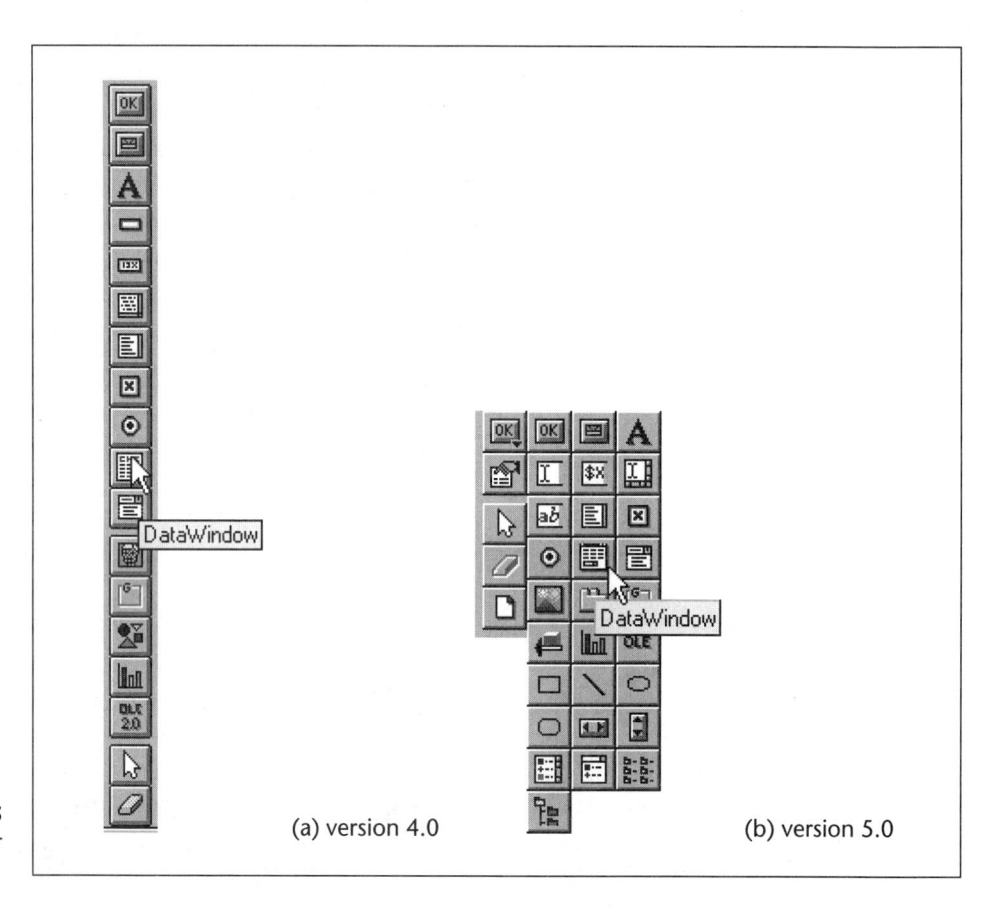

Figure 10.15
DataWindow button in the PainterBar

(a) version 4.0   (b) version 5.0

3 Click anywhere in the workspace. A square for the DataWindow control appears, as in Figure 10.16. Note that at this point, no DataWindow object has been associated with the control.

4 Drag the control's lower-right handle so that the control is wide enough to contain all the data from the DataWindow object created earlier in this chapter. Your window should look something like Figure 10.17 on page 231.

5 Drag the control so that it is approximately centered between the right and left edges of the window.

6 Double-click the control. If you are working with version 4.0, the Select DataWindow dialog box appears, containing the name of the DataWindow object that you created in the previous section of this chapter (see Figure 10.18 on page 232). Because there is currently only one DataWindow object, its name is highlighted when the dialog box is opened.

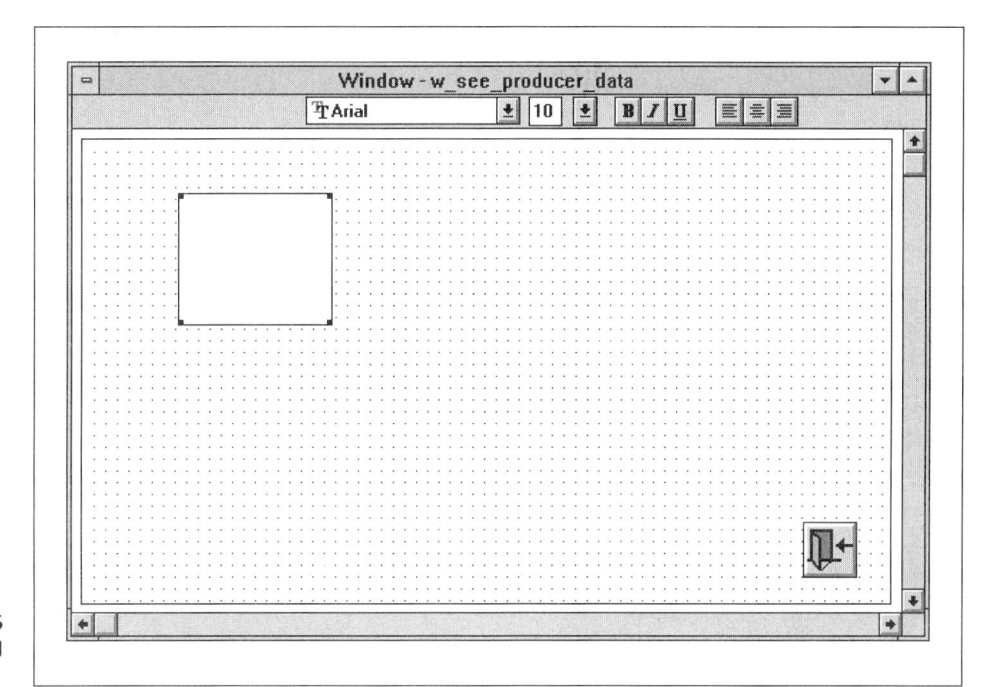

Figure 10.16
A new DataWindow control

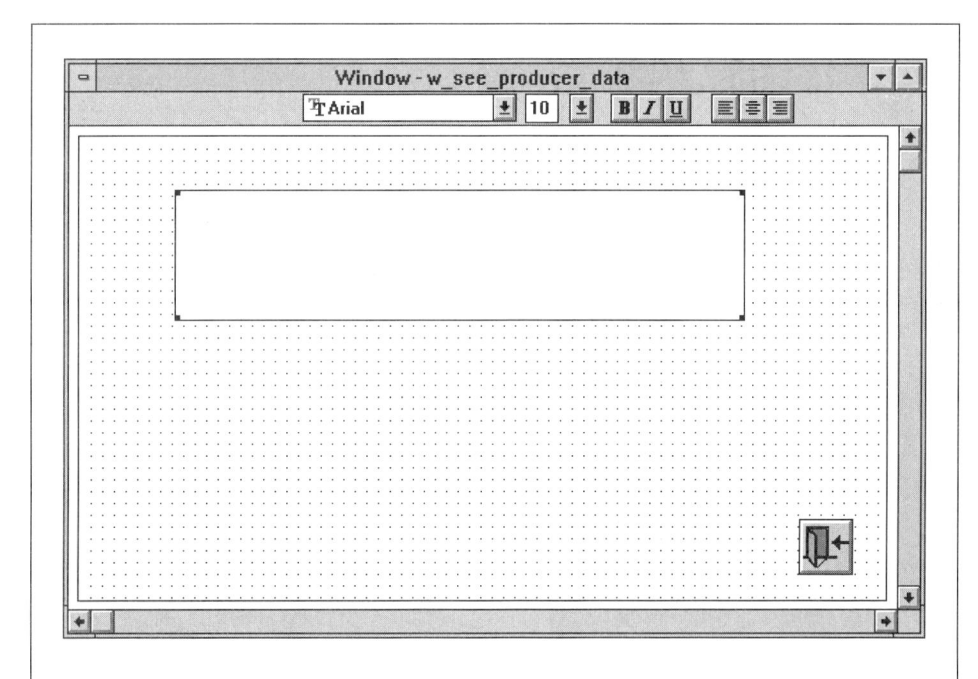

Figure 10.17
A DataWindow control after it has been enlarged

If you are working with version 5.0, double-clicking a DataWindow control opens the DataWindow properties dialog box (Figure 10.19 on page 232). To display the Select DataWindow dialog box, click the **Browse** button. In this particular example, the single DataWindow object will be highlighted.

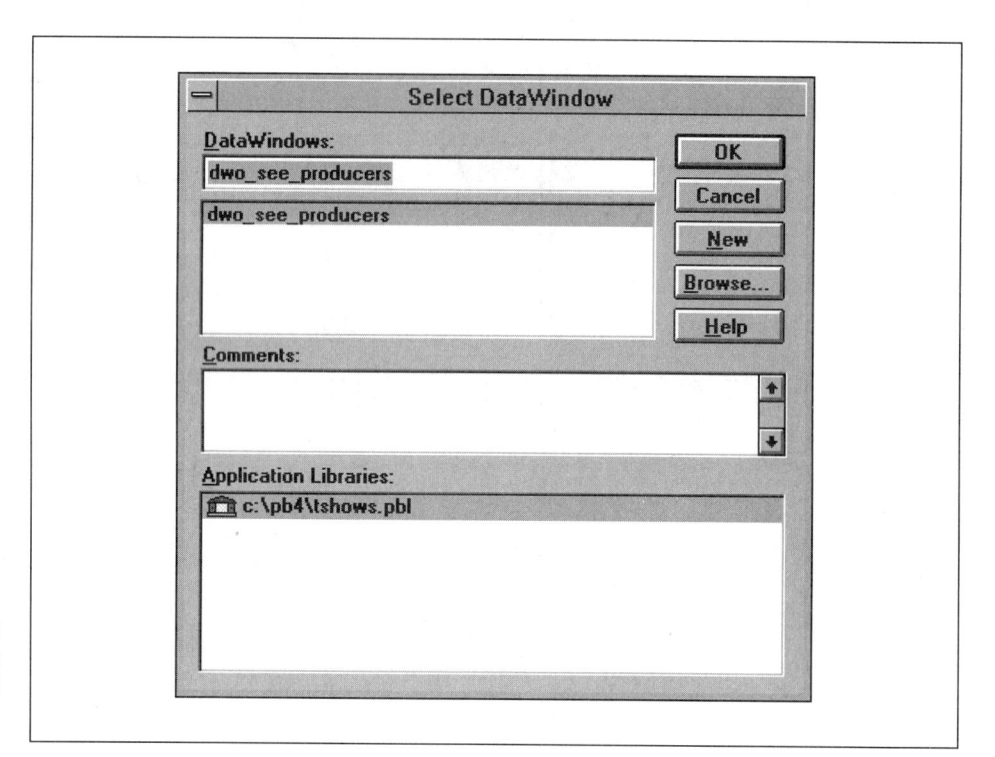

Figure 10.18
Choosing a DataWindow object to associate with a DataWindow control

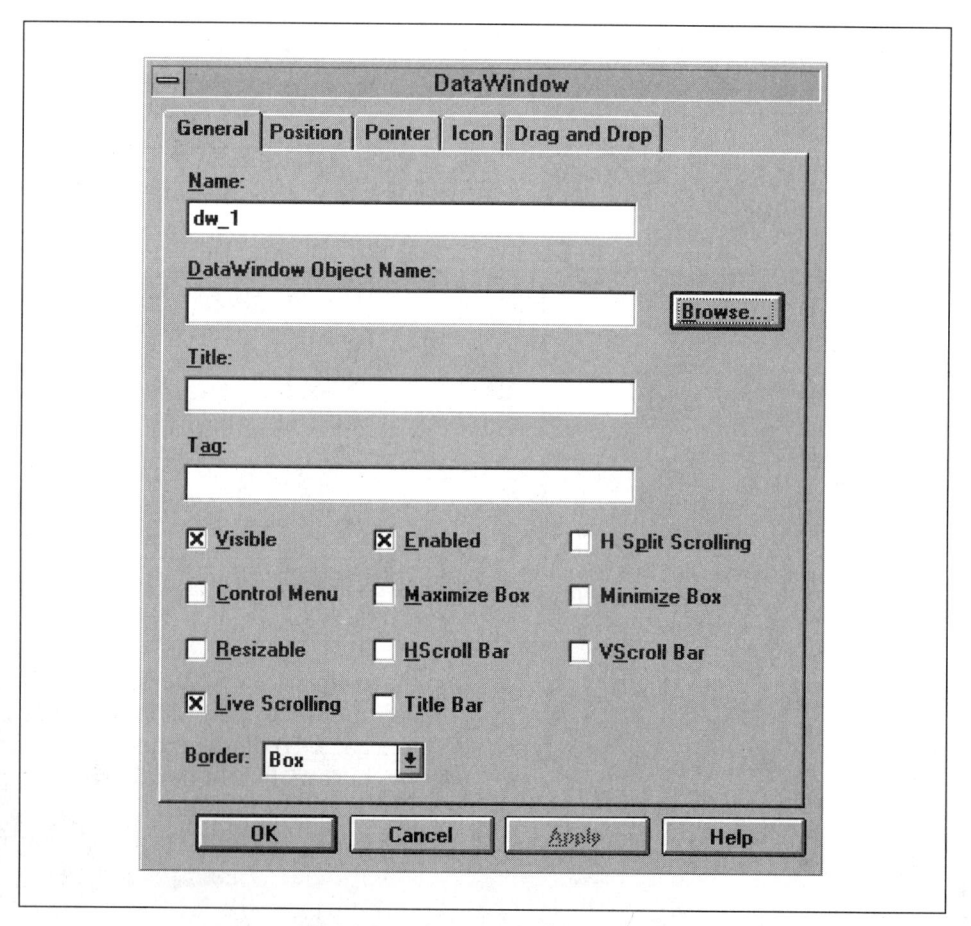

Figure 10.19
General DataWindow properties panel (5.0)

CHAPTER TEN INTRODUCING DATAWINDOWS **233**

7 Click the **OK** button to select the highlighted DataWindow object. If you are working with version 4.0, the DataWindow control dialog box appears with dwo_see_producers as part of its title.

If you are working with version 5.0, you are returned to the General panel of the DataWindow properties dialog box with dwo_see_producers inserted as the name of the DataWindow object.

8 Type **dw_see_producers** as the name of the control.

9 Click the **VScrollBar** check box to enable vertical scroll bars in the control. At this point, the version 4.0 dialog box should look like Figure 10.20. The version 5.0 should have the same characteristics.

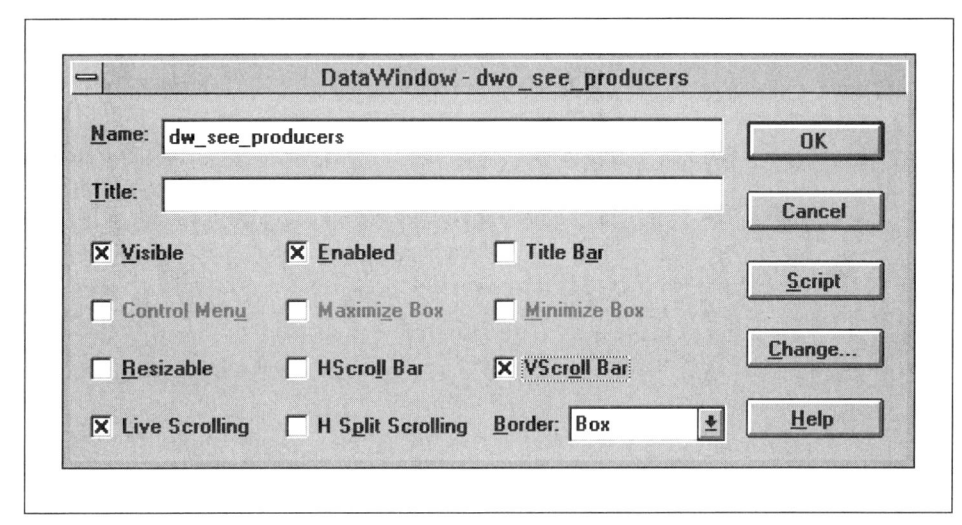

Figure 10.20
DataWindow control dialog box (4.0)

10 Click the **OK** button to return to the Window painter. PowerBuilder automatically fills in a sample of what your control will look like. Notice that the Edit format that you applied to the producer_phone column in the Database painter is used in this control.

11 If necessary, make the control wider so that the entire Producer Address can be seen. Make the control shorter so that barely two rows can be seen. This will cause a vertical scroll bar to appear at the right of the control.

If the vertical scroll bar doesn't appear, experiment with making the control taller and shorter until you find a size that does trigger the display of the scroll bar.

12 Resize the application window, moving the picture button as needed, so that the window appears similar to Figure 10.21 on page 234.

13 Preview the window so that you can see what the window will look like when it is used in the application. Don't worry if you don't see the scroll bar; it will show up when you run the application.

234 CHAPTER TEN INTRODUCING DATAWINDOWS

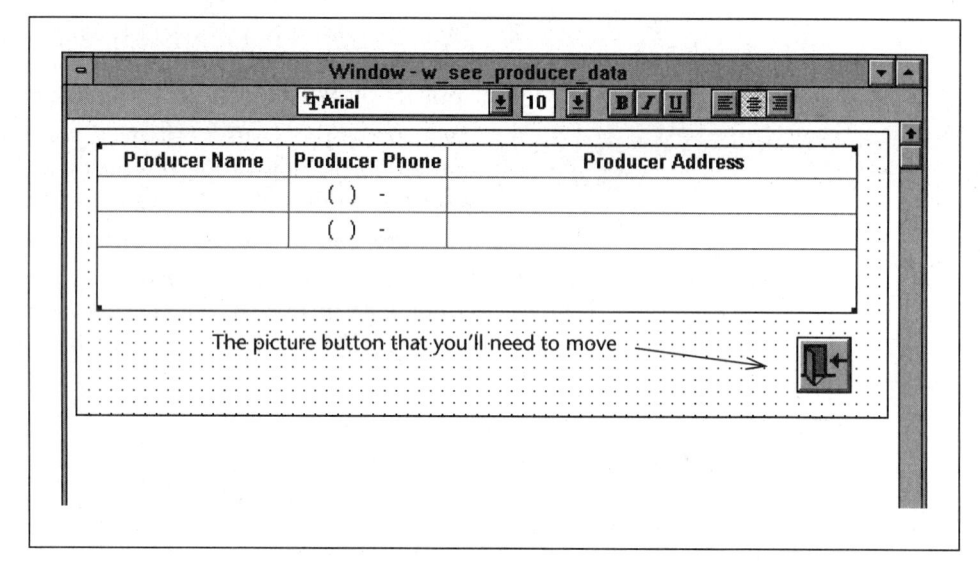

Figure 10.21
Visually completed
DataWindow control

Getting Data into a DataWindow Control

If you were to run the *tshows* application at this point, the DataWindow control would appear, but it wouldn't contain any data. It might help to understand why this is so if you think of a DataWindow object as something like the definition of a view.

A view doesn't store any data, but instead stores a query that can be executed to retrieve data. The query is executed when a SQL SELECT statement actually uses the view. By the same token, a DataWindow object stores the definition of a query. Data aren't retrieved by the query until something gives a command to execute the query. You will therefore need to add a script to the application window to associate the DataWindow control with a transaction object and to actually retrieve data.

The first decision you need to make is to decide where the script should be placed. When do you want the data retrieval to occur? In this case, data should be retrieved whenever the window on which the DataWindow control has been placed is opened. The script that you will write will therefore be triggered by the window's open event.

The script must do several things:

- Associate the DataWindow control with a transactions object using the `SetTransObject` function, which will be explained in more detail shortly.
- Execute the DataWindow's SQL query using the `Retrieve` function.
- Determine whether the query was successful. In this case, if the query retrieves one or more rows, then it was successful; if it retrieves no rows, then it is unsuccessful.
- If the query was unsuccessful, roll back the transaction.
- If the query was successful, commit the transaction and make the first row in the result table the current row using the `SetFocus` function. (This gives the row focus.) Optionally, the script can also choose an image to use as the pointer to the row that has focus with the `SetRowFocusIndicator` function.

It may seem strange that you need to commit or roll back a retrieval transaction. Certainly, no data data modifications need to be saved or undone. However, when you begin a transaction, a DBMS places locks on data as you retrieve it. In many DBMSs, such "read" locks allow other transactions to view the data while the locks are in place but prevent any transaction from modifying the data. Locks are held until a transaction ends. Therefore, even if a transaction doesn't modify data, you should explicitly end the transaction with a commit or rollback so the locks are released and other transactions can have access to the data for modification.

To enter and test the script:

1 Open the w_see_producer_data window in the Window painter.
2 Right-click in the window to display its popup menu.

Make sure you click in an area of the window that doesn't contain any controls. If you happen to right-click in a control, you'll get the control's popup menu rather than the window's popup menu.

3 Choose **Script** from the popup menu to enter the Script painter, which default's to the window's open event.
4 Type the script in Listing 10.1. (You'll learn exactly how this script works in the next section of this chapter.)

Listing 10.1
Script to retrieve data into a DataWindow object

```
// "constant" for no rows retrieved
int NO_ROWS = -1

// link to a transaction object
dw_see_producers.SetTransObject (SQLCA)

// issue a command to retrieve data into the DataWindow control
if dw_see_producers.Retrieve() = NO_ROWS then
  rollback using SQLCA;
  MessageBox ("Retrieve","Couldn't find any rows.")
else
  commit using SQLCA;
  // make DataWindow control active
  dw_see_producers.SetFocus()
  // set a hand as the indicator of the current row in the
  // DataWindow control
  dw_see_producers.SetRowFocusIndicator (Hand!)
end if
```

5 Double-click the Script painter control box to close it. PowerBuilder asks if you want to save your changes.
6 Click the **Yes** button. You are returned to the Window painter.
7 Click the **Run** button in the PowerBar. PowerBuilder asks if you want to save your changes.

8 Click the **Yes** button. PowerBuilder runs the application, hiding the development environment and displaying the application's opening screen.

9 Navigate through the application until you see the w_see_producer_data window. (*Hint*: Click the Scheduling button, followed by the Producers button and the View Producer Data button.)

10 Scroll the window to bring additional rows into view. Click in several rows to change the focus (the active row). As you click, the hand pointer moves to show you which row has focus (is active). If you scroll to the very end of the data, your screen will look something like Figure 10.22.

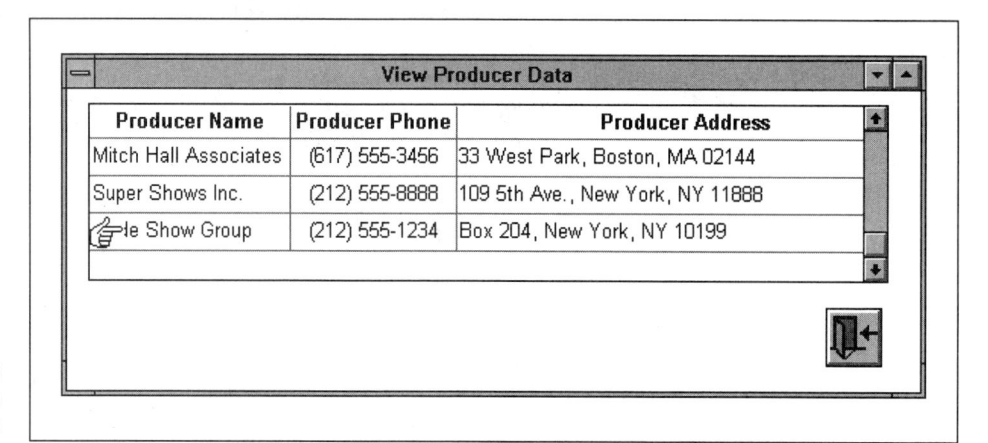

Figure 10.22
w_see_producer_data window in the running application

Although in this case the DataWindow control is being used to view data, it can also be used to modify data. You can click in any column of any row and change data as needed. However, the window has no scripts that perform data modification. You can therefore change data to your heart's content, but those changes won't be saved to the database.

NOTE

PowerBuilder has an additional painter called the Report painter. By default, its button doesn't appear in the PowerBar, although you can customize the PowerBar as discussed in Chapter 5 to include it. Reports are the same as DataWindows with one exception: they can't be updated. It is therefore up to you whether you want to use the Report painter or the DataWindow painter when creating layouts that are for data display only.

Understanding the Script

The script in Listing 10.1 uses four functions that have not been discussed in depth previously. In this section you will learn a bit more about each of those functions so that you will be able to write your own scripts.

SetTransObject   The purpose of the `SetTransObject` function is to associate a DataWindow with a database object. In other words, the SQL statement that defines the contents of a DataWindow needs to be able to determine which database it should use for its activities. That information happens to be stored in a database object. (This assumes, of course, that the application has properly initialized the transaction object.)

`SetTransObject` has the following general syntax:

dw_control_name.SetTransObject (*transaction_object_name*)

As occurs in Listing 10.1, the name of the DataWindow control is followed by a period and then the name of the function. The function's single parameter is the name of the transaction object. In most cases, this will be the default transaction object SQLCA.

Retrieve The Retrieve function is one of the functions a PowerBuilder application uses very heavily. Its purpose is to execute the SQL SELECT associated with a DataWindow. Whether it requires any input parameters depends on the way in which the SELECT was defined.

The DataWindow object you just created requires no input from the application or the user to execute. In other words, there are no variable parts of the query, no values that need to be entered for a WHERE clause. Retrieve therefore requires no parameters and has the following general syntax:

dw_control_name.Retrieve ()

Notice that although there are no parameters, the parentheses for the parameter list are still required.

You will be introduced to DataWindows that require parameters (known as arguments to PowerBuilder) in a Retrieve *function call in Chapter 11.*

Retrieve returns a long integer value to the script that called it. If the value is -1, then no rows were retrieved. Otherwise, the return value is equal to the number of rows found.

Where simple listings of data are concerned, an application only needs to determine whether *any* rows were retrieved. Therefore, the script in Listing 10.1 looks for the -1. If the call to the function returns -1, then the retrieve failed and the transaction is rolled back. Otherwise, the transaction is committed (it was successful).

If you are relatively new to computer programming, then the following syntax may seem a bit strange:

if dw_see_producers.Retrieve () = NO_ROWS then

The function call has been used as part of the logical expression in an if statement. In many high-level languages, it is legal to place an executable statement that produces some value (the function call) inside a logical expression. To evaluate this if, PowerBuilder first performs the Retrieve. The function's return value is then used in the logical expression that determines whether the if evaluates to TRUE or FALSE. In other words, when evaluating the if, PowerBuilder substitutes the function call's return value for the function call, after the actions of the function have been completed.

A script could certainly be written without embedding the call to Retrieve in the if. To do so, you might do something like the following:

```
long rows_retrieved
rows_retrieved = dw_see_producers.Retrieve()
if rows_retrieved = -1 then
```

These three lines, although functionally equivalent to embedding the function call in the `if` statement, have two drawbacks. First, they use extra memory for the variable that stores the number of rows retrieved. Second, they make the script longer. Most programmers therefore use the shorter version of the code wherever possible.

SetFocus   The purpose of the `SetFocus` function is to give some object or control focus. (Remember that when something has focus, it is the object, control, or data with which the application is currently working.) When applied to a multi-line control, such as the DataWindow control you just created, calling `SetFocus` gives focus to the first line in the control. This makes a great deal of sense to the user, who expects to view lists beginning with the first item in the list.

A call to `SetFocus` has the following general syntax:

object/control_name.SetFocus()

`SetFocus` takes no parameters. Nonetheless, the parentheses for a parameter list must be present so that PowerBuilder can distinguish between a function call and an attribute of the object.

SetRowFocusIndicator   The `SetRowFocusIndicator` function allows an application to choose the picture that PowerBuilder uses to indicate which row in a DataWindow control has focus. In its simplest form, it has the following general syntax:

dw_control_name.SetRowsFocusIndicator (*indicator_name*)

PowerBuilder provides four options for choosing the indicator's name:

- `Off!`: No indicator.
- `FocusRect!`: A dotted line rectangle appears around the row with focus.
- `Hand!`: A hand with a pointing index finger appears at the left of the row with focus.
- *picture_control*: A bitmapped image, named *picture_control* and present as a picture control somewhere on the application window, appears at the left of the row with focus.

Keep in mind that when you use one of the three first options as an input parameter, you must include the exclamation point. The exclamation point indicates that these values are part of an enumerated data type, a data type whose values are restricted to a set of values that are specified when the data type is defined. PowerBuilder associates each variable in an enumerated type with an integer. Programmers don't need to know the value of the integer; they can simply use the variable, which typically has a meaningful name that makes it easy to remember.

Overriding Edit Formats

The edit formats that you set for many columns using the Database painter establish default formats for columns when they first appear in the DataWindow painter. However, you can override the formats whenever necessary. As an example, you will next create a DataWindow object to view data from the Shows table.

To create and use the DataWindow object:

1. Click the **DataWindow** button in the PowerBar. The Select DataWindow dialog box appears.
2. Click the **New** button. The New DataWindow dialog box appears.
3. Click **Quick Select** as the data source and **Grid** as the presentation style.
4. Click the **OK** button. The Quick Select dialog box appears.
5. Click the **Shows** table. Choose all three columns in the table. Sort the query on the show_name column.
6. Click the **OK** button. The DataWindow painter appears. Notice in Figure 10.23 that the Platform column displays the radio buttons that were established for the column in the Database painter. Because this DataWindow will be used to view data rather than modify it, the radio buttons are inappropriate. In fact, you might even consider them a hindrance since they take up space that might be used to view multiple lines of data.

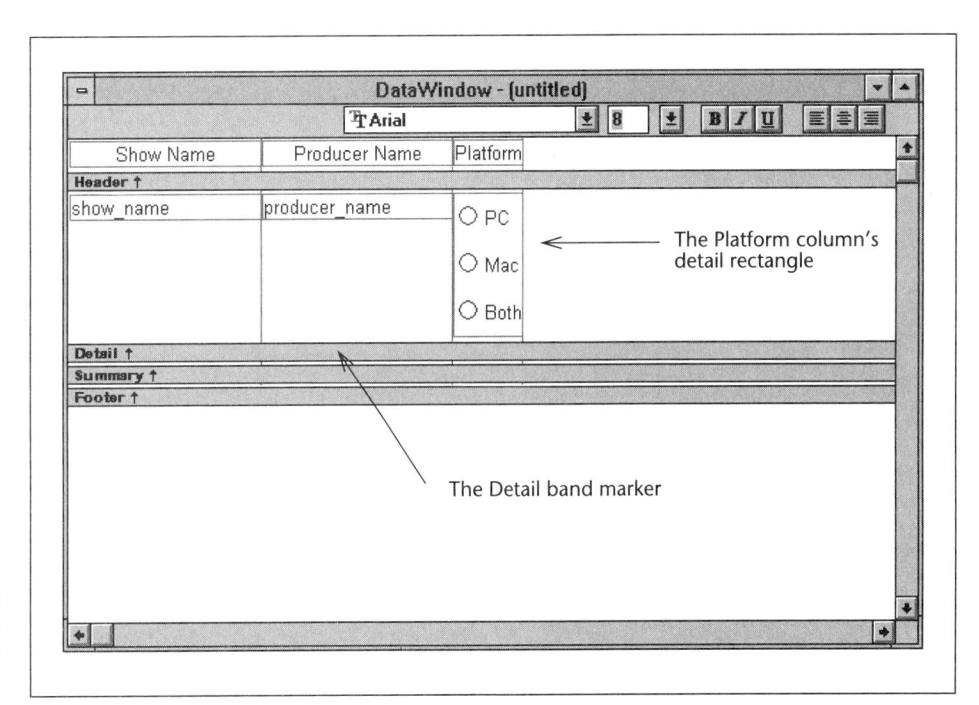

Figure 10.23
Radio button formatting in the DataWindow painter

7 Drag the detail band marker down about a half inch, leaving space at the below the Platform column's detail rectangle. (See Figure 10.23 for the location of both the detail band marker and the Platform column's detail rectangle.) This will make is easier to work with the rectangle. Notice that as you drag the band marker down, the other band markers move as well, maintain the current size of each band.

8 Right-click on the **Platform** rectangle in the detail band to display its popup menu.

9 If you are working with version 4.0, choose **Edit Styles** to display a submenu listing the types of available edit styles (Figure 10.24). Notice the check mark that indicates that the column is currently formatted as radio buttons.

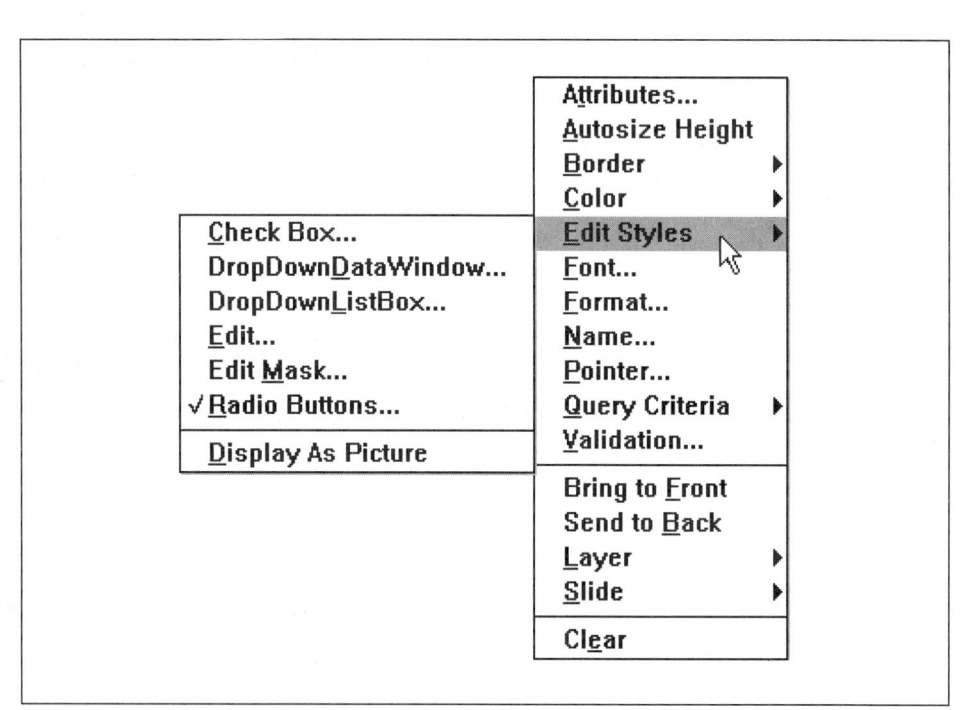

Figure 10.24
Detail column popup menu (4.0)

If you are working with version 5.0, double-click the **Platform** rectangle to display the Column Object properties dialog box. Click the **Edit** tab to display the Edit panel (Figure 10.25 on page 241).

10 If you are working with version 4.0, choose **Edit** from the submenu. As you will remember from Chapter 8, this is the default edit style for a column, which presents data in an editable rectangle. The Edit Style dialog box appears.

If you are working with version 5.0, choose **Edit** from the Style dropdown menu. The contents of the panel changes to show the default Edit style characteristics.

11 Click the **OK** button to accept the new edit style and close the dialog box. The DataWindow painter will now look like Figure 10.26 on page 241.

CHAPTER TEN INTRODUCING DATAWINDOWS **241**

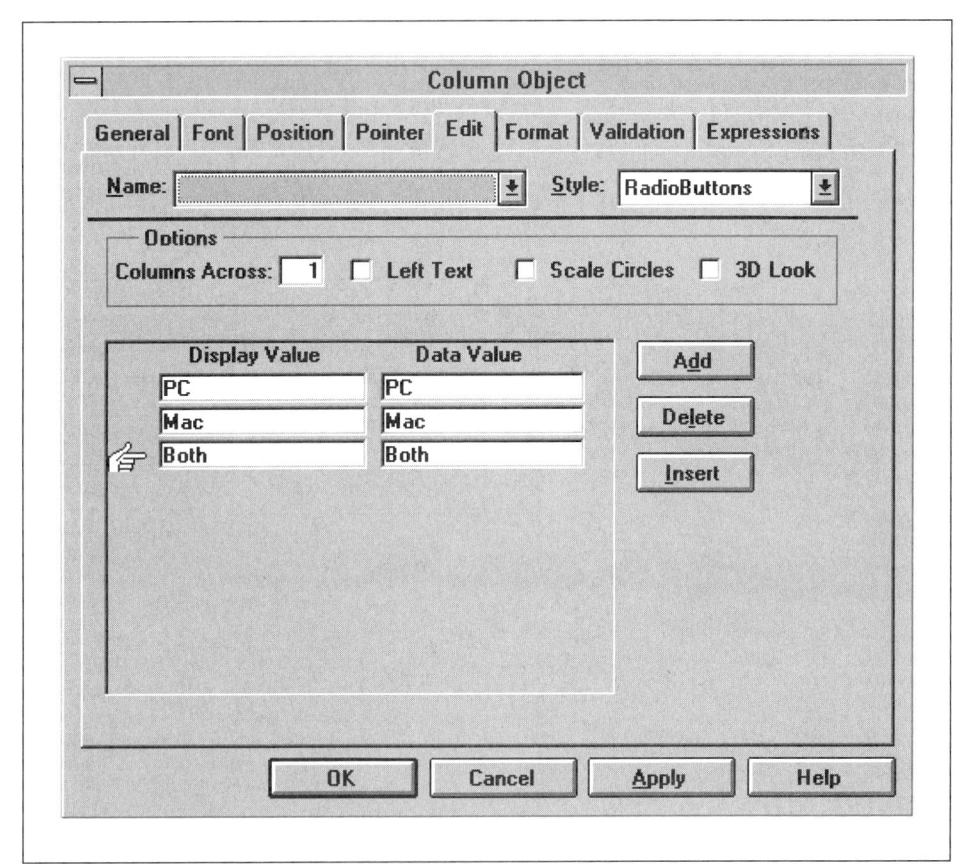

Figure 10.25
Edit panel of the Column Object properties dialog box (5.0)

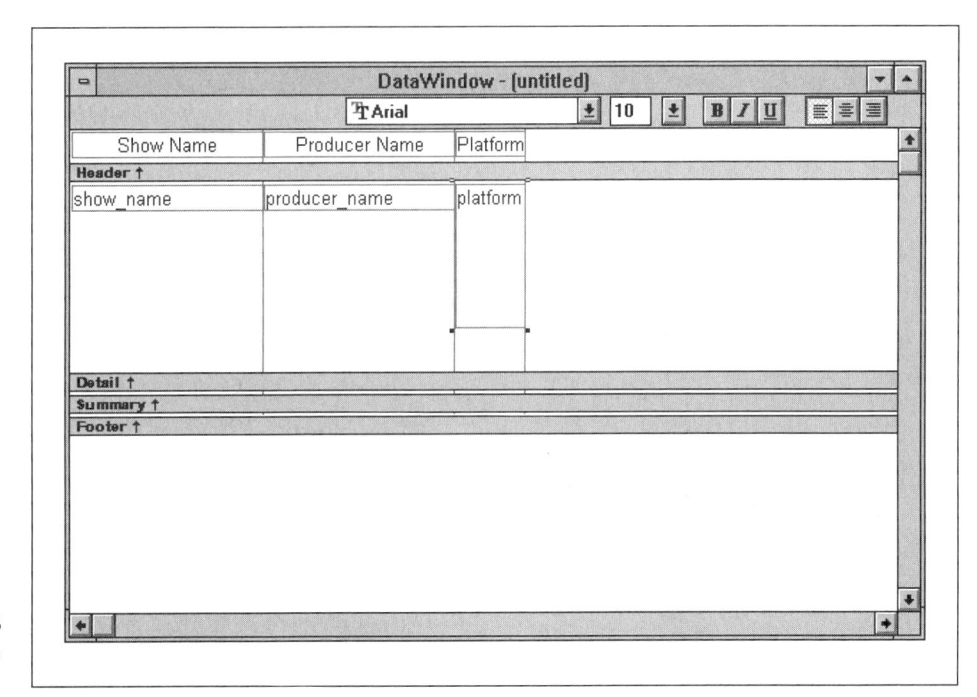

Figure 10.26
Reformatted detail column

12. Drag the bottom of the platform rectangle up until the rectangle is the same height as the show_name and producer_name rectangles.
13. The height of the detail band determines how much space each row will occupy in the DataWindow. There is currently too much space in the detail band. To make it smaller, drag the Detail band marker up until it is just under the rectangles in the band, as in Figure 10.27.

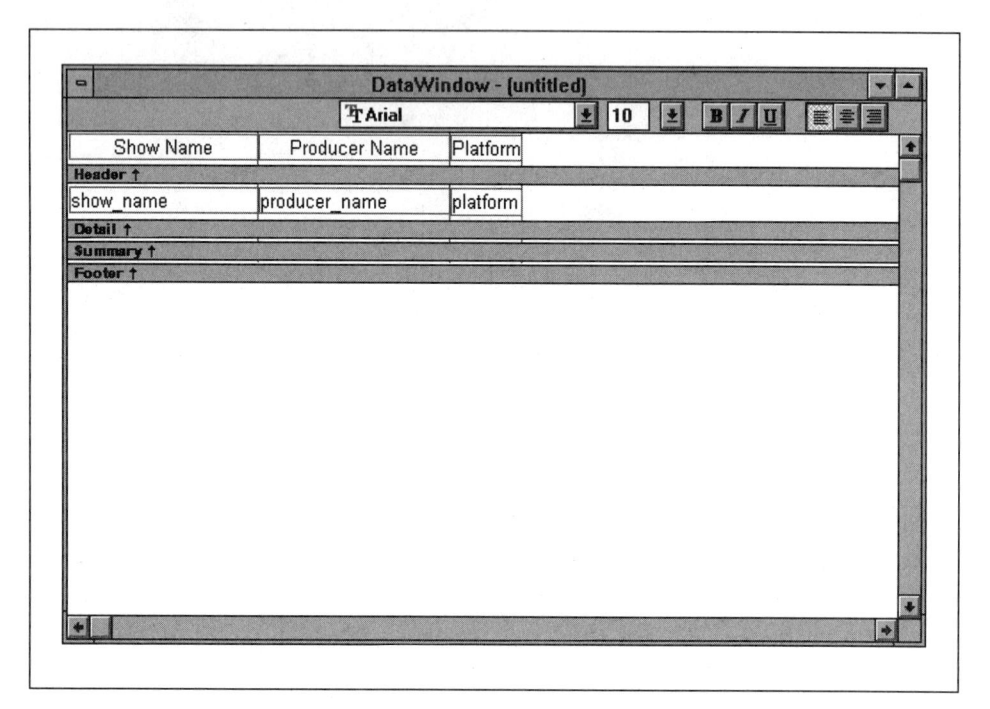

Figure 10.27
The resized detail band

14. Preview the DataWindow object to make sure that your columns are wide enough to display all of their data. Adjust column widths if necessary.
15. Save the DataWindow object as **dwo_see_shows**.
16. Place a DataWindow control based on dwo_see_shows on w_see_show_data. Name the control **dw_see_shows**. Give it a vertical scroll bar. Resize the control and window so that the window looks something like Figure 10.28 on page 243.

Copying a Script

As you know, the final step in making data appear is to write a script that retrieves the data. In this case, the script will be almost identical to that in Listing 10.1. The only difference will be the name of the DataWindow control. It therefore will save you the effort of retyping code if you can copy the script from w_see_producer_data to w_see_show_data and then simply change the name of the control.

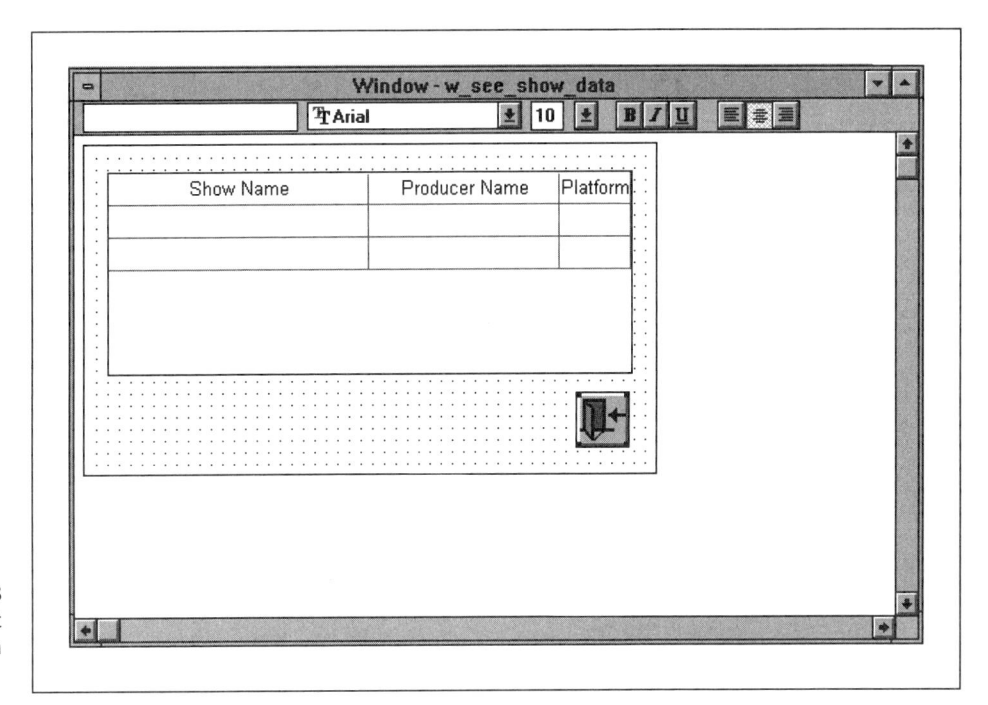

Figure 10.28
Completed window to list show data

To copy the script from one window to another:

1. Open the w_see_producer_data window. (You needn't close the w_see_show_data window if it is already open.)
2. Enter the Script painter and make sure you are looking at the open event script.
3. Drag the pointer with the right mouse button depressed across the entire script to select it, or click the **Select All** button in the PainterBar.
4. Click the **Copy** button in the PainterBar, as in Figure 10.29 on page 244.
5. Exit the Script painter.
6. Close w_see_producer_data.
7. If w_see_show_data isn't currently visible, choose its name from the Window menu.
8. Enter the Script painter for w_see_show_data.
9. Click the **Paste** button in the PainterBar (Figure 10.30 on page 244). The script appears in the Script painter workspace.
10. Modify the script, replacing "dw_see_producers" with **dw_see_shows**.
11. Save the script.
12. Run the application to make sure that your script works properly.

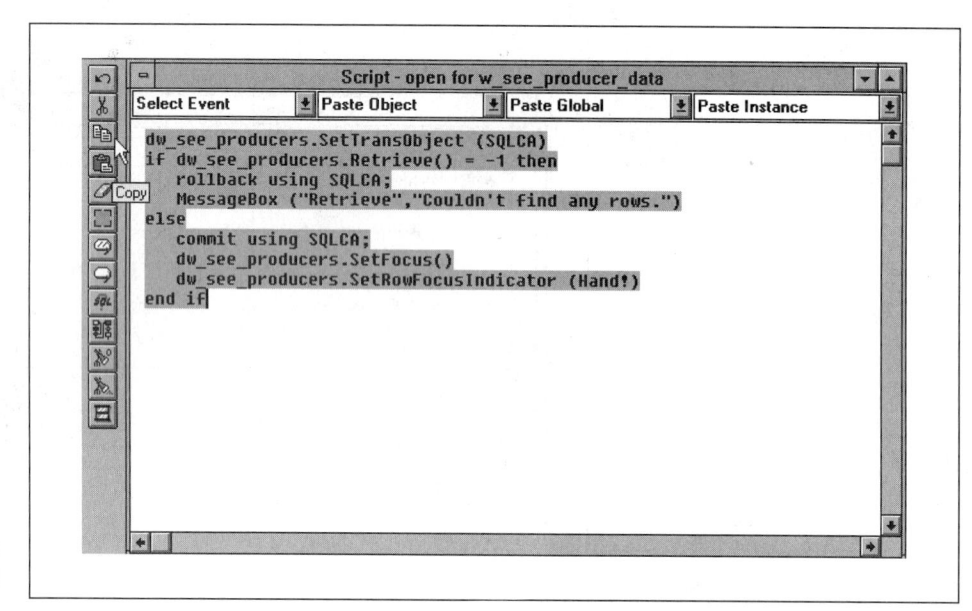

Figure 10.29
Copying a script

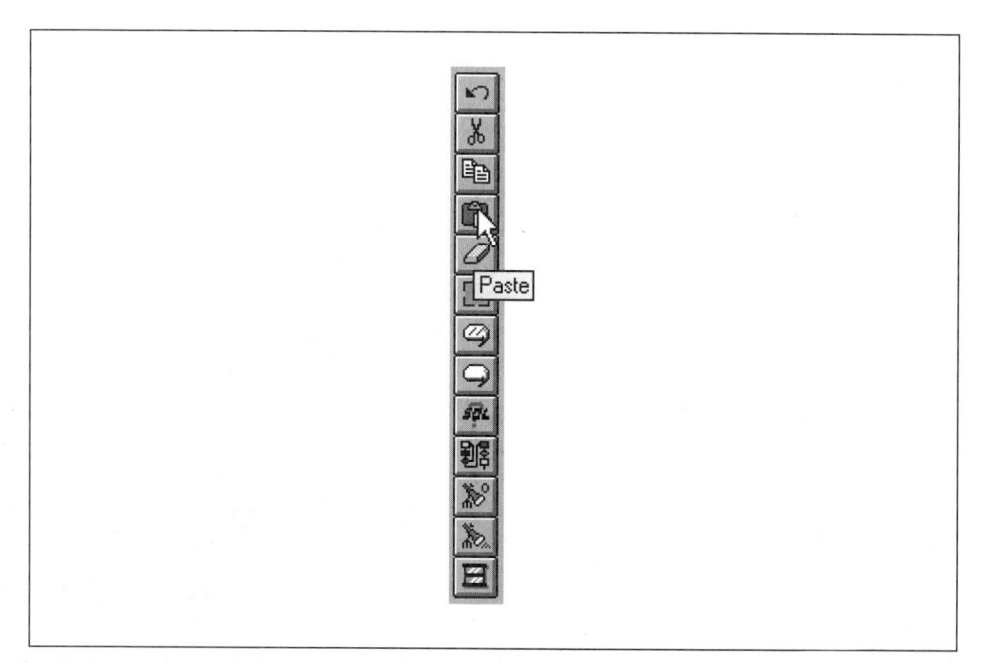

Figure 10.30
Paste button in the PainterBar

Basic Computed Fields and Duplicate Suppression

One of the things that users typically want to do with data stored in a database is to perform computations on that data. Such computations might sum quantities, increase a date by a fixed value, count the number of rows in a group, or concatenate two strings together. The result of the computations are for display only; the results aren't stored in the database.

PowerBuilder provides two ways of performing computations. One is to include the computation in the SQL Select on which a DataWindow object is built. In that case, the computations are performed by the database server when data are retrieved to populate a DataWindow control.

The alternative is to define the calculations in the DataWindow painter. Because such calculations are part of PowerBuilder, they are performed on the client workstation—not on the server—and can therefore be updated as data in the DataWindow control are changed by the user. (You will see exactly how this works in Chapter 14.)

Calculations that you define in the DataWindow painter are known as *computed fields*. The expressions that define the contents of a computed field can contain column names, arithmetic and logical operators, and DataWindow painter functions.

The DataWindow painter functions are separate from the PowerScript functions, although many DataWindow painter functions have analogs in the PowerScript function set. Nonetheless, you shouldn't assume that every PowerScript function is available in the DataWindow painter. In addition, some functions that perform actions in both sets of functions have separate names. Consult the Function Reference manual or PowerBuilder Help when you need more information about function syntax.

You will see many examples of computed fields throughout this book. However, to provide an introduction to them, you will complete a window that projects costs based on a fixed increase factor. As you work, you will also create a DataWindow object based on more than one table and learn to suppress the display of unnecessary repeating values.

Specifying a Quick Select with a Join

To create the projection of increased costs, you begin by specifying the query that will define the data in the DataWindow.

To specify the query needed to define the data in the DataWindow:

1   Click the **DataWindow** button in the PowerBar.
2   Create a new DataWindow object.
3   Choose the **Quick Select** data source and the **Tabular** presentation style.
4   In the Quick Select dialog box, choose the **Costs** and the **Calendar** tables. Because these tables are related by a primary key/foreign key, PowerBuilder automatically joins them. In this case, the join is based on the event number column, even though you haven't selected that column for display in the DataWindow.
5   Choose the following columns: **calendar.show_name**, **calendar.start_date**, **costs.cost_description**, and **costs.amount**.
6   Choose an ascending sort by Show Name and Start Date.
7   Click the **OK** button to enter the DataWindow painter.

Suppressing Duplicate Values

At this point, you can modify the appearance of the DataWindow:

1. Change the edit style of the cost_description column from DropDown-ListBox to **Edit**. (*Hint:* When the Edit dialog box or Edit panel is visible, make sure you remove the X from the Use Code Table check box.)
2. Preview the window. Notice that the show name and starting date repeat for each row that represents a cost for a given scheduled show.
3. Return to the DataWindow painter.
4. Choose **Rows -> Suppress Repeating Values**. The Specify Repeating Value Suppression List dialog box appears.
5. Drag **calendar_show_name** and **calendar_start_date** from the Source Data list to the Suppression List, as in Figure 10.31.

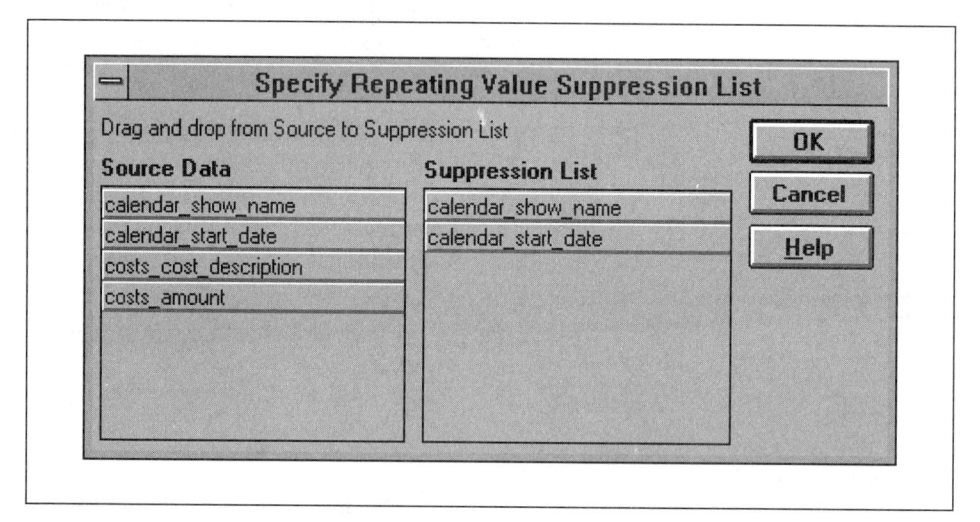

Figure 10.31
Specifying columns for duplicate suppression

6. Preview the window once more to see the effect of your changes.

Adding the Computed Field

For this example, you will be adding a computed field that shows what each cost would be if it were to increase by 10%. The computation will become part of the detail band, performed for each row in the DataWindow.

To create the computed field:

1. Click the **Compute** button in the PainterBar (Figure 10.32 on page 247) or, if the Compute button isn't present in the PainterBar, choose **Objects->Computed Field**.
2. Click in the detail band to the right of the amount rectangle. This determines the initial placement of the computed field.

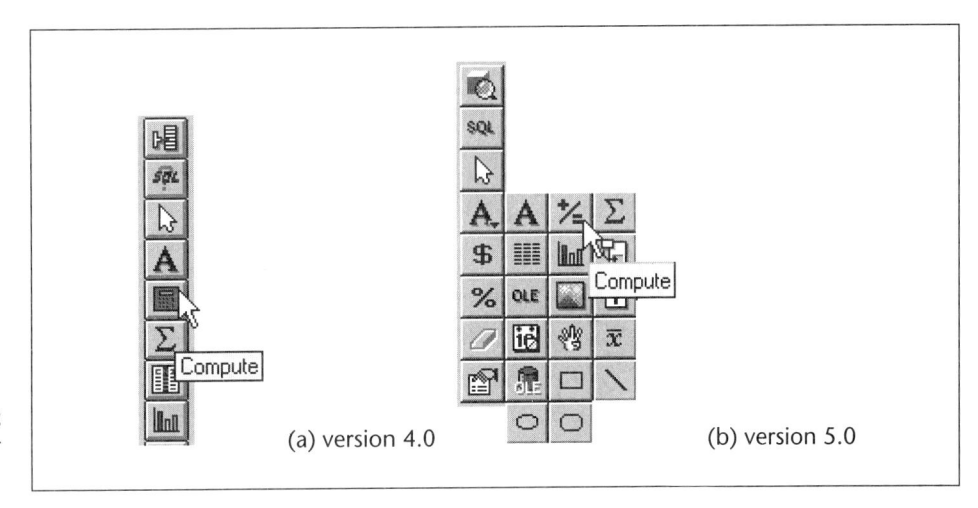

Figure 10.32
Compute button in the PainterBar

(a) version 4.0   (b) version 5.0

3   If you are working with version 4.0, the Computed Field Definition dialog box appears (Figure 10.33). This dialog box has a large edit box where you can type the expression that defines the value to be displayed in the computed field. Alternatively, you can use the buttons, functions, and columns below to create the expression.

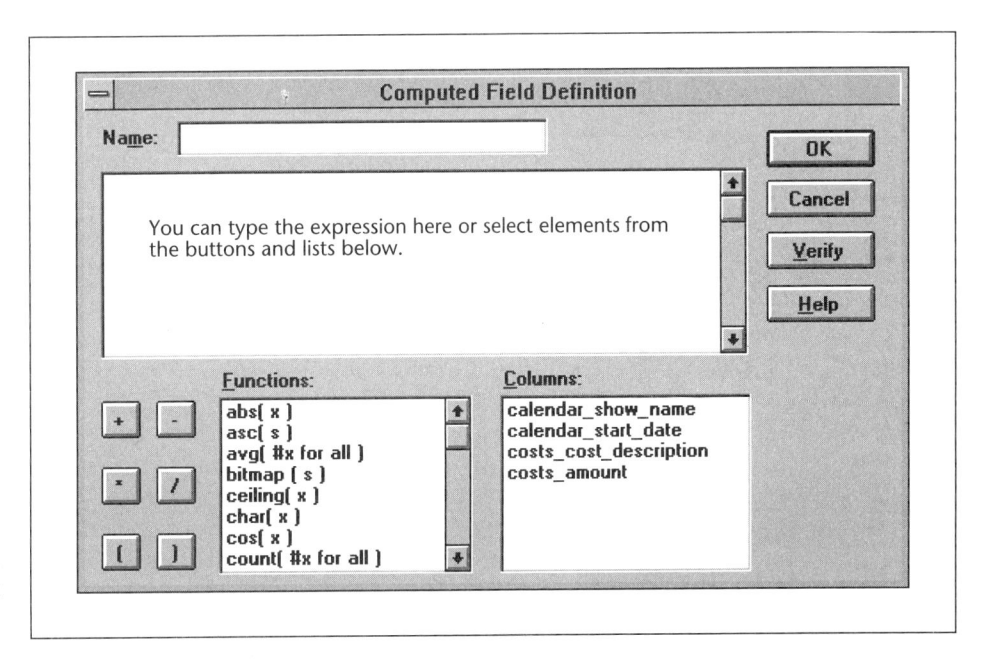

Figure 10.33
Computed Field Definition dialog box

If you are working with version 5.0, clicking in the detail band opens the Computed Object properties dialog box (Figure 10.34 on page 248). Click the **More** button to display the Computed Field Definition dialog box.

4   Type **percent_increase** as the name of the computed field.

5   Click **costs_amount** in the Columns list. The column name is transfered to the expression.

248 CHAPTER TEN INTRODUCING DATAWINDOWS

Figure 10.34
Computed Object properties dialog box (5.0)

6 Click the ***** button. The multiplication operator is transfered to the expression.

7 Type **1.1** in the expression. The completed expression should read:

```
costs_amount * 1.1
```

8 Click the **OK** button to close the Computed Field Definition dialog box. A rectangle for the computed field appears in the detail band. If you are working with version 4.0, are are now working with the DataWindow painter. If you are using version 5.0, the Computed Object properties dialog box is still visible.

9 If you are working with version 4.0, right-click the computed field rectangle to display its popup menu. Choose **Format** from the popup menu. The Display Number Formats dialog box appears.

If you are working with version 5.0, click the **Format** tab at the top of the dialog box. The Format panel appears.

10 Highlight the format shown in Figure 10.35 on page 249.

11 Click the **OK** button to close the dialog box.

12 Click the **right alignment** button in the Style Bar.

13 Make the rectangle slightly wider. (Depending on the size of your monitor, you may have to scroll the window a bit to do this.)

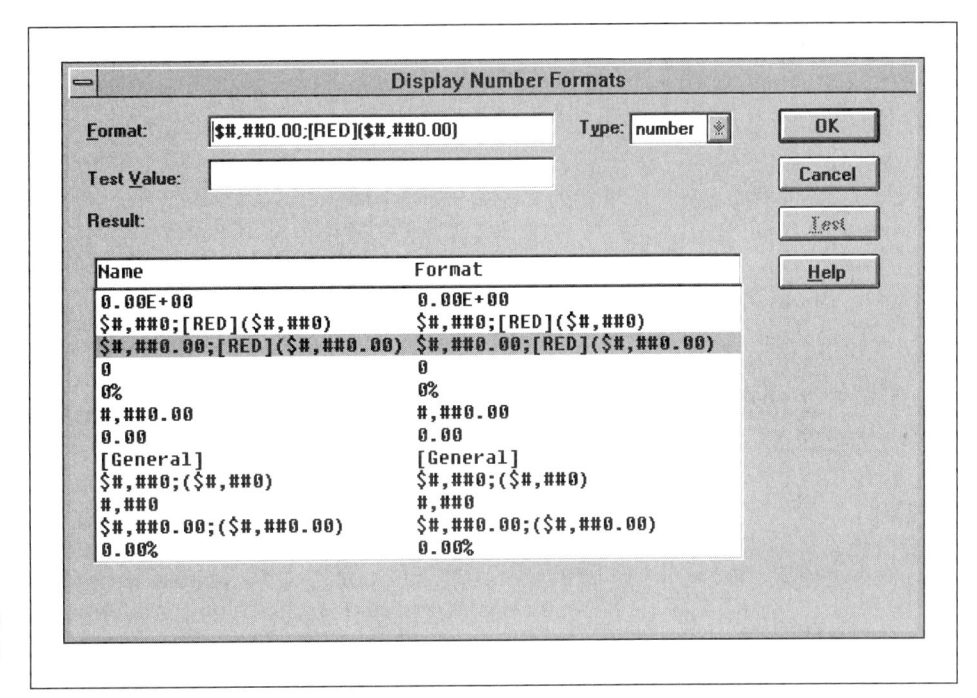

Figure 10.35
Display Number Formats dialog box

14 Click the **static text** button in the PainterBar (the button that looks like the letter A).

15 Click in the header band above the computed field. A text rectangle containing the word "text" appears.

16 Replace the default "text" in the Style Bar with **Plus 10%**.

17 Drag the text rectangle so that it is above the computed field.

To move a rectangle approximately one pixel at a time, press the arrow key that corresponds to the direction in which you want the rectangle to move.

18 Save the DataWindow object as **dwo_increased_costs**.

Placing the DataWindow Control

As you know, the final task in making this listing a part of a PowerBuilder application is to place a DataWindow control on an application window and associate it with the DataWindow object. You will then need to write scripts to associate the control with a transaction object and to retrieve data.

To complete the window:

1 Open the w_increased_costs window.

2 Place a DataWindow control in the window.

3 Associate the control with dwo_increased_costs. Name the control **dw_increased_costs**. Give it both vertical and horizontal scroll bars.

4 Enter the script in Listing 10.2 for the window's open event.

5 Run the application to test the newly completed listing.

Listing 10.2
Open event script for w_increased_costs

```
dw_increased_costs.SetTransObject (sqlca)

if dw_increased_costs.Retrieve() = -1 then
   rollback using sqlca;
   MessageBox ("Retrieve", "Couldn't retrieve any rows.")
else
   commit using sqlca;
end if
```

Looking Ahead

In this chapter you've had your first experience with using a PowerBuilder application to retrieve and display data stored in a database. You've also learned to compute and display values based on stored data. To make DataWindow controls function, you've written scripts that retrieve data, check the result of the retrieval, and modify the pointer that PowerBuilder uses to indicate the currently active row.

At this point, you're ready to learn more about creating the queries that underlie DataWindow. In Chapter 11 you will learn to develop a variety of complex queries, including those that require arguments and those that are too complex for PowerBuilder's tools.

EXERCISES

The following exercises will give you an opportunity to practice creating DataWindow objects based on simple Quick Selects. You will then create DataWindow controls from those objects and place them on application windows. You'll write the scripts needed to retrieve data into the DataWindow controls, so that you can become comfortable with the way in which PowerBuilder application data retrieval and display is performed.

1. Create a simple listing window that displays all types of merchandise in alphabetical order by merchandise description.
2. Create a simple listing window that displays all merchandise items.
3. Create a simple listing window that displays all schools.
4. Create a simple listing window that displays all customers.
5. Create a listing that displays schools and the dorms at those schools. Use duplicate suppression to stop the display of duplicate school names.
6. Create a listing that displays types of merchandise and items of merchandise owned by College and University Rentals. Use duplicate suppression to stop the display of duplicate merchandise descriptions.
7. Modify the listing of merchandise items to include two computed fields—one for the semester and one for the year—that show what the rental fees would be if the fees were to include a $3.00 service charge for each rental.

Chapter Eleven

DataWindows and Queries

IN THIS CHAPTER YOU WILL:

- Use the Select painter to create queries on which DataWindow objects are based
- Create DataWindows that require arguments
- Add summary calculations
- Use response windows to gather needed values from users
- Create queries for DataWindows that are too complex for the Select painter

The DataWindow objects that you have created to this point have been based on SQL queries that can be completely specified without user input. Although this is satisfactory for straight-forward listings, it isn't sufficient to meet many application requirements. In this chapter, for example, you will be completing the portion of the *tshows* application that displays the costs incurred while attending a single trade show. The user needs to be able to choose the show that he or she wishes to view. That choice then needs to be used as input to the Retrieve function that provides data for display.

In this chapter you will learn how to use the Select Painter to create SQL queries that accept outside values as retrieval arguments and to compute summary values with a DataWindow object. You will also learn to create response windows that can be used to collect input from a user, input which, in turn, can be passed to a DataWindow control. Finally, you will learn how to input the SQL query on which a DataWindow is based directly, so you can enter queries that the SQL ToolBox can't handle.

DataWindows and the Select Painter

The Select painter is very similar to the View painter you learned to use in Chapter 7. As you will see shortly, it provides the same SQL Toolbox for specifying the parts of a query. This means that you already know most of what you need to generate the basic structure of the SQL SELECT.

Beginning the Select

The first step in the process of working with a DataWindow that accepts arguments is to create a DataWindow object.

To create a DataWindow object that requires an argument:

1. Make sure that you are working with the *tshows* application in *tshows2.pbl* and that you are connected to the *tshows* database.
2. Click the **DataWindow** button in the PowerBar. The Select DataWindow dialog box appears.
3. Click the **New** button. The New DataWindow dialog box appears.
4. Choose **SQL Select** as the data source. Then, choose **Tabular** as the presentation style.
5. Click the **OK** button. The Select Tables dialog box appears.
6. Double-click the **Costs** table.
7. Click the **Cancel** button to dismiss the Select Tables dialog box. The Select painter appears, as in Figure 11.1 on page 253.
8. Click the **cost_description** and **amount** columns to select them both for display in the DataWindow.

NOTE: You will need to use the event# column to choose rows from the Costs table. However, there is no reason that the user needs to see these arbitrary identification numbers.

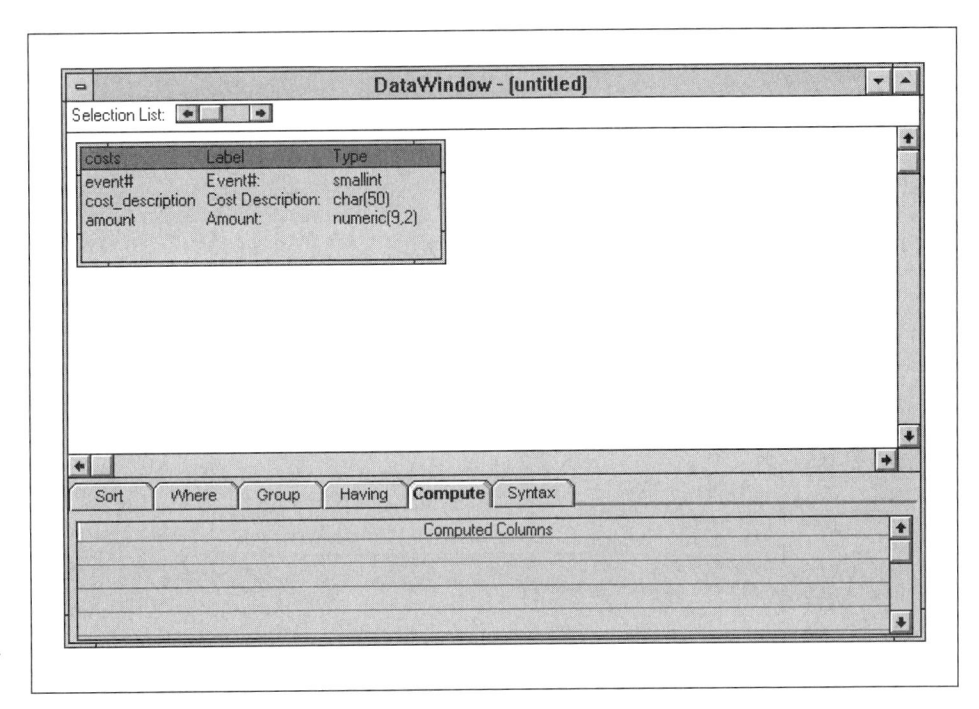

Figure 11.1
Select Painter

Creating an Input Argument

The next step is to create an input argument and use it in a WHERE clause. For this particular query, we want to select rows based on a single event#. (As you'll see when we create the response box, the user will never see the event#, even though it's being used by the application.)

The general process is to first create the argument—much like you would define a variable—and then to place it in the WHERE clause as a placeholder for data that will be passed to the DataWindow object by the `Retrieve` function.

To create and use the argument:

1 Choose **Objects -> Retrieval Arguments**. The Specify Retrieval Arguments dialog box appears (Figure 11.2 on page 254).

There are two very important features to notice about the Specify Retrieval Arguments dialog box. First, keep in mind that there is theoretically no limit to the number of arguments that you can use in a query. PowerBuilder numbers those arguments based on their position in the list in this dialog box. When arguments are placed in the `Retrieve` function's parameter list, PowerBuilder associates the parameters with the arguments based on position. In other words, data passed as the first parameter are plugged into the first argument, data passed as the second parameter are plugged into the second argument, and so on. It is up to you as a programmer to make sure that you place values in the right order in the function's parameter list.

Second, the dialog box has a place for you to give each argument a name and data type. Argument names are very much like variable names, in that they act as placeholders for data. The data type that you assign to an argument will be verified against the type of data being passed to the query. They must match.

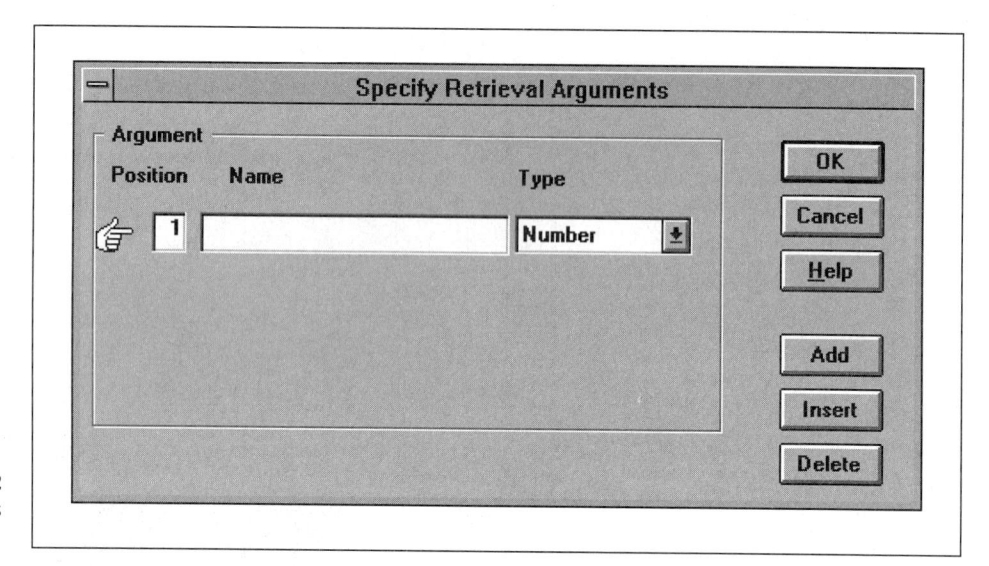

Figure 11.2
Specifying retrieval arguments

2. Type **a_event_numb** as the name of the argument.
3. Make sure its data type is Number.
4. Click the **OK** button. The argument has now been stored as part of the DataWindow object.
5. Click the **Where** tab in the SQL Toolbox.
6. Choose **"costs"."event#"** in the first row under the Column header.

If you don't want PowerBuilder to require double quotation marks around table and column names in SQL statements, change the DelimitIdentifier line in the PBOB040.INI file so that it reads:

DelimitIdentifer = 'NO'

7. Accept = as the operator.
8. Right-click in the first row under the Value header. The Value popup menu appears (Figure 11.3).

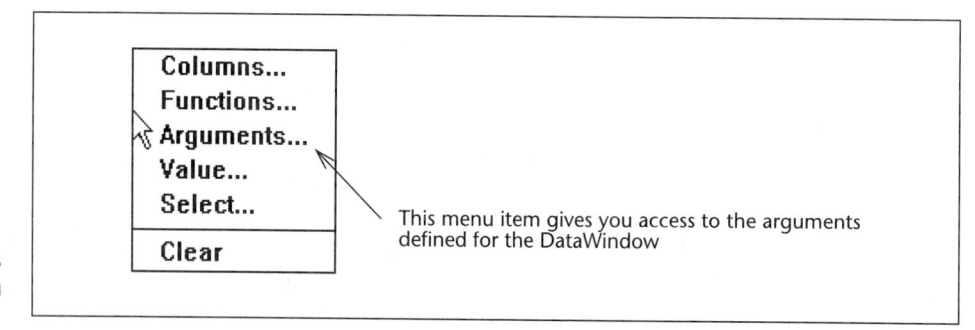

Figure 11.3
Value popup menu

9. Choose **Arguments** from the popup menu (see Figure 11.3). A list of all arguments defined for the DataWindow object appears, as in Figure 11.4 on page 255.

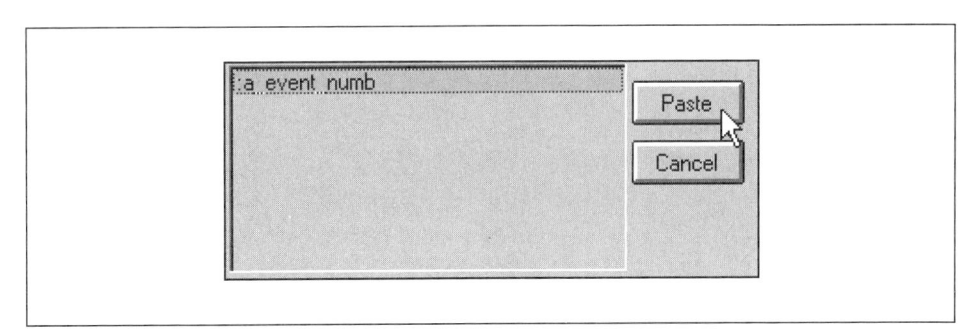

Figure 11.4
List of defined arguments

10 If necessary, click **a_event_numb** to highlight it.

11 Click the **Paste** button. PowerBuilder copies the argument into the WHERE clause. The completed WHERE clause should look like Figure 11.5.

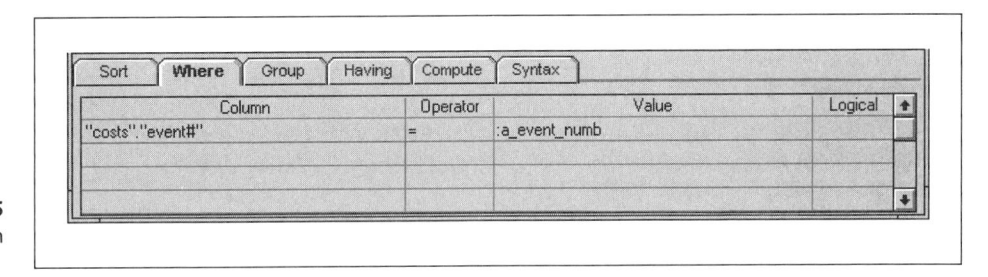

Figure 11.5
Complete WHERE clause specification

12 Click the **Design** button in the PainterBar to switch to the DataWindow painter. (*Hint:* It's the bottom button.)

Modifying the Formatting

When you switch to the DataWindow painter, you will see the default formatting for the columns that was applied in the Database Painter. Although a dropdown list works well when entering cost descriptions, it isn't appropriate for a listing.

To adjust the formatting of the DataWindow Object:

1 If you are working with version 4.0, right-click the **cost_description** rectangle in the detail band to display its popup menu. Choose **Edit Styles** -> **Edit** from the popup menu. The Edit dialog box appears. Click the **OK** button to accept the edit style, removing the DropDownListBox edit style just for this DataWindow.

If you are working with version 5.0, double-click in the **cost_description** rectangle. The Column Object properties dialog box appears. Click the **Edit** tab to display the Edit Format panel. Choose **Edit** from the Style dropdown menu. Click the **OK** button to close the dialog box to save the change.

2 Preview the DataWindow object. PowerBuilder prompts you to enter a value for the query's retrieval argument.

3 Type **2** (see Figure 11.6 on page 256).

256 CHAPTER ELEVEN DATAWINDOWS AND QUERIES

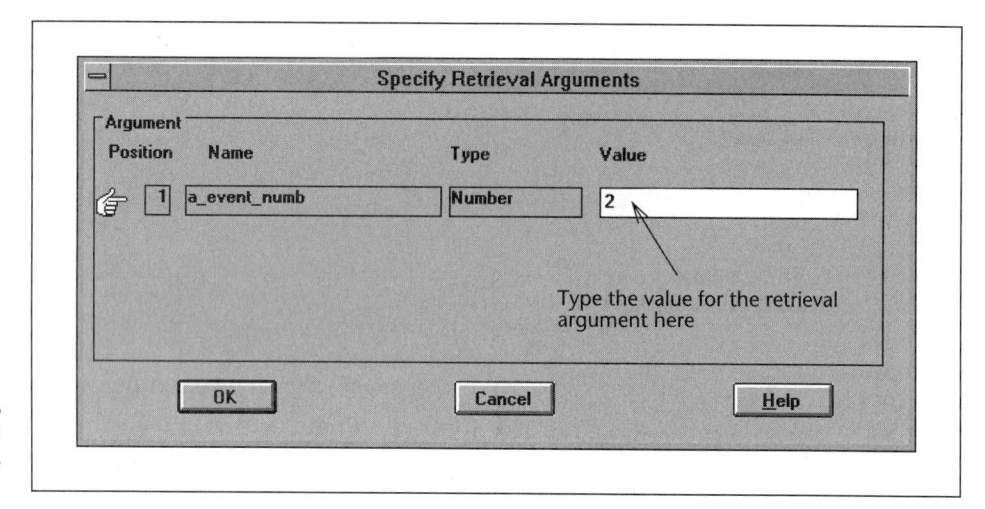

Figure 11.6
Manually entering a retrieval argument value

[Dialog: Specify Retrieval Arguments — Position 1, Name: a_event_numb, Type: Number, Value: 2. Annotation: "Type the value for the retrieval argument here"]

4 Click the **OK** button. PowerBuilder retrieves all the costs for event number 2. As you look at the preview (for example, Figure 11.7), notice that the tabular presentation style doesn't have the lines between columns and rows that were present with the grid presentation style. Notice also how awkward the DropDownListBox format is in a listing of this type.

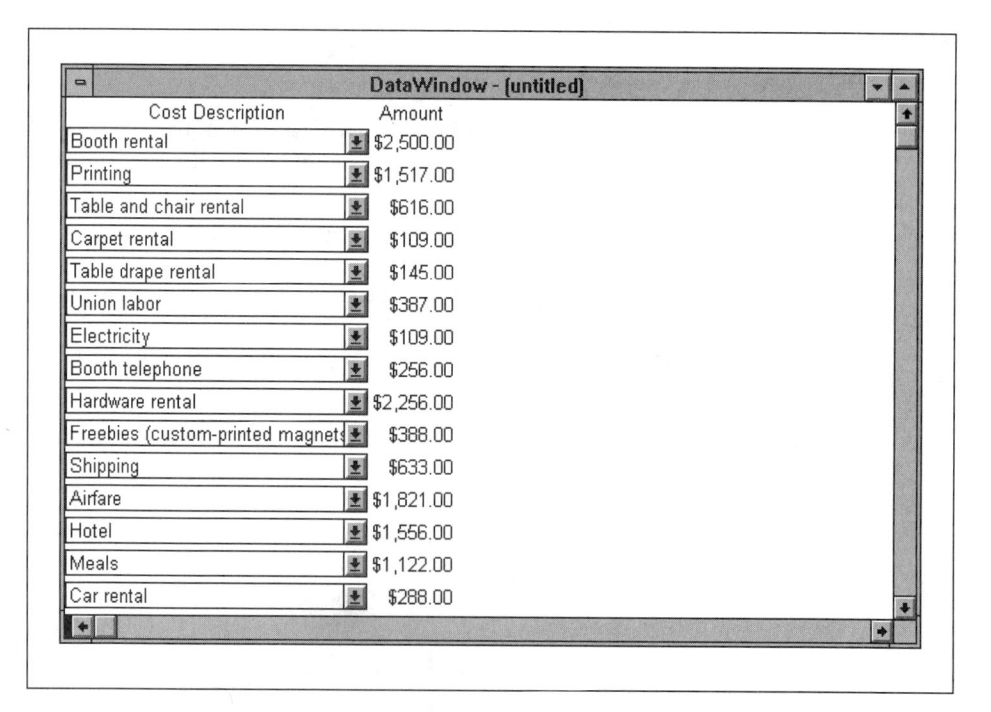

Figure 11.7
Previewing a tabular presentation sytle

Cost Description	Amount
Booth rental	$2,500.00
Printing	$1,517.00
Table and chair rental	$616.00
Carpet rental	$109.00
Table drape rental	$145.00
Union labor	$387.00
Electricity	$109.00
Booth telephone	$256.00
Hardware rental	$2,256.00
Freebies (custom-printed magnets)	$388.00
Shipping	$633.00
Airfare	$1,821.00
Hotel	$1,556.00
Meals	$1,122.00
Car rental	$288.00

5 Click the **Design** button in the PainterBar to return to the DataWindow painter. (*Hint:* Now it's at the top of the PainterBar.)

6 Make the Cost Description and Amount headers in the header band boldface. (*Hint:* Click the **B** button at the top of the workspace.)

7 Make any other formatting changes, such as moving or resizing items, that you want.

Adding a Summary Value

A sum of the costs for a single show would help the listing on which you are working provide more useful information to the user. Because this type of summing is used frequently, PowerBuilder provides a shortcut for adding summary values of number columns. A rectangle for the sum of the Amount column will appear in the summary band, indicating that the sum will appear once in the DataWindow, at the bottom of all the rows retrieved by the Data-Window's query.

To add the summary value:

1. Click the **amount** rectangle in the detail band to select it. This identifies the column on which you want to compute a summary value.
2. Click the **Sum** button in the PainterBar (Figure 11.8) or, if the Sum button isn't present in the PainterBar, choose **Objects->Sum - Computed Field**. PowerBuilder expands the summary band and places a rectangle for the computed field directly under the amount rectangle in the detail band.

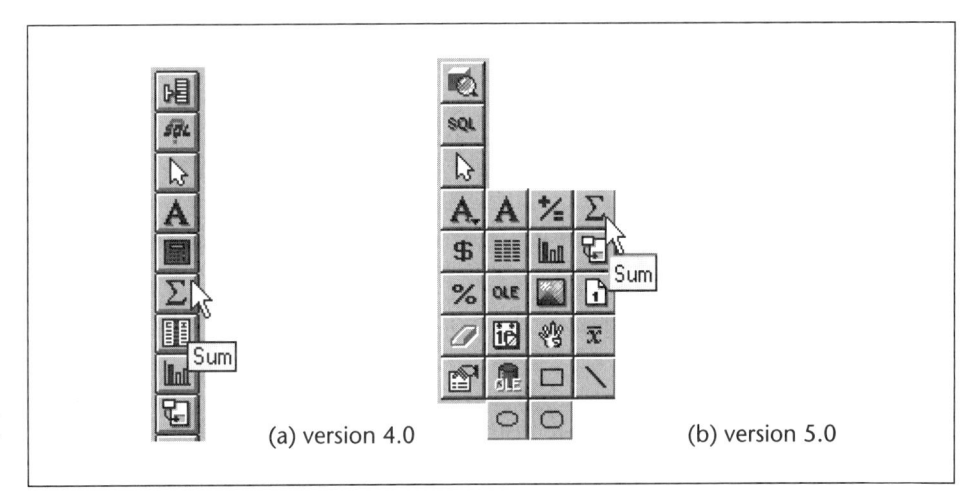

Figure 11.8
Sum button in the PainterBar

(a) version 4.0   (b) version 5.0

3. Make the summary rectangle a bit wider by dragging its left edge to the left, so that your DataWindow appears like Figure 11.9 on page 258.
4. Preview the DataWindow. Assuming you haven't left the DataWindow painter since you began working on this DataWindow, PowerBuilder remembers the retrieval argument you used the last time you previewed and therefore doesn't ask you to enter it again. Scroll the listing so that you can see the sum at the bottom.
5. Click the **Design** button to return to the DataWindow painter.
6. Save the DataWindow object under the name **dwo_one_show_costs**.
7. Exit the DataWindow painter.

258 CHAPTER ELEVEN DATAWINDOWS AND QUERIES

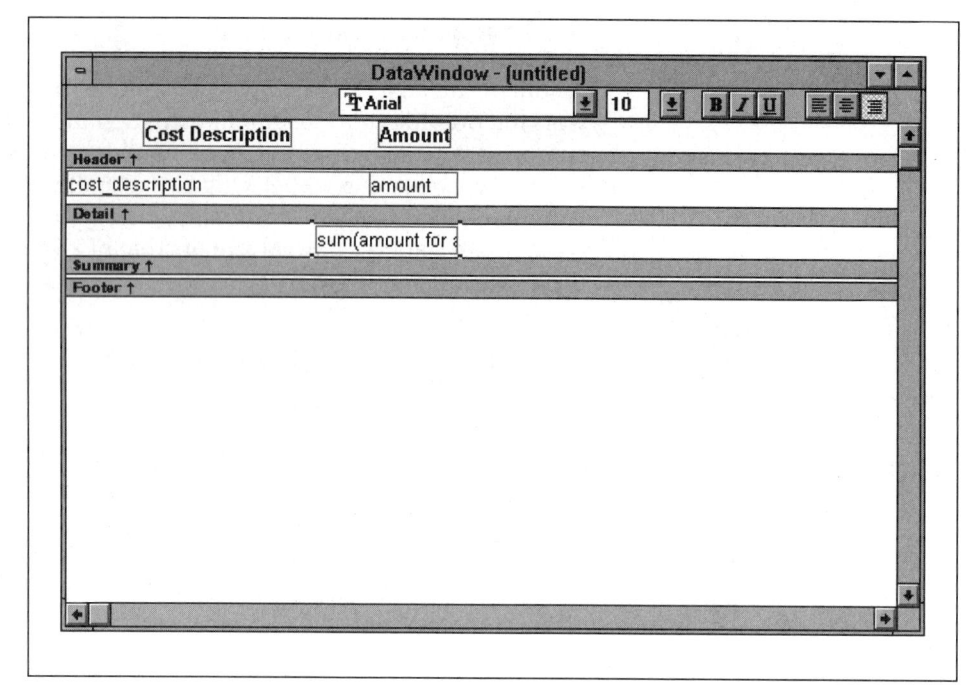

Figure 11.9
Rectangle for a column sum in the Summary band

You can generate column averages and counts much like you obtain the sum. To get an average, select the column you want to average and then choose Objects -> Average - Computed Field. To get a count of the rows in the listing, select any column and then choose Objects -> Count - Computed Field.

Placing the DataWindow Control

At this point, you can use the DataWindow object to create a DataWindow control for the application.

To place the control:

1. Open the w_see_one_show_costs window in the Window painter.
2. Place a new DataWindow control in the workspace.
3. Associate the DataWindow object named dwo_one_show_costs with the control.
4. Name the control **dw_one_show_costs**. Give it a vertical scroll bar.
5. Resize the controls and the window so that the layout is attractive, perhaps like Figure 11.10 on page 259.
6. Copy the open event script from w_see_show_data, and paste it into the open event of w_see_one_show_costs.
7. Change the name of the DataWindow control everywhere it occurs from dw_see_shows to **dw_one_show_costs**.
8. Save the script and run the application. Because you aren't supplying a retrieval argument as part of the script, PowerBuilder asks you to provide it, just as it did when you were previewing the DataWindow object.

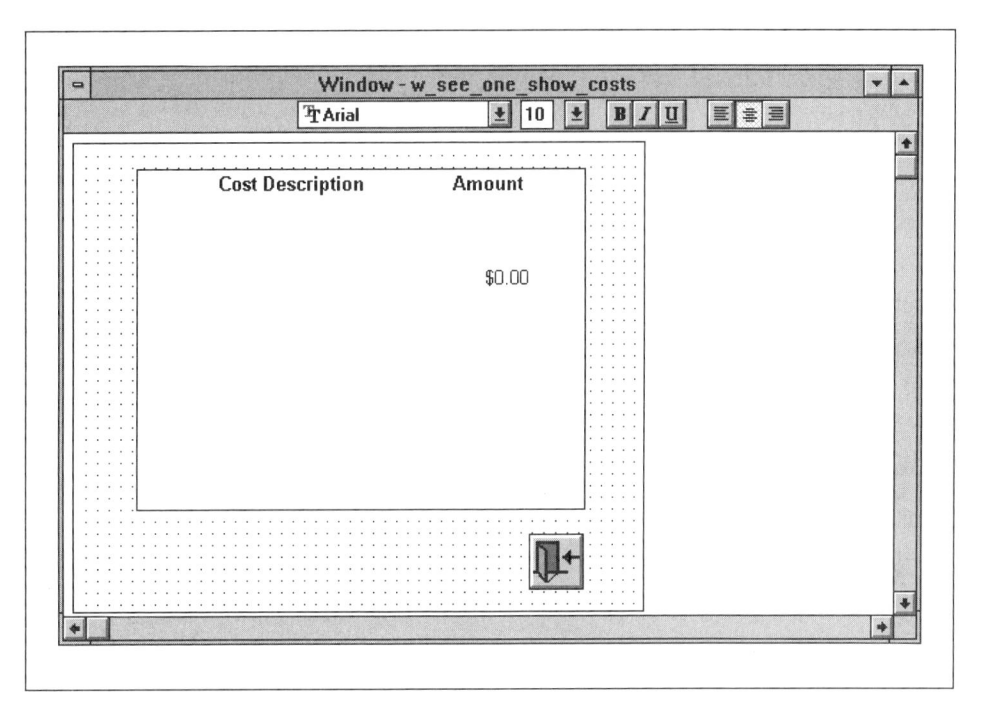

Figure 11.10
Completed window layout

> *The script you entered for the w_see_one_show_costs window's open event will be modified considerably before you're done. The way it exists now allows you to make sure that the window works properly, but it contains code that won't be needed when the response window is in place. It is also missing the retrieval argument for the DataWindow's SQL query.*

Enabling a Response Window

Although the application runs perfectly well in its current condition, the default retrieval argument window in Figure 11.6 might be confusing to users because it contains terms—for example, "Argument" and "Position"—that they might not understand. One solution is to provide a special window—a *response window*—into which a user can enter an event number, perhaps something like Figure 11.11. This window provides a better interface for a technologically unsophisticated user because it contains clear instructions and doesn't overwhelm the user with unnecessary technical language.

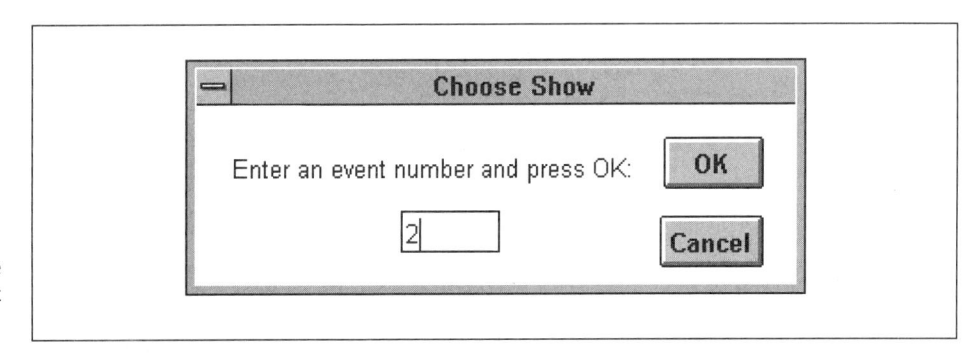

Figure 11.11
Response window to capture user input

Response windows are much like application windows. However, response windows are *modal*, meaning that they must be closed before the user can access any other application window. In this particular case, a response window is appropriate because we don't want the user attempting to display the cost summary listing without supplying a value for the retrieval argument.

There is one major problem with the solution proposed above: Users aren't likely to remember event numbers; they're more likely to remember show names and dates. The solution is to provide a window from which users can choose a show. The script underlying the window can retrieve the event number from the row the user chose and use that value as a parameter in the Retrieve function call. You'll be introduced to one technique for doing this in the next section of this chapter.

Creating the Response Window

Creating a response window is the same as creating an application window, with one exception: You change the window's type from "main" to "response." Other than that, you place items on the window in exactly the same way.

To create the response window to capture an event number:

1. Create a new window.
2. If you are working with version 4.0, right-click in the window to display its popup menu.

    If you are working with version 5.0, double-click anywhere in the window to display the Window properties dialog box.

3. If you are working with version 4.0, choose **Type** -> **Response** from the popup menu, as in Figure 11.13.

    If you are working with version 5.0, choose **Response** from the Window Type dropdown menu. PowerBuilder changes the window's type. However, you will see no effect of that change on the screen.

If you are using version 4.0, you can also display the Window Style dialog box by double-clicking anywhere in the window that isn't occupied by a control.

4. Place two command buttons on the window, one with the text **OK** and named **cb_choose_show_ok** and the second with the text **Cancel** and named **cb_choose_show_cancel**.
5. Enter **close (parent)** as the clicked event script for the Cancel button.

It is important to always give the user a chance to change his or her mind about performing some action with an application. Perhaps the user didn't intend to perform the chosen action; selecting it was a mistake. Perhaps the user realizes that he or she really doesn't need to see this data after all. You should therefore always include a Cancel button (or some equivalent menu option such as "Close") that lets the user escape and cleanly terminate a process at any appropriate point.

CHAPTER ELEVEN DATAWINDOWS AND QUERIES **261**

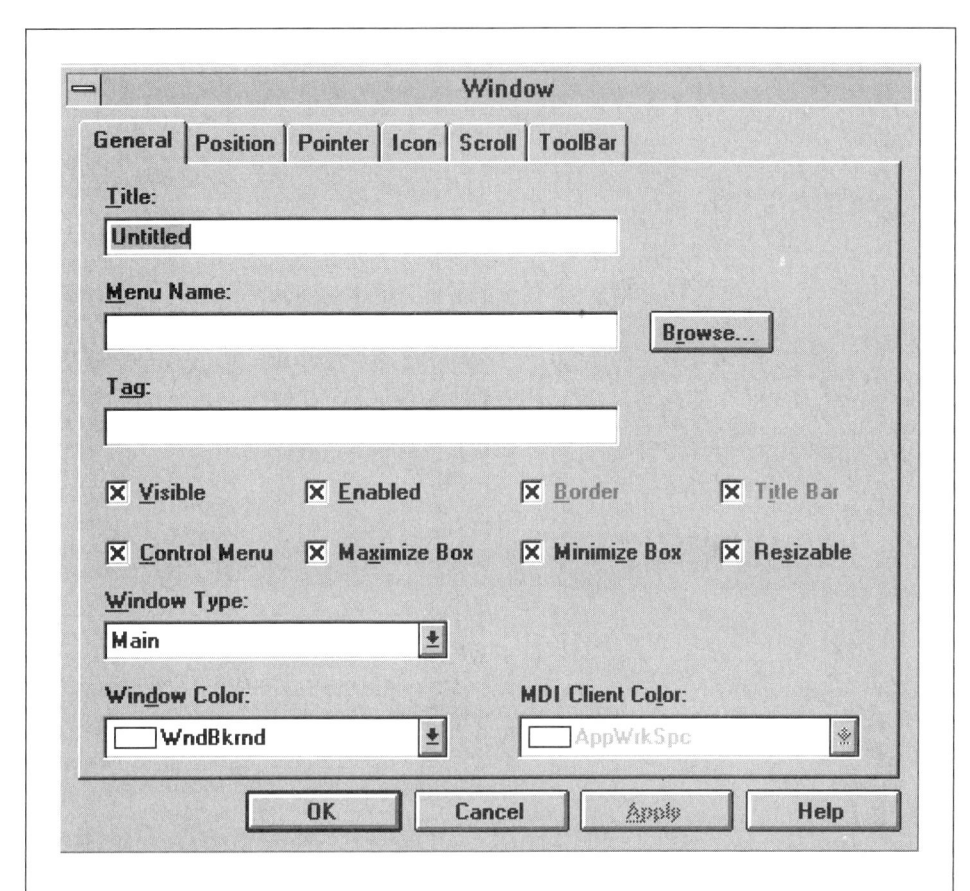

Figure 11.12
Window General properties panel (5.0)

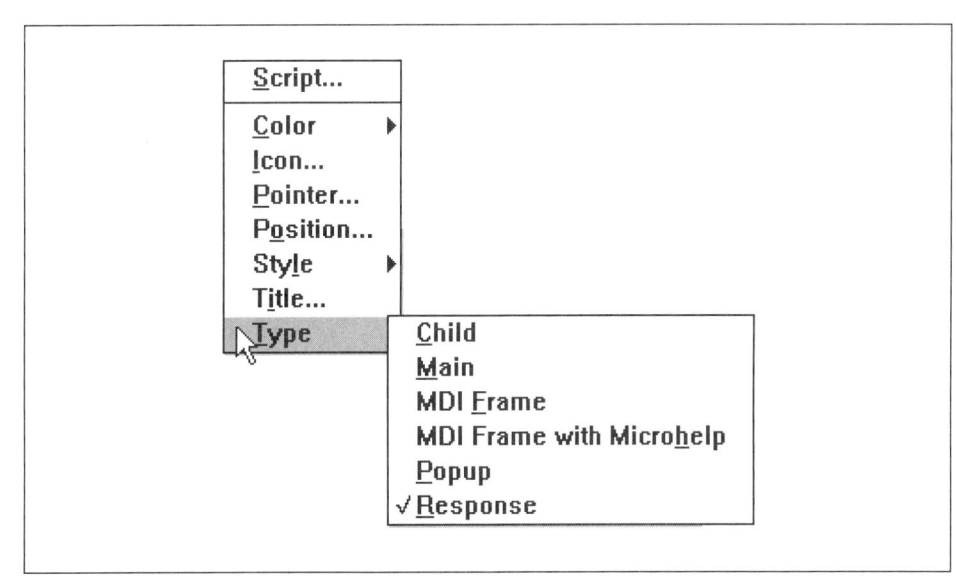

Figure 11.13
Changing a window's type

6 Click the **Text** button in the PainterBar (Figure 11.14).

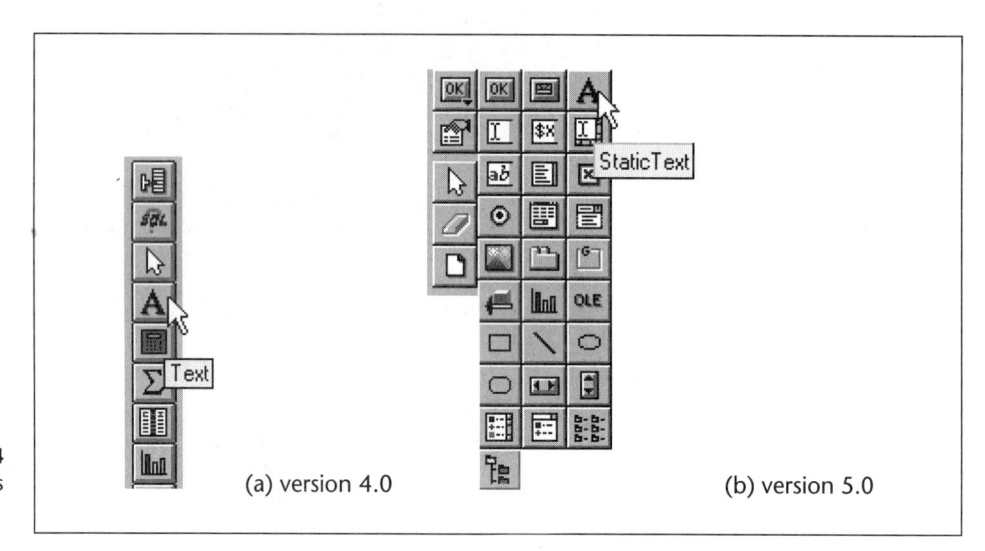

Figure 11.14
Text and Static Text buttons

(a) version 4.0 (b) version 5.0

7 Click near the upper-left corner of the window. A small static text control appears.

8 Select the default text "none" in the Style Bar. Type **Enter an event number and press OK:**. PowerBuilder expands the static text control to contain your text.

9 Resize the window and position its controls so that it appears something like Figure 11.15.

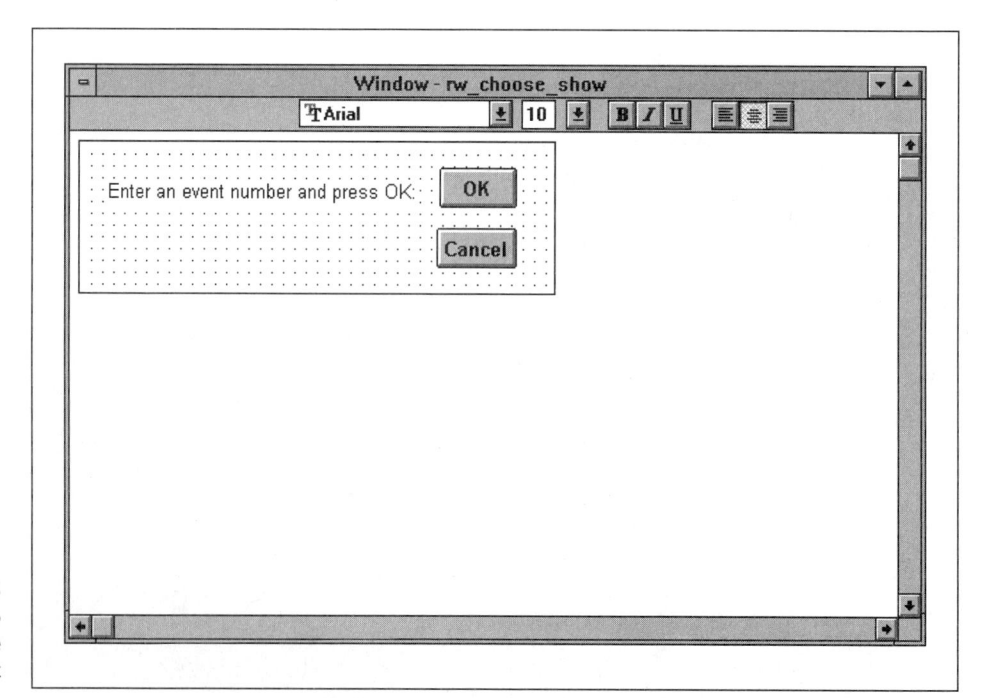

Figure 11.15
Response window with two command buttons and some static text

The final element to be placed on this response window is a control into which the user can enter an event number. When you need to capture a single value from a user, use a SingleLineEdit control. A script can then check one of the control's attributes to obtain the value entered by the user.

To create the SingleLineEdit control:

1 Click the **SingleLineEdit** button in the PainterBar (Figure 11.16).

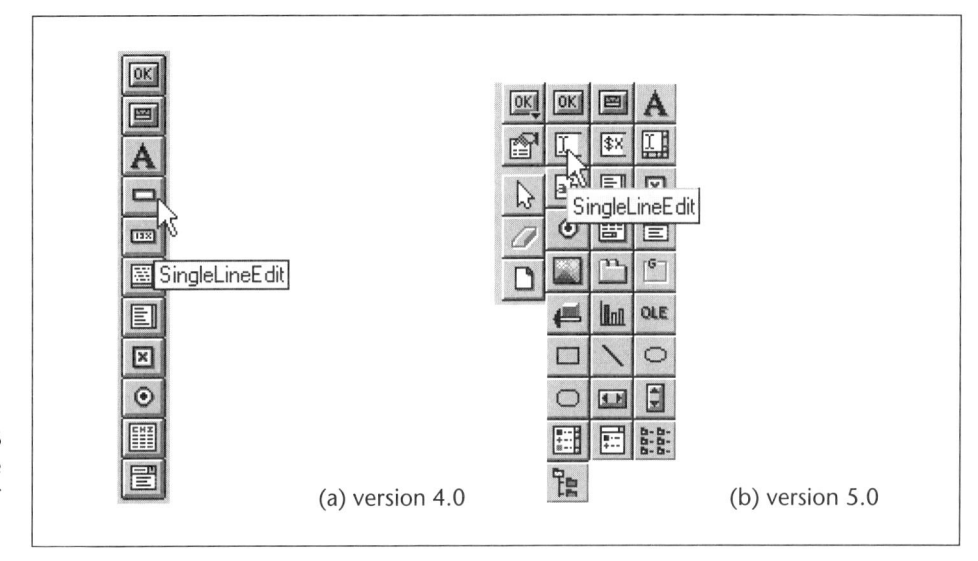

Figure 11.16
SingleLineEdit button in the PainterBar

(a) version 4.0   (b) version 5.0

2 Click in the window underneath the static text control. PowerBuilder places a rectangle for the SingleLineEdit control in the window, as in Figure 11.17.

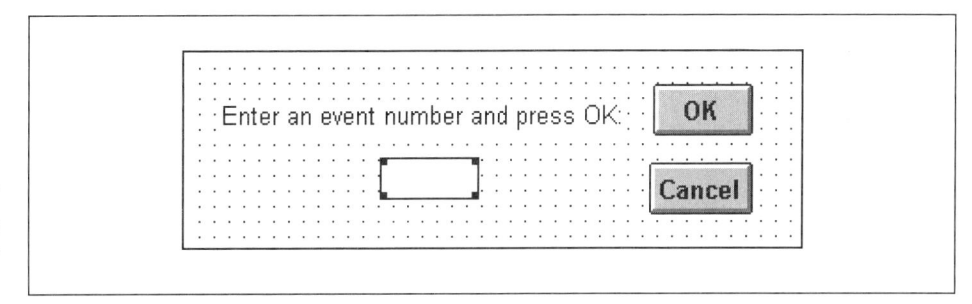

Figure 11.17
An initial SingleLineEdit control on a window

3 If you are working with version 4.0, right-click the single line edit control to display its popup menu. Choose **Name** from the popup to display the SingleLineEdit dialog box.

If you are working with version 5.0, double-click anywhere in the single line edit control to display the SingleLineEdit properties dialog box. The General panel is visible.

4 Type **sle_event_numb** as the control's name.

5 Click the **OK** button to dismiss the dialog box.

6 Save the window as **rw_choose_show**.

Writing Response Window Scripts

At this point, all the pieces of the response window are in place. All you need to do now is add the scripts that make it work. Most of the activity takes place when the user clicks the OK button. However, there is one thing that should happen when the window opens: the edit control should have focus so that the cursor flashes in the rectangle as soon as the window appears. You want to make sure that the user can start typing immediately; he or she shouldn't have to click the edit control to make it active.

To enter the script for the window's open event:

1 Open the Script painter for the window.

2 Type **sle_event_numb.SetFocus()**.

3 Close the PowerScript painter, saving the script.

To enter the script for the OK button's clicked event:

1 Open the Script painter for the OK button.

2 Type the script in Listing 11.1. This script declares a variable to hold the event number. It then converts the contents of the edit control's Text attribute to a number with the long function. That value is used as a parameter in the OpenWithParm function, which opens a window and sends one value to that window through a special object called message. Finally, the script closes the response window. (Details of all the functions used in this script will be discussed shortly.)

Listing 11.1
Clicked event script for the response window's OK button

```
long event_numb

// capture the event number from the SingleLineEdit control
event_numb = long (sle_event_numb.Text)

// open window that displays costs for one show
OpenWithParm (w_see_one_show_costs, event_numb)

// close this window
close (parent)
```

3 Exit the Script painter, saving the script.

Modifying the Application Window Script

To make the costs for one show listing work, you will need to modify the application window's script so that it takes the event number from the `message` object and uses that value as a retrieval argument in a call to `Retrieve`.

To modify the application window's script:

1. The completed open event script for the w_see_one_show_costs window can be found in Listing 11.2. Make modifications to the existing script as necessary. (You'll find a complete discussion of how this script works in the next section of this chapter.)

Listing 11.2
Modified open event script for the w_see_one_show_costs window

```
long event_numb
int NO_ROWS = -1

// associate datawindow with transaction object
dw_one_show_costs.SetTransObject (sqlca)

// extract the event number from the message object
event_numb = message.DoubleParm

// call Retrieve with the parameter
if dw_one_show_costs.Retrieve (event_numb) = NO_ROWS then
  rollback using sqlca;
  MessageBox ("Retrieve","Couldn't find any rows.")
else
  commit using sqlca;
  dw_one_show_costs.SetFocus()
  dw_one_show_costs.SetRowFocusIndicator (Hand!)
end if
```

2. Open the w_costs window. Change the clicked event script for the See Costs for One Show button so that it reads

   ```
   open (rw_choose_show)
   ```

   With this change, clicking on the See Costs for One Show button will open the response window rather than w_see_one_show_costs.

3. Run the application to test your scripts. You should be able to enter an existing event number (1 through 8, unless you have modified the data in the Costs table) and see a cost summary of that show.

Understanding the Scripts

The scripts you have just entered employ function calls and objects that provide one way of passing data between PowerBuilder objects. In addition, you have seen an example of a function that converts data types and an example of extracting data from an edit control. In this section we will look at all of these in more depth.

The Message Object The `message` object is a PowerBuilder object to which all parts of an application have access. Its primary purpose is to provide a way of communicating between objects when those objects are opened or closed or when a function explicitly triggers an event.

`Message` has three attributes that are commonly used for value passing:

- `message.DoubleParm` (any number)
- `message.String` (a string)
- `message.PowerObjectParm` (a PowerBuilder object)

Notice that you access each of the these attributes using dot notation. `Message` is the name of the object, with is followed by a period and the name of the attribute.

The drawback to using `message` for passing values between objects is that `message` can handle only one value. If you need to pass multiple values, you will have to resort to using global variables. You will remember from Chapter 3 that a global variable is a variable that is available to the entire application. You will get a chance to experiment with multiple retrieval arguments in Chapter 13.

Opening a Window with a Parameter The `OpenWithParm` function is designed to let a script open a window and make some data value available to that window through the `Message` object. The function has the following general syntax:

`OpenWithParm (window_name, parameter)`

The parameter can be a literal, such as a number or a string within double quotation marks, or it can be stored in a variable.

Edit Control Attributes Like the `message` object, a SingleLineEdit control has an attribute that stores its contents. You use dot notation to access that attribute:

`sle_control_name.Text`

The value can be assigned to a `string` variable or used as a value in another executable statement.

There is one minor difficulty with an edit control's `Text` attribute: regardless of the characters in the attribute, it is always stored as text. If you need to manipulate the data as a number, date, or time, a script will need to perform some data conversion.

Converting Data Types There are several functions that convert string data to other data types, including the following:

- `Date`: Returns a date
- `Double`: Returns a double precision floating point number
- `Dec`: Returns a decimal number
- `Integer`: Returns an integer
- `Long`: Returns a long integer
- `Real`: Returns a real number
- `Time`: Returns a time

Each function takes a single parameter: the string value to be converted. If a script is attempting to convert to a numeric value and the string doesn't constitute a valid number, the function call returns 0. An unsuccessful attempt to convert to a date returns 1900-01-01, while a unsuccessful attempt to convert to a time returns 00:00:00.

You can assign the result of a conversion function call to a variable or place the function in an executable statement, in which case PowerBuilder substitutes the result of the function for the call when evaluating the statement.

Picking From a List

As mentioned at the beginning of the previous section, a better interface for the response window would be to present the user with a list from which he or she could choose. PowerBuilder provides several methods to implement such a feature. Perhaps the easiest is to place a listing of data on a response window, let the user click or double-click on the wanted row, and then capture the data from that row. In this section you will modify the response window you just created to work in this way.

To create a DataWindow object that displays the data from which the user will choose:

1 Make sure you are working with the *tshows* application in *tshows2.pbl* and that you are connected to the *tshows* database.
2 Create a new DataWindow object using the Calendar table.
3 Include the **show_name**, **start_date**, and **event#** columns in the query.

Keep in mind that although the user won't see the event# column, the column must be present in the SQL query because event# is the value that a script needs to extract and pass through to the message object.

4 Sort the query first on **show_name** and then on **start_date**.
5 Select the rectangles in the header band. Press the **Del** key to remove them.
6 Select the **event_ rectangle** in the detail band and press the **Del** key to remove it.
7 Set the font size to **9** points. The DataWindow object should look something like Figure 11.18 on page 268.
8 Save the DataWindow object as **dwo_show_name_list**.

The next part of the process is placing a DataWindow control for the new DataWindow object on the response window.

To place a DataWindow control for the new DataWindow object on the response window:

1 Open the rw_choose_show window.
2 Select the SingleLineEdit control and press the **Del** key to remove it.

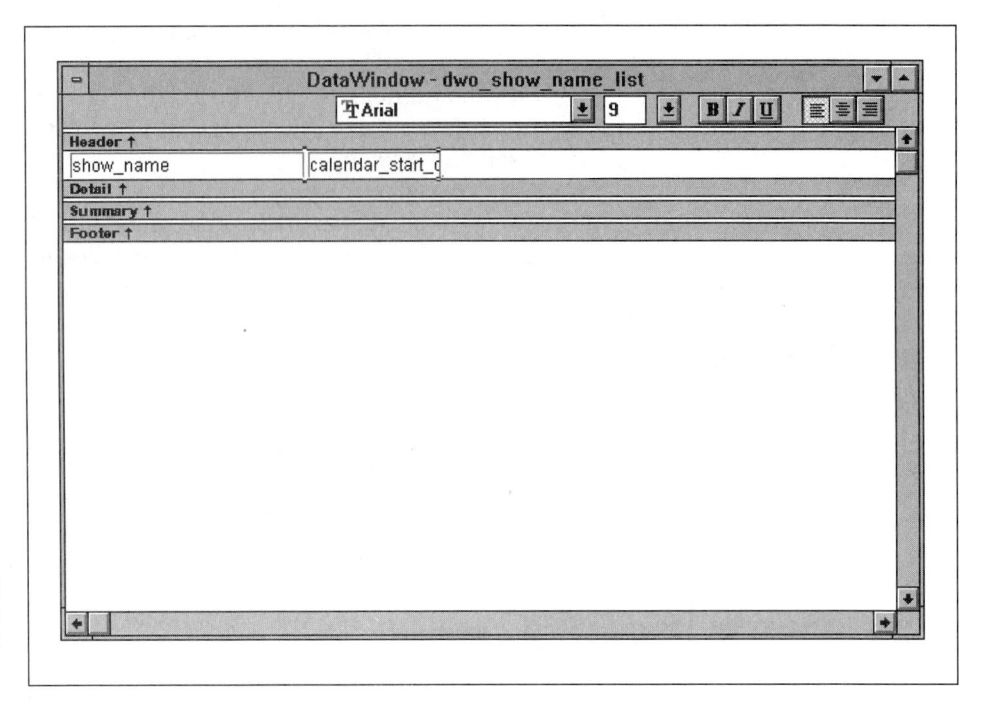

Figure 11.18
DataWindow object to be used as a list from which a user can pick

3 Enlarge the window so that it fills most of the screen.

4 Move the two command buttons to the right to get them out of the way temporarily.

5 Modify the static text control so that it reads **Choose a show and press OK or double-click on a show:**.

6 Place a DataWindow control in the window.

7 Assign dwo_show_name list to the DataWindow control. Name the control **dw_show_name_list**. Give the control a vertical scroll bar.

8 Resize the DataWindow control and the window so that it looks something like Figure 11.19.

9 Create a script for the window's open event that associates the transaction object with the DataWindow control and retrieves data for the control. (Once again, this is the same script we've been using all along to fill DataWindow controls. Only the name of the control is different.)

The actions that enable choosing from the list are part of the OK button's and DataWindow control's scripts. The final task in making this window work is therefore to add the needed scripts.

To add the necessary script:

1 Open the **OK** button's Script painter and, if necessary, choose the clicked event.

2 Create an instance variable named **row_numb**. (*Hint:* Use the Declare menu.)

3 Modify the script so that it looks like Listing 11.3 on page 269. Notice that the `OpenWithParm` function call is unchanged. However, the way

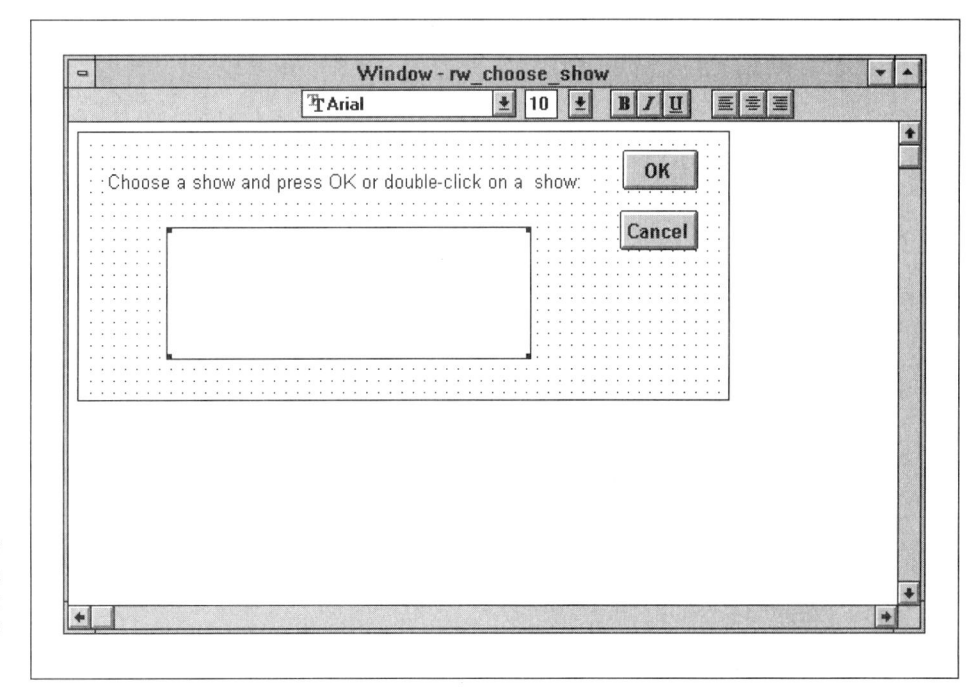

Figure 11.19
Modified response window layout with a DataWindow control for a list from which the user can pick

Listing 11.3
Script that captures the current row and a data value from that row

```
long event_numb

// get row numb
row_numb = dw_show_name_list.GetRow()

// get value in event number column for that row
event_numb = dw_show_name_list.GetItemNumber (row_numb, "event_")

// open window that displays costs and pass in event number
OpenWithParm (w_see_one_show_costs, event_numb)

// close this window
close (parent)
```

in which you obtain the event number is considerably different. (Details of how this script works appears in the next section of this chapter.)

4 Enter the following single-line script for the doubleclicked event of the DataWindow control (dw_show_name_list), the purpose of which is to trigger the clicked event script you just entered for the OK button:

cb_choose_show_ok.TriggerEvent (Clicked!)

You don't have to type the names of objects used on a given window into a script. Instead, choose a name from the Paste Object menu at the top of the PowerScript painter workspace. Doing so saves work and also helps avoid errors.

5 Run the application. Try double-clicking on a row in the listing. Try selecting a row and then clicking the OK button. (Your version of the *tshows* database has costs only for the first eight shows, although there are 16 shows in the database. To be sure that you actually see some costs, choose shows with the earliest dates.)

Understanding the Scripts

The scripts you have just seen introduce three new functions, two of which are actually part of groups of related functions. As a whole, these groups of functions give you access to the contents of DataWindow controls on windows. The third function is used to trigger an event and therefore execute a script associated with another control. The following sections discuss each of the three functions.

Finding the Current Row and Column The `GetRow` function returns an integer that represents the current row (in other words, the row that has focus) in a DataWindow control. Keep in mind that this row number is meaningful only in terms of the specific DataWindow control. If the data have been sorted or filtered for display in the control, then the row numbers will be completely independent of the rows' positions in the underlying base table or tables on which the DataWindow was based.

Related functions include the following:

- `GetClickedColumn()`: Returns an integer that represents the column clicked or double-clicked in a DataWindow control. The column number represents the column's position in the DataWindow control, not in any underlying base tables.
- `GetColumn()`: Returns an integer that represents the current column in a DataWindow control.
- `GetColumnName()`: Returns a string that represents the name of the current column in a DataWindow control.
- `GetClickedRow()`: Returns an integer that represents the row clicked or double-clicked in a DataWindow control.

All of these "Get" functions have a similar general syntax:

dw_control_name.Get*Something*( )

You can assign the result of the function to a variable or place the function in an executable statement that expects a value of the data type returned by the function.

Accessing Data in DataWindow Controls The `GetItemNumber` function retrieves a numeric value from a specific row and column of a DataWindow control. The simplest form of the function has the general syntax:

dw_control_name.GetItemNumber (*row_number*, *column*)

The row number parameter must be an integer. However, the column parameter can be either an integer or a string containing the column name. When using numbers, keep in mind that they apply to the DataWindow control, not to the underlying base tables. In fact, the call to this function is precisely why the event# column has to be present in the DataWindow object that lists show names and starting dates. PowerScript functions work on windows and their controls, not on base tables.

Although a pound sign (#) is legal as a column name, it can't be used in the PowerScript language; the language simply doesn't allow it. The string that represents the event# column name therefore appears as `event_`. *The underscore acts as a placeholder for the special character.*

There are several other functions that let you access data stored in DataWindow controls:

- `GetItemDate(row_number, column)`: Returns a date value from a date column.
- `GetItemDecimal (row_number, column)`: Returns a decimal value from a decimal column.
- `GetItemString (row_number, column)`: Returns a string value from a string column.
- `GetItemTime (row_number, column)`: Returns a time value from a time column.

As you can see, you must match the function that you use to the type of data you are trying to retrieve.

Triggering Events Under certain circumstances, you might want to explicitly trigger an event for an object, causing the script for that event to execute. You saw an example of this when you triggered the OK button script when the user double-clicked on a row in a DataWindow. This was the right behavior because double-clicking on a selection in a list is the same as selecting the item and clicking an OK button.

To trigger an event, use the `TriggerEvent` function with the following general syntax:

`control_name.TriggerEvent (event!)`

The name of the event is followed by an exclamation point, which tells PowerBuilder that the parameter is the literal name of an event rather than a variable. For example, the clicked event becomes `clicked!` and the doubleclicked event becomes `doubleclicked!`. Alternatively, you can surround the name of an event in double quotation marks, as in "`clicked`" or "`doubleclicked`".

Handling Complex Queries

Although the DataWindow painter's SQL Toolbox can handle the syntax of most queries, there are occasionally queries that are either beyond its capabilities or so complex that it is tedious to create them using the Toolbox. In either case, you can enter the query directly by typing the SQL syntax. To show you how this works, you will be completing the window that lists sales leads that have never been telephoned.

272 CHAPTER ELEVEN DATAWINDOWS AND QUERIES

Two things make this query complex. First, it requires a subquery. In other words, this query is performed by finding the difference between all sales leads and those that *have* been called. The only way to reliably perform such a query is to use the NOT IN operator with a subquery. Performing that subquery adds the second complexity: the NOT IN comparison must be based on the concatenation of lead_name and lead_company, since neither are unique by themselves.

The SQL Toolbox can handle subqueries. To create one, you choose Select from the Value column's popup menu. You are then presented with another SQL Toolbox window into which you can add specifications for subquery. However, if you are working with a subquery, it is just as easy (and often much faster) to simply type the SQL syntax.

However, the SQL Toolbox can't handle the needed concatenation. If you need a join based on concatenated keys or comparisons made on the concatenation of columns, as is the case in this example, then you have no choice but to type the SQL statement.

Under most circumstances, when you type SQL syntax directly, you can return to the SQL Toolbox and view the query in that way. However, if you use elements that the Toolbox can't handle—such as concatenation—then you won't be able to return to the Toolbox. You'll be stuck working with the SQL command syntax.

To create a DataWindow object that has a complex query behind it:

1. Make sure that you are working with the *tshows* application in *tshows2.pbl* and that you are connected to the *tshows* database.
2. Create a new DataWindow object. Choose **SQL Select** as the data source and **Tabular** as the presentation style.
3. Choose the **Leads** table and the **lead_name**, **lead_company**, and **lead_phone** columns. Make sure that you remain in the SQL Toolbox; don't exit to the DataWindow painter.
4. Choose **Options** -> **Convert to Syntax**. An editor window appears.

If your query contains syntax that the SQL Toolbox can handle, you can return to the Toolbox by choosing Options -> Convert to Graphics.

5. Type the query in Figure 11.20 on page 273.

There are some syntax differences between the query in Figure 11.20 and the SQL syntax you would typically enter if you were working interactively with a database. The DataWindow painter is very rigid about these syntax rules, which include the following:

- Surround every table name and column name with double quotation marks.
- Qualify every column name with its table name by preceding each column name with the name of its table and a period:

"`table_name`"."`column_name`"

- Place literal strings inside single quotation marks.

```
            DataWindow - dwo_leads_list
SELECT distinct "leads"."lead_name", "leads"."lead_company", "leads"."lead_phone"
    FROM "leads"
    WHERE "leads"."lead_name" || "leads"."lead_company" NOT IN
      ( SELECT "contacts"."lead_name" || "contacts"."lead_company"
        FROM "contacts"
        WHERE "contacts"."contact_type" = 'Phone call')
```

Place single quotation marks around literal strings

Place double quotation marks around each table and column name

Every column is qualified with its table name

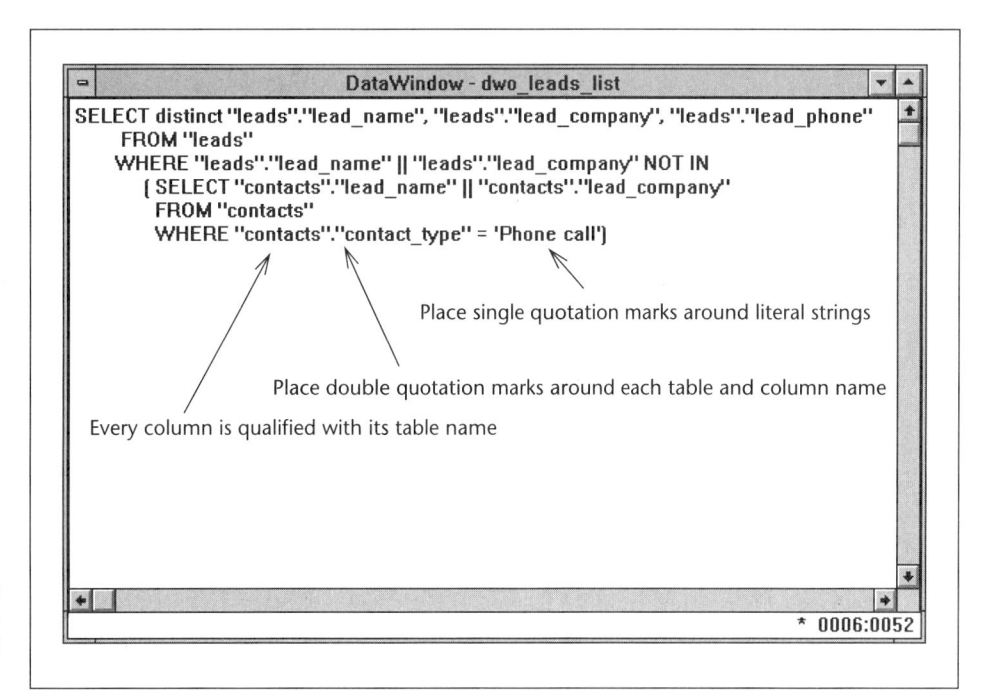

Figure 11.20
SQL query on which a DataWindow object will be based

Capitalization and spacing make no difference, although placing keywords in all caps and using indentation to show query structure usually makes the query easier to read and understand.

The query in Figure 11.20 uses || (two vertical bars) as the concatenation operator. This operator is supported by WatcomSQL and most SQL-based DBMSs. However, if you aren't using WatcomSQL, check with your DBMS's documentation to determine if you need to substitute another operator.

6 Click the **Design** button to return to the DataWindow painter.

7 Arrange the contents of the window so that you are happy with the way it looks. A simple arrangement might be that in Figure 11.21 on page 274.

The window in Figure 11.21 displays table names as prefixes to column names. Depending on the way in which your copy of PowerBuilder has been configured, you may or may not see those column names.

8 Save the window as **dwo_leads_list**.

9 Open the w_see_leads2call window.

10 Place a DataWindow control on the window and associate it with dwo_leads_list. Give the control a vertical scroll bar. Name it **dw_leads_list**. The completed window should look something like Figure 11.22.

11 Enter a script for the window's open event that associates the DataWindow control with a transaction object and retrieves data for the DataWindow control.

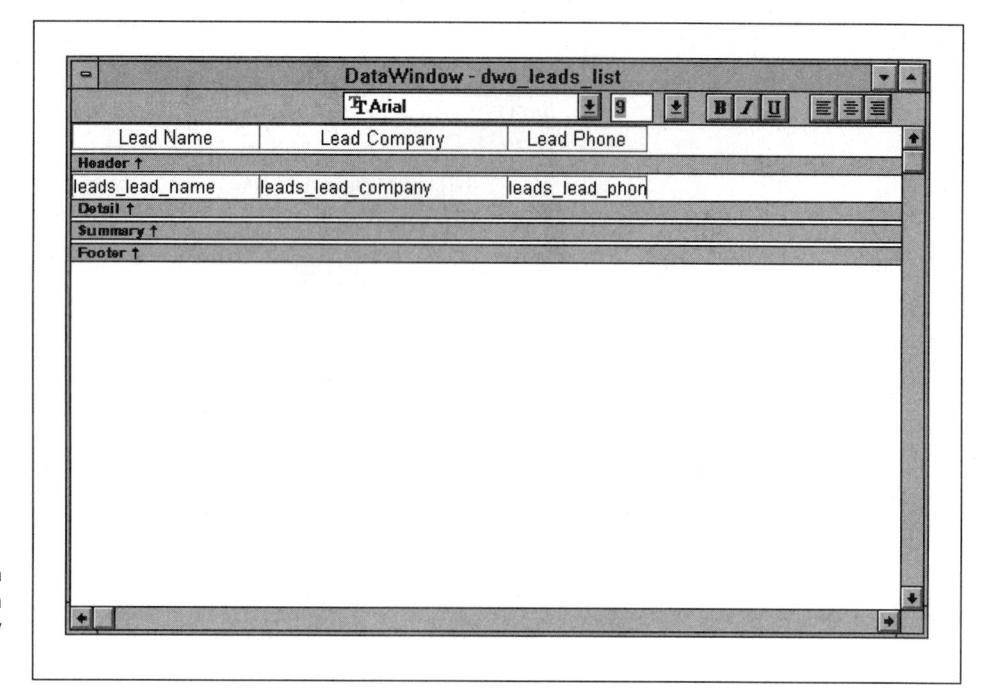

Figure 11.21
Simple arrangement of elements for a DataWindow object based on a complex query

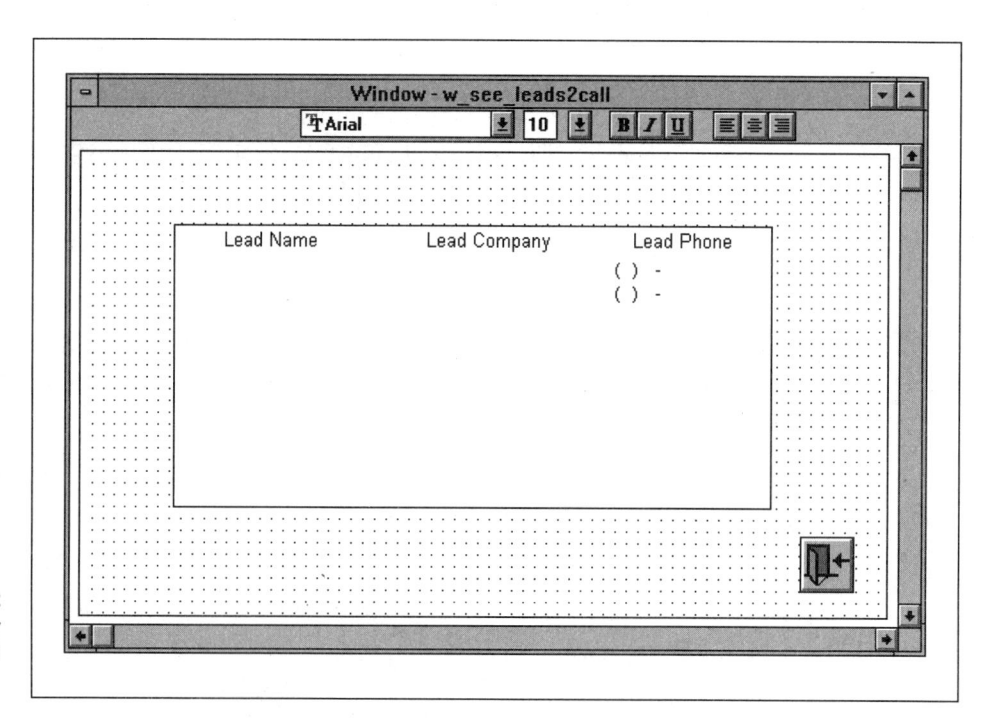

Figure 11.22
Application window that will display sales leads to be called

12 Run the application to check your work. Unless you have changed the data in either the Leads or Contacts table, 33 rows should appear in the list of leads to be called.

Looking Ahead

In this chapter you have gained experience with formulating the queries that underlie DataWindow controls. You have seen the capabilites of PowerBuilder's SQL ToolBox and learned that your ability to enter SQL syntax directly means that PowerBuilder's retrieval capabilites aren't limited by the ToolBox. At this point, you are ready to move on to more sophisticated output formatting.

One of the most common types of output provided by database applications is the control break report, a report that forms groups of data based on matching data values. Such reports typically also include summary calculations for the groups of data. You will learn how to create control break reports in Chapter 12.

EXERCISES

In these exercises, you will create many of the reports for the College and University Rentals application for which you created windows in Chapter 9. As you read through the specifications of the report, keep in mind that some of the queries require joins to obtain all the needed information.

1. Complete the window that displays a list of all items that are out for repair. Before beginning, consider how you will specify the status of the item in the query's WHERE clause. Should you hard code the value into the Select painter or should you use a retrieval argument that is supplied from a script? When you make your decision, think about the ease of modifying and reusing the DataWindow.

2. Complete the window that lists all customers at one school. Use a response box to let the user enter the name of the school. (The user can either type the name or pick it from a list.) Place the customer information (customer name, dorm, and phone number) in a scrolling list.

3. Complete the window that shows all customers who have not paid their rental fees. For each customer that meets the criteria in the SQL query underlying the DataWindow, display the customer's name, address, and phone number.

4. Complete the window that shows all rentals made by a single customer. Use a response window to let the user choose a customer. The main window opened by the response window should the rental information in a scrolling list.

5. Complete the window that shows all items of a given type that are available for rental. Use a response window to let the user enter or choose the type of merchandise. The main window opened by the response window should show each item's inventory number and description.

6. Complete a window that contains a list of all rentals that are to be returned within a given period. The window should show the name of the customer and the dorm in which the customer lives as well as what items are to be picked up. Use a response window that captures two dates: a starting date

and an ending date. Capture the dates in two separate SingleLineEdit controls. Create two global variables to hold the dates after they have been converted from text. Use the contents of the global variables as retrieval arguments. The WHERE clause for the SELECT should therefore choose rows that are greater than or equal to the first retrieval argument (the starting date) and less than or equal to the second retrieval argument (the ending date). Display an error message to the user and don't process the query if the end date isn't later than the start date. If you don't remember how to create a global variable, refer to Chapter 3.

CHAPTER TWELVE

Control Break Reports

IN THIS CHAPTER YOU WILL:

- Create control break reports that organize data in groups and compute summary values about those groups
- Use additional techniques for formatting DataWindow object layouts

In this chapter, you will be introduced to a major technique for presenting output to users. You will learn two ways to create control break reports—reports that group data and compute summary values about the groups. These reports are based on SQL queries that contain a GROUP BY clause. As you prepare the reports, you will also learn additional techniques for formatting output.

Using the Group Presentation Style

In Figure 12.1 you can see the first page of a report that contains the sales leads obtained at trade shows, organized by the company for which the leads work. If you need to create a report of this type—with a single level of grouping—you can do it directly from the DataWindow painter using the Group presentation style.

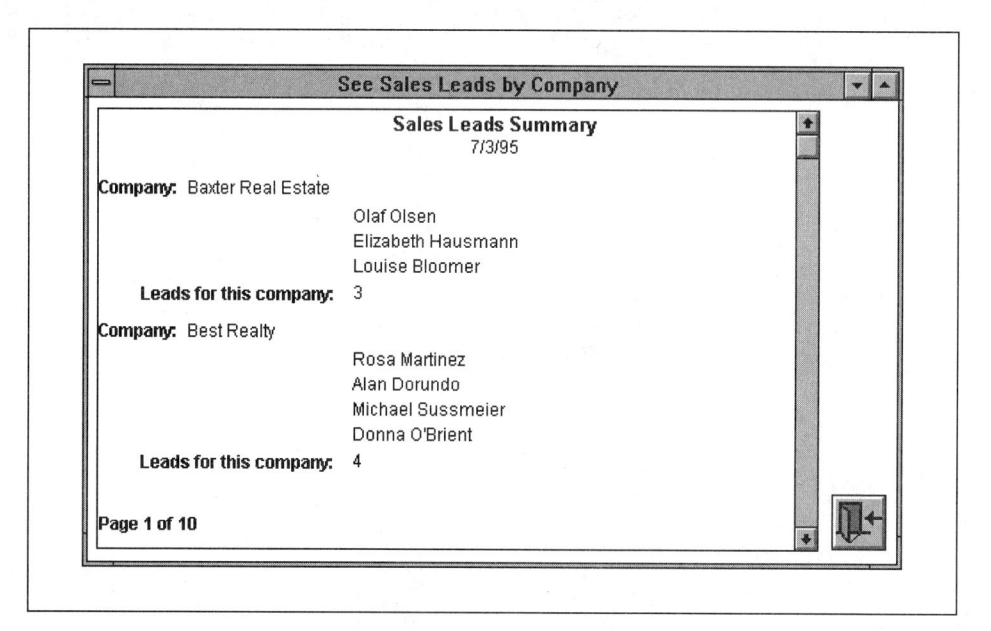

Figure 12.1
A summary report of sales lead revenue

Creating the DataWindow Object

The first step in creating a single-level control break report is to generate a DataWindow object.

To create the DataWindow object for the sales lead summary report, do the following:

1. Make sure that you are working with the *tshows* application in *tshows2.pbl* and that you are connected to the *tshows* database.
2. Create a new DataWindow object. Choose **SQL Select** as the data source and **Group** as the presentation style.
3. In the Select Tables dialog box, choose the **Leads** table.
4. Choose the **lead_name** and **lead_company** columns.

It is essential that you sort the data on the column (or columns) being used to create the groups in the report. The reason lies in the method used to create reports of this type. First, the DBMS executes the query used to define data for the report. Then, it scans the result table, beginning with the first row and moving sequentially from one row to the next. Rows that are physically next to one another with matching values for the grouping column or columns are considered to be part of the same group. The groups "break" (in other words, are separated) when a value in the grouping column(s) changes. Therefore, if the data aren't sorted properly, the groups can't be formed accurately.

5   Choose **lead_company** as the sort column.

6   Use the Design Button to enter the DataWindow painter. If you are working with version 4.0, the Specify Page Header dialog box appears. As you can see in Figure 12.2, PowerBuilder supplies a default header made up of the name of the table on which the report is based and the word "Report."

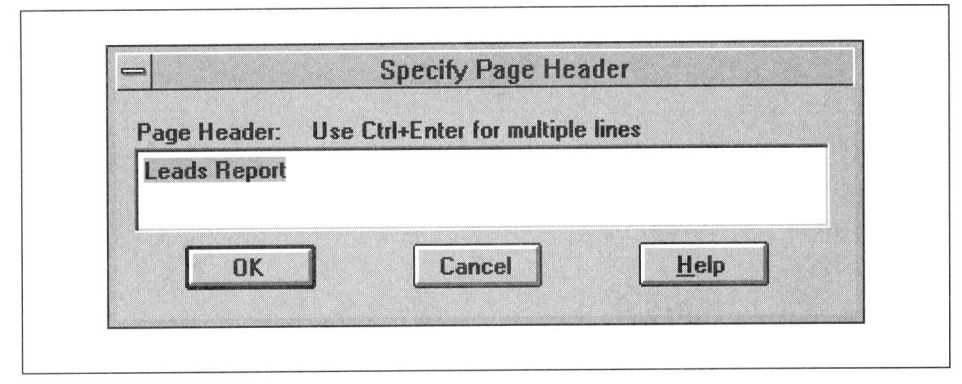

Figure 12.2
Specify Page Header dialog box

If you are working with version 5.0, the Group Report properties dialog box appears, showing you the Definition panel for specifying the column or columns that should form the report's groups (Figure 12.3 on page 280). You won't be able to specify the page header at this point—the grouping column(s) must be specified first—so skip to Step 9.

7   Type **Sales Leads Summary**. Because the default page header of Leads Report was highlighted when you began typing, your typing replaces the default.

8   Click the **OK** button. The Specify Group Columns dialog box appears (Figure 12.4).

9   Drag the **lead_company** column from the Source Data column to the Columns column. PowerBuilder creates a group based on this column and names it "group 1."

If you look again at Figure 12.3 and Figure 12.4, you'll notice that you can choose more than one grouping column. This isn't the same as having more than one grouping level. When you group by multiple columns, each group will be formed from rows that have matching values on all selected columns. A report with multiple grouping levels, however, has groups nested within one another. You'll create a report of this latter type in the next section of this chapter.

280 CHAPTER TWELVE CONTROL BREAK REPORTS

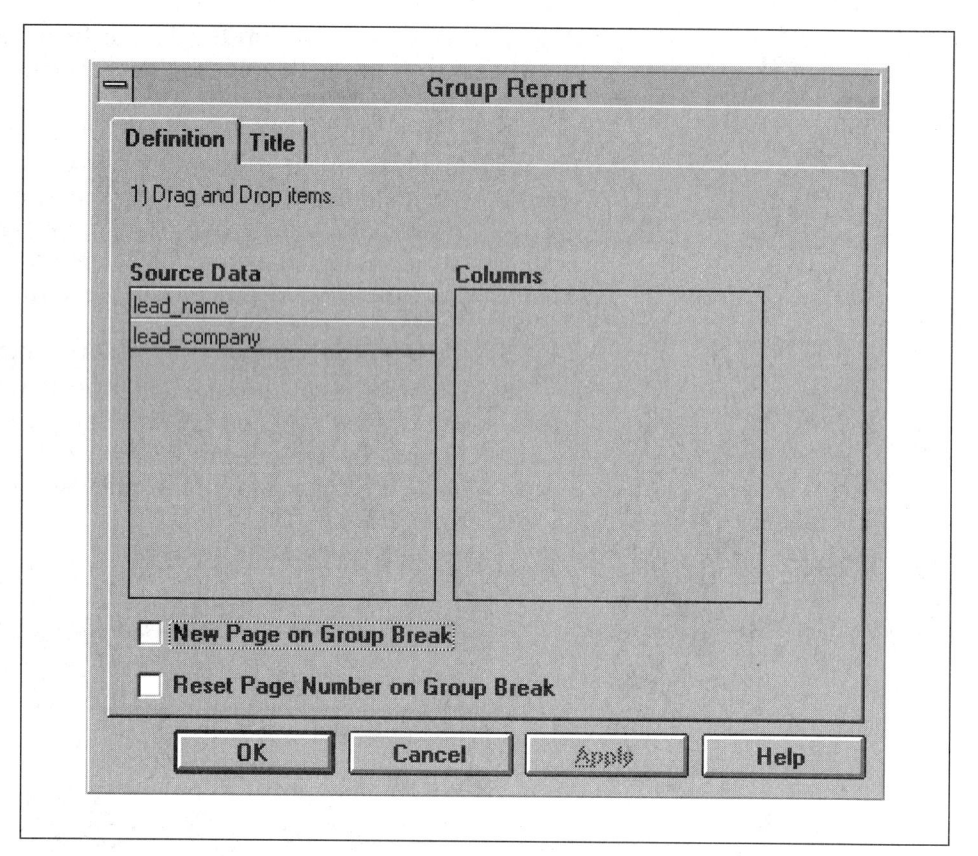

Figure 12.3
Group Report properties dialog box (5.0)

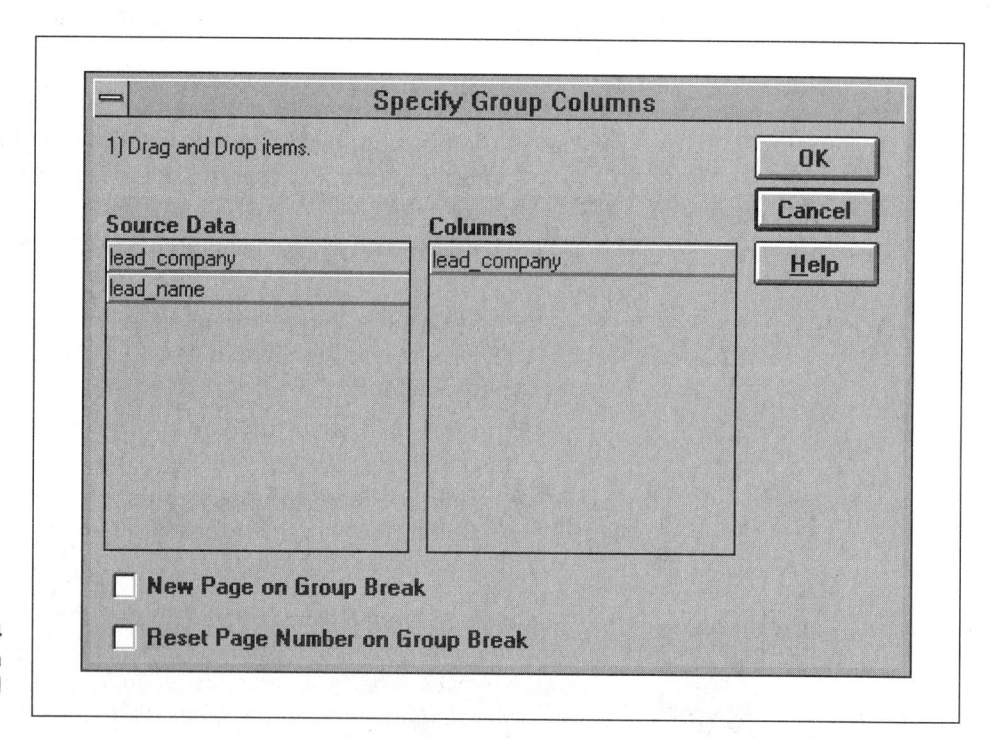

Figure 12.4
Specifying the column on which a report will be grouped

10 If you are working with version 5.0, click the **Title** tab at the top of the Group Report properties dialog box. Type **Sales Leads Summary**, replacing the highlighted default page header.

11 Click the **OK** button. PowerBuilder creates an initial DataWindow layout for you, as in Figure 12.5.

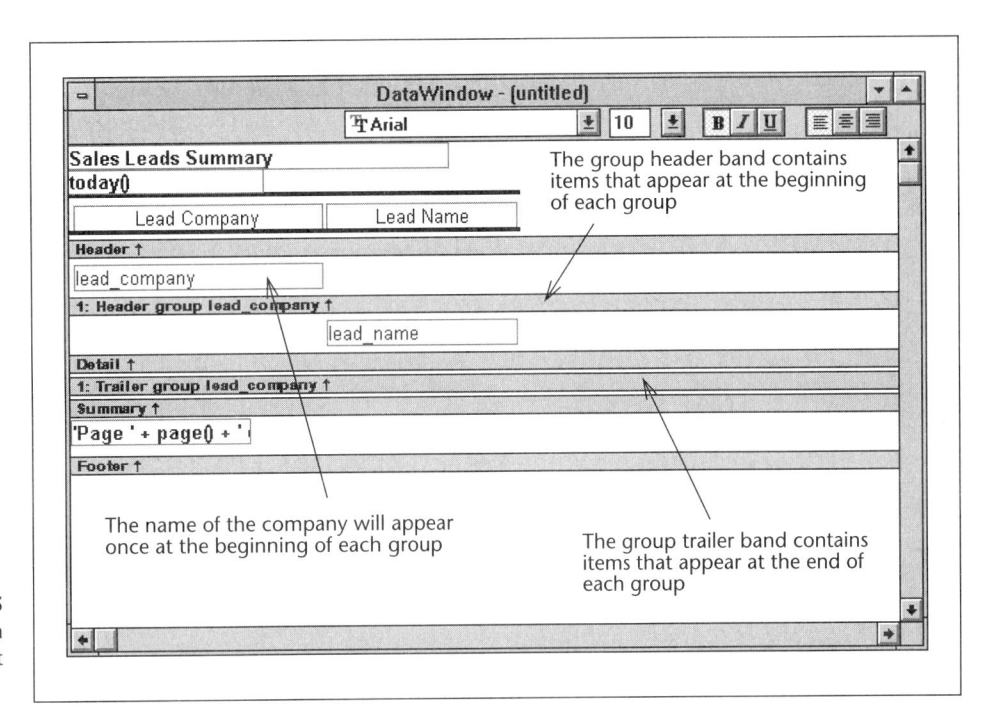

Figure 12.5
PowerBuilder's initial layout for a Group DataWindow object

Figure 12.5 contains two bands that you haven't seen before. The Header group lead_company band contains items that will appear at the beginning of each group of data. In other words, the value in the lead_company column will appear once before the names of all the people who come from that company.

The Trailer group lead_company band can be used for items that should appear below the names of all people who come from a given company. For this report, the group trailer will contain a count of the people in the group.

The default header band for this DataWindow contains the page header you entered earlier. It also contains a call to the `today()` function in a computed field, which inserts the current system date. In addition, you will find column headers that read Lead Company and Lead Name. These are *static text*, rectangles that contain text for display purposes only.

The footer band contains another computed field rectangle. As it is currently sized, you can see only part of the rectangle's expression. The entire expression is:

```
'Page' + page() + ' of ' + pagecount()
```

This means that PowerBuilder will assemble a string of text that begins with the word "Page," followed by the current page number, the word "of," and the total number of pages in the document.

The items in single quotation marks are literal text. The plus signs are the concatenation operator, which pastes one string of text on the edge of another. The two literal text strings are concatenated with the return values of two functions: `page()`, which returns the current page number, and `pagecount()`, which returns the total number of pages in the report.

Adding Summary Calculations

The report in Figure 12.1 contains a count of the number of people in each group as well as a count of the total number of people on the report. Summary values such as these that apply to each group belong in the group trailer band. Summary values that apply to the entire report go in the summary band.

To add the summary values:

1. Click the **lead_name** rectangle in the detail band to select it.
2. Choose **Objects -> Count - Computed Field**. PowerBuilder expands the group trailer band and inserts the computed field.

Once you've used the Objects menu shortcut to place a computed field of a given type on a DataWindow, PowerBuilder will ignore another command to place a computed field of that type. Therefore, you must create the row count computed field that will go in the summary band manually.

3. Drag the summary band marker down to make room for a new computed field.
4. Click the **Compute** button in the PainterBar or, if the Compute button isn't present in the PainterBar, choose **Objects->Computed Field**.
5. Click anywhere in the summary band. If you are working with version 4.0, the Computed Field Definition dialog box appears.

    If you are working with version 5.0, the Computed Object properties dialog box appears. Click the **More** button to display the Computed Field Definition dialog box.

6. Click **count(#x for all)** in the Functions list. Notice that when you do this, PowerBuilder copies the function into the dialog box's edit rectangle and highlights the **#x**. The **#x** is a placeholder for what should be counted.

The count function defaults to "for all" in this case because you are working with a summary band. If you had clicked in the group trailer band, the Functions list would have shown the count function with "for group 1."

7. Type **lead_name**. The dialog box should appear like Figure 12.6 on page 283.
8. Type **overall_count** as the name of the field.
9. Click the **OK** button to close the Computed Field Definition dialog box.

    If you are working with version 5.0, click the **OK** button to close the Computed Object properties dialog box. PowerBuilder places a rectangle for the computed field in the summary band.

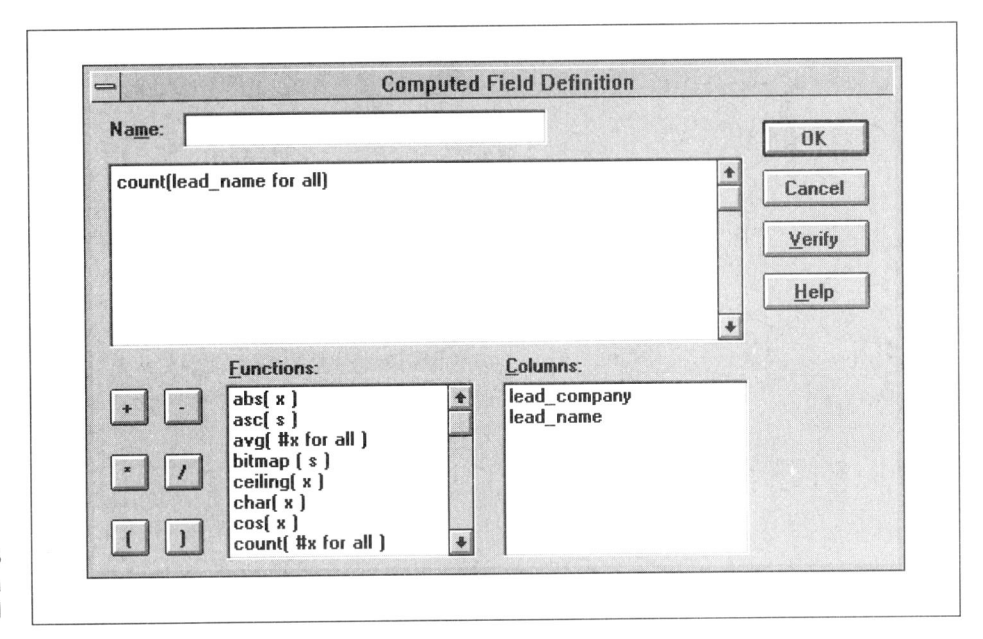

Figure 12.6
Changing the definition for a computed field

Modifying the DataWindow's Appearance

At this point, the DataWindow object can be used. However, if you preview it, you'll see that it isn't particularly attractive. In particular, the font size is too big so that very few lines appear on one page and the header, with its dark lines, should probably be modified. As you perform your modifications, you will learn several techniques for adding items to a DataWindow and for arranging those items.

To change the appearance of the data window:

1. Resize the report page header ("Sales Lead Summary") so that the rectangle is just big enough to enclose the text. Then drag the rectangle so that it is centered in the header band.

2. Select the `today()` computed field rectangle and change its font size to **9** using the dropdown menu of font sizes above the header band. Remove the boldface by clicking the **B** button in the Style Bar. Resize the rectangle so that it is just big enough to include the name of the function.

3. Ctrl-click on the report page header rectangle so that it is selected along with the `today()` computed field rectangle.

4. Choose **Edit -> Align Objects**. Choose the horizontal centering alignment from the submenu, as in Figure 12.7 on page 284. PowerBuilder centers the two objects horizontally.

5. Select one of the heavy lines in the header band. Press the **Del** key to remove it. Repeat the process with the second line.

6. Delete the Lead Company and Lead Name rectangles from the header band.

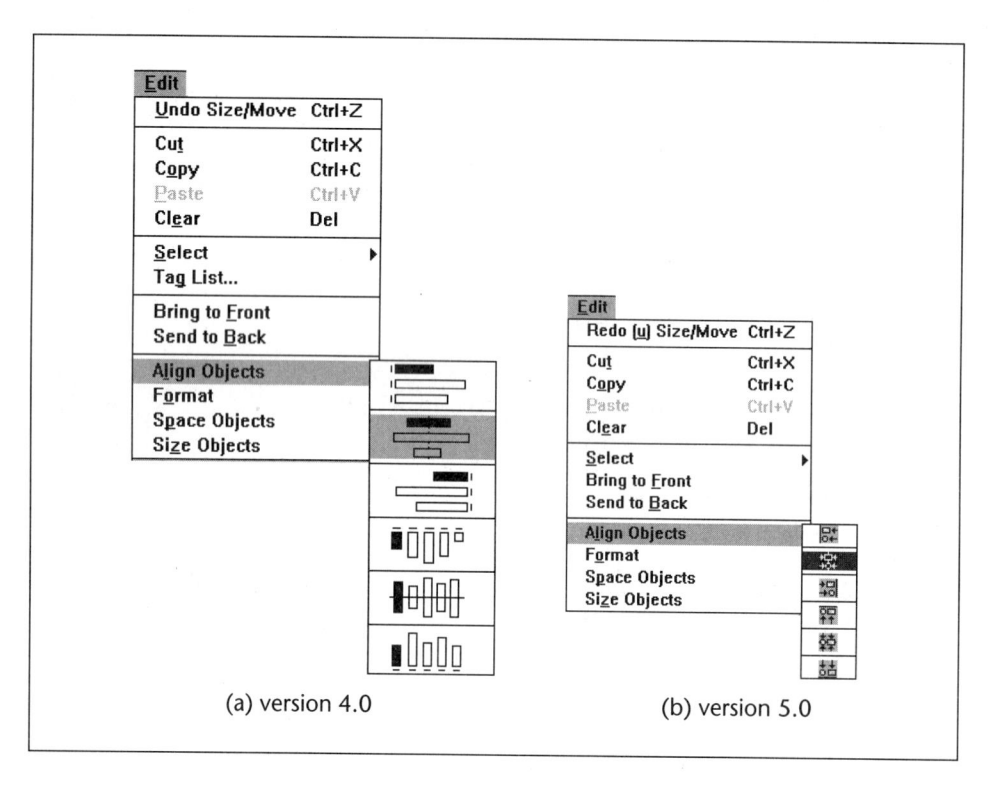

Figure 12.7
Centering objects

(a) version 4.0 (b) version 5.0

7. Move the Header band marker up until it is 1/4-inch below the contents of the band.

8. Move the rectangle in the group header band to the right to make room for some text.

9. Place a static text control at the left edge of the group header band. Type its text as **Company:**. Make the text **9** points and bold.

10. Move the text rectangle to the top left of the group header band. Move the lead_company rectangle up next to it. Align the tops of the two rectangles. (*Hint:* Select both rectangles and choose the fourth option from the Objects -> Align Objects submenu.) Move the group header band marker so the band is as small as possible.

11. Change the font size of the remaining rectangles to **9** points. (*Hint:* Ctrl-click to select all the rectangles so you can apply the change to all of them at once.)

12. Move the rectangles in the detail, group trailer, and summary bands to the top of the bands. Make the detail band as small as possible, but leave space at the bottom of the group trailer band so there will be space between groups.

13. Add static text to the left of the count (lead_name for group 1) rectangle that reads **Leads for this company:**. Add static text to the left of the count (lead_name for all) rectangle that reads **Total leads:**. Make both blocks of text boldface. Align them on their right edges. (*Hint:* Right alignment is the third option in the Edit -> Align Objects submenu.)

14 The DataWindow object is now complete. It should look something like Figure 12.8. Preview the window. If you aren't pleased with the way it looks, modify it in any way you choose. Before exiting, make sure you save the the object as **dwo_lead_summary**.

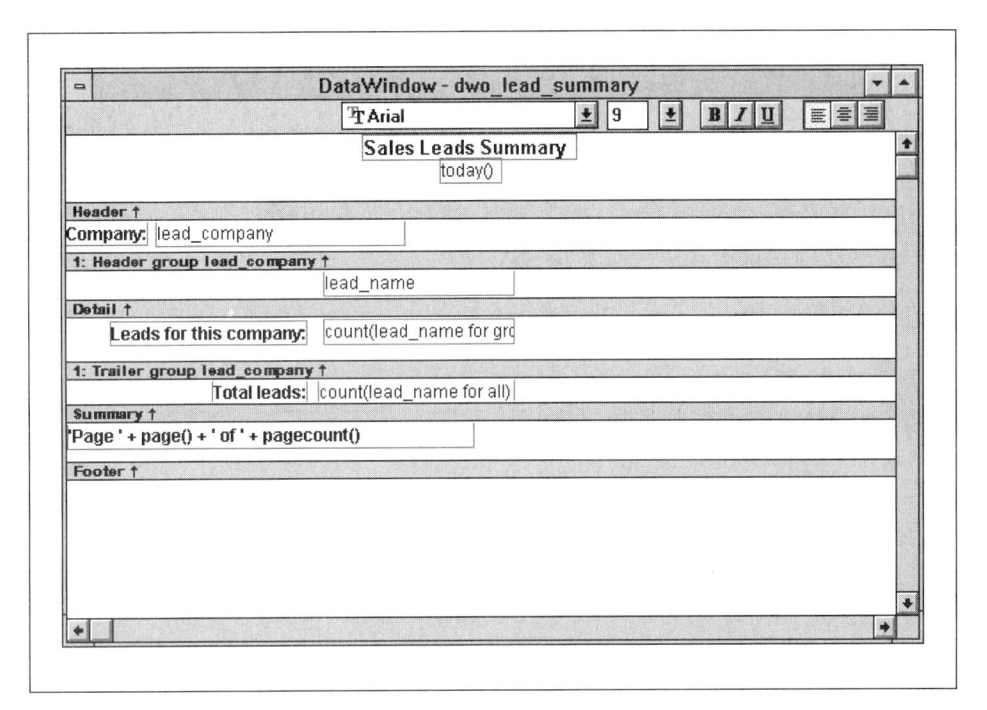

Figure 12.8
Completed DataWindow object for a report with one level of grouping

Placing the DataWindow Control

As you would expect, the next step is to attach a DataWindow control based on the new DataWindow object on an application window. Then, you'll need to add a script that retrieves data into the control.

Because you already know how to place DataWindow controls on an application window and how to write an appropriate script, the following instructions are less detailed than what you have encountered previously in this book.

To configure the DataWindow control so that you can see the control break report in the *tshows* application:

1 Open the w_leads_by_company window.

2 Place a DataWindow control on the window. Name it **dw_lead_summary**.

3 Associate the DataWindow control with the DataWindow object named dwo_lead_summary.

4 Give the control vertical scroll bars.

5 Resize the control so that it fills as much of the window as possible. Your window should look something like Figure 12.9.

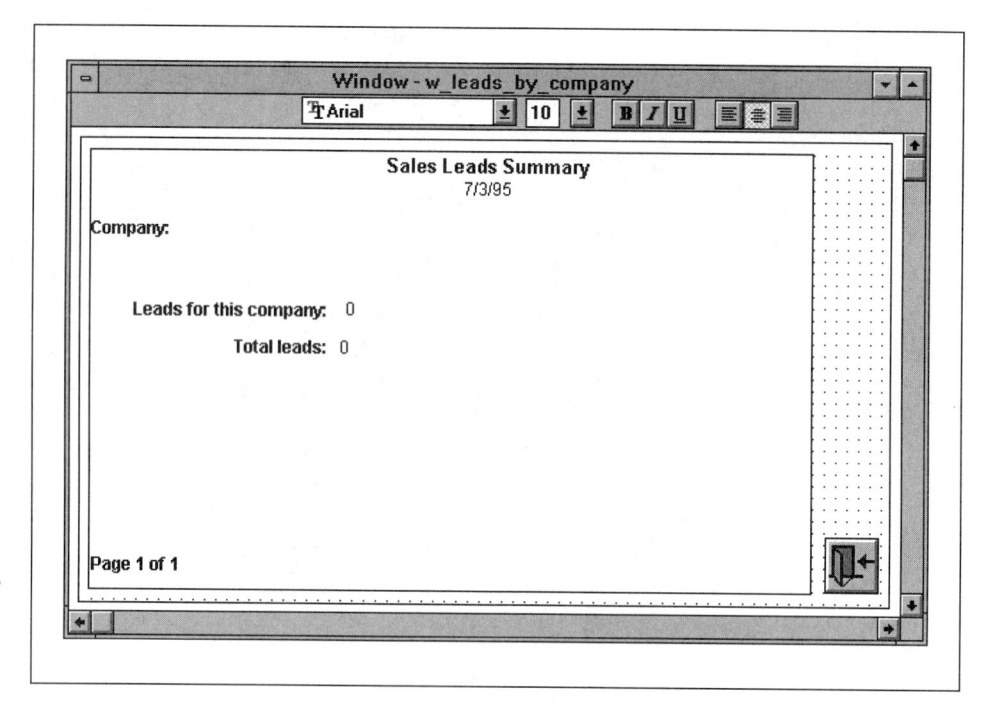

Figure 12.9
Application window with a DataWindow control for a control break report

6 Enter an open event script for the application window that does the following:

- Associates the DataWindow control with the `SQLCA` transaction object.
- Retrieves data into the DataWindow control.
- Checks to see if the retrieval succeeds.
- If the retrieval fails, rolls back the transaction.
- If the retrieval succeeds, sets the focus to the DataWindow control.

(*Hint*: This is the same script that you've used in the past to bring data into DataWindow controls. The only difference is the name of the DataWindow control.)

7 Run the application. Your output should look something like Figure 12.1. (Of course, exactly what you see depends on the data in the Leads table. If those data have been modified, your output may be different from the sample screen shot.)

Enabling Printing

Although it's useful to view reports such as the lead summary on the screen, users also often need to print reports. You might therefore want to allow them to print directly from an application. As an example, you will add a Print button to the lead summary report's window and attach a script that sends the contents of the DataWindow control to the printer.

To add printing capabilities:

1. Place a command button on the w_leads_by_company window, just above the Close button.
2. Type **Print** as the button's text. Make the text bold.
3. Enter the button's Script painter.
4. Type **Print (dw_lead_summary)** as the contents of the script.

There are several versions of the print function. In its simplest form, it sends the contents of a DataWindow control to the current default system printer. The only required parameter is the name of the DataWindow control. By default, the function displays a dialog box giving the user the opportunity to cancel printing. Should you want to suppress that dialog box, you can add a second parameter of FALSE after the name of the DataWindow control.

5. Save the script.
6. Run the application and test the Print button.

Defining Groups Through a DataWindow

The control break report in Figure 12.10 contains a summary of the costs of attending all trade shows. The report is first organized by trade show. Within each trade show, the data are organized by the starting date of the show. This report therefore has two groups: group 1 (the outer group, separated by the name of the show) and group 2 (the inner group, separated by the starting date of the show).

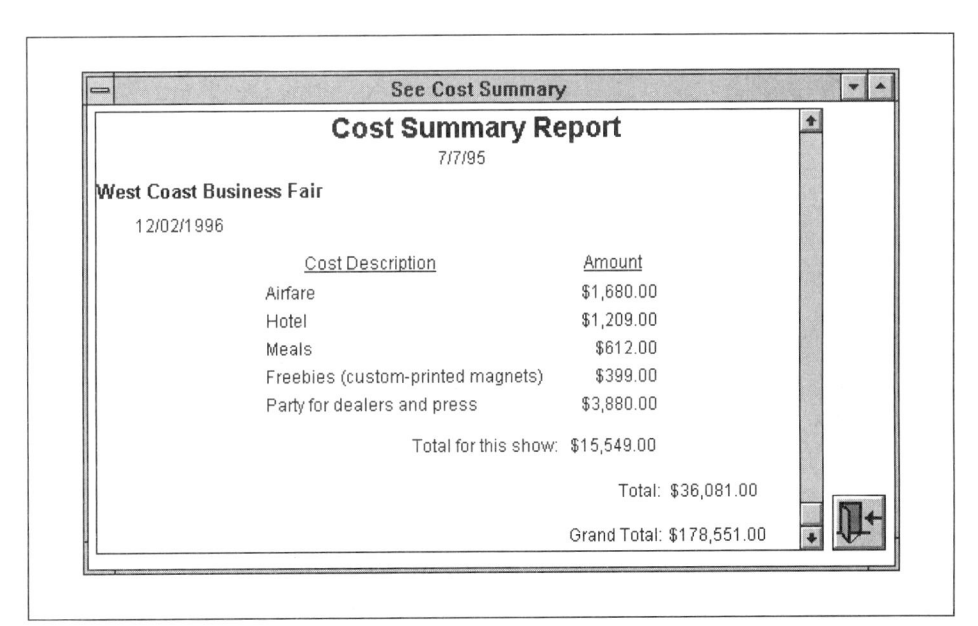

Figure 12.10
Cost Summary Report

Because the Cost Summary Report has two, nested groups, it can't be created using the Group presentation style, which can handle only a single grouping level. You must therefore add groups explicitly to a Tabular presentation style layout. In this section you will learn how to create this type of report.

Preparing the View

The data for the report in Figure 12.10 come from two tables, Calendar and Costs. Although you could build the query directly in the DataWindow painter, a view that joins Calendar and Costs might be useful for other types of output. For example, you might want to create an output window that displays costs incurred in specific year. It will therefore make the application easier to modify if you create a view on which you can base the control break report.

To create a view on which to base the control break report:

1. Enter the Database painter and, if necessary, connect to the *tshows* database.
2. Click the **View** button in the PainterBar to open the View painter.
3. Open the **Calendar** and **Costs** tables. PowerBuilder automatically joins them on the event# column.
4. Choose the **event#**, **show_name**, **start_date**, **end_date**, **cost_description**, and **amount** columns. Although the event# column appears in both tables, choose it only once. It makes no difference which table you use.
5. Click the **Return** button (the bottom button) in the PainterBar.
6. Name the view **v_calendar_costs**.

Creating the Initial DataWindow Layout

When it comes to creating DataWindow objects, using a view is just like using one or more tables. You can base a query on the view as if it were a base table, including adding retrieval arguments and joining it to other tables and views. In this particular example, however, the view contains exactly the data we need and can be used in the DataWindow object with further manipulation.

To create the DataWindow object for this report:

1. Make sure that you are using the *tshows* application in *tshows2.pbl* and that you are connected to the *tshows* database.
2. Use the DataWindow button in the PowerBar to create a new DataWindow object.
3. Choose **SQL Select** as the data source and **Tabular** as the presentation style.
4. Choose **v_calendar_costs** from the Select Tables dialog box.
5. Choose the **show_name**, **start_date**, **cost_description**, and **amount** columns.

6 Choose **show_name** as the first sort column; choose **start_date** as the second.

7 Return to the DataWindow painter.

8 Change the edit style of the cost_description column to Edit.

Adding the Groups

At this point, you have a standard tabular DataWindow object that will show one detail row for each row in the view on which the object is based. The next step therefore is to specify the columns that should be used to form the groups. You specify the outer grouping column first, followed by the inner grouping column.

To set up the groups and place data in group bands:

1 Choose **Rows** -> **Create Group**. If you are working with version 4.0, the Specify Group Columns dialog box appears.

If you are working with version 5.0, the Band Object properties dialog box appears with the Definition panel visible (Figure 12.11).

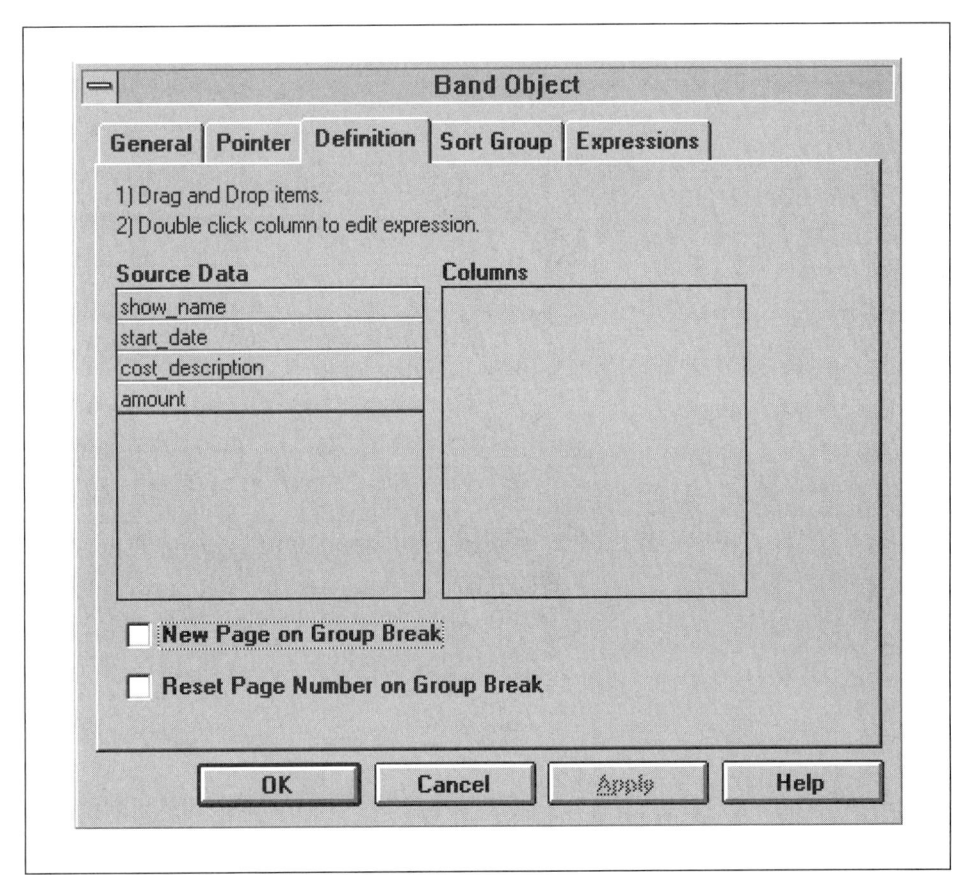

Figure 12.11
Band Object properties dialog box (5.0)

2   Drag **show_name** to the right column of the dialog box. Keep in mind that this dialog box specifies the columns that form a single level of group. The inner group must be handled separately.

3   Click the **OK** button to close the dialog box. PowerBuilder places group 1 header and trailer bands in the DataWindow painter workspace (Figure 12.12).

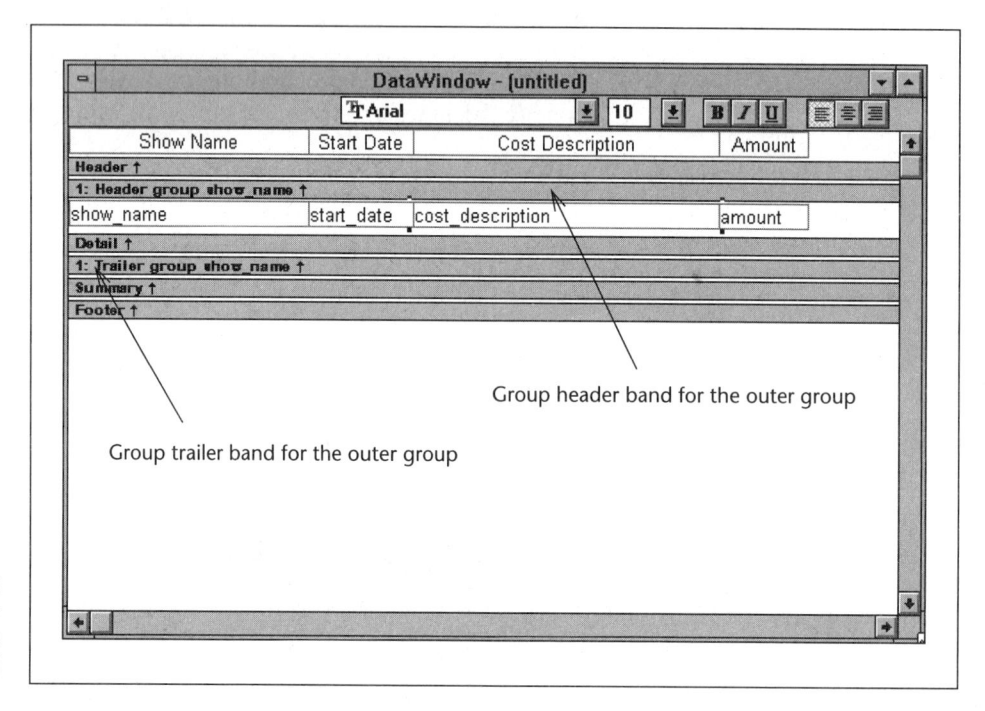

Figure 12.12
DataWindow painter workspace after bands for the first group have been added

4   Choose **Rows -> Create Group** once more to display the Specify Group Columns dialog box (version 4.0) or the Group Object properties dialog box (version 5.0).

5   Drag start_date to the right column of the dialog box.

6   Click the **OK** button to dismiss the dialog box. PowerBuilder places a group 2 header and trailer bands *inside* the group1 bands, as you can see in Figure 12.13 on page 291.

7   Drag the header band for group 1 marker down so that the band is big enough to hold a data rectangle.

8   Drag the show_name rectangle into the band. By placing it here, you ensure that the show name will display only once for each show.

9   Place the show_name rectangle at the far left of its band. Make the text bold.

10 Delete the Show Name rectangle from the header band.

11 Drag the header band for group 2 marker down so the band is about 1-inch high.

12 Drag the start_date rectangle into the group 2 header band. Place it about 1/2-inch from the left edge of the band and about 1/8-inch down from the top of the band. Make its text **9** points.

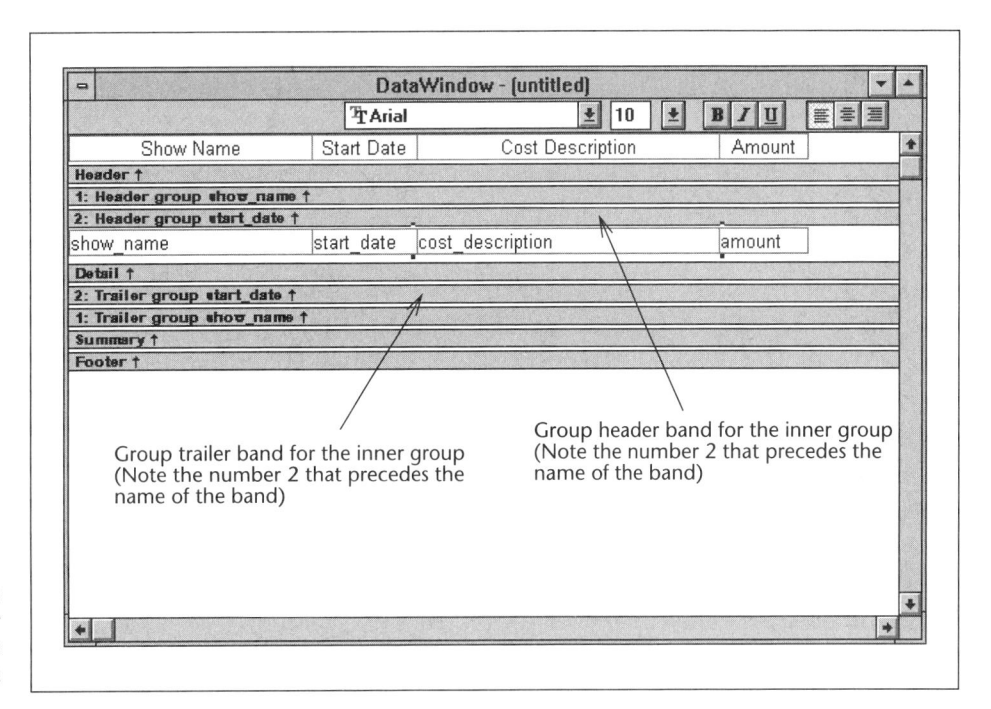

Figure 12.13
DataWindow Painter workspace after bands for the second group have been added inside bands for the first

13 Delete the Start Date rectangle from the header band.

14 Move the cost_description and amount rectangles to the center of the detail band. Make their text **9** points.

15 Move the Cost Description and Amount rectangles into the group 1 header band. Change their size to **9** points. Underline their contents by clicking the **U** button in the Style Bar. Place them above the data rectangles in the detail band, as in Figure 12.14 on page 292.

Don't forget that you can see what your DataWindow will look like at any time by clicking the Preview button in the PainterBar.

Adding Summary Calculations

The cost summary report has three levels of summary calculations: one that totals the costs of a single show (unique show name and start date), one that totals the costs of a type of show (unique show name), and a grand total. You can place the first one automatically, but because PowerBuilder will only create one computed field for a given type of calculation, you'll have to create the second two manually.

To add the group and grand totals:

1 Select the **amount** rectangle in the detail band.

2 Click the **Sum** button in the PainterBar. PowerBuilder places a computed field in the trailer band for group 2.

3 Make the group 2 trailer band about 3/4-inch high. Center the computed field in the band's height.

292 CHAPTER TWELVE CONTROL BREAK REPORTS

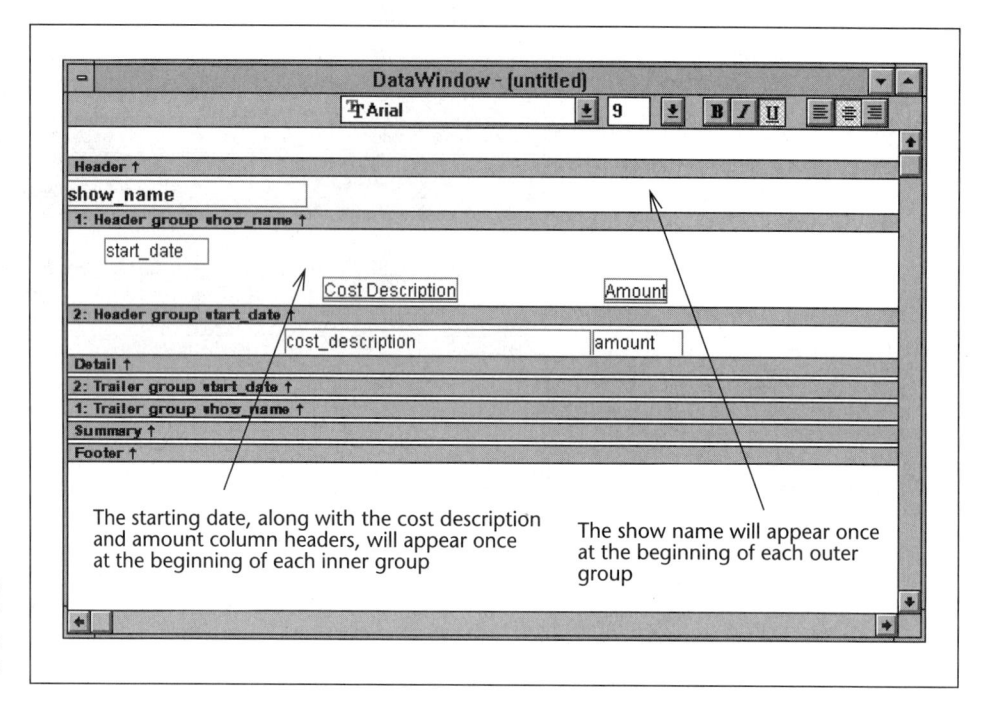

Figure 12.14
DataWindow painter workspace after contents have been placed in group header bands

4 Add text to the left of the band that reads **Total for this show:**.

5 Make the group 1 trailer band about 1/2-inch high.

6 Click the **Compute** button in the PainterBar, or if the Compute button isn't present in the PainterBar, choose **Objects->Computed Field**.

7 Click in the group 1 trailer band. If you are working with version 4.0, the Computed Field Definition dialog box appears.

If you are working with version 5.0, the Computed Object properties dialog box appears. Click the **More** button to display the Computed Field Definition dialog box.

8 Scroll the list of functions until you find the sum function. Notice that because you clicked in the group 1 trailer band, the function is written for that group.

9 Click the **sum** function in the Functions list to transfer it to the edit box at the top of the dialog box.

10 Click the **amount** column. The column name replaces the #x placeholder in the function's parameter list.

11 Click the **OK** button to close the Computed Field Definition dialog box. If you are working with version 5.0, the Computed Object properties dialog box is still visible.

12 If you are working with version 4.0, right-click on the computed field rectangle to display the rectangle's popup menu. Choose **Format** from the popup menu. The Display Number Formats dialog box appears.

If you are working with version 5.0, click the **Format** tab at the top of the Computed Object properties dialog box. The Format panel appears.

13 Choose the display format that you see in Figure 12.15. Click the **OK** button to close the dialog box.

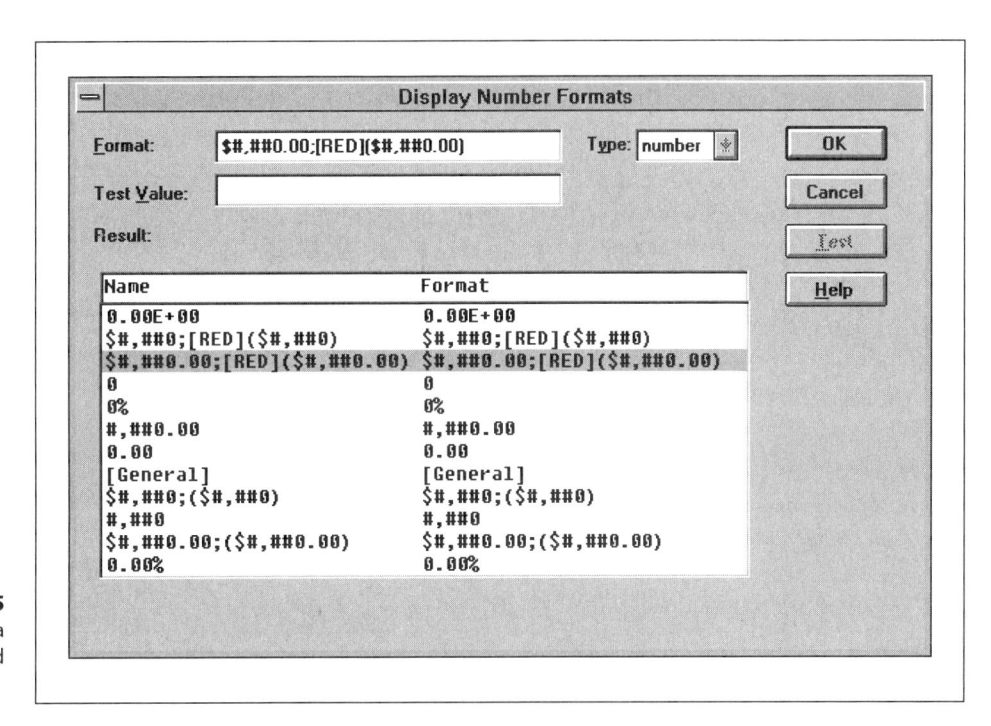

Figure 12.15
Choosing a display format for a computed field

14 Move the computed field to the right of the field column in the group 2 trailer band. Place it at the top of the band. If necessary, expand the width of the computed field so that the rectangle is 2-inches wide.

15 Add text to the group 2 trailer band that reads **Total:**. Place the text at the left of the computed field.

16 Repeat Steps 5 through 16 for the summary band. Make the text in the band read **Grand Total:**.

To finish the DataWindow object by adding a report title:

1 Place text in the header band that reads **Cost Summary Report**. Make the text 14 points and bold.

2 Add a computed field below the title that contains the `today()` function. Set the format of this computed field to the format in Figure 12.16 on page 294.

3 Save the DataWindow object as **dwo_cost_summary**.

The DataWindow object is now complete. It should look something like Figure 12.17 on page 294.

294 CHAPTER TWELVE CONTROL BREAK REPORTS

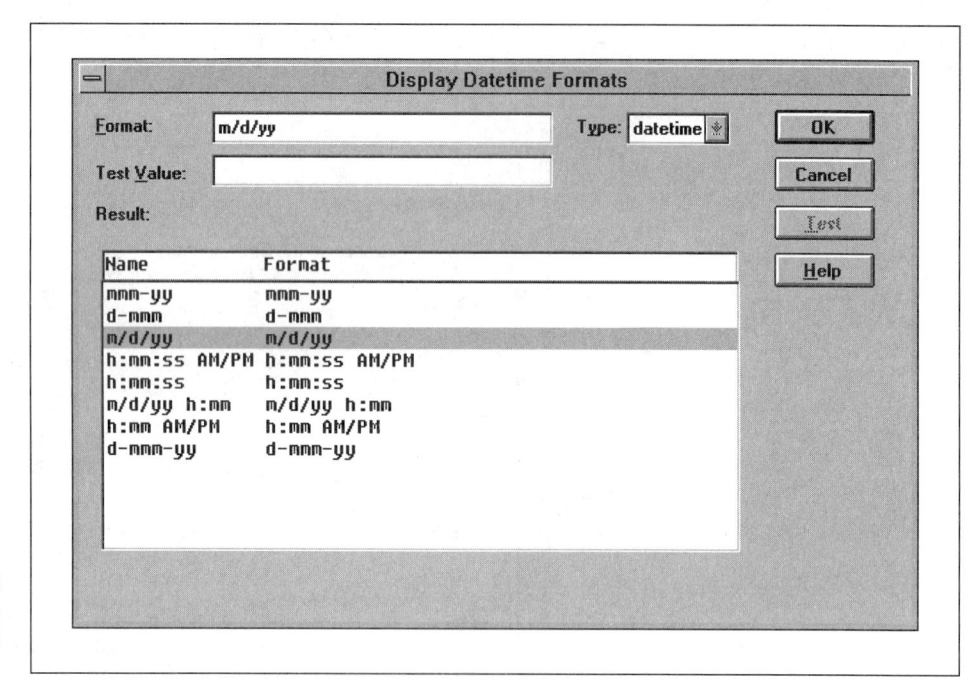

Figure 12.16
Choosing a display format for a Datetime computed field

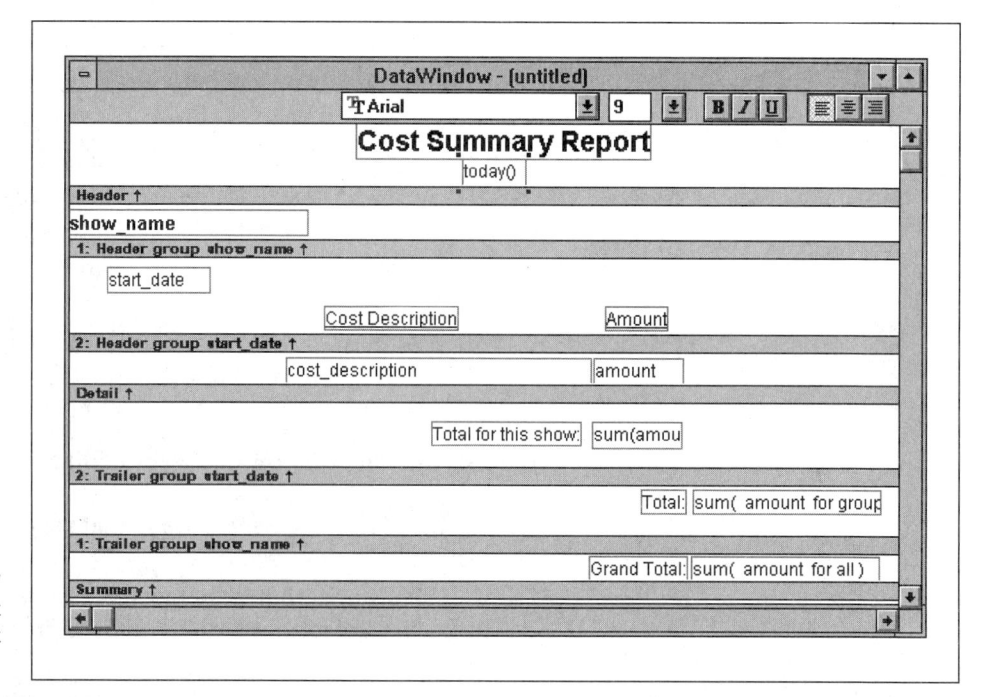

Figure 12.17
The completed cost summary report DataWindow object

Placing the DataWindow Control

As you know, to add the cost summary to the *tshows* application, you need to place a control based on the DataWindow object you just created on an application window.

To place a control on the application window:

1. Open the w_see_cost_summary window in the Window painter.
2. Place a DataWindow on the window.
3. Associate the control with dwo_cost_summary.
4. Name the control **dw_cost_summary**. Give it a vertical scroll bar.
5. Make the control as wide and tall as possible so that the user can see as much data as can fit on the screen without scrolling.
6. Add a script for the window's open event to associate the DataWindow control with a transaction object and retrieve data for the control.
7. Run the application. Make sure that you can see the group 1 and summary band computed fields. If you can't, return to the DataWindow object and move the fields to the left.

Looking Ahead

In this chapter you have explored a common type of output—the control break report—which is used to group and summarize data. Such reports are based on SQL queries with a GROUP BY clause, although you don't need to write the query directly. If you need only one level of grouping, you can use PowerBuilder's Group presentation style; if you need more than one grouping level, you can add the groups yourself in the DataWindow painter.

Although PowerBuilder has many other data presentation techniques about which you will learn in this book, the next chapter digresses a bit and focuses on inheritance. Inheritance can simplify creating DataWindows by letting you derive a new DataWindow from an existing DataWindow, in many cases, saving you a great deal of repetitive work!

EXERCISES

In these exercises you will create several control break reports for the College and University Rentals database.

1. Complete a window that lists customers by school. Base the report on the Customers table. Use school_name as the break column. Display the school name in the group header band; display customer names and phone numbers in the detail band.
2. Complete a window that displays the status of C&U Rentals merchandise. To do this you will need to:
   a. Create a view that contains the merchandise_description column from the Merchandise table and inventory_control# and status from the Item table.

b. Base the report on the view.
c. Use merchandise_description as the grouping column.
d. Display the merchandise description in the group header band.
e. Display inventory control numbers and the status of the items in the detail band.

3. Create a summary report that shows income from rentals. The report should group rentals by type of merchandise and show the total revenue for each type as well as the grant total of all merchandise. To do this you will need to:

    a. Create a view that contains merchandise_description from Merchandise, inventory_control# and fee_paid from Rentals. Restrict the view to those rows where status = 'rented.' Keep in mind that the view must use the Item table as well as Merchandise and Rentals to effect the joins.
    b. Base the report on the view.
    c. Use merchandise_description as the break column.
    d. Display the merchandise description in the group header band.
    e. Display the inventory control number and the fee collected in the detail band.
    f. Place the grand total of all rental fees in the summary band.

4. Create a report with two levels of control breaks that show the rental revenue generated by customer and by school. To do this you will need to:

    a. Create a view that contains customer_name and school from Customers, merchandise_description from Merchandise, and fee_paid from Rentals. Don't forget that you will need to use the Item table to make the necessary joins work.
    b. Base the report on the view.
    c. Use school as the group 1 break column.
    d. Display the name of the school in the group 1 header band.
    e. Use customer_name as the group 2 break column.
    f. Display the name of the customer in the group 2 break header band.
    g. Display the type of merchandise and the rental fee in the detail band.
    h. Display the total fees received from one customer in the group 2 trailer band.
    i. Display total fees received for the school in the group 1 trailer band.
    j. Display a grand total of fees received in the summary band.

5. Create a report with three levels of control breaks that can be used as a delivery schedule. To do this, you will need to:

    a. Create a view that contains customer_name, school, and dorm from Customers, and inventory_control# Rentals.
    b. Base the report on the view. Give the DataWindow object a retrieval object for the delivery_date column.
    c. Create a response window that accepts the delivery date.
    d. Use school as the first break column. Use dorm as the second break column. Use the name of the customer as the third, innermost
    e. Display the name of the school in the group 1 header; display the name of the dorm in the group 2 header; display the name of the student in the group 3 header.
    f. Place the inventory control number in the detail band.

Chapter Thirteen

Inheritance

IN THIS CHAPTER YOU WILL:

- Learn what is inherited when you derive one object from another
- Explore what you can do with a derived object
- Create windows using inheritance

As you know, inheritance provides a way of deriving objects from one another. When first created, the derived object is an exact duplicate of its ancestor. However, the descendant object can be modified in many ways to tailor it to an application's specific needs.

In this chapter you will explore inheritance, using it to create windows. You will discover what can be inherited and once inheritance has occurred, what changes you can make to the descendant object. Along the way, you will also get a chance to work with a DataWindow object that uses more than one retrieval argument and see how to change the tab order in a window.

When to Use Inheritance

Earlier in this book you duplicated windows by saving them under another name. You then changed each duplicate's title to make the window's title unique. This is one way to save time by avoiding repeated development effort. It does, however, have one major effect of which you need to be aware: The duplicated windows are completely independent of one another. If you make a change in one, it has no impact on any of the others.

In some cases, this is exactly what you want to occur. You want to take some minimally configured windows and then customize them in ways that make them unique. The windows will never share anything more than perhaps a button or two. In addition, because only windows, menus, and user objects (special objects you create and name) support inheritance, duplicating is the only way to avoid repeated actions for objects such as DataWindow objects.

However, if your application uses windows that should always behave in very similar ways, then inheritance might be appropriate. Keep in mind that unless you have modified some characteristic of a descendent, any change in the corresponding characteristic in the ancestor causes the same change to be propagated to the descendant. Inheritance therefore not only can help you avoid extra work, but can help maintain consistency in your interface.

In this chapter, you will be working with three similar windows from the *tshows* application. The first window (w_see_all_shows) displays data from the Calendar table within a range of dates. The two similar windows view past shows that have been attended (w_see_future_shows) and shows that will be attended (w_see_past_shows). The major difference among these three windows is the query on which their DataWindow object is based. The first displays all rows within a given range of dates; the second and third filter rows based on the date range and whether Pinehill Software will be attending the show.

Therefore, you can first complete the w_see_all_shows window and then create the other two using inheritance. There are two ways in which the inheritance could be implemented. You can create w_see_all_shows and derive w_see_future_shows from it. Then, you can derive w_see_past_shows from w_see_future_shows, as in Figure 13.1(a). Alternatively, you could derive both w_see_future_shows and w_see_past_shows from w_see_all_shows, as in Figure 13.1(b). You will be using the straight-line hierarchy in Figure 13.1(a) when you create your inherited windows.

All you need to do to the descendant windows is change the DataWindow object associated with the window's DataWindow control. As you modify the DataWindow object, you will also, in at least one case, need to override a script.

Script Modifications

Unless you make some modification to a script, a descendant window actually executes the scripts in its ancestor. You will see this in action when you derive a window to show future shows from a window that shows past shows. However, if the ancestor's scripts aren't exactly what you need, there are two basic ways in which you can change the scripts a descendant inherits from its ancestor:

- You can *override* the ancestor's script, in which case the descendant script runs in place of the ancestor script. Any code that you place in a script for an event in a descendant object—even a comment statement—overrides the ancestor script for that event. This means that if you simply want to prevent the ancestor script from executing, all you have to do is write a script in the descendant object that contains nothing but a comment statement. You will practice overriding an ancestor's script when you derive a window to show all past shows from a window that displays all scheduled shows.
- You can add to the ancestor's script, in which the case the descendant script runs *after* the ancestor script.

Note that there is no direct way to automatically get a descendant script to run *before* the ancestor's script. However, what you can do is override the ancestor script, write the code you want to execute, and then explicitly call the ancestor script.

To call one of the ancestor window's scripts, you use the following general syntax:

```
CALL ancestor_window_name :: event
```

To call a script attached to one of the ancestor window's controls, use the following syntax:

```
CALL ancestor_window_name `control_name :: event
```

There are two important elements in these statements. The first is the double colon (the *scope resolution operator*), which is used to show the object to which an attribute belongs. Notice that in both cases it separates the name of the event from that of the object to which it belongs. The other important feature is the character that precedes the name of the control when you are calling a control's script. That character is the left-facing single quotation mark. It is typically found to the left of the 1 key on the top row of the keyboard.

Preparing the Ancestor Application Window

The first step in creating windows using inheritance is to create the ancestor window. In the case of the *tshows* application, you already have a window with a Close button on it. You therefore need to create a DataWindow object and associate it with a DataWindow control.

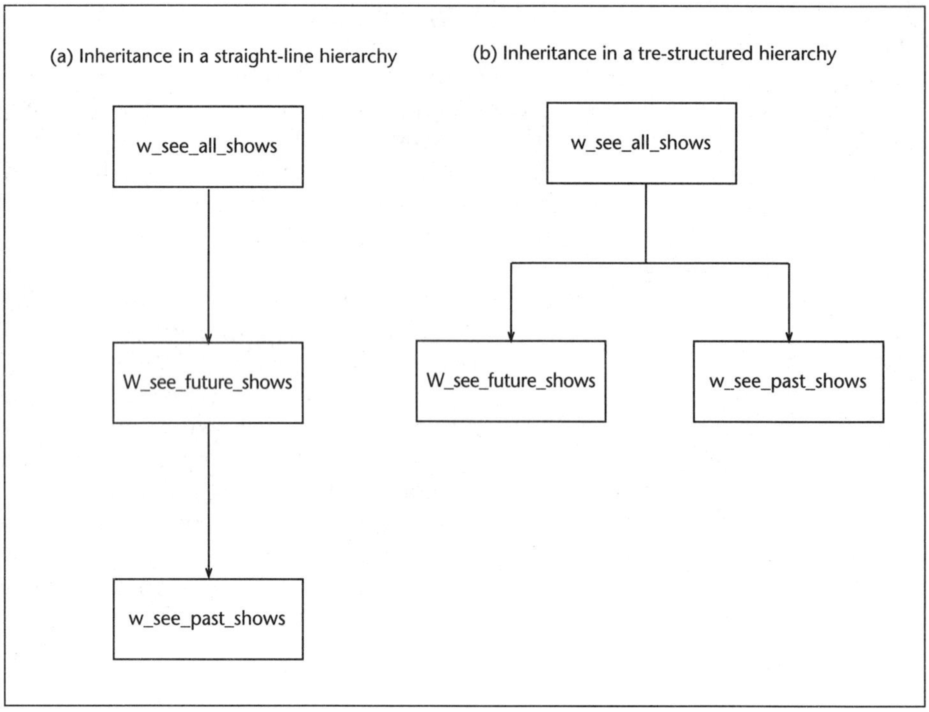

Figure 13.1
Two ways of structuring inheritance

(a) Inheritance in a straight-line hierarchy

(b) Inheritance in a tre-structured hierarchy

The ancestor window can use a response window to capture the date range for display; the descendant windows will only need one of the dates.

What You Can Do to a Descendant

When you create a new window using inheritance, the descendant window inherits everything from its ancestor, including controls placed on the window and all scripts. Because of the relationship between the ancestor and its descendants, there is a limit to the types of modifications you can make to controls and scripts in the descendant.

Control Modifications

You can make the following modifications to controls in a descendant object:

- Move controls
- Change control properties, such as name or style
- Add new controls

The one thing you *cannot* do is to delete controls. However, if you don't need a control in a descendant window, you can make it invisible so that the user can't see it.

The DataWindow Object

The initial DataWindow object for the listings of scheduled trade shows can easily be built using a SQL Select and a Tabular presentation style.

To create the DataWindow object that can accept retrieval arguments:

1. Make sure that you are working with the *tshows* application in *thsows2.pbl* and that you are connected to the *tshows* database.
2. Create a new DataWindow object using SQL Select as the data source and Tabular as the presentation style.
3. Choose the **Calendar** table and include the **show_name**, **start_date**, **end_date**, and **participation** columns.
4. Sort the output by start_date within show_name.
5. Create two retrieval arguments, one for the starting date and one for the ending date, as in Figure 13.2.

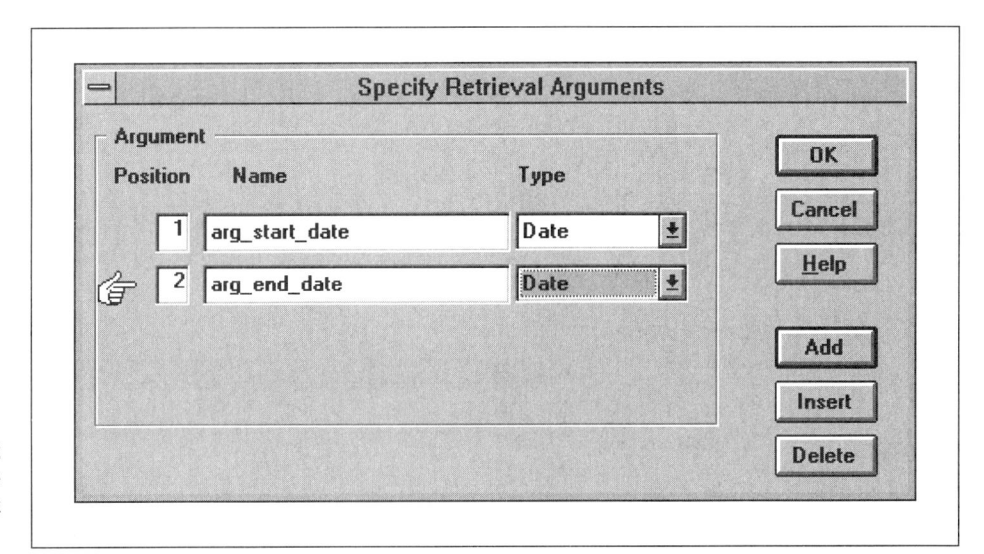

Figure 13.2
Retrieval arguments for the DataWindow object

6. Use the retrieval arguments in the WHERE clause so that the query retrieves rows that are greater than or equal to the starting date and less than or equal to the ending date, as shown in Figure 13.3.

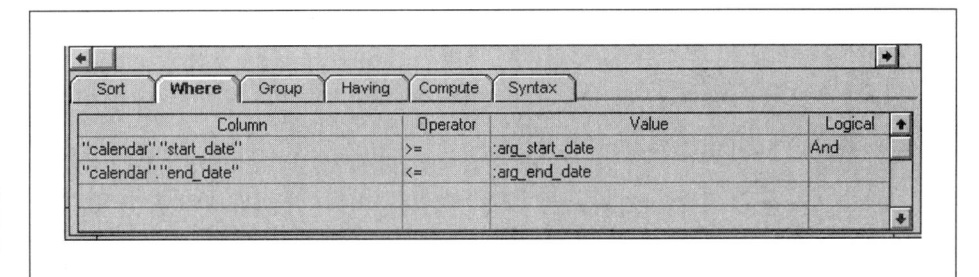

Figure 13.3
A WHERE clause using two retrieval arguments

7 Return to the DataWindow painter.

8 Remove the CheckBox edit style from the participation column; replace it with the Edit edit style. Make sure you remove the X from the Use code table check box in the Edit dialog box.

9 Format the window in any way you like.

10 Save the window as **dwo_see_all_shows**.

In its simplest form, the completed DataWindow might look like Figure 13.4.

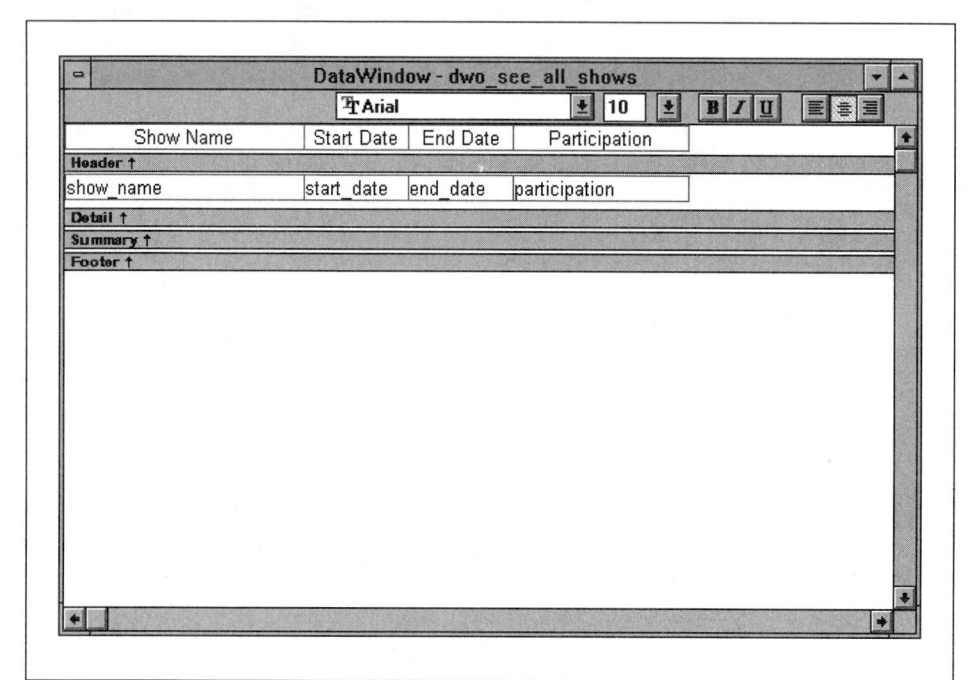

Figure 13.4
DataWindow object for the ancestor window

The Control

At this point, you can place a control for the DataWindow on the application window and write a script to populate the DataWindow control with data.

To place a DataWindow control and write a script to populate the control with data:

1 Open the w_see_all_shows window.

2 Add a DataWindow control to the window. Name it **dw_see_all_shows**. Associate it with the dwo_see_all_shows DataWindow object.

3 Resize the DataWindow control so that the window looks something like Figure 13.5 on page 303.

4 Enter the Script painter for the window's open event.

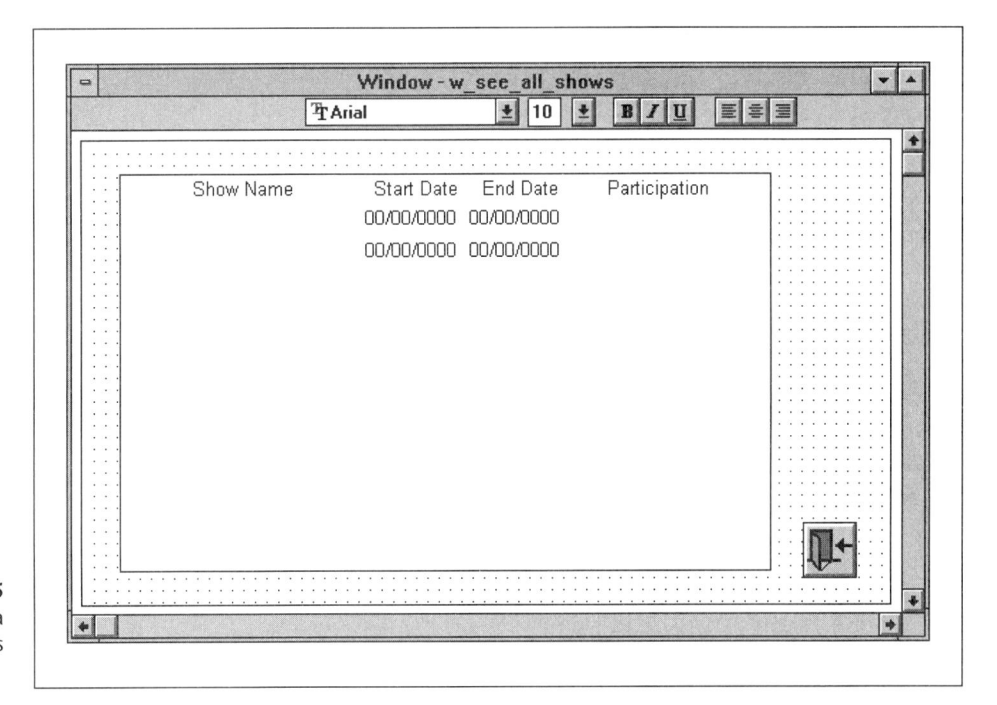

Figure 13.5
Application window that displays a listing of all scheduled shows

5 Define two global variables, as in Figure 13.6. Because the Data-Window control requires two retrieval arguments, the data must be passed between the response window and the application window through globals. (Remember that the `OpenWithParm` function can only handle one parameter because the `Message` object only has room for one value.)

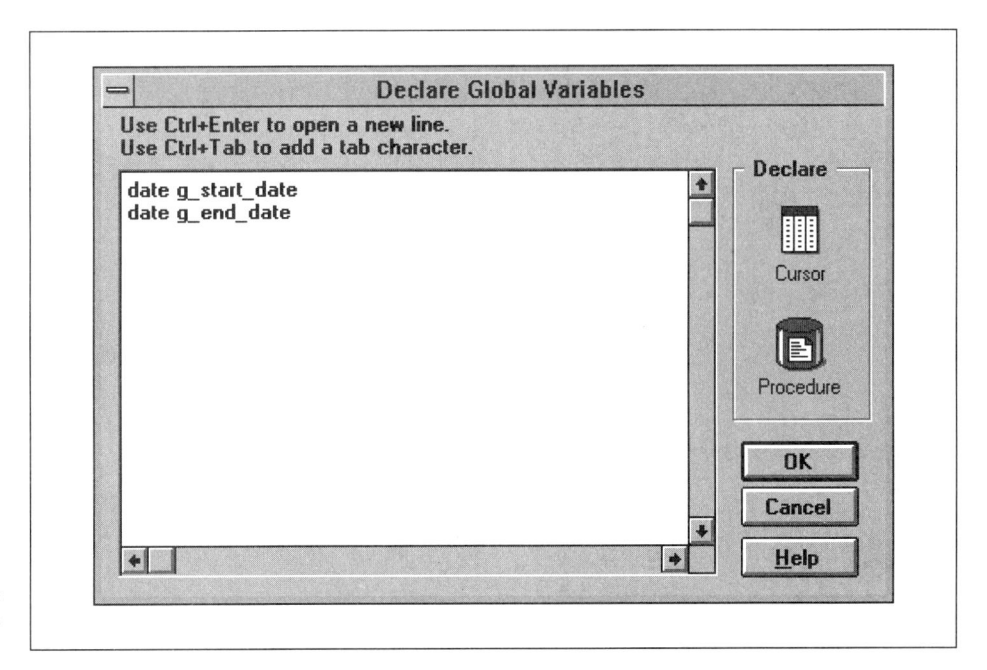

Figure 13.6
Declaring global variables

6   Enter the Script painter for the application window's open event. Enter the script in Listing 13.1. Notice that the call to Retrieve has two parameters, the starting date and the ending date. They are in the same order as they were defined in the DataWindow object.

Listing 13.1
Script for the open event for the window w_see_all_shows

```
dw_see_all_shows.settransobject (sqlca)

if dw_see_all_shows.retrieve (g_start_date,g_end_date) = -1 then
   rollback using sqlca;
   messagebox ("Retrieve","No rows were found.")
else
   commit using sqlca;
   dw_see_all_shows.setfocus()
end if
```

The application window is now ready. However, by itself it won't retrieve any rows because there's nothing that places values in the global variables that are used as retrieval arguments. The response window will take care of that problem.

Creating the Ancestor Response Window

The next step in the process is to prepare the response window that will accept the two dates that will be used as retrieval arguments.

To prepare the response window that will accept retrieval arguments from the user:

1   Create a new window.
2   Give the window the title of **Choose Calendar Report Dates**.
3   Change the window's type to **Response**.
4   Place static text toward the top of window that reads **Enter a starting and ending date and press OK:**.
5   Place two SingleLineEdit controls on the window (**sle_start_date** for the starting date and **sle_end_date** for the ending date).
6   Place static text over each edit control that reads **Starting Date** for sle_start_date and **Ending Date** for sle_end_date.
7   Create a command button with the name **cb_dates_cancel** with text that reads **Cancel** and a script that reads **close (parent)**.
8   Create a command button with the name **cb_dates_ok** with text that reads **OK**.
9   Enter the script in Listing 13.2 for the OK button's clicked event. This script takes the text stored in each SingleLineEdit control, converts it to a date, and assigns it to the appropriate global variable. Because

global variables are available to the entire application and retain their values until explicitly changed, there is no need to do anything else to make these values available to w_see_all_shows. Therefore, this script can open that window with a simple call to the Open function.

Listing 13.2
Clicked event script for the response window's OK button.

```
// need to get data from SingleLineEdit controls

g_start_date = Date (sle_start_date.Text)
g_end_date = Date (sle_end_date.Text)

// open the display window, but don't bother to pass because
// the values are global

Open (w_see_all_shows)

// close response window
close (parent)
```

10 Arrange and resize the window so that it looks something like Figure 13.7.

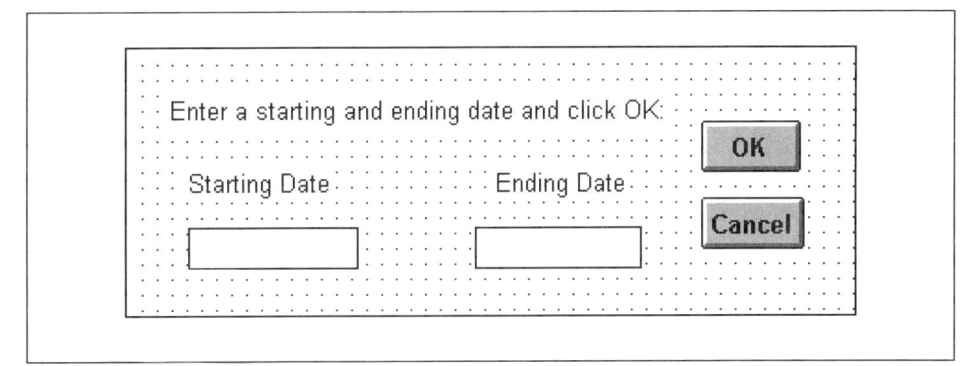

Figure 13.7
Completed design for the response window

11 Enter a script for the window's open event that reads:

```
sle_start_date.setfocus()
```

The purpose of this call to SetFocus is to place the insertion point in the first SingleLineEdit control when the window opens.

12 Save the window as **rw_enter_dates**.

13 Open the w_calendar window. Change the open script for the See All Scheduled Shows button so that it reads

```
open (rw_enter_dates)
```

Changing the Tab Order

At this point, you can run the application. When the response window appears, the cursor will flash in the starting date edit control. However, when you press the Tab key, the cursor won't jump to the ending date edit control, which is the behavior that you would expect to occur. This happens because PowerBuilder establishes a default tab order for the elements on a window based on the placement of the elements on the window. In general, the higher and more toward the left that a control is placed, the higher its place in the tab order.

To change the default tab order:

1 Choose **Design** -> **Tab Order**. Numbers that represent the current tab order appear on the window, as in Figure 13.8 The static text controls have values of 0 because they can't have focus; a user can't tab into them. The remaining numbers are relative representations of each element's tab position, lower values indicating earlier positions. In this particular window, the tab order starts with the OK button and moves to the Cancel button, the ending date edit control, and the starting date edit control.

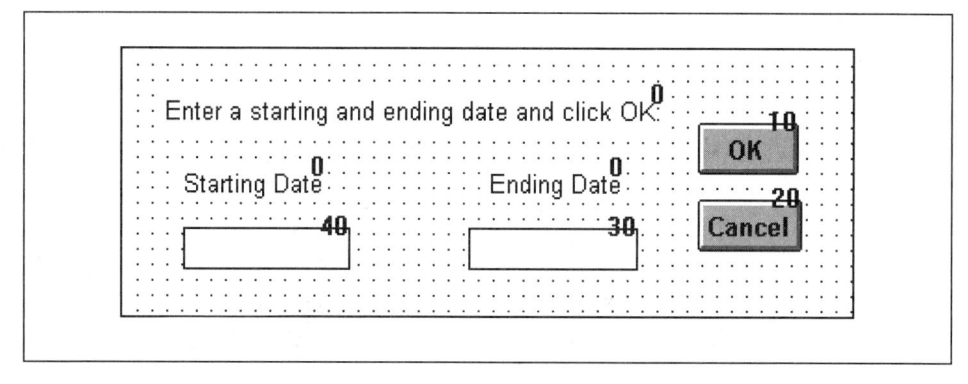

Figure 13.8
Default tab order

To change the tab order, you modify the numbers assigned to elements in the window so that their relative values place the controls in the correct order.

2 Click the number above the starting date edit control (40 in Figure 13.8) to highlight it; then type **5**.

3 Click the number above the ending date edit control (30 in Figure 13.8) to highlight it; then type **7**.

4 If necessary, change the value above the OK button to **10**.

5 If necessary, change the value above the Cancel button to **20**. Your modified window should look like Figure 13.9 on page 307.

6 Choose **Design** -> **Tab Order** once more to remove the tab order numbers.

7 Run the application again. This time, pressing the Tab key should work properly.

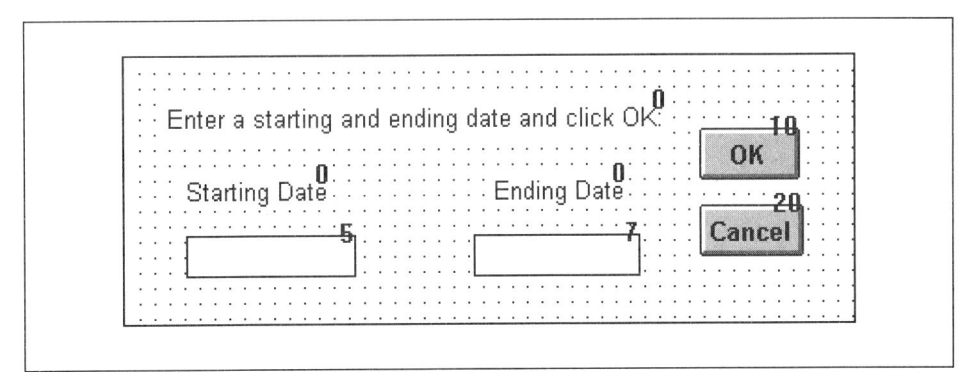

Figure 13.9
Modified tab order

Duplicating and Modifying the DataWindow Objects

Now that you have the ancestor window's developed, you can turn to the objects that you are going to derive from them. You'll work first on the application windows and then worry about the response windows.

As you've already discovered, the windows that display past and future shows are based on slightly different DataWindow objects from that used by the window that displays all scheduled shows.

Creating the First Descendant Window

You can derive many descendant windows from any single ancestor window. By the same token, a window that is itself a descendant can also become an ancestor when you derive a window from it. In this section you will be deriving one window from the ancestor you just created. Because the second descendant window is more similar to the first descendant than to the original ancestor window, you can save yourself some work by deriving the second descendant from the first descendant.

Duplicating the DataWindow Objects The first step in preparing the descendant windows is to duplicate and modify the DataWindow objects. (As you may remember, you cannot use inheritance with DataWindow objects.)

To prepare the DataWindow objects for the descendant windows:

1 Open the dwo_see_all_shows DataWindow in the DataWindow painter.
2 Save it as **dwo_see_future_shows**.
3 Click the **SQL** button in the PainterBar to enter the Query painter. (*Hint:* it's the second button from the top.)
4 Modify the query's WHERE clause so that it looks like Figure 13.10 on page 308. Notice that the second clause in this WHERE now includes an expression that retrieves only those shows that Pinehill Software will actually be attending.
5 Choose **Objects** -> **Retrieval Arguments**. The Specify Retrieval Arguments dialog box appears.

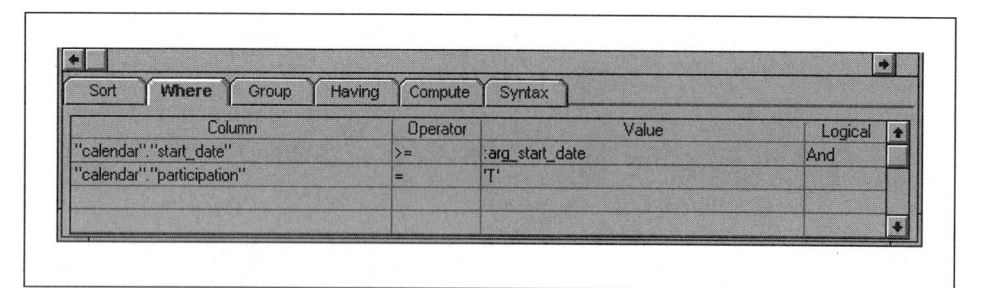

Figure 13.10
WHERE clause for dwo_see_future_shows

6   Click in the row for the second retrieval argument.
7   Click the **Delete** button to remove it.
8   Click the **OK** button to remove the dialog box.

Technically, you don't need to delete the unused retrieval argument. However, if you don't, whenever you exit the Query painter, PowerBuilder will warn you that the argument is unused and ask you if you want to proceed. It's a bit cleaner and less annoying to simply delete the argument.

9   Return to the DataWindow painter.
10 Choose **File** -> **Save** to save the change you just made.
11 Save the DataWindow object as **dwo_see_past_shows**.
12 Enter the Query painter.
13 Modify the WHERE clause by changing the >= operator in the first expression to <, as in Figure 13.11.

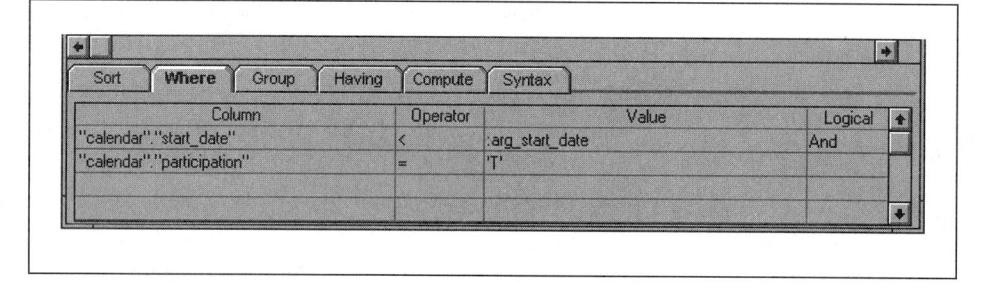

Figure 13.11
WHERE clause for dwo_see_past_shows

14 Return to the DataWindow painter and save the changes.

Creating the First Descendant Application Window   Now that the DataWindow objects have been prepared, you can turn to actually creating a descendant window. You will first derive a window for viewing future shows that will be attended from the window that displays all future shows. You will then need to change the DataWindow object with which the window's DataWindow control is associated. Because the DataWindow used in the descendant window requires only one retrieval argument, you will also need to override the ancestor window's open event script.

CHAPTER THIRTEEN INHERITANCE **309**

To create the descendant application window:

1 Click the **Window** button in the PainterBar to display the Select Window dialog box.

2 Click the **Inherit** button. The Inherit From Window dialog box appears.

3 Highlight **w_see_all_shows** in the scrolling list of window names, as in Figure 13.12.

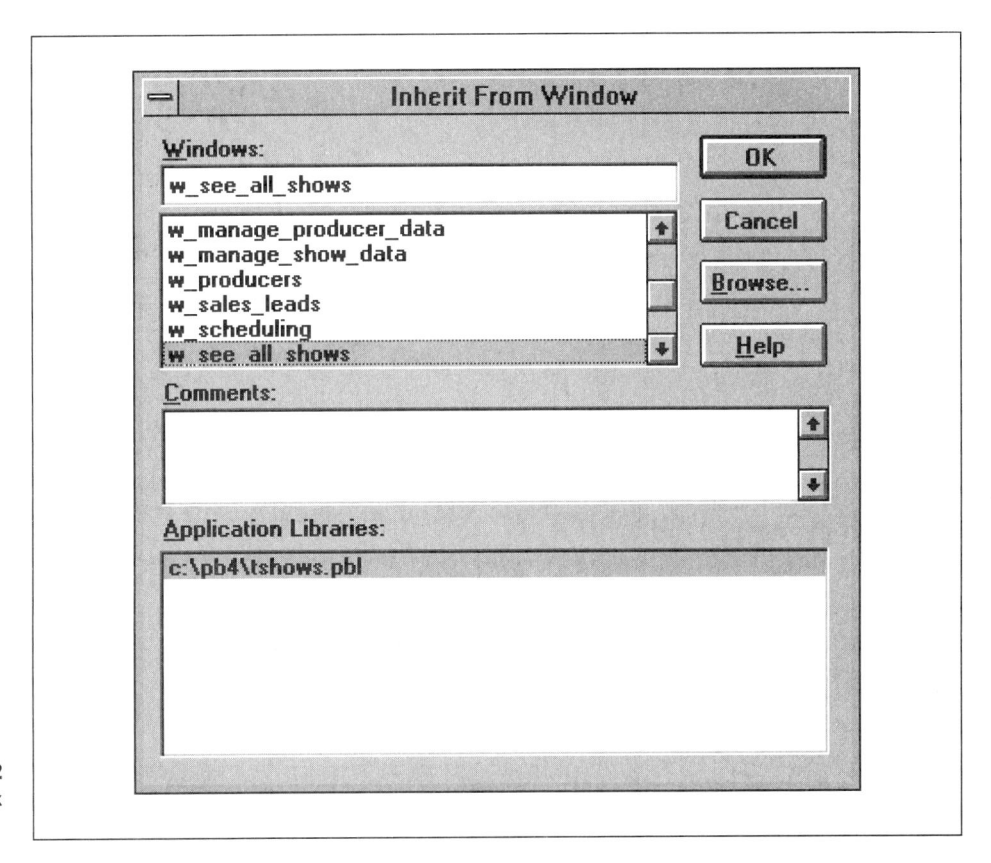

Figure 13.12
Inherit From Window dialog box

4 Click the **OK** button. A new untitled window appears. However, as you can see in Figure 13.13 on page 310, the window's title bar indicates that it is a descendant window and tells you the window from which it is derived.

5 If you are working with version 4.0, right-click the DataWindow control to display its popup menu. Choose **Change DataWindow** from the popup menu.

If you are working with version 5.0, double-click anywhere on the DataWindow control to display the DataWindow properties dialog box. Click the **Browse** button. In both versions, the Select DataWindow dialog box appears.

6 Choose **dwo_see_future_shows** from the scrolling list of DataWindow objects.

7 Click the **OK** button to close the dialog box.

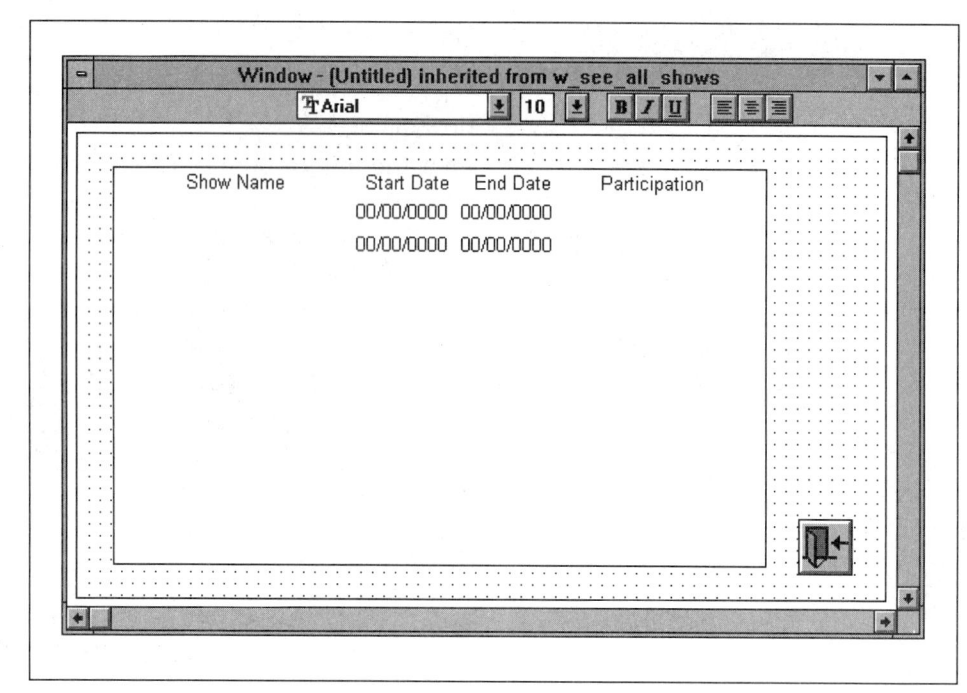

Figure 13.13
New descendant window

Although you are going to need to override the ancestor window's open event script, the script is very similar to the ancestor script. You can therefore save a lot of coding if you copy the script from the ancestor and then modify it.

8 Enter the Script painter for the window's open event.

9 Choose **Compile -> Display Ancestor Script**. The Display Ancestor Script dialog box appears (Figure 13.14).

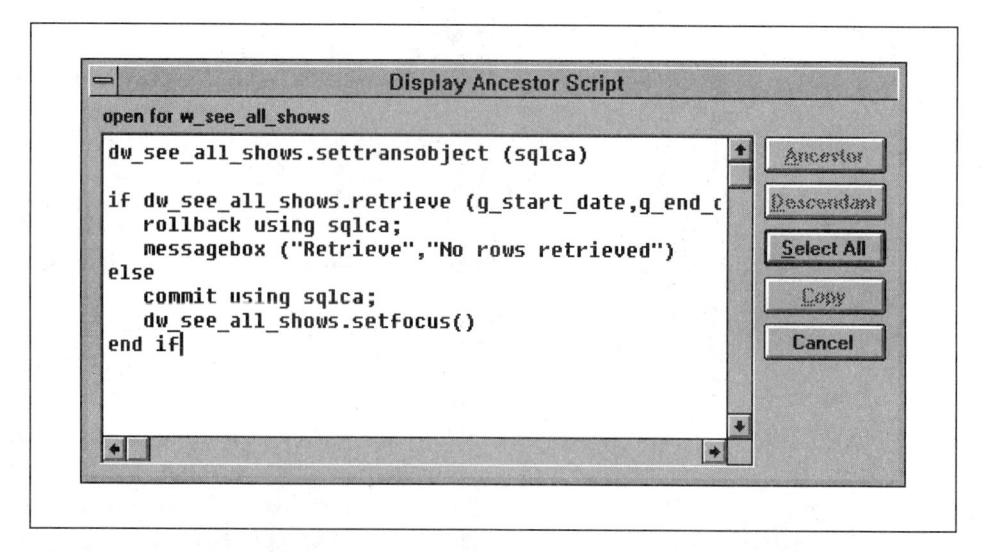

Figure 13.14
Viewing an ancestor's script

10 Click the **Select All** button to select the entire script.

11 Click the **Copy** button. PowerBuilder copies the script to the computer's Clipboard and closes the dialog box.

12 Click the **Paste** button in the PainterBar to paste the copied script into the Script painter workspace.

13 Choose **Compile -> Override Ancestor Script**. (The default is to extend the ancestor script.)

14 Remove **,g_end_date** from the parameter list of the call to the `Retrieve` function so that the function call appears as:

```
dw_see_all_shows.retrieve (g_start_date)
```

15 Exit the Script painter, saving the script.

16 Save the window as **w_see_future_shows**.

Creating the Descendant Response Window

The final piece needed to make the display of future shows work is the response window that collects the cut-off date for the display. Inheritance can again simplify the process of creating the new response window:

1 Create a new window, this time inheriting from rw_enter_dates.

2 If you are working with version 4.0, right-click on **sle_end_date** (the SingleLineEdit control for the ending date) to display its popup menu. Choose **Style -> Visible** from the popup menu. This removes the X from the Visible property, making the control invisible. (Remember that you can't delete inherited controls.)

If you are working with version 5.0, double-click **sle_end_date**. The SingleLineEdit properties dialog box appears (Figure 13.15 on page 312). To make the control invisible, remove the X from the Visible check box.

3 Repeat Steps 2 and 3 for the three static text controls.

Once you've made something invisible, you can't click on it to select it again. However, you can make invisible objects reappear by choosing Design -> Show Invisibles. Doing so doesn't change their property of being invisible: You can make the invisible objects disappear again by choose Design -> Show Invisibles once more.

4 Add static text to the top of the window that reads **Enter a cutoff date for viewing shows and click OK:**.

5 Center sle_start_date (the only visible SingleLineEdit control) under the text.

6 Move the command buttons and resize the window so that it appears something like Figure 13.16 on page 312.

Figure 13.15
Making a SingleLineEdit control invisible (5.0)

Figure 13.16
Inherited response window after being modified

The clicked event script for the OK button in the ancestor window opens w_see_all_shows. Because this is the wrong window for this response window to open, you will need to override the script. However, you can once again simplify the process by copying the script from the ancestor:

7 Open the rw_enter_dates window. Copy its OK button's clicked event script.

8 Return to the inherited response window. Paste the script into its OK button's clicked event script.

9 Choose **Compile -> Override Ancestor Script**.

> **NOTE** *The choice of whether to extend or override an ancestor script must be made individually for each script.*

10 Delete the line in the script that assigns a value to g_end_date. (You aren't using this variable.)

11 Change the parameter in the call to the Open function to w_see_future_shows.

12 Exit the Script painter, saving changes to the script.

13 Save the window as **rw_future_shows**.

Before the application will run correctly, there is one final change you need to make. You need to make sure that the window containing the button menu for calendar functions opens the correct window.

To test changes to the script:

1 Open the w_calendar window.

2 Change the open event script for the See Shows to be Attended button so that it reads:

```
open (rw_future_shows)
```

3 Run the application. (*Note:* Because the dates in the sample data are all in 1996 and 1997, enter a date toward the end of 1996.)

Creating the Second Pair of Descendants

Because the second pair of descendant windows (the windows that handle display of shows that have been attended) are so similar to the windows that handle displaying shows that will be attended, creating this second set of windows is even easier than creating the first. You won't need to override any scripts in the application window because the window's open event script is now designed to handle just a single argument. In fact, the only script that will need to be changed is the script in the response window; it will need to be overridden so that it opens the correct application window.

To create the application and response windows for displaying past shows:

1 Create a new window that inherits from w_see_future_shows.

2 Associate the DataWindow control in the new window with dwo_see_past_shows. (This is the only change you need to make to this window!)

3 Save the window as **w_see_past_shows**.

4 Create a new window that inherits from rw_future_shows.

5 Enter the PowerScript painter for the OK button's clicked event.

6 Choose **Compile -> Override Ancestor Script**.

7 Display the ancestor script and copy it.

314 CHAPTER THIRTEEN INHERITANCE

   8 Paste the ancestor script into the workspace.

   9 Change the parameter in the call to the `open` function to `w_see_past_shows`.

  10 Exit the Script painter, saving the script.

  11 Save the window as **rw_past_shows**.

  12 Open the w_calendar window.

  13 Change the clicked event script for the "See Shows that Have Been Attended" so that it reads:

```
open (rw_past_shows)
```

  14 Run the application to test your new windows.

Making Changes

As mentioned earlier, one of the benefits of inheritance is that when you make a change in an ancestor, that change is propagated through to its descendants. The only exception to this is when the descendant has made a change of its own in the specific property being changed in the ancestor. In that case, the descendant takes precedence over the ancestor.

To demonstrate the effect of changing an ancestor on its descendants:

   1 Open the rw_enter_dates window.

   2 If you are working with version 4.0, right-click the window to display its popup menu. Choose a color from the color palette submenu of the Color option, as in Figure 13.17.

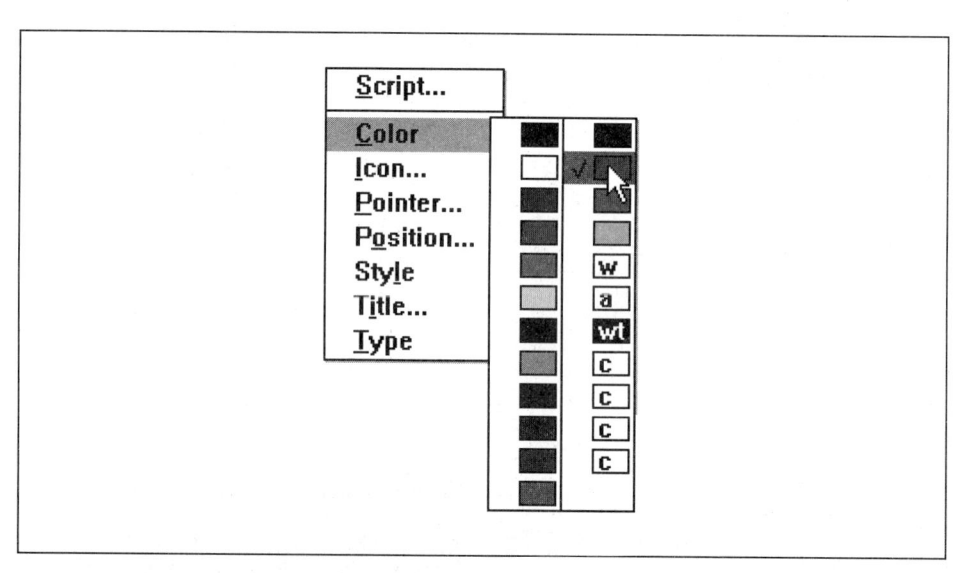

Figure 13.17
Choosing a background color for the ancestor response window (4.0)

If you are working with version 5.0, double-click anywhere in the window that isn't occupied by a control. The Window properties dialog box appears. Choose a color from the scrolling list of colors (see Figure 13.18).

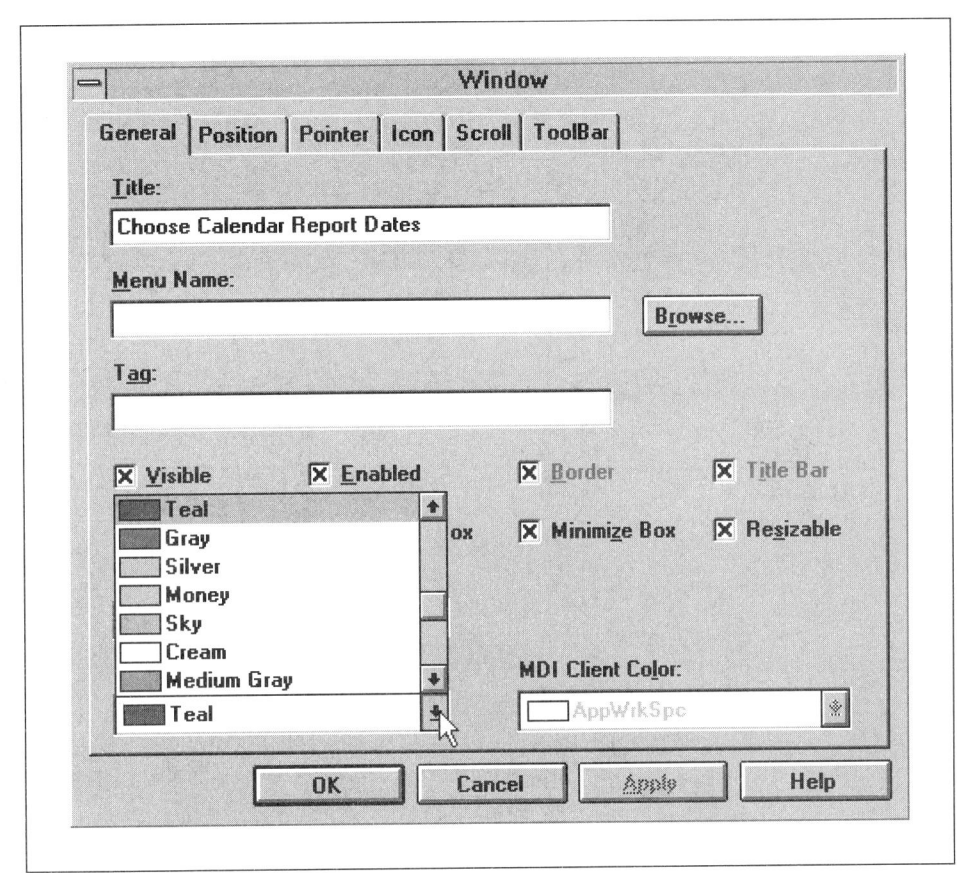

Figure 13.18
Choosing a background color for the ancestor response window (5.0)

3 Run the application and access the two descendant windows (displaying future shows and past shows). Notice that although you applied the background only to the ancestor window, it appears in the descendant windows as well.

Inherited Objects and the Object Hierarchy

Inherited objects are identified in the object hierarchy that appears in the Application painter workspace.

To view the hierarchy of objects:

1 Click the **Application** button in the PowerBar to enter the Application painter.
2 Double-click **tshows** to show its first window.

3 Double-click **opening_screen**.

4 Double-click **w_scheduling**.

5 Double-click **w_calendar**.

6 Continue to double-click the objects below w_calendar until no more appear. Your window should look something like Figure 13.19. Descendant objects appear with asterisks (*) after their names. Keep in mind that although this lets you identify which objects are inherited, you can't identify their ancestors from this display. You will need to open the object in a painter so you can read its name.

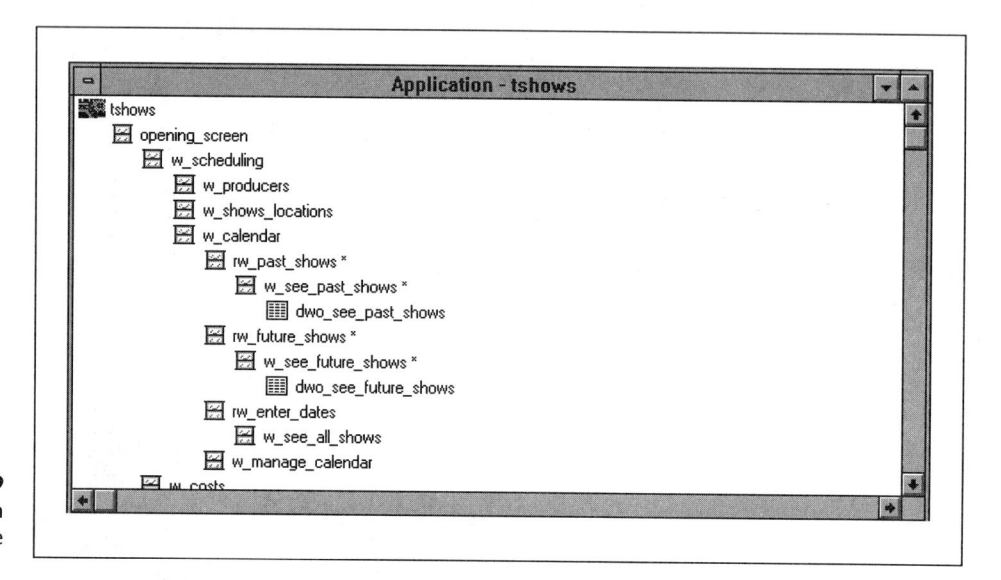

Figure 13.19
Inherited objects in the Application Painter workspace

To open an object in its painter from the Application painter workspace, highlight the object. Then press the Enter key.

Looking Ahead

In this chapter you have learned how inheritance can simply application development by allowing you to create new objects that are similar to existing objects. Although you can achieve the same effect by copying objects, inheritance has one major advantage: When an ancestor objects changes, its descendant objects reflect the change as well. The major exception to that rule is when the descendant object has modified the element that was changed in the ancestor; in that case, the descendant retains its modifications.

To this point, you have prepared windows for data display. In addition to display windows, an application needs windows that can be used to insert, update, and delete data. Such windows can provide a variety of data-entry aids for users, including lists of possible values from which they can choose. Chapter 14 will teach you how to prepare such windows. You will learn to write scripts to enable data modification, prepare lists of values from which users can choose, and autonumber columns.

EXERCISES

The following exercises will give you the chance to practice using inheritance to create windows and add them to an application. Most of these exercises involve capabilities that are new to College and University Rentals. You should therefore add command buttons to windows to access the new windows wherever necessary.

1. Using the window that shows all items that are out for a repair as an ancestor window as an ancestor, add the following capabilities to the C&U Rentals application:

    a. Show all items that are rented.
    b. Show all items that are in the warehouse.

    To be most useful to the user, these displays should include the description of the item, not just its inventory control number.

2. Using the application and response windows that let users see customers at a specific school as ancestors, add window(s) to the C&U Rentals application that let users choose the school *and* dorm.

3. Using the list of all schools as an ancestor, add the following capabilities to the C&U Rentals application:

    a. Display a list of the names, schools, and phone numbers of college housing officers.
    b. Display a list of all contacts made with college housing officers.
    c. Display a list of contacts made with the housing officer at one school.
    d. Display a list of all contacts made with college housing officers within a given range of dates.
    e. Display a list of all contacts made with the housing officer at one college within a given range of dates.

4. Using the window that provides a rental summary by school as an ancestor, add the following capabilities to the C&U Rentals application:

    a. Show a rental summary for one school only.
    b. Show a rental summary for one dorm at one school
    c. Show a rental summary for a given range of dates.

Chapter Fourteen

Enabling Data Modification Capabilities

IN THIS CHAPTER YOU WILL:

- Create one-row-at-a-time layouts for data modification
- Write scripts to enable data modification
- Add features to data entries windows that make data entry easier for the user

In theory any DataWindow control can be used for data modification. However, there are several major reasons why the windows with which you have been working to this point won't do the trick:

- There are no scripts that enable data modification activities, such as adding a new row to a table or committing a transaction.
- Many of the DataWindows don't contain every column in the table and, in some cases, don't contain the table's primary key columns, without which inserting new rows isn't possible.
- Some of the DataWindows are based on nonupdatable views or nonupdatable queries, such as those that contain joins or GROUP BY clauses.

Data management applications often contain special forms for performing data modification. These forms usually display one row at a time and include all the columns from the table. In this chapter you will learn to design DataWindows for data modification and to add scripts that perform data modification activities. In addition, you will be introduced to dropdown DataWindows and autonumbering, two techniques that can simplify the user's job during data entry.

Enabling Single-Row Modification

In Figure 14.1 you can see the window used to manage data about producers. The DataWindow object on which the window is based was created using the Freeform presentation style, which places a rectangle and label for each column in the object's detail band.

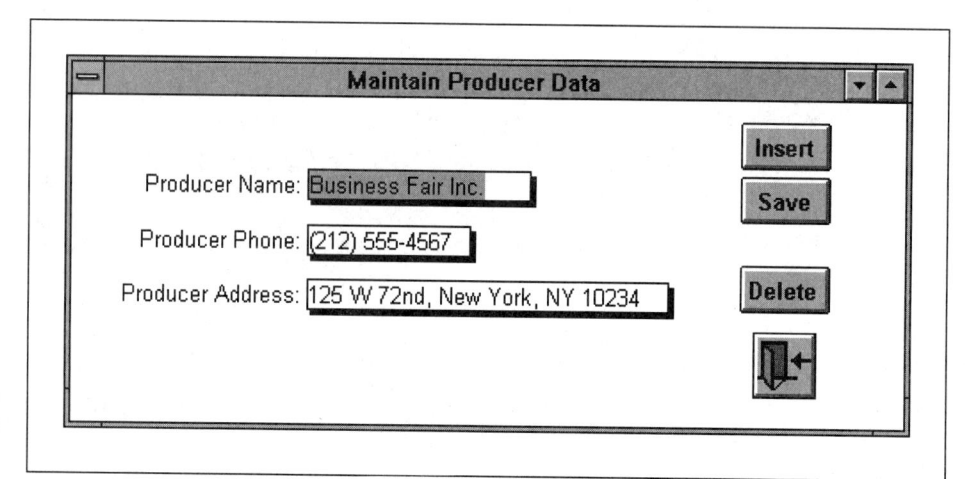

Figure 14.1
Single-row DataWindow for maintaining data about producers

Creating a Single-Row DataWindow

The first data modification window you will be creating is for managing data about producers.

To create the DataWindow object on which the window will be based:

1 Make sure that you are working with the *tshows* application in *tshows2.pbl* and that you are connected to the *tshows* database.
2 Create a new DataWindow object based with a data source of SQL Select and a presentation style of Freeform.
3 In the Select Tables dialog box, choose the **producers** table.
4 Include all three columns in the table.
5 Create a retrieval argument (`arg_producer_name`) of data type String and use it in a WHERE clause, creating the expression

   `"producers"."producer_name" = :arg_producer_name`

6 Use the Design button to enter the DataWindow painter. PowerBuilder creates a default layout that appears like Figure 14.2. As you can see, each field for data entry appears in a shadow box. The field labels have outlines that show the boundaries of their rectangles. These outlines won't appear when the DataWindow is in use.

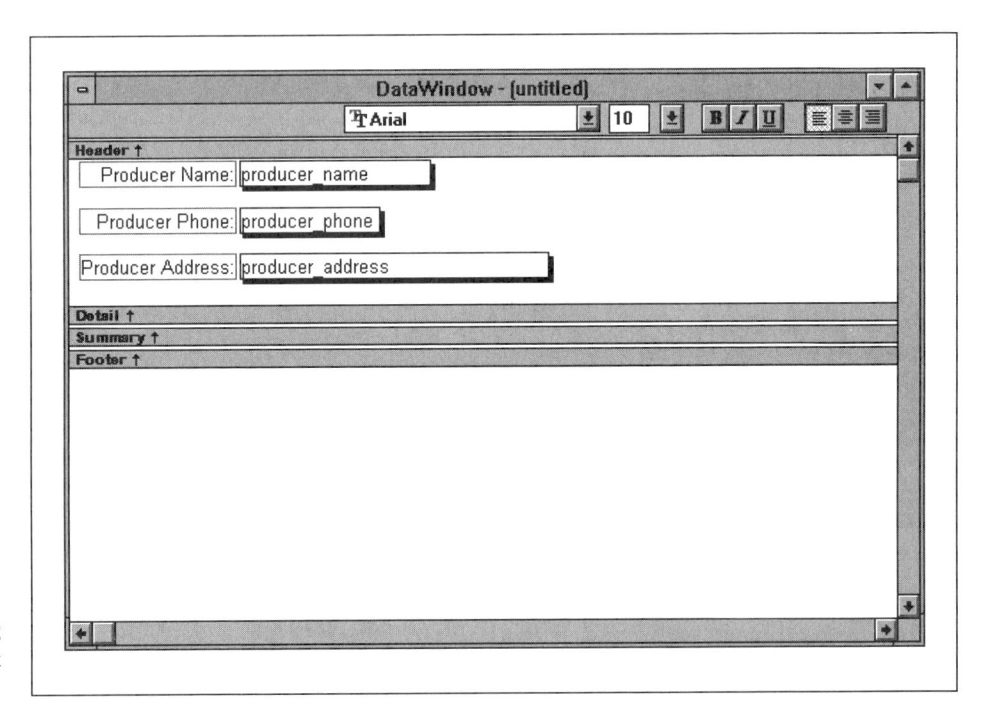

Figure 14.2
Default freeform layout

7 Make the rectangle for producer_address slightly wider by dragging to the right so that it will accommodate the longest value stored in the database.

You can change the appearance of a freeform DataWindow by moving the rectangles, changing their properties, adding color, and so on. However, to keep things moving along in this book, you'll be using the default layouts.

8 Save the DataWindow object as **dwo_manage_producers**.

Now you can complete the application window on which this DataWindow object will be used and add some scripts to enable the data modification.

To complete the application window:

1 Open the w_manage_producer_data window in the Window painter.

2 Place a DataWindow control in the window and associate it with dwo_manage_producers. Name the control **dw_manage_producers**.

3 Resize the control so that you can see all of its contents.

4 Remove the border from the control. (*Hint:* Use the control's popup menu to select Border -> None.)

5 Add three command buttons to the window:
- Name: cb_producer_insert; Text: **Insert**
- Name: cb_producer_save; Text: **Save**
- Name: cb_producer_delete; Text: **Delete**

Create just one of the command buttons; then duplicate it by pressing Ctrl-T.

6 Arrange the buttons and resize the window so that it looks something like Figure 14.3.

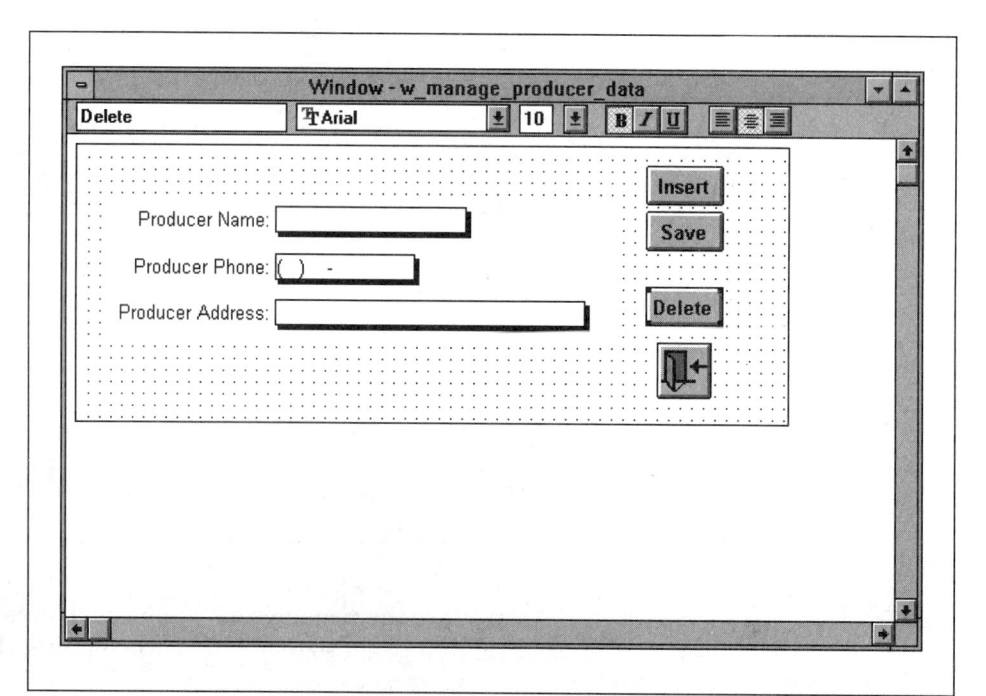

Figure 14.3
Completed layout for the window used to manage producer data

> *Place the Delete button a bit apart from the other buttons on the window. This makes it less likely that a user will click on the Delete button accidentally.*

As you would expect, the three command buttons that you added to the window in Figure 14.3 won't do anything until you add some scripts. The Insert button needs a script that inserts a new row; the Delete button needs a script that deletes a row. However, you don't need a special button or script to modify existing data. Nonetheless, any changes you make won't be submitted to the database unless PowerBuilder takes the changes that have been made and uses them to generate a SQL UPDATE command. In addition, the changes won't be permanent unless you commit the transaction. The scripts will be discussed in depth beginning on page 324.

To add the needed scripts:

1 Enter a script for the clicked event of the Insert button that reads:

```
dw_manage_producers.Reset()
dw_manage_producers.InsertRow (0)
dw_manage_producers.SetFocus ()
```

2 Enter a script for the clicked event of the Delete button that reads:

```
dw_manage_producers.DeleteRow (0)
```

3 Enter the script in Listing 14.1 for the Save button's clicked event.

Listing 14.1
Clicked event script for the producer management window's Save button

```
if dw_manage_producers.Update () = 1 then
   commit using sqlca;
   messagebox ("Save","Your changes have been saved.")
else
   rollback using sqlca;
   messagebox ("Save","Couldn't save your changes."
end if
```

4 Finally, enter a script for the window's open event that puts data into the DataWindow control (Listing 14.2 on page 324). Notice that the call to Retrieve currently doesn't include a retrieval argument. This will let you run the application without a response window to capture the argument.

5 Run the application. When the Specify Retrieval Argument dialog box appears, type **Business Fair Inc.** Modify this row and save your changes. Also try adding a new row and deleting a row.

Listing 14.2
Initial open event script for the producer management window

```
dw_manage_producers.SetTransObject (sqlca)

if dw_manage_producers.Retrieve() = -1 then
   rollback using sqlca;
   messagebox ("Retrieve","Couldn't find a matching row.")
else
   commit using sqlca;
   dw_manage_producers.SetFocus()
end if
```

Understanding the Scripts

The scripts you have just entered contain four new functions, all of which are fundamental to making data manipulation possible in a PowerBuilder application:

- `Reset`: The `Reset` function clears data from a DataWindow. Because the window retrieved a row when it first opened, that filter is still in place when you attempt insert a row. Therefore, you want to clear the retrieved row so that the newly inserted row becomes visible. (There are other ways to achieve the same result, but this is relatively easy.)

- `InsertRow`: The `InsertRow` function adds a new row to a table. It has the following general syntax:

    data_window_control.InsertRow (*row_number*)

    The function's single parameter is an integer that indicates where the new row should appear. For example, if the function call is issued as `InsertRow (10)`, then the new row appears after the current tenth row. If the function call is issued as `InsertRow (0)`, then the new row goes at the end of the table. In most cases, you can simply use 0 as the parameter.

- `DeleteRow`: The `DeleteRow` function removes one row from a table. It has the following general syntax:

    data_window_control.DeleteRow (*row_number*)

    The function's single parameter indicates which row is to be deleted. If the function call is issued as `DeleteRow (0)`, then PowerBuilder deletes the current row (the row that has focus). However, issuing the call as `DeleteRow (10)` deletes the tenth row, regardless of which row has focus.

- `Update`: The `Update` function identifies whatever changes have been made in a DataWindow control, creates one or more SQL UPDATE statements incorporating those changes, and submits the update to the database for processing. In its simplest form, it has the following general syntax:

    data_window_control.Update ()

Using a Response Window to Find a Row for Modification

Given that one of the reasons programmers create database applications in the first place is to make things easier for users, the *tshows* application should make it easy for a user to find the producer to be modified. A response window with a list from which the user can choose will do the trick. The response window should also let the user insert a new row without having to choose a producer from the list.

To prepare the response window for use:

1. Create a new response window. (*Hint*: Once the window appears in the Window painter, choose Type -> Response from the window's popup menu to change it from an application window to a response window.)
2. Place a DataWindow control on the window. Associate it with dwo_see_producers, a DataWindow object that already exists. Name the control **dw_see_producers**. Resize it so only the Producer Name column can be seen and give it a vertical scroll bar.
3. Place three command buttons on the window: OK (cb_choose_producers_ok), Insert (cb_choose_producers_insert), and Cancel (cb_choose_producers_cancel).
4. Add static text objects and arrange the window so that it looks something like Figure 14.4.

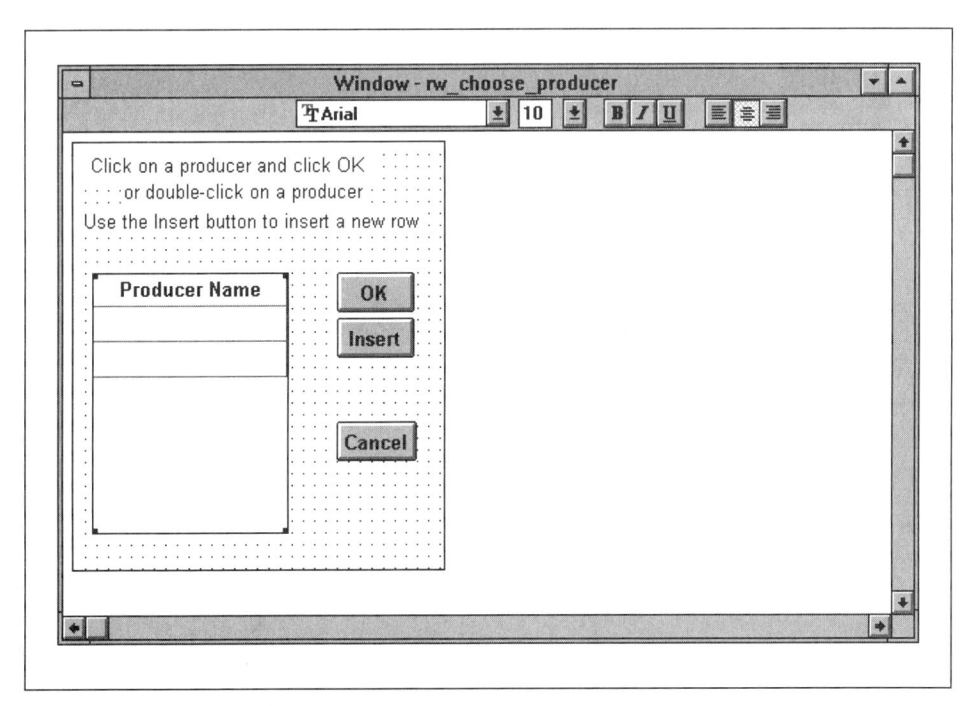

Figure 14.4
Response window from which a user can choose a producer

5. Save the window as **rw_choose_producer**.

A number of scripts need to be entered and modified to make this window work.

To enter and modify necessary scripts:

1. Enter a script for the doubleclicked event of the DataWindow control that reads:

   ```
   cb_choose_producers_ok.TriggerEvent (Clicked!)
   ```

2. Enter a script for the clicked event of the Cancel button that reads:

   ```
   close (parent)
   ```

3. Enter a script for the clicked event of the Insert button that reads:

   ```
   OpenWithParm (w_manage_producer_data,'RW')
   ```

   The parameter being sent through the message object in this case is a special value that alerts w_manage_producer_data that the window was opened by clicking this button. You will see how it is used shortly.

4. Enter the script in Listing 14.3 for the clicked event of the OK button.

Listing 14.3
Clicked event script for the OK button for the choose producer window

```
string chosen_producer
long row_numb

// get row number
row_numb = dw_see_producers.GetRow()

// get value in producer name column for current row
chosen_producer = &
    dw_see_producers.GetItemString (row_numb,"producer_name")

// open window for modifying the producer
OpenWithParm (w_manage_producer_data, chosen_producer)
```

5. Replace the first line of the Insert button's clicked event script with the following three lines:

   ```
   if message.StringParm <> 'RW' then
       dw_manage_producers.Reset()
   end if
   ```

   This avoids resetting the DataWindow object when the request to insert a new row came directly from the response window. In that case, no `Retrieve` has been performed and the DataWindow control on w_manage_producer has no current data.

6 Enter the script in Listing 14.4 for the window's open event.

Listing 14.4
Open event script for the choose producer window

```
dw_see_producers.settransobject (sqlca)

if dw_see_producers.Retrieve() = -1 then
   rollback using sqlca;
   messagebox ("Retrieve","No rows were found.")
else
   commit using sqlca;
   dw_see_producers.SetFocus()
end if
```

7 Open the w_manage_producer_data window. Modify the window's open event script to match Listing 14.5. The script now begins by retrieving a string parameter from the Message object. If the value in that parameter is RW, then the script knows that its window was opened by clicking the choose producer window's Insert button. In that case, the script triggers the script attached to its own Insert button. Otherwise, it takes the chosen producer name and uses it as a retrieval argument for the DataWindow control.

Listing 14.5
Revised open event script for the producer modification window

```
string message_text

// get text from message object
message_text = message.StringParm

dw_manage_producers.settransobject (sqlca)

if message_text = 'RW' then
   cb_producer_insert.TriggerEvent (Clicked!)
elseif dw_manage_producers.Retrieve (message_text) = -1
   rollback using sqlca;
   message box ("Retrieve","Couldn't find a matching producer.")
else
   commit using sqlca;
   dw_manage_producers.SetFocus()
end if
```

There's nothing magical about the choice of RW as the message that indicates that the open event script was triggered by the Insert button in the choose producer window. It's simply an arbitrary value that is extremely unlikely to ever be used as a producer name.

8 Open the w_producers window. Modify the clicked event script for the Maintain Producer Data button so that it reads:

```
open (rw_choose_producer)
```

9 Save all the modified windows and run the application to test it. Notice that once you make a choice from rw_choose_producer, w_manage_producer_data appears. However, rw_choose_producer doesn't go away; it's still visible on the screen. This means that after the user has finished dealing with the current row, he or she can choose another row by clicking on rw_choose_producer to make it the active window. The only thing to keep in mind is that because rw_choose_producer is a response window, it is also modal. Once the window becomes active, the user must deal with it in some (either make a choice from it or close it) before he or she can do anything else.

Picking Values From DropDown DataWindows

One way you can simplify data entry for a user is to give the user a list of values from which to pick. In Chapter 8 you learned to create a static list of values (the DropDownListBox edit style). However, in many cases you can't specify ahead of time what values should appear in a list; the list should be built dynamically from data stored in the database. For example, if a user were entering data into the Calendar table, he or she could pick a show from a list of shows retrieved from the Shows table.

Dynamic dropdown lists are implemented using the DropDownDataWindow edit style, which is different from other data styles because its appearance is determined by a DataWindow object. When you use a dropdown DataWindow, you can show the user one value yet store another value in the database. For example, when entering costs for a show, a user could choose the show by show name and starting date, yet have the event number stored in the database. This isolates the user from the arbitrary event numbers and lets the user deal with meaningful data (the show name and starting date).

Single-Column DropDown DataWindows

For your first experience with a dropdown DataWindow, you'll be creating a data entry form for the Calendar table. To create this form, you must first define a DataWindow object for the dropdown DataWindow. Then you can create a DataWindow object for the data entry form that will use the DropDownDataWindow edit style.

Creating the DropDown DataWindow Object

To create a DataWindow object for the dropdown DataWindow:

1 Create a new DataWindow object. Choose **SQL Select** as the data source and **Tabular** as the presentation style.
2 Choose the **Shows** table.
3 Choose the **show_name** column.
4 Use the Design button to enter the DataWindow painter.

5   Remove the Show Name rectangle from the header band and resize the band to that it is as small as possible.

6   Make the show_name rectangle wider. Preview the DataWindow to make sure the rectangle is wide enough to display all data. When completed, the DataWindow object should look something like Figure 14.5.

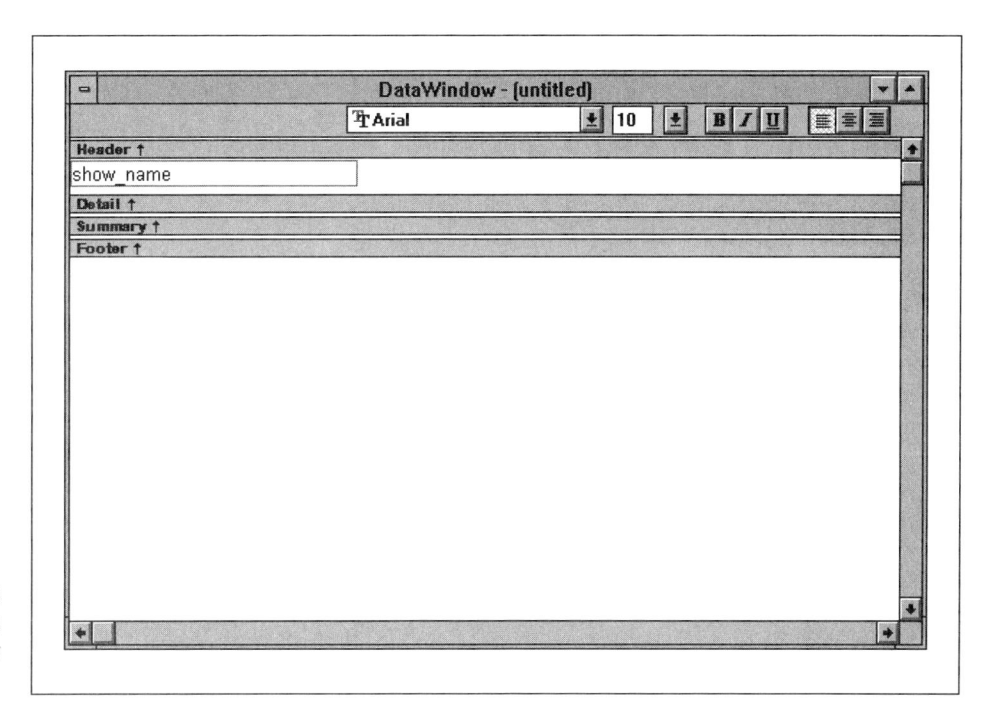

Figure 14.5
Simple DataWindow object for use as a dropdown DataWindow

7   Save the object as **dwo_show_name_dropdown**.

Creating the Data Entry Form DataWindow Object   Now you can turn to the DataWindow object to be used to enter data into the Calendar table.

To create a DataWindow object for data entry:

1   Create a new DataWindow object. Use a SQL Select as the data source and Freeform as the presentation style.

2   Choose the **Calendar** table.

3   Choose all the columns in the table.

It shouldn't be left up to the user to find a new, unique event number for a new row added to the Calendar table. You will therefore be modifying this window later in this chapter to implement autonumbering for the event number column.

4   Create two retrieval arguments: **arg_show_name** (a string for the show_name column) and **arg_start_date** (a date for the start_date column).

5 Enter a WHERE clause like that in Figure 14.6 that retrieves a row that matches the two retrieval arguments. (Data for these arguments will be collected by a response window.)

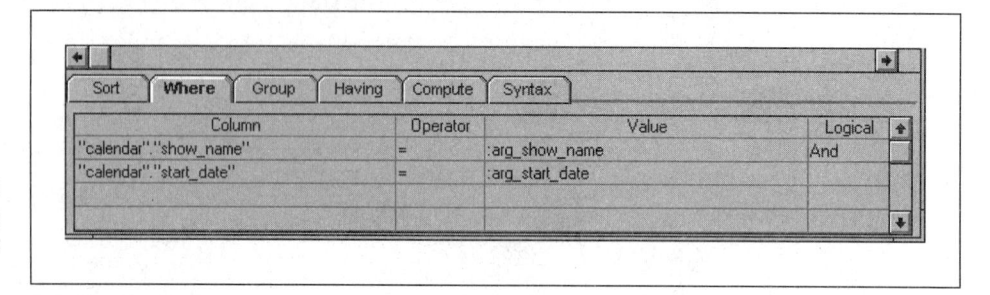

Figure 14.6
WHERE clause to use when retrieving a single calendar entry

6 Enter the DataWindow painter.
7 Remove the Participation label rectangle.
8 Use the participation column's rectangle popup menu to change its border to None. (*Hint:* The participation column has been given a default edit style of CheckBox, so its rectangle contains the check box and its display text rather than the name of the column.)
9 Move the contents of the detail band and resize the band so that the layout looks something like Figure 14.7.

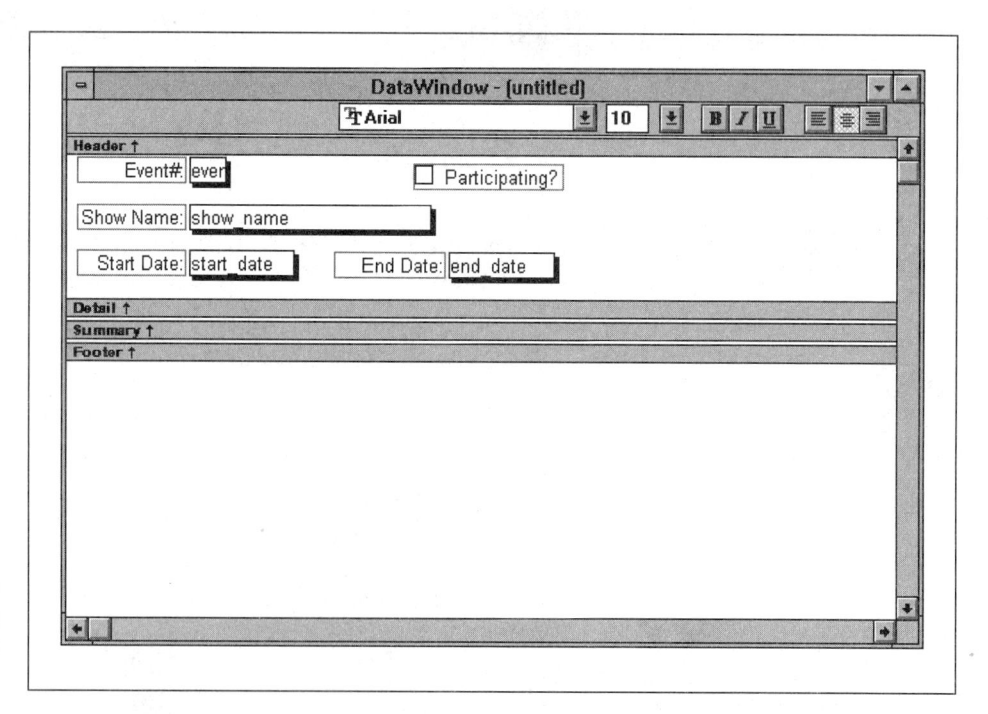

Figure 14.7
DataWindow object that can be used to schedule shows

Specifying the DropDown DataWindow Edit Style

To enable the dropdown DataWindow by choosing the DropDownDataWindow edit style for the column that will display the list:

1. If you are working with version 4.0, choose **Edit Styles -> DropDownDataWindow** from the show_name column rectangle's popup menu. The DropDownDataWindow Edit Style dialog box appears (Figure 14.8).

Figure 14.8
DropDownDataWindow Edit Style dialog box (4.0)

If you are working with version 5.0, display the show_name column rectangle's properties dialog box. Click the **Edit** tab to switch to the Edit panel. Then choose **DropDownDW** from the Style dropdown menu (Figure 14.9 on page 332).

2. Choose or type **dwo_show_name_dropdown** as the DataWindow.

The Name rectangle in the Edit Style dialog box/panel can be used to select a DropDownDataWindow edit style if a named style has been created through the Database painter and the Edit Styles dialog box.

3. Choose or type **show_name** as the display column.

Figure 14.9
Edit panel with DropDownDW style selected (5.0)

4 Choose or type **show_name** as the data column. As you might case, the display column represents the data that the user sees; the data column represents the data stored in the database when the user makes a choice from the dropdown DataWindow.

5 Click the **OK** button to close the dialog box.

6 Save the DataWindow object as **dwo_schedule_shows**.

Completing the Data Entry Window The next step is to create a DataWindow control for the DataWindow object you just created.

To create a DataWindow control for the DataWindow object:

1 Open the w_manage_calendar window.

2 Place a DataWindow control in the window and associate it with dwo_schedule_shows. Name the control **dw_schedule_shows**. Set its border to None.

3 Open the w_manage_producer_data window.

4 Highlight the **Insert** button and then press Ctrl-C to copy it to the Clipboard.

5 Return to the w_manage_calendar window, and press Ctrl-V to paste the button. Change the button's name to **cb_calendar_insert**.

6 Return to w_manage_producer_data. (*Hint:* Choose its name from the bottom of the Window menu.)

7 Copy the Delete and Save buttons from w_manage_producer_data using the procedure in Steps 4 through 6. Rename the Delete button as **cb_calendar_delete** and the Save button as **cb_calendar_save**.

When you copy a control from one window to another, the control's scripts are copied along with the rest of the control's properties. In this case, the scripts are very similar to those used in the w_manage_producer_data window. Therefore, it's easier to copy the scripts and make a few changes than to retype the scripts from scratch.

8 Close w_manage_producer_data.

9 Open the clicked event script for the Insert button. Change dw_manage_producers to **dw_schedule_shows**, everywhere the former appears.

10 Repeat Step 9 for the Save and Delete buttons.

11 Rearrange the window's elements and resize the window so that it looks something like Figure 14.10.

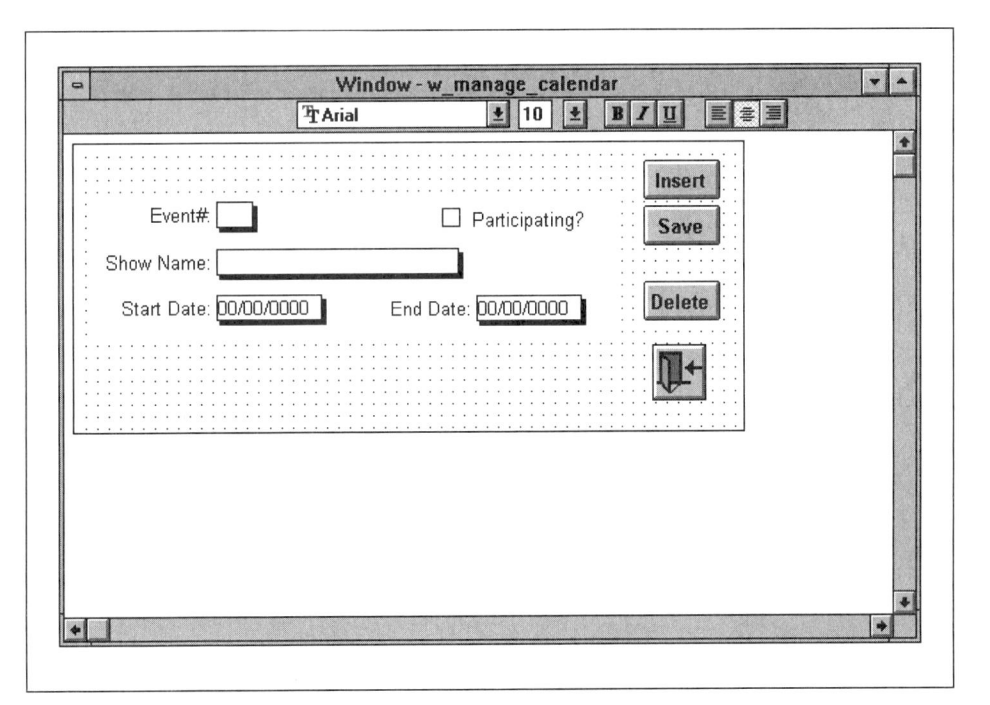

Figure 14.10
Completed window for scheduling shows

12 Enter the script in Listing 14.2 on page 324, changing the DataWindow object name to **dw_schedule_shows**, as an initial script for the open event for the window.

13 Run the application. When the Specify Retrieval Arguments dialog box appears, enter **PCExpo** for the show name and **02/12/1996** for the starting date.

14 Click the **arrow** at the right edge of the Show Name rectangle. As you can see in Figure 14.11, the dropdown DataWindow appears, showing all the shows stored in the Shows table. Notice that you didn't have to write any script to populate this list; it was handled by PowerBuilder.

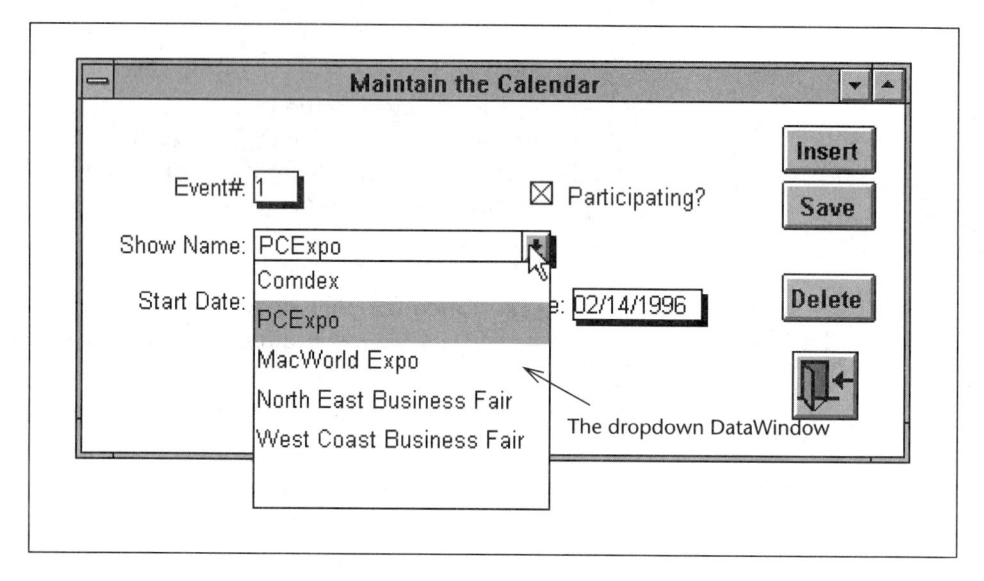

Figure 14.11
Using a dropdown DataWindow

If the dropdown DataWindow doesn't appear, try clicking first in the field to which the dropdown list is attached.

PowerBuilder assembles the contents of a dropdown DataWindow when the window that contains the dropdown is opened. In the example you have just completed, the data are drawn from the Shows table. If another user changes the contents of Shows while the Maintain the Calendar window is open, the dropdown DataWindow won't change. However, the next time Maintain the Calendar is opened, the dropdown DataWindow will be recreated using the modified contents of Shows.

Creating the Response Window To complete the portion of the *tshows* application that supports modifying the calendar, you need to create a response window that lets the user choose which scheduled show he or she wishes to modify. You can save some work by using inheritance to do so.

To create the response window:

1 Create a new window that inherits from rw_choose_producer.
2 Change its title to **Choose a Scheduled Show**.
3 Make the top static text control invisible. Type a new static text control on top of it that reads **Click a show and click OK**.
4 Make the middle static text control invisible. Type a new static text control on top of it that reads **or double-click on a show**.

5 Create a new DataWindow object based on a Quick Select data source and a Tabular presentation style. Include all rows and the show_name and start_date columns from the Calendar table. Save the DataWindow object as **dwo_show_date_list**.

6 Change the DataWindow object associated with the DataWindow control to **dwo_show_date_list**

7 Resize the window and move its contents so that it appears something like Figure 14.12.

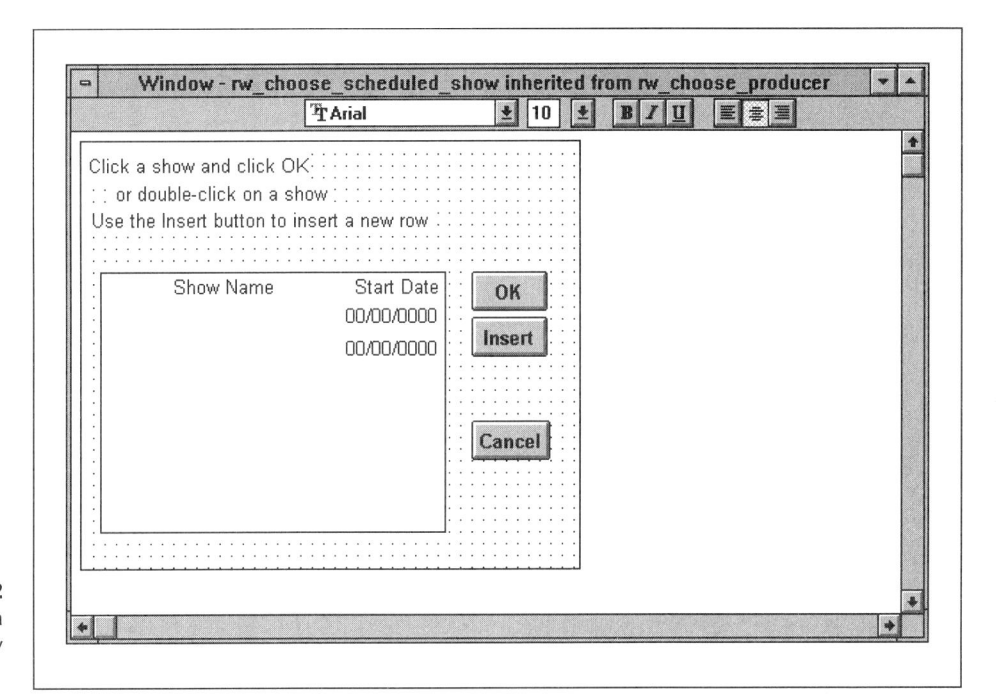

Figure 14.12
Response window for choosing a scheduled show to modify

8 Enter the Script painter for the OK button's clicked event. Copy the ancestor script.

9 Create one global variable: **g_show_name** (a string).

10 Modify the script so that it appears as in Listing 14.6 on page 336. (*Hint:* Don't forget to choose Compile -> Override Ancestor Script.)

11 Override the Insert button's ancestor script. Copy the ancestor script and change the name of the DataWindow control to **w_manage_calendar**.

12 Look carefully at the window's other scripts using Compile -> Display Ancestor Script. As you can see, none of the other scripts need to be modified.

13 Save the window as **rw_choose_scheduled_show**.

14 Open the w_calendar window. Change the clicked event script for the Maintain the Calendar button so that it reads

```
open (rw_choose_scheduled_show)
```

Listing 14.6
OK button clicked event script for the response window that chooses a scheduled show to modify

```
long row_numb

// get row number
row_numb = dw_see_producers.GetRow()

// get values in name and date columns
g_show_name = &
   dw_see_producers.GetItemString (row_numb,"show_name")
g_start_date = &
   dw_see_producers.GetItemDate (row_numb,"start_date")

// open window for modifying the calendar
OpenWithParm (w_manage_calendar,"OK")
```

15 Modify the open event script for w_manage_calendar so that it handles data coming in from the response window. Change the script so that it matches Listing 14.7.

Listing 14.7
Revised open event script for the calendar management window

```
string message_text

//get text from message object
message_text = message.StringParm

dw_schedule_shows.settransobject (sqlca)

if message_text = 'RW' then
   cb_calendar_insert.TriggerEvent (Clicked!)
elseif dw_schedule_shows.Retrieve (g_show_name,g_start_date) &
      = -1 then
   rollback using sqlca;
   message box ("Retrieve","Couldn't find any rows.")
else
   commit using sqlca;
   dw_schedule_shows.SetFocus()
end if
```

Multi-Column DropDown DataWindows

Sometimes it isn't enough to show a user a single column in a dropdown DataWindow. For example, whenever a user of the *tshows* application needs to choose a scheduled show to work with cost data or sales lead data, he or she needs to see both the name of the show and its starting date. From that information, the application can supply the appropriate event number. In this situation, the dropdown DataWindow for the event number column should display both the show name and starting date but store the event number.

There are two ways to construct the dropdown DataWindow. The first is to use a DataWindow object that has both the show_name and start_date columns. This works fine for the dropdown, but what column do you display? You can either show the event number, which doesn't mean much to the user, or you can choose *one* of the columns in the dropdown DataWindow. (You can't choose both.) Alternatively, you can create a computed field that contains the concatenation of the show_name and start_date columns, in which case the concatenated value can be displayed while the event number is stored. This latter solution is preferable because it shows the user both needed values.

As always, you begin by creating the DataWindow objects. The first task is to create a DataWindow object to be used for the dropdown DataWindow.

To create a DataWindow object for the dropdown DataWindow:

1. Open the dwo_show_date_list DataWindow object.
2. Save the object as **dwo_show_date_dropdown**.
3. Add the event# column to the DataWindow object's SQL query. This is essential: If the column isn't part of the data retrieved, you won't be able to tell PowerBuilder to store its value in the database.
4. Sort the contents of the DataWindow object by start_date within show_name.
5. Remove the show_name, start_date, and event_ column rectangles from the detail band.
6. Click the **Compute** button in the PainterBar.
7. Click anywhere in the detail band. If you are working with version 4.0, the Computed Field Definition dialog box appears.

    If you are working with version 5.0, the Computed Object properties dialog box appears. Click the **More** button to display the Computed Field Definition dialog box.

8. Name the computed field **name_and_date**.
9. Type the following expression in the text box below the name:

    ```
    show_name + ' (' + string (start_date) + ')'
    ```

    This expression (Figure 14.13 on page 338) tells PowerBuilder to take the value in the show_name column and concatenate it with a space and an opening parenthesis, followed by the starting date, followed by a closing parenthesis. Because concatenation only works with string values, the start_value date must be converted to a string with the `string` function. This function is a DataWindow function rather than a PowerScript function, although PowerScript does have an identical function.

If you don't want to type the expression, you can build it by clicking on the expression's elements, using the operator buttons, function list, and column list at the bottom of the dialog box.

10. Remove the Start Date and Event # rectangles from the header band.

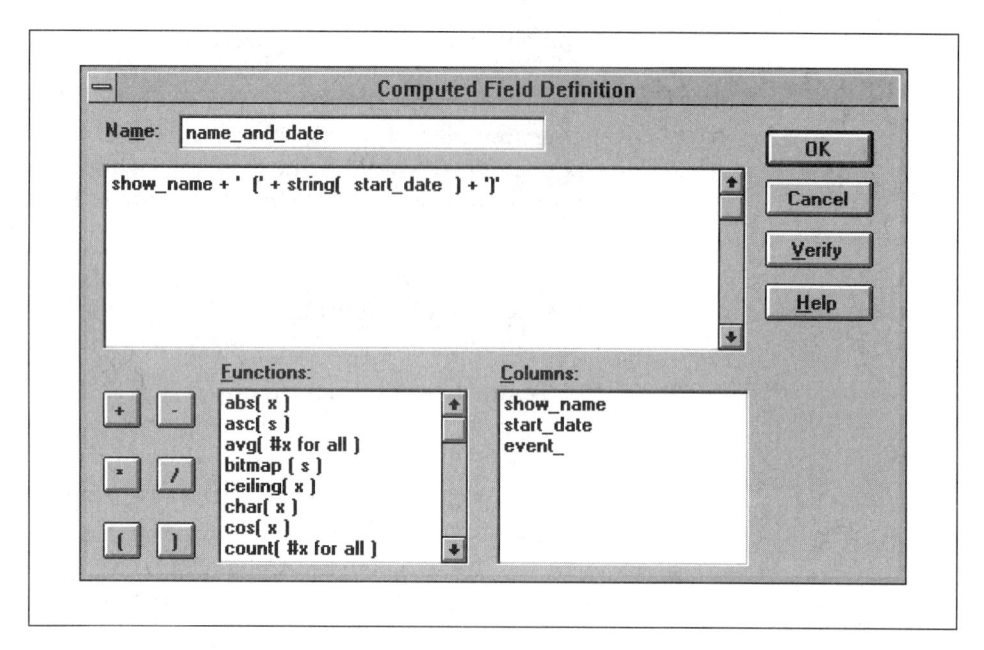

Figure 14.13
Creating a computed field to concatenate the show name and starting date

11 Add **(Starting Date)** to the Show Name rectangle in the header band. Make the text rectangle boldface and underlined.

12 Move the computed field and the text rectangle to the far left of their respective bands.

13 Save the completed dwo_show_date_dropdown.

The second task is to create a DataWindow object to be used to enter cost data. To create a DataWindow object for entering cost data:

1 Create a new DataWindow object based on the Costs table. Use a Quick Select data source and a Freeform presentation style. Include all columns in the table. No WHERE clause is needed.

The DataWindow object that PowerBuilder creates for you appears in Figure 14.14 on page 339. Notice that the DropDownListBox edit style that you added in Chapter 8 is visible for the cost_description column.

2 If you are working with version 4.0, right-click the event number rectangle in the detail band to display its popup menu. Choose **Edit Styles -> DropDownDataWindow** from the popup menu.

If you are working with version 5.0, double-click the event number rectangle in the detail band to display its properties dialog box. Then click the **Edit** tab to make the Edit panel appear. Finally, choose **DropDownDW** from the Style dropdown menu.

3 Complete the DropDownDataWindow Edit Style dialog box as in Figure 14.15 on page 339. Notice that the display column is the computed field that you created for dwo_show_date_dropdown and that the data column is the event number. Even thought the event number isn't displayed in the dropdown DataWindow, its presence in the SQL query used to create the dropdown DataWindow makes it available for use as the data column.

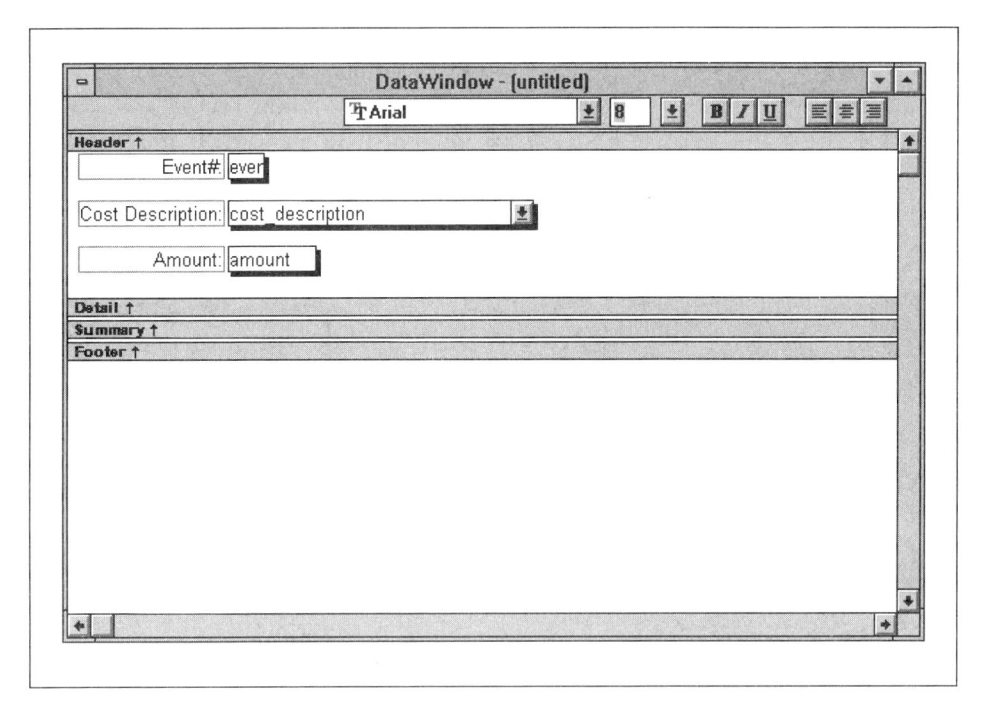

CHAPTER FOURTEEN   ENABLING DATA MODIFICATION CAPABILITIES   **339**

Figure 14.14
DataWindow object for enter the costs of attending trade shows

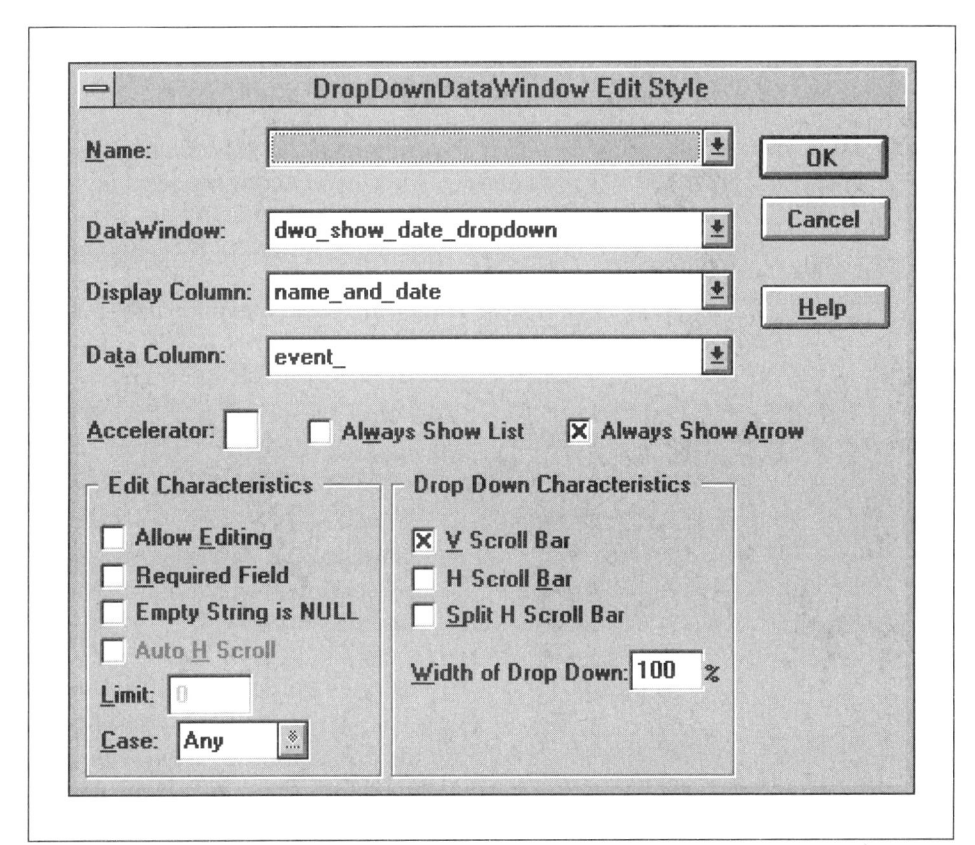

Figure 14.15
Configuring a multi-column dropdown DataWindow

4 Resize the shadowed event number rectangle (the rectangle for data entry rather than the label rectangle) so that it is approximately 1/4-inch wider than the cost_description rectangle.

5 Save the window as **dwo_enter_cost**.

Now you need to place a DataWindow control on an application window and add some scripts.

To place a DataWindow control on the window and add the scripts:

1 Open the w_enter_costs window.

2 Place a DataWindow control on the window and associate it with dwo_enter_cost. Name the control **dw_enter_cost**. Set the control's border to None.

3 Create a button named **cb_cost_insert**. Set its text to **Insert**. Write a script for the button's clicked event that reads:

```
dw_enter_cost.InsertRow (0)
dw_enter_cost.SetFocus()
```

4 Open the w_manage_producer_data window, and copy the Save button. Close the w_manage_producer_data window, and paste the button onto w_enter_costs.

TIP: You can't copy inherited objects from derived windows to paste into other objects. For example, you couldn't copy the Save button from w_manage_calendar. However, you can copy the Save button from w_manage_producer_data because that is the window on which the control was first defined.

5 Modify the clicked event script for the Save button so that it uses dw_enter_cost rather than dw_manager_producers. (*Hint:* You only need to make one change.)

6 Add a one-line script for the window's open event that reads:

```
dw_enter_cost.SetTransObject (sqlca)
```

It's not an oversight that you're not retrieving data for the window at this point. In the next section of this chapter you'll be introduced to a new way to access data, using this window.

7 Arrange the contents of the window and resize it so that it looks something like Figure 14.16 on page 341.

8 Run the application. Because there's no call to `Retrieve` when the window opens, the body of the window appears empty. However, when you click the Insert button, the contents of the DataWindow object will appear so you can enter a new row.

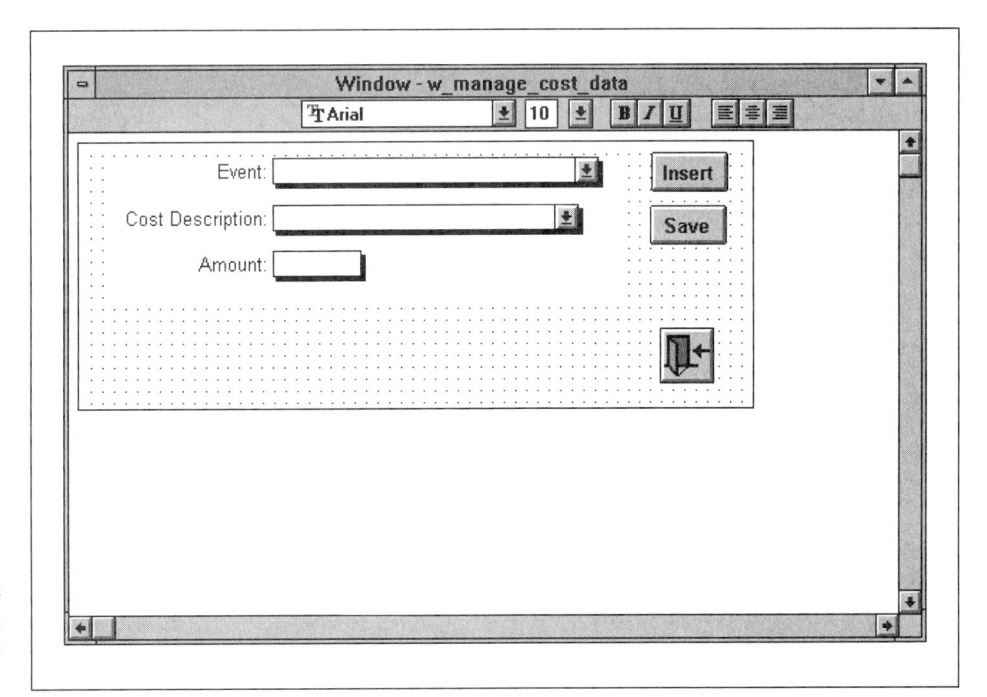

Figure 14.16
Application window for entering cost data

Implementing Sequential Access

Until now, whenever you've retrieved data for a DataWindow control, you've displayed all the data you found at once in a list. Sometimes—especially when using a window that displays only one row at a time—the user likes to be able to scroll from one row to the next. To show you how to make this possible, you'll be adding four button controls to w_enter_costs: First (display the first row), Next (display the next row), Prior (display the previous row), and Last (display the last row). You'll also be modifying the window's open event script and the Insert button's clicked event script.

To implement sequential access to data:

1 Place four command buttons evenly spaced along the bottom of w_enter_costs, much as in Figure 14.17 on page 342.

2 Enter the PowerScript painter for the window's open event.

3 Create a long integer instance variable: **rows_retrieved**. This variable will hold the total number of rows found by a call to Retrieve, which will be used by the Last button.

4 Modify the window's open event script so that it matches Listing 14.8 on page 342. The most important thing to notice about this script is that unlike previous open event scripts, which have discarded the value returned by Retrieve, this script saves the total number of rows in the instance variable you just created. This variable's contents will then be available to the rest of the controls on this window.

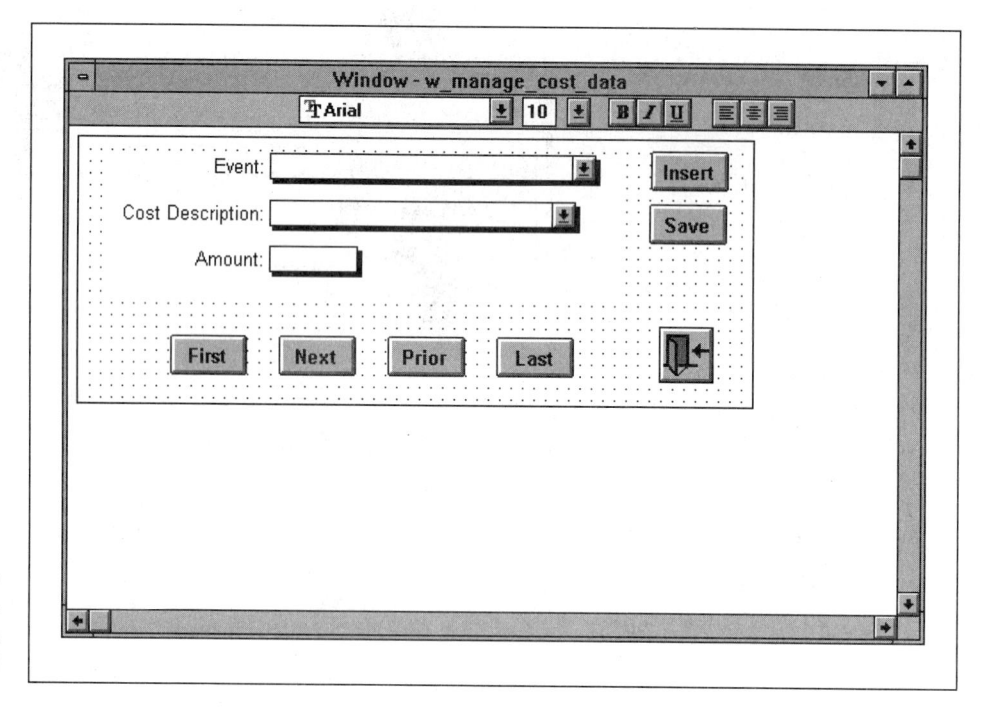

342 CHAPTER FOURTEEN ENABLING DATA MODIFICATION CAPABILITIES

Figure 14.17
Window w_manage_cost_data after sequential access buttons have been added

Listing 14.8
Revised event script for w_enter_costs's open event

```
dw_enter_cost.SetTransObject (sqlca)

// save rows retrieved for use by Last button
rows_retrieved = dw_enter_cost.Retrieve()

if rows_retrieved = -1 then
  rollback using sqlca;
else
  commit using sqlca;
  dw_enter_cost.SetFocus()
end if
```

5 Name the First button **cb_first**. Enter the following one-line script for its clicked event:

   dw_enter_cost.ScrollToRow (0)

   The ScrollToRow function makes the row whose number appears as an input parameter the current row. If necessary, it scrolls or changes a DataWindow control's display so that the new row becomes visible. If you use 0 for the row number, ScrollToRow scrolls to the first row.

6 Name the Last button **cb_last**. Enter the following one-line script for its clicked event:

   dw_enter_cost.ScrollToRow (rows_retrieved)

In this case, the `ScrollToRow` function uses the instance variable that stores the number of rows retrieved to identify the row number of the last row.

7 Name the Next button **cb_next**. Enter the following one-line script for its clicked event:

```
dw_enter_cost.ScrollNextRow()
```

As you might expect from its name, the `ScrollNextRow` function makes the next row in the DataWindow control the current row, scrolling or changing the display as needed so that the row becomes visible.

8 Name the Prior button **cb_prior**. Enter the following one-line script for its clicked event:

```
dw_enter_cost.ScrollPriorRow()
```

The `ScrollPriorRow` function does just the opposite of `ScrollNextRow`: It makes the previous row in a DataWindow control the current row, scrolling or changing the display as needed to make the row visible.

9 One of the problems with the `InsertRow` function is that it doesn't scroll to the new row. You handled the problem earlier in this chapter by resetting the query so that the new row was the only row handled by the current transaction. However, that strategy would defeat the purpose of what you are doing with this window: You want to keep the existing rows but still want to be able to see a newly inserted row. The trick is therefore to scroll to the new row. To do this, modify the Insert button's clicked event script so that it reads:

```
long new_row_numb
new_row_numb = dw_enter_cost.InsertRow (0)
dw_enter_cost.ScrollToRow (new_row_numb)
```

This script takes advantage of the `InsertRow` function's return value: the number of the inserted row. Using that value, the script can then scroll immediately to the new row.

10 Run the application to test it.

If you want this window to be a complete data entry window, consider adding a Delete button whose clicked event script contains a call to DeleteRow. However, you might decide that you don't ever want to give users the ability to delete data from this table, in which case the window is complete as it now stands.

Autonumbering Columns

One of the nastiest things a data management application can do is ask a user to generate an arbitrary, unique numeric key. The user probably doesn't know what values are in use or have any idea of what number to pick. The typical solution is to supply a value for the user, usually by adding 1 to whatever is the current maximum value.

PowerBuilder doesn't automatically supply sequence numbers, but by combining an embedded SQL statement that finds a maximum value with some simple math and a couple of PowerSoft functions, you can achieve the desired result. In this section you will learn how to do just that for the window that schedules shows (w_manage_calendar).

All of the work takes place in the Insert button's clicked event script. To implement this capability, enter the script you find in Listing 14.9. Notice that the first five lines are identical to the current script. The autonumbering code has been added to the end of it.

Listing 14.9
Script to autonumber an integer column

```
if message.StringParm <> 'RW' then
   dw_schedule_shows.Reset()
end if
dw_schedule_shows.InsertRow (0)
dw_schedule_shows.SetFocus

// declare local variables to hold maximum event number and
// current row number
long max_event_numb, row_numb

// use an embedded SELECT to find the maximum event number
// stored in the Calendar table
select max(event#)
into :max_event_numb
from calendar;

// increment the event number
max_event_numb = max_event_numb + 1

// find current row number (the new row inserted previously)
row_numb = dw_schedule_shows.GetRow()
dw_schedule_shows.SetItem (row_numb,"event_",max_event_numb)
```

The first thing the script does is to declare two local variables: max_event_numb, for the maximum event number currently stored in the Calendar table, and row_numb, for the row number of the new row inserted into Calendar. Then, it uses an embedded SQL statement to retrieve the maximum event number and place it into the previously declared max_event_numb.

NOTE: When looking at Listing 14.9, don't forget the two big differences between the syntax of PowerSoft and embedded SQL. PowerSoft statements end with a carriage return; if you break a statement onto multiple lines, each line except the last must *end with an ampersand (&), the continuation operator. On the other hand, SQL statements must end with a semicolon and therefore can be split onto multiple lines without a continuation operator.*

After retrieving the maximum event number, the script increments it by adding 1. This value must then somehow be stuffed into the event number column for the current row.

A call to the `GetRow` function provides the row number of the row just inserted. That row number, along with the name of the column and the new value for the event number, are passed as parameters to the `SetItem` function, which inserts the value into the specified column and row.

`SetItem` has the following general syntax:

`SetItem (row_number, column, value)`

The row number is an integer. The column can either be a number that represents the column's position in the DataWindow control or a string containing the column name. The value can be a constant or can be contained in a variable.

Using Related DropDown DataWindows

In Figure 14.18 you can see a window to be used for entering data about contacts made with sales leads. Both the lead name and lead company columns have dropdown DataWindows. However, on this form the two dropdowns really aren't independent. Once the user chooses a name, then the potential companies are logically limited to companies in the Leads table with a person of the same name. In other words, what we are dealing with here is a concatenated foreign key. When you choose a value for part of the key, you limit the possible values for the other.

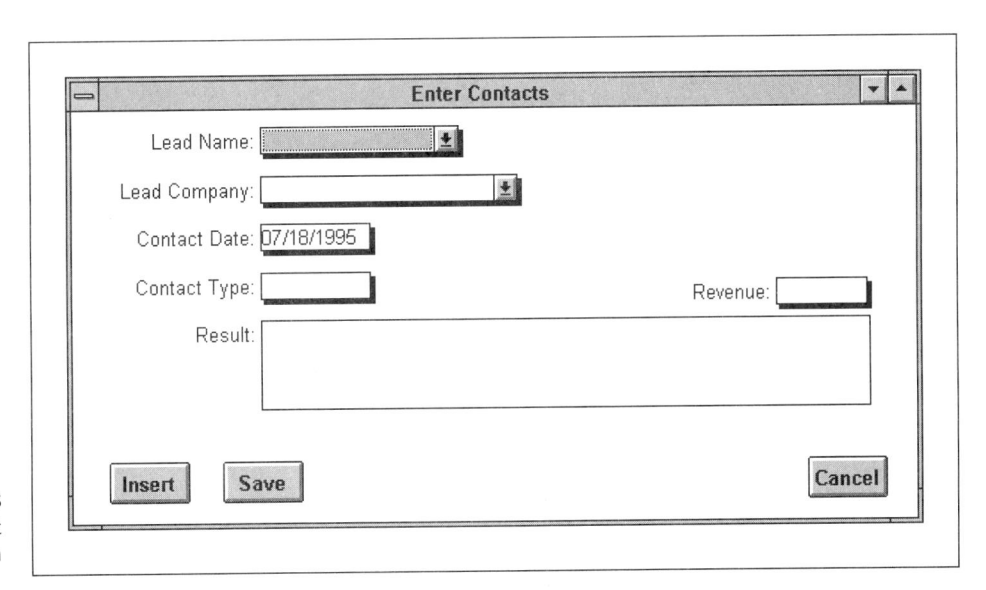

Figure 14.18
Window for entering contact information

The window in Figure 14.18 allows PowerBuilder to populate the lead name dropdown DataWindow when the window is opened. However, no values appear in the lead company dropdown until the user makes a choice for the lead name. Once the user chooses a lead name, the lead company dropdown displays those companies who have people with the chosen name in the Leads table.

PowerBuilder won't automatically link dropdown DataWindows; you have to write some scripts to do it. In this section, you will learn one way to do so. To begin, you need to understand the relationship between a dropdown DataWindow and the DataWindow control on which it is being used.

Introducing Child DataWindows

A window that is completely contained within another PowerBuilder window is called a *child* window and the window that contains the child is called a *parent*. A child window can be an application window like those with which you have been working. In that case, the child window moves only within its parent, is opened by its parent, and is closed when the parent is closed. Child windows of this type aren't used very often.

A dropdown DataWindow is a child window of the DataWindow that is using it as an edit style. Under normal circumstances, a window containing a dropdown DataWindow doesn't have access to the dropdown DataWindow. In other words, the dropdown DataWindow isn't an object that is automatically available to scripts, as other controls on the window are. This means that if a script is going to manipulate the contents of a dropdown DataWindow, the script must somehow obtain a reference to the dropdown DataWindow. The `GetChild` function will do exactly that.

To use `GetChild`, a script must first have a variable to hold the reference to the dropdown DataWindow. Such a variable has a data type of `DataWindowChild` and is declared like any other variable:

```
DataWindowChild my_dropdown
```

Then, the script can call `GetChild`, providing the name of the column to which the dropdown DataWindow is attached and the name of the variable to hold the reference:

```
dw_control.GetChild (column_name, DataWindowChildvariable)
```

Once the script has the reference to the dropdown DataWindow, it can use that reference to access the dropdown DataWindow directly, inserting rows, retrieving data, and so on, just as it would with any other DataWindow.

Creating the DataWindow Objects

To make the window in Figure 14.18 work, you will need three DataWindow objects: two for the dropdown DataWindows and one for the DataWindow control.

To create the necessary DataWindow objects:

1. Create a DataWindow object based on the Leads table (**dwo_lead_name**) that uses a Quick Select as its data source and Tabular as its presentation style. Include the lead_name column and all rows.

2. Create a DataWindow object based on the Leads table (**dwo_lead_company)** that uses SQL Select as its data source and Tabular as its presentation style. Include the lead_company column. Define a String retrieval argument (**arg_lead_name**) and create a WHERE clause that reads:

   ```
   "leads"."lead_name" = :arg_lead_name
   ```

3. Create a DataWindow object based on the Contacts table (**dwo_manage_contacts**) that uses a Quick Select as its data source and Freeform as its presentation style. Include all the columns and rows in the table.

4. Give the lead_name column in dwo_manage_contacts an edit style of DropDownDataWindow, and associate it with dwo_lead_name.

5. Give the lead_company column in dwo_manage_contacts an edit style of DropDownDataWindow, and associate it with dwo_lead_company.

6. Arrange and style the elements on dwo_manage_contacts to your own satisfaction. In Figure 14.18, for example, the rectangle for the results column was made larger; the shadow border was replaced with a box and a vertical scroll bar was added. Other elements were moved.

Putting the Window Together

Now that you have the DataWindow objects ready, you can place a DataWindow control on a window along with some buttons controls and then write the scripts to make it all work.

To place the DataWindow on a window with button controls and to write the necessary scripts:

1. Open the w_manage_contacts window.

2. Place a DataWindow control (dw_manage_contacts) on the window, and associate it with dwo_manage_contacts.

3. Add an Insert button to the window. Enter a two-line clicked event script that reads:

   ```
   dw_manage_contacts.InsertRow(0)
   dw_manage_contacts.SetFocus()
   ```

4. Add a Save button to the window. It's clicked event script needs to save any changes made, as in Listing 14.10.

Listing 14.10
Single "Save" script for the manage contacts window

```
if dw_manage_contacts.Update () = 1 then
   commit using sqlca;
   messagebox ("Save","Your changes were saved.")
else
   rollback using sqlca;
   messagebox ("Save","Couldn't save your changes.")
end if
```

5. Access the window's open event script in the Script painter.
6. Create an instance variable of type DataWindowChild named **company_dropdown**.
7. Enter the script in Listing 14.11. This script associates the DataWindow control with a transaction object. It then obtains the reference to the dropdown DataWindow and uses it to associate the dropdown DataWindow with the same transaction object. Finally, the script resorts to a bit of a trick to prevent PowerBuilder from loading data into the dropdown DataWindow—it inserts a new row.

Listing 14.11
Open event script for w_manage_contacts

```
// take care of the DataWindow controlfirst
dw_manage_contacts.SetTransObject (sqlca)

// get the reference to the child dropdown DataWindow
dw_manage_contacts.GetChild ("lead_company", company_dropdown)

// associate the child with a transaction object
company_dropdown.SetTransObject (sqlca)

// suppress retrieval into the child dropdown
company_dropdown.InsertRow (0)
```

8. The lead company dropdown DataWindow should be filled with data whenever the value in the lead company column changes. Therefore, the script should be attached to the itemchanged event for the DataWindow control. Open the Script painter for dw_manage_contacts and enter the script in Listing 14.12 on page 349. The details of this script will be discussed shortly.

9. The script in Listing 14.12 is triggered whenever a user *changes* the value in any column in dw_manage_contacts. However, the script isn't triggered if the user chooses a value from the lead name dropdown DataWindow immediately after clicking the Insert button. In this case, the value isn't "changed" because the column had no previous value to change. You therefore need one more script to handle the situation

Listing 14.12
Itemchanged event script for dw_manage_contacts

```
string column_used, chosen_value
long row_numb

// find out which column triggered the event
column_used = dw_manage_contacts.GetColumnName()

// if the column was the lead name, then populate the
// lead company column dropdown
if column_used = "lead_name" then
  row_numb = dw_manage_contacts.GetRow()
  chosen_value = &
    dw_manage_contacts.GetItemString (row_numb,"lead_name")
  company_dropdown.Retrieve (chosen_value)
end if
```

where the user clicks in the lead name column to enter an initial value. Enter the following one-line script for dw_manage_contacts's clicked event:

```
dw_manage_contacts.TriggerEvent (Itemchanged!)
```

10 Run the application to make sure that your scripts have been entered correctly and that the lead company dropdown DataWindow is working properly.

Understanding the itemchanged Event Script

An itemchanged event is triggered whenever the contents of a control change in any way. When the control is a DataWindow control, the event occurs when the user makes a change to *any* of the columns in the DataWindow. It's up to a script to figure out the column whose value actually changed.

The first thing the script in Listing 14.12 therefore must do is to identify the column using the `GetColumnName` function, which returns a string equal to the name of the current column. The function takes no parameters. Its result can be assigned to a string variable—as it is in Listing 14.12—or the function call can be placed in any statement that expects a string value.

Once the script knows which column is current, it can use an `if` statement to determine if the user modified the lead name column. If so, the script enters the body of the `if`, which contains the code to populate the lead company dropdown DataWindow.

Within the body of the `if`, the script first uses `GetRow` to identify the current row. It then uses `GetItemString` to get the value of the lead name in that row (the lead name chosen by the user from the dropdown DataWindow). Once the script has the lead name, it can use that value as a retrieval argument in a call to `Retrieve`, which places data into the lead company dropdown DataWindow.

Looking Ahead

In this chapter you have learned to create basic data entry windows. The major characteristic of these windows is that they let the user work on one row at a time. When single-row data entry windows are used in an application, their appearance is often preceded by a response window that contains a list of existing data from which a user can choose a row to modify. In addition to data entry and response windows, you have also learned to add data entry aids such as dropdown DataWindows that help users in the data entry process.

The completion of this chapter marks the end of your experience with basic PowerBuilder skills. The remaining skills you will learn will enable you to produce applications that are more capable and easier to use. In Chapter 15, for example, you will be learning about windows that contain more than one DataWindow. Such multiple DataWindows are usually connected by primary key/foreign key relationships and use the relationship to determine the data that are displayed.

EXERCISES

In these exercises you will complete a variety of data entry windows for the College and University Rentals application. As you work, try to keep the user in mind. Users should be given as much help as possible with the data entry process. The more help you give them (for example, dropdown DataWindows and autonumbering), the less likely they are to enter inaccurate data.

1. Complete a window that supports entering, modifying, and deleting data about merchandise. Use a response window to help users identify the type of merchandise to be modified.

2. Complete a window that supports entering, modifying, and deleting data about schools. Provide buttons that give users sequential access to existing rows in the Schools table.

3. Complete a window that supports entering, modifying, and deleting data about dorms. Include a dropdown DataWindow to make it easier for the user to enter the school name. Use a response window that lets the user pick the dorm (based on school name and dorm name) to be modified.

4. Complete a window that supports entering, modifying, and deleting data about customers. Use a response window so the user can choose the customer to be modified. Use a dropdown DataWindow to make it easy for users to choose the school a customer attends. Use a second dropdown DataWindow to select the dorm in which a customer lives. Restrict the listing of dorms by the school chosen from the school name dropdown DataWindow.

Chapter Fifteen

Connecting DataWindows

IN THIS CHAPTER YOU WILL:

- Create nested reports that automatically join related DataWindows
- Prepare windows that contain related, updatable DataWindows
- Use additional techniques for enhancing data entry windows that allow users to update more than one table on the same form

To this point, most of the windows you've created contain at most one DataWindow. However, sometimes an application needs to have multiple DataWindow objects on the same main window. In that case, you will probably want to connect the DataWindow objects in some way so that the rows displayed in one are logically connected to the other.

The *tshows* application might use windows with multiple DataWindow objects to:

- Display all shows and their associated costs. Although this type of output can be produced in a single DataWindow by joining tables, it's easier to do it using a *nested report*, in which two separate DataWindows are linked automatically by PowerBuilder. In this case, the second DataWindow object is embedded in the first, rather than being placed separately on an application window. The drawback to a nested report is that it is for display only; its data can't be modified.

- Display a show and costs so that costs can be modified. The window you completed in Chapter 14 was designed only for inserting new costs. However, to make it easier for the user to locate a cost for modification or deletion, he or she should be able to scroll through a list of all costs for a given show. Once found, the cost in question should be updated or deleted right on the window. Because nested reports can't be updated, you need to place two DataWindow controls on a window and then do some scripting to manually connect those controls.

- View and modify calendar detail data. The windows you have completed so far for manipulating the calendar only allow the user to change data about a scheduled show. The user has no access to data in the Shows or Producers tables. However, you can create a window that contains a list of all scheduled shows along with DataWindow controls for the related show and producer data. When the user chooses a calendar entry, the related rows from the Shows and Producers tables appear. With the needed scripts, these DataWindows can be related so they are updatable.

In this chapter you will learn to create all three types of windows using related DataWindows. You will begin with the simplest (a nested report) and then move to windows where the relationship between DataWindow controls is one-to-many. Finally, you'll work with a window where the relationships are many-to-one. As you prepare these windows, you will also discover how to control whether columns in a DataWindow are updatable, how to add running totals to updatable DataWindow, and how to warn a user that a window contains unsaved changes.

The Composite presentation style supports placing multiple DataWindows in the same DataWindow object. However, the DataWindows aren't linked in any way. They are simply independent reports that appear in the same window.

Creating Nested Reports

As mentioned earlier, a nested report is a DataWindow object in which another, related DataWindow object is embedded. Once you specify how the nested DataWindow object is related to its host, PowerBuilder automatically retrieves data for the nested object when it retrieves data for the host.

PowerBuilder needs to know how the host DataWindow object and the nested DataWindow object are related so it can retrieve the correct data for the nested object. The DataWindow object that is going to be nested must therefore have a retrieval argument for the column or columns that should be used to filter data.

To give you experience with creating a nested report, you'll be completing the window that displays all shows with their associated costs. This report uses an existing DataWindow object for summarizing cost, which is then nested within a window that displays data for one show at a time. The cost summary DataWindow has a retrieval argument based on the event number column. PowerBuilder will be instructed take the event number from the show and look for all cost rows that have matching event numbers. In other words, the relationship between the nested DataWindow object and its host is based on a primary key/foreign key relationship.

The Create the host DataWindow object for the nested report:

1 Make sure that you are working with the *tshows* application in *tshows2.pbl* and that you are connected to the *tshows* database.

2 Create a new DataWindow object (**dwo_shows_and_costs**). Choose **Quick Select** as its data source and **Freeform** as its presentation style. Base it on the Calendar table; include all columns and rows (no WHERE clause).

3 Modify the layout of the DataWindow object so that it looks something like Figure 15.1. Notice that the header band has been expanded and text to identify a scheduled show and its costs has been added.

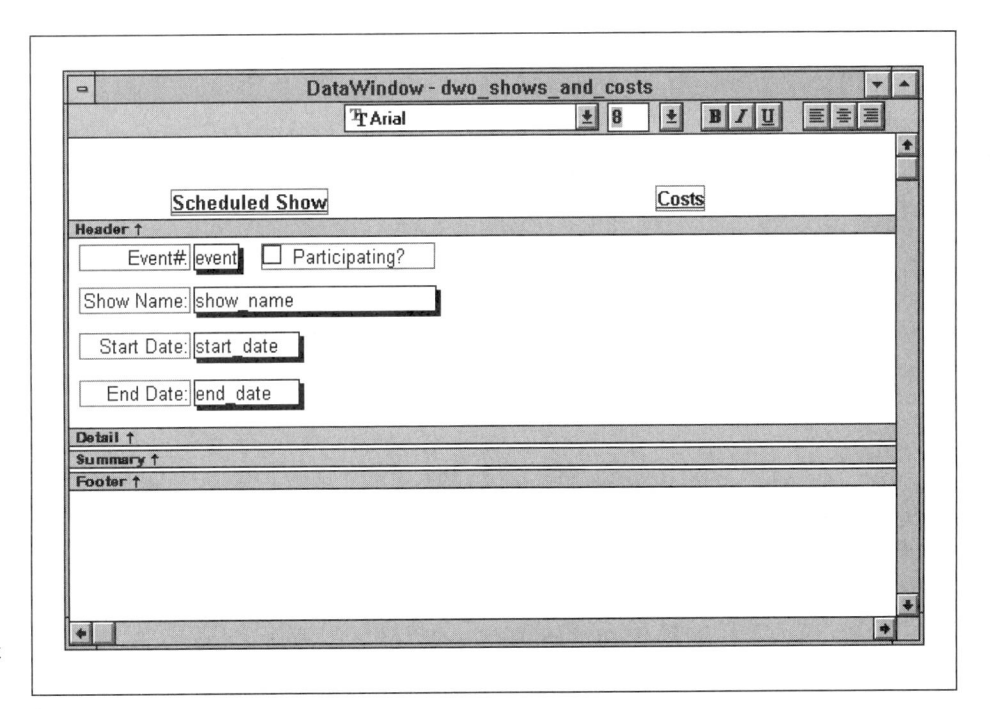

Figure 15.1
DataWindow object before adding the nested report

354   CHAPTER FIFTEEN   CONNECTING DATAWINDOWS

4   Click the **Nested Report** button in the PainterBar (Figure 15.2). If you are working with version 4.0, the Select Report dialog box appears (Figure 15.3).

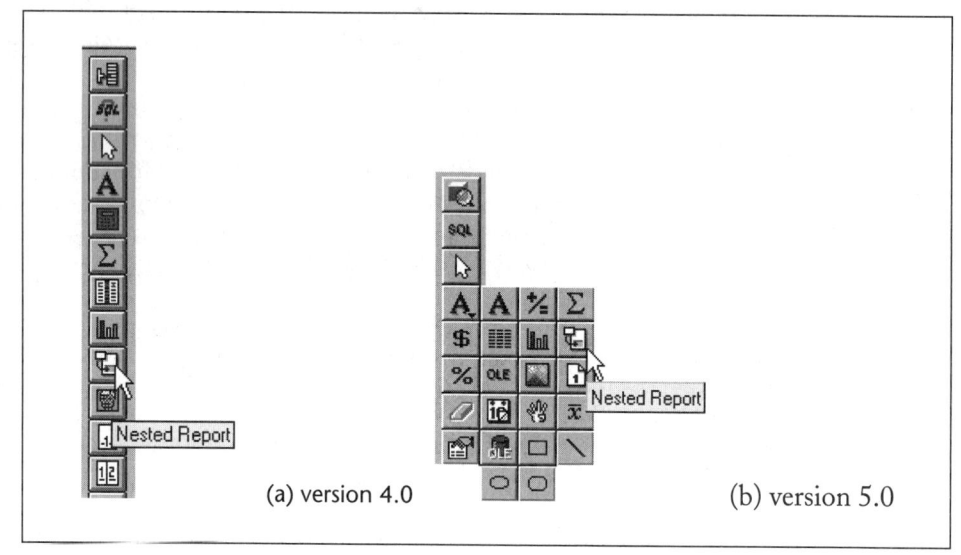

Figure 15.2
Nested Report button

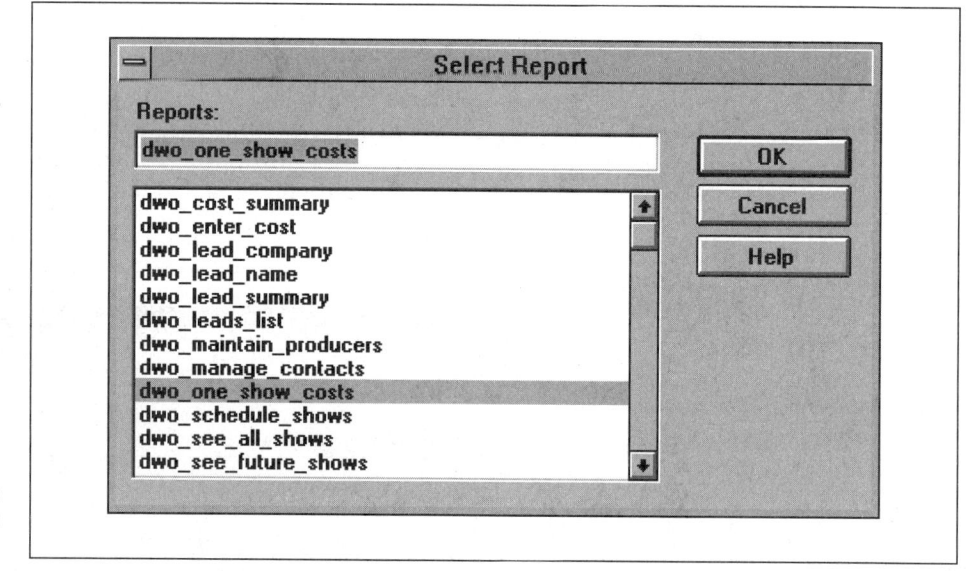

(a) version 4.0   (b) version 5.0

Figure 15.3
Select Report dialog box (4.0)

If you are working with version 5.0, click in the detail band to the right of the Participating? rectangle. The Report Object properties dialog box appears with the Select Report panel visible (Figure 15.4 on page 355).

5   Highlight **dwo_one_show_costs** and click the **OK** button to close the dialog box. PowerBuilder places a rectangle for the nested report into dwo_see_shows_and_costs (see Figure 15.5 on page 355). Notice that the details of the nested DataWindow object aren't visible. You can change the nested object's size and position, but its contents aren't directly accessible.

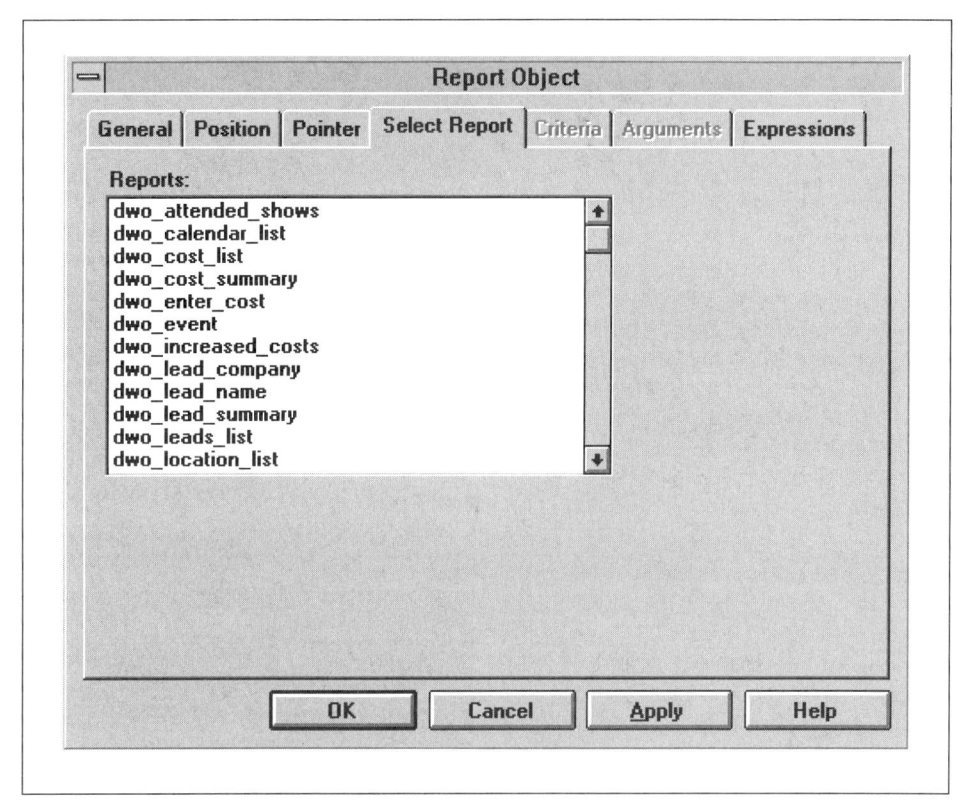

Figure 15.4
Select Report panel (5.0)

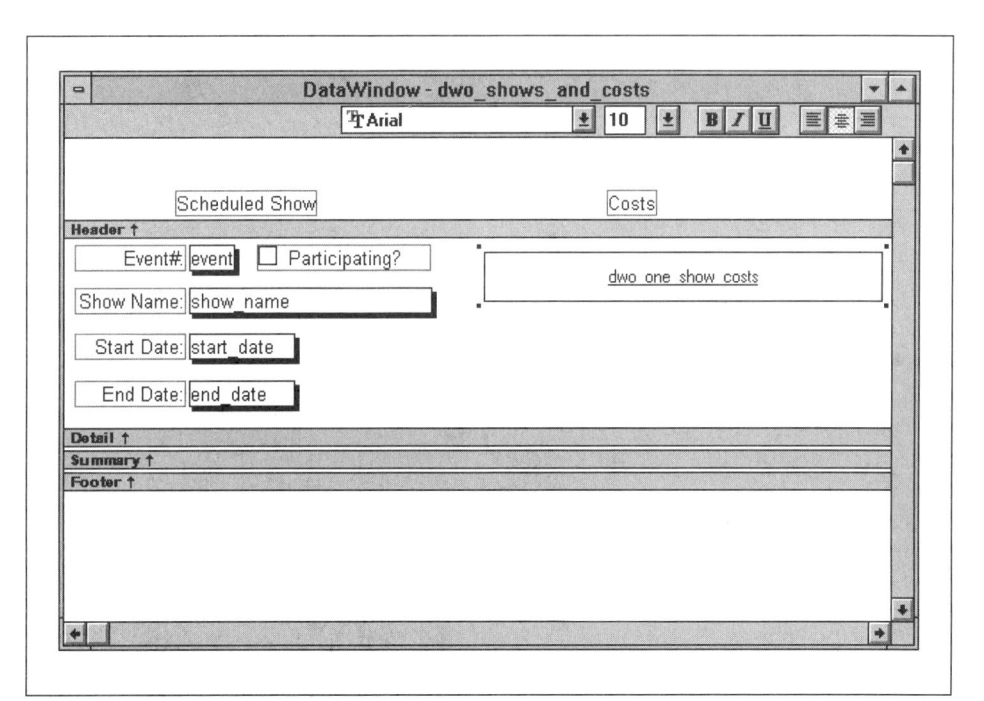

Figure 15.5
Nested report placed in a DataWindow object

To modify the contents of a nested DataWindow object, choose Modify Report from the nested object's popup menu. PowerBuilder will open the DataWindow object in the DataWindow painter so you can make any changes you desire.

356 CHAPTER FIFTEEN CONNECTING DATAWINDOWS

6 If you are working with version 4.0, right-click the nested DataWindow to display its popup menu. Choose **Retrieval Arguments** from the popup menu. The Retrieval Arguments dialog box appears. PowerBuilder fills in the retrieval arguments defined for the nested DataWindow.

If you are working with version 5.0, double-click the nested DataWindow to display its properties dialog box. Click the **Arguments** tab to display the Arguments panel. As with version 4.0, PowerBuilder fills in the retrieval arguments defined for the nested DataWindow.

7 Choose **event_** from the Expression dropdown menu, as in Figure 15.6 (version 4.0) or Figure 15.7 (version 5.0). This instructs PowerBuilder to take the value in the event number column for each row displayed in the host DataWindow and use it as a retrieval argument for the nested DataWindow. In this case, PowerBuilder retrieves one set of rows from Costs for each row in Calendar.

PowerBuilder 4.0

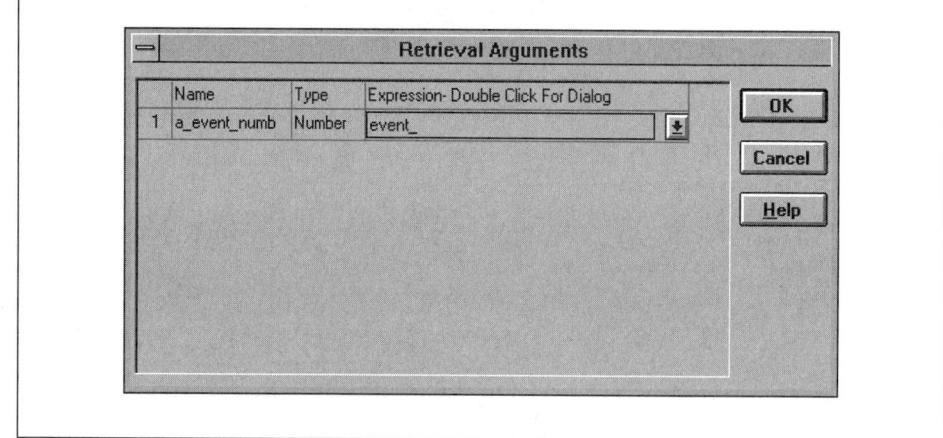

Figure 15.6
Specifying retrieval arguments to link a nested DataWindow to its host (4.0)

PowerBuilder 5.0

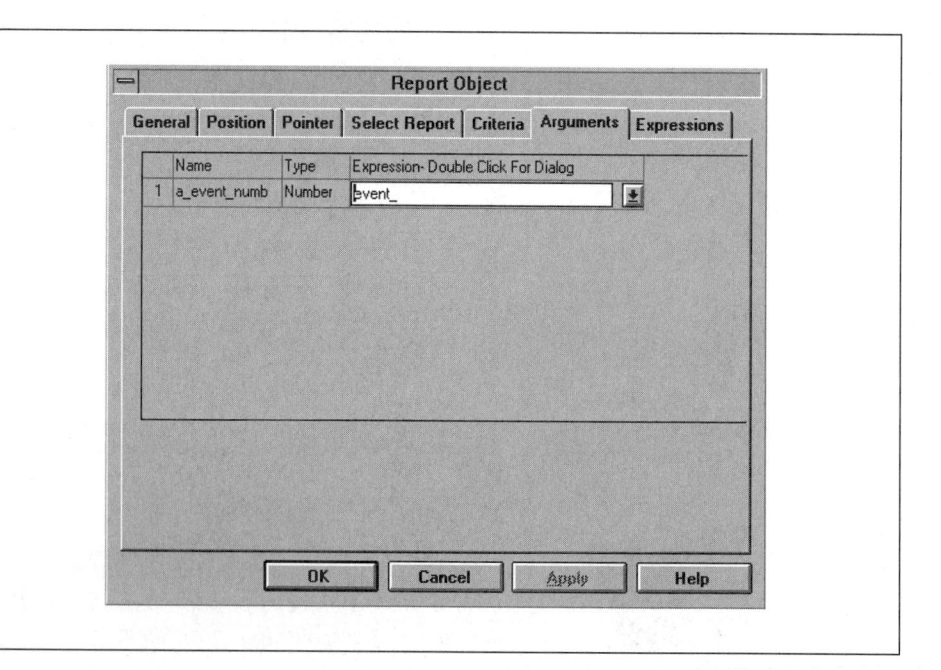

Figure 15.7
Specifying retrieval arguments to link a nested DataWindow to its host (5.0)

8 Click the **OK** button to close the dialog box.

The DataWindow object for the nested report is now complete. To make it work, all you have to do is place it on an application window and write a script to retrieve data into the control.

To place the nested DataWindow object and write the data retrieval script:

1 Open the w_see_shows_and_costs window. Make sure that the window is as large as the monitor on which you are working.

2 Place a DataWindow control on the window (dw_see_shows_and_costs). Associate it with dwo_see_shows_and_costs.

3 Resize it so that it fills the entire window. Give it both horizontal and vertical scroll bars.

4 Enter a script for the window's open event to retrieve data for the control (for example, see Listing 15.1.) Notice that this is similar to other scripts that you have written to populate simple listings. There is no call to Retrieve to obtain data for the nested DataWindow object nor is there any code that handles the nested object's retrieval argument. These simply aren't necessary when working with a nested report.

Listing 15.1
Open event script for w_see_shows_and_costs

```
int NO_ROWS = -1
dw_shows_and_costs.SetTransObject (sqlca)

if dw_shows_and_costs.Retrieve () = NO_ROWS then
   rollback using sqlca;
   messagebox ("Retrieve","Couldn't find any rows")
else
   commit using sqlca;
   dw_shows_and_costs.SetFocus()
end if
```

5 Run the application; your initial view of the report should appear something like Figure 15.8 on page 358. Notice that the report is surrounded by a box that doesn't appear in the DataWindow painter. Notice also that as hard as you try, you can't select any part of the report to display an insertion point. The report simply isn't updatable.

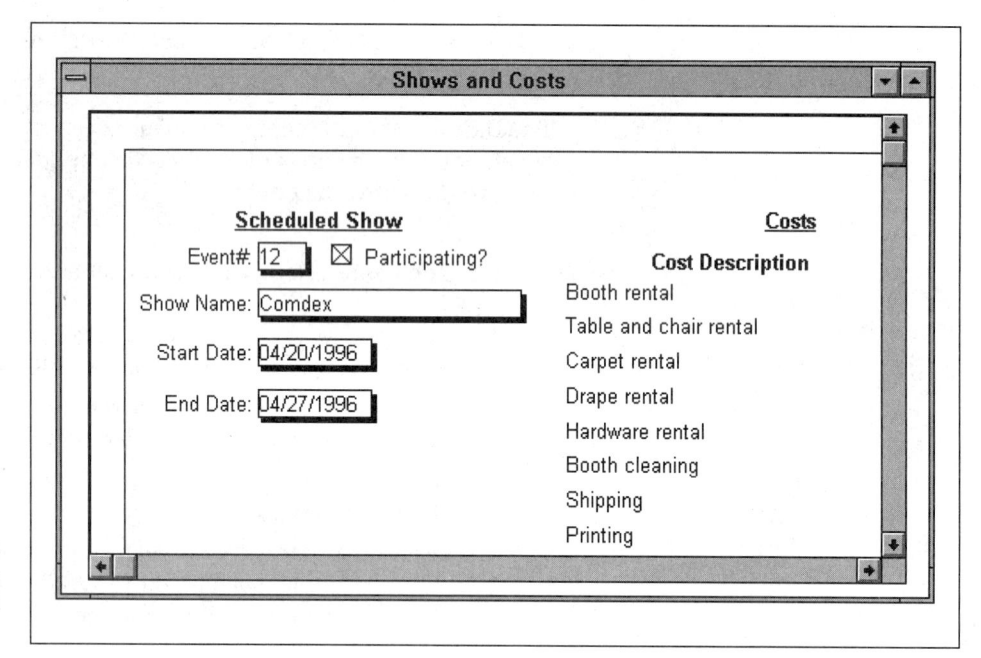

Figure 15.8
Initial view of the Shows and Costs nested report

Creating Windows with Updatable 1:M DataWindows

Although nested reports aren't updatable, there's nothing to prevent you from placing more than one DataWindow control in an application window and using scripts to manage the connection between the controls. As a first example, you'll be creating a window for modifying costs of trade shows that Pinehill Software has attended. The window will display show information along with all the costs generated by that show.

This type of window, in which many rows of detail information are displayed for a single related row from another table, occurs frequently in data management applications. In particular, this layout is useful for creating invoices, statements, or purchase orders. The row on the "one" side of the one-to-many relationship represents the header information, such as a company name, order number, date, and so on. The detail rows, those on the "many" side of the relationship, are the line items on the form.

To create the DataWindow objects:

1 Create a new DataWindow object (**dwo_attended_shows**) with a data source of SQL Select and a presentation style of Freeform. Choose the **Calendar** table. Include the event#, show name, and starting date columns. Sort the data by starting date within show name. Create a WHERE clause that reads:

```
WHERE "calendar"."participation" = 'T'
```

2 Arrange the DataWindow so that it looks something like Figure 15.9. Notice in particular that the event# column and its label have been removed from the form.

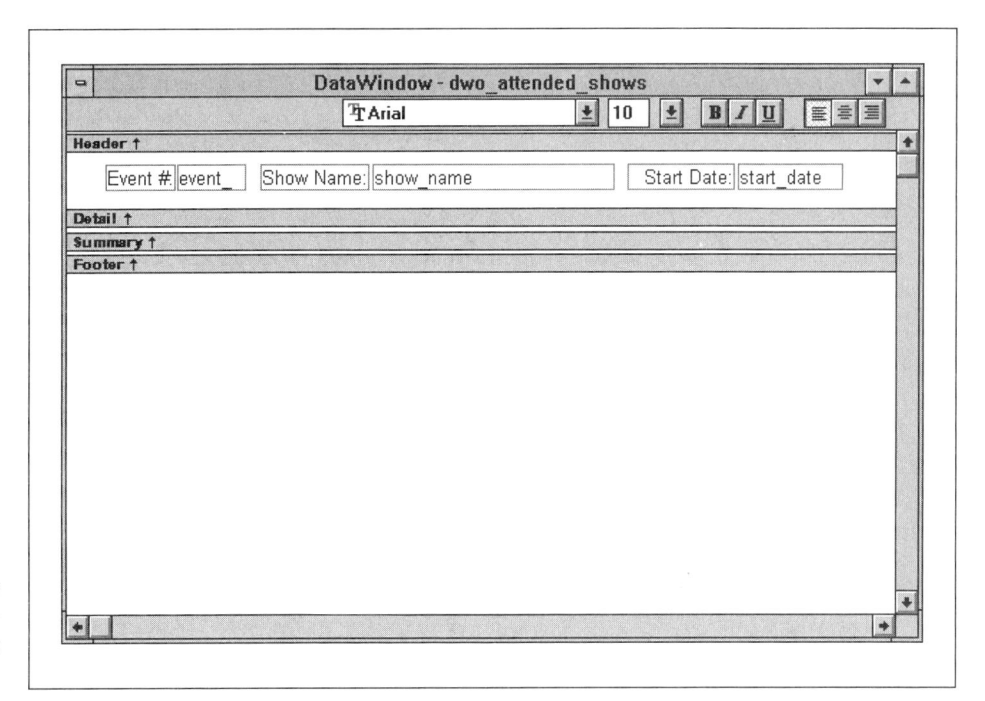

Figure 15.9
DataWindow object to display attended shows

By default, PowerBuilder decides whether a DataWindow object is updatable. DataWindow objects that are based on more than one table, based on a view, include SQL grouping commands or summary calculations, or are lacking their table's primary key columns aren't updatable. All others, including dwo_attended_shows, are updatable. However, the data from the Calendar table are for display only; they shouldn't be updated on this form. Therefore, you need to make the DataWindow nonupdatable:

3   Choose **Rows** -> **Update**. The Specify Update Characteristics dialog box appears (Figure 15.10).

4   Remove the X from the Allow Updates check box. Click the **OK** button to close the dialog box.

5   Create a second new DataWindow object (**dwo_cost_list**) with a data source of SQL Select and presentation style of Tabular. Choose the **Costs** table. Include all columns. Define a Number retrieval argument (**arg_event_numb**) and create a WHERE clause that reads:

```
WHERE "costs"."event#" = :arg_event_numb
```

6   Make all the text in the DataWindow object **9** points in size. Make the column headings bold and underlined. Resize the header and detail bands so they are as small as possible. Check the size by previewing the DataWindow. Add any other formatting that you would like, but leave the basic layout as a vertical list.

Now that the DataWindow objects have been prepared, you can place them on the application window, add some command buttons, and write the scripts to make it all work. The scripts use functions you have seen already, but in some cases use them in a different way.

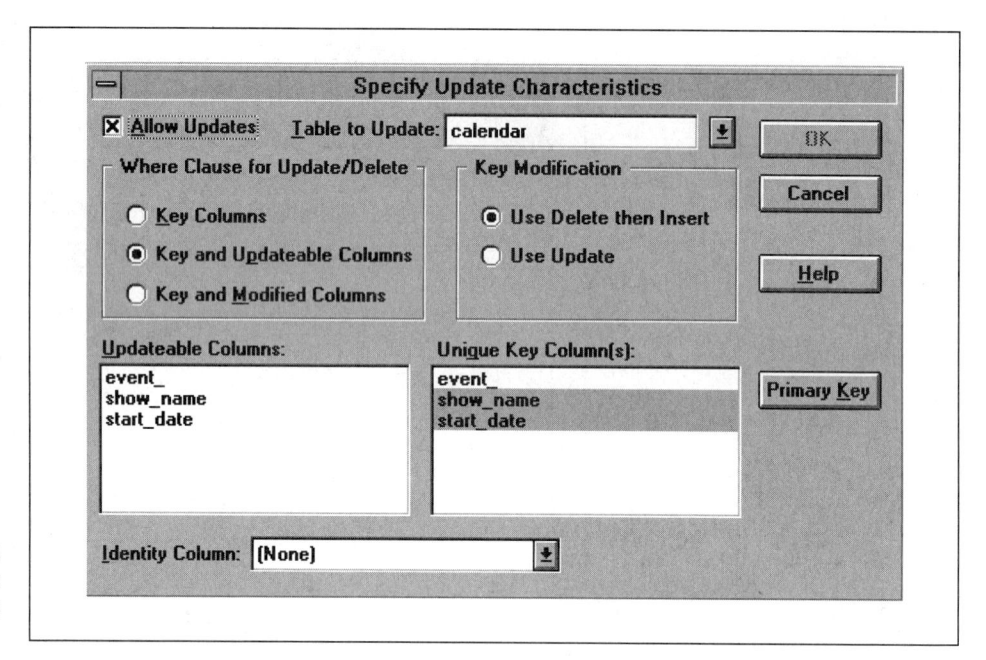

Figure 15.10
Specify Update Characteristics dialog box

To complete the window:

1 Open the w_manage_cost_data window.
2 Place a DataWindow control on the window (dw_attended_shows). Associate it with dwo_attended_shows.
3 Resize dw_attended_shows so it is just big enough to display the samples PowerBuilder provides. You only want one row to show at a time.
4 Place a second DataWindow control on the window (dw_cost_list). Associate it with dwo_cost_list. Give the control a vertical scroll bar.
5 Add command buttons and arrange objects on the window so that the window appears something like Figure 15.11 on page 361. Give the buttons names that are suggestive of their function. For example, the First Show button might be named cb_first.
6 Enter the Script painter for the window's open event.
7 Create a long integer instance variable (**i_rows_retrieved**). The value in this variable will be used by the Last Show button.
8 Enter the script in Listing 15.2 on page 361. As you can see, this script first populates dw_attended_shows and then uses the event number from the first row as a retrieval argument for dw_cost_list.
9 Enter one-line scripts for the clicked events of the sequential access command buttons, using Listing 15.3 on page 362 as a guide.
10 Enter the script in Listing 15.4 on page 362 for the clicked event of the Save button.
11 Enter the following one-line script for the Delete button:

```
dw_cost_list.DeleteRow (0)
```

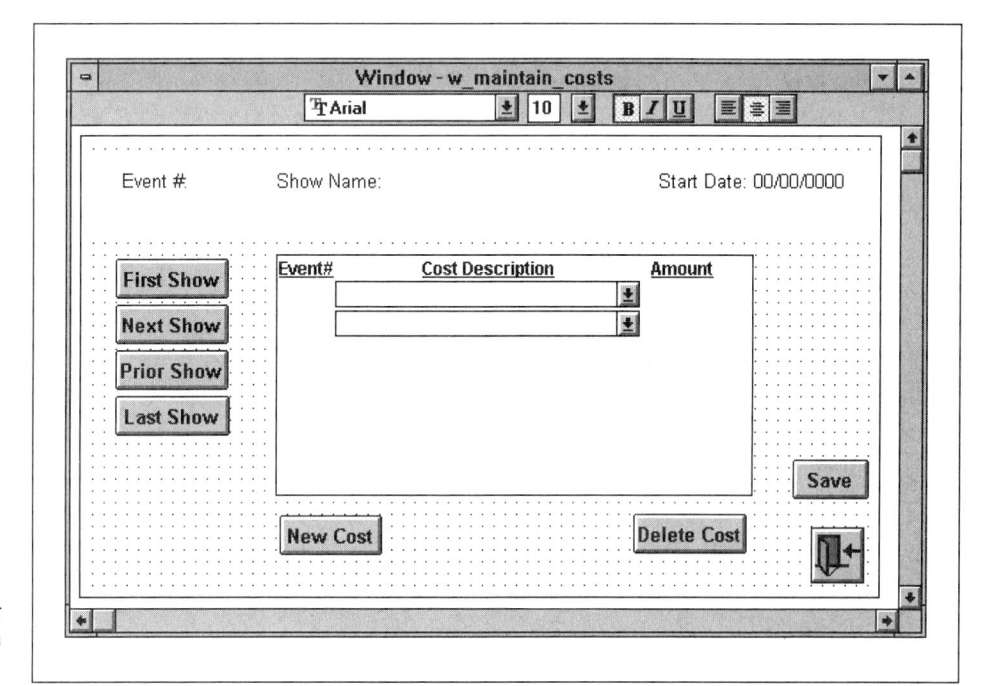

Figure 15.11
Layout of the window to be used for maintaining cost data

Listing 15.2
Open event script for the maintain costs window

```
long current_row, event_numb

// associate both DataWindow controls with a transaction object
dw_attended_shows.SetTransObject (sqlca);
dw_cost_list.SetTransObject (sqlca);

// retrieve data for dw_attended_shows and store number of rows
// retrieved for use by Last Show button
i_rows_retrieved = dw_attended_shows.Retrieve()

if i_rows_retrieved < 1 then
  rollback using sqlca;
  messagebox ("Retrieve","Couldn't find any rows.")
else
  commit using sqlca;
end if

// get row number and event number from that row
current_row = dw_attended_shows.GetRow()
event_numb=dw_attended_shows.GetItemNumber(current_row,"event_")

// retrieve data for dw_cost_list
dw_cost_list.Retrieve(event_numb)
dw_cost_list.SetFocus()
```

for the First Show button:

```
dw_attended_shows.ScrollToRow (0)
```

for the Next Show button:

```
dw_attended_shows.ScrollNextRow ()
```

for the Prior Show button:

```
dw_attended_shows.ScrollPriorRow ()
```

for the Last Show button:

```
dw_attended_shows.ScrollToRow (i_rows_retrieved)
```

Listing 15.3
Clicked event scripts for the sequential access buttons on the maintain costs window

```
if dw_cost_list.Update() = 1 then
   commit using sqlca;
   messagebox ("Save","Your changes were saved.")
else
   rollback using sqlca;
   messagebox ("Save","Couldn't save the changes.")
end if
```

Listing 15.4
Clicked event script for the Save button on the maintain costs window

12 Enter the script in Listing 15.5 for the New Cost button's clicked event. As you read through this script, notice that it takes the event number from the current row from Calendar and places it in the row inserted into Costs. This saves the user a bit of data entry and more importantly, makes data entry more accurate because it ensures that the cross reference to Calendar is accurate.

```
long row_numb, event_numb

//get current Calendar table row
row_numb = dw_attended_shows.GetRow()

// get the event number
event_numb = dw_attended_shows.GetItemNumber (row_numb,"event_")

// insert the new row and get its row number
row_numb = dw_cost_list.InsertRow (0)

// make new row visible and current
dw_cost_list.ScrollToRow (row_numb)

// stuff the event number into the new row
dw_cost_list.SetItem (row_numb, "event_", event_numb)
```

Listing 15.5
Clicked event script for the New Costs button on the maintain costs window

The maintain costs window requires one more script. Before you look at the script, you need to know why it is necessary and the event that triggers it. If you think about the open event script for the maintain costs window (Listing 15.2), you realize that it is triggered only once: when the window is opened. However, data needs to be retrieved for dw_cost_list each time the user clicks one of the sequential access buttons to change the row that appears in dw_attended_shows.

The event that occurs when the current row in dw_attended_shows changes is called rowfocuschanged, an event that is triggered by a change in the current row. (Itemchanged, which you used in Chapter 14, isn't triggered because no modification has been made to a value in dw_attended_shows.) A script to repeat the retrieval for dw_cost_list must therefore be attached to the rowfocuschanged event for dw_attended_shows.

13 Enter the script in Listing 15.6 for the rowfocuschanged event for dw_attended_shows.

Listing 15.6
rowfocuschanged event for dw_attended_shows

```
long row_numb, event_numb

// figure out which row is current and get the event number
// from that row
row_numb = this.GetRow()
event_numb = this.GetItemNumber (row_numb,"event_")

// retrieve new set of data for dw_cost_list
if dw_cost_list.Retrieve (event_numb) < 1 then
   rollback using sqlca;
else
   commit using sqlca;
   dw_cost_list.SetFocus()
end if
```

The script in Listing 15.6 doesn't mention dw_attended_shows by name. Instead, it uses a special object reference called this. The this object always refers to the current object (the object to which the script is attached). It is initialized and maintained by PowerBuilder.

14 At this point, the maintain costs window is nearly complete. Run the application to test your scripts.

Adding Running Totals

The nested report that you created at the very beginning of this chapter has one advantage over the maintain costs window as it now stands: It displays the total costs for each trade show. However, as you may remember, you can't update DataWindows that include SQL grouping commands or SQL grouping calculations. On the other hand, you *can* update windows that include PowerBuilder summary fields. This means that there is a way to keep a running total as you add and modify costs. If you adapt this type of window to invoices, statements, or purchase orders, you can see an up-to-the-minute order total as line items are added.

364 CHAPTER FIFTEEN CONNECTING DATAWINDOWS

There is another big advantage to a PowerBuilder summary field: its value is updated whenever you change data on which the summary field relies. For example, if you were to insert a new row or change the value in the amount field, the total will update. However, SQL summary computations are based on data retrieved directly from the database (not data displayed in a PowerBuilder window). The value in a SQL summary computation therefore won't change until data modifications are saved to the database and another call to `Retrieve` is issued to force the calculation to be performed again.

In Figure 15.12 you can see the final version of the maintain costs window. Notice that the total costs for a given show appears above the detail information. This computed quantity is part of dw_cost_list, even though it isn't in the summary band at the bottom of the DataWindow, where you find most summary calculations. Why not? Because you want the total to be visible at all times. If it were below all the detail lines, the user would often have to scroll the DataWindow to see it.

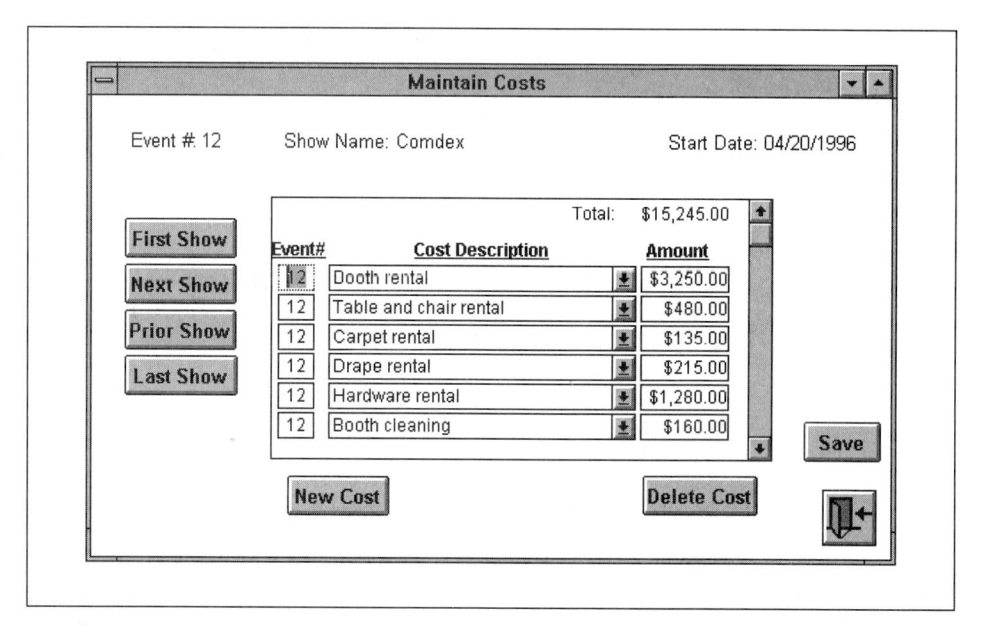

Figure 15.12
Completed Maintain Costs window

To modify dw_cost_list to include a computed field for the running total:

1. Open the dwo_cost_list DataWindow object.
2. Click the **amount** column rectangle to highlight it.
3. Click the **Sum** button in the PainterBar. A rectangle for the computed field appears in the summary band (sum(amount for all)).
4. Expand the header band so that it is approximately 1-inch high.
5. Drag the calculated field into the header band, aligning its right edge with the right edge of the amount column rectangle in the detail band below.
6. Add a static text control that reads **Total:** to label the computed field.
7. Format the computed field so that it displays as currency.

8 Save your changes and run the application. Notice as you do so that the value in the computed field is updated when data are retrieved for dw_cost_list or when you tab out of the amount column after making a change in its value.

Catching Unsaved Changes

In terms of the user interface, there is one major problem with all of the data entry windows you have completed to this point: The user receives no warning when he or she clicks the Close button without saving changes. A good user interface will warn the user that unsaved changes are pending and give the user a chance to save them, discard them, or abort the close action.

A script to manage displaying a warning alert and process the user's response to that alert is usually attached to a window's closequery event. Closequery is triggered whenever the window receives a `close` command. In our particular example, that `close` command is in the clicked event script of the Close button.

The easiest way to present users with an alert is to use an extended version of the `MessageBox` function:

```
MessageBox (title, text, icon, button(s), default_button)
```

The first two parameters—the box's title and its text—are required. (These are the parameters you've been using.) The remaining three optional parameters let you choose the icon that appears, vary the buttons that appear, and set a default button. There are five icons you can use:

- Information! (the default icon, which appears if you don't specify any other)
- StopSign! (a good choice for an alert that warns of unsaved changes)
- Exclamation!
- Question!
- None!

In addition, there are six button combinations that can appear:

- OK! (the default OK button)
- OKCancel! (OK and Cancel buttons)
- YesNo! (Yes and No buttons)
- YesNoCancel! (Yes, No, and Cancel buttons)
- RetryCancel! (Retry and Cancel buttons)
- AbortRetryIgnore (Abort, Retry, and Ignore buttons)

The buttons that appear in the message box are numbered, moving from left to right across the bottom of the box. Examples of the icons and buttons can be found in Figure 15.13 on page 366.

To set a default button, you place its number in the function call. `MessageBox` returns the number of the clicked button. (So far, you've ignored the return value because there was only one button in the box.)

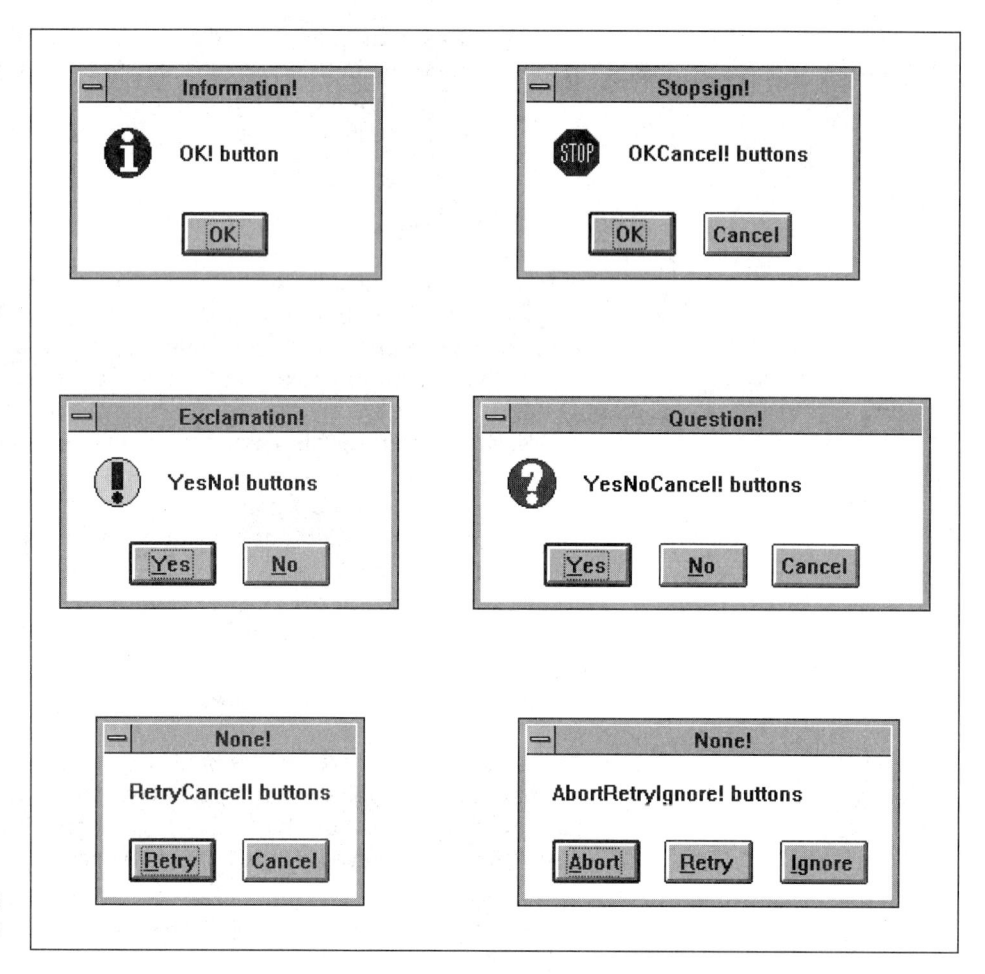

Figure 15.13
Message box icon and button options

When there is more than one button in a message box, the script that displays the box needs to include code that determines which button was clicked and takes action based on that button. (This is where the `choose case` statement comes in very handy.)

To implement the unsaved changes warning:

1   Enter the script in Listing 15.7 on page 367 for the w_manage_cost_data closequery event.

2   Run the application, making some changes that you don't save. Test the action of the three buttons in the box.

There are two items in Listing 15.7 that you haven't seen before. First is the method used to detect whether there are unsaved changes; second is the method used to stop the window from closing when the user chooses the Cancel button.

While a transaction is active, PowerBuilder keeps a count of the number of rows that have been modified (either inserted or changed) and the number of rows that have been deleted. The `ModifiedCount` function returns the

```
int chosen_button

// check to see if there are unsaved changes
if dw_cost_list.ModifiedCount() >0 or &
   dw_cost_list.DeletedCount() > 0 then

   // display the alert
   chosen_button = messagebox ("Unsaved Changes Pending", &
      "Do you want to save your changes?", StopSign!, &
      YesNoCancel!,1)

   // decide what to do
   choose case chosen_button

   // Button 1 = Yes
   case 1
      cb_save.TriggerEvent (Clicked!)

   // Button 2 = No
   case 2
      return

   // Button 3 = Cancel; must stop the close
   case 3
      message.ReturnValue = 1
      return

   end choose
end if
```

Listing 15.7
Closequery event script for w_maintain_costs

number of modified rows; the `DeletedCount` function returns the number of deleted rows. Therefore, if either of these functions returns a value greater than 0, there are unsaved changes pending.

To abort the action of the call to `close` in the Close button's clicked event script, the script in Listing 15.7 does something that at first seems totally unrelated to what is happening: It assigns a value of 1 to one of the `Message` object's attributes. There are, however, two underlying facts that explain why this has the effect it does. First, the `Message` object is not only used to pass a parameter between windows when a window is opened. In fact, its primary purpose is to communicate between PowerBuilder and Windows. Second, Windows actually takes care of opening and closing PowerBuilder windows. In other words, when PowerBuilder needs to open or close a window, it sends a request to Windows, which performs the needed operation.

The script in Listing 15.7 must therefore make Windows think that it has already processed the request to close a window. It does this by assigning the value 1 to one of the `Message` object's attributes (`ReturnValue`).

Creating Windows with Updatable M:1 DataWindows

In Figure 15.14 you can see a new window for maintaining the calendar of trade shows. At the top is a list of all current rows from the Calendar table. In addition, the form shows the row in Shows that is related to the current row in Calendar and the row in Calendar that is related to the current row in Shows. All three tables can be updated.

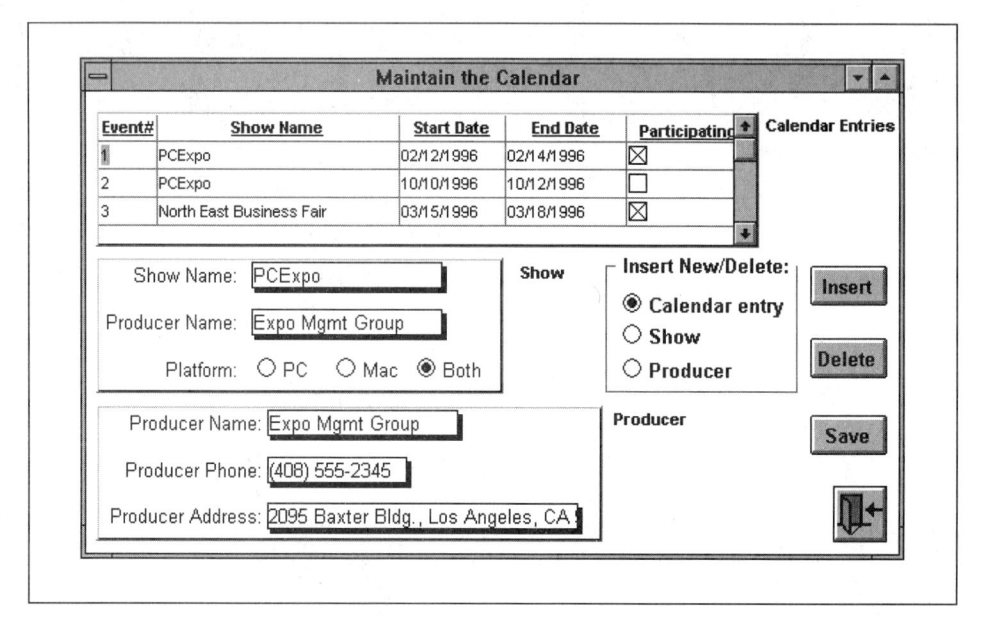

Figure 15.14
New window for maintaining the calendar

The radio buttons in the Insert New/Delete section are controls placed directly on the window; they aren't part of a DataWindow object like the radio buttons that are used to format the Platform column in the Shows table. As far as the user is concerned, the main purpose of these buttons is to identify the type of data he or she wants to insert or delete. The highlighted button changes whenever the user clicks one of the buttons or clicks in a DataWindow control. However, the radio buttons also let the window know which DataWindow control has focus so that the clicked event script of the Insert button can insert a row into the correct table or delete a row from the correct table.

There is a GetFocus function, which returns a reference to the control that has focus. Typically a script identifies which control has focus by checking the contents of the Text attribute of the object reference returned by the function call. (It won't work to simply compare the function's return value to the name of a control.) Unfortunately, DataWindow controls don't have Text attributes, so the calendar maintenance window has to resort to another method to figure out which DataWindow control has focus (in other words, the radio buttons).

The DataWindows in this version of the calendar maintenance window are related in a many-to-one manner. In other words, although many rows from the Calendar table are visible, the window shows the one row from Shows that is related to the current row from Calendar. Rather than many detail rows showing for one "master" row, as you did with the cost maintenance window, it shows one master row for a single detail row.

To work properly, a number of things must happen in this window:

- Every time the user changes the current row in the Calendar table, the rows in the both the Shows and Producers tables must update correctly.
- When the user clicks in a DataWindow control, the window should receive focus. The associated radio button should be highlighted.
- When the user chooses a radio button, the associated window should receive focus.
- When the user clicks the Insert button, the DataWindow control that has focus should receive the new row.
- When the user clicks the Delete button, the current row should be deleted from the DataWindow control that has focus.
- When the user clicks the Save button, all unsaved changes should be saved.

To make it all work together, you will need three DataWindow objects—one for each table—and a number of scripts.

This new version of the calendar maintenance window is considerably more complex than any window you have completed to this point. However, it doesn't introduce any new functions or use and PowerScript elements you haven't used before. It simply puts things you have already learned together in a new way.

Building the DataWindows

The first DataWindow that you will construct is dwo_calendar_list, which presents the contents of the Calendar table in a grid format.

To create the DataWindow object:

1 Create a new DataWindow object based on a Quick Select data source and the Grid presentation style.
2 Choose the **Calendar** table. Include all columns and rows in the table.
3 Remove the text from the participation column rectangle in the detail band. (*Hint:* You'll need to modify its edit style to do this.)
4 Set the text size for all rectangles to **8** points.
5 Make both the header and detail bands as small as possible.
6 Make the text in the header band bold and underlined. The completed object should look something like Figure 15.15 on page 370.
7 Save the DataWindow object as **dwo_calendar_list**.

The second DataWindow is laid out to display one row from the Shows table. It also needs to include an argument that will restrict which row appears based on the show name. (This argument will be supplied by the current row in the Calendar table.)

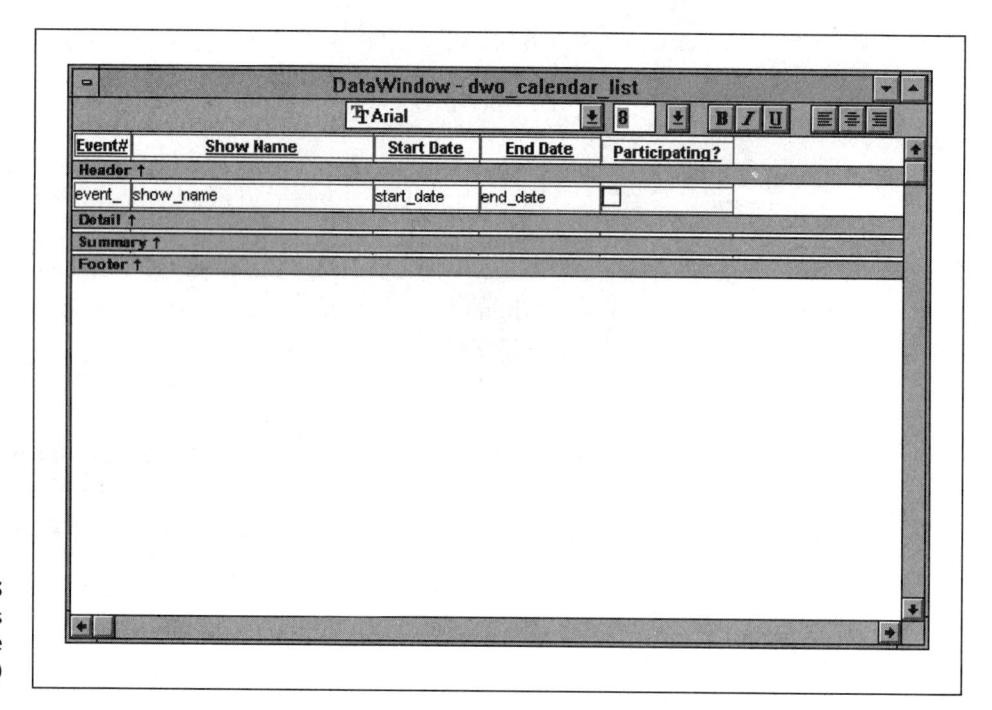

Figure 15.15
DataWindow object that displays multiple rows from the Calendar table (dwo_calendar_list)

To create dwo_manage_shows:

1. Create a new DataWindow object based on a SQL Select data source and a Freeform presentation style.
2. Choose the **Shows** table. Include all columns.
3. Create a string retrieval argument (**arg_show_name**).
4. Enter a WHERE clause with the following expression:

    "shows"."show_name" = :arg_show_name

5. Use the Design button to enter the DataWindow painter.
6. Currently, the number of columns is set to one, so the buttons appear vertically, an orientation that will take up too much room for the DataWindow object to fit on the application window. Therefore, change the edit style for the Platform column so that it displays its radio buttons in three columns across.
7. Remove the border from the radio buttons.
8. Rearrange and resize the contents of the DataWindow object so that it looks something like Figure 15.16.

The third DataWindow object, which will display one row from the Producers table, already exists. As you may remember, dwo_maintain_producers uses the Freeform presentation style and also includes the required retrieval argument to restrict rows by producer name. You can therefore use the existing object without doing any further work!

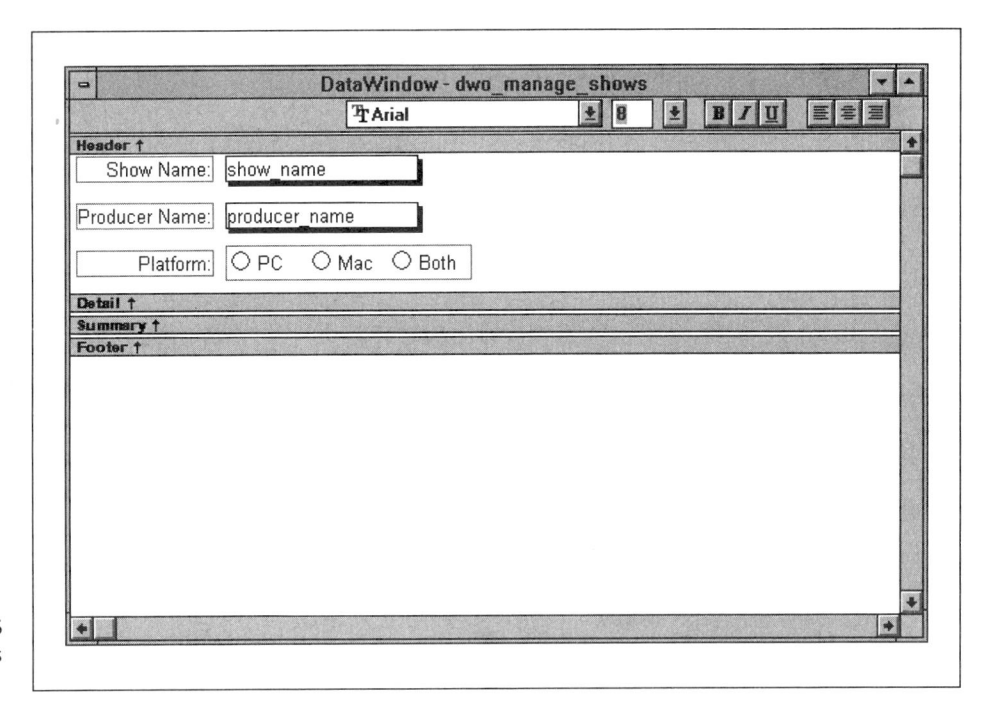

Figure 15.16
Layout for dwo_manage_shows

Laying Out the Window

Now that the three DataWindow objects are in place, you can begin to place elements on the application window. As you work, use Figure 15.14 on page 368 as a guide for placing elements on the window.

To create the window:

1 Create a new application window named **w_manage_calendar2**. Enlarge it so it fills the entire Window painter workspace.

2 Copy the Close button from w_manage_calendar and place it in the window's lower-right corner.

3 Place the first DataWindow control at the top of the window, with its upper-left corner one grid unit from the window's upper-left corner. Associate the control with dwo_calendar_list and name it **dw_calendar_list**. Give the control a vertical scroll bar. If you want to make your window look exactly like Figure 15.14, give the control a 3D Raised border and resize it so that it is wide enough to show all its columns and just less than 1/3 the height of the window.

4 Place the second DataWindow control below the first, aligning the left edges of the two controls. Associate the second control with dwo_manage_shows and name it **dw_manage_shows**. Resize it so you can see all three of its columns. Make its border match the first DataWindow control.

5 Place the third DataWindow control below the second, aligning the left edges of all three controls. Associate the third control with dwo_manage_producers and name it **dw_maintain_producers**. Resize

372 CHAPTER FIFTEEN CONNECTING DATAWINDOWS

it so you can see all three of its columns. Make its border match the first two DataWindow controls.

6 Create three command buttons: Insert (**cb_insert**), Save (**cb_save**), and Delete (**cb_delete**). For the moment, place them anywhere along the right edge of the window.

7 Add text to label each of the DataWindow controls, placing the static text controls at the upper-right corner of DataWindow controls.

Adding the Radio Buttons

Radio buttons, like other controls that you place directly on a window, are used to collect information from the user. However, unlike check boxes and edit controls, radio buttons always occur in groups. A radio button has an attribute named Checked. If Checked is TRUE, the button is highlighted. However, only one button in a group can be highlighted at a time. When the user clicks on one radio button in a group, PowerBuilder sets its Checked attribute to TRUE and the Checked attributes of all other buttons in the group to FALSE.

By default, all radio buttons on a window are part of the same group. However, you can create multiple groups by placing a group box around selected radio buttons. A group box isn't needed in the w_manage_calendar2 because there is only one group, but using the box makes it easy to put the label above the group (and gives you experience using group boxes).

To create and group the radio buttons:

1 Click the **RadioButton** button in the PainterBar (Figure 15.17).

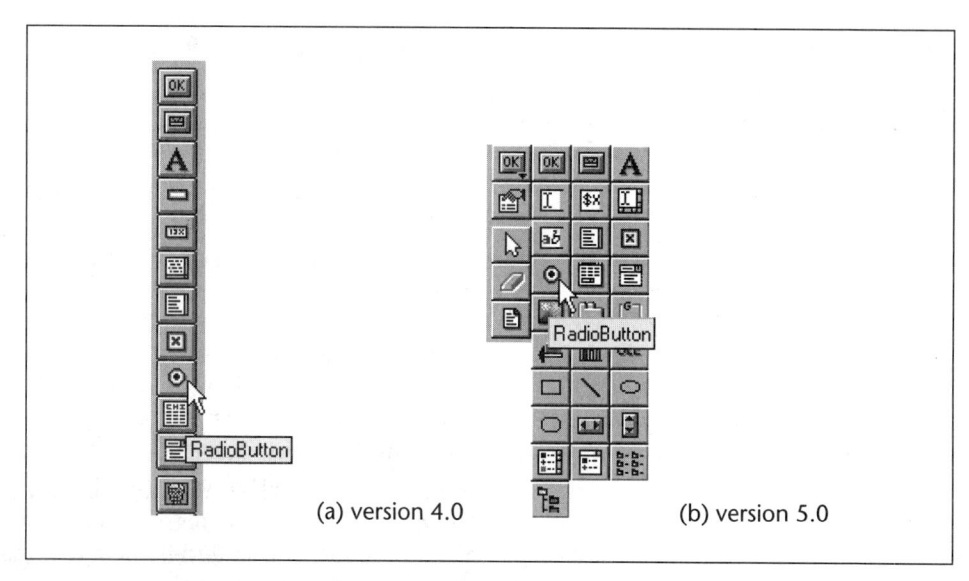

Figure 15.17
RadioButton button in the PainterBar

(a) version 4.0   (b) version 5.0

2 Click in the window to the right dw_manage_shows. A radio button with the default text of "none" appears.

3 Double-click the radio button. If you are working with version 4.0, the RadioButton dialog box appears.

If you are working with version 5.0, the RadioButton properties dialog box appears showing the General panel.

4 Name the radio button **rb_calendar**.

5 Change the radio button's text to **Calendar entry**.

6 At least one radio button in a group must be Checked when a window first opens. Therefore, place an X in the Checked check box to make this radio button the default in the group. The completed dialog box should look like Figure 15.18 (version 4.0) or Figure 15.19 (version 5.0).

Figure 15.18
Completed RadioButton dialog box (4.0)

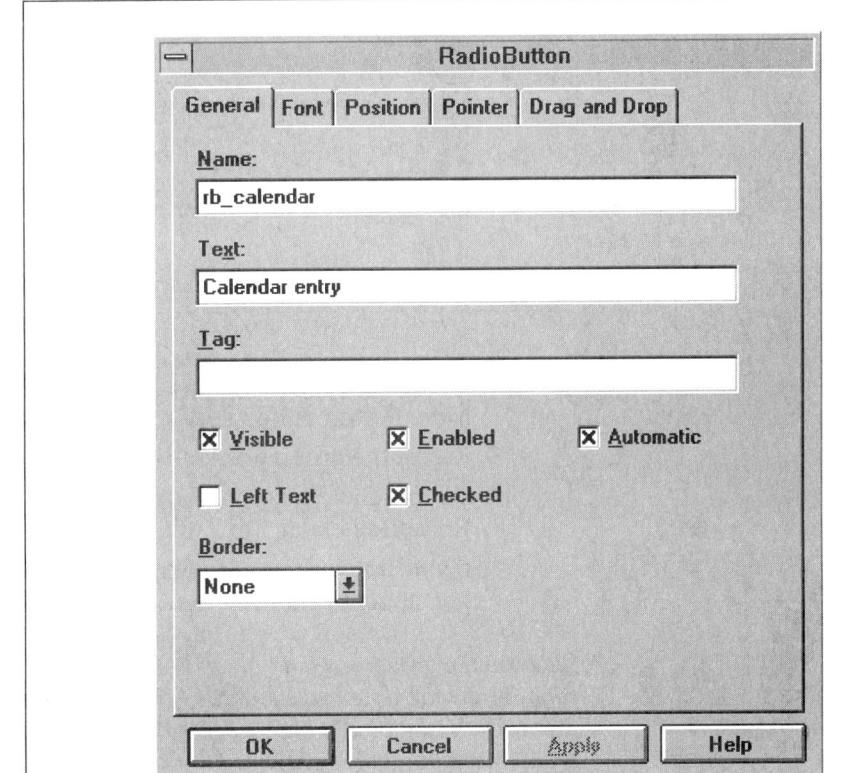

Figure 15.19
Completed RadioButton General properties (5.0)

7 Click the **OK** button to close the RadioButton dialog box.

A radio button has a popup menu that you can access by right-clicking on the button. The properties that you set in the RadioButton dialog box can be set individually using options in the popup menu.

8 Create a second radio button below the first. Name it **rb_show** and set its text to **Show**. This button should *not* be Checked.

9 Create a third radio button below the second. Name it **rb_producer** and set its text to **Producer**. This button should *not* be Checked.

10 Align the left edges of the radio buttons.

11 Click the **GroupBox** button in the PainterBar (Figure 15.20).

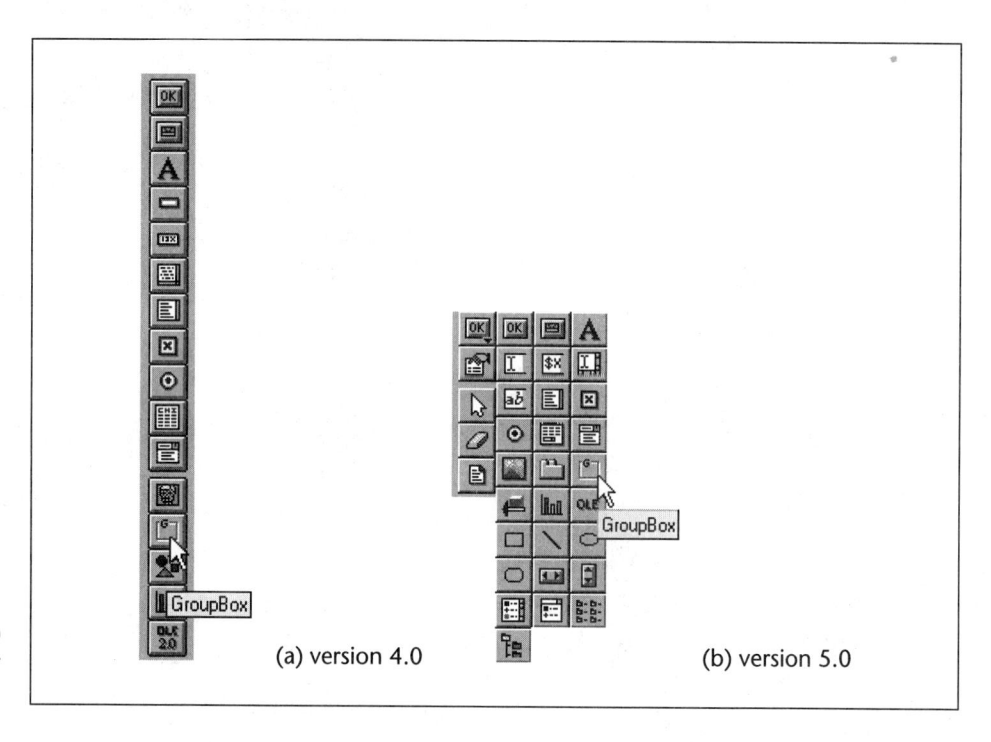

Figure 15.20
GroupBox button in the PainterBar

(a) version 4.0   (b) version 5.0

12 Click in the window above the upper-left corner of the Calendar entry radio button. A box appears where you clicked.

13 Resize the group box so that it surrounds all three radio buttons.

14 Double-click the group box. If you are working with version 4.0, the GroupBox dialog box appears.

If you are working with verison 5.0, the GroupBox properties dialog box appears showing the General panel.

Because the group box isn't much bigger than the radio buttons, it can be a bit tricky to get the double-click on the group box to work properly. It's easier if you first click on the box to highlight it and then carefully double-click just inside the group box's border. Don't worry if you accidentally open the window's or a radio button's dialog box; just close the wrong dialog box and try again.

15 Change the group box's name to **gb_choose_table**. Set its text to **Insert New/Delete:**. The completed dialog box should look like Figure 15.21 for version 4.0 and Figure 15.22 for version 5.0.

Figure 15.21
GroupBox dialog box

Figure 15.22
Completed GroupBox General properties (5.0)

16 Use the **OK** button to close the dialog box. All the visual elements of the window are now in place.

Writing the Scripts

The w_manage_calendar2 window requires more than a dozen scripts to make it behave as needed.

To enter the necessary scripts and attach them to the correct objects and events:

1. Enter the Script painter for the window's open event.
2. Create two instance variables: **row_numb** (a long integer) and **string_value** (a string).
3. Enter the script in Listing 15.8 on page 377 for the window's open event. The purpose of this script is to load all three DataWindows when w_manage_calendar2 is opened. The script begins by associating each of the DataWindow controls with a transaction object. It then retrieves data for dw_calendar_list. If the retrieval is successful, it gets the show name from the current row and uses it to retrieve a row for dw_manage_show. The script can then extract the producer name from dw_manage_show and in turn, use it to retrieve a row for dw_maintain_producers. As you can see, the principle behind handling DataWindows that are related in a M:1 manner is similar to that for handling those related in a 1:M manner: Retrieve data one DataWindow at a time, using data from a preceding DataWindow as a retrieval argument for the next.
4. Enter the script in Listing 15.9 on page 378 for dw_calendar_list's rowfocuschanged event. The purpose of this script is to reload dw_manage_show and dw_maintain_producers whenever the user chooses a new row in dw_calendar_list. It uses a very similar strategy to the window's open event script, taking a key value from a current row and using it as a retrieval argument.

    This script is also triggered when the user inserts a new row into the Calendar table. In that case, there are no related Show or Producer rows until the user enters a value for the show_name column. The script therefore checks to see if a row has been retrieved from Shows. If not, it simply resets the Producer DataWindow without attempting an invalid retrieval. As you will see when you run this window, the unsuccessful retrieval from Shows also results in an empty DataWindow, which is what you want the user to see until a valid value appears in the Calendar DataWindow's show_name column.

5. The retrieval of related show and producer data should occur as soon as the user enters a value for the show_name in the Calendar DataWindow and moves to another column. Using the Tab key to move to the next column or clicking in the next column triggers an itemfocuschanged event. To make sure that retrieval for dw_manage_shows and dw_maintain calendar occurs, enter the following one-line script for dw_calendar_list's itemfocuschanged event:

    ```
    this.TriggerEvent (rowfocuschanged!)
    ```

```
// associate each DataWindow control with a transaction object
dw_calendar_list.SetTransObject (sqlca)
dw_manage_shows.SetTransObject (sqlca)
dw_maintain_producers.SetTransObject (sqlca)

// Populate the calendar window
if dw_calendar_list.Retrieve() >=1 then

// Get show name and row number to use to populate the show window
   row_numb = dw_calendar_list.GetRow()
   string_value = dw_calendar_list.GetItemString &
     (row_numb,"show_name")

// Populate the show window
   dw_manage_shows.Retrieve (string_value)

// Get producer name to use to populate the producer window
   row_numb = dw_manage_shows.GetRow()
   string_value = dw_manage_shows.GetItemString &
     (row_numb,"producer_name")

// Populate the producer window
   dw_maintain_producers.Retrieve (string_value)

// Give focus to the calendar window
   dw_calendar_list.SetFocus()

// commit the transaction
   commit using sqlca;

else
   rollback using sqlca;
end if
```

Listing 15.8
Script for the window's open event

This script simply triggers the script in Listing 15.9. If the user hasn't entered an existing show name (in other words, attempting to store the new row in the Calendar table would cause a violation of referential integrity), then dw_manage_show and dw_maintain_producers will remain empty, letting the user know that the show name isn't valid. In that case, the user has two choices: either reenter the show name in dw_calendar_list or enter a new show.

6 This window must also manage the link between dw_manage_shows and dw_maintain_producers when inserting a new row into the Shows table or modifying an existing row. In other words, when the user makes a change to dw_manage_shows, a script needs to search for a matching row in the Producers table. If no matching row in Producers exists, the search will fail and dw_maintain_producers will remain empty, alerting the user that the producer name in dw_manage_shows isn't valid. You should therefore enter the script in Listing 15.10 on page 378 for the itemfocuschanged event of dw_manage_shows.

```
// determine which row the user chose
row_numb = this.GetRow()
string_value = this.GetItemString (row_numb,"show_name")

// get a new row for the show window
dw_manage_shows.Retrieve (string_value)

// get row retrieved from Shows table
row_numb = dw_manage_shows.GetRow()

// if there was a valid row for the Shows table, then
// get a row for the producer window
if row_numb > 0 then
  string_value = dw_manage_shows.GetItemString &
    (row_numb,"producer_name")
  dw_maintain_producers.Retrieve (string_value)
else
  dw_maintain_producers.Reset()
end if
```

Listing 15.9
Script for dw_calendar_list's rowfocuschanged event

```
// get info about current row
row_numb = this.GetRow()
string_value = this.GetItemString (row_numb,"producer_name")

dw_maintain_producers.Retrieve (string_value)
this.SetFocus()
```

Listing 15.10
Script for the itemfocuschanged event of dw_manage_shows

Why isn't there a rowfocuschanged script for dw_manage_shows, like there is for dw_calendar_list? Because the SQL query that defines the contents of dw_manage_shows only returns one row at a time. (The query is based on the table's primary key: show_name). Therefore, the only time the rowfocuschanged event is triggered for this window is when a new row is inserted. As you will see shortly, this situation is handled by the Insert button's clicked event script.

7. When the user clicks on a radio button, PowerBuilder takes care of setting the Checked attribute correctly for all buttons in the group. However, in this case, that's not enough: The DataWindow control to which the clicked button corresponds must receive focus. That action must therefore be part of the clicked event script for each button. To ensure that the focus changes correctly, enter the one-line scripts in Listing 15.11 on page 379.

8. When the user clicks in a DataWindow to give it focus, the radio button that corresponds to that DataWindow should be Checked. This won't happen automatically because there is no natural linkage between the buttons and the DataWindow controls. The window therefore needs the scripts in Listing 15.12 on page 379 to take care of it. Enter these three-line scripts for the clicked event of the appropriate DataWindow control.

Listing 15.11
Scripts for the clicked events of the three radio buttons

```
for rb_calendar:

    dw_calendar_list.SetFocus()

for rb_show:

    dw_manage_shows.SetFocus()

for rb_producer:

    dw_maintain_producers.SetFocus()
```

Listing 15.12
Scripts for the clicked events of the three DataWindow controls

```
for dw_calendar_list:

    rb_calendar.Checked = TRUE
    rb_show.Checked = FALSE
    rb_producer.Checked = FALSE

for dw_manage_shows:

    rb_calendar.Checked = FALSE
    rb_show.Checked = TRUE
    rb_producer.Checked = FALSE

for dw_maintain_producers:

    rb_calendar.Checked = FALSE
    rb_show.Checked = FALSE
    rb_producer.Checked = TRUE
```

9   Enter the script in Listing 15.13 on page 380 for the clicked event of the Insert button. Notice that this script uses the state of the Checked attribute of the radio buttons to determine which DataWindow control should receive the new row.

10 Enter the script in Listing 15.14 on page 380 for the clicked event of the Delete button. This script uses the state of the Checked attribute of the radio buttons to determine the DataWindow control from which a row should be deleted.

11 Enter the script in Listing 15.15 on page 381 for the clicked event of the Save button. Although the script could certainly check each DataWindow to determine whether there were changes pending, it's just easier to update all three. If no changes are pending for a given DataWindow, issuing the call to Update simply has no effect.

12 To catch uncommitted changes, enter the script in Listing 15.16 on page 381 for the application window's closequery event. Notice that the only major difference between the script and the one in Listing 15.7 is that this one must check for unsaved changes in three DataWindows rather than just one.

Listing 15.13 Clicked event script for the Insert button

```
long max_event_numb, new_row

// Look at the Checked attribute of the radio buttons to
// determine which DataWindow control should get the new row

// Handle a new row for the Calendar table
if rb_calendar.Checked = TRUE then

// Add the new row
   new_row = dw_calendar_list.InsertRow(0)
// Find the maximum event number
   select max(event#)
    into :max_event_numb
    from calendar;

// Add 1 to generate new event number
   max_event_numb = max_event_numb + 1

// Insert the new event number
   dw_calendar_list.SetItem (new_row,"event_",max_event_numb)

// Make the new row visible
   dw_calendar_list.ScrollToRow (new_row)

// Handle a new row for the Show table
elseif rb_show.Checked = TRUE then

// Add the new row
   new_row = dw_manage_shows.InsertRow (0)

// Make the new row visible
   dw_manage_shows.ScrollToRow (new_row)

// Clear rows from the Producers DataWindow
   dw_maintain_producers.Reset()

// Handle a new row for the Producers table
else
// Add the new row

   new_row = dw_maintain_producers.InsertRow(0)
// Make the new row visible
   dw_maintain_producers.ScrollToRow (new_row)
end if
```

Listing 15.14 Clicked event script for the Delete button

```
if rb_calendar.Checked = TRUE then
   dw_calendar_list.DeleteRow (0)
elseif rb_show.Checked = TRUE then
   dw_manage_shows.DeleteRow (0)
else
   dw_maintain_producers.DeleteRow (0)
end if
```

Listing 15.15
Clicked event script for the Save button

```
if dw_calendar_list.Update () = 1 and &
   dw_manage_shows.Update () = 1 and &
   dw_maintain_producers.Update () = 1 then
   commit using sqlca;
   messagebox ("Save","All changes have been saved.")
else
   rollback using sqlca;
   messagebox ("Save","Unable to save any changes.")
end if
```

Listing 15.16
Script for w_manage_calendar2's closequery event

```
int chosen_button

// Check to see if there are pending changes
if dw_calendar_list.ModifiedCount() > 0 or &
   dw_calendar_list.DeletedCount() > 0 or &
   dw_manage_shows.ModifiedCount() > 0 or &
   dw_manage_shows.DeletedCount() > 0 or &
   dw_maintain_producers.ModifiedCount() > 0 or &
   dw_maintain_producers.DeletedCount() > 0 then

// Display message box warning of unsaved changes
   chosen_button = messagebox ("Unsaved Changes Pending", &
   "Do you want to save your changes?", StopSign!, &
   YesNoCancel!, 1)

// Process the user's response
   choose case chosen_button

// If user wants to save, trigger the Save button's clicked
// event script
      case 1
         cb__save.TriggerEvent (Clicked!)

// If user doesn't want to save, exit script and allow
// window close to procede
      case 2
         return

// If user wants to cancel, set the message object's
// return value to 1 so that Windows won't close the
// window.
      case 3
         message.ReturnValue = 1
         return
   end choose
end if
```

13. Open the w_calendar window.
14. Change the script of the Maintain the Calendar button's clicked event to read:

    ```
    open (w_manage_calendar2)
    ```

15. Run the application. Test the various actions you can perform with this window (for example, selecting different rows in the Calendar table, adding new rows to each of the three tables, and so on) to make sure that your scripts work as expected.

Looking Ahead

In this chapter you have mastered a collection of techniques for enhancing application windows, including methods for placing multiple DataWindows on the same window. The first technique—nested reports—links DataWindows in a 1:M relationship for output only; the DataWindows aren't updatable. The second techique enables multiple updatable DataWindows on one window.

In Chapter 16 you will learn about additional ways to manipulate DataWindows while an application is running. An application can set DataWindow characteristics, such as whether the DataWindow is visible. In addition, an application can change the query that is used to populate a DataWindow.

EXERCISES

The following exercises give you a chance to add some useful, sophisticated windows to the College & University Rentals application. You will gain experience with nested reports and with several ways to design data modification windows. As you work, don't forget about the user. Use simple language to label parts of the windows. Avoid using jargon like "Commit." Also avoid using cryptic table or column names; replace them with meaningful phrases.

1. Create a nested report that shows all customers and their rentals. Include a summary of all the rental fees owed by the customer.

2. Create a nested report that shows all schools and contacts made with their house officers. Include a count of the number of contacts made at each school.

3. Complete a window that can be used to manage rentals. This window should be preceded by a response box that lets the user select the customer. Then, the window should display information about the customer in a nonupdatable DataWindow. The window should also show all outstanding rentals for the customer. The user should be able to add new rentals and modify existing rentals. When adding a new rental, use a script to copy the customer number into the new row. Include a summary field that displays a running total of how much the customer owes. Use a dropdown DataWindow for the item number of the item to be rented that shows the

merchandise type for the item. When constructing the query for the drop-DownDataWindow, include only those items whose status is "warehouse." (In other words, you want only those items that are available for rental.)

When an item is rented, you need to change its status to rented. To do this, you can use an embedded SQL UPDATE *command. Assuming that you have the number of the item being rented in a variable named* item_numb, *then the SQL can be written as:*

```
UPDATE Items SET
    status = 'rented'
    WHERE item# = :item_numb;
```

4. Complete a window that can be used to manage the item inventory (the Items table). Provide a list of merchandise in a window based on the Merchandise table. Also provide a list of items from the Items table that correspond to the current row in the Merchandise DataWindow. When the user changes the row in the Merchandise DataWindow, change the contents of the Items DataWindow. Let the user add, modify, and delete data from either window. When adding a row to the Items DataWindow, use a script to copy the merchandise number of the current type of merchandise into the new Items row.

5. Complete a window that can be used to manage the contacts made with housing officers. Use a response window to let the user choice the school with which the contact was made. Then, display the school and all contacts made at that school in the window. Allow the user to enter, modify, and delete contacts. Do no allow modification of the school data.

6. Create an alternate window for entering rentals. Provide a list of items from which the user can choose (all rows from the Items table that have a status of "warehouse"). Show data from the Merchandise table for the chosen item in a nonupdatable DataWindow. Then, include a list of customers from which the user can pick. In addition, the window will need a DataWindow into which the rental can be added. Consider carefully how you will connect the customer selected in the list of customers with the item selected for rental. (*Hint:* Your goal is to be able to enter the customer number and item number into the new rental for the user.) Don't forget to change the status of the item being rented.

CHAPTER SIXTEEN

Dynamic DataWindows

IN THIS CHAPTER YOU WILL:

- Set DataWindow characteristics while an application is running
- Change the query on which a DataWindow is based in a PowerBuilder script

386 CHAPTER SIXTEEN DYNAMIC DATAWINDOWS

To this point, you may have assumed that the characteristics of a DataWindow control are fixed while an application is running. However, that is not the case. Many of the properties of a DataWindow that you set in both the DataWindow painter and the Window painter can be changed dynamically by a script (for example, whether a control is visible). In this chapter you will be introduced to some techniques for such dynamic manipulation, including making DataWindows appear and disappear as well as changing the query on which a DataWindow is based.

> **NOTE** *DataWindow controls aren't the only controls for which you can change properties from a script. For complete information, consult the PowerBuilder manual Objects and Controls or PowerBuilder Online Help.*

Hiding and Showing DataWindows

One of the attributes of a DataWindow control—Visible—is a Boolean value that determines whether the control can be seen at any given time. Because Visible's default value is TRUE, in most cases you don't need to be concerned with it. However, there might be instances in which you want to hide or show data based on choices a user has made in a window. For example, a user might indicate that he or she wants to see detail information such as the line items on a purchase order by placing an X in a check box. If the user were to remove the X from the check box, the line item data should disappear.

To illustrate how this might work, you're going to be modifying the window that displays a listing of all shows to give the user a choice of seeing the locations where a show has or will be held. The first step is therefore to create the DataWindow object that will display the location data.

To create a DataWindow object that will display the location data:

1. Make sure that you are working with the *tshows* application in *tshows2.pbl* and that you are connected to the *tshows* database.
2. Create a new DataWindow object (**dwo_restricted_locations**). Choose a SQL Select as the data source and the Tabular presentation style.
3. Choose the **Shows**, **Calendar**, and **Locations** tables. Although this DataWindow will be displaying data only from the Locations table, it needs to restrict rows based on the name of the current show. This presents a bit of a problem: The show name isn't part of the Locations table because a show can be scheduled many times. The query must therefore find event numbers in the Calendar table for all matching shows. Then, those event numbers can be used to retrieve rows from the Locations table.
4. Choose the **venue_name** and **venue_city** columns.
5. Create a string retrieval argument (**arg_show_name**). Use the argument as part of a WHERE clause that reads:

   ```
   WHERE "shows"."show_name" = :arg_show_name
   ```

6 Sort the query by venue_name and venue_city.

7 Choose **Options** -> **Distinct** to add the keyword DISTINCT following SELECT so that duplicate rows will be removed from the display.

8 Enter the DataWindow painter and set the font size to **8** points and make both the header and detail bands as small as possible. Make the header band text bold and underlined.

9 Preview the DataWindow object to make sure its query works properly. Supply **Macworld Expo** as the retrieval argument. Assuming you haven't modified the data in the Locations table, your query should retrieve four rows.

Now that the DataWindow control is ready, you can move on to modifying the application window.

To modify the application window:

1 Open the w_see_show_data window.

2 Resize the window so that it fills the entire workspace.

3 Move the Close picture button to the lower-right corner of the window.

4 Add a second DataWindow control to the window. Associate it with dwo_restricted_locations. Name it **dw_restricted_locations**. Add a vertical scroll bar. Because this control will be visible when the window first appears, leave the X in the Visible check box.

5 Resize and place the new control so that the window appears something like Figure 16.1.

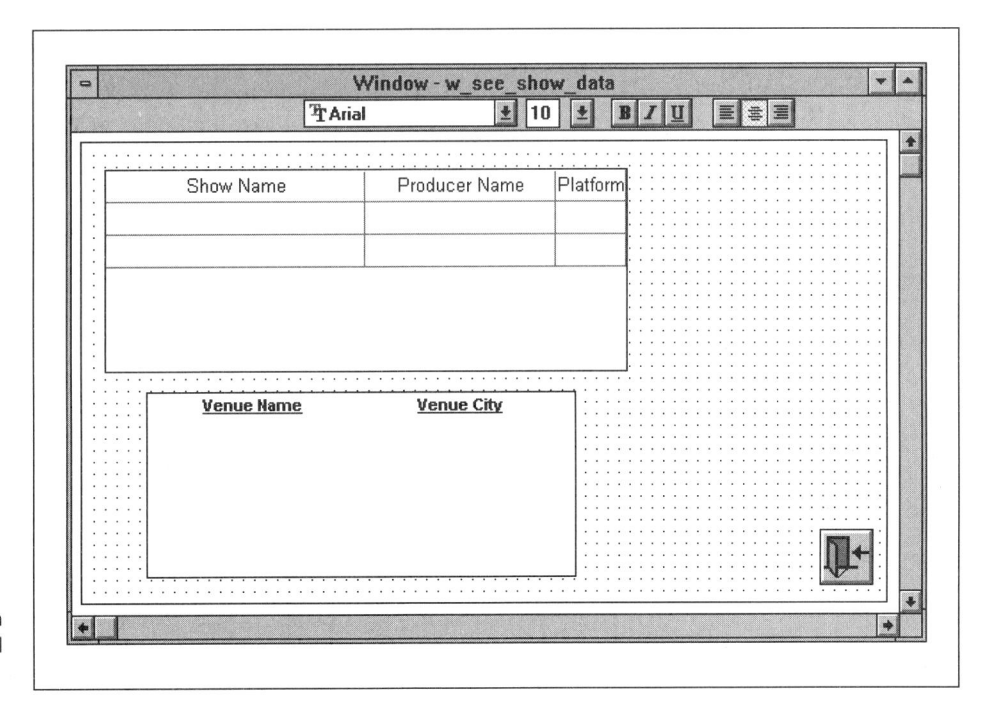

Figure 16.1
Modified Show display window with the second DataWindow control

388 CHAPTER SIXTEEN DYNAMIC DATAWINDOWS

6 Click on the **CheckBox** button in the PainterBar (Figure 16.2).

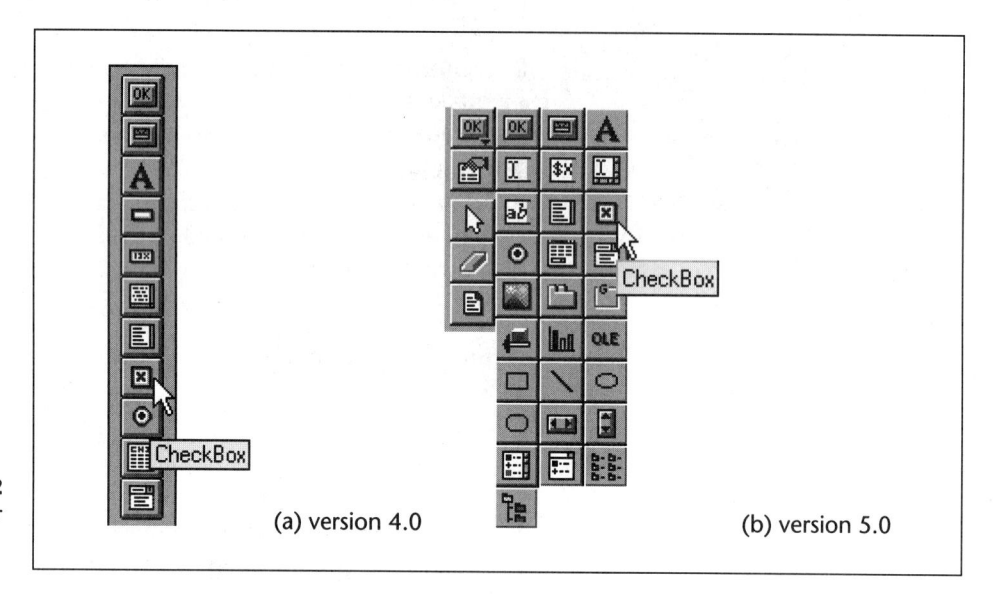

Figure 16.2
CheckBox button in the PainterBar

(a) version 4.0   (b) version 5.0

7 Click to the right of the top DataWindow control to place the check box and the default text of *none*. Like the group of radio buttons you used in Chapter 15, this check box isn't part of a DataWindow control. A script can look at the value of its Checked attribute to determine whether it contains an X.

8 Double-click the check box. Name it **cbx_show_locations**. Set its text to **Show locations**. Place an X in the Checked check box so that the Checked attribute has a value of TRUE when the window opens.

9 Preview the window. It should look something like Figure 16.3.

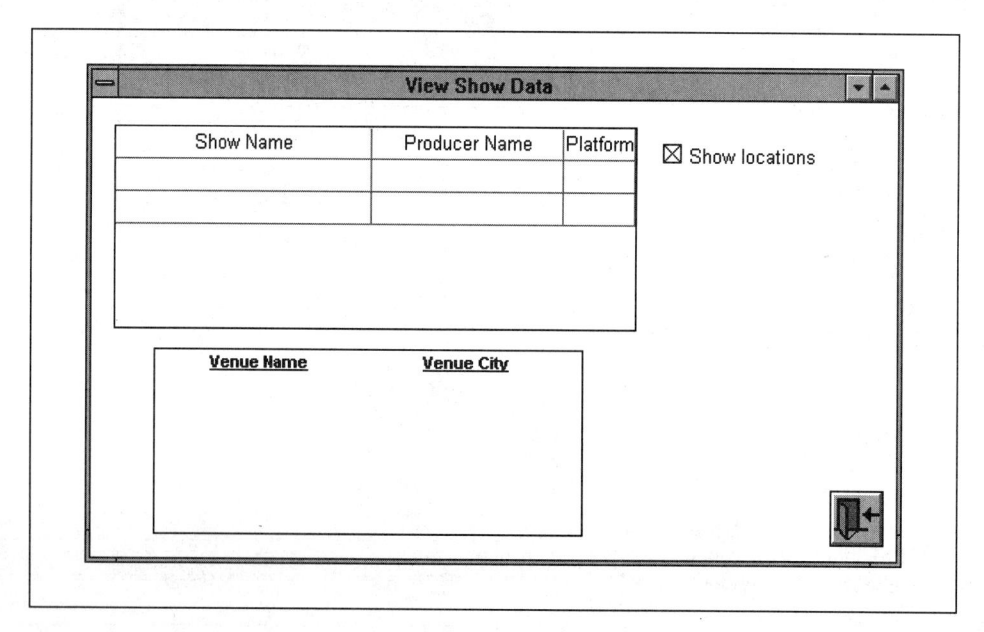

Figure 16.3
Preview of the modified window that displays show data

Finally, you need to modify the window's scripts so they retrieve data for the second DataWindow control and change the value in its Visible attribute based on the state of the Show locations check box.

To modify the window's script for retrieving data and to change the Visible attribute:

1 Create two instance variables (**show_name**, a string, and **row_numb**, a long integer).

2 Modify the window's open event script so that it matches Listing 16.1. This script populates both DataWindow controls. (Remember that the check box default to TRUE, so the location data should be visible when the window is opened.)

Listing 16.1
Modified open event script for w_see_show_data

```
dw_see_shows.SetTransObject (sqlca)
dw_restricted_locations.SetTransObject (sqlca)

if dw_see_shows.Retrieve() = -1 then
  rollback using sqlca;
  MessageBox ("Retrieve","Couldn't find any shows.")
else

// Find current row in shows table
  row_numb = dw_see_shows.GetRow ()
// Get the show name
  show_name = dw_see_shows.GetItemString (row_numb, "show_name")
// Retrieve related rows from the Locations table
  if dw_restricted_locations.Retrieve (show_name) = -1 then
    rollback using sqlca;
  else
// Give the Shows DataWindow focus and set the focus indicator
    dw_see_shows.SetFocus()
    dw_see_shows.SetRowFocusIndicator (Hand!)
    commit using sqlca;
  end if
end if
```

3 Enter the script in Listing 16.2 on page 390 for the rowfocuschanged event of dw_see_shows (the first DataWindow control). The purpose of this script is to modify the contents of the location listing whenever the current row in the show listing changes.

4 Enter the script in Listing 16.3 on page 390 for the check box's clicked event. This script looks at the value of the check box's Checked attribute to decide whether the locations DataWindow control should be visible or invisible.

5 Run the application to test your scripts and make sure they work.

Listing 16.2
rowfocuschanged event script for dw_see_shows

```
// Get current row in Shows table
row_numb = this.GetRow ()
// Get the show name
show_name = this.GetItemString (row_numb, "show_name")

// Retrieve related rows in Location table
if dw_restricted_locations.Retrieve (show_name) = -1 then
   rollback using sqlca;
else
   commit using sqlca;
end if
```

Listing 16.3
Clicked event script for cbx_show_locations

```
if this.Checked = TRUE then
// If check box is checked, make the DataWindow control visible
   dw_restricted_locations.Visible = TRUE
else
// if check box isn't checked, make the DataWindow control
// invisible
   dw_restricted_locations.Visible = FALSE
end if
```

Changing a DataWindow's Query

One of the characteristics of a DataWindow that you can change in a script is the query that determines a DataWindow control's contents. As an example, consider the complete w_calendar_query window in Figure 16.4. This window contains a listing of entries from the Calendar table. Users can fill in data that can be used to restrict rows using the radio buttons and edit controls at the bottom of the window. When the user clicks the Execute Query button, the button's script evaluates the radio buttons and edit controls and revises the DataWindow's SQL query based on the contents of those other controls. Once the query has been reset, the script can retrieve data using the new query.

The power behind the ability to reset a DataWindow's query while an application is running is the SetSQLSelect function, which takes as its sole parameter a string that comprises the new SQL query. SetSQLSelect only works with DataWindows that don't have retrieval arguments; you can add any arguments you need as part of the WHERE clause when you call the function.

To complete the calendar query window by placing all the necessary elements on the window:

1. Open the w_calendar_query window.
2. Place a DataWindow control on the window. Associate it with dwo_calendar_list (the same DataWindow object you used for w_manage_calendar2). Name the control **dw_calendar_list**. Give

CHAPTER SIXTEEN   DYNAMIC DATAWINDOWS   **391**

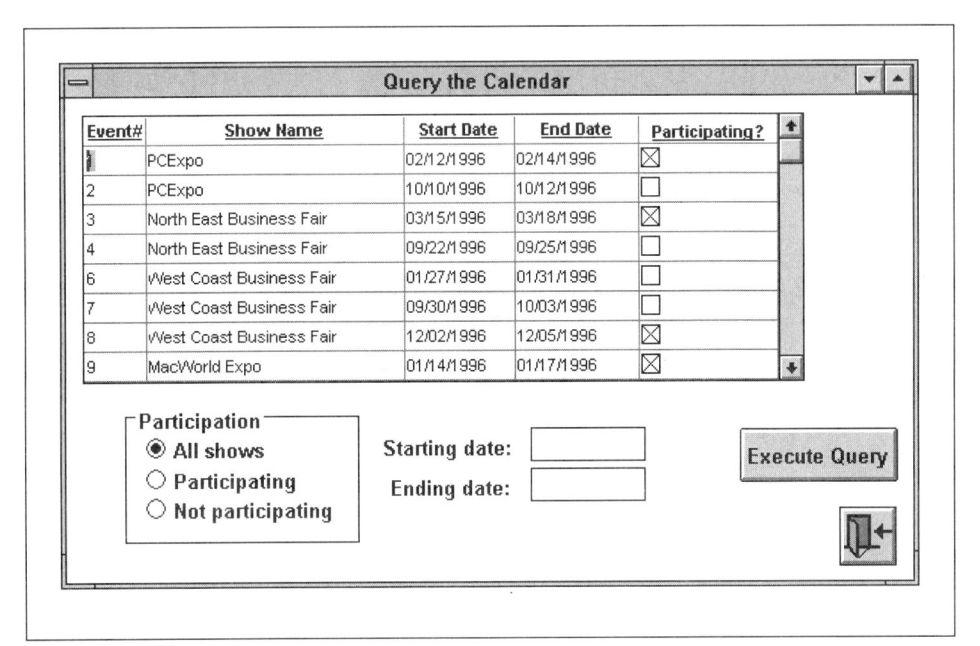

Figure 16.4
Window for querying the Calendar table

it a vertical scroll bar. Move and resize it as necessary, using Figure 16.4 as a model.

3 Create one group (**gb_partipation**, Text: **Participation**) of three radio buttons: **rb_all** (Text: **All shows**; Checked = TRUE); **rb_participating** (Text: **Participating**; Checked = FALSE); **rb_not_participating** (Text: **Not participating**; Checked = FLASE). Place the group of radio buttons in the lower left corner of the window, as in Figure 16.4.

4 Create two single line edit controls (**sle_start**, **sle_end**). Add two static text controls: **Starting date** for sle_start and **Ending date** for sle_end. Place them on the window to the right of the radio buttons, as in Figure 16.4 on page 391.

5 Add a command button above the Close picture button (**cb_execute**, with text reading **Execute Query**).

6 Preview the window to make sure you've placed the elements where you want them.

As with any PowerBuilder window, nothing will happen until you add the necessary scripts.

To add the necessary scripts:

1 Enter the script in Listing 16.4 on page 392 for the window's open event. This script populates the DataWindow control with all rows from the Calendar table. In other words, its query is based on the initial state of the window: The All shows radio button is highlighted and the two edit controls for dates are empty.

Listing 16.4
Open event script for w_calendar_query

```
dw_calendar_list.SetTransObject (sqlca)

// Retrieve data from the Calendar table using the query
// specified in the DataWindow object
if dw_calendar_list.Retrieve() = -1 then
   rollback using sqlca;
   MessageBox ("Retrieve","Retrieve error.")
else
   commit using sqlca;
end if
```

2. Most of the work for this window takes place in the clicked event script for the Execute Query button. You can find this script in Listing 16.5 on page 393. Enter it carefully, paying special attention to where spaces appear within quotation marks. Also copy single and double quotation marks exactly as you see them. Because this script is very complex, you'll look at it in depth shortly.

The script in Listing 16.5 is based on the way in which Watcom SQL expects dates to be used in SQL statements (year-month-day). If you are working with a DBMS other than Watcom SQL, you should do two things before attempting to use this script. First, check to see how dates need to be formatted for use in SQL WHERE *clauses. Then, read through the Understanding the Script section that follows so that you understand it well enough to figure out how you need to modify the script to make it acceptable to your DBMS.*

3. Run the application and test the scripts. Make sure you enter invalid dates as well as valid ones so you can test the error trapping in the Execute Query button's script.

Understanding the Script

A large part of the complexity in the script in Listing 16.5 comes from the need to manipulate strings and in particular, to deal with dates that are entered as strings in a format that Watcom SQL can't understand. However, because the dates are the trickiest part of the script, you'll look at the rest of it first.

Calling SetSQLSelect   The call to SetSQLSelect, which actually changes the query, is very nearly the last thing in the script. (Only the Retrieve statement and the error checking that surrounds it follows.) SetSQLSelect's parameter can be anything that generates a valid string. In other words, it could be a single string variable, a single string constant, or the concatenation of any number of either. Functions that return string values are also valid in the string expression.

In this case, the string parameter is the concatenation of the part of the string that doesn't vary throughout the script (stored in string1) and the part of the string that is assembled based on data found in the radio buttons and edit controls (stored in string2). The concatenation is placed within the parameter list:

```
dw_calendar_list.SetSQLSelect (string1 + string2)
```

```
string string1, string2
int i_month, i_day, i_year

// set the first part of the query, which doesn't change
string1 = "select event#, show_name, start_date, end_date," + &
  "participation from calendar "

// check the radio buttons
if rb_participating.Checked = TRUE then
   string2 = "where participation = 'T'"
elseif rb_not_participating.Checked = TRUE then
   string2 = "where participation = 'F'"
end if

// check for dates
if len(sle_start.Text) > 0 then

  // make sure dates are valid
  if IsDate(sle_start.Text) = FALSE then
    MessageBox ("Date Problem","The starting date isn't valid.")
    return
  elseif IsDate(sle_end.Text) = FALSE then
    MessageBox ("Date Problem","The ending date isn't valid.")
    return
  end if

  // set the first part of the variable half of the query
  if len(string2) > 0 then
    string2 = string2 + " and "
  else
    string2 = "where "
  end if

  // pull out parts of starting date
  i_month = month(date(sle_start.Text))
  i_day = day(date(sle_start.Text))
  i_year = year(date(sle_start.Text))

  // add to string2
  string2 = string2 + "(start_date >= '" + string(i_year) + &
    "/" + string(i_month) + "/" + string(i_day) + &
    "' and end_date <= "

  // pull out parts of ending date
  i_month = month(date(sle_end.Text))
  i_day = day(date(sle_end.Text))
  i_year = year(date(sle_end.Text))

  // add to string2
  string2 = string2 + "'" + string(i_year) + "/" + &
    string(i_month) + "/" + string(i_day) + "')"
end if
```

Listing 16.5
Clicked event script for the Execute query button

Continued on next page

Listing 16.5
Clicked event script for the Execute query button (Continued)

```
// use the strings to change the query
dw_calendar_list.SetSQLSelect (string1 + string2)

// retrieve new data
if dw_calendar_list.Retrieve() = -1 then
   rollback using sqlca;
   MessageBox ("Retrieve","Retrieve error")
else
   commit using sqlca;
end if
```

When using SetSQLSelect, you can place anything in the parameter list that constitutes a valid string expression, regardless of how or where the parts of the expression are assembled. However, the function works properly only when the parameter is actually a SQL query! The query must adhere to the syntax of the DBMS to which it is being submitted. Unlike embedded SQL, this query *doesn't* end with a semicolon.

Checking the Radio Buttons The first part of the WHERE clause for this query depends on the settings in the group of radio buttons. The script therefore identifies which radio button is Checked and adds the correct characters to string2 for that button. Notice, however, that if the All shows button is checked, no WHERE clause is added at all.

Verifying Valid Dates Once the radio buttons have been handled, the script turns to the issue of the dates. It first determines whether any characters have been entered into the Starting date edit control: If this box is empty, there's no point in examining the dates any further.

The simplest way to find out if something has been entered in the Starting date edit control is to check the length of the edit control's text, using the function Len, which returns an integer indicating the number of characters in the string. If Len returns a value greater than 0, then something has been entered into sle_start, and further processing is required to determine whether both the starting and ending dates are valid. This is an essential step, because if invalid dates are included in the new SQL query and the query is sent to the database, the DBMS will respond with an error message, presenting the user with a dialog box that he or she isn't likely to understand.

The PowerBuilder IsDate function examines a string and returns a Boolean value indicating whether the characters constitute a valid date. The script therefore examines the Text attribute of both sle_start and sle_end. If the dates aren't valid, the script displays an error message to the user and ends.

Extracting Parts of Dates Assuming the script has valid dates, then it can turn to formatting the dates for the query, a process that is highly DBMS specific. WatcomSQL, the DBMS we have been using throughout this book, expects dates to be quoted by either single or double quotation marks and in a year-month-day format. Of all the date formats available, year-month-day is one of the least likely to be entered by an English-speaking user. It is therefore unrealistic for the script to assume dates are entered in that way.

The script handles the problem by extracting the individual parts of each date and then reassembling them in the correct order. There are three functions that perform the extraction:

- `Month`: Returns an integer from 1 to 12 corresponding to the month from a value of type Date.
- `Day`: Returns an integer from 1 to 31 corresponding to the day from a value of type date.
- `Year`: Returns a four-digit integer corresponding to the year from a value of type date.

Because the preceding functions require a parameter of type Date, the Text attribute of an edit control must first be converted to a date with the `Date` function. The script therefore embeds the function calls, as in:

```
i_month = month(date(sle_start.Text))
```

Putting the Query Together   The irony of all the conversions the script does with the parts of the dates is that to concatenate the parts onto `string2`, the integers must be converted back to strings. Each piece of the query is therefore handled separately, using the `String` function to convert a number. After all the concatenation—assuming the Participating radio button is highlighted and the dates are 1/1/96 and 12/31/96—the contents of `string2` will look like the following:

```
where participation = 'T" and
    (start_date >= '96/1/1' and end_date <= '96/12/31')
```

Keep in mind that the preceding statement has been broken onto two lines so you can see it more easily. The actual string in one, unbroken line.

Looking Ahead

In this chapter you have mastered two techniques for manipulating DataWindows while an application is running. The first technique involves hiding and showing DataWindow controls; the second technique changes the query on which the contents of a DataWindow control are based.

The final part of your study of PowerBuilder is creating menus to provide users with another way to access an application's features. In Chapter 17 you will learn to generate menus from scratch and to derive menus using inheritance.

EXERCISES

The following exercises will give you a chance to implement the techniques you have learned in this chapter in the College and University Rentals application. At this point in your PowerBuilder experience, you have a significant amount of knowledge about manipulating DataWindows. You will therefore find only a broad suggestion of what a window should do in each exercise. Use your knowledge and experience to design windows that are easy for a user to understand.

1. Modify the window that lists customers so that it includes a listing of the current customer's rentals. Give the user the choice of whether he or she wants to see the rental data.

2. Modify the list of merchandise items so that the use can enter a type of merchandise on the window. The type of merchandise should then be used in a query to restrict the rows that appear in the listing. (*Hint:* You're going to need a join between the Merchandise and Items tables to do this.)

3. Modify the window from Exercise 2 so that it allows the user to choose merchandise items by status as well as by type of merchandise.

4. Modify the list of deliveries that are to be made so that the user can enter a range of dates directly on the listing form. Use those dates to restrict the rows that appears. In addition, let the user choose the school to which the deliveries will be made. (*Hint:* Try a dropdown DataWindow control based on the Schools table to make it easier for the user to choose the school.)

CHAPTER SEVENTEEN

Creating Menus

IN THIS CHAPTER YOU WILL:

- Integrate menus into a PowerBuilder application's user interface
- Create and use menu objects
- Attach accelerator keys and shortcut keys to menu options

Although menus have been left for the last chapter in this book, they are an important part of the interface of any PowerBuilder application. In most cases, you want to give a user two, three, or four ways to perform any action:

- Use the mouse to make a choice from a menu.
- Use an *accelerator key*—a character key pressed in combination with the Alt key—to make a choice from a menu when the menu is visible. Theoretically, every menu option should have an accelerator key so that users who don't have a mouse can still work with the Windows interface. When assigning accelerator keys, keep in mind that the letter needs to be unique only within each menu.
- Use a *shortcut key*—a function key or a combination of a modified key and a character key—to make a choice from a menu when the menu isn't visible.
- Use the mouse to click on a command button.

As you may have noticed when working with PowerBuilder's interface, all the commands represented by buttons in the PowerBar and PainterBars are duplicated by menu commands. The menus also contain commands that aren't available in the toolbars. The general principle is that every application window should have menus, and that all functions should be available through those menus, even if the functions are also available through command buttons.

Menus are created using the Menu painter. You can create a menu from scratch or use inheritance to derive a menu from another, saving some work in the process.

In this chapter you will learn to create menu objects and to attach them to windows. You will also learn how to write scripts that are triggered when a menu option is chosen.

Creating a Main Application Menu

The *tshows* application will have two types of menus. The first is a main menu attached to the opening_screen window that takes the user to any of the windows that contain DataWindow objects. If the user chooses to use the menu rather than the command buttons, he or she doesn't need to navigate through the secondary button menu windows. The menus can use menu options and, in the case of the Scheduling functions, cascading submenus to provide complete navigation through the application.

The second type of menu is one that is attached to a window that contains a DataWindow. These menus control the actions that the user can take in the window, such as inserting new rows or closing the window.

Setting Up Menu Items and Options

For your first experience with menus, you'll be creating the main application menu for navigation through the application.

CHAPTER SEVENTEEN   CREATING MENUS   **399**

To enter the menu items and options for navigating through an application:

1. Make sure that you are working with the *tshows* application in *tshows2.pbl* and that you are connected to the *tshows* database.
2. Click the **Menu** button in the PowerBar (Figure 17.1). The Select Menu dialog box appears, as in Figure 17.2.

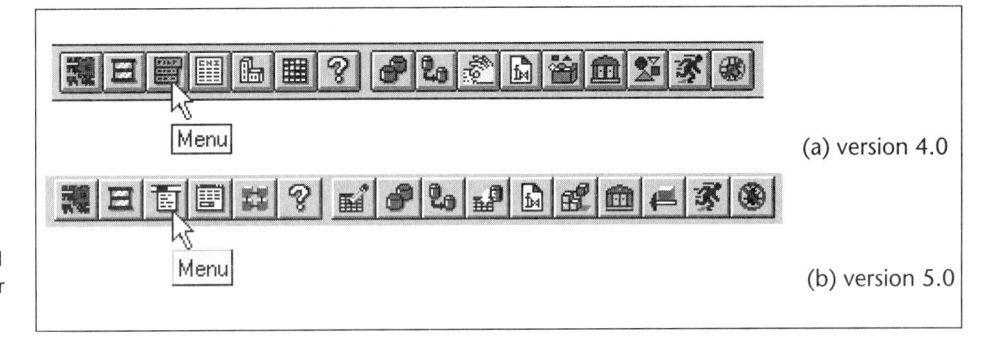

Figure 17.1
Menu button in the PowerBar

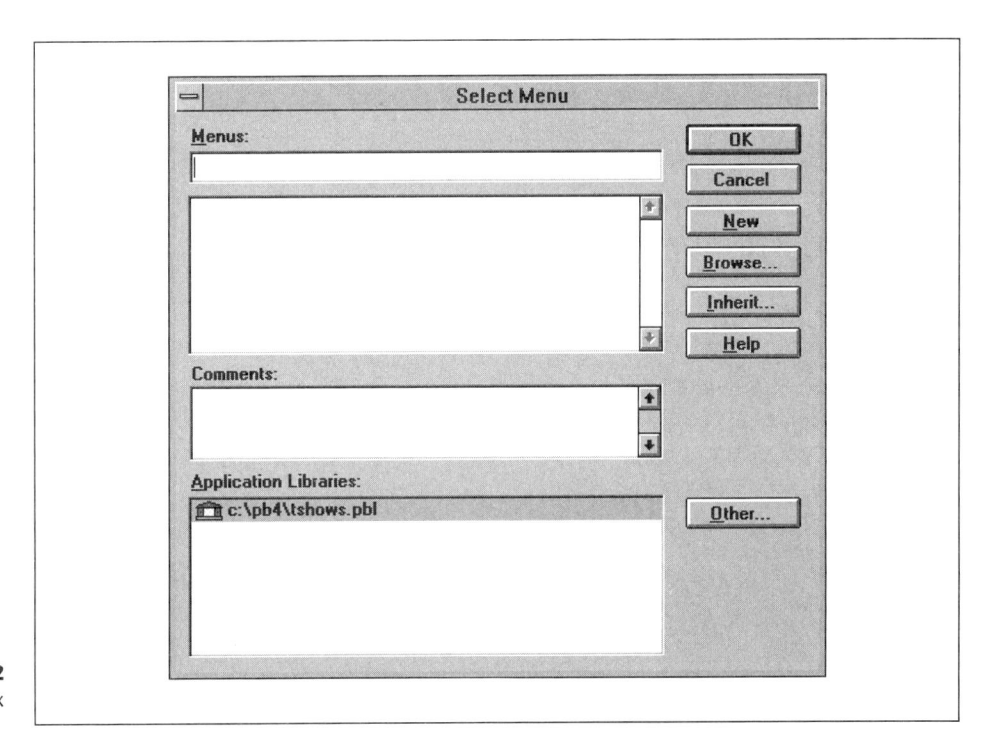

(a) version 4.0
(b) version 5.0

Figure 17.2
Select Menu dialog box

3. Click the **New** button to dismiss the dialog box and to create a new menu from scratch. The Menu painter workspace appears. As you can see in Figure 17.3 on page 400 (version 4.0) and Figure 17.4 on page 400 (version 5.0), this workspace looks quite different from other painter workspaces.

400 CHAPTER SEVENTEEN CREATING MENUS

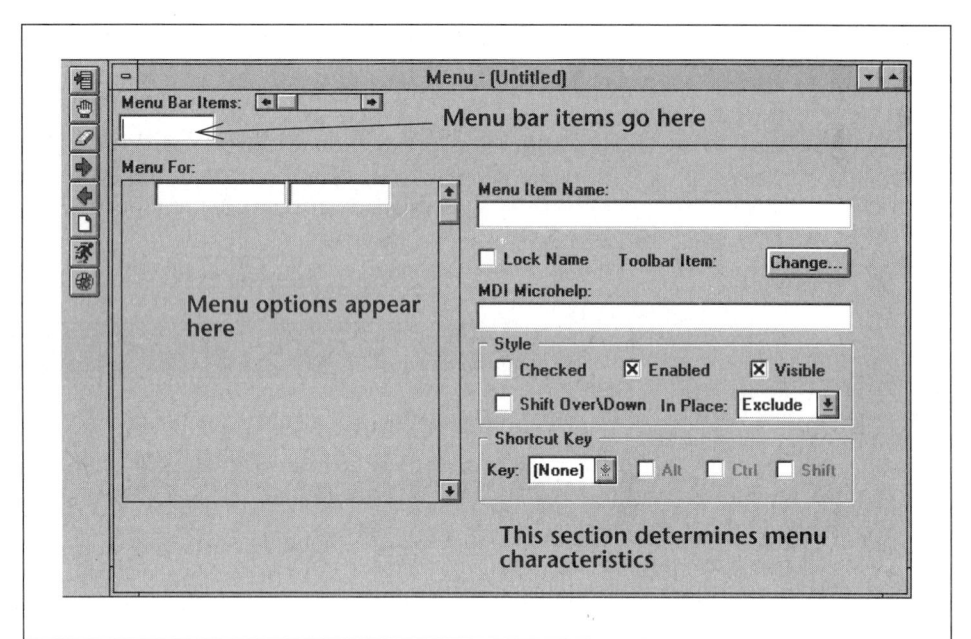

Figure 17.3
Menu painter workspace (4.0)

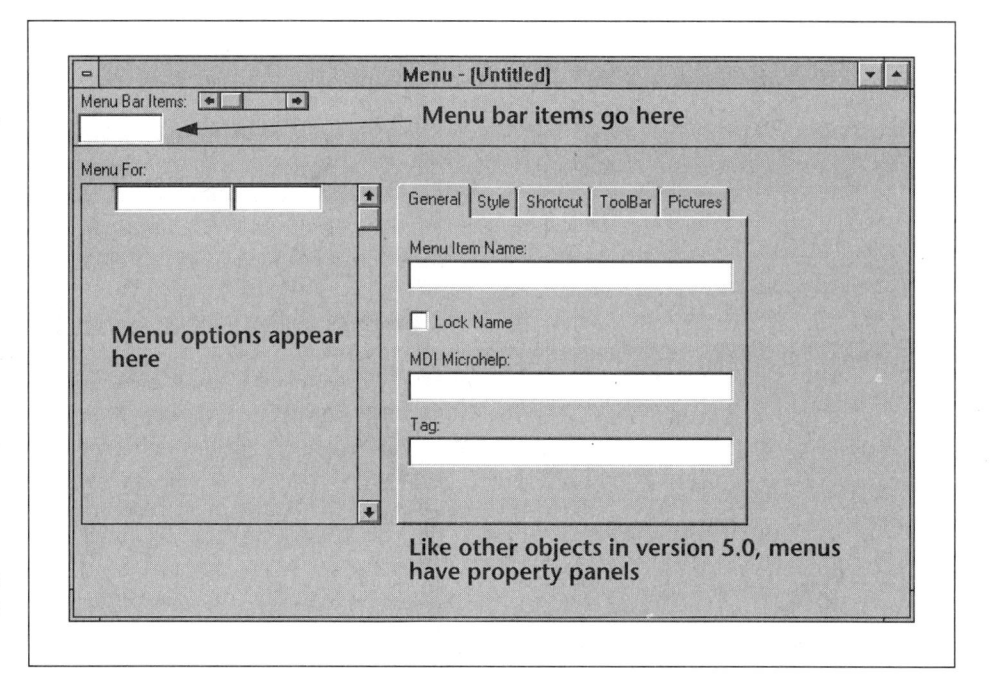

Figure 17.4
Menu painter workspace (5.0)

Items for the menu bar appear in a horizontal list at the top of the window. The options for whichever menu bar item is highlighted appear in the list at the left of the workspace. The right of the workspace is used to configure the way in which a menu option appears and behaves.

   4   Save the menu as **m_main**.
   5   Click in the box under Menu Bar Items.

6 Type **&File** as the name of the first item in the menu bar. By convention, File is always the leftmost menu. Its options deal with opening and closing files, saving changes, and exiting an application or window. The ampersand (&) in front of the F indicates that F will be the item's accelerator key. When the item appears in the menu bar, the F will be underlined (File).

Notice that as you type the name of the menu item, PowerBuilder automatically fills in a name for the item. By default, the name starts with m_ and includes the text of the item. If there are spaces in the item's name, PowerBuilder simply leaves then out.

7 Click in the box on the left under Menu For.

8 Type **&Quit** as the menu option. Because all other file operations (for example, saving changes to the database) are handled in windows with DataWindows, this is the only option needed by this File menu. At this point, your Menu painter workspace should look like Figure 17.5.

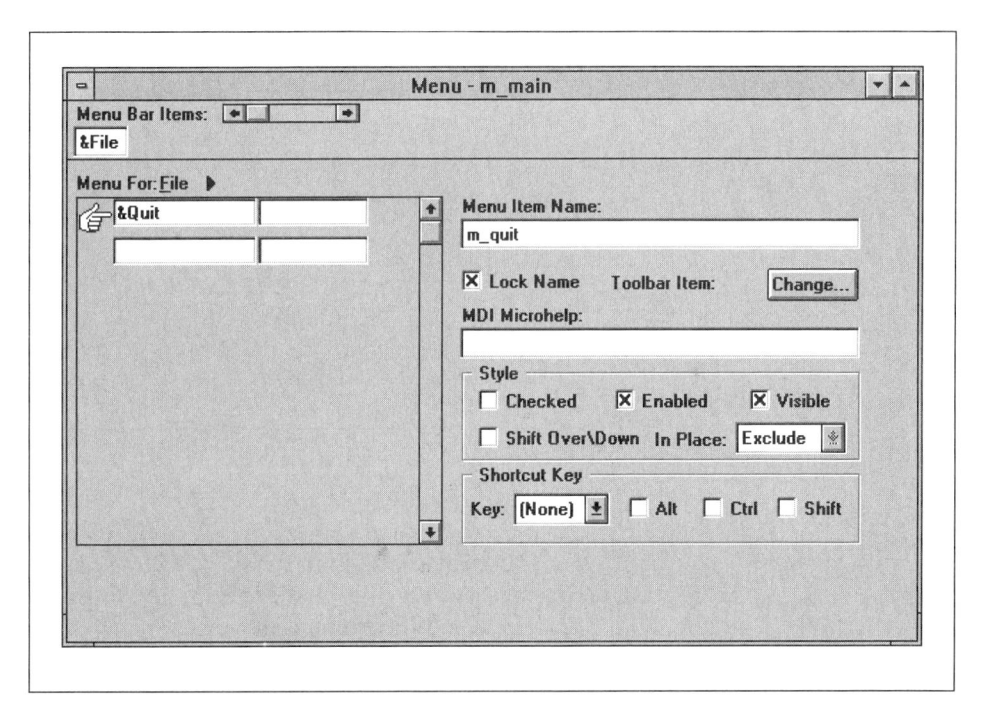

Figure 17.5
Complete File menu

9 Click to the right of &File. A new space for a menu bar item appears.

10 Type **&Scheduling**. Don't enter any menu options right now. Because this menu requires cascading menus (menus with suboptions), you'll take care of it in the next section.

11 Click to the right of &Scheduling to create another space for a menu bar time.

12 Type **&Costs**.

13 Type **&Enter Costs** as the first menu option.

14 Press the Tab key to make space for a second menu option.

15 Enter the following for the remaining options in the Costs menu: **&Maintain Costs, &Costs for One Show, S&hows and Costs, C&ost Summary, &Increased Costs**.

16 Create a final item in the menu bar: **Sales &Leads**.

17 Enter the following options for the Sales Leads menu: **Maintain &Sales Leads, Maintain &Contacts, Leads to C&all, Leads by C&ompany, Leads &Revenue Summary**. Your completed menu should look like Figure 17.6.

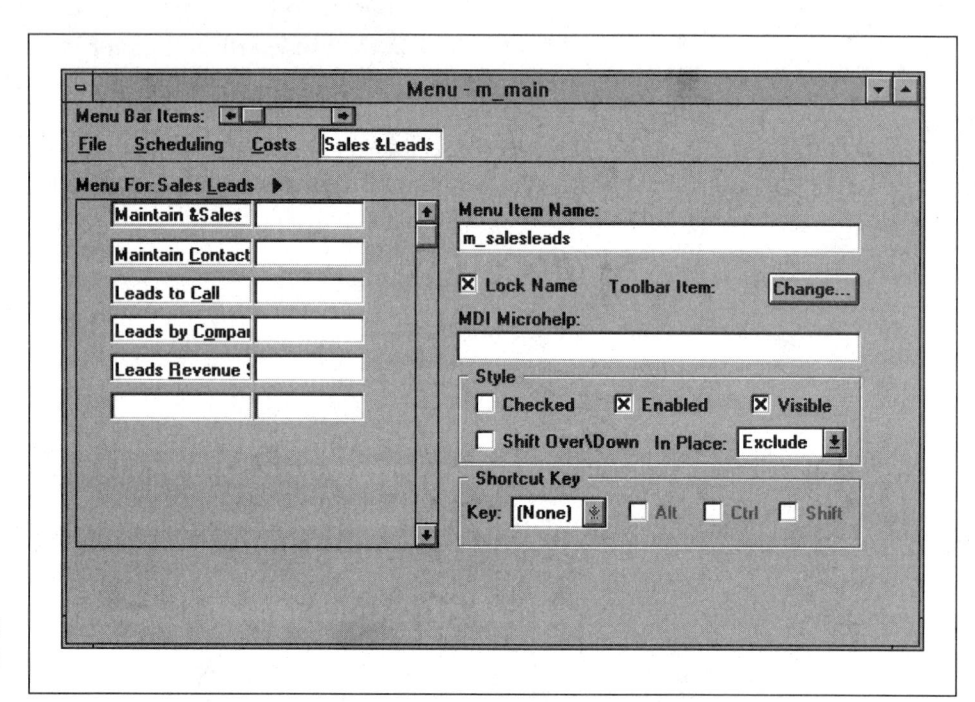

Figure 17.6
Complete Sales Leads menu

Previewing the Menu

You can preview a menu to see how it will appear. Although you won't be able to trigger any scripts that are attached to the menu options, you can check the organization of the menu options.

To preview the menu:

1 Choose **Design** ->**Preview** or press Ctrl-W. A window with the menu bar appears.

2 Click the **Costs** menu to make its options visible, as in Figure 17.7 on page 403.

3 Display the File and Sales Leads menus to check your work.

4 Double-click the window's control box to return to the Menu painter.

CHAPTER SEVENTEEN   CREATING MENUS   **403**

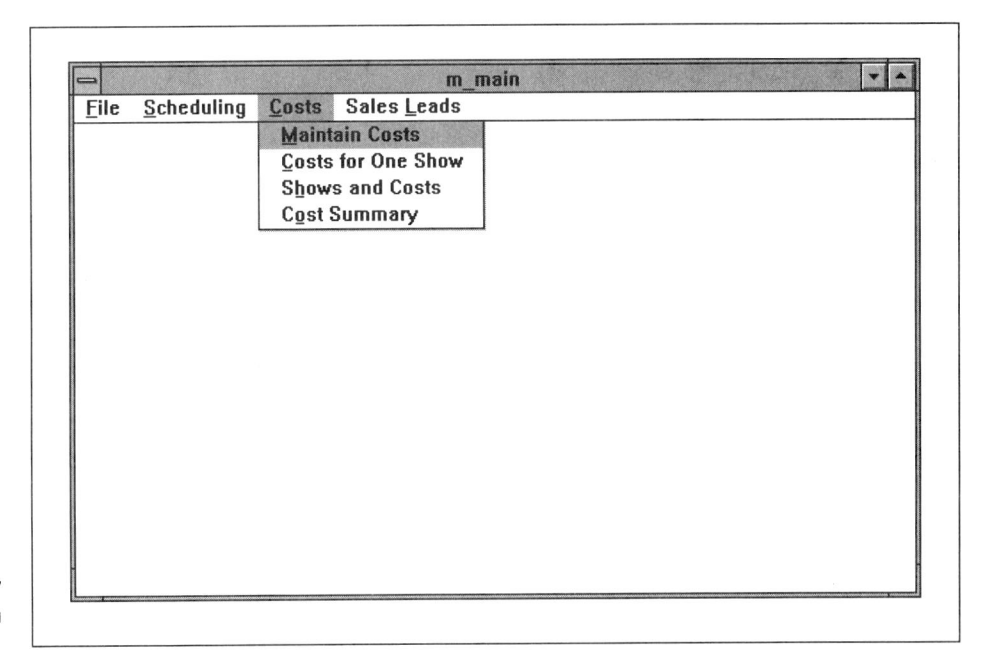

Figure 17.7
Previewing a menu

Adding Cascading Menus

As mentioned earlier, the Scheduling menu requires cascading submenus. It therefore takes some extra steps to configure the menu options.

To complete the Scheduling menu's options:

1. Click in the Scheduling menu bar item to make it current. (It will have a white box behind it.
2. Type **&Producers** for the first menu option.
3. Click the **Next Level** button in the PainterBar (Figure 17.8). The workspace changes to provide you with a blank list into which you can enter submenu items. Notice in Figure 17.9 on page 404 that you can keep track of where you are by looking at the menu path, which follows Menu For.

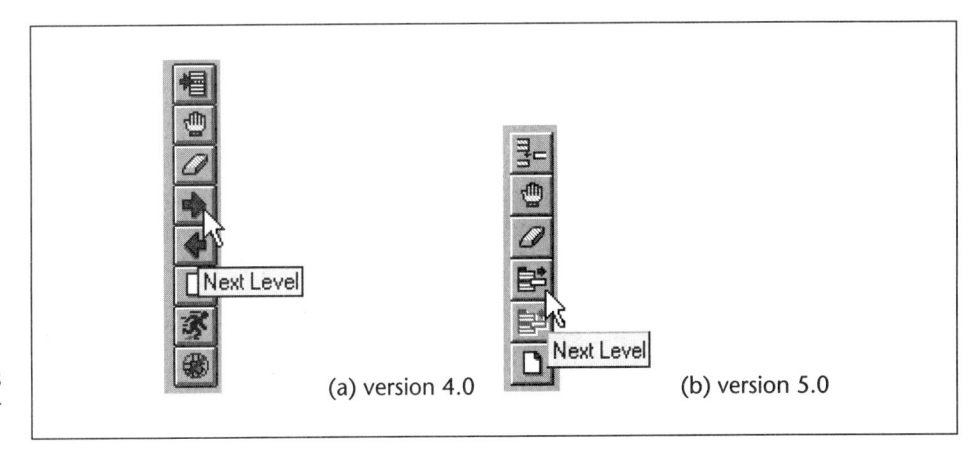

Figure 17.8
Next Level button in the PainterBar

(a) version 4.0   (b) version 5.0

404 CHAPTER SEVENTEEN CREATING MENUS

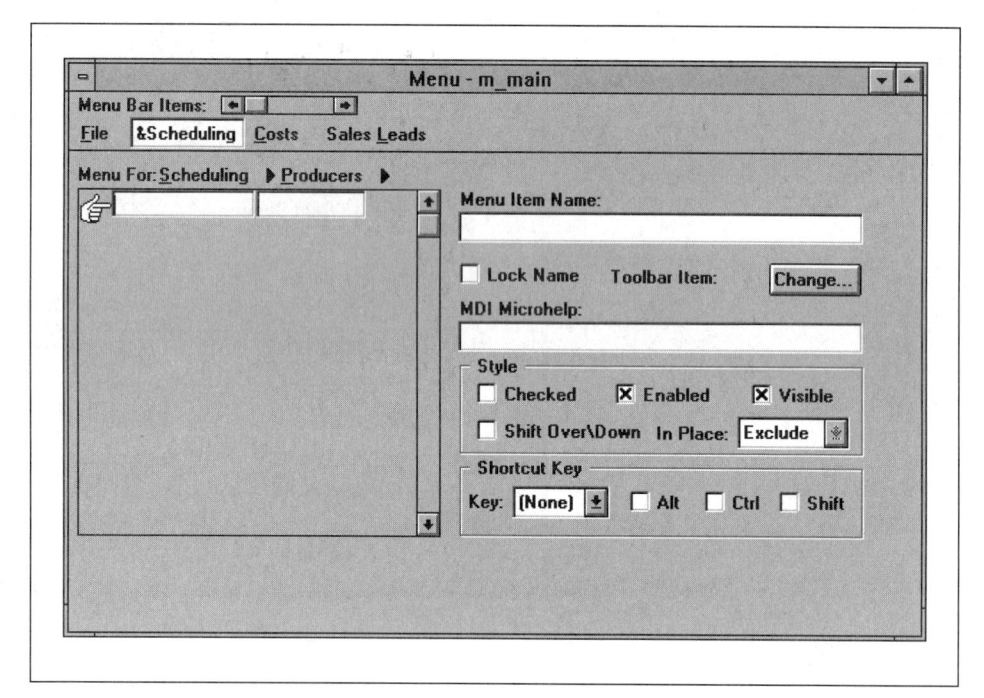

Figure 17.9
Entering items for a cascading submenu

4. Enter the following options for the Producers submenu: **&Maintain Producers** and **&See Producers**.
5. Click the **Prior Level** button in the PainterBar (Figure 17.10).

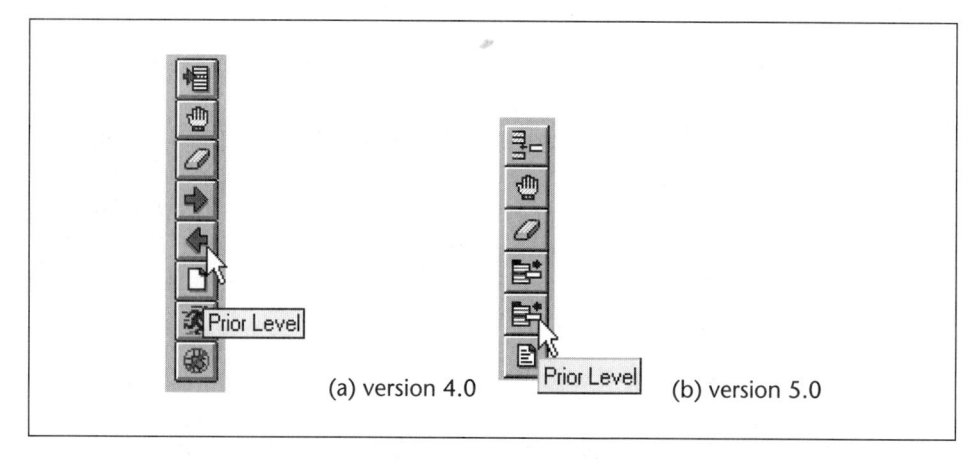

Figure 17.10
Prior Level button in the PainterBar

(a) version 4.0   (b) version 5.0

6. Type **S&hows and Locations** as the second option in the Scheduling menu.
7. Enter the following as submenu options for the Shows and Locations menu: **Maintain &Shows**, **Maintain &Locations**, **&Assign Locations**, **S&ee Shows**.
8. Type **C&alendar** as the third option in the Scheduling menu.

9 Enter the following as submenu options for the Calendar menu: **&Maintain the Calendar**, **&Query the Calendar**, **&Scheduled Shows**, **&Future Shows** and **&Past Shows**.

10 Preview the menu bar once more to see how your cascading menus look.

Writing Scripts for Menu Options

Menu bar items and menu options respond to only two events: clicked, which is triggered whenever the user choose a menu option, either with the mouse or the keyboard, and selected, which is triggered whenever the menu option is highlighted but not chosen. In most cases, you will be writing scripts just for the clicked event.

A window knows the names of the controls that have been placed on it. Therefore, whenever a window script needs to reference a control, the script needs to include only the name of the object. In contrast, a menu object doesn't know anything about the contents of the window to which it is attached. (In theory, you could attach the same menu object to more than one window.)

This means that when you write a menu script that refers to a control on a window, you must name the window as well as the control. The rules for referring to windows and window controls in a menu script are:

- When referring to a window, use the window's name:

```
open (w_maintain_calendar2)
```

- When referring to the window to which a menu is attached, use `ParentWindow`:

```
close (ParentWindow)
```

- When referring to a control on a window, use the window name, a dot, followed by the control name:

```
w_maintain_calendar2.cb_save.TriggerEvent (Clicked!)
```

When menu options duplicate command buttons, you can attach a script to the command button and have the menu option script trigger the command button event. Alternatively, you can attach the script to the menu option and have the command button trigger the menu event. To refer to a menu option, you must use the name of the menu, a dot, followed by the name of the menu item, another dot, and the name of the menu option, as in:

```
m_main.m_costs.m_maintaincosts.TriggerEvent (Clicked!)
```

One of the biggest problems in writing scripts for menus is that the Script painter's Paste Object menu lists only parts of the menu, not objects such as windows. What can you do if you can't remember the names of the windows and controls on those windows that make up your application? The solution is the Script painter's Browse Objects dialog box. To display the dialog box, click the Browse Objects button in the PainterBar (Figure 17.11 on page 406) to display the Browse Objects dialog box. If you are working with version 4.0, choose the type of object and the characteristic of the object that you want to see. Figure 17.12 on page 406, for

406 CHAPTER SEVENTEEN CREATING MENUS

example, is browsing the names of window objects. Highlight the object you want and click the Paste button to paste the value into a script. If you are working with version 5.0, click the tab that corresponds to the type of object you want to see. Then select the object in the scrolling list at the left and the characteristic of the object from the list at the right (see Figure 17.13 on page 407).

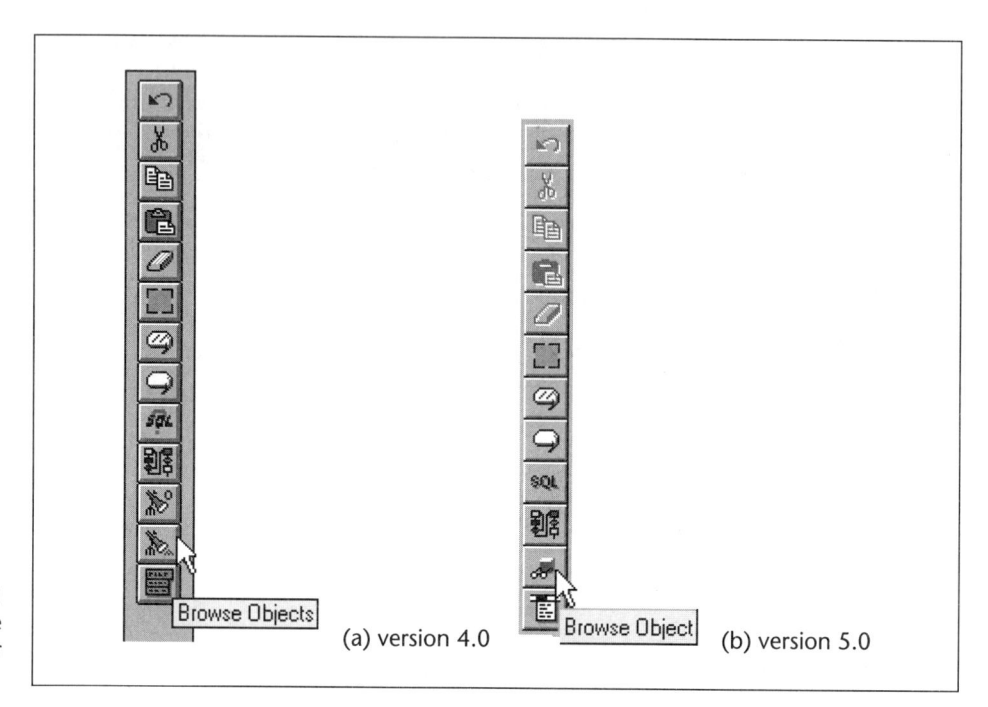

Figure 17.11
Browse Objects button in the PainterBar

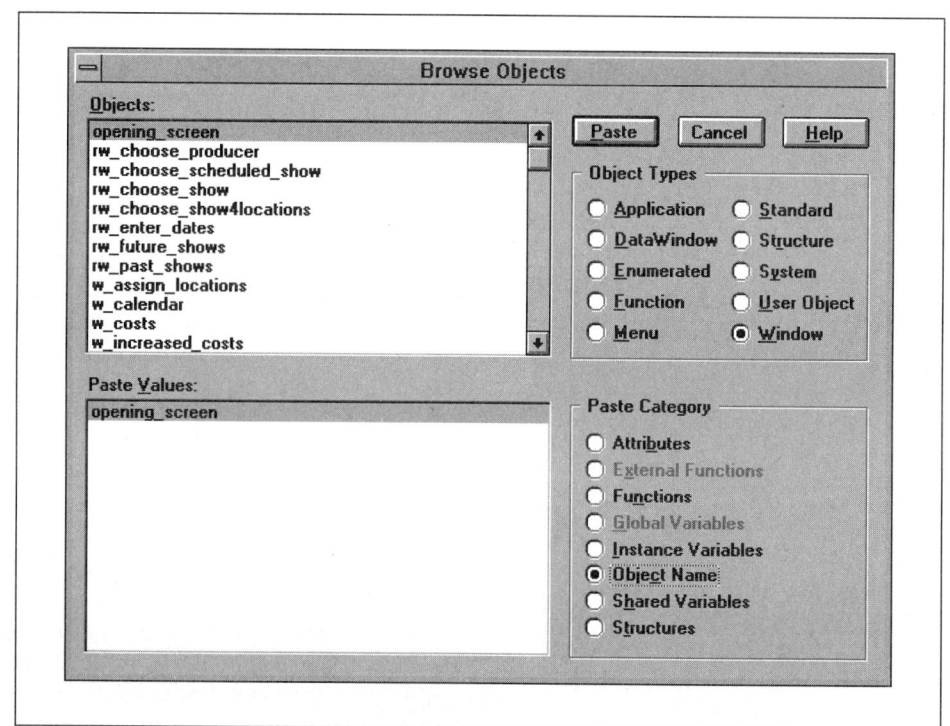

(a) version 4.0   (b) version 5.0

Figure 17.12
Browse Objects dialog box (4.0)

CHAPTER SEVENTEEN   CREATING MENUS   **407**

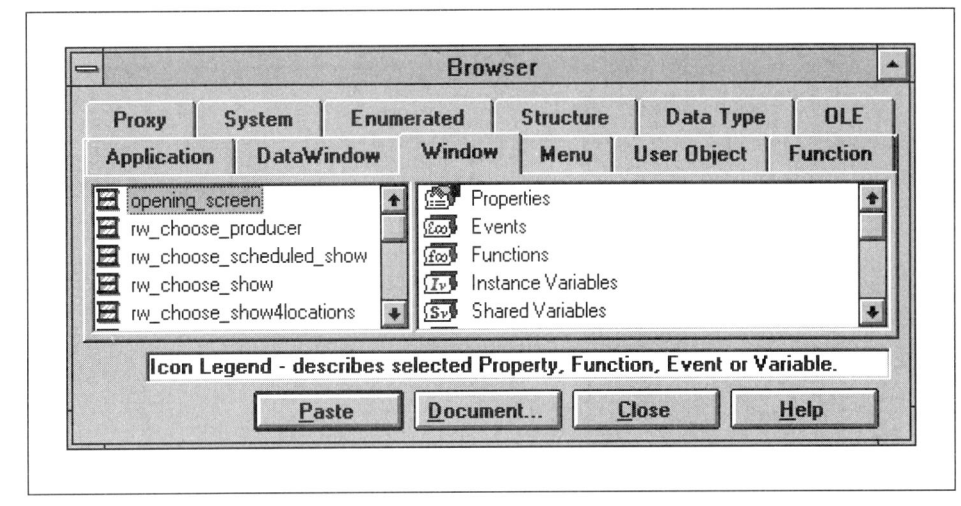

Figure 17.13
Object Browser (5.0)

For the *tshows* application's main menu, all the menu options (other than Quit) open other windows. All options therefore require only a one-line script, most with a call to the `open` function.

To enter the scripts for the main menu:

1. Click **&File** in the list of menu bar items.
2. Click the **Quit** option.
3. Click the **Script** button in the PowerBar (Figure 17.14). The Script painter appears.

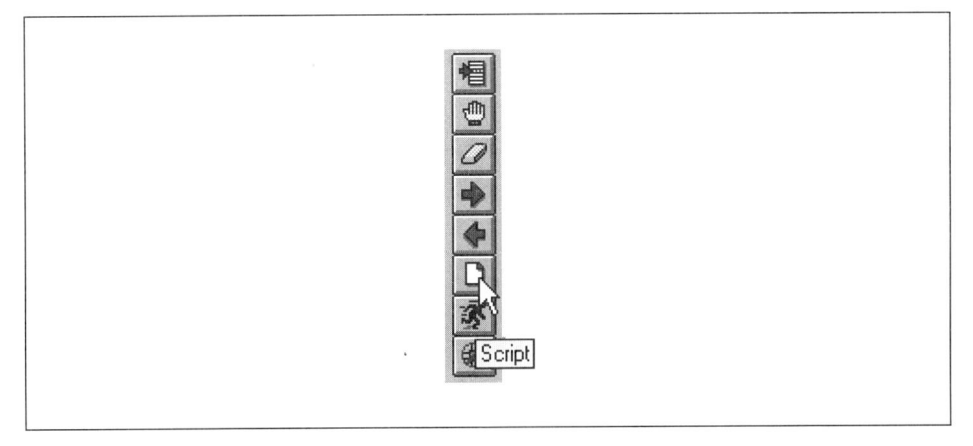

Figure 17.14
Script button in the PainterBar

4. Type the following one-line script:

    ```
    close (ParentWindow)
    ```

5. Enter scripts for the remaining menu options, using Table 17.1 on page 408 as a guide.

MENU OPTION	SCRIPT
Scheduling -> Producers -> Maintain Producer Data	open(rw_choose_producer)
Scheduling -> Producers -> See Producers	open(w_see_producer_data)
Scheduling -> Shows and Locations -> Maintain Shows	open(w_manage_show_data)
Scheduling -> Shows and Locations -> Maintain Locations	open(w_manage_location_data)
Scheduling -> Shows and Locations -> Assign Locations	open(w_assign_locations)
Scheduling -> Shows and Locations -> See Shows	open(w_see_show_data)
Scheduling -> Calendar -> Maintain the Calendar	open(w_manage_calendar2)
Scheduling -> Calendar -> Scheduled Shows	open(rw_enter_dates)
Scheduling -> Calendar -> Future Shows	open(rw_future_shows)
Scheduling -> Calendar -> Past Shows	open(rw_past_shows)
Costs -> Enter Costs	open(w_enter_costs)
Costs -> Maintain Costs	open(w_maintain_costs)
Costs -> Costs for One Show	open(rw_choose_show)
Costs -> Shows and Costs	open(w_see_shows_and_costs)
Costs -> Cost Summary	open(w_see_cost_summary)
Sales Leads -> Maintain Sales Leads	open(w_manage_lead_data)
Sales Leads -> Maintain Contacts	open(w_manage_contacts)
Sales Leads -> Leads to Call	open(w_see_leads2call)
Sales Leads -> Leads by Company	open(w_leads_by_company)
Sales Leads -> Leads Revenue Summary	open(w_leads_revenue_summary)

Table 17.1 Menu option scripts for m_main

At this point, the menu object is complete, but it needs to be attached to a window before it will operate.

Attaching the Menu Object to a Window

To attach a menu object to a window using the Window painter:

1. Open the opening_screen window.
2. Double-click in the window (anywhere that isn't occupied by a control), or choose **Design -> Window Style**. The Window Style dialog box appears.
3. Click the **Menu** check box to place an X in it.

4   Choose the name of the menu you want to use from the dropdown list of menus. In this case, because there is currently only one menu, m_main automatically appears when you click the Menu check box.

5   Click the **OK** button to close the dialog box.

6   Run the application to make sure that your menu scripts open the correct windows.

Creating a Menu for an Application Window

When a window contains one or more DataWindow controls, the scripts that manage menu options that duplicate command or picture button actions only need to include calls to `TriggerEvent`. This assumes, of course, that the complete scripts have been attached to the buttons.

For your first experience with creating a menu for a window that contains DataWindow controls, you will develop the menu bar for w_manage_calendar2.

To create and implement the menu object:

1   Create a new menu object.

2   Save it as **m_manage_calendar**.

3   Define menu bar items, menu options, and scripts based on what you find Table 17.2. Notice that the scripts for the Insert and Delete menus trigger two events. First, they trigger the clicked event for the DataWindow control being modified. This takes care of the radio buttons so that the insert and delete scripts will work properly. In addition, the highlighting in the group of radio buttons changes to give the user the added visual cue about the type of data being modified. The second call to `TriggerEvent` actually performs the insert or delete.

MENU BAR ITEMS AND OPTIONS	SCRIPT
&File	
File -> &Save	`w_manage_calendar2.cb_save.TriggerEvent (Clicked!)`
File -> &Return	`close (ParentWindow)`
&Insert	
Insert -> New &Calendar entry	`w_manage_calendar2.dw_calendar_list.TriggerEvent (Clicked!)` `w_manage_calendar2.cb_insert.TriggerEvent (Clicked!)`
Insert -> New &Show	`w_manage_clanedar2.dw_manage_shows.TriggerEvent (Clicked!)` `w_manage_calendar2.cb_insert.TriggerEvent (Clicked!)`
Insert -> New &Producer	`w_manage_calendar2.dw_maintain_producers.TriggerEvent (Clicked!)` `w_manage_calendar2.cb_insert.TriggerEvent (Clicked!)`
&Delete	
Delete -> &Calendar entry	`w_manage_calendar2.dw_calendar_list.TriggerEvent (Clicked!)` `w_manage_calendar2.cb_delete.TriggerEvent (Clicked!)`
Delete -> &Show	`w_manage_clanedar2.dw_manage_shows.TriggerEvent (Clicked!)` `w_manage_calendar2.cb_delete.TriggerEvent (Clicked!)`
Delete -> &Producer	`w_manage_calendar2.dw_maintain_producers.TriggerEvent (Clicked!)` `w_manage_calendar2.cb_delete.TriggerEvent (Clicked!)`

Table 17.2   Menu items, menu options, and scripts for m_manage_calendar

4 Attach the completed menu to w_manage_calendar2.
5 Run the application and test the menu scripts.

Using Inheritance to Create a Menu

As with windows, using inheritance to create menus can simplify the developer's job a bit. To give you a taste of using inheritance, you'll first create a menu object that implements data modification for a listing window. Then, you'll use inheritance to adapt that menu object for use with another similar window.

Developing the Ancestor Menu

The first task is to create the ancestor menu object. In this case, it will be for the window that currently lists all the data in the Producer table.

To create an ancestor menu object:

1 Create a new menu object.
2 Save it as **m_see_producers**.
3 Use the data in Table 17.3 to create the menu items, menu options, and scripts for the clicked events. Notice that the major difference between these scripts and those you would write for buttons is that all references to controls (for example, DataWindow windows) must be preceded by the name of the window on which they reside.

MENU BAR ITEMS AND OPTIONS	SCRIPT
&File	
File -> &Save	```if w_see_producer_data.dw_see_producers.Update () = 1 then
commit using sqlca;
messagebox ("Save","Changes have been saved."
else
rollback using sqlca;
messagebox ("Save","Couldn't save changes."
end if```
File -> &Return	`close (ParentWindow)`
&Data	
Data -> &Insert new row	```long new_row

new_row = w_see_producer_data.dw_see_producers.InsertRow (0)
w_see_producer_data.dw_see_producers.ScrollToRow (new_row)``` |
| Data -> &Delete current row | `w_see_producer_data.dw_see_producers.DeleteRow (0)` |

Table 17.3 Menu item, menu options, and scripts for m_see_producers

CHAPTER SEVENTEEN CREATING MENUS **411**

4 Add a shortcut key to the Insert new row menu option. To do so, click in the Insert new row menu option.

If you are working with version 5.0, click the **Shortcut** tab to display the Shortcut properties dialog box.

For both versions, choose **F2** from the Shortcut Key dropdown menu, as in Figure 17.15 (version 4.0) or Figure 17.16 (version 5.0).

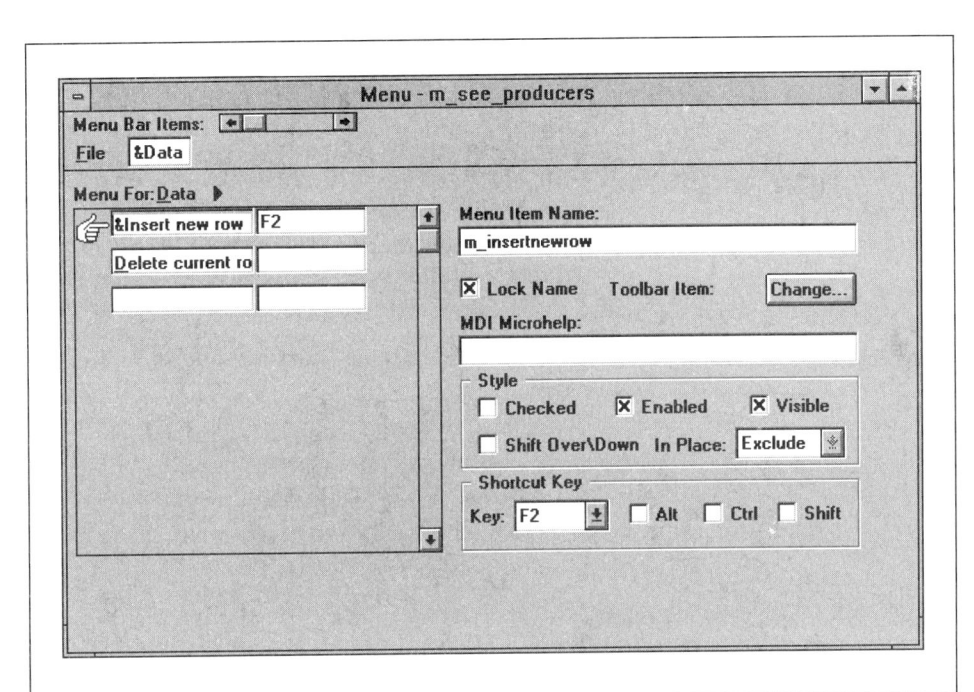

Figure 17.15
Entering a shortcut key (4.0)

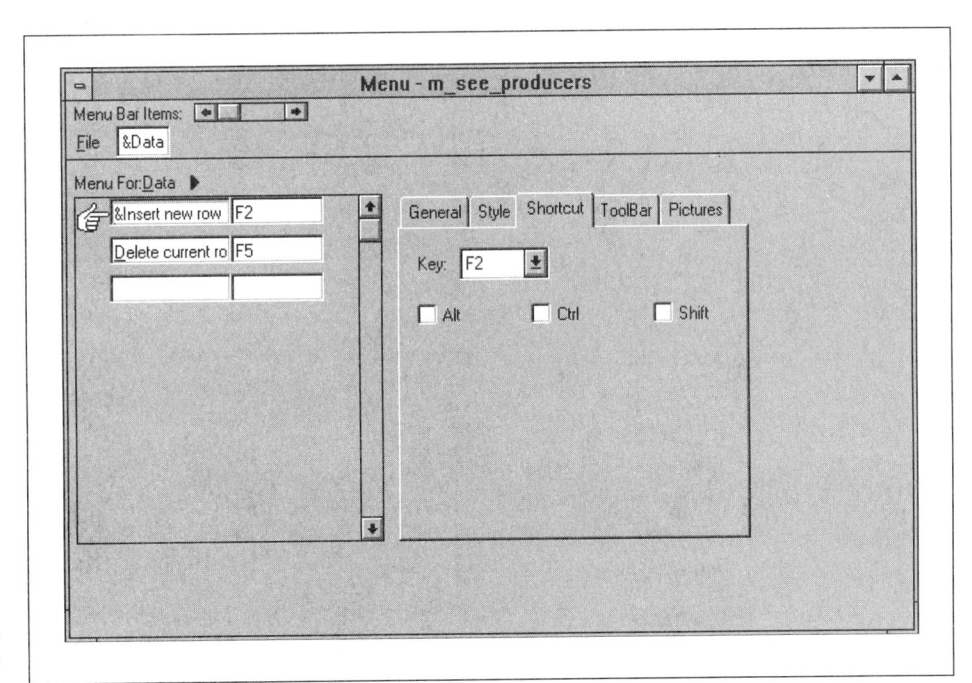

Figure 17.16
Entering a shortcut key (5.0)

5   Set **F3** as the shortcut key for Save. Set **F5** as the shortcut key for Delete.

6   Attach m_see_producers to w_see_producer_data.

7   If you wish, remove the Close picture button from the window—it isn't strictly necessary any more because the window has both a control box and a Return option in the File menu—and enlarge the Data-Window control so that more rows can be seen at one time.

8   Run the application and test your scripts to make sure that they work properly.

Developing the Descendant Menu

Now that you have the ancestor menu, you can use inheritance to create other, similar menus. In this case, you will be creating a menu for w_see_show_data, which provides a list of all the rows in the Shows table.

To create and use the descendant menu:

1   Click the **Menu** button in the PowerBar. The Select Menu dialog box appears.

2   Click the **Inherit** button. The Inherit From Menu dialog box appears.

3   Choose **m_see_producers** in the list of menus, as in Figure 17.17.

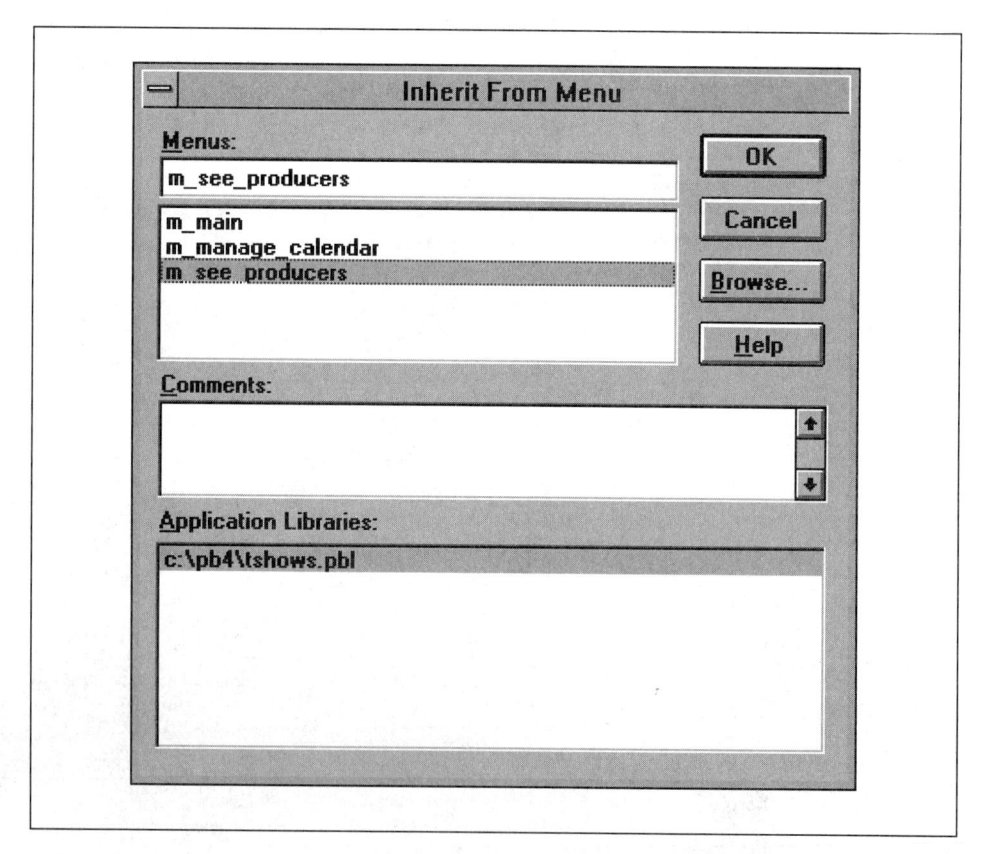

Figure 17.17
Inherit From Menu dialog box

4 Click the **OK** button to close the dialog box. The inherited menu appears in the Menu painter, looking exactly like its ancestor.

5 Save the menu as **m_see_shows**.

In this example, the menu bar items and the menu options should remain unchanged. However, the scripts need to be changed to reflect the window to which this menu is going to be attached.

You can insert new items into an inherited menu, change a menu item's text, and modify scripts (add new scripts, override ancestor scripts, extend ancestor scripts). However, you can't change the order items in an inherited menu or delete items.

6 Enter the Script painter for the clicked event of File -> Save.

7 Choose **Compile** -> **Override Ancestor Script** to instruct Power-Builder to use the descendant object's script rather than the ancestor's script.

8 Choose **Compile** -> **Display Ancestor Script**.

9 Use the Select All button to select the entire ancestor script.

10 Use the Copy button to place the ancestor script on the clipboard.

11 Paste the ancestor script into the Script painter.

12 Replace w_see_producer_data.dw_see_producers with w_see_show_data.dw_see_shows.

13 Repeat Steps 7 through 13 for Data -> Insert new row and Data -> Delete current row.

14 Attach the menu object to w_see_show_data.

15 Run the application to test the inherited menu.

Wrapping Up

In this chapter you have learned to create menus, the final piece of a PowerBuilder application's user interface. You have created menus from scratch and used inheritance to derive child menus from parent menus. As a result, a user has several ways to initiate each action in your PowerBuilder applications: clicking a button, making a menu choice with the mouse, use a function key, or using an accelerator key.

This chapter concludes your study of PowerBuilder. The remainder of the book provides additional support for projects you may be completing for your coursework. For example, Appendix A discusses creating executables—PowerBuilder applications that can be run without the presence of the PowerBuilder development environment. You will also find PowerScript language support and reference material for the functions used in the scripts in this book.

EXERCISES

The following exercises will let you complete the College and University Rentals application by creating the menus needed by the program. Don't forget to keep the user in mind when you write menu options. The options should be short but understandable and free of jargon.

1. Create a main menu object for the C&U Rentals application. Attach it to the application's opening screen.

2. Create a menu object for the window that supports entering, modifying, and deleting data about merchandise.

3. Create a menu object for the window that supports entering, modifying, and delete data about schools. Can you use inheritance to build this menu, perhaps using the menu object from Exercise 2? Or are the two menu objects so different that you might as well start from scratch?

4. Create menu objects for all other windows that are designed to let you modify one row in a table at a time. Consider carefully whether you will use inheritance or whether you will create the menus from scratch.

5. Create a menu object for the window that lists types of merchandise. Add insert, delete, and save functions to that menu.

6. Use the menu object that you created in Exercise 5 as the ancestor for menus for the windows that list all schools and customers.

7. Create a menu object that can be used on a report menu, such as the report that summarizes revenue by type of merchandise. Consider carefully exactly what functions are appropriate for a menu object that will be attached to a nonupdatable window.

8. Use the menu object that you created in Exercise 7 as the ancestor for menus for all report windows (in other words, windows that aren't updatable).

Appendix A

Building Executables

When PowerBuilder compiles a script, it compiles each script separately. Unlike a general-purpose high-level programming language such as Pascal or C++, PowerBuilder compilation doesn't generate a single binary file that can easily be moved from one computer to another. You can however, in a series of separate steps, create a PowerBuilder executable, a binary file with a .EXE extension accompanied optionally by binary libraries and collections of resources. This latter strategy is useful when a single binary file is too large to fit on a single floppy disk and would therefore be difficult to transport from one computer to another.

A PowerBuilder executable isn't a stand-alone program. It must be accompanied by the Database Development and Deployment Kit, which ships along with PowerBuilder 4. There are no fees for distributing this set of dynamic link libraries (DLLs) that are needed to run a PowerBuilder application without the presence of the development environment.

A DLL is a collection of compiled program modules that provide a support environment for another program. Typically, the modules in a DLL contain code for language functions. PowerBuilder DLLs, for example, need to provide the code to execute PowerBuilder functions.

Why should you bother to create a PowerBuilder executable? There are at least three reasons:

- You can distribute multiple copies of an application to users, without requiring each user to have a copy of the PowerBuilder development environment.
- An executable provides a known, small set of files that can easily be moved from one computer to another.
- An executable cannot be opened, examined, or modified by the PowerBuilder development software. The executable therefore provides security for the scripts written to support your application.

In this appendix you will be introduced to two methods for creating executables. The first is an easy method that creates a single, self-contained .EXE file suitable for small applications. The second is a bit more complex, but splits an application into multiple files (an .EXE file and accompanying DLLs) that are easier to transport on media such as floppy disks.

Creating a Quick Executable

The easiest way to create an executable is to let PowerBuilder create it for you, in which case PowerBuilder figures out which objects in the application are actually being used. All objects, scripts, and graphics end up in one file. To create a quick and simple executable, do the following:

1. Make sure that you are working with the *tshows* application in *tshows2.pbl*.
2. Enter the Application painter.

3 Choose File -> Create Executable. The Select Executable File dialog box appears (Figure A.1). Notice that PowerBuilder fills in a default file name for the executable, based on the application's name.

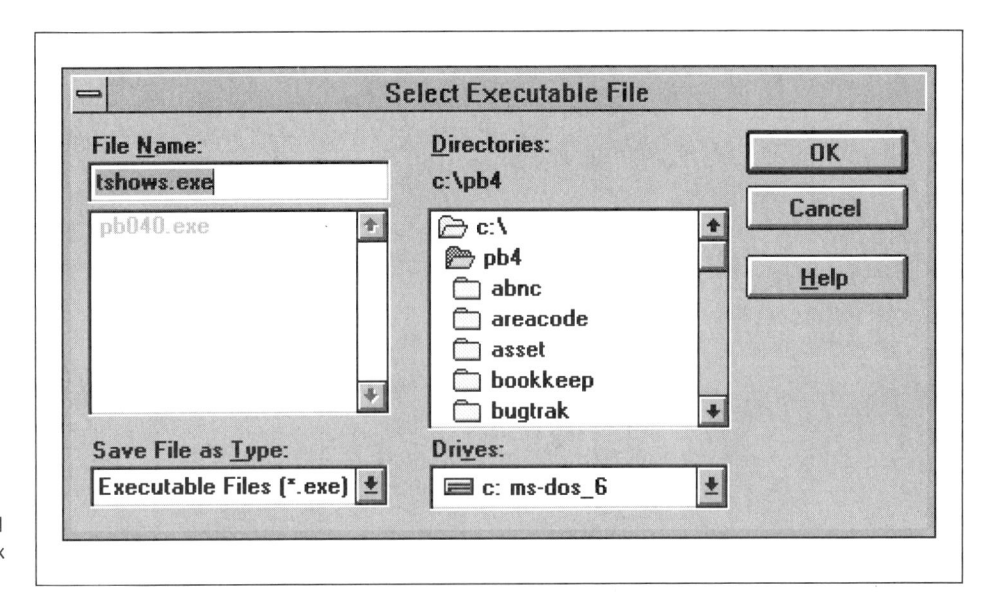

Figure A.1
The Select Executable File dialog box

4 Click the OK button to close the dialog box. The Create Executable dialog box appears (Figure A.2). PowerBuilder fills in the current application library in the Dynamic Libraries list. If there are other libraries that should be part of the application, you would add them at this time.

5 Click the OK button to close the dialog box. PowerBuilder closes the dialog box and generates the executable file. Assuming you have completed the application as directed throughout this book, the executable file should be between 450K and 500K in size.

6 To test this executable, exit PowerBuilder. Make sure that the Database Development and Deployment Kit is installed. If it is installed, run the executable just like you would run any other windows application.

The executable file generated in this manner is less than 500K and will easily fit on a single floppy disk for transporting between computers. So what's the problem with it? There are at least two potential problems:

- As applications become more complex, the executable file can grow rapidly in size, making it too big to distribute easily on a floppy disk.
- Each time you modify the application, you must recreate the entire application. Even libraries that haven't been modified are regenerated into the executable. As an application grows larger, this takes up unnecessary time.

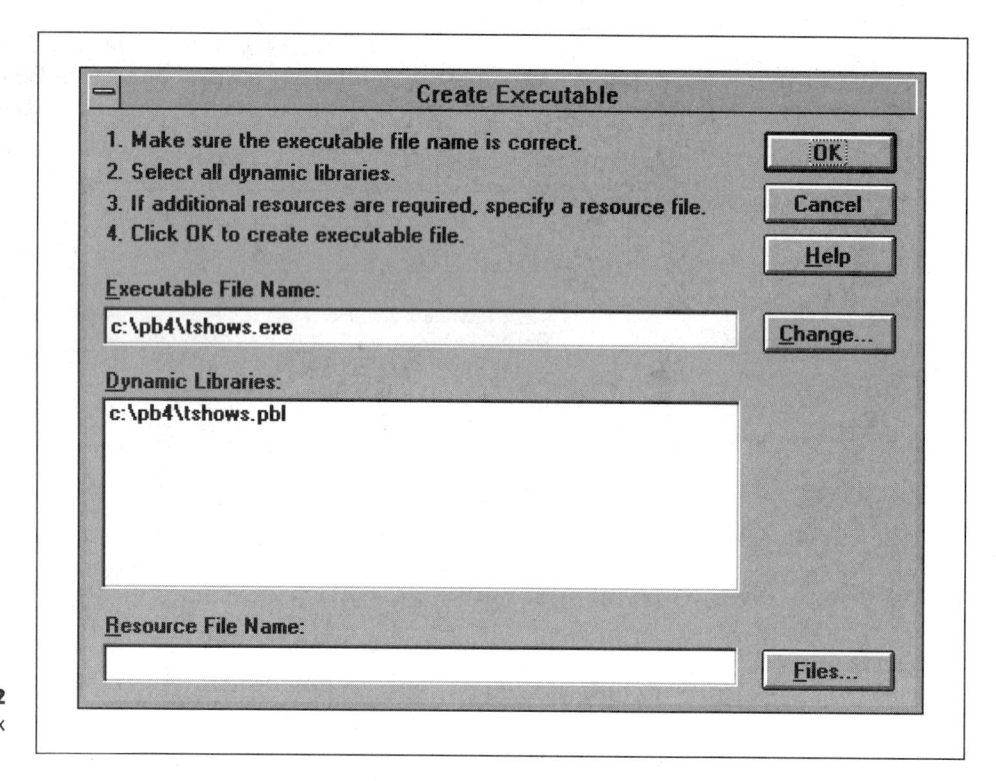

Figure A.2
The Create Executable dialog box

Creating Executables Using the Project Painter

The alternative to generating a single executable file is to build executables using the Project painter, which lets you split a large application into many files: an executable, one or more dynamic libraries, and one or more resource files. A project also keeps track of which parts of the project have been modified since the last time the executable was generated. It therefore only needs to regenerate those items, cutting down on the time it takes to produce the executable.

A *dynamic library* is a PowerBuilder library that is linked to a PowerBuilder executable when needed during the application's run. It can be generated from an existing .pbl file or it can be a new library created to store just the objects needed by a particular executable. Dynamic libraries contain DataWindow objects and other objects used by an executable.

NOTE

If an executable contains a significant number of bit-mapped graphics, those graphics can be separated into resource files, which can also become parts of a project.

To see how the Project painter works, try the following:

1. Click the Project button in the PowerBar (Figure A.3). The Select Project dialog box appears, as in Figure A.4.
2. Click the New button to create a new project. The Select Executable File dialog box appears, with PowerBuilder's suggestion for a name of the executable file.

APPENDIX A   BUILDING EXECUTABLES   **419**

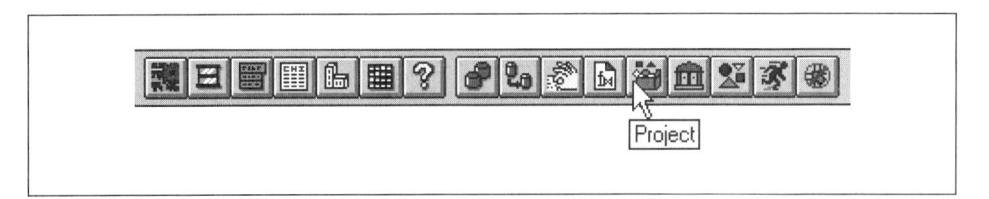

Figure A.3
The Project button

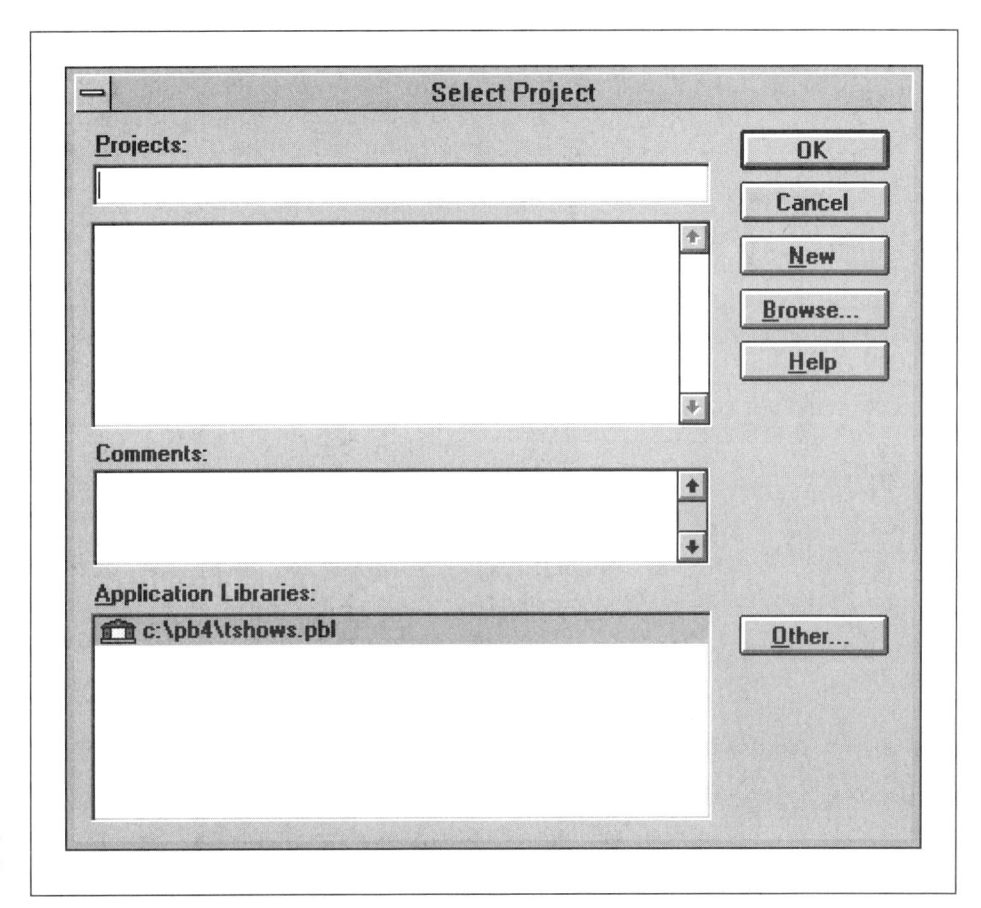

Figure A.4
The Select Project dialog box

3 If necessary, change the name of the executable. However, in this case *tshows.exe* is the name you want to use. Therefore, click OK to accept PowerBuilder's suggestion and close the dialog box. The Project workspace appears. As you can see in Figure A.5, it adds all libraries used by the application to the project automatically.

4 By default, all libraries are included in the executable file. (In other words, they aren't dynamic.) To make a library a dynamic library that is stored in a separate file, click the check box under PBD ("Power-Builder Dynamic"). For this example, make *tshows2.pbl* dynamic.

5 Click the Build button in the PainterBar to create the executable file and the separate dynamic library. (*Hint*: It's the only button in the PainterBar.) Notice that PowerBuilder displays its actions as it works at the bottom left of the window.

6 Save the project object as **p_tshows**.

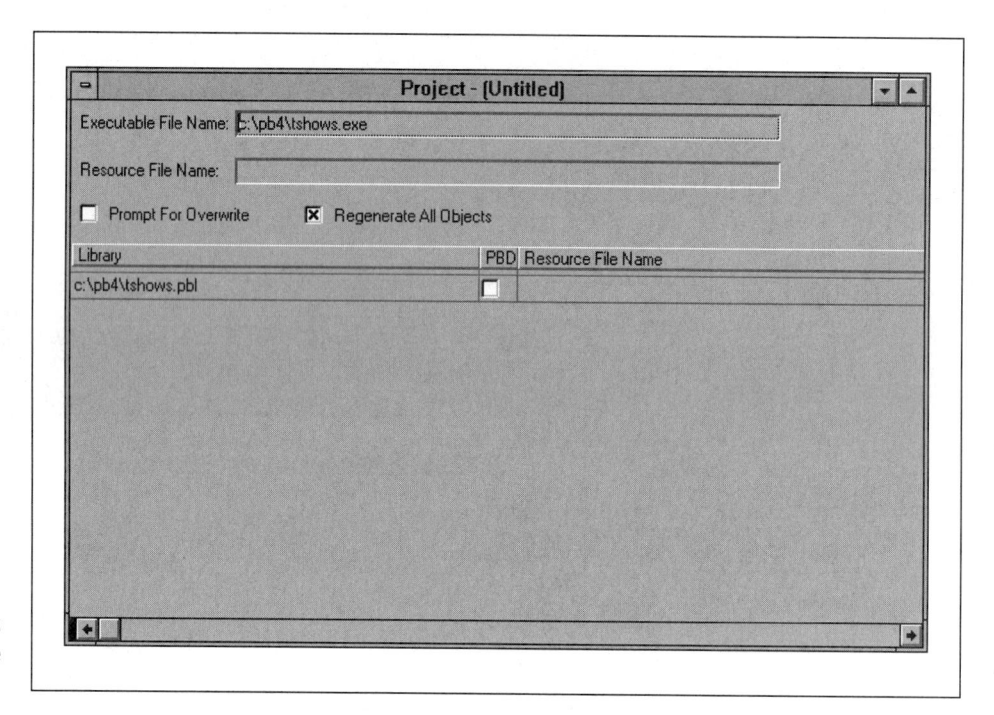

Figure A.5
The Project painter workspace

When you've finished generating an executable from the project, you will discover that *tshows.exe* is now only about 10K in size. However, the dynamic library—*tshows.pbd*—is about 450K.

When you create an executable, PowerBuilder includes only those objects that it can identify as being used in an application. Objects that are referenced as literal strings (for example, "dw_my_datawindow") aren't included. If an application happens to set object attributes equal to object names in this way (tshows does not), then you will need to add those objects to a dynamic library manually. To do so, open the library containing the objects in the Library painter. Then, create a new dynamic library by choosing Library -> Create. Use the Entry -> Move command to transfer the objects from their original library to the new dynamic library. Once transferred, you can add the new library to the project.

APPENDIX B

Using PowerBuilder Macintosh

The Macintosh version of PowerBuilder 4.0 is extremely compatible with PowerBuilder Windows 4.0. You can copy the Windows applications that accompany this text to the Macintosh and they will run, unmodified. Unfortunately, the price of that compatibility is a number of compromises with the Macintosh user interface.

In this appendix you will read about the adjustments a Macintosh user needs to make to work with PowerBuilder, including global keyboard equivalance changes and differences found in specific painters. Throughout, we will also be looking at some of the issues that application developers need to keep in mind when designing cross-platform applications.

This appendix has been written specifically for Macintosh users. It assumes that you are familiar with the Macintosh user interface and operating system.

PowerBuilder Macintosh is written in 680x0 code; it is not native on the Power Macintosh. Be prepared for performance that is slower than what you'd expect from most Macintosh applications. For example, connecting to a database is especially slow. However, when you switch painters, the Painterbar of the new painter should appear fairly quickly. If you are trying to enter the Window, DataWindow, or User Object painters and the Painterbar doesn't switch within 30 seconds, you may have too many font bit maps for PowerBuilder to handle; it will be unable to build the font menu necessary for those painters. In that case, you will need to reboot your system, because it will be crashed beyond recovery even with a forced quit.

You may find that there are some significant INIT conflicts with PowerBuilder Macintosh. For example, on this author's PowerMac 8100/80 and System 7.5.1 it is incompatible with QuicKeys. (You can have QuicKeys loaded when PowerBuilder Macintosh is running, but look out for a crash if you try to execute a QuicKeys macro!)

Keyboard Changes for Macintosh Users

If you are working with PowerBuilder Macintosh, the following are the keyboard adjustments you will need to make:

- Whenever the documentation and this book refer to clicking the right mouse button, hold down CTRL and click the mouse button.
- Whenever you see a reference to the CTRL key, use ⌘.
- Whenever you see a reference to the ALT key, use Option.

Keep in mind that the PowerBuilder documentation has not been rewritten to support the Macintosh user interface. It is therefore up to you to make the keyboard substitutions wherever appropriate.

PowerBuilder Macintosh uses keyboard equivalents differently from most Macintosh applications. You can't count on any of the standard keyboard equivalents to work consistently. For example, ⌘-S doesn't save your work; it usually opens the script painter. In addition, in the PowerScript painter ⌘-Q appears in two menus: the File menu (where you would expect to find it associated with the Quit option) and the Edit menu (where it invokes Paste SQL). If you press ⌘-Q in the PowerScript painter, it invokes the Edit menu option rather than Quit.

Window Painter Changes

As you are aware, the geography of a Macintosh window is somewhat different from that of a Windows window. However, if you look at Figure B.1, you can see that the Window Style dialog box is a direct copy of the Windows version.

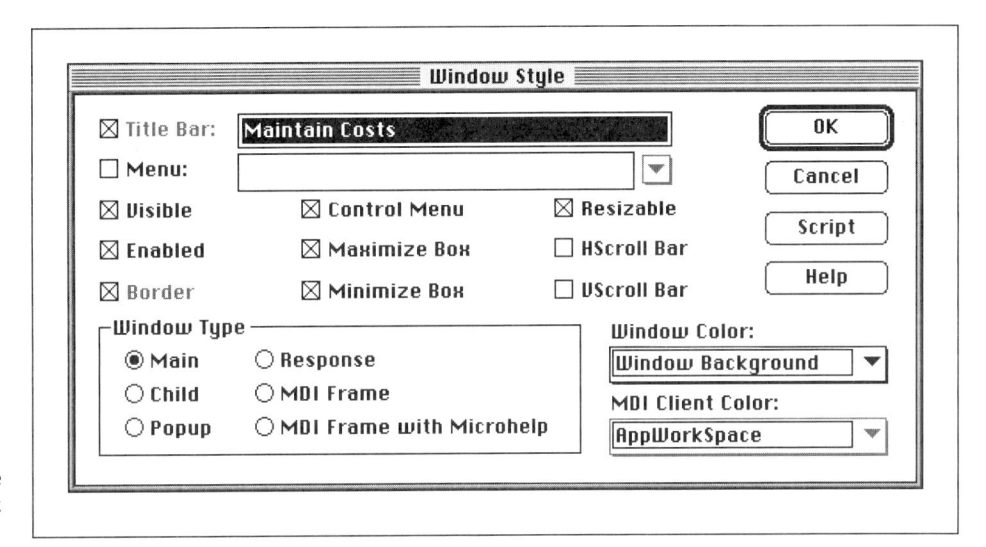

Figure B.1
The Macintosh Window Style dialog box

> **NOTE:** *This copying of a Windows dialog box without modifying it to make it reflect the Macintosh environment is typical of PowerBuilder Macintosh. Everything still has the Windows terminology, even if options aren't available on the Mac or if some Macintosh option is missing.*

The check boxes in the dialog box map to the Macintosh in the following way:

- The Control Menu check box places a close box in a Macintosh window's title bar.
- The Maximize Box and Minimize Box check boxes are ignored because they represent Windows features not shared by the Macintosh.
- The Resizable check box places a grow box in the lower-right corner of a Macintosh window.

The Window Types also correspond to Macintosh window types:

- A Main window is a standard document window with a title bar and optionally a close box, grow box, and scroll bars. A menu that is "attached" to this window will appear in the Macintosh's menu bar, not on top of the window as it would under Windows.
- A Response window is a dialog box. If it has a title bar, it is a movable modal dialog box; if it has no title, it is a typical modal dialog box that cannot be moved. In either case, the dialog box must be closed before the user can work with any other window within an application.

- A Popup window is a modeless dialog box. Although a popup's parent window cannot overlay it and a popup closes when its parent is closed, it behaves much like a standard document window.

There are two window types that don't map directly between Windows and the Macintosh:

- PowerBuilder Macintosh has no direct equivalent for alerts. Use a MessageBox instead.
- Child windows are not a typical part of the Macintosh user interface. However, they are supported with PowerBuilder Macintosh and act just as they do in PowerBuilder Windows.

Font Issues

Although both the Macintosh and Windows machines use bit-mapped fonts for screen display, if you port a Windows application directly to the Macintosh you may find that Windows-only fonts such as Arial don't look particularly attractive on the screen. Therefore, when designing a window that will be used on both Windows and Macintosh machines, try to use a font that is available on both platforms.

PowerBuilder provides a set of fonts (the AccuFonts) that correspond to some typical Macintosh screen fonts. For example, the Macintosh's Geneva font looks particularly good on the screen. The Windows equivalent is Accujen. For the best appearance, use 9, 10, 12, 14, or 18 point type. The Macintosh fonts are TrueType fonts and will be scaled, but the Windows versions aren't TrueType and won't be scaled to other sizes.

If you develop an application under Windows and port it to the Macintosh, the Macintosh correctly maps the Windows AccuFonts to Macintosh fonts. However, if you develop on the Macintosh, the same substitution won't occur.

Menu Painter Changes

The Macintosh menu painter workspace looks exactly like that found in the Windows version. As you can see in Figure B.2, the "shortcut key" reference still exists, including check boxes for the ALT and CTRL keys. When working with this painter, keep in mind that the ALT key maps to Option and that the CTRL key maps to ⌘.

The other major difference between Windows menus and Macintosh menus is where a menu appears. In the Windows environment, menus are attached at the top of a window (right under the title bar), rather than across the top of the screen as they are on the Macintosh. In addition, if a Windows window has a control box, some standard functions (for example, closing the window) are part of the control box's menu.

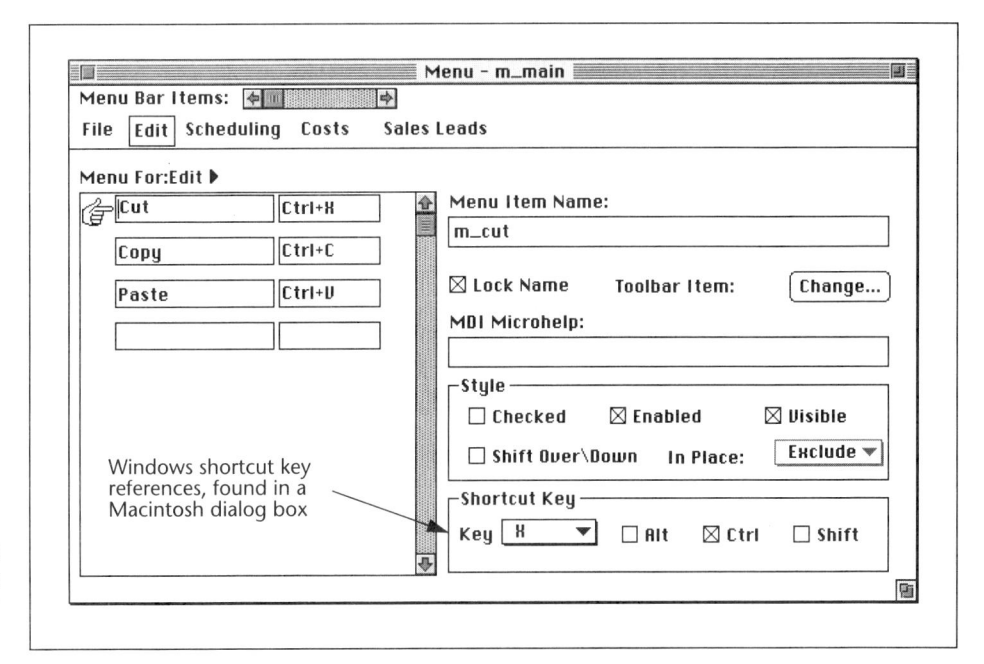

Figure B.2
The PowerBuilder Macintosh menu painter

[Screenshot showing the PowerBuilder Macintosh menu painter with Menu Bar Items: File, Edit, Scheduling, Costs, Sales Leads. Menu For: Edit shows Cut (Ctrl+X), Copy (Ctrl+C), Paste (Ctrl+V). Menu Item Name: m_cut, with Lock Name checked, Style options (Checked, Enabled, Visible, Shift Over\Down), In Place: Exclude, and Shortcut Key: X with Ctrl checked. Annotation: "Windows shortcut key references, found in a Macintosh dialog box"]

Cross-Platform Menu Issues

When a PowerBuilder menu is displayed on a Macintosh, it *replaces* the entire Macintosh menu bar with the exception of the menu. This means that you are responsible for including standard File and Edit menu options in the menu and for writing scripts that support those options.

If you want your application to look and feel like a normal Macintosh application, then the File menu will typically contain Open, Close, Save, Save As, Print, and Quit options. The Edit menu will usually contain Cut, Copy, Paste, Clear, and Undo. You will use the typical Macintosh keyboard equivalents for these options.

Windows menus, however, are different. As mentioned earlier, some of the operations that appear in the Macintosh menu bar are found in a Windows control menu and therefore don't need to be included in a PowerBuilder menu. In addition, Windows menus have accelerator keys (key combinations that provide keyboard access to menu items), which aren't used on the Macintosh.

The bottom line is that there is no way to satisfactorily design one set of menus for both a Macintosh and Windows application. The solution is to have separate menus for both platforms and then, when the program runs, determine the platform on which the program is running and use a script to select the correct menu object.

To find the platform on which an application is running, first declare an integer global variable to hold the operating system (theOS in the sample code in Listing B.1). Then, place code like that in Listing B.1 in the application's open event script:

Listing B.1
Identifying the platform on which an application is running

```
integer returnValue
environment theEnvironment

returnValue = GetEnvrionment (theEnvironment)
IF returnValue <> 1 THEN RETURN // error trapping
theOS = theEnvrionment.OSType
```

Whenever your application opens a main window, you will need to check the operating system and install the appropriate menu. To switch a menu, use the `ChangeMenu` function, which has the general syntax:

windowname.ChangeMenu (*menuname*)

As an example, consider Listing B.2. This code should be placed in a window's open event script. It uses the `theOS` global variable to select which menu object is to be used.

Listing B.2
Switching menus on the fly

```
CHOOSE CASE theOS
   CASE Macintosh!
      this.ChangeMenu (w_Mac_enter_data)
   CASE Windows!
      this.ChangeMenu (w_Win_enter_data)
END CHOOSE
```

Project Painter Changes

There are two minor differences between creating an executable with the project painter for a Windows platform and for a Macintosh platform. The first concerns the use of a Macintosh resource file. If you have a resource file (perhaps containing PICT resources that you are using as icons or for background illustrations), you can attach that resource file to the executable with the Options -> Paste Macintosh Resource menu option.

The second difference can be seen in Figure B.3. Notice that there is a space to enter a four-character creator string for the executable. This gives the executable a unique identity within a Macintosh system. (With a traditional Macintosh application, a creator string links documents with the application that created it.) Creator strings that will be used outside the Macintosh on which they are generated should be registered with Apple Developer Services. There is no fee for doing so, but it is essential to ensure that no two applications have duplicate strings. (See http://www.apple.com for details.)

Your best chance at avoiding a creator string conflict is to create one that includes at least one uppercase letter.

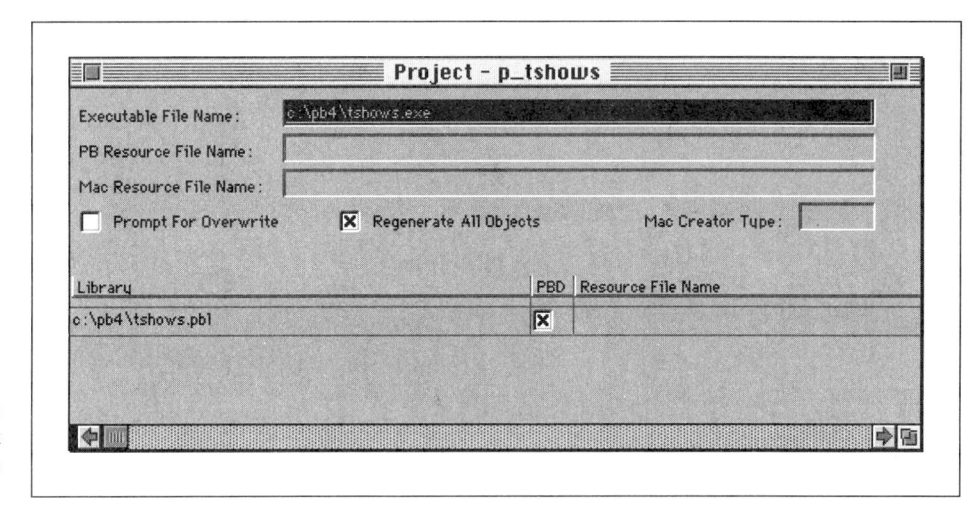

Figure B.3
PowerBuilder Macintosh's project painter workspace

Appendix C

Function Reference

PowerScript Functions

Close

Description   Closes a window or an OLE storage or stream. There are several syntaxes:

- To close a window, use Syntax 1.
- To save the object in the specified OLEStorage object variable and clear any connections between it and a storage file or object, use Syntax 2. Close also severs connections with any OLE 2.0 controls that have opened the object. Calling Close is the same as calling Save and then Clear.
- To close the stream associated with the specified OLEStream object variable, use Syntax 3.

Applies to

(Syntax 1) Window objects
(Syntax 2) OLEStorage objects
(Syntax 3) OLEStream objects

Syntax 1

`Close (windowname)`

Parameter	Description
windowname	The name of the window you want to close

Return Value 2

Integer. Returns 1 if it succeeds and −1 if an error occurs. The return value is usually not used.

Syntax 2

`olestorage.Close()`

Parameter	Description
olestorage	The OLEStorage object variable that you want to save and close

Return value 2

Integer. Returns 0 if it succeeds and one of the following negative values if an error occurs:

- −J The storage is not open
- −9 Other error

Syntax 3

`olestorage.Close()`

Parameter	Description
olestorage	The OLEStorage object variable that you want to close

Return value 3	Integer. Returns 0 if it succeeds and one of the following negative values if an error occurs: ■ −J The storage is not open ■ −9 Other error
Usage	Use Syntax 1 of Close to close a window and release the storage occupied by the window and all the controls in the window. When you call Close, PowerBuilder removes the window from view, closes it, executes the scripts for the CloseQuery and Close events (if any), and then executes the rest of the statements in the script that called the Close function. After a window is closed, its attributes, instance variables, and controls can no longer be referenced in scripts. If a statement in the script references the closed window or its attributes or instance variables, an execution error will result. ***Preventing a window from closing.*** *You can prevent a window from being closed by setting* `Message.ReturnValue` *to 1 in the script for the CloseQuery event. You must make the setting in the last statement in the script.*

Examples	These statements close the window w_employee and then open the window w_departments:
	
	``
	Close (w_employee)
	Open (w_departments)
	``
	
	The following statements in the script for the CloseQuery event prompt the user for confirmation before they exit the application:
	
	``
	IF MessageBox('ExitApplication', &
	'Exit?', Question!, YesNo!) = 1 THEN
	  // If yes, close the window. If no, no action.
	  Close (w~employee)
	END IF
	``

Syntax 2	This example saves and clears the object in the OLEStorage object variable olest_stuff. It also leaves any OLE 2.0 controls that have opened the object in olest_stuff empty too: ``` integer result result = olest_stuff.Close( ) ```

Date

Description	Converts DateTime, string, or numeric data to data of type date. It also extracts a date value from a blob. You can use one of three syntaxes, depending on the data type of the source data:

432 APPENDIX C FUNCTION REFERENCE — DATE

- To extract the date from DateTime data, or to extract a date stored in a blob, use Syntax 1.
- To convert a string to a date, use Syntax 2.
- To combine numeric data into a date, use Syntax 3.

Syntax 1

Date (*datetime*)

Parameter	Description
datetime	A DateTime value or a blob in which the first value is a date or DateTime value. The rest of the contents of the blob is ignored.

Return value 1

Date. Returns the date in *datetime* as a date. If *datetime* does not contain a valid date, Date returns 1900-01-01.

Syntax 2

Date (*string*)

Parameter	Description
string	A string whose value is a valid date (such as January 1, 1998, or 12-31-99) that you want returned as a date

Return value 2

Date. Returns the date in *string* as a date. If *string* does not contain a valid date, Date returns 1900-01-01.

Syntax 3

Date (*year, month, day*)

Parameter	Description
year	The 4-digit year (-9999 to 9999) of the date
month	The 1- or 2-digit integer for the month (1 to 12) of the year
day	The 1- or 2-digit integer for the day (1 to 31) of the month

Return value 3

Returns the date specified by the integers for year, month, and day, as a date data type. If any value is invalid (that is, out of the range of values for dates), Date returns 1900-01-01.

Usage

Valid dates in strings can include any combination of day (1 to 31), month (1 to 12 or the name or abbreviation of a month), and year (2 or 4 digits). Leading zeros are optional for month and day. If the month is a name or an abbreviation, it can come before or after the day; if it is a number, it must be in the month location specified in the Windows control panel. PowerBuilder assumes a 4-digit number is a year.

Date literals, which do not need to be converted with the Date function, have the format yyyy-mm-dd.

Examples

After a value for the DateTime variable 1dt_StartDateTime has been retrieved from the database, this example sets 1d_StartDate equal to the date in 1dt_StartDateTime:

```
DateTime ldt_StartDateTime
date ld_StartDate

ld_StartDate = Date(ldt_StartDateTime)
```

Suppose that the value of a blob variable ib_blob contains a DateTime value beginning at byte 32. The following statement converts it to a date value.

```
date ld_date
ld_date = Date(HlobMid(ib_blob, 32))
```

Syntax 2

These statements all return the date data type for text expressing the date July 4, 1994 (1994-07.04). The system setting for the month location is in the center:

```
Date("1994/07/04")
Date("1994 July 4")
Date("July 4, 1994")
```

The following groups of statements check to be sure the date in sle_start_date is a valid date and display a message if it is not. The first version checks the result of the Date function to see if the date was valid. The second uses the IsDate function to check the text before using Date to convert it.

Version 1:

```
// Windows Control Panel date format is FY/MM/DD date ld~my_date

ld_my_date = Date( sle_start_date.Text )
IF ld_rnydate = Date("1900-01-01") THEN
  MessageBox("Error", "This date is invalid: "
  +sle_start_date.Text)
END IF
```

Version 2:

```
date ld_my_date

IF IsDate(sle_start_date.Text) THEN
  ld_my_date = Date(sle_start_date.Text)
Else
  MessageBox("Error", "This date is invalid: " &
  +sle_start_date.Text)
END IF
```

Syntax 3

These statements use integer values to set ld_my_date to 1994-10-15:

```
date ld_my_date
ld_my_date = Date(1994, 10, 15)
```

Day

Description   Obtains the day of the month in a date value.

Syntax   Day (*date*)

Parameter	Description
date	A date value from which you want the day

Return value   Integer. Returns an integer (1 to 31) representing the day of the month in date.

Examples   These statements extract the day (31) from the date literal 1994-01-31 and set li_day_portion to that value:

```
integer li_day_portion
li_day_portion = Day(1994-01-31)
```

These statements check to be sure the date in sle_date is valid and, if so, set li_day_portion to the day in the sle_date:

```
integer li~day~portion

IF IsDate(sle_date.Text) THEN
  li_day_portion = Day(Date( sle_date Text))
ELSE
  MessageBox("Error",  &
    "This date is invalid: "  &
    +sle_date.Text)
END IF
```

Dec

Description   Converts a string to a decimal number or obtains a decimal value stored in a blob.

Syntax   Dec (*stringorblob*)

Parameter	Description
stringorblob	The string whose value you want returned as a decimal value or a blob in which the first value is the decimal you want. The rest of the contents of the blob is ignored.

Return value   Decimal. Returns the value of *stringorblob* as a decimal. If *stringorblob* is not a valid PowerScript number, Dec returns 0.

Examples   This statement returns 24.3 as a decimal data type:

```
Dec("24.3")
```

This statement returns the contents of the SingleLineEdit sle_salary as a decimal number:

```
Dec(sle_salary.Text)
```

DeletedCount

Description Reports the number of rows that have been marked for deletion in the database.

Syntax *datawindowname*.DeletedCount()

Parameter	Description
datawindowname	The name of the DataWindow control or child DataWindow for which you want the number of rows that have been deleted, but not updated, in the associated database table

Return value Long. Returns the number of rows that have been deleted from *datawindowname* but not updated in the associated database table.

Returns 0 if no rows have been deleted or all the deleted rows have been updated in the database table. Returns –1 if it fails.

Usage An updatable DataWindow control has several buffers. The primary buffer stores the rows currently being displayed. The delete buffer stores rows that the application has marked for deletion by calling the DeleteRow function. These rows are saved until the database is updated. You can use DeletedCount to find out if there are any rows in the delete buffer.

Examples If two rows in dw_employee have been deleted but have not been updated in the associated database table, then these statements set ll_Del to 2:

```
Long ll_Del
ll_Del = dw_employee.DeletedCount()
```

The following example tests whether there are rows in the delete buffer and, if so, updates the database table associated with dw_employee:

```
Long ll_Del
ll_Del = dw_employee.DeletedCount()
If ll_Del <> 0 then dw_employee.Update()
```

DeleteRow

Description Deletes a row from a DataWindow control or child DataWindow.

Applies to DataWindow controls and child DataWindows

Syntax

datawindowname.DeleteRow (*row*)

Parameter	Description
datawindowname	The name of the DataWindow control or child DataWindow in which you want to delete a row.
row	A long identifying the row you want to delete. To delete the current row, specify 0 for row.

Return value

Integer. Returns 1 if the row is successfully deleted and -1 if an error occurs.

Usage

DeleteRow deletes the row from the DataWindow's primary buffer.

If the DataWindow control is not updatable, all storage associated with the row is cleared. If the DataWindow is updatable, DeleteRow moves the row to the DataWindow's delete buffer; PowerBuilder uses the values in the delete buffer to build the SQL DELETE statement.

The row is not deleted from the database table until the application calls the Update function. After the Update function has updated the database and the update flags are reset, then the storage associated with the row is cleared.

Examples

This statement deletes the current row from dw_employee:

```
dw_employee.DeleteRow( 0)
```

These statements delete row 5 from dw_employee and then update the database with the change:

```
dw_employee.DeleteRow( 5)
dw_employee.Update
```

Double

Description

Converts a string to a double or obtains a double value that is stored in a blob.

Syntax

Double (*stringorblob*)

Parameter	Description
stringorblob	The string whose value you want returned as a double or a blob in which the first value is the double value. The rest of the contents of the blob is ignored.

Return value

Double. Returns the contents of *stringorblob* as a double. If *stringorblob* is not a valid PowerScript number, Double returns 0.

Usage

To distinguish between a string whose value is the number 0 and a string whose value is not a number, use the IsNumber function before calling the Double function.

GetChild

Examples

This statement returns 24.372 as a double:

```
Double("24.372")
```

This statement returns the contents of the SingleLineEdit sle_distance as a double:

```
Double(sle_distance Text)
```

After assigning blob data from the database to lb_blob, the following example obtains the double value stored at position 20 in the blob. (The length you specify for BlobMid must be at least as long as the value but can be longer):

```
double lb_num
lb_num = Double(BlobMid(lb_blob, 20, 40))
```

GetChild

Description

Provides a reference to a child DataWindow or to a report in a composite DataWindow, which you can use in DataWindow functions to manipulate that DataWindow or report.

Applies to

DataWindow controls

Syntax

datawindowname.GetChild (*name, dwchildvariable*)

Parameter	Description
datawindowname	The name of the DataWindow control that contains the child DataWindow or report
name	A string that names the column containing the child DataWindow or that names the report in the composite DataWindow
dwchildvariable	A variable of type DataWindowChild in which you want to store the reference to the child DataWindow

Return value

Integer. Returns 1 if it succeeds and –1 if an error occurs. The reference to the child DataWindow or report is stored in *dwchildvariable*.

Usage

A child DataWindow is a DropDownDataWindow in a DataWindow object.

A report is a DataWindow that is part of a composite DataWindow. A report is read-only. When you define the composite DataWindow in the DataWindow painter, make sure you give each report a name so that you can refer to it in the GetChild function.

Use GetChild when you need to explicitly retrieve data for a child DataWindow or report. Although PowerBuilder retrieves data for the child or report automatically when the main DataWindow is displayed, you need to explicitly retrieve data when there are retrieval arguments or when conditions change and you want to retrieve new rows.

When you insert a row or retrieve data in the main DataWindow, PowerBuilder automatically retrieves data for the child DataWindow. If the child DataWindow has retrieval arguments, PowerBuilder will display a dialog box asking the user for values for those arguments. To suppress the dialog box, you can explicitly retrieve data for the child before changing the main DataWindow. (See the example.)

Example

This example retrieves data for the child DataWindow associated with the column emp_state before retrieving data in the main DataWindow. The child DataWindow expects a region value as a retrieval argument. Because you populate the child DataWindow first, specifying a value for its retrieval argument, there is no need for PowerBuilder to display the retrieval argument dialog box:

```
Datawindowchild state_child
integer rtncode

rtncode = dw_1.GetChild('emp_state', state_child) IF rtncode = -1 &
 THEN MessageBox ("Error", "Not a Datawindowchild")

// Establish the connection if not already connected
CONNECT USING SQLCA;

// Set the transaction object for the child
state_child.SetTransobject(SQLCA)

// Populate the child with values for eastern states
state_child.Retrieve("East")

// Set transaction object for main DW and retrieve
dw_1.SetTransobject ( SQLCA)
dw_1.Retrieve()
```

In a composite DataWindow there are two reports: orders and current inventory. The orders report has a retrieval argument for selecting the order status. This report will display open orders. The composite DataWindow is displayed in a DataWindow control called dw_news and the reports are named open_orders and current_inv. The following code in the Open event of the window that contains dw_news provides a retrieval argument for open_orders:

```
Datawindowchild dwc_orders
dw_news.GetChild("open_orders", dwc_orders)
dwc_orders. SetTransobject ( SQLCA)
dwc_orders.Retrieve("open")
```

GetClickedColumn

Description

Obtains the number of the column the user clicked or double-clicked in a DataWindow control.

Applies to

DataWindow controls and child DataWindows

GETCLICKEDROW   APPENDIX C FUNCTION REFERENCE **439**

Syntax   *datawindowname*.GetClickedColumn()

Parameter	Description
datawindowname	The name of the DataWindow control or child DataWindow for which you want the number of the column the user clicked or double-clicked

Return value   Integer. Returns the number of the column that the user clicked or doubleclicked in *datawindowname*. Returns 0 if the user did not click or doubleclick a column (for example, the user double-clicked outside the data area, in text or spaces between columns, or in the header, summary, or footer area).

Usage   Call GetClickedColumn in the Clicked or DoubleClicked event for a DataWindow control.

When the user clicks on the column, that column becomes the current column after the Clicked or DoubleClicked event is finished. During those events, GetColumn and GetClickedColumn can return different values.

If the user arrived at a column by another means, such as tabbing, GetClickedColumn will not tell you that column. Use GetColumn instead to find out the current column.

Example   These statements return the number of the column the user clicked or double-clicked in dw_employee:

```
integer li_ColNbr
li_ColNbr = dw_employee.GetClickedColumn()
```

GetClickedRow

Description   Obtains the number of the row the user clicked or double-clicked in a DataWindow control.

Applies to   DataWindow controls and child DataWindows

Syntax   *datawindowname*.GetClickedRow()

Parameter	Description
datawindowname	The name of the DataWindow control or child DataWindow for which you want the number of the row the user clicked or double-clicked

Return value   Long. Returns the number of the row that the user clicked or double-clicked in datawindowname. Returns 0 if the user did not click or double-click a row (for example, the user double-clicked outside the data area, in text or spaces between rows, or in the header, summary, or footer area).

Usage

Call GetClickedRow in the Clicked or DoubleClicked event for a DataWindow control.

When the user clicks on the row, that row becomes the current row after the Clicked or DoubleClicked event is finished. During those events, GetRow and GetClickedRow can return different values.

If the user arrived at a row by another means, such as tabbing, GetClickedRow will not tell you that row. Use GetRow instead to find out the current row.

Example

These statements return the number of the row the user clicked or double-clicked in dw_Employee:

```
long ll_RowNbr
ll_RowNbr = dw_Employee.GetClickedRow()
```

GetColumn

Description

Obtains the number of the current column. The current column is the column that has the focus.

Applies to

DataWindow controls and child DataWindows

Syntax

datawindowname.GetColumn()

Parameter	Description
datawindowname	The name of the DataWindow control or child DataWindow for which you want the number of the current column

Return value

Integer. Returns the number of the current column in datawindowname. Returns 0 if no column is current (because all the columns have a tab value of 0, making all of them uneditable), and –1 if an error occurs.

Usage

GetColumn and GetClickedColumn, when called in the Clicked or DoubleClicked event, can return different values. The column the user clicked doesn't become current until after the event.

Use GetColumnName, instead of GetColumn, when you need the column's name. Use SetColumn to change the current column.

> **NOTE** *A column becomes the current column after the user tabs to it or clicks it or if a script calls the SetColumn function. A column cannot be current if it cannot be edited, that is, if it has a tab value of 0.*
>
> *A DataWindow always has a current column, even when the control is not active, as long as there is at least one editable column.*

Example

These statements return the number of the current column in dw_Employee:

```
Integer li_ColNbr
li_ColNbr = dw_Employee.GetColumn( )
```

GetColumnName

Description	Obtains the name of the current column. The current column is the column that has the focus.
Applies to	DataWindow controls and child DataWindows
Syntax	*datawindowname*.GetColumnName( )

Parameter	Description
datawindowname	The name of the DataWindow control or child DataWindow for which you want the name of the current column

Return value	String. Returns the name of the current column in *datawindowname*. Returns the empty string ("") if no column is current or if an error occurs.
Usage	See GetColumn for information on the current column.
Example	These statements return the name of the current column in dw_Employee:

```
string ls_ColName
ls_ColName = dw_Employee.GetColumnName( )
```

GetFocus

Description	Determines the control that currently has focus.
Syntax	GetFocus( )
Return value	GraphicObject. Returns the control that currently has focus. Returns a null control reference if an error occurs.
Example	These statements set which_control equal to the data type of the control that currently has focus, and then set text_value to the text attribute of the control:

```
Graphicobject which_control
SingleLineEdit sle_which
CommandButton cb_which
string text_value

which_control = GetFocus( )

CHOOSE CASE TypeOf(which_control)

CASE CommandButton!
  cb_which = which_control
  text_value = cb_which.Text
```

```
CASE SingleLineEdit
  sle_which = which_control
  text_value = sle_which.Text

CASE ELSE
  text_value =
END CHOOSE
```

> **Note:** Not all controls have a Text attribute (for example, the DataWindow control does not). For those controls, you could assign text to the Tag attribute, which is available for all controls, and access the Tag attribute instead of the Text attribute that is shown in this example.

GetItemDate

Description Gets data whose type is Date from the specified buffer of a DataWindow control. You can obtain the data that was originally retrieved and stored in the database from the original buffer, as well as the current value in the primary, delete, or filter buffers.

Applies to DataWindow controls and child DataWindows

Syntax

datawindowname.GetItemDate (*row, column* &
  {, *dwbuffer, originalvalue* })

Parameter	Description
datawindowname	The name of the DataWindow control or child DataWindow in which you want to obtain the date data contained in a specific row and column.
row	A long identifying the row location of the data.
column	The column location of the data. The data type of the column must he date. *Column* can be a column number (integer) or a column name (string). **Tip** To get the contents of a computed field, specify the name of the computed field for *column*. Computed fields do not have numbers.
dwbuffer (optional)	A value of the dwBuffer enumerated data type identifying the DataWindow buffer from which you want to get the data: ■ PRIMARY!—(Default) The data in the primary buffer (the data that has not been deleted or filtered out). ■ DELETE!—The data in the delete buffer (data deleted from the DataWindow). ■ FILTER!—The data in the filter buffer (data that was filtered out).

Parameter	Description
originalvalue (optional)	A boolean indicating whether you want the original or current values for *row* and *column*: ■ TRUE—Return the original values, that is, the values initially retrieved from the database. ■ FALSE—(Default) Return the current values. If you specify *dwbuffer*, you must also specify *originalvalue*.

Return value

Date. Returns NULL if the column value is NULL. Returns 1900-01-01 if an error occurs.

Usage

Use GetItemDate when you want to get information from the DataWindow's buffers. When you want to find out what the user entered in the current column before that data is accepted, use GetText.

To access a row in the original buffer, specify the buffer that the row currently occupies (primary, delete, or filter) and the number of the row in that buffer. When you specify TRUE for *originalvalue*, the function gets the original data for that row from the original buffer.

An execution error occurs when the data type of the DataWindow column does not match the data type of the function; in this case date.

Examples

These statements set HireDate to the current Date data in the third row of the primary buffer in the column named first_day of dw_employee:

```
Date HireDate
HireDate = dw_employee.GetItemDate(3, "first_day")
```

These statements set HireDate to the current Date data in the third row of the filter buffer in the column named first_day of dw_employee:

```
Date HireDate
HireDate = dw~employee.GetItem(LDate(3, "first_day", Filter1)
```

These statements set HireDate to original Date data in the third row of the primary buffer in the column named hdate of dw_employee:

```
Date HireDate
HireDate = dw_employee.GetItemDate(3, "hdate", Primary !, TRUE)
```

GetItemDecimal

Description

Gets data whose type is Decimal from the specified buffer of a DataWindow control. You can obtain the data that was originally retrieved and stored in the database from the original buffer, as well as the current value in the primary, delete, or filter buffers.

Applies to
DataWindow controls and child DataWindows

Syntax
datawindowname.GetItemDecimal (*row, column* &
  {, *dwbuffer, originalvalue* })

Parameter	Description
datawindowname	The name of the DataWindow control or child DataWindow in which you want to obtain the decimal data contained in a specific row and column.
row	A long identifying the row location of the data.
column	The column location of the data. The data type of the column must be date. *Column* can be a column number (integer) or a column name (string). **Tip** To get the contents of a computed field, specify the name of the computed field for *column*. Computed fields do not have numbers.
dwbuffer (optional)	A value of the dwBuffer enumerated data type identifying the DataWindow buffer from which you want to get the data: ■ PRIMARY!—(Default) The data in the primary buffer (the data that has not been deleted or filtered out). ■ DELETE!—The data in the delete buffer (data deleted from the DataWindow). ■ FILTER!—The data in the filter buffer (data that was filtered out).
originalvalue (optional)	A boolean indicating whether you want the original or current values for *row* and *column*: ■ TRUE—Return the original values, that is, the values initially retrieved from the database. ■ FALSE—(Defiult) Return the current values. If you specify *dwbuffer*, you must also specify *originalvalue*.

Return value
Decimal. Returns NULL if the column value is NULL. Returns 0 if an error occurs.

Usage
Use GetItemDecimal when you want to get information from the DataWindow's buffers. When you want to find out what the user entered in the current column before that data is accepted, use GetText.

To access a row in the original buffer, specify the buffer that the row currently occupies (primary, delete, or filter) and the number of the row in that buffer. When you specify TRUE for originalvalue, the function gets the original data for that row from the original buffer.

NOTE

An execution error occurs when the data type of the DataWindow column does not match the data type of the function, in this case a decimal data type.

GETITEMSTRING   APPENDIX C FUNCTION REFERENCE **445**

Examples   These statements set salary_amt to the current decimal data in the primary
                     buffer for row 4 of the column named emp_salary of dw_employee:

```
decimal salary_amt
salary_amt = dw_employee.GetItemDecmnal(4, "emp_salary")
```

These statements set salary_amt to the current decimal data in the filter
buffer for row 4 of the column named emp_salary of dw_employee:

```
decimal salary_amt
salary_amt = dw_employee.GetItemDecimal (4, "emp_salary", Filter!)
```

These statements set salary_amt to the original decimal data in the primary buffer for row 4 of the column named emp_salary of dw_employee:

```
decimal salary_amt
salary_amt = dw_employee.GetItemDecimal(4,"emp_salary", &
  Primary!, TRUE)
```

GetItemString

Description   Gets data whose type is String from the specified buffer of a DataWindow
                     control. You can obtain the data that was originally retrieved and stored in
                     the database from the original buffer, as well as the current value in the pri-
                     mary, delete, or filter buffers.

Applies to   DataWindow controls and child DataWindows

Syntax   *datawindowname*.GetItemString (*row, column* &
                       {, *dwbuffer, originalvalue* })

Parameter	Description
datawindowname	The name of the DataWindow control or child DataWindow in which you want to obtain the string data contained in a specific row and column.
row	A long identifying the row location of the data.
column	The column location of the data. The data type of the column must he date. *Column* can be a column number (integer) or a column name (string). **Tip** To get the contents of a computed field, specify the name of the computed field for *column*. Computed fields do not have numbers.

446 APPENDIX C FUNCTION REFERENCE

GetItemString

Parameter	Description
dwbuffer (optional)	A value of the dwBuffer enumerated data type identifying the DataWindow buffer from which you want to get the data: ■ PRIMARY!—(Default) The data in the primary buffer (the data that has not been deleted or filtered out). ■ DELETE!—The data in the delete buffer (data deleted from the DataWindow). ■ FILTER!—The data in the filter buffer (data that was filtered out).
originalvalue (optional)	A boolean indicating whether you want the original or current values for *row* and *column*: ■ TRUE—Return the original values, that is, the values initially retrieved from the database. ■ FALSE—(Defiult) Return the current values. If you specify *dwbuffer*, you must also specify *originalvalue*.

Return value

String. Returns NULL if the column value is NULL. Returns the empty string ("") if an error occurs.

Usage

Use GetItemString when you want to get information from the DataWindow's buffers. When you want to find out what the user entered in the current column before that data is accepted, use GetText.

To access a row in the original buffer, specify the buffer that the row currently occupies (primary, delete, or filter) and the number of the row in that buffer. When you specify TRUE for *originalvalue*, the function gets the original data for that row from the original buffer.

An execution error occurs when the data type of the DataWindow column does not match the data type of the function, in this case String.

Examples

These statements set LName to the current string in the primary buffer for row 3 of in the column named emp_name in the DataWindow dw_employee:

```
String LName
LName = dw_employee.GetItemString(3, "emp_name")
```

These statements set LName to the current string in the delete buffer for row 3 of the column named emp_name of dw_employee:

```
String LName
LName = dw_employee.GetItemString(3, "emp_name", Delete!)
```

The following statements set LName to the original string in the delete buffer for row 3 of the column named emp_name of dw_employee:

```
String LName
LNane = dw_employee.GetItemString(3, "emp_name", Delete!, TRUE)
```

GetItemTime

Description   Gets data whose type is Time from the specified buffer of a DataWindow control. You can obtain the data that was originally retrieved and stored in the database from the original buffer, as well as the current value in the primary, delete, or filter buffers.

Applies to   DataWindow controls and child DataWindows

Syntax
datawindowname.GetItemTime (*row, column* &
    {, *dwbuffer, originalvalue* })

Parameter	Description
datawindowname	The name of the DataWindow control or child DataWindow in which you want to obtain the time data contained in a specific row and column.
row	A long identifying the row location of the data.
column	The column location of the data. The data type of the column must be date. *Column* can be a column number (integer) or a column name (string). **Tip** To get the contents of a computed field, specify the name of the computed field for *column*. Computed fields do not have numbers.
dwbuffer (optional)	A value of the dwBuffer enumerated data type identifying the DataWindow buffer from which you want to get the data: ■ PRIMARY!—(Default) The data in the primary buffer (the data that has not been deleted or filtered out). ■ DELETE!—The data in the delete buffer (data deleted from the DataWindow). ■ FILTER!—The data in the filter buffer (data that was filtered out).
originalvalue (optional)	A boolean indicating whether you want the original or current values for *row* and *column*: ■ TRUE—Return the original values, that is, the values initially retrieved from the database. ■ FALSE—(Defiult) Return the current values. If you specify *dwbuffer*, you must also specify *originalvalue*.

Return value   Time. Returns NULL if the column value is NULL. Returns 00:00:00.000000 if an error occurs.

Usage

Use GetItemTime when you want to get information from the DataWindow's buffers. When you want to find out what the user entered in the current column before that data is accepted, use GetText.

To access a row in the original buffer, specify the buffer that the row currently occupies (primary, delete, or filter) and the number of the row in that buffer. When you specify TRUE for *originalvalue*, the function gets the original data for that row from the original buffer.

An execution error occurs when the data type of the DataWindow column does not match the data type of the function, in this case time.

Examples

These statements set Start to the current Time data in the primary buffer for row 3 of the column named title in dw_employee:

```
Time Start
Start = dw_employee.GetItemTime(3, "title")
```

These statements set Start to the current Time data in the filter buffer for row 3 of the column named start_time of dw_employee:

```
Time Start
Start = dw_employee.GetItemTime(3, "start_time", Filter!)
```

These statements set Start to the original Time data in the primary buffer for row 3 of the column named start_time of dw_employee:

```
Time Start
Start = dw_employee.GetItemTime(3, "start_time", Primary!, TRUE)
```

GetRow

Description

Reports the number of the current row in a DataWindow control.

Applies to

DataWindow controls and child DataWindows

Syntax

datawindowname.GetRow()

Parameter	Description
datawindowname	The name of the DataWindow control or the child DataWindow for which you want the number of the current row

Return value

Long. Returns the number of the current row in datawindowname. Returns 0 if no row is current and -1 if an error occurs.

The current row is not always a row displayed on the screen. For example, if the cursor is on row 7 column 2 and the user uses the scroll bar to scroll to row 50, the current row remains row 7 unless the user clicks row 50.

Example

This statement returns the number of the current row in dw_Employee:

```
dw_employee.GetRow( )
```

InsertRow

Description

Inserts a row in a DataWindow. If any columns have default values, the row is initialized with these values before it is displayed.

Applies to

DataWindow controls and child DataWindows

Syntax

datawindowname.InsertRow (*row*)

Parameter	Description
datawindowname	The name of the DataWindow control or child DataWindow in which you want to insert a row
row	A long identifying the row before which you want to insert the row. To insert a row at the end, specify 0.

Return value

Long. Returns the number of the row that was added if it succeeds and -1 if an error occurs.

Usage

InsertRow simply inserts the row without changing the display or the current row. To scroll to the row and make it the current row, call ScrollToRow. To simply make it the current row, call SetRow.

Examples

This statement inserts an initialized row before row 7 in dw_Employee:

```
dw_Employee. InsertRow( 7)
```

This example inserts an initialized row after the last row in dw_employee, then scrolls to the row, which makes it current:

```
long ll_newrow
ll_newrow = dw_employee.InsertRow(0)
dw_employee. ScrollToRow( ll_newrow)
```

IsDate

Description

Tests whether a string value is a valid date.

Syntax

IsDate (*datevalue*)

Parameter	Description
datevalue	A string whose value you want to test to determine whether it is a valid date

Return value

Boolean. Returns TRUE if *datevalue* is a valid date and FALSE if it is not.

Usage

You can use IsDate to test whether a user-entered date is valid before you convert it to a date data type. To convert a value into a date value, use the Date function.

Examples

This statement returns TRUE:

```
IsDate("Jan 1, 95~)
```

This statement returns FALSE:

```
IsDate('Jan 32, 1997')
```

If the SingleLineEdit sle_Date_Of_Hire contains 7/1/91, these statements store 1991-07-O1 in HireDate:

```
Date HireDate
IF IsDate(sle_Date_Of_Hire.text) THEN
  HireDate = Date(sle_Date_Of_Hire.text)
END IF
```

Len

Description

Reports the length of a string or a blob.

Syntax

Len (*stringorblob*)

Parameter	Description
stringorblob	The string or blob for which you want the length

Return value

Long. Returns a long whose value is the length of *stringorblob* if it succeeds and -1 if an error occurs.

Usage

Len counts the number of characters in a string. The NULL that terminates a string is not included in the count.

If you specify a size when you declare a blob, that is the size reported by Len. If you don't specify a size for the blob, PowerBuilder assigns it a size the first time you assign data to the blob, which becomes the size reported by Len. Initially, Len reports that the blob's length is 0.

Examples

This statement returns 0:

```
Len("")
```

These statements store in the variable s_address_len the length of the text in the SingleLineEdit slc_address:

```
long s_address_len
s_address_len = Len(sle_address.Text)
```

The following scenarios illustrate how the declaration of blobs affects their length, as reported by Len.

In the first example, an instance variable called ib_blob is declared but not initialized with a size. If you call Len before data is assigned to ib_blob Len returns 0. After data is assigned, Len returns the blob's new length.

The declaration of the instance variable is:

```
blob ib_blob
```

The sample code is:

```
long ll_len
ll_len = Len(ib_blob)   // ll_len set to 0
ib_blob = Blob ("Test String")
ll_len = Len(ib_blob)   // ll_len set to 11
```

In the second example, ib_blob is initialized to the size 100 when it is declared. When you call Len for ib_blob, it always returns 100. This example uses BlobEdit, instead of Blob, to assign data to the blob because its size is already established. The declaration of the instance variable is:

```
blob{100} ib_blob
```

The sample code is:

```
long ll_len
ll_len = Len(ib_blob)   // ll_len set to 100
BlobEdit(ib_blob, 1, "Test String")
ll_len = Len(ib_blob)   // ll_len set to 100
```

Long

Description Converts data into data of type long. There are two syntaxes:

- To combine two unsigned integers into a long value, use Syntax 1.
- To convert a string whose value is a number into a long or to obtain a long value stored in a blob, use Syntax 2.

Syntax 1 Long (*lowword, highword*)

Parameter	Description
lowword	An UnsignedInteger to be the low word in the long
highword	An UnsignedInteger to be the high word in the long

Return value 1 Long. Returns the long if it succeeds and -1 if an error occurs.

Syntax 2

Long (*stringorblob*)

Parameter	Description
stringorblob	The string you want returned as a long or a blob in which the first value is the long value. The rest of the contents of the blob is ignored.

Return value 2

Long. Returns the value of *stringorblob* as a long if it succeeds and 0 if *stringorblob* is not a valid PowerScript number.

Usage

Use Syntax 1 to pass values to external C functions or to specify a value for the LongParm attribute of PowerBuilder's Message object.

To distinguish between a string whose value is the number 0 and a string whose value is not a number when using Syntax 2, use the IsNumber function before calling the Long function.

Examples

These statements convert the Unsignedintegers nLow and nHigh into a long value:

```
Unsignedint nLow   //Low integer 16 bits
UnsignedInt nHigh  //High integer 16 bits
long Lvalue    //Long value 32 bits

nLow = 12345
nHigh = 0
Lvalue = Long(nLow, nHigh)
MessageBox("Long Value", Lvalue)
```

This statement returns 2167899876 as a long:

```
Long("2167899876")
```

Syntax 2

After assigning blob data from the database to lb_blob, the following example obtains the long value stored at position 20 in the blob:

```
long lb_num
lb_num = Long(BlobMid(lb_blob, 20, 4))
```

MessageBox

Description

Displays a system MessageBox with the title, text, icon, and buttons you specify.

Syntax

MessageBox (*title*, *text* {, *icon* {, *button* {, *default*} }})

Parameter	Description
title	A string specifying the title of the message box, which appears in the box's title bar.
text	The text you want to display in the message box. The text can be a numeric data type, a string, or a boolean value.

Parameter	Description
icon (optional)	A value of the long enumerated data type indicating the icon you want to display on the left side of the message box. Values are: ■ Information! (Default) ■ StopSign! ■ Exclamation! ■ Question! ■ None!
button (optional)	A value of the Button enumerated data type indicating the set of CommandButtons you want to display at the bottom of the message box. The buttons are numbered in the order listed in the enumerated data type. Values are: ■ OK! (Default) OK button ■ OKCancel! OK and Cancel buttons ■ YesNo! - Yes and No buttons ■ YesNoCancel! Yes, No, and Cancel buttons ■ RetryCancel! Retry and Cancel buttons ■ AbortRetryIgnore! Abort, Retry, and Ignore buttons
default (optional)	The number of the button you want to be the default button. The default is 1. If you specify a number larger than the number of buttons displayed, MessageBox uses the default.

Return value

Returns the number of the selected button (1, 2, or 3) if it succeeds and -1 if an error occurs.

Usage

If the value of title or text is NULL, the MessageBox does not display.

Unless you specify otherwise, PowerBuilder continues executing the script when the user clicks the button or presses ENTER, which is appropriate when the MessageBox has one button. If the box has multiple buttons, you will need to include code in the script that checks the return value and takes an appropriate action.

Before continuing with the current application, the user must respond to the MessageBox. However, the user can switch to another application without responding to the MessageBox.

When MessageBox doesn't work (Windows 3.1 only)

Controls capture the mouse in order to perform certain operations For instance, CommandButtons capture during mouse clicks, Edit controls capture for text selection, and scrollbars capture during scrolling. If a MessageBox is invoked while the mouse is captured, Windows becomes unstable. Therefore PowerBuilder won't display a MessageBox in the ScrollVertical and ScrollHorizontal events and in similar situations. Instead, you can display text in a text control or in the window's title. (Note: Although the mouse is captured during clicking, the click is complete when the Clicked event script is run, so MessageBox works.)

Because MessageBox grabs focus, you should not use it when focus is changing, such as in a LoseFocus event. Instead, you might display a message in the window's title or a MultiLineEdit.

Examples

This statement displays a MessageBox with the title Greeting, the text Hello User, the default icon (Information!), and the default button (the OK button):

```
MessageBox("Greeting", "Hello User")
```

The following statements display a Message Box titled Result and containing the result of a function, the Exclamation icon, and the OK and Cancel buttons (the Cancel button is the default):

```
integer Net
long Distance = 3.457

Net = MessageBox("Result ", Abs(Distance),  Exclamation!, &
   OKCancel!, 2)
IF Net = 1 THEN
...   // Process OK.
ELSE
...   // Process CANCEL.
END IF
```

ModifiedCount

Description

Reports the number rows that have been modified but not updated in a DataWindow.

Applies to

DataWindow controls and child DataWindows

Syntax

datawindowname.ModifiedCount ( )

Parameter	Description
datawindowname	The name of the DataWindow control or child DataWindow for which you want the number of rows that have been modified but not updated in the associated database table

Return value

Long. Returns the number of rows that have been modified in the primary buffer. Returns 0 if no rows have been modified or if all modified rows have been updated in the database table. Returns -1 if an error occurs.

Usage

ModifiedCount reports the number of modified rows in the primary buffer. If a row is modified and then filtered out, PowerBuilder no longer includes it in the count. If the data is filtered again so that the row returns to the primary buffer, PowerBuilder then includes it in the count.

The DeletedCount function counts the number of rows in the deleted buffer. The RowCount function counts the total number of rows in the primary buffer.

Examples

If five rows in dw_Employee have been modified but not updated in the associated database table or filtered out of the primary buffer, the following code sets ll_Rows equal to 5:

```
long ll_Rows ll_Rows = dw_Employee.ModifiedCount( )
```

If any rows in dw_Employee have been modified but not updated in the associated database table, this statement updates the database table associated with the dw_employee DataWindow control:

```
IF dw_employee.ModifiedCount( ) > 0 THEN dw employee.Update()
```

Month

Description

Determines the month of a date value.

Syntax

Month (*date*)

Parameter	Description
date	The date from which you want the month

Return value

Integer. Returns an integer (1 to 12) whose value is the month portion of date.

Examples

This statement returns 1:

```
Month(1994-01-31)
```

These statements store in start_month the month entered in the SingleLine-Edit sle_start_date:

```
integer start_month
start_month = Month(date(sle_start_date.Text )
```

Open

Description

Opens a window or an OLE object.

For windows, Open displays a window and makes all its attributes and controls available to scripts. There are two syntaxes:

- To open an instance of a particular window data type, use Syntax 1.
- To allow the application to select the window's data type when the script is executed, use Syntax 2.

For OLE objects, Open loads an OLE object contained in a file or storage into an OLE 2.0 control or storage object variable. The source and the target are now connected for the purposes of saving work. There are several syntaxes:

- To open an OLE object in a file and load it into an OLE 2.0 control, use Syntax 3.
- To open an OLE object in a storage object in memory and load it into an OLE 2.0 control, use Syntax 4.
- To open an OLE object in an OLE storage file and load it into a storage object in memory, use Syntax 5.
- To open an OLE object that is a member of an open OLE storage and load it into a storage object in memory, use Syntax 6.
- To open a stream in an OLE storage object in memory and load it into a stream object, use Syntax 7.

Applies to

(Syntax 1 and 2) Window objects
(Syntax 3 and 4) OLE 2.0 controls
(Syntax 5 and 6) OLE storage objects
(Syntax 7) OLE stream objects

Syntax 1

`Open (windowvar {,parent})`

Parameter	Description
windowvar	The name of the window you want to display. You can specify a window object defined in the Window painter (which is a window data type) or a variable of the desired window data type. Open places a reference to the opened window in windowvar.
parent (child and popup windows only)	The window you want make the parent of the child or popup window you are opening. If you open a child or popup window and omit parent, PowerBuilder associates the window being opened with the currently active window.

Return value 1

Integer. Returns 1 if it succeeds and -1 if an error occurs.

Syntax 2

`Open (windowvar, windowtype {,parent})`

Parameter	Description
windowvar	A window variable, usually of data type window. Open places a reference to the opened window in windowvar.
windowtype	A string whose value is the data type of the window you want to open. The data type of windowtype must be the same or a descendant of windowvar.
parent (child and popup windows only)	The window you want to make the parent of the child or popup window you are opening. If you open a child or popup window and omit parent, PowerBuilder associates the window being opened with the currently active window.

Return value 2

Integer. Returns 1 if it succeeds and -1 if an error occurs.

Syntax 3

`ole2control.Open ( OLEsourcefile )`

Parameter	Description
ole2control	The name of the OLE 2.0 control into which you want to load an OLE object.
OLEsourcefile	A string specifying the name of an OLE storage file containing the object. The file must already exist and contain an OLE 2.0 object. OLEsourcefile can include a path for the file, as well as path information inside the OLE storage.

Return value 3

Integer. Returns 0 if it succeeds and one of the following negative values if an error occurs:

- -1   The file is not found or its data has an invalid format
- -9   Other error

Syntax 4

`ole2control.Open ( sourcestorage, substoragename )`

Parameter	Description
ole2control	The name of the OLE 2.0 control into which you want to load an OLE object.
sourcestorage	The name of an object variable of OLEStorage containing the object you want to load into ole2control.
substoragename	A string specifying the name of a substorage that contains the desired object within storagename.

Return value 4

Integer. Returns 0 if it succeeds and one of the following negative values if an error occurs:

- -2   The parent storage is not open
- -9   Other error

Syntax 5

`olestorage.Open ( OLEsourcefile {, readmode {, sharemode }} )`

Parameter	Description
olestorage	The name of an object variable of type OLEStorage into which you want to load the OLE object.
OLEsourcefile	A string specifying the name of an OLE storage file containing the object. The file must already exist and contain OLE 2.0 objects. *OLEsourcefile* can include the file's path, as well as path information within the storage.

Parameter	Description
readmode (optional)	A value of the enumerated data type stgReadMode that specifies the type of access you want for OLEsourcefile. Values are: ■ stgReadWrite!—(Default) Read/write access. If the file does not exist, Open creates it. ■ stgRead!—Read-only access. You can't change *OLEsourcefile*. ■ stgWrite!—Write access. You can rewrite *OLEsourcefile* but not read its current contents. If the file does not exist, Open creates it.
sharemode (optional)	A value of the enumerated data type stgShareMode that specifies how other attempts, by your own or other applications, to open *OLEsourcefile* will fare. Values are: ■ stgExclusive!—(Default) No other attempt to open *OLEsourcefile* will succeed. ■ stgDenyNone!—Any other attempt to open *OLEsourcefile* will succeed. ■ stgDenyRead!—Other attempts to open *OLEsourcefile* for reading will fail. ■ stgDenyWrite—Other attempts to open *OLEsourcefile* for writing will fail.

Return value 5

Integer. Returns 0 if it succeeds and one of the following negative values if an error occurs:

- -1 The file is not an OLE 2.0 storage file
- -3 The file is not found
- -9 Other error

Syntax 6

`olestorage.Open ( substoragename, readmode, sharemode, sourcestorage )`

Parameter	Description
olestorage	The name of an object variable of type OLEStorage into which you want to load the OLE object.
substoragename	A string specifying the name of the storage member within sourcestorage that you want to open. Note the reversed order of the *sourcestorage* and *substoragename* arguments from Syntax 4.

Parameter	Description
readmode	A value of the enumerated data type stgReadMode that specifies the type of access you want for *substoragename*. Values are: ■ stgReadWrite!—Read/write access. If the member does not exist, Open creates it. ■ stgRead!—Read-only access. You can't change *substoragename*. ■ stgWrite!—Write access. You can rewrite *substoragename* but not read its current contents. If the member does not exist, Open creates it.
sharemode	A value of the enumerated data type stgShareMode that specifies how other attempts, by your own or other applications, to open *substoragename* will fare. Values are: ■ stgExclusive!—(Default) No other attempt to open *substoragename* will succeed. ■ stgDenyRead!—Other attempts to open *substoragename* for reading will fail. ■ stgDenyWrite—Other attempts to open *substoragename* for writing will fail.
sourcestorage	An open OLEStorage object containing *substoragename*.

Return value 6

Integer. Returns 0 if it succeeds and one of the following negative values if an error occurs:

- -2   The parent storage is not open
- -3   The member is not found (when opened for reading)
- -9   Other error

Syntax 7

olestream.Open (*sourcestorage, streamname* {, *readmode* {, *sharemode* } })

Parameter	Description
olestream	The name of an object variable of type OLEStream into which you want to load the OLE object.
sourcestorage	An OLE storage that contains the stream to be opened.
streamname	A string specifying the name of the stream within *sourcestorage* that you want to open.
readmode (optional)	A value of the enumerated data type stgReadMode that specifies the type of access you want for *streamname*. Values are: ■ stgReadWrite!—Read/write access. If *streamname* does not exist, Open creates it. ■ stgRead!—Read-only access. You can't change *streamname*. ■ stgWrite!—Write access. You can rewrite *streamname* but not read its current contents. If *streamname* does not exist, Open creates it.

Parameter	Description
sharemode (optional)	A value of the enumerated data type stgShareMode that specifies how other attempts, by your own or other applications, to open *streamname* will fare. Values are: ■ stgExclusive!—No other attempt to open *streamname* will succeed. ■ stgDenyNone!—Any other attempt to open *streamname* will succeed. ■ stgDenyRead!—Other attempts to open *streamname* for reading will fail. ■ stgDenyWrite—Other attempts to open *streamname* for writing will fail.

Return value 7

Integer. Returns 0 if it succeeds and one of the following negative values if an error occurs:

- -1 Stream not found
- -2 Stream already exists
- -3 Stream is already open
- -4 Storage not open
- -5 Access denied
- -6 Invalid name
- -9 Other error

Usage

You must open a window before you can access the attributes of the window. If you access the window's attributes before you open it, an execution error will occur.

To reference an open window in scripts, use *windowvar*.

Tip for Syntax 1: If you call Syntax 1 of the Open function twice for the same window, PowerBuilder activates the window twice; it does not open two instances of the window.

When you use Syntax 2, the window object specified in *windowtype* must be the same data type as *windowvar* (the data type includes data types inherited from it). The data type of *windowvar* is usually window, from which all windows are inherited, but it can be any ancestor of *windowtype*. If it is not the same type, an execution error will occur.

Use Syntax 2 to open an array of windows when each window in the array will have a different data type. See the last example, in which the window data types are stored in one array and are used for the *windowtype* argument when each window in another array is opened.

Tips for Syntax 2: When you use Syntax 2, PowerBuilder opens an instance of a window of the data type specified in windowtype and places a reference to this instance in the variable windowvar.

If windowtype is a descendant window, you can only reference attributes, events, functions, or structures that are part of the definition of windowvar. For example, if a user event is declared for windowtype, you cannot reference it.

The object specified in windowtype is not automatically included in your executable application. To include it, you must save it in a PBD file (PowerBuilder dynamic library) that you deliver with your application.

Parent windows for the opened window

Generally, if you are opening a child or a popup window and specify *parent*, the window identified by *parent* is the parent of the opened window (*windowname* or *windowvar*). When a parent window is closed, all its child and popup windows are closed too.

Not all types of windows can be parent windows. Only a window whose borders are not confined within another window can be a parent. A child window or a window opened as a sheet cannot be a parent. If you specify a "confined" window as a parent, PowerBuilder will check its parent, and that window's parent, until it finds a window that it can use as a parent. Therefore if you open a popup window and specify a sheet as its parent, PowerBuilder will make the MDI frame that contains the sheet its parent.

If you don't specify a parent for a child or popup window, the active window becomes the parent. Therefore, if one popup is active and you open another popup, the first popup is the parent, not the main window. When the first popup is closed, PowerBuilder closes the second popup too.

Remember though, that, in an MDI application, the active sheet is not the active window and cannot be the parent. In Windows, it is clear that the MDI frame, not the active sheet, is the active window—its title bar is the active color and it displays the menu. On the Macintosh, it is not obvious because the frame is not visible, but the frame is still the active window.

On the Windows platform, Windows enforces this hierarchy of parent and child windows. On the Macintosh, PowerBuilder implements the hierarchy so that cross-platform applications have the same behavior.

OLE storage files

An OLE storage file is structured like a directory. Each OLE object can contain other OLE objects (substorages) and other data (streams). You can open the members of an OLE storage belonging to a server application if you know the structure of the storage. However, PowerBuilder's functions for manipulating storages are provided so that you can build your own storage files for organizing the OLE objects used in your applications.

The whole file can be an OLE object and substorages within the file can also be OLE objects. More frequently, the structure for a storage file you create is a root level that is not an OLE object but contains independent OLE objects as substorages. Any level in the storage hierarchy can contain OLE objects or be simply a repository for another level of substorages.

Opening nested objects: Because you can specify path information within an OLE storage with a backslash as the separator, you can open a deeply nested object with a single call to Open. However, there is no error checking for the path you specify and if the Open fails, you won't know why. It is strongly recommended that you open each object in the path until you get to the one you want.

Examples

This statement opens an instance of a window named w_employee:

```
Open(w_employee)
```

The following statements open an instance of a window of the type w_employee:

```
w_employee w_to_open
Open(w_to_open)
```

The following code opens an instance of a window of the type child named cw_data and makes w_employee the parent:

```
child cw_data
Open(cw_data, w_employee)
```

The following code opens two windows of type w_emp:

```
w_emp w_e1, w_e2
Opein (w_e1)
Open (w_e2)
```

Syntax 2

This example opens a window of the type specified in the string s_w_name and stores the reference to the window in the variable w_to_open. The SELECT statement retrieves data specifying the window type from the database and stores it in s_w name.

```
window  w_to_open
string  s_w name

SELECT next_window INTO :s_w_name FROM routing_table WHERE . . .;
Open(w_to_open, W_w_name)
```

This example opens an array of ten windows of the type specified in the string is_w_empl and assigns a title to each window in the array. The string is_w_empl is an instance variable whose value is a window type:

```
integer n
window Win_array[10]

FOR n = 1 to 10
  open(win_array[n], is_w_empl)
  win_array[n].title = "Window " + string(n)
NEXT
```

The following statements open four windows. The type of each window is stored in the array w_stock_type. The window reference from the Open function is assigned to elements in the arrow w_stock_win:

```
window w_stock_win[ ]
String w stock-type14]

w_stock_type[1] = "w_stock_wine"
w_stock_type[2] = "w_stock_scotch"
w_stock_type[3] = "w_stock_beer"
w_stock_type[4] = "w_stock_soda"

FOR n = 1 to 4
  open(w_stock win[n], w_stock_type[n])
NEXT
```

| Syntax 3 | This example opens the object in the file MYSTUFF.OLE in the control ole_1.<br><br>```
integer result
result = ole_1.open("c:\ole2\mystuff.ole")
``` |
| Syntax 4 | This example opens the object in the substorage excel_obj within the storage variable stg_stuff and loads it into the control ole_1. Olest_stuff is already open:<br><br>```
integer result
result = ole_1.Open(stg_stuff, "excel_obj")
```<br><br>This example opens a substorage in the storage variable stg_stuff and loads it into the control ole_1. The substorage name is specified in the variable stuff_1. Olest_stuff is already open:<br><br>```
integer result
string stuff_1 = "excel_obj"
result = ole_1.Open(stg_stuff, stuff_1)
``` |
| Syntax 5 | This example opens the object in the file MYSTUFF.OLE and loads it into the OLEStorage variable stg_stuff:<br><br>```
integer result
OLEStorage stg_stuff

stg_stuff = CREATE OLEStorage
result = stg_stuff.Open("c:\ole2\mystuff.ole")
```<br><br>This example opens the same object for reading:<br><br>```
integer result
OLEStorage stg_stuff

stg_stuff = CREATE OLEStorage
result = stg_stuff.Open("c:\ole2\mystuff.ole", stgRead!)
``` |
| Syntax 5 and 6 | This example opens the object in the file MYSTUFF.OLE and loads it into the OLEStorage variable stg_stuff, as in the previous example. Then it opens the substorage drawing_1 into a second storage variable. (This example does not include code to close and destroy any of the objects that were opened):<br><br>```
integer result
OLEStorage stg_stuff, stg_drawing

stg_stuff = CREATE OLEStorage
result = stg_stuff.Open("c:\ole2\mystuff.ole")

IF result >= 0 THEN
  stg_drawing = CREATE OLEStorage
  result = opest_drawing.Open("drawing_1", stgRead!, &
    stgDenyNone!, stg_stuff) END IF
``` |

Syntax 5 and 7

This example opens the object in the file MYSTUFF.OLE and loads it into the OLEStorage variable stg_stuff. Then it checks whether a stream called info exists in the OLE object, and if so, opens it with read access. (This example does not include code to close and destroy any of the objects that were opened):

```
integer result
boolean str_found
OLEStorage stg_stuff
OLEStream mystream

stg_stuff = CREATE OLEStorage
result = stg_stuff.Open("c:\ole2\mystuff.ole")
IF result < 0 THEN RETURN

result = stg_stuff.MemberExists("info", str_found)
IF result < 0 THEN RETURN

IF str_found THEN
  mystream = CREATE OLEStream
  result = mystream.Open(stg_stuff, "info",  stgRead!, stgDenyNone!)
  IF result < 0 THEN RETURN
END IF
```

OpenWithParm

Description

Displays a window and makes all its attributes and controls available to scripts, as Open does. OpenWithParm also stores a parameter in the system's Message object so that it is accessible to the opened window.

There are two syntaxes. Syntax 1 opens an instance of a particular window data type. Syntax 2 allows the application to select the window's data type when the script is executed.

Applies to

Window objects

Syntax 1

OpenWithParm (*windowvar*, *parameter* {, *parent*})

Parameter	Description
windowvar	The name of the window you want to display. You can specify a window object defined in the Window painter (which is a window data type) or a variable of the desired window data type. Open places a reference to the open window in *windowvar*.
parameter	The parameter you want to store in the Message object when the window is opened. Parameter must have one of these data types: ■ String ■ Numeric ■ PowerObject

OPENWITHPARM

APPENDIX C FUNCTION REFERENCE **465**

Parameter	Description
parent (child and popup windows only)	The window you want make the parent of the child or popup window you are opening. If you open a child or popup window and omit *parent*, PowerBuilder associates the window being opened with the currently active window.

Return value 1   Integer. Returns 1 if it succeeds and -1 if an error occurs.

Syntax 2   OpenWithParm (*windowvar, parameter, windowtype* {, *parent* })

Parameter	Description
windowvar	A window variable, usually of data type window. Open places a reference to the open window in *windowvar*.
parameter	The parameter you want to store in the Message object when the window is opened. *Parameter* must have one of these data types: ■ String ■ Numeric ■ PowerObject
windowtype	A string whose value is the data type of the window you want to open. The data type of *windowtype* must be the same or a descendant of *windowvar*.
parent (child and popup windows only)	The window you want to make the parent of the child or popup window you are opening. If you open a child or popup window and omit *parent*, PowerBuilder associates the window being opened with the currently active window.

Return value 2   Integer. Returns 1 if it succeeds and -1 if an error occurs.

Usage   The system Message object has three attributes for storing data. Depending on the data type of the parameter specified for OpenWithParm, your scripts for the opened window would check one of the following attributes.

Message object attribute	Parameter data type
Message.DoubleParm	Numeric
Message.PowerObjectParm	PowerObject (PowerBuilder objects, including user-defined structures)
Message.StringParm	String

In the opened window, it is a good idea to access the value passed in the Message object right away because some other script may use the Message object for another purpose.

Avoiding null object references: *When you pass a PowerObject as a parameter, you are passing a reference to the object. The object must exist when you refer to it later or you will get a null object reference. For example, if you pass the name of a control on a window that is being closed, that control will not exist when a script accesses the parameter.*

Passing several values as a structure: *To pass several values, create a user-defined structure to hold the values and access the PowerObjectParm attribute of the Message object in the opened window. The structure is passed by value, not by reference, so you can access the information even if the original structure has been destroyed.*

Examples

This statement opens an instance of a window named w_employee and stores the string parameter in Message.StringParm. The script for the window's Open event uses the string parameter as the text of a StaticText control st_empname. The script that opens the window has the following statement:

```
OpenWithParm(w_employee, "James Newton")
```

The window's Open event script has the following statement:

```
st_empname.Text = Message.StringParm
```

The following statements open an instance of a window of the type w_to_open. Since the parameter is a number it is stored in Message.DoubleParm:

```
w_employee w_to_open
integer age = 50
OpenWithParm(w_to_open, age)
```

The following statement opens an instance of a child window named cw_data and makes w_employee the parent. The window w_employee must already be open. The parameter benefit_plan is a string and is stored in Message.StringParm

```
OpenWithParm(cw_data, "benefit_plan", w_employee)
```

Syntax 2

These statements open a window of the type specified in the string s_w_name and store the reference to the window in the variable w_to_open. The script gets the value of s_w_name, the type of window to open, from the database. The parameter in e_location is text, so it is stored in Message.StringParm.

```
window w_to_open
string s_w_name, e_location
e_location = sle_location.Text
SELECT next_window INTO :s_w_name
   FROM routing_table
   WHERE ... ;
OpenWithParm(w_to_open, e_location, s_w_name)
```

The following statements open a window of the type specified in the string c_w_name, store the reference to the window in the variable wc_to_open, and make w_emp the parent window of wc_to_open. The parameter is numeric, so it is stored in Message.DoubleParm:

```
window wc to_open
string c_w_name integer
age = 60

c_w_name = "w_c_emp1"

OpenWithParm(wc_to_open, age, c_w name, w_emp)
```

Print

Description

Sends data to the current printer (or spooler, if the user has a spooler set up). There are several syntaxes:

- To send the contents of a DataWindow control to the printer as a print job, use Syntax 1.
- To include a visual object, such as a window or a graph control in a print job, use Syntax 2.
- To send one or more lines of text as part of a print job, use Syntax 3. The text can be preceded or followed by tab settings, which control the text's horizontal position on the page.

Applies to

(Syntax 1) DataWindow controls and child DataWindows
(Syntax 2) Any object
(Syntax 3) Not object-specific

Syntax 1

datawindowname.Print ({ *canceldialog* })

Parameter	Description
datawindowname	The name of the DataWindow control or child DataWindow that contains the information to be printed.
canceldialog (optional)	A boolean value indicating whether you want to display a non-modal dialog that allows the user to cancel printing. Values are: ■ TRUE—(Default) Display the dialog ■ FALSE—Do not display the dialog

Return value 1

Integer. Returns 1 if it succeeds and -1 if an error occurs.

Syntax 2

objectname.Print (*printjobnumber*, *x*, *y* {, *width*, *height*})

Parameter	Description
objectname	The name of the object that you want to print. The object must either be a window or an object whose ancestor type is DragObject, which includes all the controls that you can place in a window.

Parameter	Description
printjobnumber	The number the PrintOpen function assigns to the print job.
x	An integer whose value is the x coordinate on the page of the left corner of the object, in thousandths of an inch.
y	An integer whose value is the y coordinate on the page of the left corner of the object, in thousandths of an inch.
width (optional)	An integer specifying the printed width of the object in thousandths of an inch. If omitted, PowerBuilder uses the object's original width.
height (optional)	An integer specifying the printed height of the object in thousandths of an inch. If omitted, PowerBuilder uses the object's original height.

Return value 2

Integer. Returns 1 if it succeeds and -1 if an error occurs.

Syntax 3

```
Print ( printjobnumber, { tab1, } string {, tab2 } )
```

Parameter	Description
printjobnumber	The number the PrintOpen function assigned to the print job.
tab1 (optional)	The position, measured from the left edge of the print area in thousandths of a inch, to which the print cursor should move before string is printed. If the print cursor is already at or beyond the position or if you omit *tab1*, Print starts printing at the current position of the print cursor.
string	The string you want to print. If the string includes carriage return-newline character pairs (~r~n), the string will print on multiple lines. However, the initial tab position is ignored on subsequent lines.
tab2 (optional)	The new position, measured from the left edge of the print area in thousandths of a inch, of the print cursor after string printed. If the print cursor is already at or beyond the specified position, Print ignores *tab2* and the print cursor remains at the end of the text. If you omit *tab2*, Print moves the print cursor to the beginning of a new line.

Return value 3

Integer. Returns 1 if it succeeds and -1 if an error occurs.

Usage

PowerBuilder manages print jobs by opening the job, sending data, and closing the job. When you use Syntax 1, print job management happens automatically. When you use Syntax 2 and 3, you must call the PrintOpen function and the PrintClose or PrintCancel functions yourself to manage the process.

Use Syntax 1 to print the contents of a DataWindow object. The Print function prints all the rows that have been retrieved. To print several DataWindows as a single job, don't use Print. Instead, open the print job with PrintOpen, call the PrintDataWindow function for each DataWindow, and close the job.

Events for DataWindow printing: *When you use Print for DataWindow controls, it triggers a PrintStart event just before any data is sent to the printer (or spooler), a PrintPage event for each page break, and a PrintEnd event when printing is complete.*

The PrintPage event has action codes that let you control whether the page about to be formatted is printed. You can skip the upcoming page by calling SetActionCode in the PrintPage event and setting the action code to 1.

Print cursor in a print job: *PowerBuilder uses a print cursor to keep track of the print location. The print cursor stores the coordinates of the upper-left corner of the location at which print will begin. PowerBuilder updates the print cursor after printing text with Print.*

Line spacing when printing text: *Line spacing in PowerBuilder is proportional to character height. The default line spacing is 1.2 times the character height. When Print starts a new line, it sets the x coordinate of the cursor to 0 and increases the y coordinate by the current line spacing. You can change the line spacing with the PrintSetSpacing function, which lets you specify a new factor to be multiplied by the character height.*

Because Syntax 3 of Print increments the y coordinate each time it creates a new line, it also handles page breaks automatically. When the y coordinate exceeds the page size, PowerBuilder automatically creates a new page in the print job. You don't need to call the PrintPage function, as you would if you were using the printing functions that control the cursor position (for example, PrintText or PrintLine).

Print area and margins: *The print area is the physical page size minus any margins in the printer itself. Depending on the printer, you may be able to change margins using PrintSend and printer-defined escape sequences.*

Using fonts: *You can use PrintDefineFont and PrintSetFont to specify the font used by the Print function when you are printing a string. When you use Syntax l to print a DataWindow, PowerBuilder uses the fonts and layout that appear in the DataWindow.*

Examples

This statement sends the contents of dw_employee to the current printer:

```
dw_employee.Print( )
```

Syntax 2

This example prints the CommandButton cb_close in its original size at location 500, 1000:

```
integer Job
Job = PrintOpen( )
cb_close.Print(Job, 500,1000)
PrintClose(Job)
```

Syntax 2 and 3

This example opens a print job, which defines a new page, then prints a title and a graph on the first page and a window on the second page:

```
integer Job
Job = PrintOpen( )
Print(Job, "Report of Year-to-Date Sales")
gr_sales1.Print(Job, 1000,PrintY(Job)+500, 6000,4500)
PrintPage(Job)
w_sales.Print(Job, 1000,500, 6000,4500)
PrintClose(Job)
```

Syntax 3

This example opens a print job, prints the string Powersoft Corporation in the default font, and then starts a new line:

```
integer Job

// Define a blank page and assign the job an ID
Job = PrintOpen( )

// Print the string and then start a new line
Print(Job, "Powersoft Corporation")
...
PrintClose(Job)
```

This example opens a print job, prints the string Powersoft Corporation in the default font, tabs 5 inches from the left edge of the print area but does not start a new line:

```
integer Job

// Define a blank page and assign the job an ID
Job = PrintOpen( )

// Print the string but do not start a new line
Print(Job, "Powersoft Corporation", 5000)
...
PrintClose(Job)
```

The first Print statement below tabs half an inch from the left edge of the print area, prints the string Powersoft Corporation, and then starts a new line. The second Print statement tabs one inch from the left edge of the print area, prints the string Directors:, and then starts a new line:

```
integer Job

// Define a blank page and assign the job an ID
Job = PrintOpen( )

// Print the string and start a new line
```

```
Print(Job, 500, "Powersoft Corporation")

// Tab 1 inch from the left edge and print
Print(Job, 1000, "Directors:")
...
PrintClose(Job)
```

The first Print statement below tabs half an inch from the left edge of the print area prints the string Powersoft Corporation, and then tabs 6 inches from the left edge of the print area but does not start a new line. The second Print statement prints the current date and then starts a new line:

```
integer Job

// Define a blank page and assign the job an ID
Job = PrintOpen( )

// Print string and tab 6 inches from the left edge
Print(Job, 500, "Powersoft Corporation", 6000)

// Print the current date on the same line
Print(Job, String(Today()))
...
PrintClose(Job)
```

In a window that displays a database error message in a MultiLineEdit mle_message, the following script for a Print button prints a title with the date and time and the message:

```
integer li_prt
li_prt   = PrintOpen("Database Error")

Print(li_prt, "Database error  - " &
   + String(Today(), "mm/dd/yyyy")  &
   + " - "   &
   + String(Now(), "HH:MM:SS"))
Print(li_prt, " ")
Print(li_prt, mle_message.text)

PrintClose(li_prt)
```

Real

Description

Converts a string value to a real data type or obtains a real value that is stored in a blob.

Syntax

Real (*stringorblob*)

Parameter	Description
stringorblob	The string whose value you want returned as a real value or a blob in which the first value is the real value. The rest of the contents of the blob is ignored.

Return value

Real. Returns the value of stringorblob as a real. If stringorblob is not a valid PowerScript number, Real returns 0.

Examples

This statement returns 24 as a real:

```
Real ( " 2 4 " )
```

This statement returns the contents of the SingleLineEdit sle_Temp as a real:

```
Real ( sle_Temp.Text )
```

The following example, although of no practical value, illustrates how to assign real values to a blob and how to use Real to extract those values. The two BlobEdit statements store two real values in the blob, one after the other. In the statements that use Real to extract the values, you have to know where the beginning of each real value is. Specifying the correct length in BlobMid is not important because the Real function knows how many bytes to evaluate:

```
blob{20} lb_blob
real r1, r2
integer len1, len2

len1 = BlobEdit(lb_blob, 1, 32750E0)
len2 = BlobEdit(lb_blob, len1, 43750E0)

// Extract the real value at the beginning and
// ignore the rest of the blob
r1 = Real(lb_blob)
// Extract the second real value stored in the blob
r2 = Real(BlobMid(lb_blob, len1, len2 - len1))
```

Reset

Description

Clears data from a control. There are three syntaxes, depending on the target object:

- To clear the data from a DataWindow control, use Syntax 1.
- To delete all items from a list, use Syntax 2.
- To delete all the data, and, optionally, the series and categories, from a graph, use Syntax 3.

Applies to

(Syntax 1) DataWindow controls and child DataWindows
(Syntax 2) ListBox and DropDownListBox controls
(Syntax 3) Graph controls in windows and user objects. Does not apply to graphs within DataWindow objects because their data comes directly from the DataWindow.

Syntax 1

datawindowname.Reset ( )

Parameter	Description
datawindowname	The name of the DataWindow control or child DataWindow you want to clear

RESET

APPENDIX C FUNCTION REFERENCE 473

Return value 1 Integer. Returns 1 if it succeeds and -1 if an error occurs. The return value is usually not used.

Syntax 2

```
listboxname.Reset ( )
```

Parameter	Description
listboxname	The name of the ListBox or DropDownListBox from which to delete all items

Return value 2 Integer. Returns 1 if it succeeds and -1 if an error occurs. The return value is usually not used.

Syntax 3

```
controlname.Reset ( graphresettype )
```

Parameter	Description
controlname	The name of the graph object in which you want to delete all the data values or all series and all data values
graphresetype	A value of the grResetType enumerated data type specifying whether you want to delete only data values or all series and all data values: ■ All!—Delete all series, categories, and data in *controlname* ■ Category!—Delete categories and data in *controlname* ■ Data!—Delete data in *controlname* ■ Series!—Delete the series and data in *controlname*

Return value 3 Integer. Returns 1 if it succeeds and -1 if an error occurs. The return value is usually not used.

Usage Reset (Syntax 1) is not the same as deleting rows from the DataWindow object or child DataWindow. Reset affects the application only, not the database. If you delete rows and then call the Update function, the rows are deleted from the database table associated with the DataWindow object. If you call Reset and then call Update, no changes are made to the table.

Use Syntax 3 of Reset to clear the data in a graph before you add new data.

This statement completely clears the contents of dw_employee:

Examples
```
dw_employee.Reset( )
```

Syntax 2 This statement deletes all items in the ListBox portion of ddlb_Actions:

```
ddlb_Actions.Reset( )
```

Syntax 3 This statement deletes the series and data, but leaves the categories, in the graph gr_product_data:

```
gr_product_data.Reset(Series!)
```

Retrieve

Description Retrieves rows from the database for a DataWindow control. If arguments are included, the argument values are used for the retrieval arguments in the SQL SELECT statement for the DataWindow object or child DataWindow.

Applies to DataWindow controls and child DataWindows

Syntax *datawindowname*.Retrieve ({, *argument*, *argument*. . . })

Parameter	Description
datawindowname	The name of the DataWindow control or child DataWindow that you want to cause to retrieve rows from the database.
argument (optional)	One or more values that you want to use as retrieval arguments in the SQL SELECT statement defined in *datawindowname*.

Return value Long. Returns the number of rows displayed (that is, rows in the primary buffer) if it succeeds and -1, if it fails.

Usage After rows are retrieved, the DataWindow object's filter is applied. Therefore, any retrieved rows that don't meet the filter criteria are immediately moved to the filter buffer and are not included in the return count.

Before you can retrieve rows for a DataWindow control, you must specify a transaction object with SetTransObject or SetTrans. If you use SetTransObject, you must also use an SQL CONNECT statement to establish a database connection.

Normally, when you call Retrieve, any rows that are already in the DataWindow control are discarded and replaced with the retrieved rows. You can set the action code for the RetrieveStart event to 2 to prevent this. In this case, Retrieve adds any retrieved rows to the ones that are already in the DataWindow's buffers. (See the last example.)

Events Retrieve may trigger these events:

- DBError
- RetrieveEnd
- RetrieveRow
- RetrieveStart

Examples This statement causes dw_empl to retrieve rows from the database:

```
dw_emp 1 . Retrieve ()
```

This example illustrates how to set up a connection and then retrieve rows in the DataWindow control. A typical scenario is to establish the connection in the application's Open event and to retrieve rows in the Open event for the window that contains the DataWindow control.

The following is a script for the application open event. SQLCA is the default transaction object. The ProfileString function is getting information about the database connection from an initialization file:

```
// Set up Transaction object from the INI file
SQLCA.DBMS = ProfileString("PB.INI", &
  "Database", "DBMS", " ") SQLCA.DbParm = ProfileString("PB.INI", &
  "Database", "DbParm", " ")

// Connect to database
CONNECT USING SQLCA;

// Test whether the connect succeeded
IF SQLCA.SQLCode <> 0 THEN
  MessageBox("Connect Failed", &
   "Cannot connect to database. " + SQLCA.SQLErrText)
  RETURN
END IF
Open(w_main)
```

To continue the example, the open event for w_main sets the transaction object for the DataWindow control dw_main to SQLCA and retrieves rows from the database. If no rows were retrieved or if there is an error (that is, the return value is negative), the script displays a message to the user:

```
long ll_rows
dw_main.SetTransObject( SQLCA )

ll_rows = dw_main.Retrieve( )
IF ll_rows < 1 THEN MessageBox( &
 "Database Error", &
 "No rows retrieved." )
```

This example illustrates the use of retrieval arguments. Assume dw_emp contains this SQL SELECT statement:

```
SELECT Name, emp.sal, sales.rgn From Employee
WHERE emp.sal = :Salary and sales.rgn = :Region
```

:Salary and :Region are declared as arguments in the DataWindow painter. To modify the SQL SELECT statement, choose Edit Data->Source from the Design menu in the DataWindow painter.

Then this statement causes dw_empl to retrieve employees from the database who have a salary greater than $50,000 and are in the northwest region:

```
dw_empl.Retrieve(50000, "NW")
```

This example also illustrates retrieval arguments. Assume dw_EmpHist contains this SQL SELECT statement and emps is defined as a number array:

```
SELECT EmpNbr, Sal, Rgn From Employee
    WHERE EmpNbr IN (:emps)
```

These statements cause dw_EmpHist to retrieve Employees from the database whose employee numbers are values in the array emps:

```
Double emps[3]
emps[1] = 100
emps[2] = 200
emps[3] = 300
dw-EmpHist.Retrieve(emps)
```

This example illustrates how to use Retrieve twice to get data meeting different criteria. Assume the SELECT statement for the DataWindow object requires one argument, the department number. Then these statements retrieve all rows in the database in which department number is 100 or 200.

The script for the RetrieveStart event in the DataWindow control sets the return code to 2 so the rows and buffers of the DataWindow control will not be cleared before each retrieval:

```
This.SetActionCode(2)
```

The script for the Clicked event for a Retrieve CommandButton retrieves the data with two function calls. The Reset function clears any previously retrieved rows, normally done by Retrieve. Here, Retrieve is prevented from doing it by the action code setting in the RetrieveStart event:

```
dw_1.Reset( )
dw_1.Retrieve(100)
dw_1.Retrieve(200)
```

ScrollNextRow

Description Scrolls a DataWindow control to the next row (forward one row). ScrollNextRow changes the current row, but not the current column.

Applies to DataWindow controls and child DataWindows

Syntax *datawindowname*.ScrollNextRow ( )

Parameter	Description
datawindowname	The name of the DataWindow control or child DataWindow you want to scroll to the next row.

Return value Long. Returns the number of the row displayed at the top of the DataWindow control when the scroll is complete or if it tries to scroll past the last row. ScrollNextRow returns -1 if an error occurs.

Usage After you call ScrollNextRow, the row after the current row becomes the new current row. If that row is already visible, the displayed rows do not change. If it is not visible, the displayed rows move up to display the row.

ScrollNextRow does not highlight the row. Use SelectRow to let the user know what row is current.

SCROLLPRIORROW　　　　　　　　　　　　　　　　　　　APPENDIX C　FUNCTION REFERENCE　**477**

Events	ScrollNextRow may trigger these events: ■ ItemChanged ■ ItemError ■ ItemFocusChanged ■ RowFocusChanged
Example	This statement scrolls dw_employee to the next row: `dw_employee.ScrollNextRow( )`

ScrollPriorRow

Description	Scrolls a DataWindow control backward one row. ScrollPriorRow changes the current row but not the current column.
Applies to	DataWindow controls and child DataWindows
Syntax	*datawindowname*.ScrollPriorRow ( )

Parameter	Description
datawindowname	The name of the DataWindow control you want to scroll backward one row.

Return value	Long. Returns the number of the row displayed at the top of the DataWindow control when the scroll is complete or if it tries to scroll past the first row. ScrollPriorRow returns -1 if an error occurs.
Usage	After you call ScrollPriorRow, the row before the current row becomes the new current row. If that row is already visible, the displayed rows do not change. If it is not visible, the displayed rows move down to display the row. 　　ScrollPriorRow does not highlight the row. Use SelectRow to let the user know what row is current.
Events	ScrollPriorRow may trigger these events: ■ ItemChanged ■ ItemError ■ ItemFocusChanged ■ RowFocusChanged
Example	This statement scrolls dw_employee to the prior row: `dw_employee.ScrollPriorRow( )`

ScrollToRow

Description
Scrolls a DataWindow control to the specified row. ScrollToRow changes the current row but not the current column.

Applies to
DataWindow controls and child DataWindows

Syntax
datawindowname.ScrollToRow (*row*)

Parameter	Description
datawindowname	The name of the DataWindow control or child DataWindow you want to scroll to a specific row.
row	A long identifying the row to which you want to scroll. If *row* is 0, ScrollToRow scrolls to the first row. If *row* is greater than the last row number, it scrolls to the last row.

Return value
Integer. Returns 1 if it succeeds and -1 if an error occurs.

Usage
After you call ScrollToRow, the specified row becomes the new current row. If that row is already visible, the displayed rows do not change. If it is not visible, the displayed rows change to display the row.

ScrollToRow does not highlight the row. Use SelectRow to let the user know what row is current.

Events
ScrollToRow may trigger these events:

- ItemChanged
- ItemError
- ItemFocusChanged
- RowFocusChanged

Example
This statement scrolls to row 10 and makes it current in the DataWindow control dw_employee:

```
dw_Employee.ScrollToRow(10)
```

SetFocus

Description
Sets the focus on the specified object or control.

Applies to
Any object

Syntax
objectname.SetFocus ( )

Parameter	Description
objectname	The name of the object or control in which you want to set the focus.

Return value

Integer. Returns 1 if it succeeds and -1 if an error occurs.

Usage

If objectname is a ListBox, SetFocus displays the focus rectangle around the first item. If objectname is a DropDownListBox, SetFocus highlights the edit box. To select an item in a ListBox or DropDownListBox, use SelectItem.

Drawing objects cannot have focus. Therefore, you cannot use SetFocus to set focus to in a Line, Oval, Rectangle, or RoundRectangle.

Example

This statement in the script for the Open event in a window moves the focus to the first item in lb_Actions:

```
lb_Actions . SetFocus ()
```

SetItem

Description

Sets the value of a row and column in a DataWindow control to the specified value.

Applies to

DataWindow controls and child DataWindows

Syntax

datawindowname.SetItem (*row, column, value*)

Parameter	Description
datawindowname	The name of the DataWindow control or child DataWindow in which you want to set a specific row and column to a value.
row	A long whose value is the row location of the data.
column	The column location of the data. Column can be a column number (integer) or a column name (string).
value	The value to which you want to set the data at the row and column location. The data type of the value must be the same data type as the column.

Return value

Integer. Returns 1 if it succeeds and -1 if an error occurs.

Usage

SetItem sets a value in a DataWindow buffer. It does not affect the value currently in the edit control over the current row and column, which is the data the user has changed or may change. The value in the edit control does not become the value of the DataWindow item until it is validated and accepted (see AcceptText). In a script, you can change the value in the edit control with the SetText function.

You can use SetItem when you want to the set the value of an item in a DataWindow control that has script as the source.

You can also use SetItem to set the value of an item when the data the user entered is not valid. When you set an action code that rejects the data the user entered but allows the focus to change (action code of 2 in the script of the ItemChanged event or action code of 3 in the ItemError event), you can call SetItem to put valid data in the row and column.

If PowerBuilder cannot convert the string the user entered properly, you will have to include statements in the script for the ItemChanged or ItemError event to convert the data and use SetItem with the converted data. For example, if the user enters a number with commas and a dollar sign (for example, $1,000), PowerBuilder is unable to convert the string to a number and you will have to convert it in the script.

If you use SetItem to set a row and column to a value other than the value the user entered, you can use SetText to assign the new value to the edit control so that the user sees the current value.

Examples

This statement sets the value of row 3 of the column named hire_date of the DataWindow control dw_order to 1993-06-07:

```
dw_order.setItem(3, "hire_date", 1993-06-07)
```

When a user starts to edit a numeric column and leaves it without entering any data, PowerBuilder tries to assign an empty string to the column. This fails the data type validation test. In this example, code in the Item-Error event sets the column's value to NULL and allows the focus to change.

This example assumes that the data type of column 2 is numeric. If it is date, time, or datetime, replace the first line (integer null_num) with a declaration of the appropriate data type.

```
integer null_num    //to contain null value
integer col_no

SetNull(null_num)
col_no = This.GetColumn()

// Special processing for column 2
IF col_no = 2 THEN
  // If user entered nothing (""), set to null
  IF This.GetText() = "" THEN
    This.SetItem(This.GetRow(), col_no, null_num)
    This.SetActionCode(2)
    RETURN
  END IF
END IF
```

The following example is a script for a DataWindow's ItemError event. If the user specifies characters other than digits for a numeric column, the data will fail the data type validation test. You can include code to strip out characters such as commas and dollar signs and use SetItem to assign the now valid numeric value to the column. The action code of 3 causes the data in the edit control to be rejected because the script has provided a valid value:

```
string s, snum, c
integer cnt

s = This.GetText()

// Extract the digits from the user's data
FOR cnt = 1 to Len(s)
 c = Mid(s, cnt, 1)
 IF IsNumber(c) THEN snum = snum + c
NEXT

This.SetItem(This.GetRow(), This.GetColumn(),  &
   Long(snum))
This.SetActionCode(3)
```

SetRowFocusIndicator

Description Specifies the visual indicator that identifies the current row in the Data-Window control. You can use Windows' standard dotted-line rectangle, PowerBuilder's pointing hand, or an image stored in a Picture control.

Applies to DataWindow controls and child DataWindows

Syntax *datawindowname*.SetRowFocusIndicator (*focusindicator* {, & *xlocation* {, *ylocation* }})

Parameter	Description
datawindowname	The name of the DataWindow control or child DataWindow in which you want to set the row focus indicator.
focusindicator	The visual indicator for the current row. Valid values are a RowFocusInd enumerated data type or the name of a Picture control, as follows: ■ Off!—No indicator. ■ FocusRect!—Put a dotted line rectangle around the row. FocusRect! has no effect on the Macintosh. ■ Hand!—Use the PowerBuilder pointing hand. ■ Name of a Picture control—Use the specified Picture control.
xlocation (optional)	An integer whose value is the x coordinate in PowerBuilder units of the position of the hand or bitmap relative to the upper-left corner of the row.
ylocation (optional)	An integer whose value is the y coordinate in PowerBuilder units of the position of the hand or bitmap relative to the upper-left corner of the row.

Return value Integer. Returns 1 if it succeeds and -1 if an error occurs.

Usage Sets the current row indicator in datawindowname to focusindicator. If you select Hand or a Picture control as the indicator, PowerBuilder displays the indicator at the left side of the body of the DataWindow unless you specify location coordinates (xlocation, ylocation). The default location is 0,0 (the left side of the body of the DataWindow control).

Pictures as row focus indicators: To use a picture as the row focus indicator, set up the Picture control in the Window painter. Place the Picture control in the window that contains the DataWindow control and then reference it in the SetRowFocusIndicator function. You can hide the picture or place it under the DataWindow control so the user doesn't see the control itself.

Examples This statement sets the row focus indicator in dw_employee to the pointing hand:

```
dw_employee.SetRowFocusIndicator(Hand!)
```

If p_arrow is a Picture control in the window, the following statement sets the row focus indicator in dw_employee to p_arrow:

```
dw_employee.SetRowFocusIndicator(p_arrow)
```

SetSQLSelect

Description Specifies the SQL SELECT statement for a DataWindow control.

Applies to DataWindow controls and child DataWindows

Syntax *datawindowname*.SetSQLSelect (*statement*)

Parameter	Description
datawindowname	The name of the DataWindow control or child DataWindow for which you want to change the SELECT statement.
statement	A string whose value is the SELECT statement for the DataWindow object. The statement must structurally match the current SELECT statement (that is, it must return the same number of columns, the columns must be the same data type, and the columns must be in the same order).

Return value Integer. SetSQLSelect returns 1 if it succeeds and -1 if the SELECT statement cannot be changed.

Usage Use SetSQLSelect to dynamically change the SQL SELECT statement for a DataWindow object in a script.

If the DataWindow is updatable, PowerBuilder validates the SELECT statement against the database and DataWindow column specifications when you call the SetSQLSelect function. Each column in the SQL SELECT statement must match the column type in the DataWindow object. The statement is validated only if the DataWindow object is updatable.

You must use the SetTrans or SetTransObject function to set the DataWindow control's internal transaction object before the SetSQLSelect function will execute.

If the new SELECT statement has a different table name in the FROM clause and the DataWindow object is updatable, then PowerBuilder must change the update information for the DataWindow object. PowerBuilder assumes the key columns are in the same positions as in the original definition. The following conditions will make the DataWindow not updatable:

- There is more than one table in the FROM clause.
- A DataWindow update column is a computed column in the SELECT statement.

If changing the SELECT statement makes the DataWindow object not updatable, the DataWindow control cannot execute an Update function call for the DataWindow object in the future.

Limitations to using SetSQLSelect: *Use SetSQLSelect only if the data source for the DataWindow object is a SQLSELECT statement without arguments and you want PowerBuilder to modify the update information for the DataWindow object are changing the UPDATE statement. If the SELECT statement has arguments, use Modify. For example:*

dw_1.Modify("Datawindow.Table.select='select...'")

However, Modify will not verify SELECT statement or change the update information, making it faster but more susceptible to user error.

Example

If the current SELECT statement for dw_emp retrieves no rows, the following statements replace it with the syntax in NewSyn:

```
string OldSyn, NewSyn

OldSyn = &
'SELECT employee.EMP_Name FROM employee' &
   + 'WHERE salary < 70000'
NewSyn = 'SELECT employee.EMP_Name FROM employee' &
   + 'WHERE salary < 100000'

IF dw_emp.Retrieve( ) = 0 THEN
   dw_emp.SetSQLSelect(NewSyn)
   dw_emp.Retrieve()
END IF
```

SetTransObject

Description   Causes a DataWindow control to use a programmer-specified transaction object. The transaction object provides the information necessary for communicating with the database.

Applies to   DataWindow controls and child DataWindows

Syntax   *datawindowname*.SetTransObject (*transaction*)

Parameter	Description
datawindowname	The name of the DataWindow control or child DataWindow in which you want to use a programmer specified transaction object rather than the DataWindow control's internal transaction object.
transaction	The name of the transaction object you want to use in the datawindowname.

Return value   Integer. Returns 1 if it succeeds and -1 if an error occurs.

Usage   A programmer-specified transaction object gives you more control over the database transactions and provides efficient application performance. You control the database connection by using SQL statements such as CONNECT, COMMIT, and ROLLBACK.

Since the DataWindow control does not have to connect to the database for every RETRIEVE and UPDATE statement, these statements run faster. You are responsible for committing and rolling back transactions after you call the Update function, using code like the following:

```
IF dw_Employee.Update()>0 THEN
   COMMIT USING emp_transobject;
ELSE
   ROLLBACK USING emp_transobject;
END IF
```

You must set the parameters required to connect to your DBMS in the transaction object before you can use the transaction object to connect to the database. PowerBuilder provides a global transaction object called SQLCA, which is all you need if you are connecting to one database. You can also create additional transaction objects, as shown in the examples.

To use SetTransObject, write code that does the following tasks:

1 Set up the transaction object by assigning values to its fields (usually in the application's Open event).

2 Connect to the database using the SQLCONNECT statement and the transaction object (in the Open event for the application or window).

3 Call SetTransObject to associate the transaction object with the DataWindow control (usually in the window's Open event).

4 Check the return value from the Update function and follow it with an SQL COMMIT or ROLLBACK statement, as appropriate.

SETTRANSOBJECT
APPENDIX C FUNCTION REFERENCE 485

If you change the DataWindow object associated with the DataWindow control or if you disconnect and reconnect to a database, the connection between the DataWindow control and the transaction object is severed. You must call SetTransObject again to reestablish the connect.

SetTransObject versus SetTrans: *In most cases, use the SetTransObject function to specify the transaction object because it is efficient and gives you control over when transactions are committed.*

The SetTrans function provides another way of managing the database connection. SetTrans, which sets transaction information in the DataWindow control's internal transaction object, manages the connection automatically. You do not explicitly connect to the database; the DataWindow connects and disconnects for each database transaction, which is less efficient but necessary in some situations..

Examples

This statement causes dw_employee to use the default transaction object SQLCA:

```
dw_employee.SetTransObject(SQLCA)
```

This statement causes dw_employee to use the programmer-defined transaction object emp_TransObj. In this example, emp_TransObj is an instance variable, but your script must allocate memory for it with the CREATE statement before you use it:

```
emp_TransObj = CREATE transaction
    . . .  // Assign values to the transaction object
dw_employee.SetTransObject(emp_TransObj)
```

This example has two parts. The first script, for the application's Open event, reads database parameters from an initialization file called MYAPP.INI and stores the values in the default transaction object (SQLCA). The Database section of MYAPP.INI has the same keywords as Power-Builder's own PB.INI file. The parameters shown are for a SQLServer, ORACLE, or SQLBase database. The second script, for the window's Open event, establishes a connection and retrieves data from the database.

The application's Open event script populates SQLCA:

```
SQLCA.DBMS = ProfileString("myapp.ini", &
    "database", "DBMS", " ")
SQLCA.Database = ProfileString("myapp.ini", &
    "database", "Database", " ")
SQLCA.LogId = ProfileString("myapp.ini", &
    "database", "LogId", " ")
SQLCA.LogPass = ProfileString("myapp.ini", &
    "database", "LogPassword", " ")
SQLCA.ServerName = ProfileString("myapp.ini", &
    "database", "ServerName", " ")
SQLCA.UserId = ProfileString("myapp.ini", &
    "database", "UserId", " ")
SQLCA.DBPass = ProfileString("myapp.ini", &
    "database", "DatabasePassword", " ")
SQLCA.lock = ProfileString("myapp.ini", &
    "database", "lock", " ")
```

The Open event script for the window that contains the DataWindow control connects to the database, assigns the transaction object to the DataWindow, and retrieves data:

```
long RowsRetrieved
 string LastName

// Connect to the database.
CONNECT USING SQLCA;

// Test whether the connect succeeded.
IF SQLCA.SQLCode <> 0 THEN
   MessageBox("Connect Failed", &
      "Cannot connect to database " &
      + SQLCA.SQLErrText)
   RETURN
END IF

// Set the transaction object to SQLCA.
dw_employee.SetTransObject(SQLCA)

// Retrieve the rows.
LastName = . . .
RowsRetrieved = dw_employee.Retrieve(LastName)

// Test whether the retrieve succeeded.
IF RowsRetrieved < 0 THEN
   MessageBox("Retrieve Failed", &
      "Cannot retrieve data from the database.")
END IF
```

String

Description

String has two syntaxes:

- Syntax 1 formats data as a string according to a specified display format mask. You can convert and format date, DateTime, numeric, and time data. You can also apply a display format to a string.
- Syntax 2 converts a blob to a string.

Syntax 1

String (*data*, { *format* })

Parameter	Description
data	The data you want returned as a string with the specified formatting. Data can have a date, DateTime, numeric, time, or string data type.
format (optional)	A string whose value is the display masks you want to use to format the data. The masks consist of formatting information specific to the data type of data. If data is type string, format is required. The format can consist of more than one mask, depending on the data type of data. Each mask is separated by a semicolon. See Usage for details on each data type.

Return value 1   String. Returns data in the specified format if it succeeds and the empty string ("") if the data type of data does not match the type of display mask specified or *format* is not a valid mask.

Syntax 2   String (*blob*)

Parameter	Description
blob	The blob whose value you want returned as a string.

Return value 2   String. Returns the value of blob as a string if it succeeds and the empty string ("") if it fails. It the blob does not contain string data, String interprets the data as characters, if possible, and returns a string.

Usage   For date, DateTime, numeric, and time data, PowerBuilder uses the system's default format for the returned string if you don't specify a format. For numeric data, the default format is the [General] format.

For string data, a display format mask is required. (Otherwise, the function would have nothing to do.)

The format can consist of one or more masks:

- Formats for date, DateTime, string, and time data can include one or two masks. The first mask is the format for the data; the second mask is the format for a null value.
- Formats for numeric data can have up to four masks. A format with a single mask handles both positive and negative data. If there are additional masks, the first mask is for positive values, and the additional masks are for negative, zero, and NULL values.

If the display format doesn't match the data type, PowerBuilder will try to apply the mask, which can produce unpredictable results.

You can also use String to extract a string from the Message object after calling TriggerEvent or PostEvent. See those events for more information.

Examples   This statement applies a display format to a date value and returns Jan 31, 1998:

```
String(1998-01-31, "mmm dd, yyyy")
```

This example applies a format to the value in order_date and sets date1 to 6-11-95:

```
Date order_date = 1995-06-11
string date1
date1 = String(order_date,"m-d-yy")
```

This example includes a format for a NULL date value so that when order_date is NULL, date1 is set to none:

```
Date order_date = 1995-06-11
string date1
SetNull(order_date)
date1 = String(order_date,"m-d-yy;'none'")
```

This statement applies a format to a DateTime value and returns Jan 31, 1998 6 hrs and 8 min:

```
String(DateTime(1998-01-31, 06:08:00), &
    'mmm dd, yyyy h "hrs and" m "min"')
```

This example builds a DateTime value from the system date and time using the Today and Now functions. The String function applies formatting and sets the text of sle_date to that value, for example, 6-11-95 8:06 pm:

```
DateTime sys_datetime
string datetime1
sys_datetime = DateTime(Today(), Now())
sle_date.text = String(sys_datetime,
    & "m-d-yy h:mm am/pm;'none'")
```

This statement applies a format to a numeric value and returns $5.00:

```
String(5,"$#,##0.00")
```

These statements set stringl to 0123:

```
integer nbr = 123
string stringl
stringl = String(nbr,"0000;(000);****;empty")
```

These statements set stringl to (123):

```
integer nbr = -123
string stringl
stringl = String(nbr,"000;(000);****;empty")
```

These statements set stringl to * * * *:

```
integer  nbr = 0
string stringl
stringl = String(nbr,"0000;(000);****;empty")
```

These statements set stringl to "empty":

```
integer nbr
string stringl
SetNull(nbr)
stringl = String(nbr,"0000;(000);****;empty")
```

This statement formats string data and returns A-B-C. The display format assigns a character in the source string to each @ and inserts other characters in the format at the appropriate positions:

```
String(" ABC ", " @ - @ - @ " )
```

This statement returns A*B:

```
String("ABC ", " @ * @ " )
```

This statement returns ABC:

```
String(" ABC ", " @ @ @ " )
```

This statement returns a space:

```
String( "ABC", " " )
```

This statement applies a display format to time data and returns 6 hrs and 8 min:

```
String(06:08:02,'h "hrs and" m "min"')
```

This statement returns 08:06:04 pm:

```
String(20:06:04,"hh:mm:ss am/pm")
```

This statement returns 8:06:04 am:

```
String(08:06:04,"h:mm:ss am/pm")
```

Syntax 2

This example converts the blob instance variable ib_sblob, which contains string data, to a string and stores the result in sstr:

```
string sstr
sstr = String(ib_sblob)
```

This example stores today's date and test status information in the blob bb. Pos1 and pos2 store the beginning and end of the status text in the blob. Finally, BlobMid extracts a "sub-blob" that String converts to a string. Sle_status displays the returned status text:

```
blob{100} bb
long pos1, pos2
string test_status
date test_date

test_date = Today()
IF DayName(test_date) = "Wednesday" THEN  &
    test_status = "Coolant Test"
IF DayName(test_date) = "Thursday" THEN  &
    test_status = "Emissions Test"

// Store data in the blob
pos1 = BlobEdit( bb, 1, test_date)
pos2 = BlobEdit( bb, pos1, test_status )
. . . // Some processing

// Extract the status stored in bb and display it
sle_status.text = String(  & BlobMid(bb, pos1, pos2 - pos1))
```

Time

Description

Converts DateTime, string, or numeric data to data of type time. It also extracts a time value from a blob. You can use one of three syntaxes, depending on the data type of the source data:

- To extract the time from DateTime data, or to extract a time stored in a blob, use Syntax 1.
- To convert a string to a time, use Syntax 2.
- To combine numbers for hours, minutes, and seconds into a time value, use Syntax 3.

Syntax 1

Time (*datetime*)

Parameter	Description
datetime	A DateTime value or a blob in which the first value is a time or DateTime value. The rest of the contents of the blob is ignored.

Return value 1

Time. Returns the time in datetime as a time. If datetime does not contain a valid time, Time returns 00:00:00.000000. If datetime is NULL, Time returns NULL.

Syntax 2

Time (*string*)

Parameter	Description
string	A string whose value is a valid time (such as 8AM or 10:25) that you want returned as a time. Only the hour is required; you do not have to include the minutes, seconds, or microseconds of the time or AM or PM. The default value is 00 for minutes and seconds and 000000 for microseconds. PowerBuilder determines whether the time is AM or PM based on a 24-hour clock.

Return value 2

Time. Returns the time in string as a time. If string does not contain a valid time, Time returns 00:00:00.000000.

Syntax 3

Time (*hour, minute, second* {*, microsecond*})

Parameter	Description
hour	The integer for the hour (00 to 23) of the time.
minute	The integer for the minutes (00 to 59) of the time.
second	The integer for the seconds (O to 59) of the time.
microsecond (optional	The integer for the microseconds (0 to 599999) of the time.

Return value 3

Time. Returns the time as a time data type and *00:00:00* if the value in any argument is not valid (out of the specified range of values). If any argument is NULL, Time returns NULL.

Usage

Valid times can include any combination of hours (00 to 23), minutes (00 to 59), seconds (00 to 59), and microseconds (0 to 599999).

Examples

After StartDateTime has been retrieved from the database, this example sets StartTime equal to the time in StartDateTime:

```
DateTime StartDateTime
time StartTime
...
StartTime = Time( StartDateTime )
```

Suppose that the value of a blob variable ib_blob contains a DateTime value beginning at byte 32. The following statement extracts the time from the value:

```
time lt_time
lt_time = Time(BlobMid(ib_blob, 32))
```

Syntax 2 These statements set What_Time to NULL:

```
Time What_Time
string null_string

SetNull ( null_string
What_Time = Time(r.ull_ string)
```

This statement returns a time value for 45 seconds before midnight (23:59:15), which is specified as a string:

```
Time("23:59:15")
```

This statement converts the text in the SingleLineEdit sle_Time_Received to a time value:

```
Time(sle_Time_Received.Text)
```

Syntax 3 These statements set What_Time to 10:15:45:234 and display the resulting time as a string in st_1. The default display format doesn't include microseconds, so the String function specifies a display format with microseconds:

```
Time What_Time
What_Time = Time(10, 15, 45, 234)
st_1.Text = String(What_Time, "hh:mm:ss:ffffff")
```

These statements set What_Time to 10:15:45:

```
Time What_Time
What_Time = Time(10, 15, 45)
```

TriggerEvent

Description Triggers an event associated with the specified object, which executes the script for that event immediately.

Syntax *objectname*.TriggerEvent (*event* {, *word*, *long* })

Parameter	Description
objectname	The name of any PowerBuilder object or control that has events associated with it.

Parameter	Description
event	A value of the TrigEvent enumerated data type that identifies a PowerBuilder event (for example, Clicked!,Modified!, or DoubleClicked!) or a string whose value is the name of an event. The event must be a valid event for *objectname* and a script must exist for the event in *objectname*.
word (optional)	A long value to be stored in the WordParm attribute of the system's Message object. If you want to specify a value for *long*, but not *word*, enter 0. (For cross-platform compatibility, WordParm and LongParm are both longs.)
long (optional)	A long value or a string that you want to store in the LongParm attribute of the system's Message object. When you specify a string, a pointer to the string is stored in the LongParm attribute, which you can access with the String function (see Usage).

Return value

Integer. Returns 1 if it is successful and the event script runs and -1 if the event is not a valid event for objectname, or no script exists for the event in objectname.

Usage

If you specify the name of an event instead of a value of the TrigEvent enumerated data type, enclose the name in double quotation marks.

It is a good idea to check the return code to determine whether TriggerEvent succeeded and, based on the result, perform the appropriate processing.

You can pass information to the event script with the word and long arguments. The information is stored in the Message object. In your script, you can reference the WordParm and LongParm fields of the Message object to access the information.

If you have specified a string for long, you can access it in the triggered event by using the String function with the keyword "address" as the format parameter. Your event script might begin as follows:

```
string PassedString
PassedString = String(Message.LongParm, "address")
```

To trigger system events that are not PowerBuilder-defined events, use Post or Send, instead of PostEvent and TriggerEvent. Although Send can send messages that trigger PowerBuilder events, as shown below, you have to know the codes for a particular message. It is easier to use the PowerBuilder functions that trigger the desired events.

Equivalent syntax

Both of the following statements click the CheckBox cb_OK. The following call to the Send function:

```
Send(Handle(Parent), 273, 0, Long(Handle(cb_OK), 0))
```

is equivalent to:

```
cb_OK.TriggerEvent(Clicked!)
```

Examples

This statement executes the script for the Clicked event in the CommandButton cb_OK immediately:

```
cb_OK.TriggerEvent(Clicked!)
```

This statement executes the script for the user-defined event cb_exit_request in the parent window:

```
Parent.TriggerEvent("cb_exit_request")
```

This statement executes the script for the Clicked event in the MenuItem m_File on the menu m_Appl:

```
m_Appl.m_File.TriggerEvent(Clicked!)
```

Update

Description

Updates the database with the changes made in a DataWindow control. Update can also call AcceptText for the current row and column before it updates the database.

Applies to

DataWindow controls and child DataWindows

Syntax

datawindowname.Update ({ *accept* {, *resetflag* } })

Parameter	Description
datawindowname	The name of the DataWindow control or child DataWindow that contains the information you want to use to update the database.
accept (optional)	A boolean value specifying whether the DataWindow control should automatically perform an AcceptText prior to performing the update: ■ TRUE—(Default) Perform AcceptText ■ FALSE—Do not perform AcceptText
resetflag (optional)	A boolean value specifying whether datawindowname should automatically reset the update flags: ■ TRUE—(Default) Reset the flags ■ FALSE—Do not reset the flags

Return value

Integer. Returns 1 if it succeeds and -1 if an error occurs.

Usage

If *accept* is TRUE, the update is performed only if the data passes validation.
    You must use the SetTrans or the SetTransObject function to specify the database connection before the Update function will execute. When you use SetTransObject, the more efficient of the two, you must do your own transaction management, which includes issuing the SQL COMMIT or ROLLBACK statement to finalize the update.
    By default, Update resets the update flags after successfully completing the update. However, you can prevent the flags from being reset until you

perform other validations and commit the changes. When you are satisfied with the update, call ResetUpdate to clear the flags so that items are no longer marked as modified.

Use SetTransObject when resetflag is FALSE: *You would typically use Set-TransObject, not SetTrans, to specify the DataWindow control's transaction object when you plan to update with the resetflag argument to FALSE. Only SetTransObject gives you control of when changes are committed.*

If you want to update several tables in one DataWindow control, you can use Modify to change the Update attribute of columns in each table. To preserve the status flags of the rows and columns, set the resetflag argument to FALSE. Because the updates all occur in the same DataWindow control, you cannot allow the flags to be cleared until all the tables have used them. When all the updates are successfully completed and committed, you can call ResetUpdate to clear the changed flags in the DataWindow. See Modify for an example of this technique.

If you are updating multiple DataWindow controls as part of one transaction, set the resetflag argument to FALSE. This will prevent the DataWindow from "forgetting" which rows to update in case one of the updates fails. You can roll back, try to correct the situation, and update again. Once all of the DataWindows have been updated successfully, use COMMIT to finalize the transaction and use ResetUpdate to reset the DataWindow's status flags.

If you call Update with the resetflag argument set to FALSE and do not call ResetUpdate, the DataWindow will attempt to issue the same SQL statements again the next time you call Update.

If you call Update in an ItemChanged event, be sure to set the accept argument to FALSE to avoid an endless loop and a stack fault. Because AcceptText triggers an ItemChanged event, you cannot call it in that event (see AcceptText).

If you call Update in the ItemChanged event, then the item's old value is updated in the database, not the newly entered value. The newly entered value in the edit control is still being validated and won't become the item value until the ItemChanged event is successfully completed. If you want to include the new value in an update in the ItemChanged event, use the appropriate SetItem function first.

Events

Update may trigger these events:

- SQLPreview
- UpdateEnd
- UpdateStart

If AcceptText is performed, it may trigger these events:

- ItemChanged
- ItemError

Examples

This example connects to the database, specifies a transaction object for the DataWindow control with SetTransObject, and then updates the database with the changes made in dw_employee. By default, AcceptText is performed on the data in the edit control for the current row and column and the status flags are reset:

```
CONNECT USING SQLCA;
dw_employee.SetTransObject(SQLCA) . . .
  // Some processing
dw_employee.Update( )
```

This example connects to the database, specifies a transaction object for the DataWindow control with SetTransObject, and then updates the database with the changes made in dw_employee. The update resets the status flags but does not perform AcceptText before updating the database:

```
CONNECT USING SQLCA;
dw_employee.SetTransObject(SQLCA) . . .
// Some processing
dw_Employee.Update(FALSE, TRUE)
```

As before, this example connects to the database, specifies a transaction object for the DataWindow control with SetTransObject, and then updates the database with the changes made in dw_employee. After Update is executed, the example checks the return code and depending on the success of the update, executes a COMMIT or ROLLBACK:

```
integer   rtn

CONNECT USING SQLCA;
dw_employee.SetTransObject(SQLCA)
rtn = dw_employee.Update( )
IF rtn = 1 THEN
   COMMIT USING SQLCA;
ELSE
   ROLLBACK USING SQLCA;
END IF
```

Year

Description

Determines the year of a date value.

Syntax

Year (*date*)

Parameter	Description
date	The date from which you want the year.

Return value

Integer. Returns an integer whose value is a 4-digit year adapted from the year portion of date if it succeeds and 1900 if an error occurs.

When you convert a string that has a two-digit year to a date, then PowerBuilder chooses the century, as follows. If the year is between 00 to 49, PowerBuilder assumes 20 as the first two digits; if it is between 50 and 99, PowerBuilder assumes 19.

496 APPENDIX C FUNCTION REFERENCE COUNT

Usage   PowerBuilder handles years from 1000 to 3000 inclusive.

If your data includes date before 1950, such as birth dates, always specify a 4-digit year so that Year and other PowerBuilder functions, such as Sort, interpret the date as intended.

Example   This statement returns 1995:

```
Year(1995-01-31)
```

DataWindow Painter Functions

Count

Description   Calculates the total number of rows in the specified column.

Syntax   Count (column { for range { DISTINCT {expres1{, expres2 {, ...}}}}})

Parameter	Description
column	The column for which you want the number of rows. *Column* can be the column name or the column number preceded by a pound sign (#). *Column* can also be an expression that includes a reference to the column.
for range (optional)	If you specify *range*, you must precede it with the keyword *for*. Values for *range* are: ■ (Default) The total number of rows in column. ■ Crosstab—(Crosstabs only) The total number of rows in column in the crosstab. ■ Graph—(Graphs only) The total number of rows in column for the graph. This value for range has effect only when you specify Page in the Rows option in the Graph Data window. ■ GroupNbr—The number of rows in column in the specified group. Specify the keyword group followed by the group number. For example: for group 1. ■ Page—The number of rows in column on a page.
DISTINCT (optional)	Causes Count to consider only the distinct values in column when counting the rows. For a value of column, the first row found with the value is used and other rows that have the same value are ignored.

Parameter	Description
expresn (optional)	One or more expressions that you want to evaluate to determine distinct rows. *Expresn* can be the name of a column, a function, or an expression.

Return value

Long. Returns the total number of rows in range.

Usage

If you specify *range*, Count determines the number of rows in *column* in *range*. If you specify DISTINCT, Count returns the number of the distinct rows displayed in *column*, or if you specify *expresn*, the number of rows displayed in *column* where the value of *expresn* is distinct.
Null values in the column are ignored and are not included in the count.

Not in validation rules or filter expressions: *You cannot use this or other aggregate functions in validation rules or filter expressions.*

Examples

This expression returns the number of rows in the column named emp_id that are not NULL:

```
Count(emp_id)
```

This expression returns the number of rows in the column named emp_id of group 1 that are not NULL:

```
Count(emp_id for group 1)
```

This expression returns the number of dept_ids that are distinct:

```
Count(dept_id for all DISTINCT)
```

This expression returns the number of regions with distinct products:

```
Count(region_id for all DISTINCT Lower(product_id))
```

This expression returns the number of rows in column 3 on the page that are not NULL:

```
Count(#3 for page)
```

Page

Description

Determines the number of the current page.

Syntax

```
Page ( )
```

Return value

Integer. Returns the number of the current page

> ***Calculating the page count:*** *The vertical size of the paper less the top and bottom margins is used to calculate the page count. When the print orientation is landscape, the vertical size of the paper is the shorter dimension of the paper.*

Examples This expression returns the number of the current page:

```
Page ()
```

This expression for a computed field in the DataWindow's footer band displays a string showing the current page number and the total number of pages in the report. The result has the format **Page** *n* **of** *total*:

```
' Page ' + Page ( ) + ' of ' + PageCount ()
```

PageCount

Description Determines the total number of pages.

Syntax PageCount ( )

Return value Integer. Returns the total number of pages.

> ***Calculating the page count:*** *The vertical size of the paper less the top and bottom margins is used to calculate the page count. When the print orientation is landscape, the vertical size of the paper is the shorter dimension of the paper.*

Example This expression returns the number of pages:

```
PageCount ()
```

This expression for a computed field in the DataWindow's footer band displays a string showing the current page number and the total number of pages in the report. The result has the format Page n of total:

```
'Page ' + Page( ) + ' of ' + PageCount( )
```

Sum

Description Calculates the sum of the values in the specified column.

Sum

Syntax

```
Sum ( column {for range {DISTINCT {expres1 {, expres2 {, ...}}}}} )
```

Parameter	Description
column	The column for which you want the sum of the data values. *Column* can be the column name or the column number preceded by a pound sign (#). *Column* can also be an expression that includes a reference to the column. The data type of *column* must be numeric.
for range (optional)	If you specify *range*, you must precede it with the keyword *for*. Values for *range* are: ■ (Default) The sum of the values of the rows of column. ■ Crosstab—(Crosstabs only) The sum of the values in the rows of column in the crosstab. ■ Graph—(Graphs only) The sum of the values in the rows of column for the graph. This value for range has effect only when you specify Page in the Rows option in the Graph Data window. ■ GroupNbr—The sum of the values of the rows of column in the specified group. Specify the keyword group followed by the group number. For example: for group 1. ■ Page—The sum of the values of column on a page.
DISTINCT (optional)	Causes Sum to consider only the distinct values in column when determining the sum. For a value of column, the first row found with the value is used and other rows that have the same value are ignored.
expresn (optional)	One or more expressions that you want to evaluate to determine distinct rows. *Expresn* can be the name of a column, a function, or an expression.

Return value

The appropriate numeric data type. Returns the sum of the data values in column.

Usage

If you specify *range*, Sum returns the sum of the values in *column* within *range*. If you specify *DISTINCT*, Sum returns the sum of the distinct values in *column*, or if you specify *expresn*, the sum of the values of *column* where the value of *expresn* is distinct.

NULL values are ignored and are not included in the calculation.

Not in validation rules or filter expressions: You cannot use this or other aggregate functions in validation rules or filter expressions.

Examples

This expression returns the sum of the values in group 1 in the column named salary:

```
Sum(salary for group 1)
```

This expression returns the sum of the values in column 4 on the page:

```
Sum(#4 for page)
```

Assume the report displays the order number, amount, and line items for each order. This computed field returns the sum of the order amount for the distinct order numbers:

```
Sum(order_amt for all DISTINCT order_nbr)
```

Today

Description Obtains the system date.

Syntax `Today ( )`

Return value DateTime. Returns the current system DateTime.

Example This expression returns the current system date:

```
Today ()
```

APPENDIX D

PowerScript Language Reference

Language Basics

This section describes the conventions and techniques PowerScript uses for:

- Comments
    - Identifier names
    - Labels
    - ASCII characters
    - NULL values
    - Reserved words
    - Statement continuation and separation
- White space

Comments

You can use comments to document your scripts and to prevent statements within a script from executing.

There are two ways to designate comments in PowerScript: the **double slash** method and the **slash and asterisk** method.

In the PowerScript painter and the Function painter, you can use the Comment Selection icon or Comment Selection on the Edit menu to comment out the line containing the cursor or a selected group of lines.

Double Slash Method

You use the double slash method to designate a single line comment. The comment can be the entire line or part of the line. When the compiler encounters double slashes, it ignores everything following double slashes and on the same line. When you use this method to designate a comment, the comment *cannot* extend to multiple lines.

Examples

The following examples show how to use the double slash method to designate comments:

```
// This entire line is a comment.
// This entire line is another comment.

amt = qty * cost   // Rest of the line is comment.

// The following statement was commented out so it
// would not execute.
// SetNull(amt)
```

Slash and Asterisk Method

The slash and asterisk method uses a slash followed by an asterisk (/*) to identify the start of a comment and an asterisk followed by a slash (*/) to identify the end of the comment. The compiler ignores everything between the slash asterisk and the asterisk slash. When you use this method to designate a comment, you can:

- Make all or part of a line a comment
- Extend a comment to multiple lines
- Nest comments

Continuing Comments: *Multiline comments do not require a continuation character.*

Examples

```
/* This is a single-line comment.*/

/* This comment starts here,
continues to this line,
and finally ends here. */

A = B + C  /* This comment starts here.
/* This is the start of a nested comment. The nested comment ends here. */
The first comment ends here.  */ + D + E + F
```

Summary

Delimiter	Use to
//	Designate all or part of a line as a comment
/* ... */	Designate all or part of a line as a comment or multiple lines as a single comment
	Nest comments

Identifier Names

You use identifiers to name variables, labels, functions, windows, controls, menus, and anything else you refer to in scripts.

Rules

Identifiers:

- Must start with a letter
- Can have up to 40 characters, but no spaces
- Are case insensitive (PART, Part, and part are identical)
- Can include any combination of letters, numbers, and these special characters:
    -   Dash
    - _ Underscore
    - $ Dollar sign
    - # Number sign
    - % Percent sign

Prohibiting Dashes in Variable Names

By default, PowerBuilder allows you to use dashes in all identifiers, including variable names in a script. This means that when you use the subtraction operator or the operator in a script, you must surround it with spaces (otherwise, PowerBuilder thinks the expression is an identifier name).

If you want to disallow dashes in variable names in scripts (and not have to surround the subtraction operator and -- with spaces), you can set the DashesInIdentifiers preferences variable to 0 in the [pb] section of PB.INI.

```
[pb]
DashesInIdentifiers=0
```

By default, DashesInIdentifiers equals 1, which allows dashes.

But be careful: if you do set the variable to 0 and have previously used dashes in variable names, you will get errors the next time you compile.

Using Multiword Names

Since PowerScript does not allow spaces in identifier names, you can use any of the following techniques for multiword names:

- Initial caps (for example, FirstWindow)
- Dashes, except in variable names if you set DashesInIdentifiers to 0 (for example, customer-name)
- Underscores (for example, quantity_on_hand)

Examples

Here are some valid identifiers:

```
ABC_Code
Child-Id
FirstButton
response35
pay-before-%deductions$
ORDER_DATE
Actual-$-amount
Part#
```

Here are some invalid identifiers:

```
2nd-quantity // Does not start with a letter
ABC Code // Contains a space
Child'sId // Contains invalid special character
```

Labels

You can include labels in scripts for use with GOTO statements. A label can be any valid identifier followed by a colon (:). You can enter it on a line by itself or at the start of the line preceding a statement. (For information about the GOTO statement, see "Statements" later in this appendix.)

Examples

The label shown below is on its own line and above the statement:

```
FindCity:
if city=cityname[1] then ...
```

The label shown below is on same line as the statement:

```
FindCity: If city=cityname[1] then ...
```

ASCII characters

You can include special ASCII characters in strings. For example, you may want to include a tab in a string to ensure proper spacing or a bullet to indicate a list item.

Common ASCII characters

To specify this ASCII character	Enter
Newline	~n
Tab	~t
Vertical tab	~v
Carriage return	~r
Formfeed	~f
Backspace	~b
Double quote	~"
Single quote	~'
Tilde	~~

Where is the tilde key? To type a tilde on most U.S. keyboards, press and hold down the SHIFT key, then press the key just to the left of the 1 key.

String	Description
`"dog~n"`	A string containing the word dog followed by a newline character
`"dog~tcat~tfiger"`	A string containing the word dog, a tab character, the word cat, another tab character, and the word tiger

ASCII Values

You can specify *any* ASCII character (including the characters in the previous table) by typing a tilde (~) followed by the decimal, hexadecimal, or octal ASCII value for the character:

ASCII value	Enter
Decimal	A tilde followed by three digits from 000 to 255
Hexadecimal	A tilde followed by a lowercase h, followed by a two-digit hexadecimal number from 01 to FF
Octal	A tilde followed by a lowercase o, followed by a three-digit octal number from 000 to 377

Examples

The following table shows how to indicate a bullet (•) in a string by using the decimal, hexadecimal, and octal ASCII values:

Value	Description
~249	The ASCII character with decimal value 249
~hF9	The ASCII character with hexadecimal value F9
~o371	The ASCII character with octal value 371

NULL Values

Although PowerBuilder supports NULL values for all variable data types, it does not initialize variables to NULL. Instead, when a variable is not set to a specific value when it is declared, PowerBuilder sets it to the default initial value for the data type. For example. zero for a numeric value, FALSE for boolean, and the empty string ("") for a string.

Typically, you work with NULL values only with respect to database values.

NULL Variables

A variable can become NULL only if one of the following occurs:

- A NULL value is read into it from the database. If your database supports NULL and a SQL INSERT or UPDATE statement sends a NULL to the database, it is written to the database as NULL and can be read into a variable by a SELECT or FETCH statement.

When a NULL value is read into a variable, the variables remains NULL unless it is changed in a script.

- The SetNull function is used in a script to set the variable explicitly to NULL. For example:

```
string city  // city is an empty string.

SetNull(city)  // city is set to NULL.
```

What NULL Means

NULL means undefined. Think of NULL as unknown. It is not the same as an empty string or zero or a date of 0000.00-00. For example, NULL is neither 0 nor not 0.

Any function that has a NULL value for any argument returns NULL. Any expression that has a NULL variable results in NULL.

Examples

None of the following statements will make the computer beep. The variable `nbr` is set to NULL, so each statement evaluates to NOT TRUE:

```
int  Nbr
// Set Nbr to NULL.
SetNull (Nbr)
if Nbr =1 then Beep(1)
if Nbr <> 1 then Beep(1)
if NOT (Nbr = 1) then Beep(1)
```

In the following `IF...THEN` statement, the expression evaluates to NOT TRUE, so the `ELSE` is executed:

```
int  a
SetNull (a)
If a = 1 Then
    MessageBox("Value", "a = 1")
Else
    MessageBox("value","a = NULL")
End If
```

This is very useful. For example, the following statement displays a message if no control has focus (if no control has focus, GetFocus returns a null object reference):

```
If GetFocus() Then
.
. // Some processing
.
Else
    MessageBox("Important", "Specify an option!")
End If
```

Testing for NULL

To test whether a variable or expression is NULL, use the IsNull function. You *cannot* use an equal sign (=) to test for NULL.

Examples

These statements show the correct and incorrect way to test for NULL:

```
if IsNull(a) then . . .   // This is correct.
if a = NULL then  ...   // This is not valid.
```

Reserved Words

The words PowerBuilder uses internally are called reserved words and generally cannot be used as identifiers. The exceptions are *Parent*, *This*, *ParentWindow*, and *Super*. You can use these pronouns to make general references in scripts to objects and controls.

Parent, This, ParentWindow, and Super

When you use Parent, This, ParentWindow, or Super to make a general reference to an object or control, the reference is correct even if the name of the object or control changes.

You can use these pronouns in functions to cause an event in an object or control, or to manipulate or change an object or control. You can also use these pronouns to obtain or change the setting of an attribute.

Each of these pronouns has a specific meaning and use.

Parent

You can use the pronoun Parent in the following scripts:

- Scripts for a control in a window
- Scripts for a custom user object
- Scripts for a MenuItem

Where you use Parent determines what it references.

Window Controls

When you use Parent in a script for a control (such as a CommandButton), Parent refers to the window that contains the control. For example, if you include the following statement in the script for the Clicked event in a CommandButton within a window, clicking the button closes the window containing the button:

```
Close (Parent)
```

If you include the following statement in the script for the CommandButton, clicking the button displays a horizontal scroll bar within the window (sets the HScrollBar attribute of the window to TRUE):

```
Parent.HScrollBar = TRUE
```

User Object Controls

When you use Parent in a script for a control in a custom user controls object, Parent refers to the user object. For example, if you include the following statement in a script for the Clicked event for a CheckBox in a user object, clicking the CheckBox hides the user object:

```
parent.Hide()
```

If you include the following statement in the script for the CheckBox, clicking the CheckBox disables the user object (sets the Enabled attribute of the user object to FALSE):

```
parent.Disable()
```

If you include the following statement in the script for the Clicked event in the MenuItem Select All, clicking Select All checks the MenuItem Select:

```
Parent.Checked = TRUE
```

This

The pronoun This refers to the window, user object, MenuItem, application object, or control itself. For example, if you include the following statement in the script for the Clicked event for a CommandButton, clicking the button changes the horizontal position of the button (changes the button's X attribute):

```
This.x = This.x+50
```

Similarly, the following statement in a script for a MenuItem places a checkmark next to the MenuItem:

```
This.Check()
```

Why Include This

In the script for an object or control, you can refer to the attributes of the object or control without qualification. However, it is good programming practice to include This to make the script easy to read and to add clarification.

For example, if you omit This in the statement shown above, the statement accomplishes the same result but looks like this:

```
x = x + 50
```

However, if you omit This and there is a variable named x within the scope of the script, the variable takes precedence (the script adds 50 to the variable x, not to the x attribute of the control).

Also, you can use This in a function call to pass a reference to the object containing the script, such as:

```
ReCalc (This)
```

ParentWindow

The pronoun ParentWindow refers to the window that a menu is associated with at execution time. ParentWindow can be used only in scripts for MenuItems.

For example, the following statement in a script for a MenuItem closes the window the menu is associated with at execution time:

```
Close (Parentwindow)
```

This statement in the script for a MenuItem reduces the height of the window the menu is associated with at execution time:

```
Parentwindow.Height = Parentwindow.Height/2
```

However, the following statement in the script for a MenuItem is not valid. You cannot use ParentWindow to qualify a reference to a control:

```
Parentwindow.sle_Result.text = ... // INVALID
```

Super

When you write a script for a descendant object or control, you can call scripts written for any ancestor. You can directly name the ancestor in the call, or you can use the reserved word Super to reference the immediate ancestor (parent).

For example, to call the parent's Clicked script, code:

```
Call Super::Clicked
```

Summary

Reserved word	In a script for a	Refers to the
Parent	Control in a window	Window containing the control
	Control in a custom user object	Custom user object containing the control
	MenuItem	MenuItem on the level above the item the script is for
This	Window, custom user object, MenuItem, application object, or control	Object or control itself
ParentWindow	MenuItem	Window the MenuItem is associated with at execution time
Super	A descendant object or control	Parent

Statement Continuation and Separation

Although you typically put one statement on each line, you will occasionally want to continue a statement to more than one line or combine multiple statements on a single line.

Continuation Character

The PowerScript continuation character is the ampersand (&). To continue a statement to another line, insert an ampersand wherever there is white space at the end of a line and then start the new line. The ampersand must be the last nonwhite character on the line (or the compiler will consider it part of the statement). White space is discussed at the end of this section.

Examples

This statement is continued across two lines:

```
IF INDEX = 3 AND &
COUNT =4 THEN BEEP(4)
```

This statement is continued across three lines:

```
Total-Cost = Price&
   * Quantity +&
(Tax + Shipping)
```

Continuing a Quoted String

You can continue a quoted string by simply placing an ampersand in the middle of the string and continuing the string on the next line:

```
If Employee_District = "Eastern United State and&
Eastern Canada" Then ...
```

However, a better way to continue a quoted string is to enter a quotation mark before the continuation character ('& or "& depending on whether the string is delimited by single or double quotation marks) at the end of the first line of the string and a plus sign and a quotation mark (+' or +") at the start of the next line.

This method ensures that you do not inadvertently include unwanted characters (such as tabs) or spaces in the string literal. The examples in the PowerBuilder documentation and online Help use this method to continue quoted strings.

Examples

The following statement uses only the ampersand to continue the quoted string in the `IF...THEN` statement to another line. Note that a tab was used at the start of the second line to make the script easier to read:

```
If Employee~District = "Eastern United States and&
    Eastern Canada" Then ...'
```

When you use the method shown above to continue the string, the compiler includes the tab in the string, which may result in an error. When you use the recommended method (shown below), the tab is not included in the string:

```
If Employee_District = "Eastern United States and "&
    +" Eastern Canada" Then ...
```

Continuing a Variable Name

You *cannot* split a line by inserting the continuation character within a variable name. This will cause an error.

Examples

The following statement will fail, because the continuation character splits the variable name (Quantity):

```
Total-Cost = Price * Quan&
    tity + (Tax + Shipping)
```

The following statement is valid, because "Price * Quantity + (Tax + Shipping) is a quoted string, so Quantity can be split:

```
Total-Cost = "Price * Quan" &
    +"tity + (Tax + Shipping)"
```

Continuing a Comment

Do not use a continuation character to continue a comment. The continuation character is considered part of the comment and is ignored by the compiler.

Continuing a SQL Statement

Do not use a continuation character to continue a SQL statement. In PowerBuilder, SQL statements always end with a semicolon (;). The compiler considers everything from the start of the SQL statement until it encounters a semicolon to be part of the SQL statement. A continuation character in a SQL statement is considered part of the statement and usually causes an error.

Statement Separator

The PowerScript statement separator is the semicolon (;). Use it to separate multiple statements on a single line to conserve space when there are a number of short, related statements in a script.

Example

The following line contains three short statements:

```
A = B + C;  D = E + F;  Count = Count + 1
```

White Space

Blanks, tabs, formfeeds, and comments are forms of white space. The compiler ignores them unless they are part of a string literal (enclosed in single or double quotation marks).

Examples

In this example, the spaces and the comment in the expression are white space, so the compiler ignores them:

```
A + B /*Adjustment factor */+C
```

However, the spaces in the following are within a string literal, so the compiler does not ignore them:

```
"The value of A + B is:"
```

The subtraction operator: *Unless you have prohibited the use of dashes in identifiers, you must surround the subtraction operator (minus sign) with spaces. If you don't, PowerBuilder will consider the operator part of a variable name:*

```
Order - Balance  // Subtracts Balance from Order
Order-Balance    // A variable named Order-Balance
```

For information on the use of dashes in names, see "Identifier names" earlier in this appendix.

Data Types

This section describes the three kinds of data types provided by PowerScript:

- Standard data types
- System object data types
- Enumerated data types

The Standard Data Types

The standard data types are the familiar data types that are used in many programming languages, including char, integer, decimal, long, and string. In PowerScript, you use these data types when you declare variables or arrays.

This section:

- Lists all standard PowerScript data types
- Describes the use of literals
- Describes the string and char data types

Listing of the Standard Data Types

The following table lists all standard PowerScript data types.

Data Type	Description
Blob	Binary large object. Used to store an unbounded amount of data (for example, generic binary image, or large text, such as a word processing document).
Boolean	Contains TRUE or FALSE.
Char or character	A single ASCII character.
Date	The date, including the full year (1000 to 3000), the number of the month (01 to 12), and the day (01 to 31).
DateTime	The date and time in a single data type, used only for reading and writing DateTime values from and to a database. To convert DateTime values to data types that you can use in PowerBuilder, use: - The Date(datetime) function to convert a datetime value to a PowerBuilder date value after reading from a database - The Time(datetime) function to convert a datetime value to a PowerBuilder time value after reading from a database - The DateTime (date, time) function to convert a date and (optional) time to a DateTime before writing to a DateTime column in a database PowerBuilder supports microseconds in the database interface for any DBMS that supports microseconds.
Decimal or Dec	Signed decimal numbers with up to 18 digits. You can place the decimal point anywhere within the 18 digits. For example 123.456, 0.000000000000000001, or 12345678901234.5678.

Data Type	Description
Double	A signed floating-point number with 15 digits of precision and a range from 2.2E-308 to 1.7E+308.
Integer or Int	16-bit signed integers from -32768 to +32767.
Long	32-bit signed integers, from -2,147,483,648 to +2,147,483,647.
Real	A signed floating-point number with six digits of precision and a range from 1.17 E -38 to 3.4 E +38.
String	Any ASCII characters with variable length (0 to 60,000).
Time	The time in 24-hour format, including the hour (00 to 23), minute (00 to 59), second (00 to 59), and fraction of second (up to six digits) with a range from 00:00:00 to 23:59:59.999999.
UnsignedInteger, UnsignedInt, or UInt	16-bit unsigned integers, from 0 to 65,535.
UnsignedLong or ULong	32-bit unsigned integers, from 0 to 4,294.967,295.

Using Literals

You use literals to assign values to variables of the standard data types. PowerScript supports the following types of literals: date, decimal, integer, real, string, and time.

You use integer literals to assign values to data types that can contain only whole numbers and real literals to assign values to the data types real and double.

The following table describes each type of literal:

Type	Description

Date	The date, including the full year (1000 to 3000), the number of the month (01 to 12), and the day (01 to 31), separated by hyphens. For example:
	
	`1992-12-25 // December 25, 1992`
	`1995-02-06 // February 6, 1995`

Decimal	Any number with a decimal point and no exponent. The plus sign is optional (95 and +95 are the same). For numbers between zero and one, the zero to the left of the decimal point is optional (for example, 0.1 and .1 are the same). For whole numbers, zeros to the right of the decimal point are optional (32.00. 3 2.0. and 32. are all the same). For example:
	
	`12.34 0.005 14.0 15`
	`16. -6500 +3.555`

Type	Description
Integer	Any whole number (positive, negative, or zero). The leading plus sign is optional (18 and +18 are the same). For example: `1 123 1200 +55 -32`

Real	A decimal value, followed by E, followed by an integer; no spaces are allowed. The decimal number before the E follows all the conventions specified above for decimal literals. The leading plus sign in the exponent (the integer following the E) is optional (3E5 and 3E+5 are the same). For example:
	
	`2E4 2.5E78 +6.02E3 -4.1E-2`
	`-7.45E16 7.7E+8 3.2E-45`

String	As many as 1024 characters enclosed in single or double quotes, including a string of zero length or an empty string. For example: `"CAT" "123" 'C:\WEST94' ""`

Time	The time in 24-hour format, including the hour (00 to 23), minute (00 to 59), second (00 to 59), and fraction of second (up to six digits) with a range from 00:00:00 to 23:59:59.999999. You separate parts of the time with colons, except for fractional sections, which should be separated by a decimal point. For example:
	
	`21:09:15 // 15 seconds after 9:09 pm`
	`06:00:00 // Exactly 6 am`
	`10:29:59 // 1 second before 10:30 am`
	`10:29:59.9 // 1/10 second before 10:30 am`

Using Strings and Chars

PowerBuilder provides tow character-based data types: char and string. Chars contain one character; strings can contain multiple characters. You can define arrays of either type.

Using Strings

Most of the character-based data in your application, such as names, addresses, and so on, will be defined as strings. PowerScript provides many functions that you can use to manipulate strings, such as a function to convert characters in a string to uppercase and functions to remove leading and trailing blanks.

Using Chars

If you have character-based data that you will want to parse in an application, you might want to define it as an array of type char. Parsing a char array is easier and faster than parsing strings. Also, if you will be passing character-based data to external functions, you might want to use char arrays instead of strings.

Using Quotation Marks

You can use either single or double quotation marks with strings and chars. For example, these two assignments are equivalent:

```
String s1
s1 = "This Is a string"
s1 = 'This is a string'
```

Similarly, these two assignments are equivalent:

```
char c
c = "T"
c = 'T'
```

You can embed a quotation mark in a string literal if you enclose the literal with the other quotation mark. For example:

```
string s1
s1 = "Here's a String."
```

results in the string *Here's a string*.

Otherwise, you must use a tilde (~) to embed a quotation mark in a string literal. For example:

```
string s1 = 'He said, "It~'s good!"'
```

Converting Between Strings and Chars

There is no explicit char literal type. String literals convert to type char using the following rules:

- When a string literal is assigned to a char variable, the first character of the string literal is assigned to the character. For example:

```
char c = "xyz"
```

results in the character *x* being assigned to the char c.
- Special characters (such as newline, formfeed, octal, hex, and so on) can be assigned to char variables using string conversion, such as:

```
char c = "~n"
```

Also, string variables assigned to char variables convert using the same rules. A char variable assigned to a string variable results in a one-character string.

Assigning Strings to Char Arrays

As with other data types, you can use arrays of chars. Assigning strings to char arrays follows these rules:

- If the char array is unbounded (that is, if it is defined as a variable-size array), the contents of the string are copied directly into the char array.
- If the char array is bounded and its length is less than or equal to the length of the string, the string is truncated in the array.
- If the char array is bounded and its length is greater than the length of the string, the entire string is copied into the array along with its zero terminator. Remaining characters in the array are undetermined.

Assigning Char Arrays to Strings

When a char array is assigned to a string variable, the contents of the array are copied into the string up to a zero terminator, if found, in the string.

Using both Strings and Chars in an Expression

Expressions using both strings and char arrays promote the chars to strings before evaluation. For example:

```
char c
.
.
.
if (c = "x") then
```

promotes the contents or c to a string before comparison with the string "x".

Using Chars in PowerScript Functions

PowerScript functions that take strings also take chars and char arrays, subject to the conversion rules described above.

The System Object Data Types

In PowerBuilder applications, you manipulate objects such as windows, menus, command buttons, listboxes, and graphs. Internally, PowerBuilder defines each of these kinds of objects as a data type. Usually you don't need to concern yourself with these objects as data types—you simply define the objects in a PowerBuilder painter and use them.

But there are times when you need to understand how PowerBuilder maintains its system objects in a hierarchy of data types. For example, when you need to define instances of a window, you will define variables whose data type is window. When you need to create an instance of a menu to pop up in a window, you will define a variable whose data type is menu.

This section describes the PowerBuilder system object hierarchy.

Using the Class Browser

The easiest way to understand the hierarchy of system objects is to use the Class browser.

To open the Class browser:

1 Open the Library painter.
2 Select Browse Class Hierarchy from the Utilities menu.

    The Class browser displays:

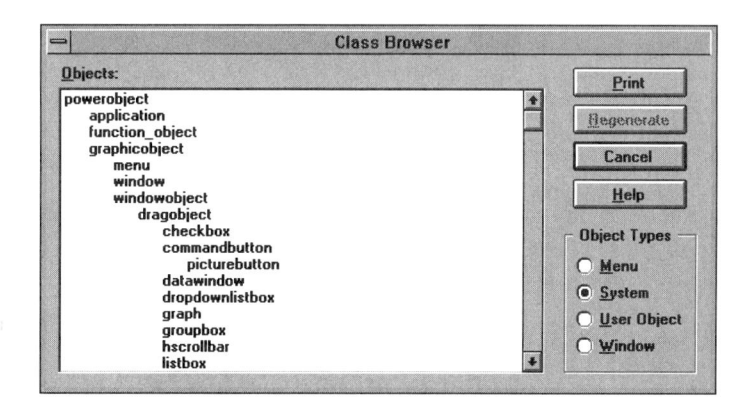

3 To see the system objects, make sure the System button is selected in the Object Types box. (Clicking any of the other buttons displays the inheritance hierarchy of objects that have been created in the current application.)

About the System Object Hierarchy

PowerBuilder maintains its system objects in a class hierarchy. Each type of object is a class. The classes form an inheritance hierarchy of ancestors and descendants.

Looking at the Hierarchy

By scrolling through the list of classes in the Class browser, you can see the hierarchy. The Class browser uses indentation to show inheritance. In the preceding screen, for example, you can see that at the top of the hierarchy is PowerObject—all PowerBuilder system objects are derived from PowerObject.

Looking further down, you see GraphicObject, which is the class that serves as the ancestor to all the graphical objects you use in PowerBuilder applications. For example, Menu is a type of GraphicObject—that is, the Menu class is derived from the GraphicObject class. Window is also a type of GraphicObject.

Objects as Data Types

All the classes shown in the Class browser are actually data types that you can use in your applications. You can define variables whose type is any class.

Examples

For example, to define a window variable, you could code:

```
window mywin
```

To define a menu variable, you could code:

```
menu mymenu
```

If you have a series of buttons in a window and for some reason need to keep track of one of them (for example, the last one clicked), you could declare a variable of type CommandButton and assign it the appropriate button in the window:

```
// Instance variable in a window commandbutton
LastClicked
// In Clicked event for a button in the window.
// Indicates that the button was the last one
// clicked by the user.
LastClicked = This
```

Being a CommandButton, the LastClicked variable has all the attributes of a CommandButton. After the last assignment above, LastClicked's attributes have the same values as the most recently clicked button in the window.

The Enumerated Data Types

Like the system object data types, enumerated data types are specific to PowerScript. These data types are used in two ways:

- As arguments in functions
- To specify the attributes of an object or control

About Enumerated Data Types

Each enumerated data type can be assigned a fixed set of values. Values of enumerated data types always end with an exclamation point (!).

For example, the enumerated data type Alignment, which specifies the alignment of text, can be assigned one of the following three values: Center!, Left!, and Right!.

When you enter enumerated data type values, do not enclose the value in quotation marks:

```
// This is correct.
mle_edit.Alignment = Left!
// The following statement will NOT compile.
// "Left!" is a string and the compiler
// expects an enumerated data value.
mle_edit.Alignment="Left!"
```

Advantage of Enumerated Types

Enumerated data types have the following advantage over standard data types: when an enumerated data type is required, the compiler checks the data and makes sure it is the correct type.

For example, to set the alignment of text in a line edit in a script, set the Alignment attribute to one of the Alignment enumerated data values, such as:

```
mle_edit .Alignment = Right!
```

If you set the Alignment attribute to any other data type or value, the compiler will not allow the value.

Listing the Enumerated Data Types

You can list all the enumerated data types and their values in the Object browser.

To list the enumerated data types:

1 Do one of the following:

- Open the PowerScript painter and click the Browse icon or select Browse Objects from the Edit menu.
- Open the Library painter and select Browse Objects from the Utilities menu.

The Object browser opens.

2 Select Enumerated as the Object Type and Attributes as the Paste Category.

PowerBuilder lists all enumerated data types in the Objects box and the valid values of the selected data type in the Paste Values box.

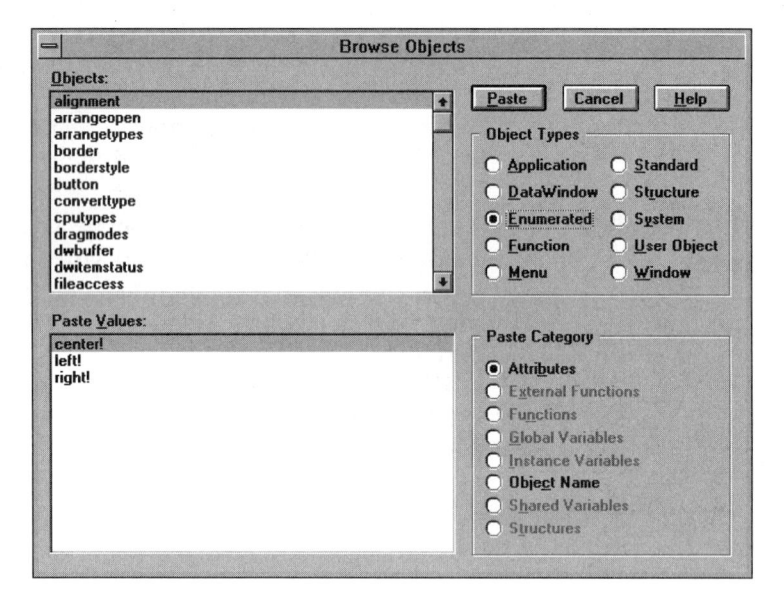

Declarations

Before you use a variable or array in a script, you must declare it (give it a type and a name). For example, before you can use an integer variable, you must identify it as an integer and assign it a name.

This section explains how to declare variables and arrays.

Types of Variables

PowerScript recognizes four types of variables:

- Global variables, which are accessible anywhere in an application
- Instance variables, which are associated with one instance of an object, such as a window
- Shared variables, which are associated with a type of object
- Local variables, which are accessible only in one script

Global Variables

You use global variables when you have data that needs to be available anywhere: global variables can be used without qualification in any script in an application.

For example, if you have defined a global integer variable named WinCount, you can reference the variable directly in any script, such as:

```
Wincount = Wincount + 1
```

To declare global variables:

1 Select Global Variables from the Declare menu in the Window, User Object, Menu, or PowerScript painter.

Instance Variables

You use instance variables when you have variables that need to be accessible in more than one script within an object, but that don't need to be global throughout the entire application. For example, several scripts for a window might reference an employee ID. You can declare EmpID as an instance variable for that window; all scripts in that window have access to that variable. In effect, instance variables are attributes of the object.

Instance variables can be application-level, window-level, user-object-level, or menu-level variables:

- Application-level variables are declared within the application object. They are always available in any scripts for the application object. In addition, you can choose to make access to them available throughout the application.
- Window-level variables are declared within a window. They are always available in any scripts for the window in which they are declared and the controls in that window. In addition, you can choose to make access to them available throughout the application.
- User-object-level variables are declared within a user object. They are always available in any scripts for the user object in which they are declared and the controls in that user object. In addition, you can choose to make access to them available throughout the application.
- Menu-level variables are declared within a menu. They are always available in any scripts for the menu in which they are declared and its MenuItems. In addition, you can choose to make access to them available throughout the application.

Declaring Instance Variables

To declare instance variables:

1 Select Instance Variables from the Declare menu in the Window, User Object, Menu, or PowerScript painter.

Specifying Access to Instance Variables

When you declare an instance variable you can also specify the access level for the variable—that is, you can specify which scripts have access to the instance variable:

Access	You can reference the instance variable in
Public	Any script in the application.
Private	Scripts for events in the object for which the variable is declared. You cannot reference the variable in descendants of the object.
Protected	Scripts for the object for which the variable is declared and its descendants.

To specify an access level when you declare an instance variable, include the access level in the declaration. If you don't specify an access level, the variable is defined as Public.

Two Ways to Specify Access

You can specify the access level using one of two formats. In the first format, you include the access specifier on the same line as the declaration, before the data type:

```
access-specifier type variable
access-specifier type variable
...
```

For example:

```
private int X,Y
public int Subtotal
protected int WinCount
```

In the second format, you can group declarations by including the access specifier on its own line, followed by a colon:

```
access-specifier:
    type variable
    type variable
```

For example:

```
Private:
    int X=10, Y=24
    string Name, Address1
Protected:
    int Units
    double Results
    string Lname
Public:
    int Weight
    string  Location="Home"
```

In the preceding example. X, Y, Name, and Address1 are Private variables: Units, Results, and Lname are Protected variables; and Weight and Location are Public variables.

How Instance Variables Are Initialized

When you define an instance variable for a window, menu, or application object, the instance variable is initialized when the object is opened. Its initial value is the default value for its data type or the value specified in the variable declarations.

When you close the object, the instance variable ceases to exist. If you open the object again, the instance variable is initialized again.

If you need a variable that continues to exist after the object is closed, use a shared variable, described next.

When Using Multiple Instances of Windows

When you build a script for one of multiple instances of a window, instance variables can have a different value in each instance of the window. For example, to set a flag based on the contents of the instance of a window, you would use an instance variable.

If you need a variable that keeps the same value over multiple instances of an object, use shared variables, described next.

Referring to Instance Variables

You can refer to instance variables in scripts if there is an instance of the object open in the application. Depending on the situation, you might need to qualify the name of the instance variable with the name of the object defining it.

Using Unqualified Names

You can refer to instance variables without qualifying them with the object name in the following cases:

- For application-level variables, in scripts for the application object
- For window-level variables, in scripts for the window itself and in scripts for controls in that window
- For user-object-level variables, in scripts for the user object itself and in scripts for controls in that user object
- For menu-level variables, in scripts for the menu itself and in scripts for the MenuItems in that menu

For example, if W_Emp has an instance variable EmpID, in any script for W_Emp or its controls, you can reference EmpID without qualification, such as:

```
sle_id.Text = EmpID
```

Using Qualified Names

In all other cases, you need to qualify the name of the instance names variable with the name of the object using dot notation:

```
object.instance-variable
```

(Of course, this applies only to Public or Protected instance variables. You cannot reference Private instance variables outside the object at all.)

For example, to refer to the w_emp instance variable EmpID from a script outside the window, you need to qualify the variable with the window name, such as:

```
sle_ID.Text = w_emp.EmpID
```

There is another situation in which references must be qualified: suppose that W_Emp has an instance variable EmpID and that in W_Emp there is a command button that declares a local variable EmpID in its Clicked script. In that script, you must qualify all references to the instance variable, such as:

```
Parent.EmpID
```

Shared Variables

Shared variables, like instance variables, can be application level, window-level, user-object level, or menu-level variables. Shared variables are associated with the object definition, rather than an instance of the object. Therefore, all instances of the object type have the shared variable in common.

For example, if you define a shared variable for the window W_Emp, each instance of W_Emp open in the application uses the same variable: the value of the shared variable is the same in each instance of W_Emp.

Shared variables retain their value when an object is closed and then opened again.

To declare shared variables:

1 Select Shared Variables from the Declare menu in the Window, User Object, Menu, or PowerScript painter.

You declare access to and reference shared variables the same way you do for instance variables, described above.

How Shared Variables Are Initialized

When you use a shared variable in the script for a window or menu, the variable is initialized when the first instance of the window is opened. When you close the window, the shared variable continues to exist until you exit the application. If you open the window again without exiting the application, the shared variable will have the value it had when you closed the window.

For example, if in the script for a window you set the shared variable Count to 20 and close the window, and then reopen the window without exiting the application, Count will be equal to 20.

When using multiple instances of windows *If you have multiple instances of the window in the example above, Count will be equal to 20 in each instance. Since shared variables are shared among all instances of the window, changing Count in any instance of the window changes it for all instances.*

Local Variables

Use local variables when you need a temporary variable to hold some value. Local variables are declared in a script and can be used only in that script.

How PowerBuilder Looks for Variables

When PowerBuilder executes a script and finds an unqualified reference to a variable, it looks for the variable in the following order:

1 A local variable
2 A shared variable
3 A global variable
4 An instance variable

As soon as PowerBuilder finds a variable with the specified name, it uses the variable's value.

Declaring Variables

There are two sets of syntax for declaring variables: a standard syntax for all variable data types except blob and decimal, and a syntax for blob and decimal variables.

Standard Declarations

To declare any variable except a blob or decimal, enter the data type followed by one or more spaces and the variable name:

```
int count                // Declares count as an integer
long comment-length      // Declared comment-length
                         // as a long
string first-name        // Delcares first-name as
                         // a string
                         // Strings do not have
                         // predefined sizes.
```

You can declare multiple variables of the same data type on one line. To declare additional variables of the same type on the same line, enter a comma and the next variable name:

```
int a, b, c              // Declares a, b, and c
```

Blob Declarations

To declare a blob variable, enter **Blob** followed by the length of the blob (in bytes) enclosed in braces ({}) and the variable name. The length is optional, and braces are required only if you specify the length.

If you enter the length and exceed the declared length in a script, PowerBuilder will truncate the blob. If you do not enter the length in the declaration, the blob has an initial length of 0 and PowerBuilder will define its size by use at execution time.

Blobs cannot be initialized.

Examples

```
blob           Emp_Picture    // Declares Emp_Picture
                              // as a blob with 0 length
blob (100)     Emp_Picture    // Declares Emp_Picture
                              // a blob with a length of
                              // 100 bytes
```

Decimal Declarations

To declare a decimal variable, enter **Dec** or **Decimal** followed by the number of digits after the decimal point (the **precision**) enclosed in braces ({ }) and the variable name. The braces are required only if you enter the precision.

If you do not enter the precision in the declaration, the variable takes the precisions assigned to it in the script.

Examples

```
decimal {2}    Amount         // Declares Amount as a
                              // decimal number with 2
                              // digits after the
                              // decimal point

dec {4}        Rate1, Rate2   // Declares Rate1 and
                              // Rate2 as decimal
                              // numbers with 4
                              // digits after the
                              // decimal point
```

```
                    decimal {0}    Balance          // Declares Balance as a
                                                    // decimal with 0 digits
                                                    // after the decimal point

                    dec            Result
                    dec {2}        Op1, Op2
                    Result = Op1 * Op2              // Result now has 4 digits
                                                    // after the decimal point.
```

Initial Values

When you declare a variable, you can assign an initial value to the variable or accept the default initial value.

Assigning Values

To assign a value to a variable when you declare it, place an equal sign (=) and a literal appropriate for that variable data type after the variable.

Examples

```
                    int count = 5                   // Declares count as an integer
                                                    // and assigns 5 to it

                    int a = 5, b = 10               // Declares a and b as integers
                                                    // and assigns 5 to a and 10 to b

                    string methods = "UPS"          // Declares method as a
                                                    // string and assigns "UPS" to it

                    int a = 1, b, c = 100           // Declares a, b, and c as
                                                    // integers, assigns 1 to a, lets
                                                    // b default to 0, and assigns
                                                    // 100 to c.

                    date StartDate = 1993-02-01     // Declares StartDate as a
                                                    // date and assigns
                                                    // Feb 1, 1993 to it
```

NOTE

Assignment using a variable of an existing variable, such as: You can also initialize a variable with the value

```
int i
...
int j = i
```

When you do this, the variable is assigned the value the existing variable has when the script is compiled.

Using Default Values

If you do not assign a value to a variable when you declare it, PowerBuilder sets the variable to the default value for its data type.

The following table lists the default values for variable data types:

Variable data type	Default value
Blob	A blob of 0 length; an empty blob
Char	ASCII value 0
Boolean	FALSE
Date	1900-01-01 (January 1, 1900)

Variable data type	Default value
DateTime	1900-01-01 00:00:00
Numeric (integer, long, decimal, real, double, UnsignedInteger, and UnsignedLong	0 (zero)
String	Empty string ("")
Time	00:00:00 (midnight)

Declaring Arrays

An array is an indexed collection of elements of a single data type. An array can be single- or multidimensional. Single-dimensional arrays can have a fixed or variable size, and single-dimensional arrays without a range can have as many as 65,534 elements. Each dimension of a multidimensional array can have 65,534 (-32,767 to +32,767) elements.

To declare an array, enclose the sizes of the array in square brackets after the variable name. Here is an example of a single-dimensional array of three integers named TaxCode:

```
int TaxCode[3]  // Delcares an array of 3 integers
```

To refer to individual array elements, use square brackets and the element number, such as TaxCode[1], TaxCode[2], and TaxCode [3].

Array Defaults

PowerBuilder initializes each element of an array to the same default value as its underlying data type. For example, in the integer array TaxCode[3], the elements TaxCode[1], TaxCode[2], and TaxCode[3] are all initialized to zero.

To override the default values, initialize the elements of the array when you declare the array by specifying a comma-separated list of values enclosed in braces. Here is an example of an initialized one-dimensional array of three variables:

```
real Rate[3] = {1.20, 2.40, 4.80}
```

You can also assign values after declaring an array using the same syntax:

```
int Arr[]
Arr = {1, 2, 3, 4}
```

Array Element Numbering

Array elements start counting at 1 (TaxCode[1]). To override this default, use the TO notation:

```
real Rate[2 to 5]             // Declares array of 4 real
                              // numbers:  Rate[2], Rate[3],
                              // Rate[4] and Rate[5]
```

```
int Qty[0 to 2]           // Declares array of 3 integers
string Test[-2 to 2]      // Declares 5 strings
```

In an array dimension, the second number must be greater than the first. These declarations are invalid:

```
int   count[10 to 5]      // INVALID because 10 is
                          // greater than 5

int   price[-10 to -20]   // INVALID because -10 is
                          // greater than -20
```

Variable-Size Arrays

A variable-size array consists of a variable name followed by square brackets but no number. PowerBuilder defines it *by use* at execution time (subject only to memory constraints). Only one-dimensional arrays can be variable-size arrays.

Examples

```
long price[ ]             // Declares a variable-size
                          // array of any quantity of
                          // decimal numbers

price [100] =2000
price[50] =3000
price [110] =5000
```

When the statements above first execute, they allocate memory as follows:

- The statement price[l00]=2000 will allocate memory for 100 long numbers price[1] to price[100], then assign 0 (the default for numbers) to price[1] through price[99] and assign 2000 to price[100].
- The statement price[50]=3000 will not allocate more memory, but will assign the value 3000 to the 50th element of the price array.
- The statement price[110]=5000 will allocate memory for 10 more long numbers named price[101] to price[110], then assign 0 (the default for numbers) to price[101] through price[109] and assign 5000 to price[110].

Example

To initialize a variable-size array, list all required values in braces. The following statement sets code[1] equal to 11, code[2] equal to 242, and code[3] equal to 27:

```
INT code[ ]={11,242,27}
```

Multidimensional Arrays

A fixed-size array can have more than one dimension. To specify additional dimensions, use a comma-separated list. The amount of memory in your system is the only limit to the number of dimensions for an array. You cannot initialize multidimensional arrays.

Example

Here is an example of a declared six-element two-dimensional integer array:

```
int score[2,3]            // Declares a 6-element,
                          // 2-dimensional array
```

The individual elements are score[1,1], score[1,2], score[1,3], score[2, 1], score[2,2], and score[2,3].

Index Values

By default, all index values of a multidimensional array start at 1, but you can override the default with the TO notation.

Example

The array declarations below are valid:

```
// 2-dimensional 75-element array
int RunRate[1 to 5, 10 to 25]
// 3-dimensional 45,000-element array
long days[3,300,50]
// 3-dimensional 20,000-element array
int staff[100,0 to 20,-5 to 5]
```

String Arrays

You declare string arrays the same way you declare numeric arrays.

Examples

```
string day[7]              // Declares a one-dimensional array
                           // of 7 strings

string name[-10 to 15]     // Declares a one-dimensional array
                           // of 26 strings

string plant[3,10]         // Declares a 2-dimensional array
                           // of 30 strings

string [city]              // Declares an array that can hold
                           // any number of strings and each
                           // string can be any length
```

Decimal Arrays

To declare a decimal array, enter Dec or Decimal, followed by the number of digits after the decimal point (the precision) enclosed in braces ({}), the array name, and the dimensions of the array enclosed in square brackets.

If you do not enter the precision in the declaration, the variable takes the precisions assigned to it in the script.

Examples

```
dec{2} Cost[10]            // Declares an array of 10 decimal
                           // numbers each with 2 digits
                           // following the decimal point

decimal price[20]          // Declares an array of 20 decimal
                           // numbers where each takes the
                           // assigned precision; no
                           // precision specified

dec{8} limit[]             // Declares a variable-size array
                           // of decimal numbers each with 8
                           // digits following the decimal
                           // point

dec limit[]                // Declares a variable-size array
                           // of decimal numbers and does not
                           // specify the precision so each
                           // element will take the
                           // precision assigned
```

```
                 dec{2} rate[3,4]               // Declares a 2-dimensional array
                                                // of 12 decimal numbers each
                                                // with 2 digits after the
                                                // decimal point

                 decimal{3} first[10], second[15,5],third[]
                                                // The line above declares 3
                                                // decimal arrays. Every number
                                                // in each array has 3 digits
                                                // after the decimal point.
```

Array Errors

Referring to array elements outside the declared size causes an error during execution. For example:

```
int test[10]
test[11] = 50                   // This causes an execution error.
test[0] = 50                    // This causes an execution error.
int trial[5,10]
trial [6,2] = 75                // This causes an execution error.
trial [4,11] = 75               // This causes an execution error.
```

Accessing a variable-size array above its largest assigned value or below its lowest assigned value also causes an error during execution:

```
int stock[]
stock[50] = 200

if stock[51] = 0 then Beep(1)   // This causes an
                                // execution error.

if stock[0] = 0 then Beep(1)    // This causes an
                                // execution error.
```

Operators and Expressions

Operators perform arithmetic calculations: compare numbers, text, and boolean values; execute logical operations on boolean values; and manipulate text strings.

This section describes the operators supported in PowerScript and shows how you can manipulate strings in expressions.

Operators

PowerScript supports the following types of operators:

- Arithmetic operators
- Relational operators
- Logical operators

Arithmetic Operators

The following table lists the arithmetic operators:

Operator	Meaning	Example
+	Addition	`Total = Sub/Total+Tax`
-	Subtraction	`Price = Price - Discount` Unless you have prohibited the use of dashes in identifier names, you must surround the minus sign with spaces.
*	Multiplication	`Total = Quantity * Price`
/	Division	`Factor = Discount / Price`
^	Exponentiation	`Rank = Rating ^ 2.5`

Multiplication and Division

Multiplication and division are carried out to full precision (16–18 digits). Decimal numbers are rounded (not truncated) on assignment.

Examples

```
decimal {4} a,b,c,d,e,f
decimal {3} c
a = 20.0/3              // a contains 6.6667.
b = 3 * a               // b contains 20.0001.
c = 3 * a               // c contains 20.000.
d = 3 * (20.0/3)        // d contains 20.000.
e = truncate(20.0/3,4)  // e contains 6.6666.
e = truncate(20.0/3,5)  // e contains 6.6667.
```

Calculations with NULL

When you form an arithmetic expression that contains a NULL value, the expression becomes NULL.

Thinking of NULL as undefined makes this easier to understand.

Examples

```
int a, b = 100, c
SetNull(c)
a = b + c               // a is NULL.
a = b - c               // a is NULL.
a = b * c               // a is NULL.
a = b / c               // a is NULL.
```

For more information about NULL values, see "Language Basics."

Errors and Overflows

Division by zero, exponentiation of negative values, and so on cause errors during execution.
   Overflow of real, double, and decimal values cause errors during execution. Overflow of signed or unsigned integers and longs cause results to wrap.

Example

```
int i
i = 32767
i = i + 1                    // i is now -32768.
```

Relational Operators

PowerBuilder uses relational operators in relational expressions to evaluate two or more operands. The result is always TRUE or FALSE.

The following table lists the relational operators:

Operator	Meaning	Example
=	Equals	if Price=100 then Rate=.05
>	Greater than	if Price>100 then Rate=.05
<	Less than	if Price<100 then Rate=.05
<>	Not equal	if Price<>100 then Rate=.05
>=	Greater than or equal to	if Price>=100 then Rate=.05
<=	Less than or equal to	if Price<=100 then Rate=.05

Logical Operators

PowerBuilder uses logical operators to form boolean expressions. The result of evaluating a boolean expression is always TRUE or FALSE.

The following table lists the logical operators:

Operator	Meaning	Example
NOT	Logical negation	if NOT Price=100 then Rate=.05
AND	Logical and	if Tax>3 AND Ship<5 then Rate=.05
OR	Logical or	if Tax>3 OR Ship<5 then Rate=.05

Null Value Evaluations

When you form a boolean expression that contains a NULL value, the AND and OR operators behave differently. Thinking of NULL as undefined (neither TRUE nor FALSE) makes the results easier to calculate.

Examples

```
boolean d, e = TRUE, f
SetNULL(f)
d = e and f                  // d is NULL
d = e or f                   // d is TRUE
```

For more information about NULL values, see "Language Basics."

Operator Precedence

To ensure predictable results, all operators in a PowerBuilder expression are evaluated in a specific order of precedence. When the operators have the same precedence, PowerBuilder evaluates them left to right.

The following table lists the operators in descending order of precedence:

Operator	Purpose
()	Grouping (see note below)
+, -	Unary plus and unary minus
^	Exponentiation
*, /	Multiplication and division
+, -	Addition and subtraction; string concatenation
=, >, <. <=, >=, <>	Relational operators
NOT	Negation
AND	Logical and
OR	Logical or

Grouping expressions *To override the order, enclose expressions in parentheses. This identifies the group and order in which PowerBuilder will evaluate the expressions. When there are nested groups, the groups are evaluated from the inside out.*

Example

In the expression, (x+(y*(a+b))), a+b is evaluated first. The sum of a and b is then multiplied by y, and this product is added to x.

Strings

You can concatenate and compare strings.

String Concatenation

To concatenate strings, use the plus sign (+) operator between the strings.

Example

```
string Test
Test = "over" + "stock"  // Test contains "overstock"

string Lname, Fname, FullName
FullName = Lname + ', ' + Fname
    //FullName contains last name and first name,
//separated by a comma and space.
```

String Comparison

When PowerBuilder compares strings, the comparison is case-sensitive. Trailing blanks are significant.

Case-Sensitive Examples

```
City1 = "Austin"
City2 = "AUSTIN"
if City1 = City2 ...              // Will return FALSE

City1 = "Austin"
City2 = "AUSTIN"
if UPPER(City1) = UPPER(City2) ...// Will return TRUE
```

534 APPENDIX D POWERSCRIPT LANGUAGE REFERENCE

To compare strings regardless of case, use the Upper of Lower function.

Trailing Blanks Examples

```
City1 = "Austin"
City2 = "Austin      "
if City1 = City ...              // Will return FALSE
```

To remove trailing blanks, use the RightTrim function. To remove leading blanks, use the LeftTrim function. To remove leading and trailing blanks use the Trim function.

Statements

You can use the following statements in a script:

- Assignment statements
- CALL
- CHOOSE CASE
- CONTINUE
- CREATE
- DESTROY
- DO...LOOP
- EXIT
- FOR...NEXT
- GOTO
- HALT and RETURN
- IF...THEN

This section describes each statement and how to use it in a script.

Assignment Statements

Use assignment statements to assign values to variables. To assign a value to a variable anywhere in a script use the equal sign (=). For example:

```
String1 = "Part is out of stock"
TaxRate = .05
```

No Multiple Assignments

Since the equal sign is also a logical operator, you cannot assign more than one variable in a single statement. For example. the following statement does not assign the value 0 to A and B:

```
A = B = 0 // This will not assign 0 to A and B.
```

The above statement first evaluates B = 0 to TRUE or FALSE and then tries to assign this boolean value to A. When A is not a boolean variable, this line produces an error when compiled.

Assigning Array Values

You can assign multiple array values with one statement, such as:

```
int Arr[]
Arr = {1,2,3,4}
```

You can also copy array contents. For example:

```
Arr1 = Arr2
```

copies the contents of Arr2 into array Arr1.

Shortcuts

Shortcuts PowerScript provides the following shortcuts you can use to assign values to variables. They have slight performance advantages over their equivalents:

Assignment	Example	Equivalent to
++	i++	i = i + 1
--	i--	i = i - 1
+=	i += 3	i = i + 3
-=	i -= 3	i = i - 3
*=	i += 3	i = i * 3
/=	i /= 3	i = i / 3
^=	i ^= 3	i = i ^ 3

Unless you have prohibited the use of dashes in variable names, you must leave a space before – and -= (otherwise, PowerScript thinks the minus sign is part of a variable name). For more information, see "Identifier names" in "Language Basics."

Here are some examples of assignments:

```
int i = 4
i ++                         // i is now 5.
i --                         // i is 4 again.
i += 10                      // i is now 14.
i /= 2                       // i is now 7.
```

These shortcuts can be used only in pure assignment statements. They cannot be used with other operators in a statement. For example, the following is invalid:

```
int i, j
i = 12
j = i ++                     // INVALID
```

The following is valid, because ++ is used by itself in the assignment:

```
int i, j
i = 12
i ++
j = i
```

Using Dot Notation

To assign a value to an attribute of an object, use PowerScript dot notation to identify the object and attribute:

```
object.attribute
```

where object is the name of the object (or the reserved word Parent, ParentWindow, or This), and attribute is the attribute to which you assign the value. You also use dot notation to test for or obtain the value of an object.

Examples

This example makes a CheckBox invisible:

```
Chkbox_on.Visible = FALSE
```

This example calculates the value of the string in the SingeLineEdit sle_emp:

```
string Text1
Text1 = sle_emp.Text + ".DAT"
```

Call

CALL calls an ancestor script from a script for a descendant object.

Syntax

```
CALL ancestorobject {`controlname}::event
```

Parameter	Description
ancestorobject	An ancestor of the descendant object
controlname	The name of a control in an ancestor window or custom user object
event	An event in the ancestor object

Examples

The following statement calls a script for an event in an ancestor window:

```
CALL w_emp::Open
```

The following statement calls a script for an event in a control in an ancestor window:

```
CALL w_emp`cb_close::Clicked
```

CHOOSE CASE

Use the CHOOSE CASE control structure to direct program execution based on the value of a test expression (usually a variable).

Syntax

```
CHOOSE CASE textexpression
CASE expressionlist
    statementblock
{CASE expressionlist
    statementblock
    .
    .
    .
CASE expressionlist
    statementblock}
{CASE ELSE
    statementblock}
END CHOOSE
```

Parameter	Description
testexpression	The expression on which you want to base the execution of the script.
expressionlist	One of the following expressions: ■ A single value ■ A list of values separated by commas (for example, 2, 4, 6, 8) ■ A TO clause (for example, 1 TO 30) ■ IS followed by a relational operator and comparison value (for example, IS > 5) ■ Any combination of the above with an implied OR between expressions (for example, 1, 3, 5, 7, 9, 27 TO 33, IS > 42)
statementblock	The block of statements you want PowerBuilder to execute if the text expression matches the value in *expressionlist.*

At least one CASE clause is required. You must end a CHOOSE CASE control structure with END CHOOSE.

Description

- If *testexpression* at the beginning of the CHOOSE CASE statement matches a value in *expressionlist* for a CASE clause. the statements immediately following the CASE clause are executed. Control then passes to the first statement after the END CHOOSE clause.
- If multiple CASE expressions exist, then testexpression is compared to each expressionlist until a match is found or the CASE ELSE or END CHOOSE is encountered.
- If there is a CASE ELSE clause and the test value does not match any of the expressions, statementblock in the CASE ELSE clause is executed. If no CASE ELSE clause exists and a match is not found, the first statement after the ENDCHOOSE clause is executed.

538 APPENDIX D PowerScript Language Reference

Examples

```
CHOOSE CASE Weight
CASE IS < 16
    Postage = Weight * 0.30
    Method = "USPS"
CASE 16 to 48
    Postage = 4.50
    Method = "UPS"
CASE ELSE
    Postage = 25.00
    Method = "FedEx"
END CHOOSE

CHOOSE CASE Real (sle_real.Text)
CASE is < 10.99999
    sle_message.Text = "Real Case < 10.99999"
CASE 11.00 to 48.99999
    sle_message.Text = "Real Case 11 to 48.99999"
CASE is > 48.99999
    sle_message.Text = "Real Case > 48.99999"
CASE ELSE
    sle_message.Text = "Cannot evaluate."
END CHOOSE
```

CONTINUE

Use the CONTINUE statement in a DO... LOOP or a FOR...NEXT control structure. CONTINUE takes no parameters.

In a DO...LOOP Structure

When PowerBuilder encounters a CONTINUE statement in a DO... LOOP, control passes to the next LOOP statement. The statements between the CONTINUE statement and the LOOP statement are skipped in the current iteration of DO... LOOP. In a nested DO...LOOP structure, a CONTINUE statement bypasses statements in the current DO...LOOP structure.

Example

The following statements display a message box twice: when B equals 2 and when B equals 3. As soon as B is greater than 3, the statement following CONTINUE is skipped during each iteration of the loop:

```
int A=1, B=1
DO WHILE A < 100
    A = A+1
    B = B+1
    if B > 3 then CONTINUE
Messageaox("Hi", "B is " + String(B)
LOOP
```

In a FOR...NEXT Structure

When PowerBuilder encounters a CONTINUE statement in a FOR...NEXT control structure, control passes to the following NEXT statement; the statements between the CONTINUE statement and the NEXT statement are skipped in the current iteration of FOR...NEXT.

Example

The following statements stop incrementing B as soon as Count is greater than 15:

```
int A=0, B=0, Count
FOR Count = 1 to 100
    A=A+ 1
    IF Count > 15 then CONTINUE B=B+1
NEXT
// Upon completion, a=100 and b=15.
```

CREATE

The CREATE statement generates an object instance for a specified object type. You usually use CREATE to create a new transaction object. After a CREATE statement, attributes of the created object instance can be referenced using dot notation.

The CREATE statement returns an object instance which can be stored in a variable of the same type.

Syntax

CREATE *object_type*

Parameter	Description
object_type	The object data type

Example

This example creates a new transaction object and stores the object in the variable DBTrans:

```
transaction DBTrans
DBTrans = CREATE transaction
DBTrans.DBMS = 'ODBC'
```

DESTROY

DESTROY eliminates an object instance that was created with the CREATE statement. After a DESTROY statement, attributes of the deleted object instance can no longer be referenced.

Syntax

DESTROY *object_variable*

Parameter	Description
object_variable	A variable containing a PowerBuilder object

Example

The following statement destroys the transaction object DBTrans that was created with a CREATE Statement:

```
DESTROY DBTrans
```

DO...LOOP

The DO...LOOP control structure is a general-purpose iteration statement. Use DO...LOOP to execute a block of statements while or until a condition is true. DO...LOOP has four formats.

In all four formats of the DO...LOOP control structure, DO marks the beginning of the statement block that you want to repeat. The LOOP statement marks the end.

You can nest DO...LOOP control structures.

Using as DO UNTIL

Syntax

```
DO UNTIL condition
    statementblock
LOOP
```

Parameter	Description
condition	The condition you are testing
statementblock	The block of statements you want to repeat

Description

This format of the DO...LOOP executes *statementblock* until *condition* is TRUE. If *condition* is TRUE on the first evaluation, *statementblock* does not execute.

Using as DO WHILE

Syntax

```
DO WHILE condition
    statementblock
LOOP
```

Parameter	Description
condition	The condition you are testing
statementblock	The block of statements you want to repeat

Description

This format of the DO...LOOP executes *statementblock* while *condition* is TRUE. If *condition* is FALSE on the first evaluation, *statementblock* does not execute.

Using as LOOP UNTIL

Syntax

```
DO
    statementblock
LOOP UNTIL condition
```

Parameter	Description
condition	The condition you are testing
statementblock	The block of statements you want to repeat

Description | This format of the DO...LOOP executes *statementblock* at least once and continues until *condition* is TRUE.

Using as LOOP WHILE

Syntax
```
DO
    statementblock
LOOP WHILE condition
```

Parameter	Description
condition	The condition you are testing
statementblock	The block of statements you want to repeat

Description | This format of the DO...LOOP executes *statementblock* at least once and continues while *continue* is TRUE.

When to Use the Different Forms

Use DO WHILE or DO UNTIL when you want to execute a block of statements *only* if a condition is TRUE (for WHILE) or FALSE (for UNTIL). DO WHILE and DO UNTIL test the condition before executing the block of statements.

Use LOOP WHILE or LOOP UNTIL when you want to execute a block of statements at least once. LOOP WHILE and LOOP UNTIL test the condition after the block of statements has been executed.

Examples

The following DO UNTIL executes a block of Beep functions until A is greater than 15:

```
Int    A = 1, B = 1

DO UNTIL A>15
    Beep (A)
    A = (A + I) * B
LOOP
```

The following DO WHILE executes a block of BEEP functions only while A less than or equal to 15:

```
Int A, B = 1

DO WHILE A<=15
    Beep (A)
    A = (A + 1) + B
LOOP
```

The following LOOP UNTIL executes a block of Beep functions and then continues to execute the functions until A is greater than 15:

```
Int A = 1, B = 1

DO
    Beep (A)
    A = (A + 1) * B
```

```
                LOOP UNTIL A>15
```

The following LOOP WHILE executes a block of Beep functions while A is less than or equal to 15:

```
Int A = 1, B = 1

DO
    Beep (A)
    A = (A + 1) * B
LOOP WHILE A<=15
```

EXIT

Use the EXIT statement in a DO...LOOP or a FOR...NEXT control structure to pass control out of the current loop. EXIT takes no parameters.

Using in DO...LOOP

An EXIT statement in a DO...LOOP control structure causes control to pass to the statement following the LOOP statement. In a nested DO...LOOP structure, an EXIT statement passes control out of the current DO...LOOP structure.

Example

The following EXIT statement causes the loop to terminate if an element in the Nbr array equals 0:

```
int Nbr[10]
int Count = 1
// Assume values get assigned to Nbr array...

DO WHILE Count < 11
    IF Nbr[Count] = 0 THEN EXIT
    Count = Count + 1
LOOP

Messagebox("Hi", "Count is now " + String (Count))
```

Using in FOR...NEXT

An EXIT statement in a FOR...NEXT control structure causes control to pass to the statement following the NEXT statement.

Example

The following EXIT statement causes the loop to terminate if an element in the Nbr array equals 0:

```
int Nbr[10]
int Count
// Assume values get assigned to Nbr array...

FOR Count = 1 to 10
    IF Nbr[Count] = 0 THEN EXIT
NEXT

Messagebox("Hi", "Count is now " + String(Count))
```

FOR...NEXT

The FOR...NEXT control structure is a numerical iteration. Use FOR...NEXT to execute one or more statements a specified number of times.

Syntax

```
FOR varname = start TO end (STEP increment)
    statement
NEXT
```

Parameter	Description
varname	The name of the iteration counter variable. It can be any numerical type (integer, double, real, long, or decimal), but integers provide the fastest performance.
start	Starting value of varname.
end	Ending value of varname.
increment	(Optional) The increment value or variable. increment must be the same data type as varname. If you enter an increment, STEP is required. +1 is the default increment.
statementblock	The block of statements you want to repeat

Description

- For a positive *increment*, *end* must be greater than *start*. For a negative *increment*, *end* must be less than *start*.
- When *increment* is positive and *start* is greater than *end*, *statementblock* does not execute. When *increment* is negative and *start* is less than *end*, *statementblock* does not execute.
- You can nest FOR NEXT statements. You must have a NEXT for each FOR.

Examples

These statements add 10 to A as long as n is >=5 and <=25:

```
FOR n=5 to 25
    A=A+10
NEXT
```

These statements add 10 to A and increment n by 5 as long as n is >= 5 and <=25:

```
FOR N=5 TO 25 STEP 5
    A=A+10
NEXT
```

These statements contain two lines that will never execute because increment is negative and start is less than end:

```
FOR Count = 1 to 100 STEP-1
    If Count < 1 then EXIT // These 2 lines
    Box [Count] =10 // will never execute.
NEXT
```

These are nested FOR...NEXT statements:

```
Int Matrix[100,50,200]
FOR X=1 to 100
    FOR Y=1 to 50
    FOR z = 1 to 200
    Matrix [x, y, z] =1
    NEXT
    NEXT
NEXT
```

GOTO

Use the GOTO statement to transfer control from one statement in a script to another statement that is labeled.

Syntax

GOTO *label*

Parameter	Description
label	The label associated with the statement to which you want to transfer control. A label is an identifier followed by a colon (such as OK:). Do not use the colon with a label in the GOTO statement.

Examples

The following GOTO statement skips over the Taxable=FALSE line:

```
Goto Nextstep
Taxable=FALSE   //This statement will never
     //execute.
NextStep:
Rate=Count/Count4
```

The following statement transfers control to the statement associated with the label OK:

```
GOTO OK
.
.
.
OK:
.
.
.
```

HALT and RETURN

Use the HALT statement without associated keywords to terminate the application immediately. Use the RETURN statement to stop the execution of a script or function immediately.

Using HALT

Syntax

```
HALT {CLOSE}
```

Description

When PowerBuilder encounters HALT without the keyword CLOSE, it immediately terminates the application.

When PowerBuilder encounters HALT with the keyword CLOSE, it immediately executes the script for the Close event for the application and then terminates the application. If there is no script for the Close event at the application level, PowerBuilder immediately terminates the application.

Examples

In the following example, the script stops the application if the user enters a password in the SingleLineEdit named sle_password that does not match the value stored in a string named CorrectPassword:

```
if sle_password.Text <> Correctpassword then HALT
```

The following statement executes the script for the close event for the application before it terminates the application if the user enters a password in the sle_password that does not match the value stored in the string CorrectPassword:

```
if sle_password.Text <> Correctpassword &
    then HALT CLOSE
```

Using RETURN

Syntax

In a script:

```
RETURN
```

In a function:

```
RETURN expression
```

Parameter	Description
expression	Any value (or expression) you want the function to return. The return value must be the data type specified as the return type in the function.

Description
When PowerBuilder encounters RETURN in a script, it terminates execution of that script immediately and waits for the next user action. When PowerBuilder encounters RETURN in a function, RETURN transfers (returns) control to the point at which the function was called.

Examples
This script causes the system to beep once: the second beep in a string statement will not execute:

```
Beep (1)
RETURN
HALT // This statement will not execute.
```

These statements in a user-defined function return the result of dividing Arg1 by Arg2 if Arg2 is not equal to 0; they return -1 if Arg2 is equal to 0:

```
IF Arg2<>0 THEN
    RETURN Arg1/Arg2
ELSE
    RETURN -1
END IF
```

IF...THEN

Use the IF...THEN control structure to cause the script to perform a specified action if a stated condition is true. IF...THEN has a single-fine format and a multiline format.

Using the Single-Line Format

Syntax

```
IF condition THEN action1 {ELSE action2}
```

Parameter	Description
condition	The condition you want to test
action1	The action you want performed if the condition is TRUE. The action must be a single statement on the same line as the rest of the IF statement.
action2	(Optional) The action you want performed if the condition is FALSE. The action must be a single statement on the same line as the rest of the IF statement.

You can use continuation characters to place the "single-line" format on more than one physical line in the script.

Examples
The following single-line IF...THEN statement opens window w_first if Num = 1; otherwise, w_rest is opened:

```
IF Hum = 1 THEN Open(w_first) ELSE Open(w_rest)
```

The following single-line IF...THEN statement displays a message if the value in the SingleLineEdit sle_State is TX. It uses the continuation character to continue the single-line statement across two physical lines in the script:

```
IF sle_State.text="TX" THEN    &
MessageBox("Hello", "Tex")
```

Using the Multiline Format

Syntax

```
IF condition1 THEN
    action1
{ELSEIF condition2 THEN
    action2
    .
    .
    .}
{ELSE
    action3}
END IF
```

Parameter	Description
condition1	The first condition you want to test.
action1	The action you want performed if *condition1* is TRUE. The action can be a statement or multiple statements that are separated by semicolons or placed on separate lines. At least one action is required.
condition2	(Optional) The condition you want to test if *condition1* is FALSE. You can have multiple ELSEIF...THEN statements in an IF...THEN control statement.
action2	The action you want performed if *condition2* is TRUE. The action can be a statement or multiple statements that are separated by semicolons or placed on separate lines.
action3	(Optional) The action you want performed if none of the preceding conditions is true. The action can be a statement or multiple statements that are separated by semicolons or placed on separate lines.

You must end a multiline IF...THEN control structure with END IF (which is two words).

Examples

The following multiline IF...THEN compares the horizontal positions of windows w_first and w_second. If w_first is to the right of w_second, w_first is moved to the left side of the screen:

```
IF w_first.X > w_second.X THEN
    w_first.X = 0
END IF
```

The following multiline IF...THEN causes the application to:

- Beep twice if X equals Y
- Display the Parts listbox and highlight item 5 if X equals Z
- Display the Choose listbox if X is blank
- Hide the Empty button and display the Full button if none of the above conditions is TRUE

```
IF X=Y THEN
    Beep (2)
ELSEIF X=Z THEN
    Show (lb_parts); lb_parts.Setstate(5,TRUE)
ELSEIF X=" " THEN
    Show (lb_choose)
ELSE
    Hide(cb_empty)
    Show(cb_full)
END IF
```

APPENDIX E

Complete Design for C&U Rentals

550 APPENDIX E COMPLETE DESIGN FOR C&U RENTALS

This appendix contains the design of the College and University Rentals database (*rents*). The entity-relationship diagram in Figure E.1 presents the relationships between the data objects in the database. Figure E.2 contains bubble diagrams illustrating the functional dependencies between the attributes. The relations, with primary keys underlined, follow the diagrams. These relations are used in the exercises that appear in Parts II and III of this book.

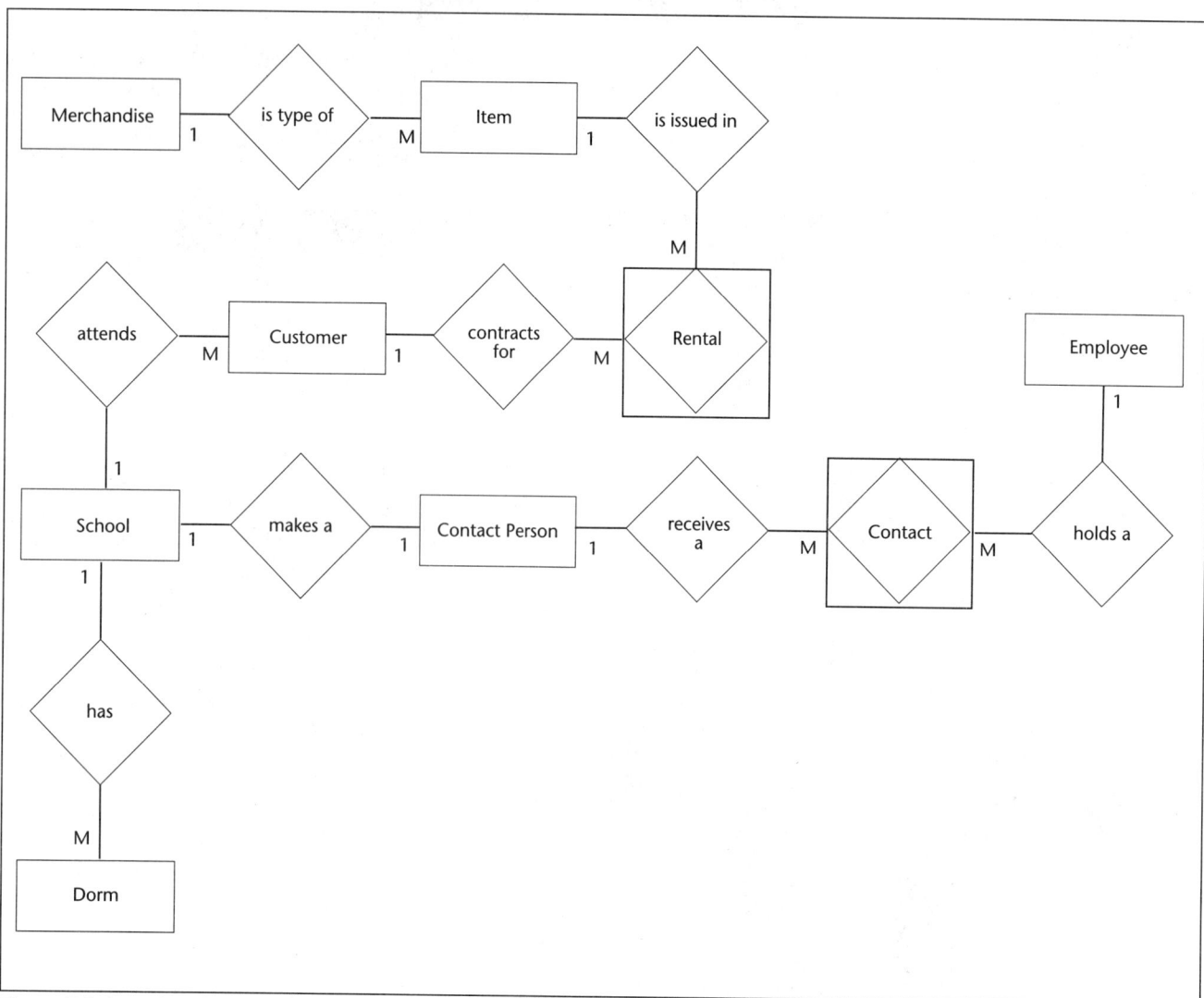

Figure E.1 An entity-relationship diagram for the *rents* database

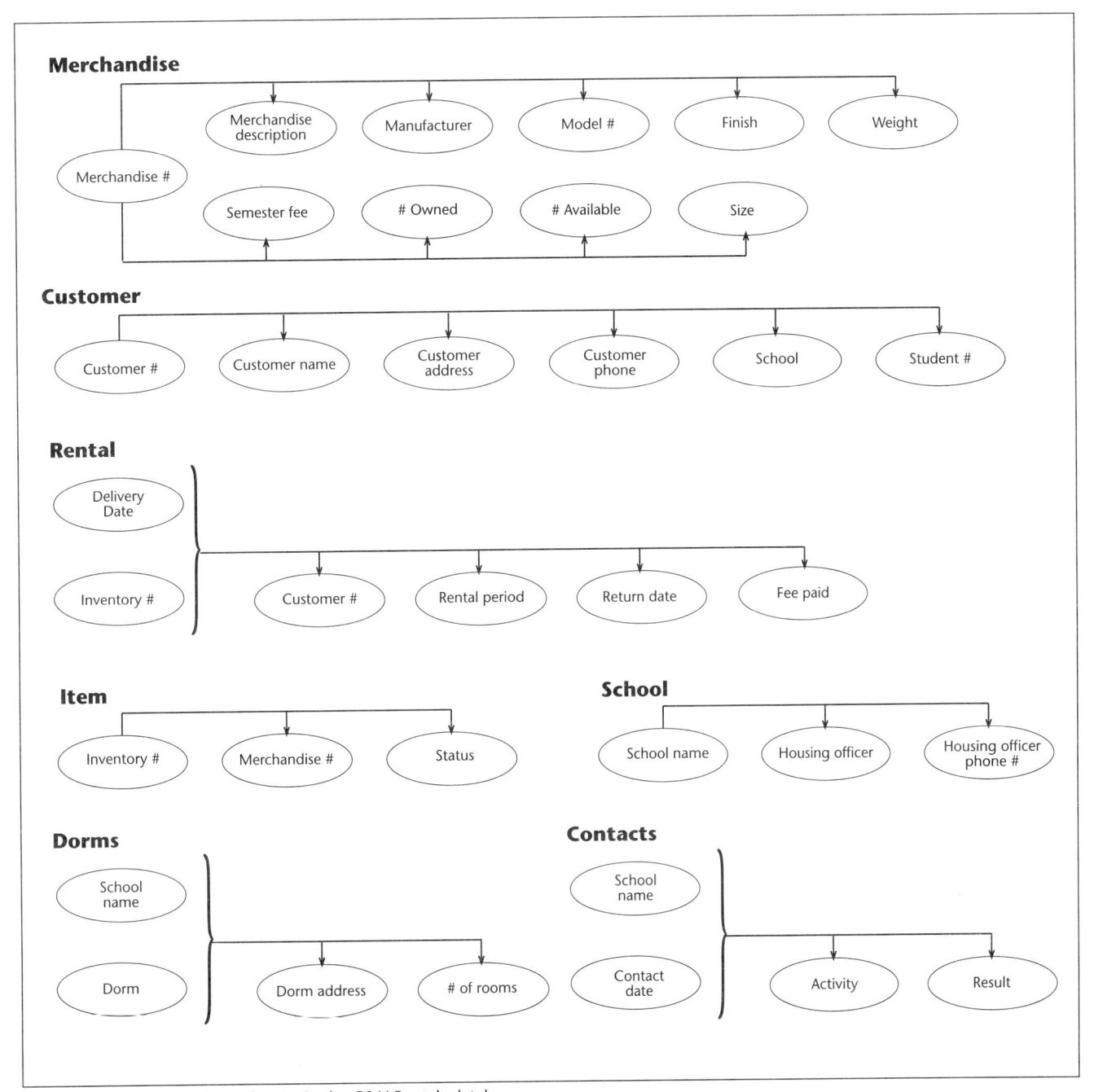

Figure E.2 Functional dependencies in the C&U Rentals database

The relations in the C&U Rentals database are as follows:

- Merchandise (<u>Merchandise #</u>, Merchandise description, Manufacturer, Model #, Finish, Weight, Size, Semester fee, # Owned, # Available)

The # Owned and # Available columns are actually computed quantities. It is possible to count the number of rows in the Item table with a given Merchandise # to arrive at the # Owned. The number of items available for rental can be computed by counting the number of rows in the Item table that have a Status of 'warehouse.' However, as the number of items in the database grows, the time needed to compute # Owned and # Available will rise. Because C&U Rentals uses these quantities so frequently, they are actually stored in the database and updated whenever the Item table is updated.

Computed quantities such as # Owned and # Available present an interesting database design trade-off. Storing the computed quantities requires extra disk space and takes extra time during data modification. However, data retrieval is faster because the computations do not have to be performed. In most cases, the decision whether to store computed quantities is based on the amount of disk storage required, the time required to update the stored quantities during data modification, and how often the computed quantities will be used. The more frequently the computed quantities are used relative to the amount of disk storage and update time required, the more advantageous it is to store the computed quantities.

- Item (<u>Inventory #</u>, Merchandise #, Status)

- Customers (<u>Customer #</u>, Customer name, Customer address, Customer Phone, School, Student #)

- Rentals (<u>Inventory #</u>, <u>Delivery date</u>, Customer #, Rental period, Return date, Fee paid)

- Schools (<u>School name</u>, Housing officer, Housing officer phone)

- Dorms (<u>School name</u>, <u>Dorm name</u>, Dorm address, # of rooms)

- Contacts (<u>School name</u>, <u>Contact date</u>, Activity, Result)

Glossary

Accelerator key: A character key pressed in combination with the ALT key to make a choice from a menu.

Ancestor: An object from which a descendent object is derived.

Anomaly: An unexpected and usually undesirable property of a relation, including the inability to store data when desired or the deletion of data that should be kept.

Application library: A disk file with a .pbl (pronounced "pibble") extension that contains data about one or more applications.

Attributes: Containers for the data that describe PowerBuilder objects.

Base class: In an object-oriented environment, a class from which other classes inherit.

Base table: A tables in which data are stored in a database.

Before-image file: A file that contains data about every action taken by transactions that are currently in progress.

Blob (binary large object): A column defined to store binary data such as a graphic image.

Candidate key: An attribute or combination of attributes that could be selected to serve as the primary key of a relation.

Child window: A window that is completely contained within another window.

Class: A template from which objects are creating, specifying the types of data that describe objects of that class and describing the behaviors the object knows how to perform.

Client-server: A data management environment in which the processing of data is distributed among many computers linked by a data communications network.

Client-server architecture: The way in which the components of a client-server environment are configured.

Column headers: Words that appear at the top of a column on the Preview screen or on a list of data in a DataWindow object.

Commit a transaction: Make permanent the changes made by a transaction to a database.

Composite entity: An entity that represents the relationship between two other entities.

Computed column: A column whose contents aren't stored in the database but are assembled for output by manipulating data according to the formula that defines the column.

Computed field: A field in a DataWindow object whose contents are computed by PowerBuilder on the client workstation.

Concatenated key: A primary or foreign key made up of the combination of two or more columns.

Continuation character: A character used to indicate that a statement is continued on the following line; in PowerScript, an ampersand (&).

Control break report: A report that forms groups of data based on matching data values and usually computes summary values for its groups.

Controls: Elements placed in windows that accept input from a user and present output for a user to see, such as places to enter data and buttons.

Data source: A repository of data that PowerBuilder can use.

Database: A collection of data and definitions of the relationships between those data.

Database profile: PowerBuilder's record of a known database, including the database file's path name and the user name and password to be used to connect to the database.

Database server: A DBMS designed to accept queries from clients and return the result of the query to the client for further processing; (hardware) A computer dedicated to running database server software.

DataWindow control: A control that is linked to a DataWindow object.

Deadlock: A database condition in which transactions are unable to proceed because two or more transactions are each waiting for data to which the others have been given exclusive access.

Decompose a relation: Break the relation into a set of smaller relations, eliminating design problems.

Default value: A common value that a database application assigns automatically to a column.

Deletion anomaly: The requirement to delete data that should be kept because part of the row's primary key has become null.

Derived class: In an object-oriented environment, a class that inherits from another class.

Descendant: An object that is derived from another object, inheriting all of the parent object's properties.

Determinant: An attribute or combination of attributes on which another attribute is functionally dependent.

Display mask: A pattern used to specify the display format for data.

Domain constraint: An expression of the permissible values for a column.

Dot notation: Notation used to identify the object to which an attribute or function call relates: object_name.attribute_or_function_name

Drop: Delete a table, view, or index from a database.

Dynamic library: A PowerBuilder library that is linked to a PowerBuilder executable when needed during the application's run.

Encapsulation: In object-oriented programming, keeping the details of a function hidden from the rest of the program.

Entity: An object about which a database stores data (a physical object, a person, a place, an event, or the relationship between other entities).

Entity integrity: A constraint on a relation that states that no part of the primary key can be null.

Event: A type of behavior that occurs in an application environment, such as clicking on a button or opening a window.

Extended attributes: PowerBuilder properties applied to columns (for example, comments, labels, column headers, display formats, and validation rules) independent of the DBMS being used.

Focus: The row and column that PowerBuilder is currently using in a DataWindow.

Foreign key: An attribute that is part of the primary key of its table or a non-key attribute that is the same as the entire primary key of another table.

Handle: A small square at the corner of an object that can be dragged to resize the object.

Index: An ordered list of key values that can be searched quickly to provide fast data access.

Information hiding: In object-oriented programming, keeping the details of a function hidden from the rest of the program.

Insertion anomaly: The inability to insert a row into a table because data for a complete primary key aren't available.

Instance: A specific occurrence of an object.

Labels: Words that appear on freeform DataWindow objects

MDI (multiple document interface) frame: A window used as a container for other windows (sheets).

Member function: A declaration of the behavior that an object knows how to perform.

Message: The communication mechanism used by objects and other program elements.

Method: A declaration of the behavior that an object knows how to perform.

Middleware: Software that translates data manipulation requests from a client DBMS into syntax that a database server can understand.

Modal: A property of a window in which no other activity can take place as long as the window is open; the user must close the window before proceeding with the application.

Modification anomaly: The tendency of unnecessary duplicated data to become inconsistent when those data are updated.

Nested report: A report that contains two or more DataWindows that are linked automatically by PowerBuilder.

Normal forms: A set of increasingly stringent rules to which relations must conform.

Normalization: Decomposing relations into sets of smaller relations to remove anomalies, improving the design of the database.

Glossary

Object: A data structure that contains data that describe the object along with definitions of procedures the object knows how to perform.

Object-oriented paradigm: A method of organizing the elements of an application environment where data and the operations data can perform are stored together.

Open Database Connectivity (ODBC): An interface that allows PowerBuilder to interact with a SQL-based database server.

Override a script: Create a script in a descendant object that runs in place of the ancestor object's script.

PainterBar: An button bar that contains buttons specific to the current painter.

Parameter: Data passed into a member function so that the function can perform its task.

Parent (window): A window that opens and therefore controls another window; the owner of a popup or child window.

Polymorphism: Having objects of different classes in the same inheritance hierarchy responding differently to the same message.

PowerBar: The button bar that appears by default at the top of the PowerBuilder window, providing navigation between painters.

PowerTip: Text that appears when the mouse pointer moves over a button in the PowerBar or a PainterBar.

Private elements of a class: Parts of a class that are not accessible except within the class.

Prototype: A working model of an application that is modified as users test it.

Public elements of a class: The parts of a class that are accessible to other parts of the program.

Referential integrity: An integrity constraint that states that every nonnull foreign key must reference an existing primary key.

Relational data model: A data model in which all data and data relationships are represented as two-dimensional tables.

Response window: A modal window that must be dismissed before any other actions can be taken with an application.

Roll back a transaction: Undo the changes made by a transaction to the database, restoring the database to the state it was in before the transaction began.

Scope resolution operator: An operator (::) that is used to identify the object to which an attribute belongs.

Script: A module of program code attached to an object and triggered by an event in the PowerBuilder environment.

Sheet: A window opened within an MDI frame.

Shortcut key: A function key or a combination of a modified key and a character key used to make a choice from a menu.

SQLCA (SQL Communications Area): The default transaction object, used to allow an application to connect to a database.

Static text: Text for display only on a DataWindow.

Tab-delimited text file: A text file in which columns are separated by tab characters and each row ends with a carriage return.

Transaction object: An object that stores information about the database with which an application is interacting.

Transaction: A series of data manipulation activities that are presented to a database as a unit.

Transitive dependency: A functional dependency in which attribute A determines B and B determines C; therefore A determines C.

Validation rule: A logical expression against which data in a column are checked. Only data that meet the criteria in the expression can be stored in the database.

Variable: In a class, a container for data that describes an object.

View: A virtual table that is the result of executing a relational query.

Virtual function: A function first declared in a base class that is redefined in derived classes.

Virtual table: A table that exists temporarily in main memory.

Workspace: The area between the scroll bars in a painter, used to define the contents of an object.

Index

Symbols
& 47, 510–511
: : 300
; 512

A
Access 9
Aligning 283
Alter Table dialog box 104, 149, 154, 168
Anomalies
    causes of 23–24
    deletion 22
    insertion 21–22
    modification 23
Application
    events 194
    open event 194–196
    opening 52–54
Application libraries
    definition of 41
Application objects
    definition of 42
Application painter
    entering 53
    keyboard eqivalent for 73
    object hierarchy in 315–316
Application planning 180–181
Applications
    creating 54–56
    running 66
Arguments 253–255
Attributes 43
Autonumbering 344–345

B
Bands 225
Base tables 26
Before-image file 46
`binary` 96
`Blob` 96, 513
`Boolean` 513
Boyce-Codd normal form 26
Browser 517
Button controls
    creating 202–206
    events 201, 206–207
Buttons, picture *see* Picture buttons

C
Calculated fields 291–293
`Call` 300, 536
Catalogs 28
Catching unsaved changes 365–367
Changing tab order 306
`Char` 95, 96, 513
Check box controls 388
Check boxes 164–165
Child DataWindows
    definition of 346
    retrieving data into 348
    suppressing retrieval into 348
    transaction objects for 348
    variables for 346
Child windows 185
`Choose case` 366, 537–538
Class browser 517
Classes
    declaring 39
    definition of 38–39
    information hiding 39
    inheritance 40–41
    member functions 39
    polymorphism 41
    variables 39
    virtual functions 41
Clicked events 198, 201, 271, 379
Client-server database management
    benefits of 7–8
    characteristics of 5–6
    drawbacks to 8
    PowerBuilder and 9–10
    switching to 7
`Close` 207, 326, 430–431
Close events 194, 198, 199–200
Column comments 149–151
Column data types 95–96
Column Header dialog box 152
Column Properties dialog box 152, 164, 166, 169, 172, 174
Column Validation dialog box 172, 174
Column validation *see* Validation
Command buttons 341–343
Committing a transaction 45, 323
Computed Field Definition dialog box 247
Computed fields 257–258, 282, 363–365
    adding to a DataWindow object 246–249
    definition of 245
Computed Object properties dialog box 247
Concatenation 47
Configuring ODBC 58–62
connect 199
Connecting to a database 58–62, 184, 199
Constructor events 201

Continuation character 47, 510–511
`Continue` 538–539
Control break reports
    group bands 281
    group presentation style 278–287
    grouping queries for 287–295
    page headers 279
    specifying grouping columns 279, 289–290
    totals for 291–293
Controls
    making invisible 311
Controls *see* specific types of controls
`Count` 496–497
`Create` 539
Create Index dialog box 114
Create Local Database dialog box 93
Creating
    applications 54–56
    button controls 202–206
    databases 92–94
    DataWindow objects 239–242, 245–249
    indexes 114–116
    main windows 186–188
    picture buttons 207–212
    primary keys 98–101
    response windows 260–264
    tables 94–103
    views 136–142
    windows 200–201

D

Data dictionaries 28
Data formatting *see* Extended attributes
Data Manipulation painter 124–125
Data modification
    catching unsaved changes 365–367
    DataWindows for 321–323
    deleting rows 323
    finding rows for 325–328
    inserting rows 323
    interactive 128–129, 130–131
    saving changes 323
    sequential access to rows 341–343
Data relationships 14–15
Data retrieval 234–238
Data sources 52
Data types 95–96, 266, 513–514, 519–520
Database
    connecting to 184, 199
        creating 92–94
        definition of 14

    disconnecting from 184, 200
Database Development and Deployment Kit 416
Database management
    centralized 4
    client-server 5–6, 7, 9–10
Database painter
    creating tables 94–103
    entering 59
    keyboard equivalent for 73
Databases
    connecting to 58–62
    designing 21–26
DataWindow controls
    associating with objects 229–233, 258
    changing the underlying query 390–395
    definition of 220
    formatting 233
    linked retrieval between 360–363, 368–382
    making invisible 389
    menus and 409–410
    nested reports and 357
    retrieving data into 234–238
DataWindow objects
    aligning objects in 283
    arguments 253–255
    associating with controls 229–233, 258
    bands 225
    computed fields 245–249, 257–258
    copying 307–308
    data modification layouts 321–323
    definition of 42
    duplicate suppression 246
    formatting 225–229, 239–242, 255–256
    grouping queries 287–295
    joins for 245–249
    Macintosh 423–424
    making updatable 359
    nested reports and 353–357
    Quick Select for 220–225, 245
    SQL Select for 252–255, 271–274
    summary fields 257–258
    updatability 359
DataWindow painter 73
DataWindow properties dialog box 231
DataWindows *see also* Child DataWindows
DataWindows *see also* Dropdown DataWindows
`Date` 95, 266, 395, 431–433, 513
Dates 394–395
`DateTime` 513
`Day` 395, 434
DB2/2 9
dBASE 9

`Dec` 266, 434–435, 513
`Decimal` 95, 513
Default values 174
`DeletedCount` 367, 435
`DeleteRow` 323, 324, 435–436
Deleting objects 80–81
Deleting rows 131, 323
Deletion anomalies 22
Descendants *see* Inheritance
`Destroy` 539
Destructor events 201
Determinants 23
disconnect 200
Disconnecting from a database 184, 200
Display formats
    definition of 155
    numeric columns 156–157
Display masks 155
Display Number Formats 248
DLLs 416
`Do...until` 540–542
`Do...while` 540–542
Domain constraints 20–21
Domain-Key normal form 26
Dot notation 43, 536
`Double` 95, 266, 436–437, 514
Doubleclicked event 269, 271
Doubleclicked events 198
Dropdown DataWindows
    adding to DataWindow objects 331–332
    DataWindow objects for 328–329
    definition of 328
    multi-column 336–340
    related 345–350
    single-column 328–336
    using 334
Dropdown lists 169–171
Dropping
    indexes 118
    tables 112–113
    views 142
Duplicate supression 246
Dynamic libraries 418
Dynamic Link Libraries 416

E

Edit Formats
    character columns 162–164
Edit formats
    check boxes 164–165
    date columns 160–162
    default edit style 157–160
    definition of 157
    Dropdown lists 169–171
    radio buttons 166–168
Edit Mask dialog box 162
Edit masks *see also* Edit formats
Edit Style dialog box 157, 161, 162, 164, 169
Edit styles 240–242
Edit Styles dialog box 166
Editing data
    interactive 128–129
Embedded SQL 48
Entering data
    interactive 130–131
Entity integrity 18–19
Entity, definition of 14
Enumerated data types 519–520
Events
    application 194
    button controls 201
    clicked 198, 201, 271, 379
    close 194, 198, 199–200
    constructor 201
    definition of 44
    destructor 201
    doubleclicked 198, 269, 271
    idle 194
    itemchanged 363
    itemfocuschanged 376, 377
    key 198
    mousedown 198
    mousemove 198
    open 194, 194–196, 198, 198–199
    rbuttondown 198, 201
    resize 198
    rowfocuschanged 363, 376, 378
    systemerror 194
    window 198
Executables
    definition of 416
    Macintosh 426
    project painter for 418–420
    quick 416–417
`Exit` 542–544
Exiting PowerBuilder 57
Extended attributes
    alignment 154–155
    column comments 149–151
    column headers 151–154
    definition of 148
    labels 151–154
    width 154–155

F

Fifth normal form 26
Filtering data 125–127
First normal form 26
`Float` 95
Foreign Key Definition dialog box 105
Foreign keys 19–20, 103–107
Formatting *see* Display formats
Formatting *see* Edit formats
Formatting *see* Extended attributes
Fourth normal 26
FoxPro 9
Function objects 42
Function painter 73
Functional dependencies 23

G

`GetChild` 346, 348, 437–438
`GetClickedColumn` 270, 438–439
`GetClickedRow` 270, 439–440
`GetColumn` 270, 440
`GetColumnName` 270, 349
`GetFocus` 368, 441–442
`GetItemDate` 271, 442–443
`GetItemDecimal` 271, 443–445
`GetItemNumber` 270
`GetItemString` 271, 349, 445–446
GetItemTime 271
`GetItemTime` 447–448
`GetRow` 270, 349, 448–449
Getting help
    launching PowerBuilder Help 82
    Microhelp 72
    searching for 86–87
    view help history 85
    viewing help topics 82
Global variables 48
`Goto` 544
Group box controls 374–375
Group presentation style 278–287
GroupBox dialog box 374
GroupBox properties dialog box 374
Grouping queries 287–295

H

`Halt` 545–546
Halt 198
Headers 279
Help
    launching 82
    Microhelp 72

searching 86–87
viewing history 85
viewing topics 82

I

Idle events 194
if 198
`If...then` 183, 198, 546–548
Importing data 132–133
Index 559
Indexes
    creating 114–116
    description of 113–114
    Dropping 118
Information hiding 39
Informix 9
Inherit From Window dialog box 309
Inheritance
    ancestors 44
    controls and 299
    copying ancestor scripts 310
    creating descendants 307–314
    definition of 40–41, 44, 298
    descendants 44
    menus and 410–413
    modifying descendants 300, 314–315
    object hierarchy 315–316
    overriding ancestor scripts 311, 312
    scripts and 300
Input Validation dialog box 172
Inserting rows 323
Insertion anomalies 21–22
`InsertRow` 323, 324, 340, 343, 449
Instance variables 48
`Int` 95, 514
`Integer` 95, 266, 514
Integrity rules 17–21
Interactive data manipuation
    deleting 131
Interactive data manipulation
    entering data 130–131
    importing data 132–133
    modification 128–129
    retrieval 125–127
    sorting 127–128
    SQL commands 133–135
Interactive SQL 133–135
`IsDate` 394, 449–450
Itemchanged events 349, 363
Itemfocuschanged events 376, 377

J
Joins 245

K
Key events 198

L
Launching PowerBuilder 52
`Len` 394, 450–451
Libraries *see* Application libraries
Library painter
    deleting objects 80–81
    keyboard equivalent for 73
Linking DataWindow controls 360–363, 368–382
Literals 514–517
Loading data 132–133
Local variables 48
`Long` 264, 266, 451–452, 514
long binary 96
long varchar 95
Loop until 540–542

M
Macintosh *see* PowerBuilder Macintosh
Main windows 185, 186–188
Many-to-many relationships 15
MDI windows 185
Member functions
    calling 43, 536
    definition of 39
Menu objects
    accelerator keys 401–402
    attaching to windows 408–409
    cascading 403–405
    DataWindow controls and 409–410
    definition of 42
    inheritance and 410–413
    menu items for 399–400
    object references in 405
    options for 401–402
    previewing 402
    scripts for 405–408
    using 66
Menu painter 73
Menus
    Macintosh 424–426
`Message` object 264, 265, 266, 303, 327, 367
`MessageBox` 183, 199, 365, 452–454
Messages 41
Microhelp 72
Middleware 9–10

Modification anomalies 23
`ModifiedCount` 366, 454–455
`Month` 395, 455
Mousedown events 198
Mousemove events 198

N
Nested reports
    DataWindow controls for 357
    definition of 352
    host DataWindow objects for 353–357
    scripts for 357
New DataWindow dialog box 221, 239
Normal forms 25–26
Normalization 24–26
NULL 506–507
`Numeric` 95

O
Objects
    accessing attributes 43
    aligning 283
    application 42
    DataWindow 42
    definition of 38–39
    deleting 80–81
    function 42
    hierarchy of 315–316
    inheritance 40–41
    invoking member functions 43
    menu 42
    `Message` 264, 265, 266, 327
    project 42
    structure 42
    system 517–518
    transaction 42, 182–184
    user 42
    viewing hierarchy of 216–217
    window 42
ODBC
    configuring 58–62
    definition of 9–10
ODBC.INI 58, 94
ODBCINST.INI 58
One-to-many relationships 15
One-to-one relationships 14–15
`Open` 305, 327, 455–464
open 196, 207
Open events 194, 194–196, 198, 198–199
Opening
    applications 52–54

`OpenWithParm` 264, 266, 303, 326, 464–467
Oracle 9

P
`Page` 281, 497–498
Page headers 279
`PageCount` 498
`Pagecount` 281
PainterBar 74
Painters 72
    keyboard equivalents for 73
Painters *see also* Names of specific painters
Paradox 9
`parent` 207, 508
`ParentWindow` 509
Password 92
PB.INI 58, 60, 62, 94, 183
Picture buttons 207–212
Polymorphism 41
Popup windows 185
PowerBar 71
PowerBuilder
    exiting 57
    launching 52
    quitting 57
    starting 52
PowerBuilder Help *see* Help
PowerBuilder Macintosh
    configuring menus for 424–426
    configuring windows with 423–424
    executables 426
    fonts 424
    keyboard substitutions 422
PowerScript
    arithmetic operators 531–532
    assignment statements 534–536
    blanks 512
    comments 502–503
    concatenation 47
    continuation character 47, 510–511
    data types 47–48
    enumerated data types 519–520
    identifiers 503–504
    labels 504–505
    literals 514–517
    logical operators 532
    NULL 506–507
    precedence 532–533
    relational operators 532
    reserved words 507–510
    special characters for 505–506
    statement continutation 510–511
    statement separator 512
    statement syntax 47
    strings 533–534
    variable names 503–504
    variables 47–48, 520–530
    white space 512
PowerScript *see also* individual PowerScript statements
PowerScript *see also* Variables
Powersoft 9
PowerTips 79
Precision 95
Previewing tables 124
Primary Key Definition dialog box 99
Primary keys 98–101
Primary keys *see* Tables, primary keys
`Print` 287, 467–471
Printing 286–287
Project painter 418–420, 426
Projects 42
Prototypes 180

Q
Query languages 27–28
Query painter 73
Quick executables 416–417
Quick Select 220–225, 245
Quick Select dialog box 239
Quitting PowerBuilder 57

R
Radio button controls 372–375, 378, 394
Radio buttons 166–168
RadioButton dialog box 372
RadioButton properties dialog box 373
Rbuttondown events 198, 201
`Real` 95, 266, 471–472, 514
Referential integrity 19–20
Relational data model 16–21
Relations
    adding columns 111
    adding rows 132–133
    candidate keys 17
    concatenated keys 16
    creating 94–103
    data types 101–103
    deleting rows 131
    designing 21–26
    domain constraints 20–21
    dropping 112–113

editing rows 128–129
foreign keys 103–107
inserting rows 130–131
modifying 110–111
normalizing 24–26
previewing 124
primary key constraints 18–19
primary keys 16–17, 98–101
referential integrity 19–20
Relationships *see* Data relationships
Reports, control break *see* Control break reports
Reports, nested *see* Nested reports
`Reset` 323, 324, 326, 472–473
Resize events 198
Response windows 185, 325–328, 334–336
    creating 260–264
    inheritance and 311–313
    inhertitance and 313–314
    lists on 267–271
    scripts for 264
    uses of 259
Retrieval arguments 253–255
`Retrieve` 234, 237–238, 265, 304, 323, 326, 340, 341, 349, 474–476
`Return` 183, 198, 545–546
`Rollback` 200
Rolling back a transaction 45, 323
Rowfocuschanged events 363, 376, 378
Rows *see* Tables
Running an application 66
Running totals 363–365

S
Scale 95
Scope resolution operator 300
Script painter
    dropdown menus 76–77
    entering 75
    features of 77
Scripting *see* PowerScript
Scripts
    copying 242–243
    defintion of 44
    overriding ancestor scripts 313
`ScrollNextRow` 343, 476–477
`ScrollPriorRow` 343, 477
`ScrollToRow` 342, 343, 478
Second normal form 26
Select DataWindow dialog box 221, 230, 239
Select Executable File dialog box 417
Select Menu dialog box 399

Select painter 252–255
Select Tables dialog box 92
Select Window dialog box 186
Sequential access 341–343
`SetFocus` 234, 238, 323, 340, 478–479
`SetItem` 344, 345, 479–481
`SetRowFocusIndicator` 234, 238, 481–482
`SetSQLSelect` 392–394, 482–483
`SetTransObject` 234, 236–237, 340, 484–486
Shared variables 48
SingleLineEdit controls 263–264, 266
`Smallint` 95
Sorting 127–128, 140–141
Specify Group Columns dialog box 279
Specify REpeating Value Suppression List dialog box 246
Specify Retrieval Arguments dialog box 253
Specify Update Characteristics dialog box 359
SQL 27
    concatenation in 272
    embedded 48
    grouping queries 287–295
    interactive 133–135
    removing duplicates 387
    subqueries 272
SQL Anywhere 60
SQLBase 9
`SQLCA` 183, 196, 237
`SQLCODE` 183
`SQLERRTEXT` 184
SQLServer 9
Starting PowerBuilder 52
`String` 395, 486–489, 514
Structure editor 73
Structure objects 42
StyleBar 74
`Sum` 498–500
Summary fields 257–258, 282, 291–293, 363–365
`Super` 509
Sybase 9
Systemerror events 194

T
Tab order 306
Table Properties dialog box 99
Tables
    adding columns 111
    adding rows 132–133
    base 26
    candidate keys 17
    concatenated keys 16

creating 94–103
data types 101–103
deleting rows 131
designing 21–26
domain constraints 20–21
dropping 112–113
editing rows 128–129
foreign keys 103–107
formatting *see* Display formats
formatting *see* Edit formats
formatting *see* Extended attributes
inserting rows 130–131
modifying 110–111
normalizing 24–26
previewing 124
primary key constraints 18–19
primary keys 16–17, 98–101
referential integrity 19–20
virtual 26
`Text` 266
Text files 132–133
Third normal form 26
`this` 363, 508–509
`Time` 95, 266, 489–491, 514
`Timestamp` 96
`Today` 281, 500
Toolbars
    displaying as palettes 79
    displaying button text 78–79
    moving 80
    PowerTips 79
Totals 363–365
Transaction
    before-image file 46
    committing 45
    definition of 45–46
    rolling back 45
Transaction objects 182–184
    definition of 42
Transitive dependencies 24
Trasaction
    rolling back 200
`TriggerEvent` 269, 271, 326, 349, 409, 491–493
`Type` 401

U
`UInt` 514
Unsaved changes 365–367
`UnsignedInt` 514
`UnsignedInteger` 514
`Update` 324, 493–495

User ID 92
User object painter 73
User objects 42

V
Validation
    definition of 171
    rules for 172–174
`Varchar` 95, 96
Variables
    arrays 527–530
    declaring 525–526
    default values 526
    global 48, 520–521
    initializing 526
    instance 48, 521–523
    local 48, 524
    shared 48, 524
Views
    choosing columns for 138–139
    choosing rows for 139–140
    creating 136–142, 288
    definition of 26–27, 136
    dropping 142
    grouping queries with 143–145
    naming 141–142
    saving 141–142
    sorting rows in 140–141
    updatability 136, 142, 145
    viewing data through 142
Virtual functions 41
Virtual tables 26

W
WatcomSQL 9
WatcomSQL 4.0 60
Window objects
    definition of 42
Window painter 73
Window painter *see* Windows
Window Properties dialog box 189
Window Style dialog box 189
Windows
    aborting close of 367
    attaching menus to 408–409
    changing tab order 306
    child 185
    close events 199–200
    creating 186–188, 200–201
    events 198
    inheritance and 308–311

inhertance and 313–314
main 185
making resizable 190
MDI 185
naming 193
open events 198–199
popup 185
response 185
saving 193
saving a copy of 213
setting color 190
setting screen position 190–192
setting title 190
setting type 190
styles 189–192
types of 185–186
Workspace 74

Y
Year 395, 495–496